Gilled Mushrooms

(Agaricaceae) of Michigan and

the Great Lakes Region

Calvin Henry

C. H. KAUFFMAN

IN TWO VOLUMES

VOLUME TWO

D0988962

DOVER PUBLICATIONS, INC.

NEW YORK

Published in Canada by General Publishing Company, Ltd.,
30 Lesmill Road, Don Mills, Toronto, Ontario.
Published in the United Kingdom by Constable and Company,
Ltd., 10 Orange Street, London WC 2.

This Dover edition, first published in 1971, is an unabridged
republication of the work originally published in 1918 by the
Wynkoop Hallenbeck Crawford Company for the Michigan
Geological and Biological Survey as Publication 26 of Biological
Series 5 under the title *The Agaricaceae of Michigan.*
In the original edition, the first volume contained the complete
text and the second volume contained all 172 plates; in the
present reprint, each volume contains approximately half of the
text together with the corresponding plates.
The publisher gratefully acknowledges the cooperation of The
Milton S. Eisenhower Library of The Johns Hopkins University,
which supplied a copy of this work for the purpose of
reproduction.

International Standard Book Number: 0-486-22397-3
Library of Congress Catalog Card Number: 74-142877

Manufactured in the United States of America
Dover Publications, Inc.
180 Varick Street
New York, N. Y. 10014

TABLE OF CONTENTS

TABLE OF CONTENTS

PLATES

Inocybe Fr.

(From the Greek *is,* a fibre, and *kybe,* a head, referring to the silky-fibrillose covering of the pileus.)

Ochre-brown-spored. Pileus conical or campanulate at first, *innately silky, fibrillose or fibrillose-scaly;* the cuticle continuous to the stem in the form of a more or less evanescent, fibrillose cortina. Volva none. Gills and spores pale and sordid; *edge of gills provided with cystidia or saccate, sterile cells.*

Putrescent, mostly terrestrial, often with a characteristic odor. *Mostly small or medium-sized plants;* intermediate between Hebeloma and Cortinarius, lacking mostly the viscid pileus of the former, and the delicate, cobwebby cortina and the darker brown or rusty spores of the latter; formerly joined with the genus Hebeloma. They are usually omitted from the list of edible species on account of their mostly disagreeable odor and taste. Some

are known to be markedly poisonous, e. g., *I. infida* Pk., *I. infelix*
Pk., *I. fibrosa* Bres., etc.

The PILEUS has a cuticle composed of radiating, *parallel* fibrils,
which breaks up more or less during development and in age, so
as to form minute radiating cracks (rimose), or still more so, to
form fibrillose scales, which in some species become recurved (squarrose-scaly) ; in others, the surface fibrils remain more or less interwoven and do not become rimose; in a few species the cuticle is at
first viscid. These different modes of .adjustment of the fibrils
form a basis for a division of the species into sections. The color
of the cap is rarely bright, it is mostly of whitish, ochraceous, grayish or brownish shades; *I. frumentacea* and its variety *jurana,*
have sometimes a beautiful vinaceous or purple color, and
are well-marked by it. Others, like *I. pyriodora,* have a
characteristic pinkish tint to the flesh as they grow older.
In most cases, however, color-descriptions are apt to be
confusing, as the shades of brown, fawn, gray, or ochraceous vary in the same species and the same plants. For a
satisfactory study of this group, the interested student should
attempt to make colored sketches of the species he finds, accompanied by spore and cystidia drawings. It is practically impossible
to be sure of a species of this genus without the use of the microscope. The GILLS may be adnexed or almost free, occasionally
entirely free; adnate to subdecurrent in a few species. The color
of the mature gills is usually of a dull, sordid or pale fuscous, hard
to describe, but characteristic for many of the species, so that one
soon learns to distinguish an Inocybe by the tints of the gills. The
color of the gills is very similar to that of the genus Hebeloma.
However, it may vary in some species to brown, yellow or olivaceous
shades, and in one species becomes dingy purplish. A few have
been described with pale violet or blue gills when young, but
usually the young gills are whitish. The STEM is fibrous, usually
rather rigid at maturity, its surface varying from slightly silky
to fibrillose or squarrose-scaly. In the last case the stem is somewhat peronate or sheathed by the remains of the fibrillose-scaly
covering which was continuous in the young plant from cap to
stem; such species belong to the "Squarrosae" section. The apex
of the stem is usually mealy or scurfy. It may be stuffed and later
hollow, but most species have a solid stem. Some species are well
marked by the striking color of the lower part of the stem. The stem
of *I. calamistrata* Fr. has a dark greenish-blue base. The base of
the stem of *I. hirsuta* Lasch., is said to be bright green; this species
has not been found with us. In *I. cincinnata* Fr., the apex of the

stem as well as the young gills are said to be dark violet. The FLESH is characterized in some species by changing to a reddish color in age, e. g., *I. pyriodora* Bres., *I. repanda* Bres., *I. trinii* Bres., *I. incarnata* Bres. and *I. bongardii* Weinn. Some of these have not been found here. The SPORES are of great importance in the diagnosis of species. They may be spiny, angular or smooth. For the convenience of the student, each *section* may therefore be divided into the rough-spored and the smooth-spored species. Some authors have gone so far as to suggest the use of this character to establish genera. In some species, however, the spores are scarcely angular, i. e., they are intermediate between the smooth and angular shapes; an example of this condition is *I. decipiens*. In two of our species, *I. calospora* and *I. asterospora,* the spores are spiny, i. e., the surface of the spores is covered with slender, rod-like tubercles producing a pretty effect when seen under the microscope. Even the smooth spores often vary sufficiently in size and shape so as to provide means for the identification of species. CYSTIDIA are present in many species on the sides and edge of the gills; they are usually ventricose-lanceolate, mostly obtuse and covered at the apex by crystal-like deposits. In other species the cystidia are lacking, and only the edge of the gills is provided with differentiated structures; these are inflated-rounded at the apex in the form of obclavate or saccate, *sterile cells,* somewhat longer than the basidia. Ricken has used the rough and smooth characters of the spores, and the presence or absence of cystidia in such a way as to group the species under three divisions: (a) those with rough spores; (b) those with smooth spores and cystidia and; (c) those with smooth spores and without true cystidia. I have preferred to retain the more natural Friesian arrangement, modified so as to use the spore character under the sections.

The species included below have been interpreted from the point of view of the eminent mycologist, Ab. Bresadola, who has revised the older conceptions, and cleared up the complicated mass of synonyms for the European forms. The recent work of Ricken, which is also based on Bresadola's opinions, has helped not a little to arrive at definite conclusions.

Key to the Species

(A) Spores angular, tubercular or spiny.
  (a) Pileus viscid, small, tawny-ochraceous. 493. *I. trechispora* Berk.
  (aa) Pileus not viscid.
    (b) Pileus squarrose-scaly, fuscous to cinnamon.
      (c) Spores spherical, with rod-like spines. 468. *I. calospora* Quel.
      (cc) Spores subrectangular or wedge-shape in outline, irregular. 467. *I. leptophylla* Atk.
    (bb) Pileus not squarrose-scaly.
      (c) Pileus appressed fibrillose-scaly.
        (d) Stem fulvous-tinged; pileus 3-6 cm. broad, umbo fulvous. 487. *I. repanda* Bres.
        (dd) Stem whitish; pileus brownish-ochraceous, large; spores elongated-oblong in outline. 474. *I. decipientoides* Pk.
      (cc) Pileus soon rimosely cracked, fibrillose or silky.
        (d) Disk of pileus white and glabrous, pale grayish-lilac or grayish-drab on the margin. 485. *I. albodisca* Pk.
        (dd) Disk not sharply marked in color.
          (e) Pileus creamy-white or tinged ochraceous, large, 4-8 cm. 484. *I. fibrosa* Bres.
          (ee) Pileus not whitish.
            (f) Spores subglobose, with blunt spines; pileus brown or rufous-brown. 486. *I. asterospora* Quel.
            (ff) Spores irregularly-angular; pileus dark fuscous-brown. 483. *I. radiata* Pk.
(AA) Spores smooth, (i. e., not angular, etc.).
  (a) Cystidia present on sides of gills.
    (b) Stem squarrose-scaly or floccose-scaly; pileus brown, squarrose-scaly.
      (c) Spores 10-13 micr. long; stem squarrose-scaly. 463. *I. hystrix* Fr.
    (bb) Pileus not squarrose-scaly.
      (c) Pileus fibrillose-scaly, rarely or not at all rimose.
        (d) Spores elongated-subcylindrical, 11-18 x 4-6 micr.; pileus brown, umber, etc. 471. *I. lacera* Fr. 472. *I. infelix* Pk.
        (dd) Spores not markedly elongated.
          (e) Small plants; pileus 1-2.5 cm. broad, tawny-brown; stem tinged rufous-brown. 473. *I. flocculosa* Berk.
          (ee) Larger; pileus 2-6 cm. broad.
            (f) Flesh tinged reddish or pinkish in age; pileus whitish then sordid brownish-ochraceous; taste sweetish. 469. *I. pyriodora* Bres.
            (ff) Flesh not changing to reddish.
              (g) Pileus and mature gills smoky-brown; spores 7-8 x 5 micr. 470. *I. scaber* Fr.
              (gg) Pileus dark brown or rufous-brown, umbo darker; stem faintly rufous-tinged; spores 8-10 x 5-5.5 micr. 477. *I. destricta* Fr.
      (cc) Pileus at length rimose, fibrillose or subscaly. [See also (ccc).]
        (d) Spores obscurely angular, or almost even; pileus large, whitish, 4-8 cm. broad. 484. *I. fibrosa* Bres.
        (dd) Spores smooth; pileus not whitish.
          (e) Pileus dark brown or rufous-brown with chestnut-brown umbo; stem rufous-tinged. 477. *I. destricta* Fr.
          (ee) Pileus paler; stem not rufous-tinged.
            (f) Gills, when young, pale violaceous; pileus grayish-buff; spores 8-10 x 5-6 micr. *I. violaceifolia* Pk.
            (ff) Gills not violaceous; pileus fawn-color, almost chestnut-brown when young and cortinate, often appressed-scaly. 482. *I. eutheloides* Pk.

    (ccc) Pileus neither scaly, nor rimose, but persistently silky or fibrillose.
      (d) Pileus violaceous-lilac. 491. *I. lilacina* Pat.
      (dd) Pileus some other color.
        (e) Pileus small, 1-2.5 cm. broad.
          (f) Pileus and stem white, glossy-shining. 490. *I. geophylla* Fr.
          (ff) Pileus and slender stem rufous; in wet places. 492. *I. scabella* Fr. var. *rufa.*
        (ee) Pileus larger, 2-6 cm. broad.
          (f) Pileus whitish to straw-color or tinged ochraceous, woolly-fibrillose; stem white. 488. *I. sindonia* Fr.
          (ff) Pileus ochraceous or ochraceous-yellow, fibrillose-sub-scaly; stem pale ochraceous in age. 489. *I. subochracea* Pk.
(aa) Cystidia lacking on sides of gills; edge of gills provided with sac-shaped sterile cells.
  (b) Pileus when fresh squarrose-scaly or floccose-warty; stem sheathed by floccose or fibrillose scales.
    (c) Gills purplish-red; pileus smoky-brown, stem blood-red within; mostly in gardens and greenhouses. (See 236. *Psalliota echinata.*)
    (cc) Gills not red.
      (d) Stem dark greenish-blue towards base; pileus coffee-brown to wood-brown. 465. *I. calamistrata* Fr.
      (dd) Stem and pileus fulvous-yellowish or ochraceous; stem at length tubular. 466. *I. caesariata* Fr.
  (bb) Pileus not squarrose-scaly.
    (c) Pileus appressed-scaly.
      (d) Pileus large, 3-8 cm., smoky-purple, tinged wine-color, broadly umbonate. 475. *I. frumentacea* (Fr.) Bres.
      (dd) Pileus olivaceous-fulvous; gills at first olive or fawn-yellow; flesh citron-yellowish; cortinate; spores 10-11 x 5.5-6.5 micr. *I. dulcamera* Schw.
    (cc) Pileus at length rimose, fibrillose or subglabrous.
      (d) Pileus smoky-purple, vinaceous, conico-campanulate. 475. *I. frumentacea* Bres. var. *jurana* Pat.
      (dd) Pileus not purplish.
        (e) Pileus whitish, tawny, ochraceous or yellowish.
          (f) Center of pileus covered with white hoary-silky fibrils, convex and obtuse. 481. *I. lanatodisca* sp. nov.
          (ff) Not hoary-silky.
            (g) Spores 9-12 x 5-6 micr.; pileus conic-campanulate, pheasant-yellow to ochraceous-tan, virgate. 478. *I. fastigiata* Bres.
            (gg) Spores smaller.
              (h) Pileus pale yellow to straw color, lutescent; stem lutescent. 480. *I. cookei* Bres.
              (hh) Pileus ochraceous to tawny-yellowish, gibbous; stem irregularly clavate. 479. *I. curreyi* Berk.
        (ee) Pileus some shade of brown.
          (f) Pileus glabrous, sublubricous on umbo, sordid livid-brown, putrescent. 494. *I. glaber* sp. nov.
          (ff) Pileus fibrillose-virgate and very rimose, brown; spores 7-9 x 5-6 micr. 476. *I. rimosa* Fr. (Sense of Ricken.)

Section I. Squarrosae. Pileus at first densely scaly or squarrose-scaly; stem concolor.

**Spores smooth.*

463. Inocybe hystrix Fr.

Epicrisis, 1836.

Illustrations: Fries, Icones, Pl. 106.
Cooke, Ill., Pl. 424.

PILEUS 2-5 cm. broad, convex-expanded, broadly umbonate, *clothed* with *dense wood-brown, pointed or squarrose scales,* not rimose, nor striate; flesh white. GILLS adnate, not broad, close, pallid-alutaceous then brown, edge white-floccose. STEM 4-8 cm. long, 3-6 mm. thick, equal or enlarged below, *peronate to above the middle by squarrose scales,* concolor. SPORES elliptic-ovate, inequilateral, 9-13 x 5-5.5 micr., *smooth,* brown. CYSTIDIA on sides and edge of gills, ventricose below, obtuse, 70-90 x 12-17 micr. ODOR none.

Scattered or solitary. On the ground in mixed woods of northern Michigan. Marquette, Ishpeming. August. Rare.

Known by the dense recurved scales on the stem and by the large spores.

465. Inocybe calamistrata Fr.

Syst. Myc., 1821.

Illustrations: Fries, Icones, Pl. 106.
Gillet, Champignons de France, No. 360.

PILEUS 1-4 cm. broad, campanulate-convex, obtuse, surface soon broken up into dense, coffee-brown, squarrose scales, not rimose; flesh thin, *tinged dilute reddish,* darker in age. GILLS adnate-seceding or becoming sinuate, *broad,* close, soon cinnamon, at length ferruginous-sprinkled, edge thickish, white-flocculose. STEM firm, 4-8 cm. long, 2-5 mm. thick, tapering upward, *smoky-greenish-blue below,* fuscous or tinged rufous-brown above, *clothed with recurved fibrillose scales,* at length merely fibrillose, solid. SPORES ellipticoblong, subreniform, obtuse at ends, 10-12 x 5-6 micr., *smooth,* ferruginous-brown in mass. CYSTIDIA none. STERILE CELLS on

edge of gills obclavate, rounded-inflated above, about 30 x 12 micr.
ODOR slight.

Scattered or subcaespitose. On the ground in low woods,
throughout the State. Marquette, Houghton, Bay View, New Richmond, Detroit, Ann Arbor. July-September. Infrequent and never
plentiful.

Known by the smoky-blue lower part of the stem. The flesh
turns pinkish-red in young fresh specimens where cut. When old or
dry the stem is almost black below.

466. Inocybe cæsariata Fr.

Epicrisis, 1836.

Illustrations: Fries, Icones, Pl. 109.
Ricken, Die Blätterpilze, Pl. 31, Fig. 4, 1911.

PILEUS 2-5 cm. broad, broadly convex and obtuse, *at first covered by dense, leather-yellow, ochre-yellowish or fulvous, tomentose-
fibrillose or erect warts or scales,* becoming loosely fibrillose
scaly, appressed fibrillose on margin, not rimose, margin
incurved and at first connected with stem by a dingy-
white or ochraceous fibrillose cortina. FLESH white or
whitish, at length sub-ochraceous, *thick and compact on disk,*
thin on margin. GILLS rounded-ascending behind, adnate-
seceding or at length subdecurrent by tooth, rather broad,
ventricose, dull ochraceous-yellowish then ferruginous-ochraceous or
cinnamon, edge white-flocculose. STEM 1.5-4 cm long, 2-6 mm.
thick, *usually rather stout and short,* equal, at first floccose-scaly
below, usually densely floccose-fibrillose, *concolor,* apex flocculose-
scurfy, *soon definitely tubular,* ochraceous-whitish within. SPORES
short oblong, rounded-obtuse at both ends, subreniform, 8-10 x 5-6
micr., ochraceous-cinnamon in mass, *smooth.* CYSTIDIA none;
sterile cells on edge of gills variable, from inflated-pyriform to
flexuous-cylindrical. ODOR none. TASTE mild.

Gregarious, usually many individuals in favorable spots, as
if sown. On the ground in moist places, naked soil or among short
grass, near springs, lakes or water courses. Spring and autumn.
Ann Arbor, New Richmond. Not infrequent locally.

A rather variable plant when found under different weather
conditions. In the luxuriant state or when fresh the cuticle of
the pileus is broken up into dense floccose warts the bases of which

radiate and connect with one another by silky white fibres; after being exposed for some time to rain or wind, the scales become more appressed-fibrillose, straw color or paler. The color is well shown in Fries' figures, but the scales on the cap and stem are more highly developed at times, so that it should be referred to this section, to which Ricken also referred it. It is easily mistaken for a Cortinarius. *I. unicolor* Pk., *I. subtomentosa* Pk., *I. subdecurrens* E. & E. and *I. squamosodisca* Pk. are related to it.

**Spores tubercular-spiny.

467. *Inocybe leptophylla Atk.

Amer. Jour. of Bot., Vol. V, p. 212, 1918.

PILEUS 1-4 cm. broad, convex-expanded, obtuse, *covered with dense, cinnamon or umber, squarrose or pointed scales,* fibrillose on margin; flesh thin, whitish. GILLS rounded behind, adnexed, broad, *ventricose,* pallid becoming ferruginous-cinnamon, *edge white-crenulate.* STEM 2-4 cm. long, 2-4 mm. thick, equal, solid, *floccose-fibrillose* to tomentose-scaly, concolor, paler within, apex pruinose. SPORES subrectangular in outline, almost twice as long as wide, varying in shape, *with scattered obtuse tubercles* which are wider at base, 7-11 x 5-7 micr., ferruginous-brown. CYSTIDIA lacking; sterile cells on edge of gills, short, rounded-obclavate.

Solitary or gregarious. On the ground, in coniferous woods, or in swamps. Bay View, New Richmond, Ann Arbor. June-September. Rare.

This is apparently one of the American forms of *I. lanuginosa* (Fr.) Bres., to which Peck referred his species in his monograph of the New York Inocybes. (N. Y. State Mus. Bull. 139, p. 51.) But this seems unwarranted in view of the spore-measurements of *I. lanuginosa* given by such authorities as Bresadola and Schroeter who agree that the spores of the European species are much larger, about 11-15 x 8-9 micr. Specimens from three widely different localities in Michigan and New York yielded the same, smaller-sized spores. Schroeter has described a similar species, *I. lanuginella,* of which the spores are given the same size as ours, but have "prominent angles;" this may be our plant.

---

* This species was reported as *I. entomospora,* (see Mich. Acad. Sci. Rep. 8, p. 26) but became a *nomen nuda* by the publication of the above name by Atkinson after this report was in press.

468. Inocybe calospora Quel.

Bresadola, Fungi Trid., 1881.

Illustrations: Ibid, Pl. 21.
　　Plate XCI of this Report.

PILEUS 1-3 cm. broad, conic-campanulate at first, then expanded, umbonate, fuscous-rufescent, fading to ochraceous, umbo darker, covered, except umbo, by loose or recurved fibrillose scales, margin fibrillose and paler; flesh thin, pale. GILLS adnexed to almost free, rather narrow, subventricose, pallid then pale fuscous-cinnamon, edge white-fimbriate. STEM 3-6 cm. long, 1.5-2.5 mm. thick, firm, rigid-elastic, subequal, stuffed then hollow, pale brown, rufescent, sprinkled with a delicate pruinosity, bulbillate. SPORES spherical or nearly so, 9-12 micr. diam. (incl. aculeae), *covered with cylindrical, blunt aculeae*, 2-3 micr. long. CYSTIDIA few or scattered on sides, numerous on edge of gills, subventricose, apex granulate, 40-55 x 8-12 micr. ODOR none.

Gregarious. On the ground in low frondose woods. Ann Arbor. June-September. Rather frequent locally.

This pretty little plant usually occurs in patches of about a dozen. There is a slight rufescent tinge developed as the plant dries. Our specimens had longer and more slender stems as a rule than those shown in Bresadola's figure. *I. rigidipes* Pk. is said to approach it, but to "differ in the tawny-gray color, slightly adnexed lamellae, solid flexuous stem and larger spores." N. Y. State Mus. Bull. 139, p. 59.

Section II. Lacerae. Cuticle of pileus appressed-scaly or fibrillosely-lacerate, not rimose. Stem pallid at first.

*Spores smooth.

469. Inocybe pyriodora Fr.

Syst. Myc., 1821.

Illustrations: Gillet, Champignons de France, No. 368.
　　Bresadola, Fungi Trid., Vol. I, Pl. 52.
　　Patouillard, Tab. Analyt., No. 528.

PILEUS 3-5 cm. broad, campanulate then plane-expanded and *umbonate*, sometimes irregularly lobed on margin, whitish when

young, *soon dingy ochraceous or pale fuscous-clay color,* at length
here and there *faintly stained with pinkish-red,* at first silky-fibrillose, at length appressed fibrillose-scaly, radially split on
margin in age. FLESH white at first, slowly pale red
where cut, thick on disk. GILLS sinuate-adnexed, medium
broad, close, whitish then sordid cinnamon, in age diluted
with a rufous tinge, edge white-flocculose. STEM 4-7 cm. long, 4-10
mm. thick, subequal, at the very first white-cortinate, subfibrillose,
apex furfuraceus, strict, subbulbous at base, white at first, becoming
light-red in age, solid but soon cavernous from grubs. SPORES
broadly elliptical, subreniform, smooth, 8-10.5 x 5-6 micr. CYS-
TIDIA rather abundant on sides and edge of gills, ventricose above
the short pedicel, broadly cylindrical above, 45-55 x 12-18 micr.
ODOR *sweet,* spicy or like bumble-bee honey, becoming disagreeable.

Gregarious. On the ground in frondose woods of oak, etc. Ann
Arbor. August. Infrequent.

This Inocybe is well described by Bresadola, and can be recognized by its peculiar light-red stains, especially between the gills
or where they have been removed by snails or slugs. On the cap
this color-change is not very marked. The odor has been described
as being like that of ripe pears or clove pinks, and is quite characteristic. Except that the pileus is usually fully expanded, Patouillard's figure shows the old stage, which is most often found.
The gills are sometimes narrow instead of broad, as indicated by
Bresadola.

470. Inocybe scaber Fr.

Syst. Myc., 1821.

Illustrations: Ricken, Die Blätterpilze, Pl. 30, Fig. 1, 1911.
Patouillard, Tab. Analyt., No. 539.
Gillet, Champignons de France, No. 375.

"PILEUS 5-8 cm. broad, conical-campanulate, at length plane
and broadly umbonate, *pale smoky,* with smoky, almost overlapping,
fibrillose scales, the disk olive-blackish, at times tesselated, at the
very first with a white-woolly cortina on margin, *fleshy.* Gills pale
clay-color, finally almost smoky, close, broad, ventricose, emarginate-
adnate, seceding. STEM 5-8 cm. long, 7-10 mm. thick, solid, subequal, *stout,* pallid or streaked with reddish-brown, silky-fibrillose
with a slightly pruinose apex. SPORES almond-shaped, small,
7-8 x 5 micr., *smooth.* CYSTIDIA on sides and edge of gills, flask-

shaped, 50-65 x 15-25 micr., sparse. ODOR weak, somewhat like pears, agreeable."

Reported by Longyear. The description has been adapted from Ricken, who gives the characters most fully. Ricken's diagnosis agrees in microscopic details with most other authors, except that his plants are very large. Patouillard gives the same spores as Ricken, but figures a small plant. Cooke (Ill., Pl. 391) figures a plant whose spores measured 11 x 6 micr. Cooke's spore-size has been copied by Massee and Schroeter. Thus, there seem to be two species at present confused under this name. I have not seen a plant which could be referred to either.

471. Inocybe lacera Fr.

Syst. Myc., 1821.

Illustrations: Ricken, Die Blätterpilze, Pl. 30, Fig. 4, 1911.
Patouillard, Tab. Analyt., No. 531.
Cooke, Ill., Pl. 583.

"PILEUS 3-5 cm. broad, umbonate-expanded, at times depressed, umbo obtuse, *fawn-brown to mouse-gray,* at first almost glabrous-fibrillose, soon fibrillose-scaly, becoming ragged around the umbo; FLESH thin, whitish. GILLS rounded-adnexed, broad, ventricose, subdistant, brownish-clay color, at length concolor. STEM 3-4 cm. long, 4-5 mm. thick, subequal, *brownish,* with red-brown fibrils, *apex naked,* white-mycelioid at base, stuffed, *reddish within.* SPORES almost *cylindrical, long and narrow,* straight, 12-18 x 4-6 micr., smooth. CYSTIDIA on sides and edge of gills, narrow-lanceolate, 54-70 x 14-17 micr., rounded above. ODOR slight; *taste* mild."

Reported by Longyear.

Apparently well-marked by the long, cylindrical spores. Patouillard gives the spores of somewhat different size, 10-13 x 6-7 micr. The above description is adapted from Ricken. An unusual mark of this species is the naked apex of the stem; in most species this is pruinose or scurfy. A form occurred at New Richmond, which agreed except that the spores were the size of those of *I. infelix.*

472. Inocybe infelix Pk. (POISONOUS)

N. Y. State Mus. Rep. 32, 1879.

PILEUS 1-2.5 cm. broad, *rather small,* campanulate then expanded-plane, *umbonate,* grayish-brown, *umbo cinnamon or umber,* fibrillose at first, becoming fibrillose-scaly or floccose-scaly, flesh thin, whitish. GILLS adnexed, rather broad, ventricose, close, whitish becoming cinnamon. STEM 2-5 cm. long, 2-3 mm. thick, equal, stuffed, silky-fibrillose, whitish or faintly violaceous at apex, becoming dingy brown below, white within. SPORES *elongated-oblong,* smooth, 10-14 x 4-6 micr. CYSTIDIA flask-shaped, 50-70 x 15-20 micr., apex crystallate. ODOR slight.

Solitary or gregarious. On low, wet ground. Ann Arbor, Bay View. May-July. Frequent.

Scarcely differs from preceding except in size. In those plants which grow in wet places the stem is hollow. Peck says the cuticle of the pileus is more lacerated in wet weather than in dry weather.

473. Inocybe flocculosa Berk.

Eng. Flora.

Illustration: Cooke, Ill., Pl. 393.

PILEUS 1-2 cm. broad, subcampanulate, expanded-umbonate, *tawny-brown with tinge of fuscous,* fibrillose-scaly, not rimose. GILLS rounded-adnate, broad, *ventricose,* almost subdistant, brownish-ashy then concolor, edge fimbriate-crenulate. STEM 1-2 cm. long, 1-2 mm. thick, equal, hollow, pruinose-hoary, scurfy at apex, *tinged brown.* SPORES 8-9 x 4-6, elliptical-ovate, *smooth.* CYSTIDIA on sides and edge of gills, flask-shaped, apex crystallate, about 60 micr. long.

Among spruce needles and on the ground in swamps. Bay View. New Richmond. August.

This little species is usually found in low, wet places. The stem is tinged rufous-brown in most cases.

**Spores angular.*

474. Inocybe decipientoides Pk.

Torr. Bot. Club Bull. 34, p. 100, 1907.

PILEUS 1-4 cm. broad, campanulate-convex, expanded-umbonate, umbo subconic, *silky-floccose,* then scaly-diffracted, dry, brownish-ochraceous; flesh thin, pallid. GILLS adnate, broad, close, whitish at first then *lurid-cinnamon,* edge white-fimbriate. STEM 4-5 cm. long, 2-5 mm. thick, equal, usually slender, glabrous to subfibrillose, slightly striate, whitish or pallid, apex white-pruinose, base bulbil-late, stuffed. SPORES irregularly wedge-shape, subrectangular, etc., *tuberculate,* 9-13 x 5-7 micr. CYSTIDIA on sides and edge of gills, ventricose-elliptical, slender pediceled, 50-60 x 12-18 micr. ODOR and TASTE slight.

Gregarious. On the ground, grassy places in low frondose woods. Detroit. June. Rare.

This is a species very clearly marked by the peculiar spores.

Section III. Rimosae. Pileus radiately fibrous, soon *rimose,* sometimes subscaly or adpressed-scaly.

***Spores smooth.**

475. Inocybe frumentacea Bres.

Fung. Trid., Vol. II, 1892.

Illustrations: Ibid, Pl. 200.
> Bres., Fung. Trid., Vol. I, Pl. 87 (as *I. rhodiola* Bres.).
> Patouillard, Tab. Analyt., No. 551 (as *I. jurana* Pat.).
> Plate XCII of this Report.

PILEUS large, 3-8 cm. broad, rigid-firm, campanulate at first, then expanded and broadly umbonate, fibrillose, becoming rimose or scaly, *fibrils and scales brown-purplish to reddish-chestnut with a dark vinaceous tint,* umbo darker; flesh thick, white, vinaceous under cuticle. GILLS adnexed, at length emarginate-uncinate, close, not broad, thickish, white at first, then grayish-brown, edge white-flocculose, becoming rufescent-spotted. STEM 3-8 cm. long, rather stout, 6-12 mm. thick, equal, terete or compressed, sometimes twisted, fibrillose, apex glabrous or sub-floccose, whitish, *rufous-vinaceous below,* becoming spotted with the same color where handled, solid. SPORES broadly elliptic-subreniform, *smooth,* epispore strongly colored, 10-13 x 6-7 micr. CYSTIDIA none. *Sterile cells* on edge of gills obclavate, or subcylindrical, rounded-inflated above, 45-60 x 9-12 micr. ODOR and TASTE slight, of meal.

Gregarious. On the ground in low places under frondose trees in Belle Isle Park, Detroit and near Ann Arbor. August and July.

This large, wine-colored Inocybe was found in abundance in the above localities during two seasons. It corresponded accurately to the figures of Bresadola, Plate 200, in shape and stoutness. In age or after lying for a day, the characteristic dark vinaceous color becomes more marked. The umbo is broad and in half-expanded caps a gibbous condition is not unusual. It has the appearance of a Tricholoma.

I. jurana Pat. seems to be a distinct plant, although referred to by Bresadola as a synonym of *I. frumentacea.* Our photograph shows the shape and habit well. The pileus is at first conic-elliptical, then campanulate. The stem is more slender than that of *I. frumentacea,* and the spores are smaller, 9-10 x 5-6 micr. There are no cystidia, and the sterile cells on the edge of the gills are of the same size. The other characters are very similar.

Gregarious. On the ground, in low frondose woods. Ann Arbor. August.

476. Inocybe rimosa Pk. (Sense of Ricken)

Syst. Myc., 1821.

Illustrations: Gillet, Champignons de France, No. 371.
Cooke, Ill., Plate 384.
Ricken, Die Blätterpilze, Pl. 30, Fig. 8.
Murrill, Mycologia, Vol. 4, Pl. 56, Fig. 7.

PILEUS 3-6 cm. broad, oval-campanulate then expanded and obtuse or subumbonate, silky-fibrillose, *at length rimose* and virgate, often split on the margin, *brown,* tinged yellowish in age, margin at length recurved; FLESH pallid, fragile. GILLS almost free, *narrow,* scarcely ventricose, crowded, cinereous-clay color, edge white-fimbriate. STEM 4-8 cm. long, 5-7 mm. thick, equal, straight or curved at base, whitish or pallid, solid, subglabrous, apex white-mealy, *base usually with a marked rounded or subdepressed bulb.* SPORES *short,* reniform, very obtuse at ends, *smooth,* 7-9 x 5-6 micr. CYSTIDIA none; STERILE CELLS on edge of gills, saccate, 30-40 x 12 micr. ODOR after crushing rather strong and nauseous; TASTE disagreeable.

Gregarious. On the ground, in low frondose woods. Ann Arbor. August. Infrequent.

Dark individuals of this species have the appearance of non-scaly forms of *I. destricta* and a microscopic examination is usually necessary to distinguish them. In age the color of different caps varies considerably in intensity. It is probably widely distributed, but I have few collections. The figure of Patouillard (Tab. Analyt., No. 114) shows the presence of cystidia and belongs elsewhere.

477. Inocybe destricta Fr. (MINOR)

Epicrisis, 1836-38. (As var. *I. rimosa.*)

Illustrations: Fries, Icones, Pl. 108.
    Cooke's Ill., Pl. 387.
    Ricken, Die Blätterpilze, Pl. 29, Fig. 9.

PILEUS 2-4 cm. broad, conic-campanulate, then expanded-umbonate, at length depressed around the darker abrupt umbo, dark brown, rufous-brown or ochraceous-brown, *umbo persistently dark chestnut* or umber, fibrillose at first, *at length lacerate-scaly or rimose, or both;* FLESH thin, whitish. GILLS sinuate-adnexed or deeply emarginate, uncinate, *ventricose,* medium broad, close to subdistant, whitish then *pale brownish-ashy,* edge white-fimbriate. STEM 2.5-5 cm. long, 2.5-5 mm. thick, equal, scarcely bulbillate, *pallid, tinged with rufous,* varying flocculose-fibrillose to glabrous, apex pruinate, solid, white within. SPORES subreniform, inequilateral, *smooth,* 8-10 x 5-5.5 micr. CYSTIDIA abundant on sides and edge of gills, ventricose, stout above, apex crystallate, 50-65 x 15-18 micr. ODOR at first slight then somewhat nauseous.

Gregarious. On the ground in coniferous forests of pine and hemlock. Bay View, New Richmond. August-September. Frequent.

This is a variable plant, and when developed under moist weather conditions the cap becomes lacerate-scaly and often excoriate in part, and is then non-rimose; in dry weather it becomes markedly rimose and less scaly. When young or freshly expanded the pileus is usually densely fibrillose and its edge minutely appendiculate by the remains of the rather copious, white cortina. At first the pileus is dark brown, but in age it becomes somewhat ochraceous-brown beyond the umbo. The faint tinge of rufous on the older stems is a well-marked character, duly noted by Fries. The spores are markedly subreniform in one view, short fusiform-ovate in the other view. Our collections contain mostly plants with a rather longer stem and narrower cap than shown by the figures of Cooke and·Fries. It is easily confused in some of its forms with *I. rimosa,* but differs in possessing abundant cystidia. Occasionally a troop of dwarf forms occurs, which, however, scarcely differ except in the shorter stem.

478. Inocybe fastigiata Bres.

Fung. Trid., Vol. I, 1881.

Illustrations: Ibid, Pl. 57.
   Cooke, Ill., Pl. 383.
   Patouillard, Tab. Analyt., No. 343.
   Fries, Icones, Pl. 108.
   Ricken, Die Blätterpilze, Pl. 31, Fig. 1.
   Plate XCIII of this Report.

PILEUS 2-7 cm. broad, *typically very conical or conico-campanulate,* sometimes oval-campanulate, at length subexpanded, *usually with a prominent umbo,* radially fibrillose, *rimose,* virgate, *rich yellowish-fuscous,* ochraceous-tan or straw-color, margin at length split or lobed; FLESH white. GILLS adnexed, becoming sinuate-free, and narrower behind, not broad, ventricose, close, whitish at first, soon tinged *olive or gray,* darker in age. STEM 4-8 cm. long, 4-10 mm. thick, equal or tapering upwards, solid, more or less fibrillose or scurfy, white or slightly fuscescent, sometimes twisted or obscurely striate. SPORES elliptic-subreniform, *smooth* (not angular), obtuse at ends, 9-12 x 5-6 micr. CYSTIDIA none. STERILE CELLS on edge of gills saccate. ODOR strong and disagreeable or entirely lacking.

Gregarious. On the ground, in low, moist places in frondose or conifer woods. Throughout the State. July-September. Frequent.

This is a striking species, and quite variable. The stem may be dull whitish to pale ochraceous. Small forms occur with cap less campanulate and at length papillate. The odor may be very strong or altogether absent. All these forms agree in having the same size spores, gills of the same color and no cystidia. The color of the pileus is sometimes a rich pheasant-yellow, sometimes fulvous-ochraceous, at other times much paler. The English authors, Massee and Berkley, were in error when they assigned rough, nodulose spores to this species. (British Fungus Flora and Outlines.)

479. Inocybe curreyi Berk.

Outlines of Brit. Fung., 1860.

Illustration: Cooke, Ill., Pl. 398.

PILEUS 2-4 cm. broad, irregularly convex-campanulate, obtuse, not umbonate, gibbous at times, appressed-fibrillose, at length rimose, *pale tawny-yellowish,* edge undulate; FLESH white. GILLS slightly adnexed, rather broad, close, *becoming smoky-olivaceous,* edge white-fimbriate. STEM 2-4 cm. long, variously curved, *tapering upward from a subclavate base,* not bulbous, solid, slightly fibrillose, glabrescent, whitish at first, furfuraceus-scaly at apex. SPORES elliptic-subreniform, obtuse .at ends, 7-9.5 x 5-5.5 micr., *smooth,* fuscous-cinnamon in mass. CYSTIDIA none. STERILE CELLS on˙edge of gills saccate. ODOR strongly earthy when crushed.

Gregarious. On the ground among grass in frondose woods. Ann Arbor. July-August. Not infrequent.

This plant is referred to this form with some hesitation as published details of Berkley's species, especially as to the microscopic characters, are insufficient. The color of the pileus approaches *I. fastigiata* rather closely, but it is not conical nor truly umbonate, and the spores are constantly smaller. From the following it is distinguishable by the very different form of the stem and by the color of the pileus. Patouillard gives the spores 6 x 4 micr., in which he is quite at variance with the British authors.

480. Inocybe cookei Bres.

Fung. Trid., Vol. 2, 1892.

Illustration: Ibid, Pl. 121.

PILEUS 1.5-4 cm. broad, subconic-campanulate, expanded-umbonate, silky-fibrillose, at length rimose, glabrous on center, *straw-yellow, becoming sordid lutescent,* margin at length wavy or split; FLESH whitish. GILLS sinuate-adnexed or almost free, scarcely ventricose, narrow, close, whitish at first, soon tinged ashy-ochraceous-cinnamon, edge white-fimbriate. STEM 2.5-5 cm. long, 3-5 mm. thick, equal, solid, silky-fibrillose, pruinose at apex, *with a marginate distinct bulb,* whitish at first, *lutescent.* SPORES 8-9.5 x 4.5-5.5 micr., elliptic-subreniform, obtuse at ends, *smooth.*

CYSTIDIA none. STERILE CELLS on edge of gills, inflated-obclavate, 30 x 12-15 micr.

Gregarious. On moist ground in frondose and coniferous woods. Ann Arbor, Bay View, New Richmond. August-September. Infrequent.

The uniform pale yellow color of the pileus which becomes deeper in age, the lutescent stem and margined bulb are characters which separate this from the two preceding species. The odor is scarcely noticeable at times but occasionally it is rather strong of rancid meal.

481. Inocybe lanotodisca sp. nov.

PILEUS 2-4 cm. broad, rarely broader, convex-campanulate, obtuse or broadly umbonate, ground-color pale ochraceous-brownish or pale tawny, *at first covered by a white, mouldy-like silkiness on the center, when expanded subzonate by the subconcentric arrangement of the downy-silky fibrils,* at length rimose; FLESH white, rather thick on disk. GILLS adnexed-emarginate, moderately broad, close, at length cinereous-alutaceous, edge white-fimbriate. STEM 3-5 cm. long, 4-6 mm. thick, equal or subequal, solid, glabrescent, apex pruinate-scaly, white, becoming pale sordid yellowish in age. SPORES elliptic-subreniform, *smooth,* obtuse at ends, 9-10.5 x 5-6 micr. CYSTIDIA none. STERILE CELLS on edge of gills, obclavate, attenuated downward. BASIDIA clavate, 33 x 9 micr., 4-spored. ODOR nauseous on crushing the plant.

Gregarious to subcaespitose. On the ground in low frondose woods. Ann Arbor. August-September. Infrequent.

A well-marked species; to be known by the hoary-silkiness on the central portion of the pileus and by the lack of cystidia. It approaches *I. sindonia* in appearance, but that species has abundant cystidia, the cap is not rimose, and the covering of the pileus is differently disposed. The habit varies from rather slender forms to those quite stout. As the pileus expands the white fibrils are disposed over a larger area.

482. Inocybe eutheloides Pk.

N. Y. State Mus. Rep. 32, 1879.

PILEUS 1-2.5 cm. broad, conico-campanulate, then expanded-umbonate, *fawn-color to grayish-fawn,* darker to chestnut when young or on the *distinct umbo,* silky-fibrillose, at length rimose, sometimes appressed-scaly. GILLS adnexed, rather broad, ventricose, close, whitish then brownish-cinnamon, white-fimbriate on edge. STEM 2-5 cm. long, 2-4 mm. thick, equal, subbulbillate at base, solid, densely white-fibrillose when young, subglabrescent, apex scurfy-pruinate. SPORES 8-10 (rarely longer) x 4.5-5.5 micr., variable in shape, subreniform-fusoid, ends somewhat narrowed, *smooth.* CYSTIDIA *rather abundant* on sides and edge of gills, narrowly flask-shaped, apex crystallate, 50-70 x 12-16 micr. BASIDIA 30 x 9 micr., 4-spored. ODOR slight.

Gregarious. Common in southern Michigan; on the ground in low frondose woods. June-September.

This is closely allied to *I. destricta,* form *minor,* in its microscopic characters. The colors are, however, constantly distinct, and *I. destricta* seems limited to coniferous regions. *I. eutheloides* also approaches *I. eutheles* as interpreted by some authors, e. g., Massee. But according to Patouillard that species is devoid of cystidia. The stem is usually markedly silky-fibrillose, and the umbo is dark chestnut in young and fresh specimens. In young specimens the margin of the pileus is often crenately fringed by the white cortina.

**Spores angular-tuberculate.

483. Inocybe radiata Pk. (POISONOUS)

Torr. Bot. Club Bull. 22, p. 488, 1895.

PILEUS 1.5-5 cm. broad, campanulate, fuscous-brown to ochraceous-brown, *very umbonate by an obtuse, dark umber umbo,* which remains glabrous; elsewhere appressed-fibrillose with brown fibrils, not at all viscid, becoming rimose; FLESH white, thickish on disk. GILLS *adnate,* broad, at length sinuate-uncinate, close, becoming ochraceous-cinnamon to subferruginous, edge white, flocculose. STEM 3-6 cm. long, 2-4 mm. thick, equal, stuffed, silky-fibrillose, *becoming umber-fuscous-brown,* apex paler, subbulbillate and white-myceliod at base. SPORES irregularly oblong-rectangular to sub-wedge shape in outline, angular and with few scattered tubercles, 7-9 x 5-6 micr. CYSTIDIA few or scattered, on sides and edge of gills, 55-65 x 12-18 micr., broadly ventricose, apex somewhat pointed and crystallate, on slender pedicel. ODOR earthy. TASTE mild.

Gregarious. On the ground, in frondose woods. August. Ann Arbor.

This seems to be intermediate between *I. carpta* Bres. and *I. umbrina* Bres. in its microscopic characters. The umbo does not become warty nor scaly and is not subviscid as in the latter species. The same species has been received from Massachusetts; it was sent by Simon Davis, who reports it poisonous.

484. Inocybe fibrosa Bres. (Poisonous)

Fung. Trid., Vol. I, 1881.

Illustrations: Ibid, Pl. 56.
    Cooke, Ill., Pl. 454.
    Ricken, Die Blätterpilze, Pl. 29, Fig. 8.
    Plate XCIV of this Report.

PILEUS 4-8 cm. broad, *large,* obtusely campanulate, then broadly umbonate and expanded, dry, *creamy-white or tinged straw-color,* sometimes ochraceous-stained, silky, at length rimose and margin lobed, split or recurved; FLESH white, *thick,* thin on margin. GILLS free, rounded behind, *ventricose,* broader toward front, close, whitish at first, then ashy-cinnamon, edge white-fimbriate. STEM 4-8 cm. long, 6-15 mm. thick, fibrous, splitting longitudinally, subequal, striatulate to subsulcate, glabrescent, apex pruinate, white then sordid, base often subbulbous. SPORES angular-oblong, *with obscure, scattered tubercles,* 9-13 x 5-7 micr., epispore reddish under the microscope. CYSTIDIA fusoid, crystallate at apex, abundant on sides and edge of gills, 60-75 x 10-15 micr. ODOR earthy. TASTE mild.

Gregarious. On the ground, in low, moist, frondose woods. June-August. Ann Arbor. Infrequent.

Apparently our largest species. The spores are inclined to be more or less sinuate-tuberculate, but the angularity is not as marked as in many others. The character of the surface of the pileus is much like *I. fastigitata* except in color. It appears earlier than most Inocybes, and is said to be *poisonous.* (See Bresadola, Fung. Trid.)

485. Inocybe albodisca Pk.

N. Y. State Mus. Rep. 51, 1898.

PILEUS 1.5-3.5 cm. broad, conical at first, soon campanulate-umbonate or expanded, *umbo lubricus-glabrous, obtuse and whitish*, elsewhere silky, at first pale lilac-flesh color, at length *grayish-drab* and rimose; FLESH whitish, not changing color. GILLS rather narrow, close, narrowly adnate, whitish at first, then subferruginous, edge minutely white-flocculose. STEM 3-5 cm. long, 3-5 mm. thick, equal, subbulbillate to somewhat marginate-bulbous, solid, *glabrous* or upper part pruinate, at first tinged by color of pileus, fading, even. SPORES *sinuate-angular*, subrectangular to subglobose in outline, shape variable, 7-8 x 5-6 micr., nucleate. CYSTIDIA very abundant on sides and edge of gills, crystallate at apex, fusoid-ventricose, about 50 x 15 micr. Basidia 33 x 9 micr., 4-spored. ODOR slight, subnauseous.

Gregarious-scattered. On the ground, clay soil of hemlock and beech woods. New Richmond. September. Infrequent.

Known by its glabrous, whitish, obtuse umbo, submarginate bulb, and the peculiar shade of pale lilac-incarnate color when young. This color disappears in older specimens where the cap takes on a grayish shade and becomes rimose. The spores distinguish it sharply from *I. lanatodisca*, and the smaller size of the plant and spores separate it from *I. fibrosa*. It is closely related to *I. umbratica* Bres. and *I. fallax* Pk.

486. Inocybe asterospora Quel.

Bull. Soc. Bot. France, Vol. 26, p. 50, 1879.

Illustrations: Ricken, Die Blätterpilze, Pl. 29, Fig. 1.
          Cooke, Ill., Pl. 385.
          Patouillard, Tab. Analyt., No. 546.

PILEUS 2-5 cm. broad, conic-campanulate to convex-umbonate, brown or rufous-brown, *very rimose*, fibrillose-scaly; FLESH pallid, rather thin. GILLS narrowly adnate, emarginate, ventricose, close, at length olivaceous-cinnamon or grayish-brown. STEM 4-6 cm. long, 2.5-6 mm. thick, equal above the subemarginate or rounded bulb, *rufescent*, innately striatulate, *mealy-pubescent*, fibrous, solid. SPORES subsphoeroid, slightly longer than broad, covered with blunt, subcylindrical tubercles which are broader toward base, 9-11 micr. CYSTIDIA abundant on sides and edge of gills, 50-75 x 15-24 micr., ventricose, apex crystallate. ODOR slight or subnauseous.

Gregarious. In low, sandy, frondose woods. Ann Arbor. June-August.

It is rather difficult to keep *I. asterospora* and *I. calospora* distinct. The rimose and scaly characters by which they are set apart may vary under certain weather conditions so as to be obliterated. The spores are very similar, but those of *I. asterospora* are not as truly spherical as in *I. calospora*. With us this species tends to be smaller than the figures show it. It is at once separable from the other red-brown species by the spiny-tuberculate spores.

Section IV. Velutinae. Pileus not rimose, cuticle of interwoven fibrils, glabrescent or appressed-scaly.

*Spores angular-tuberculate.

487. Inocybe repanda Bres.

Fung. Trid., Vol. II, 1892.

Illustrations: Ibid, Pl. 119.
Plate XCV of this Report.

PILEUS 3-5 cm. broad, obtusely conic-campanulate, then expanded and broadly umbonate, umbo fulvous and glabrous, *elsewhere covered with orange-fulvous fibrils on a whitish foundation,* sublubricous, margin at length split or subrimose, sometimes scaly-cracked. FLESH white, rather fragile, thick on disk. GILLS adnexed or almost free, broad, subventricose, close, at first white, *rufescent,* finally argillaceous-cinnamon, edge white-fimbriate. STEM 3-6 cm. long, strict, 5-6 mm. thick, equal above the abrupt or rounded bulb, stuffed, terete, even, slightly silky fibrillose, *the fibrils fulvous-tinged toward base,* apex white-pruinose. SPORES angular, 7-9.5 x 6-7 micr., longer than wide, sometimes rectangular in outline, *with minute papillate tubercles.* CYSTIDIA moderately abundant on edge and sides of gills, ventricose-fusiform, apex crystallate, 60-75 x 12-18 micr. ODOR and TASTE mild.

Gregarious. On the ground, in low frondose woods. Ann Arbor. July-August. Infrequent.

This is one of our larger Inocybes and is well-marked. The flesh does not readily become rufescent in our plants, yet there is little doubt that the plant is the one described by Bresadola.

**Spores smooth.*

488. Inocybe sindonia Fr.

Epicrisis, 1836-38.

Illustrations: Cooke, Ill., Pl. 400.
Ricken, Die Blätterpilze, Pl. 30, Fig. 7.

PILEUS 2-6 cm. broad, at first obtusely conic-oval, then campanulate-expanded and *broadly umbonate, cortinate, at first woolly-fibrillose from dense white fibrils,* later subglabrescent, not rimose, *whitish* becoming straw-yellow to dingy ochraceous in age. FLESH compact, thick on disk, white. GILLS emarginate-adnexed or almost free, moderately broad, ventricose, close, at first pale grayish-white then grayish-clay color. STEM 3-6 cm. long, 4-9 mm. thick, equal above the subemarginate bulb, *white,* stuffed, often striate, silky shining, at first fibrillose, flesh satiny-shining. SPORES subreniform, *smooth,* relatively broad, 8-10 x 5-6 micr. CYSTIDIA abundant on sides and edge of gills, ventricose-lanceolate to subcylindrical, apex crystallate, 60-75 x 15-20 micr. ODOR rather strong, somewhat nauseous.

Gregarious. On the ground, in low, rich, frondose woods. Ann Arbor. August-September. Infrequent.

Without an examination of the microscopic characters, this species might easily be confused with *I. lanatodisca.* In the young stage the white woolly-fibrillose cortina is continuous with the fibrils on the margin of the cap. At maturity the pileus becomes glabrous, especially on the disk, while in *I. lanatodisca* the disk is marked at last by the white fibrils. It is probable that Hard's Fig. 218, p. 269, Mushroom Book, of *I. subochracea* var. *burtii* Pk. is referable to this species.

489. Inocybe subochracea Pk.

N. Y. State Mus. Rep. 23, 1872 (as Hebeloma).

Illustration: N. Y. State Mus. Rep. 54, Pl. H. (as var. *burtii*).

PILEUS 2-3.5 cm. broad, *conical at first,* then convex-campanulate, umbonate, *ochraceous or ochraceous-yellow,* appressed fibrillose subscaly, darker and more scaly on disk, *not rimose*. FLESH *white, thin.* GILLS sinuate-adnexed, scarcely close, moderately broad, whitish then pale ochraceous-brown to rusty-brown. STEM 2.5-5 cm. long, 2-4 mm. thick, *equal,* solid, subglabrous, whitish, pallid ochraceous in age. SPORES broadly elliptic-subreniform, 7-9 x 4.5-5 micr., *smooth.* CYSTIDIA scattered on sides and edge of gills, apex crystallate, lanceolate, stipitate, *yellowish,* 70-90 x 12-20 micr. ODOR and TASTE mild.

Gregarious. On the ground, frondose woods. August-September. Ann Arbor.

This species has a smaller and more yellowish pileus than *I. sindonia;* the spores and cystidia are similar. A variety has been described by Peck with a distinct, webby cortina and more fibrillose stem, as var. *brutii.*

490. Inocybe geophylla Fr.

Syst. Myc., 1821.

Illustrations: Cooke, Ill., Pl. 401.
Gillet, Champignons de France, No. 364.
Patouillard, Tab. Analyt., No. 228.

PILEUS 1.5-2.5 cm. broad, conical at first, then expanded-umbonate, *very silky and glossy, white or whitish,* not rimose; FLESH white, thin. GILLS adnexed, close, rather broad, ventricose, whitish then pale grayish-clay color. STEM 2-5 cm. long, 2-3 mm. thick, slender, equal, firm, stuffed, *white,* silky, apex pruinose. SPORES elliptic-subreniform, *smooth,* 8-9 x 5 micr. CYSTIDIA fusiform, 40-55 x 12-15 micr. ODOR "slightly nauseous."

Gregarious or scattered. On the ground in frondose and conifer woods. Throughout the State. July-October. Common.

One of our commonest Inocybes, although not often found in abundance at one place. The clear, white, glossy cap and stem are characteristic. Other white species which have been described are: *I. comatella* Pk., a smaller plant, which has a hairy pileus and at times a reddish-brown stem, but the spores and cystidia are the same, usually grows on rotten wood; *I. fallax* Pk., with angular or nodulose spores; *I. infida* Pk., also with nodulose spores and a subscaly, reddish-brown umbo. Both the latter species have cystidia.

491. Inocybe lilacina (variety of preceding by authors)

Illustrations: Patouillard, Tab. Analyt., No. 545.
Ricken, Die Blätterpilze, Pl. 30, Fig. 2.
Hard, Mushrooms, Fig. 219, p. 270, 1908.

PILEUS lilaceous-violet, the umbo darker, almost smoky-purple at first. STEM pale lilac-violaceous to whitish. Otherwise like *I. geophylla.*
Gregarious. On the ground, in frondose and conifer woods. Throughout the State. August-October. Less frequent than *I. geophylla* Fr.
This is a pretty little plant, and is usually combined with *I. geophylla.* It is usually found in gregarious groups of several individuals and not mixed with *I. geophylla.* This fact and its constantly independent color, leads me to believe that it does not arise from the same mycelium as *I. geophylla.* The general appearance during development and the character of the surface of the cap, although not easily differentiated in words, seem sufficiently different from the white species.

492. Inocybe scabella Fr.

Syst. Myc., 1821.

Illustrations: Fries, Icones, Pl. 110, Fig. 1.
Bresadola, Fung. Trid., Vol. I, Pl. 86, Fig. 1.
Patouillard, Tab. Analyt., No. 229.

PILEUS 1.5-2.5 cm. broad, conico-campanulate, then expanded and *with a naked, glabrous, obtuse, rather small umbo,* silky elsewhere, dry, cinnamon-brown to sordid alutaceous, at length minutely appressed-fibrillose-scaly. FLESH thin, pallid. GILLS sinuate-adnexed, *subdistant, ventricose,* pale grayish-white, then sordid cinnamon, edge white-fimbriate. STEM 2.5-3.5 cm. long, 2-4 mm. thick, equal, stuffed, subfibrillose, *soon glabrescent, pallid or slightly fuscous, slightly rufous upwards.* SPORES almond-shaped, almost golden-yellow in microscope, *smooth,* 10-13 x 5-6 micr. CYSTIDIA fuscoid-ventricose, on sides and edge of gills, apex crystallate, 60-70 x 13-14 micr. ODOR slightly rancid-subfarinaceous. TASTE sweetish.
Var. *rúfa:* Whole plant pale rufous to sordid brick color. STEM more slender, 5-6 cm. long, 1-2 mm. thick. SPORES inequilateral,

elongated-elliptic, subacute at ends, smooth. CYSTIDIA abundant, ventricose flask shaped.

Gregarious. The variety is common in swampy or mossy wet places on rich soil, of cedar and hemlock woods. It scarcely differs except in color from the typical form as described by Bresadola. The wet habitat easily accounts for the more slender stem. The color, however, is constant in young and old plants, or may become brownish on the cap. The typical form is less easily distinguished, and approaches *I. trechispora,* an angular-spored species. In fact, Bresadola has pointed out that Patouillard's figure No. 547, and Cooke's Plate 402 are illustrations of *I. trechispora.* June-September. In coniferous regions. Houghton, Bay View, New Richmond.

Section V. Viscidae. Pileus viscid, more or less silky when dry.

*Spores angular-tubercular.

493. Inocybe trechispora Berk.

Outlines of Brit. Fung., 1860.

Illustrations: Ibid, Pl. 8, Fig. 6.
Cooke, Ill., Pl. 403 (Pl. 402 as *I. scabella*).

PILEUS 2-2.5 cm. broad, convex, expanded-umbonate, *viscid,* silky when dry, *umbo tawny* and naked, elsewhere tawny-ochraceous and paler. GILLS sinuate-adnexed, moderately broad, ventricose, close, white then grayish-brown, edge white-fimbriate. STEM 2.5-5 cm. long, 2-3 mm. thick, subequal, usually tapering upwards, *marginate-bulbous at base,* glabrous, apex pruinose, solid, *white.* SPORES tubercular-angular, slightly longer than wide, irregular in outline, 6-8 x 4-6 micr. CYSTIDIA ventricose, flask-shaped, 50 x 16-18 micr., apex crystallate and obtuse.

Gregarious. On the ground, among debris, in conifer swamps. Houghton, Bay View, New Richmond. August-September. Infrequent.

A small species, known by its viscid pileus with shining, naked and tawny umbo, by the rather abruptly marginate bulb of the stem and by the tuberculate spores. Our plant agrees with Berkeley's species in the spore character as given by Massee. Ricken has applied the name to a plant with spores 14-15 x 6-7 micr.

**Spores smooth.*

494. Inocybe glaber sp. nov.

PILEUS 1.5-3.5 cm. broad, at first narrowly elliptic-oval, then campanulate-expanded and umbonate, *umbo glabrous-sublubricous,* sordid ochraceous-brown or livid-brown, at length darker on margin, paler on umbo, at first glabrous, at length subfibrillose, moist and shining, *becoming soft and fragile in moist weather.* FLESH thin. GILLS almost free, rather narrow, close, pallid then pale fuscous-brown, edge white-fimbriate. STEM 3-5 cm. long, 2.5-4 mm. thick, equal above the bulbillate base, glabrous, even, solid, white or pallid. SPORES subreniform, *smooth,* 7-9 x 4-5 micr. CYSTIDIA *none.* STERILE CELLS on edge of gills subcylindrical to rounded-enlarged at apex. ODOR nauseous to slightly radishy.

Gregarious. On the ground, in low frondose woods. Saginaw, Ann Arbor. July-September. Infrequent.

This species approaches the genus Hebeloma in some of the characters. The pileus becomes soft and watery at maturity and is easily crushed, and the odor is obsoletely of radish. The shape of the young pileus is however distinctly Inocybe-like, and the plants were found growing with a number of other Inocybes. It seems to approach *Hebeloma discomorbidum* Pk., but lacks the reddish tint on the cap, the hollow stem and the spores of that species. It is not truly viscid, even in moist weather, although the umbo is somewhat lubricous.

Hebeloma Fr.

(From the Greek, *hebe,* the vigor of youth, and *loma,* a fringe, referring to the presence of the cortina in the young plant.)

Ochre-brown-spored. Stem continuous with the pileus, *without a membranous annulus;* fleshy to fibrous; *partial veil in the form of a fibrillose cortina or lacking; no volva;* gills adnexed or emarginate; pileus *viscid or subviscid,* its margin at first incurved; *spores alutaceous,* never ferruginous.

Putrescent, *terrestrial,* often with a strong odor. They approach the terrestrial Pholiotas on the one hand, but without the membranous annulus, and Inocybe, Flammula and Cortinarius on the other. Inocybe differs in its silky or fibrillose-scaly pileus and verrucose-pointed cystidia; Flammula, in its non-emarginate, subdecurrent or broadly adnate gills, and mostly lignicolous habit; Cortinarius, in having a more delicately woven, spider web-like cortina and darker brown to ferruginous spores. Hebeloma corresponds to the genus Tricholoma of the white-spored group. Their *edibility* is not established and a number of species are under suspicion.

The PILEUS is glabrous, somewhat viscid, mostly with pale colors: whitish, tan, brownish, dingy ochraceous or rufous, often with shades of these colors variously distributed. The small amount of variation in the colors of different species makes it difficult to become rapidly acquainted with them, and often one has to rely on somewhat minute or variable characters to distinguish them. The young plants should always be examined for the fibrillose *veil or cortina* which disappears in most mature specimens and which is entirely wanting in one section. The viscidity should also be established before referring a plant to this genus since this is hardly noticeable in dry weather. The GILLS at length become emarginate, and this character, as in the genera Tricholoma and Entoloma, limits the genus. Variations sometimes occur in individual specimens, where the gills are adnate-decurrent or arcuate, and hence a single specimen is very unsatisfactory for a definite diagnosis. The edge of the gills is sometimes minutely fimbriate on account of the long sterile cells or cystidia and in a few species the edge distills drops of liquid which give it a beaded appearance under a lens; in many cases the edge remains white or whitish after the spores have colored the rest of the gills. The STEM often has a distinct outer, fleshy or fibrous rind which varies in thickness, while the interior, which is of varying diameter in different species, is stuffed by a white pith. While the stem is developing this pith breaks down leaving a hollow axis, although in some species the pith persists a long time. When no pith is present, the stem is said to be *solid* and is then composed of a fibrous texture which does not disappear. In both cases, however, grubs nearly always hollow out the stem at maturity, a condition which must be clearly distinguished from the term "hollow stem," which is not applied in that case. The SPORES are usually pale in color, ochraceous, brownish or alutaceous, coloring the mature gills a similar shade. The paler color of the gills and spores usually provides the means of separation from the genus Cortinarius. The shape of the spores varies but is generally elliptical-ovate, inequilateral and apiculate at one end; they are almost smooth except in a few species in which they are obscurely rough. CYSTIDIA are rather rare in this genus on the

sides of the gills, *H. albidulum* being the only one known to me
with cystidia. *Sterile cells,* usually elongated beyond the hymenium,
are found on the edge of the gills, and furnish important microscopic
details for the certain identification of many of the species of this
genus. Their shape and size vary, and at maturity they give to
the edge of the gills a white, fimbriate or flocculose appearance. The
ODOR is often like that of radish, especially when the flesh is
rubbed or bruised. The TASTE also is sometimes radishy or bitter
and disagreeable. McIlvaine, who studied the *edibility* of so many
mushrooms, has given us little information on this genus. Some are
probably poisonous, and as far as known, even where a species
has been proved harmless, the taste when cooked is not found to be
appetizing, so that the Hebelomas are hardly to be considered of
much value for the table. This is a difficult genus for the amateur,
and much uncertainty is prevalent, even in the minds of mycologists,
as to the limits of the species.

The genus may be divided into two sections, those with a cortina
when young, Indusiati; and those without a visible cortina, Denudati. It does not seem to me that Fries' section "Pusilli," which
included the smaller species, is a satisfactory grouping, and the
species which have been placed in "Pusilli" are distributed under
Indusiati and Denudati. Even the two divisions retained run into
each other imperceptibly.

Key to the Species

(A) Stem solid, rarely becoming cavernous.
  (a) Cortina present when young.
    (b) Edge of gills beaded with drops in moist weather; pileus pale
        yellowish-tan; odor of radish. 496. *H. fastibile* Fr.
    (bb) Edge of gills not beaded.
      (c) Cystidia numerous on gills; spores 6-7 x 3-4.5 micr.; gills
         arcuate-adnate, rather narrow; pileus yellowish-tan, etc. (See
         513. *Flammula lenta.*)
      (cc) Cystidia lacking; spores larger.
        (d) Pileus conical when young, 2-3 cm. broad, pale yellowish,
          clay-color, darker on disk; stem slender. 497. *H. mesopha-*
          eum Fr.
        (dd) Pileus soon convex, umbonate or subumbonate.
          (e) Growing in open woods, fields, bare places, etc.; pileus
            2-5 cm., brownish-clay-color, rufescent. 499. *H. pascuense*
            Pk.
          (ee) In coniferous woods; pileus 5-7 cm., mature gills dark.
            H. firmum Fr.
  (aa) Cortina not present.
    (b) Stem stout, scaly-torn, white; pileus large, sordid grayish-
        brown to pale tan, odor of radish. 500. *H. sinapizans* Fr.
    (bb) Stem flexuous, silky fibrillose, base enlarged by adhering sand;
        pileus alutaceous to tan. 508. *H. colvini* Pk.

(AA) Stem stuffed by a pith, or hollow.
  (a) Cortina present at first.
    (b) Pileus glutinous (wet), sprinkled with superficial white scales. *H. glutinosum* Fr. (See also *Flammula lenta*.)
    (bb) Pileus glabrous; gills whitish at first; odor of radish.
      (c) Cortina cottony-fibrillose, somewhat persistent on stem or on margin of pileus; pileus chestnut, reddish-gray or grayish. 495. *H. velatum* Pk.
      (cc) Cortina fugacious; pileus brick-red to reddish-ochraceous; spores 10-13 x 6-7 micr. *H. testaceum* Fr.
      (ccc) Cortina fugacious; stem slender; pileus 2-3 cm. broad, pale ochraceous-tan. 498. *H. gregarium* Pk.
  (aa) Cortina not present.
    (b) Gills bright flesh-colored or pink, turning brown only in extreme age; pileus chalk-white to dingy-white. 506. *H. sarcophyllum* Pk.
    (bb) Gills not pinkish.
      (c) Edge of gills beaded with drops in moist weather; odor strong; pileus pale tan, darker on disk. 501. *H. crustuliniforme* Fr.
      (cc) Edge of gills not beaded.
        (d) Stem short, 2-4 cm. in length.
          (e) Spores 12-13 x 6-7 micr.; pileus pale tan. 502. *H. hiemale* Bres.
          (ee) Spores 6-9 x 4-5 micr.
            (f) Pileus brick-red (moist), umbonate; spores 7-9 x 4-5 micr. 510. *H. magnimamma* Fr.
            (ff) Pileus yellowish-white, not umbonate; in pastures, etc. *H. sociale* Pk.
        (dd) Stem long and rather stout in normal specimens, white.
          (e) Stem bulbous; cystidia long, slender, cylindrical; pileus whitish. 504. *H. albidulum* Pk.
          (ee) Stem equal or attenuated downward.
            (f) Stem fragile, partially hollow; pileus whitish to tan; odor not of radish. 503. *H. longicaudum* Fr.
            (ff) Stem firm.
              (g) Pileus white or whitish, tinged tan.
                (h) Gills narrow, adnexed; pileus white; spores 12-16 x 6-8 micr. 507. *H. album* Pk.
                (hh) Gills rather broad, adnate at first; sterile cells on edge of gills clavate-thickened at apex; stem floccose; spores 11-13 x 6-7 micr. 505. *H. simile* sp. nov.
              (gg) Pileus darker colored.
                (h) Gills intervenose, costate; pileus ochraceous to tawny-ochraceous; edge of gills with clavate, sterile cells. Spores 12-15 x 7-8 micr. *H. neurophyllum* Atk.
                (hh) Gills not costate; pileus tinged reddish to ferruginous, with a viscid separable pellicle; spores 9-11 x 5-6 micr. 509. *H. syrjense* Karst.

Section I. Indusiati. Cortina present in young stage.

495. Hebeloma velatum Pk.

N. Y. State Mus. Bull. 139, 1909.

PILEUS 2-6 cm. broad, bullate-convex at first, then expanded, obtuse or umbonate, viscid (moist), glabrous, *becoming appressed-*

silky on drying, livid-bay, fading to tan with reddish disk, *margin decorated by the remains of cortina,* even.   FLESH white, thin, hygrophanous, soft and pliant.   GILLS adnexed-seceding, close, rather narrow, subventricose, whitish then alutaceous, edge minutely white-fimbriate.   STEM 3-6 cm. long, 4-6 mm. thick, equal, stuffed then hollow, *white at first then dingy ochraceous,* fibrous-fleshy, flexuous, twisted at times, pruinose-floccose at apex, *floccose above middle from the subpersistent cortina,* at length fibrillose, splitting longitudinally in age.   SPORES 10-12 x 5-7 micr., narrowly elliptic, acute at one end, subobtuse at distal end.   CYSTIDIA none; sterile cells on edge of gills short, slender, 30-45 x 6 micr.   ODOR and TASTE slight.

Gregarious.   Ground, in mixed woods.   New Richmond.   September.   Infrequent.

Peck says it is very variable in color and in the development of the cortina.   Sometimes a distinct annulus adheres to the stem and is then easily mistaken for a Pholiota, other specimens show a slight development of the cortina.   The odor of radish was slight in our specimens and the gills were hardly ventricose and rather narrow. It appears as a plant of small stature at times.   The colors of the pileus, the rather floccose stem, and the short sterile cells of the gills distinguish it.

496.   Hebeloma fastibile Fr.   (Suspected)

Syst. Myc., 1821.   Epicrisis, 1836.

Illustrations: Fries, Icones, Pl. 111.
        Patouillard, Tab. Analyt., No. 342.
        Ricken, Blätterpilze, Pl. 32, Fig. 1.

PILEUS 3-7 cm. broad, compact, convex-plane, often wavy, obtuse, viscid (moist), glabrous, *yellowish-ochraceous to alutaceous-whitish,* margin pubescent and incurved.   FLESH white.   GILLS *emarginate, subdistant,* unequal, whitish then argillaceous-cinnamon, *edge* white-fimbriate and *beaded with aqueous drops in moist weather.*   STEM 4-6 cm. long, 5-10 mm. thick, solid or slightly hollow, *firm,* bulbous, fibrillose, *white,* decorated above by the remains of the cortina which is sometimes annular.   SPORES 10-12 x 5-6 micr., elliptical-ovate, smooth.   CYSTIDIA clavate.   ODOR *disagreeable.*   TASTE *bitter.*

Gregarious. In woods. New Richmond, etc. Frequency unknown. September.

The beaded gills, color of pileus, subdistant to distant gills, odor and taste are the distinguishing features. The odor is somewhat of radish.

497. Hebeloma mesophæum Fr.

Epicrisis, 1836.

Illustrations: Cooke, Ill., Pl. 411.
        Ricken, Blätterpilze, Pl. 32, Fig. 3.

PILEUS 1-3 cm. broad, *campanulate or subconical at first,* then convex-expanded and subumbonate, sometimes wavy on margin, slightly viscid, buff to whitish on margin, brownish to chestnut or rufous on disk, glabrous, silky-shining, even, the margin at times decorated with the delicate remnants of the dingy-white cortina. GILLS soon emarginate, adnate, close, rather broad, whitish at first then pale rusty-alutaceous, edge white-fimbriate. STEM 4-6 cm. long, 3-5 mm. thick, mostly slender, fleshy-fibrous, *equal, silky-fibrillose,* sometimes twisted, mealy at apex, whitish, becoming dingy, with a small tubule. ODOR and TASTE slight.

Gregarious to subcaespitose. On sandy ground among grass or on bare ground in woods, fields, etc. Ann Arbor. October. Sometimes frequent.

Known by its rather small, subconical pileus when young, its tough, equal stem, peculiar cast to the pileus and lack of a distinctive odor. The spores are rather larger than the size given by Massee, but otherwise it agrees well with Fries' description. The stem is at first solid but develops a slight tubule in age. It differs from *H. hiemale* in the presence of a cortina which sometimes forms a slight, fugacious ring on the stem. Dried, the cap and stem remain whitish-tan. The surface of the cap is often quite silky. Ricken says it is known by its rusty-brown flesh when old, a character I have not noticed.

498. Hebeloma gregarium Pk.

N. Y. State Mus. Rep. 49, 1896.

PILEUS 1.5-3 cm. broad, *convex,* obtuse, slightly viscid, isabelline to ochraceous-tan, sometimes darker on disk, glabrous, even.

FLESH rather thin, *whitish*. GILLS adnate at first, then emarginate, close, thin, rather broad, subventricose, whitish at first then rusty-cinnamon. STEM 4-10 cm. long; 2-4 mm. thick, slender, equal, *stuffed then hollow*, subcartilaginous, fibrillose below, slightly mealy at apex, pallid, at length dingy-brown. SPORES 9-12 x 5-6 micr., variable, elliptical, smooth, alutaceous-cinnamon in mass. CYSTIDIA none. ODOR strong, radishy or almost lacking. TASTE slightly disagreeable. CORTINA scanty, fibrillose, evanescent.

(Dried: Pileus rusty-tan to brown, gills cinnamon-brown, stem sordid brownish.)

Gregarious. Under shrubbery or trees, on lawns, etc. Ann Arbor, East Lansing. May, June, September, October. Infrequent.

This species is closely related to *H. mesophaeum*. Its spores are the same, and usually it has a similar stature. As far as I can see, *H. gregarium* is distinguished from *H. mesophaeum* only by its darker gills and spores, its truly convex pileus and sometimes by its odor. Specimens identified by Peck as his species were compared with the above. It has been reported by Peck and others as occurring in October and November although I have seen it also in early spring, a seasonal distribution quite frequent in the case of certain species of mushrooms. Its cortina and general appearance suggest a Cortinarius; it is clearly not distantly related to that genus and I suspect has been referred to it more often than to Hebeloma. On drying it becomes much darker than *H. mesaphaeum,* as the latter is diagnosed above. It has slender sterile cells on the edge of the gills.

499. Hebeloma pascuense Pk.

N. Y. State Mus. Rep. 53, 1900.

Illustrations: Ibid, Pl. C, Fig. 21-27.
Hard, Mushrooms, Fig. 222, p. 274.

PILEUS 2-5 cm. broad, convex then plane, obtuse, viscid when moist, *brownish-clay color,* tinged rufous on disk, becoming pale (dry), subhygrophanous, glabrous, *innately streaked* or *variegated by fibrils,* margin whitish at first from the cortina. FLESH whitish. GILLS adnexed, becoming ventricose and sinnuate, *rather broad,* close, pallid then pale ochraceous-cinnamon, edge white-fimbriate at first. STEM 2-5 cm. long, 3-6 mm. thick, solid or apex hollow, sometimes with a tubule, cortex subcartilaginous, fibrillose or subfloccose, apéx floccose-scurfy, often somewhat twisted or curved, pallid but soon darker or tinged umber toward base. COR-TINA cobwebby, evanescent, slight remnants at apex of stem or on margin of pileus. SPORES 8-10 x 4-6 micr. (mostly 8-9 x 4-5), ellip-tical, smooth, pale ochraceous-cinnamon in mass. CYSTIDIA none; *sterile cells* on edge of gills are prominent, *cylindrical.* 40-50 x 4-5 micr. ODOR radishy.

Gregarious or subcaespitose. On denuded or grassy soil in open, pastured woods or similar places, often on sterile, gravelly soil. Washtenaw County. May and June (as early as May 3). Frequent locally.

This Hebeloma loves sterile or gravelly soil which has scanty grass. It is early with us, although Peck reports it for October. In its seasonal habit it corresponds, therefore, with *H. gregarium* from which it differs in size, color, and its smaller spores. Peck says it is closely related to *H. fastibile* but is smaller, with a more slender stem, differently colored pileus and more crowded gills. The margin of the pileus sometimes shows a differentiated brown zone. Small forms are easily confused with *H. hiemale,* except for the spores and the presence of a cortina.

Section II. Denudati. Cortina lacking.

500. Hebeloma sinapizans Fr.

Epicrisis, 1836.

Illustrations: Cooke, Ill., Pl. 413.
Plate XCVII of this Report.

PILEUS 6-12 cm. broad, *compact,* convex-expanded, obtuse, *viscid* (moist), glabrous, even, somewhat irregular, *ashy-brown to clay-color* or whitish-tan, sordid. FLESH thick, soft in age. GILLS adnexed to deeply emarginate, *broad,* close, dry, pallid then pale alutaceous-cinnamon, *edge entire and concolor.* STEM stout, 6-12 cm. long, 1.5-2.5 cm. thick, rigid, *equal,* even or striate above, fibril-lose, upper part *becoming squarrose-scaly* from the tearing of the cuticle, stuffed but soon cavernous, *white* then dingy, apex squamu-lose-floccose. SPORES broadly elliptical, hyaline-apiculàte at both ends, obscurely rough, 11-13 x 7-8 micr., pale-cinnamon in mass. CYSTIDIA none. ODOR and TASTE usually strongly of radish.

In troops, subcaespitose or gregarious. On the ground, wooded hillsides, oak, maple and beech woods. Washtenaw County. September. Infrequent.

This is one of our largest and most luxurious Hebelomas, appearing after heavy rains. The stout, scaly-torn white stem, lack of cortina, broad gills and large spores, distinguish it. In age and in wet weather it decays rapidly. Fries says it is solitary, but with us it grows in troops as described by Stevenson, often forming dense rows along hillsides where Cortinarii flourish. Cooke's figures illustrate our plant well. It approaches *H. sinuosum* Fr. (sense of Ricken).

501. Hebeloma crustuliniforme Fr.

Epicrisis, 1836.

Illustrations: Michael, Führer f. Pilzfreunde, Vol. II, No. 69.
Engler and Prantl. I, 1**, Fig. 117, p. 242.
Swanton, Fungi, Pl. 40, Fig. 5-6, 1909.
Cooke's Illus., Pl. 507.
Ricken, Blätterpilze, Pl. 32, Fig. 2.
Plate XCVII of this Report.

PILEUS 4-8 cm. broad, broadly convex, then plane, subrepand, slightly viscid (moist), glabrous, even, *pale whitish-tan, disk reddish* or yellowish, *zoneless,* margin at first incurved. FLESH thickish, rather firm, white. GILLS adnexed, *crowded,* narrow, rounded behind, thin, whitish then watery cinnamon-brown, *edge crenulate and beaded with drops* when young or moist. STEM 4-8 cm. long, 4-6 mm. thick, equal or subbulbous, stuffed then hollow, somewhat *floccose-squamulose,* glabrous below, white or whitish, pruinose at apex. SPORES 10-12 x 5-7 micr., apiculate, ovoid elliptical, smooth, pale brown. Sterile cells on edge of gills, cylindric-saccate, 24-30 x 6 micr., abundant. ODOR strong of radish. TASTE disagreeable. Said to be *poisonous.*

Solitary or gregarious, sometimes forming interrupted rings. In frondose grassy woods. Washtenaw County. October. Infrequent.

The description given above is that of the continental mycologists. My own notes and specimens were lost.

Form *minor:* is smaller, pileus 2-3 cm. broad. It has no cystidia on the sides of the gills, and the spores measure 8-10 x 5-7 micr. Sterile cells on the edge of the gills are clavate at the apex. The edge of the gills exudes drops. Found in the same woods as the type.

Form *sphagnophilum:* These plants grew on dense sphagnum. PILEUS 4-7 cm. broad. STEM 7-9 cm. by 5-8 mm. There are no cystidia on the sides of the gills; the sterile cells on the edge are slender, slightly thickened below, cylindrical above. The edge of the gills distils drops. The odor, when the plants are fresh, is similar to alcohol ethers. Otherwise as the type. See Plate XCVII of this Report.

The most striking characteristic of this species and its varieties is their habit of distilling drops from the gills when fresh or moist. In this respect it imitates *H. fastibile,* but lacks the cortina and has more crowded gills. It is considered poisonous, and is said to be called "poison-pie" in England, no doubt because the color of the cap simulates a baked pie crust. In dry weather it is easily confused with other species, and the occurence of the forms mentioned above shows that it needs further study. It does not seem to be as common here as in Europe.

502. Hebeloma hiemale Bres.

Fungi Tridentini, 1892.

Illustration: Ibid, Pl. 160.

"PILEUS rather fleshy, 2-4.5 cm. broad, convex-subhemispherical then plane and gibbous or depressed, viscid, glabrous, margin at first involute and white flocculose, pale alutaceous, marked by a crustuline center or broad zone. GILLS crowded, white then argillaceous-subcinnamon, edge white-floccose, sinuate-adnate or adnexed and almost free. STEM 2-3 cm. long, 5-7 mm. thick, white, becoming yellowish below, stuffed then somewhat hollow, equal, subfibrillose, apex white-furfuraceous. Spores obversely pyriform, 12-13 x 6-7 micr., golden-yellow under the microscope; basidia clavate, 30-35 x 7-8 micr. ODOR scarcely any. TASTE somewhat bitter.

"Approaching nearest to *H. crustuliniforme,* from which it differs by its constantly smaller stature and scarcely noticeable odor."

The description is that of Bresadola, as my own notes are not full enough. It is with some hesitancy included under Michigan species but is said to occur in the United States and is easily confused with the preceding. It is at least of value to make Bresadola's description accessible in English.

503. Hebeloma longicaudum Fr.

Syst. Mycol., 1821.

Illustrations: Cooke, Ill., Pl. 415.
   Gillet, Champignons de France, No. 309.
   Berkeley, Outlines, Pl. 9, Fig. 2.
   Ricken, Blätterpilze, Pl. 33, Fig. 2.

PILEUS 3-6 cm. broad, convex-expanded, subumbonate, glabrous, viscid (moist), even, somewhat irregular, *pale ochraceous-tan,* becoming whitish. FLESH soft, watery, white. GILLS *arcuate-adnate* then emarginate, medium broad, narrowed behind, crowded, whitish then pale clay-color, edge minutely fimbriate. STEM 5-10 cm. long, 4-9 mm. thick, *white,* equal, subbulbous below, stuffed then somewhat hollow, *fragile,* fibrillose-striate, mealy at apex or throughout. SPORES obliquely-elliptical, inequilateral, narrow at one end, smooth, 12-15 x 6-7 micr. CYSTIDIA none. *Sterile cells* slender, slightly enlarged at base, numerous on edge of gills. ODOR scarcely noticeable or none. TASTE mild, not of radish.

Gregarious. In or near cedar and tamarack swamps, sometimes on sphagnum, sometimes on rich humus. Ann Arbor, New Richmond. September-November. Infrequent.

The white stem, medium size, lack of cortina and large spores distinguish this species. The white-stemmed species of Hebeloma are quite distinct from those with sordid or brownish stems, although the former may become dingy or brownish by handling. The gills are at first adnate-decurrent and often do not become emarginate until late maturity, a character found in several other species. European authors do not agree upon the size of the spores for this species and usually give smaller spores; but our plant agrees so well with descriptions and the figures referred to above that it seems best to place it here. It differs from *H. elatum,* for which Massee gives large spores, by its lack of a radish odor, and the smaller average size of the pileus. Two other related species with persistently white stems were found at New Richmond: (a) had a more slender stem up to 9 cm. long, tapering downward, flocculose at apex, elsewhere innately fibrillose-striate; its pileus was up to 7 cm. broad, yellowish ochre on disk and white on margin; gills rather broad; odor none. (b) was smaller, with a stem about 5 cm. long, hollow and torn-scaly as in *H. sinapizans;* its cap was testaceous-tan and it had a radishy odor. Both forms had spores 9-12 x 5-6 micr. in size. They need further study.

504. Hebeloma albidulum Pk.

N. Y. State Mus. Rep. 54, 1901.

PILEUS 3-6 cm. broad, convex-expanded, obtuse, *glabrous,* viscid (moist), dingy-white, buff, or tinged ochraceous or grayish, even. FLESH white, thick on disk. GILLS adnexed, emarginate, *narrow, crowded,* whitish then isabelline to pale rusty-brownish, minutely white-fimbriate on edge. STEM 3-9 cm. long, 4-10 mm. thick, equal or subbulbous at base, glabrous and innately *silky-shining,* stuffed then hollow, *white,* pruinose at apex. SPORES elliptical, inequilateral, 10-12.5 x 5-7 micr., pale-brownish under the microscope, smooth. CYSTIDIA rather abundant on sides and edge of gills, *cylindrical,* slender, obtuse, about 75 x 5-6 micr. Odor none; taste mild.

(Dried: Pileus rufous-brown to tan; gills rusty-brown; stem pallid to dingy white.)

Gregarious to subcaespitose. On the ground, mixed or frondose woods. Ann Arbor, New Richmond. September-October. Infrequent.

Definitely known by its peculiar cylindrical cystidia; its dingy-white or ochraceous-buff pileus, white stem and narrow gills also help to place it. It is related to *H. album* Pk. which has larger spores, measuring 12-16 x 6-8 micr., and a more persistent white pileus and stem. Both *H. albidulum* and *H. album* can be easily distinguished from *H. sarcophyllum* which is also a pure white species, by the pink gills of the latter. *H. neurophyllum* Atk. may also be confused with it. Some of our specimens had a rather abrupt, oblique and marginate bulb, in this respect approaching Cortinarii, but fresh young specimens lack the cortina. The gills and spores have a peculiar shade of brown, showing their relation to *H. sarcophyllum.*

505. Hebeloma simile sp. nov.

PILEUS 2-6 cm. broad, convex-expanded, whitish tinged ochraceous, subviscid (moist), lustre dull (dry), glabrous, even. FLESH thick on disk, white. GILLS adnate at first, becoming emarginate, *rather broad,* not crowded, ventricose, thin, whitish then alutaceous, edge minutely floccose-denticulate, not costate. STEM 3-8 cm. long, 2-5 mm. thick, *slender,* equal, *not bulbous, white, floccose to mealy throughout,* glabrescent, at length innately fibrillose-striatulate, *stuffed with a persistent pith,* white within and without, texture fibrous. SPORES fusiform-elliptical, inequilateral, smooth or obscurely rough, apiculate, 11-13 x 6-7 micr. CYSTIDIA none. *Sterile cells* on edge of gills, *clavate-thickened at apex,* 55-65 micr. long. ODOR and TASTE slightly of radish.

(Dried: Pileus and stem whitish, dingy; gills cinnamon-brown.)

Gregarious. On the ground, in copses, woods, etc., among grass. Ann Arbor, Detroit. September-October. Infrequent.

Differs from *H. neurophyllum* Atk. in the lack of costate gills, the persistent pith of the stem, smaller spores and broader gills. Its *sterile cells* are clavate-thickened like the upper portion of many paraphyses among the Pezizaceae, a character which is said to belong to the sterile cells on the gills of *H. neurophyllum* Atk. It differs from *H. album* Pk. by the broader gills, floccose-mealy stem and smaller spores; and from *H. albidulum* by the lack of cystidia, broader gills, etc.

506. Hebeloma sarcophyllum Pk.

N. Y. State Cab. Rep. 23, 1872.

Illustrations: Ibid, Pl. I, Fig. 7-11.

PILEUS 3-6 cm. (or more) broad, *chalk-white,* becoming dingy white, convex, obtuse, glabrous, subviscid (moist), soon dry, even. FLESH white, thickish. GILLS rather narrow, adnexed, *deeply emarginate,* close, *deep rose to flesh color,* edge minutely fimbriate. STEM 3-8 cm. long, 4-8 mm. thick, equal or tapering upward, clavate-bulbous at first,*white,* firm, stuffed by a persistent pith, finally hollow, fibrillose, glabrescent, minutely scurfy-mealy at apex, subshining. SPORES ventricose-elliptical, subinequilateral, ovate-pointed at both ends, obscurely rough, at first *deep-flesh color in mass,* but changing to dark brown, 9-12 x 5-6 micr. STERILE CELLS on edge of gills, cylindrical, slender, 5-6 micr. diam. CYSTIDIA similar, rarely found. ODOR subfarinaceous, TASTE bitterish.

Solitary, scattered or gregarious. On grassy ground, in frondose or mixed woods. Ann Arbor, Huron Mountains. June-August. Infrequent.

Remarkable for the deep pinkish color of the mature gills and spores which simulate those of a Psalliota. There is no cortina, else the shape and structure of the spores would indicate a Cortinarius. The spores lose their pink color in the herbarium. Luxuriant specimens, with caps 15 cm. across, have been found, whose surface was minutely silky-floccose. When fresh the plants present a beautiful appearance because of their chalky whiteness of cap and stem as contrasted with the deep flesh-colored gills. It is an aberrant species and approaches the genus Entoloma.

507. Hebeloma album Pk.

N. Y. State Mus. Rep. 54, 1901.

Illustrations: Ibid, Pl. G, Fig. 1-7.
  N. Y. State Mus. Bull. 139, Pl. 117, Fig. 1-6, 1910.

"PILEUS 2.5-5 cm. broad, fleshy, firm, convex becoming nearly plane, or concave by the margin curving upward, glabrous, subviscid, *white or yellowish-white.* FLESH white. GILLS thin, *narrow,* close, sinuate, adnexed, whitish *becoming brownish-ferruginous.* STEM 3.5-7 cm. broad, 4-6 mm. thick, equal, firm, rather long, *solid or stuffed,* slightly mealy at the top, *white.* SPORES subellipsoid, pointed at both ends, 12-16 x 6-8 micr."

Specimens sent from Detroit have been referred by Peck to this species. Its large spores, narrow gills and white or almost white cap distinguish it from related species. Compare *H. albidulum, H. simile* and *H. sarcophyllum.*

508. Hebeloma colvini Pk.

N. Y. State Mus. Rep. 28, 1876.

"PILEUS 2-7.5 cm. broad, convex or nearly plane, sometimes gibbous or broadly umbonate, rarely centrally depressed, glabrous, grayish or alutaceous with an ochraceous tint. GILLS close, broad, sinuate, adnexed, whitish, becoming brownish-ochraceous. STEM 2-8 cm. long, 2-6 mm. thick, equal, flexuous, silky-fibrillose, stuffed or hollow above, solid toward the base, whitish. SPORES ellipsoid, 10-12 x 5-6 micr. Sandy soil in open places. The mycelium binds the sand into a globose mass which adheres to the base of the stem."

The description is that of Peck. One collection at New Richmond is closely related. The plants grew in sand which adhered to the cap and stem. Our plants varied from the type in having narrow gills and a solid stem which becomes cavernous.

509. Hebeloma syrjense Karst.

PILEUS 2-5.5 cm. broad, convex-expanded, firm, glabrous, *viscid,* provided with a gelatinous, separable pellicle, even, *rufous or brick-red,* fading to ochraceous-brown, margin at first incurved. FLESH toughish, pallid or tinged rufous-brown. GILLS adnate at first, then emarginate, close, moderately broad, whitish then rufous-brown to cinnamon-brown, edge obscurely flocculose. STEM 4-6 cm. long, 3-5 mm. thick, subequal or attenuated downward, *floccose-scaly above,* glabrescent below, *toughish,* elastic, stuffed then hollow, whitish, becoming sordid brownish below, even. SPORES elliptical, inequilateral, apiculate, smooth, 8-10.5 x 5-6 micr., pale rusty-cinnamon in mass. CYSTIDIA none. *Sterile cells* short, slender, cylindrical, on edge of gills. ODOR slight. TASTE slightly astringent.

Gregarious or caespitose. On the ground in frondose woods. Ann Arbor. September-October. Infrequent.

This species has the appearance of a Cortinarius, but no cortina is present in the young stage; on this account it is also to be distinguished from *H. testaceum.* The brick-red color, caespitose stems and separable pellicle are characteristic features. The somewhat tough texture is also a marked character. When young, the pileus is often bay-brown and in age may become irregular or repand.

510. Hebeloma magnimamma Fr.

Hymen. Europaei, 1874.

Illustration: Cooke, Ill., Pl. 508.

PILEUS 1-2 cm. broad, *umbonate,* convex, *brick-red* (moist), paler on margin, fading, glabrous, viscid (moist), even. GILLS adnate, close, thin, narrow, width uniform, ochraceous-isabelline, edge white-fimbriate. STEM 3-4 cm. long, 1-2 mm. thick, equal, even, *glabrous,* narrowly fistulose, pallid-ochraceous, apex pruinose. SPORES elliptical, smooth, mostly with a large nucleus, 7-9 x 4-5 micr. *Sterile cells* on edge of gills numerous, narrow-cylindrical, about 65 x 4-5 micr.

Gregarious. Ground in cedar swamp. New Richmond. September. Rare.

Flammula Fr.

(From the Latin, *flamma,* a flame.)

Ochre-brown to rusty-spored. Stem central, continuous with the pileus, without an annulus, *fleshy or fibrous;* partial veil in the form of a fibrillose or subarachnoid cortina, evanescent. Gills *adnate or subdecurrent at first.* Spores *dark brown, rusty-brown or rusty-yellow.* Pileus viscid or dry. Mostly *on wood.*

Fleshy, putrescent, lignicolous, rarely terrestrial fungi, characterized by the habitat and the spore-color. To be separated from Pholiota by the non-membranous inner veil; from Hebeloma by the darker brown or rusty-yellow gills and spores; from Naucoria by the fleshy-fibrous stem; from Continarius by the habitat on wood. It corresponds to Hypholoma of the purple-spored group in habit. By reason of the bitter taste or odor, the Flammulas are not attractive for food, and although no definite information is available to prove that they are not edible, they are usually considered unpalatable and looked upon with suspicion. The genus is difficult and the species appear to run into one another. They occur mostly in the northern forests.

The PILEUS is often very viscid, with a separable pellicle, or, in the section Sapineae, with a dry adnate cuticle; it is usually tinged with yellowish, olivaceous or fuscous hues. The margin or surface is sometimes dotted with thin, fibrillose scales but becomes denuded in age or after rains; it is therefore important to obtain fresh plants for study. The fibrillose *cortina* is more copious in some species than in others and this fact must be kept in mind. The GILLS are referred to by authors as adnate-decurrent and some emphasize the decurrent character as a means of recognizing the genus; there is, however, considerable variation in this respect, and more often the gills are adnate or slightly rounded behind and in age may become emarginate as in related genera. The color of the gills at maturity is conditioned by the spores and is markedly different in the first and last section. *F. polychroa* is unique by the gray and purplish hues which cloud them. *F. carbonaria* has dark dirty-brown gills. In the last section they are bright rusty-ochre or yellow. The STEM is fleshy or fibrous, usually more or less fibrillose, glabrescent, mostly naked at the apex and with a tendency to become darker, sordid, brown or rusty in age, especially at or toward the base. The SPORES are usually elliptical or oval, smooth or slightly rough under high magnification. A spore-print is very important for the diagnosis of species, because of the considerable difference in the color. CYSTIDIA are present and rather abundant on the sides and edge of the gills. The ODOR is an important character and was frequently employed by Fries, especially in the Monographia, to separate the species. The TASTE is often bitter, sometimes strong, and tends to turn away the searcher who is after edible mushrooms.

The species are not yet well understood, especially in this country. Peck has described some twenty-five species but most of these are poorly known. Only about half of my different collections have been included here since the rest are still doubtfully determined. Few species seem to be common at least in the southern part of the State but it is likely that more species occur in the north during favorable seasons.

Key to the Species

(A)   Pileus dry, golden-tawny, minutely floccose-scaly; gills chrome-yellow. 519. *F. sapinea* Fr.

(AA) Pileus glutinous, viscid, subviscid or moist.
  (a)   Gills grayish to olive-purplish-fuscous; pileus glutinous, with superficial scales. 511. *F. polychroa* Berk.
  (aa) Gills without gray or purple tints.
    (b)   Pileus 6-12 cm. or more broad, viscid, flesh white. 512. *F. lubrica* Fr.
    (bb) Pileus 3-8 cm. broad, glutinous; flesh white. 513. *F. lenta* Fr.
    (bbb) Pileus 2-7 cm. broad; flesh yellowish.
      (c)   Gills smoky-brown to fuscous-brown; pileus not truly yellow. 514. *F. carbonaria* Fr. var.
      (cc) Gills yellow or pallid-ochraceous.
        (d)   Pileus with viscid or glutinous separable pellicle.
          (e)   Pileus sulphur-yellow, with fulvous center; stem slender; flesh thin. 515. *F. spumosa* Fr.
          (ee) Pileus pale ochraceous-olivaceous-buff; flesh thick. 517. *F. gummosa* Fr.
        (dd) Pileus without a viscid pellicle.
          (e)   Odor strong, bitter; pileus pale, cadmium-yellow, lubricous; stem elongated. 518. *F. alnicola* Fr.
          (ee) Odor slight or none; pileus bright yellow, glabrous, margin cortinate; 516. *F. flavida* Fr.

Section I.   Phaeotae. Spore mass sordid brown. Pileus with a more or less viscid or glutinous, separable pellicle.

511.   Flammula polychroa Berk.

Lea's Catalog, Plants, Cinn. 1844.

Illustrations: Atkinson, Mushrooms, Fig. 147, p. 156, 1900.
    Moffatt, Chicago, Nat. Hist. Surv., Bull. No. VII, Part I, Pl. 10, Figs. 1-2, 1909.

PILEUS 3-7 cm. broad, broadly convex, then expanded, obtusely depressed, sometimes broadly umbonate, very viscid, *varying dull orange to yellowish on disk, paler yellowish toward the olive or greenish margin,* in age variegated yellowish-olivaceous-brown, at first *decorated toward margin by wedge-shaped, creamy to vina- ceous, fibrillose, detersile, delicate scales,* concentrically arranged, the outermost forming an interrupted fringe at the edge of the pileus, glabrescent in age, margin even, at first incurved. FLESH soft, moist, thick on disk, thin on margin, yellowish-white. GILLS adnate, rounded behind or sinuate, often seceding or subdecurrent in age, rather broad behind, tapering anteriorly, close to crowded, at the very first creamy-buff, soon grayish-fuscous, *finally dark olive purplish-gray,* edge white-flocculose. STEM 3-6 cm. long, 3-5 mm. thick, *slender,* rigid-tough, subequal, curved, solid-fibrous with- in, in age hollow, fibrillose and *dotted with small, recurved scales up to the evanescent annulus,* yellowish above, becoming dull red- dish-brown below. VEIL rather well-developed at the first, vary- ing white to vinaceous, lilac or purplish-tinged, floccose-fibrillose. SPORES oval or short oblong, 6-7.5 x 3.5-4.5 micr., smooth, dark, fuscous-brown *with a slight purplish tinge in mass.* CYSTIDIA numerous on sides and edge of gills, subventricose below, lanceolate above, about 55 micr. long.

Solitary to subcaespitose. On logs, sticks, dead branches, etc., frondose and mixed coniferous woods.

Marquette, New Richmond, Ann Arbor, etc. Throughout the State. July-October. Rather frequent.

This species is distinguished from all the other Flammulas by the peculiar color of the gills and spores; the tint of gray and purple which these possess may easily lead the student into plac- ing it among the purple-spored genera. The other characters, however, ally it to the genus Flammula. The colors of the pileus are, furthermore, quite variable, but there is nearly always an olivaceous tint present, especially on the margin when young. The pelliculose cap is usually glutinous and when fresh dotted with the triangular, hairy, appressed scales. It is apparently indigenous to America.

512.   Flammula lubrica Fr.

Syst. Myc., 1821.

Illustrations: Fries, Icones, Pl. 116, Fig. 1.
 Ricken, Blätterpilze, Pl. 57, Fig. 4.

PILEUS 6-12 cm. broad, tough, broadly convex, then expanded, obtuse or depressed, *tawny-orange or fulvous on disk,* yellowish on margin, sometimes paler, with a separable, *viscid* pellicle, loosely *scaly-dotted,* glabrescent, even.   FLESH whitish, moist, rather thick, tinged yellow under pellicle.   GILLS adnate, then emarginate or seceding, sometimes subdecurrent or uncinate, medium broad, close to crowded, sulphur-yellow to greenish-yellow, *then dingy-ochre to olive-brown,* edge minutely fimbriate.   STEM 4-6 cm. long, 8-15 mm. thick, equal or slightly tapering downwards, curved or straight, subbulbous at base, spongy-solid or hollowed by grubs, at first *whitish within and without,* tinged yellowish or at base rusty-brown in age, fibrillose.   SPORES minute, elliptical, 5-6 x 3-3.5 micr., smooth, pale rusty-brown in mass.   CYSTIDIA very abundant on sides and edge of gills, ventricose, obtuse, 45 x 12-15 micr., rarely longer.   ODOR and TASTE mild or very slightly of radish.

Gregarious or subcaespitose.   On decaying logs in mixed or frondose, low woods.   Bay View, New Richmond.   September.   Infrequent or local.

Our plant departs slightly from the accepted characters for the species.   It is known by its large size, viscid or glutinous, scaly-dotted, yellow-tawny cap and whitish stem when fresh.   The colors of the pileus are shown in the figures of Fries, although a form, such as is shown in Ricken's figure, has been found in the same locality with the Friesian plant.   The flesh of both forms is white in the fresh plant.   The color of the spore-mass indicates the next section; but it must not be confused with *F. spumosa* which is a smaller plant, whose cap is not dotted with scales, and whose flesh is greenish-yellow.   *F. lubrica* appears to be limited to the coniferous regions of the State.

513. Flammula lenta Fr.

Syst. Myc., 1821.

Illustrations: Cooke, Ill., Pl. 439 and 440.
Gillet, Champignons de France, No. 284.
Ricken, Blätterpilze, Pl. 57, Fig. 3.

PILEUS 3-7 cm. broad, firm, convex-expanded, obtuse, *glutinous,* dotted toward margin with scattered, concentric, superficial, fibrillose scales, or glabrous and white-silky on the incurved margin, *dingy white to buff,* brownish-tan on disk, even. FLESH pallid, slightly thick. GILLS adnate-subdecurrent, rather narrow, close, white at first then pale alutaceous, buff-color, edge minutely white-flocculose. STEM 4-7 cm. long, 8-11 mm. thick, varying equal, tapering down or subbulbous, stuffed then narrowly tubular, firm, floccose-pruinose at apex, floccose-scaly up to the obsolete annulus, white, becoming brownish toward base in age. SPORES elliptical, slightly curved, smooth, pale, 5-7 x 3.5-4 micr., grayish-brown in mass. CYSTIDIA abundant on sides and edge of gills, lanceolate, ventricose, obtuse at apex, 50-55 x 12 micr., deep in the subhymenium. ODOR and TASTE slight.

On decaying logs or on the ground among debris in conifer woods. New Richmond. September. Infrequent.

Known by its pale color, glutinous cap and the remnants of the whitish cortina on the margin of the cap or on the stem. It differs from *F. lubrica* mainly in color, especially in the color of the gills. It is seldom reported in this country, although very abundant in Europe. The flesh is white. *Hebeloma glutinosum* also has a glutinous, scaly-dotted pileus, but the gills are said to be emarginate, and the flesh of the stem to become blackish toward the base. (Ricken, Blätterpilze.) In drier weather the pileus is less viscid and may appear to be entirely naked. It is easily mistaken for a Hebeloma because of its pale gills and its frequent development on the ground. *Hebeloma parvifructum* Pk. may be a form of this species, although Peck does not report any cystidia.

514. Flammula carbonaria Fr. var.

Syst. Myc., 1821.

Illustration: Cooke, Ill., Pl. 442.

PILEUS 2-6 cm. broad, pliant, convex, *then plane,* usually de-pressed in age, more or less viscid or subviscid, pellicle somewhat separable, dull crustuline to fulvous-yellowish, *dull dingy-rufous-brown in age,* disk rusty-yellow, glabrous, even, at first with rem-nants of cortina on edge. FLESH pallid then tinged yellowish, rather thin. GILLS adnate-subdecurrent, sinuate in age, crowded, rather narrow, at first pallid, *finally pale smoky-brown or fuscous-brown,* edge white-fimbriate. STEM 3-5 cm. long, 3-5 mm. thick at apex, *tapering downwards,* tough, rigid-elastic, flexible, dilated and cavernous at apex, elsewhere soon *hollowed in form of tubule,* fibrillose, at length *dark sordid-brown or smoky-fuscous,* curved or bulbillose at attached base. SPORES elliptic-oblong, smooth, 6-7.5 x 3.5-4 micr., pale ochraceous under microscope, *solid fuscous-brown in mass.* CYSTIDIA on sides and edge of gills, scattered, flask-shaped to subcylindrical, variable, 30-55 x 10-15 micr. ODOR and TASTE slight or mild.

Solitary, gregarious or caespitose, on roots, sticks, stumps, etc., in low, swampy woods or wet places. New Richmond, Ann Arbor. September-October. Infrequent.

At least two forms have been referred here: a small plant, with cap 2-3 cm. broad, growing on burnt-over ground, and a larger plant not always on charcoal remains, to which I have referred my collections. Cooke's figures illustrate our plants well except in the slightly smaller size. The principal characteristic is the color of gills and spores, in which it approaches *F. fuscus.* No critical notes of such a plant other than the description of *F. carbonarius* are at hand, and authors vary considerably in their conception of it except that they hold closely to the idea that it occurs always on charred soil or wood. Hard illustrates what appears to be the small form, and Ricken likewise emphasizes the small size in which respect they follow the Friesian tradition. Under this name Peck has described a still different form, whose spores measure 7-10 x 4-5 micr., and which also grows on charcoal beds. The species clearly needs further study in this country, as it is not likely that either Peck's or my plants represent the Friesian species. *F. high-landensis* Pk. may represent the true species.

Section II. *Caespitose,* spores rusty-brown in mass. Caespitose or crowded. Pileus with subviscid, subseparable pellicle.

515. Flammula spumosa Fr.

Syst. Myc., 1821.

Illustrations: Fries, Icones, Pl. 116, Fig. 3.
Cooke, Ill., Pl. 475.
Ricken, Blätterpilze, Pl. 57, Fig. 5.

PILEUS 2-5 cm. broad, convex-plane, with viscid, separable pellicle, *sulphur-yellow,* sometimes greenish-tinged, fulvous on center, paler on margin, glabrous, even, sometimes obscurely virgate, provided when young with a yellowish-white cortina on the margin. FLESH *yellowish or greenish-yellowish,* rather thin. GILLS adnate-emarginate or decurrent by a tooth, close, moderately broad, *sulphur-yellow or greenish-yellow at first,* finally pale ferruginous. STEM 3-7 cm. long, 3-7 mm. thick, *often slender,* equal, hollow by a narrow tubule which is at first stuffed, *fibrillose,* yellowish above, soon sordid rusty-fulvous toward base. SPORES elliptic-oval, smooth, 6-8 x 4-5 micr., contracted toward one end. CYSTIDIA on sides and edge of gills, 60-70 x 12 micr., lanceolate-ventricose. ODOR slight or of radish.

Gregarious or scattered. On the ground among forest debris or on mossy logs, etc., in coniferous regions in moist places. Marquette, Houghton, Bay View, New Richmond, Detroit. July-September. Rather frequent.

This is probably as common as any of the Flammulas but is to be sought in the regions once covered with hemlock or pine. The color of the pileus and flesh varies from youth to age, becoming darker or more dingy, and individual specimens vary from sulphur-yellow to greenish-yellow but are never as green on the margin of the cap as *F. polychroa.* The usual distinguishing marks are the sulphur-yellow margin of the cap, its fulvous to tawny disk, the marked viscidity, the slender, fibrillose stem and the yellowish or citron-yellow flesh. The spores have a rather characteristic shape as compared with nearly related species.

516.   Flammula flavida Fr.

Syst. Myc., 1821.

Illustrations: Cooke, Ill., Pl. 444.
Ricken, Blätterpilze, Pl. 58, Fig. 1.

"PILEUS 4-7 cm. broad, campanulate-expanded, subumbonate, moist, *not viscid,* even, *glabrous,* rather regular, *bright yellow* (flavus), sometimes almost sulphur-yellow with pale fulvous disk, decorated *along the margin by the adherent, white or pallid remains of the cortina.* FLESH white then yellowish. GILLS adnate, close, thin, rather narrow, at first white, soon yellowish *then rusty-fulvous,* edge white-fimbriate. STEM 5-10 cm. long, 6-10 mm. thick, either narrowed or enlarged toward base, stuffed then hollow, fibrillose, flavus-yellow, rusty toward base, at length entirely rusty-brown, *sometimes with evanescent annulus.* CORTINA whitish. SPORES elliptical, 8-9 x 4-5 micr., smooth, ferruginous. CYSTIDIA clavate, 36-40 x 8-9 micr."

Reported by Lonygear from Chandlers, Michigan. The description is adopted from the Monographia of Fries, with additions from Ricken. It seems to be well-marked by the non-viscid pileus, the shreds of the cortina on its margin or on the apex of stem and the spores.

517.   Flammula gummosa Fr.

Epicrisis, 1836-38.

Illustrations: Cooke, Ill., Pl. 441.
Fries, Icones, Pl. 116, Fig. 2.
Ricken, Blätterpilze, Pl. 57, Fig. 1.

PILEUS 3-7 cm. broad, convex-plane, at length subdepressed or subumbonate, with a *glutinous,* separable pellicle, even, *pale ochraceous mixed with buff and olivaceous hues,* glabrescent. FLESH thick on disk, concolor when moist, paler when dry. GILLS adnate-subdecurrent, broad behind, tapering in front, close, *pale ochraceous-cinnamon,* edge minutely flocculose. STEM 4-6 cm. long, 4-10 mm. thick, rather firm, subequal, *floccose-scaly above,* fibrillose below, stuffed, *pallid above,* umber downwards, dull reddish-umber when bruised at base. SPORES oblong-elliptical, 6-7 x 3-4 micr., smooth, pale rusty-brown. CYSTIDIA scattered, ventricose, tapering, 45-50 x 15 micr. ODOR and TASTE mild.

Solitary or subcaespitose and crowded. At the base of stumps in mixed woods. New Richmond. September. Rare.

Our specimens are well illustrated by Cooke's figures. The species differs from *F. lubrica* in its usually glabrous pileus and the rusty-red base of stem; the spores are slightly smaller.

518. Flammula alnicola Fr.

Syst. Myc., 1821.

Illustrations: Cooke, Ill., Pl. 443.
      Gillet, Champignons de France, No. 282.
      Grevillea, Vol. VI, Pl. 90.
      Ricken, Blätterpilze, Pl. 58, Fig. 5.

"PILEUS 5-7 cm. broad, convex then expanded, obtuse, *not truly viscid*, lubricous, at first superficially fibrillose toward margin, sometimes minutely scaly, *cadmium-yellow*, becoming rusty and sometimes greenish. FLESH slightly compact, concolor. GILLS subadnate, at times decurrent or rounded behind, broad, plane, *at first dingy-pallid* or yellowish-pallid, at length ferruginous. STEM 5-10 cm. long, 6-12 mm. thick, attenuated-rooting at base, commonly curved or flexuous, *fibrillose*, at first cadmium yellow then becoming rusty. CORTINA manifest, fibrillose or arachnoid. SPORES elliptical, 9 x 4 micr. ODOR *strong and pungent, bitter*. TASTE *bitter*.

"On old stumps of frondose trees especially of alder and willow."

This has been reported from the State, but I have found no typical specimens. Ricken describes and figures a plant with smaller spores, which departs considerably from the figures of Cooke, Gillet and those in Grevillea. The description given above is adopted from that of Fries in Monographia, and the figures of Cooke, etc., fit it well. *F. alnicola* should be recognized by its long, rooting, caespitose stems, by the color and by the strong bitter odor. Peck reports it from the Catskill and Adirondack Mountains only.

Section III.   Sapineae.   Spore mass ochre-yellow.   Gills fulvous-golden yellow.   Pileus dry or nearly so.

519.   Flammula sapinea Fr.

Syst. Myc., 1821.

Illustrations: Fries, Icones, Pl. 118, Fig. 3.
    Cooke, Ill., Pl. 447.
    Michael, Führer f. Pilzfreunde, Vol. III, No. 90.
    Moffatt, Chicago Nat. His. Surv., Bull. 7, Part I, Pl. 9, Fig. 2,

PILEUS 2-7 cm. broad, *firm,* convex, then subexpanded, obtuse, golden-yellow to tawny, paler toward margin, velvety or *minutely floccose-scaly, dry,* at length fading and rimose-cracked.   FLESH thick, *yellowish.*   GILLS adnate, plane, rather narrow, thin, *chrome-yellow* then rusty-yellow, edge minutely fimbriate.   STEM 4-7 cm. long, 6-12 mm. thick, rather stout, stuffed then hollow, *sometimes compressed and irregular,* fibrous, innately fibrillose, yellowish, brownish below when handled.   CORTINA yellowish, scanty.   SPORES elliptical, 6-8 x 4-5 micr., smooth, rusty-yellow. ODOR strong.

Subcaespitose, scattered or solitary.   On wood of conifers in the north; on tamarack stumps and logs in the southern part of the State.   Bay View, New Richmond, Ann Arbor, Detroit.   August-October.   Infrequent.

This is a rather variable plant, not yet sufficiently studied.   The forms on tamarack are apparently the same as the species in pine and hemlock woods but often the pileus is almost glabrous.   In the young state the colors are rich, in age they often fade.

Galera Fr.

(From the Latin, *Galera, a little helmet.*)

Ochre-brown or rusty-yellow spored.   Stem *subcartilaginous,* tubular, slender.   Partial veil none or fibrillose; volva lacking. Pileus thin, conical, campanulate or oval, *its margin at first straight and appressed on the stem.*   Spores elliptical or oval, usually smooth.   Cystidia lacking.

Putrescent, fragile, small mushrooms, growing on dung, mosses, grass or on the ground.   They correspond to Mycena of the white-spored group in the nature of the stem, the straight margin of the young pileus and in the slender habit; they also correspond to Nolanea of the pink-spored group. Their small size, growth on dung and scarcity in number makes them useless for food.

The PILEUS is thin and membranous, either conical, oval or elliptical when very young, becoming campanulate, or, in a few species, expanded. It is hygrophanous and in many species is striatulate on the margin when moist. The color varies within narrow limits, mostly rusty, ochraceous, brownish, yellowish or whitish; when dry they usually fade to a much paler shade. Many develop an atomate or delicate silky surface after losing their moisture, such "atoms" being due to microscopic erect cells.

The GILLS are never decurrent, but are either narrowly adnate or adnexed to the stem within the cone of the pileus. They are more generally narrow and linear, although some species possess ventricose, rather broad gills. *Galera ovalis,* described in European works, has very broad gills, and seems to be a rarity with us, if it is not entirely lacking. It has been reported from the United States but may have been confused with others. Ricken omits it from the list of German Galeras. The mature gills of this genus are usually a pale rusty-yellow which is a convenient mark of recognition; sometimes this color shades into cinnamon. The edge of the gills is provided with microscopic sterile cells. In the first section they have the shape of nine-pins or Indian clubs, with a rounded knob at the apex, i. e., capitate, but with a more narrowed base. These can scarcely be seen, unless a portion of a gill is mounted sideways under the microscope. In the other groups, these cells vary in shape from lanceolate to filiform, and are never capitate. True cystidia are wanting. The *trama* of the gills is usually composed of large-celled hyphae, and a careful comparative study may bring out good specific characters here. The STEM is always slender, hollow, and usually fragile. In some species, however, it is toughish or flaccid as in certain Mycenas. In texture it is somewhat cartilaginous. It is usually equal throughout but species are known where a marked thickening occurs at the base in the form of a bulb; others may develop a slight bulblet or even a long root-like prolongation as in *G. antipus.* The CORTINA is lacking in most or all of the section Conocephalae. In the second group there is a delicate, fibrillose cortina which disappears early. Another section, of which no examples are included below, includes species which have a more highly developed superficial veil whose delicate remnants are visible after the pileus has expanded. Some of these, e. g., *G. pellucida* Fr., *G. stagnina* Fr. and *G. paludosa* Fr., are now placed in the genus Tubaria, because of their decurrent or broadly adnate gills.   *G. rufipes* Pk. seems at present the only species of this third section likely to be found within our limits.

About 24 species of Galera have been reported or newly described for the United States east of the Rocky Mountains. Some of these will probably be found to be synonyms. Several unnamed species are included below whose identity is not established and which as yet seem to be distinct from the others. This genus needs considerably more microscopic study in order to place its species on a firm basis. Special pains were taken to obtain material throughout the course of this study but a comparatively small number of the described American species came to hand. See Plate XCVII for habit.

Key to the Species

(A) Edge of gills provided with microscopic, capitate, sterile cells. (Growing on dung, or on the soil among grass of manured lawns, gardens, fields and pastures.)
   (a) Stem long, rooting below the enlarged base; primarily on dung-hills. 520. *G. antipus* Lasch.
   (aa) Stem without root-like prolongation.
     (b) Stem bulbous-enlarged at base; gills narrow; on dung-hills. 522. *G. bulbifera* sp. nov.
     (bb) Stem equal.
       (c) Gills very broad, almost free, ferruginous; plants large, very fragile; rare. *G. ovalis* Fr.
       (cc) Gills narrow to medium broad.
         (d) Stem striatulate and pubescent; spores 10-12 x 6-7 micr. 523. *G. pubescens* Gill.
         (dd) Stem not markedly striatulate.
           (e) Spores small, 7-8.5 x 4-5 micr., pileus soft and very fragile, finally expanded. 527. *G. teneroides* Pk.
           (ee) Spores 10 micr. or more in length.
             (f) Pileus markedly cylindric-conical, longer than wide, pale isabelline. 521. *G. lateritia* Fr.
             (ff) Pileus not narrowed-conical.
               (g) On cow-dung; spores 15-18 x 9-10 micr; pileus not striatulate when moist. 524. *G.* sp.
               (gg) In grassy places, lawns, etc.
                 (h) Stem tough, filiform; spores 9-12 x 6-7 micr. 528. *G. capillaripes* Pk.
                 (hh) Stem fragile.
                   (i) Gills crisped and interveined. 526. *G. crispa* Longyear.
                   (ii) Gills not crisped; very common on lawns. 525. *G. tenera* Fr.
(AA) Edge of gills with sterile cells of a different form. (Growing attached to mosses, grass, sedges, etc., in moist places.)
   (a) Stem bluish to greenish-gray; on mosses in swamps. 529. *G. cyanopes* sp. nov.
   (aa) Stem whitish or pallid.
     (b) Pileus sulcate, convex; gills narrow; on grass. 530. *G. plicatella* Pk.
     (bb) Pileus even or striatulate when moist; gills broad.

(c) Spores 8-10 x 5-6 micr., pileus conic-campanulate; very common on mosses; small. 531. *G. hypnorum* Fr.
(cc) Spores 10-12 x 6 micr., pileus hemispherical-convex; on grass. *G.* sp.

Section I. Conocephalae. Pileus conico-campanulate at first; gills ascending and on the edge with microscopic differentiated, capitate cells; cortina none. Habitat on dung or manured ground.

520. Galera antipus Lasch.

Illustrations: Fries, Icones, Pl. 128, Fig. 2.
Gillet, Champignons de France, No. 293.
Ricken, Die Blätterpilze, Pl. 60, Fig. 9.

PILEUS 1.5-2.5 cm. broad (rarely up to 5 cm.), *broadly campanulate*, dingy ferruginous-cinnamon (moist), hygrophanous, yellowish-isabelline (dry), glabrous or subpruinose, not striatulate, atomate when dry, subflaccid. FLESH submembranous, slightly fleshy on disk. GILLS narrowly adnate, ascending, *crowded, narrow*, sublinear, pale cinnamon-ochraceous, finally dark ferruginous. STEM 3-5 cm. long and 2-4 mm. thick above substratum, *subfusiform-enlarged at base, and with a very long, subhorizontal, thickish, flexuous, whitish root-like prolongation*, pruinose or scurfy, *striate or twisted*, concolor or paler than pileus. SPORES lemon-shaped, obscurely 6-angled, otherwise smooth, 8-9 x 6 micr. BASIDIA 18-25 x 7-8 micr.; *sterile cells* on edge of gills, small, capitate. ODOR none.

Gregarious on dung-hills in beech and pine woods. New Richmond. September. Locally abundant.

This is often a large-capped species, known by its long root-like prolongation, which may extend 5-8 cm. below the point of entrance. Dung-hills on which the plants are plentiful, are often penetrated by a thick mass of these "roots" which interweave in a horizontal position. The stem appears clavate or fusiform where it enters the substratum, and easily separates at this point, so that the "root" is easily overlooked. All stages of development were observed; the very young pileus is oval and whitish, and is scarcely broader than the stout young stem; it becomes campanulate and finally is broadly expanded. No cortina is present at any stage. The spores are very characteristic and agree entirely with Ricken's description. Cooke gives the spores entirely too large in connection with Plate 463 of the Illustrations.

521. Galera lateritia Fr.

Syst. Myc., 1821.

Illustrations: Fries, Icones, Pl. 127.
>   Michael, Führer f. Pilzfreunde, Vol. III, No. 94.
>   Ricken, Die Blätterpilze, Plate 60, Fig. 11.
>   Cooke, Ill., Plate 460.

PILEUS 2.5-3 cm. high, 2-2.5 cm. wide, almost *cylindrical-conical,* later subcampanulate, *pale isabelline,* hygrophanous, glabrous, fine-ly striate on margin. FLESH membranous. GILLS nearly free, *narrow,* linear, ascending, crowded, fulvous-rusty-ochraceous. STEM 5-10 cm. long, 2-3 mm. thick, rigid, equal, hollow, *fragile, pure white,* mealy-frosted. SPORES elliptical, ferruginous, 12-15 x 8-9 micr., smooth. STERILE CELLS on edge of gills capitate.

On dung or rich grassy places. Reported by Longyear as abund-ant; rarely seen by the writer. June-September.

The color of the cap is not as dark as in some of the Friesian figures; a fact noted by European as well as American observers. The narrow, elongated pileus is unique among the Galeras.

522. Galera bulbifera sp. nov.

PILEUS .5-2.5 cm. broad, oval-campanulate, obtuse, *ferruginous-cinnamon* when moist, hygrophanous, ochraceous and atomate when dry, rivulose-reticulate. GILLS ascending-adnate, *narrow, sub-linear,* close to crowded, ferruginous-cinnamon, sprinkled by fer-ruginous spores. STEM 6-15 cm. long, 1.5-3 mm. thick, strict when moist, equal above the bulbous base, pale ferruginous, hollow, glab-rous-shining when dry, sometimes faintly striatulate. SPORES elliptical, obtuse at ends, smooth, ferruginous in mass, 12-15 x 8-9 micr. CYSTIDIA none. STERILE CELLS on edge of gills small, capitate. ODOR none.

On horse dung; dung-hills in mixed woods. New Richmond. September.

Variable in size; solitary specimens attain the large size, while a patch of them is apt to be composed of smaller sizes. It has the appearance, in the large condition, of *G. ovalis,* but differs by the narrow gills, etc. It is well marked by the gills, the bulblet at base of stem, and the spores. The whole plant is ferruginous-cinnamon when moist, and in large plants the pileus is finely rugose-reticu-late.

523. Galera pubescens Gill.

Champignons de France, 1874.

Illustrations: Ibid, No. 296.

PILEUS 1-4 cm. broad, *oval-campanulate* or obtusely conical-campanulate, *ferruginous-cinnamon* to rufous-brown when moist, hygrophanous, buff to ochraceous-tan when dry, sometimes reticulate-rivulose or obscurely rugulose, atomate when dry. FLESH submembranous. GILLS ascending-adnate, *rather narrow, close,* subventricose, cinnamon-ochraceous. STEM 3-10 cm. long, 1-3 mm. thick, *equal,* often *striatulate, minutely pubescent or glabrous,* hollow, brownish-ochraceous, becoming pallid and shining. SPORES elliptical, smooth, obtuse, 10-12 x 5.5-7 micr. CYSTIDIA none. STERILE CELLS capitate, on edge of gills.

Common locally on cow-dung, cultivated fields, etc. Ann Arbor, New Richmond. June-September.

This differs from *G. bulbifera* in the size of the spores and of the stem which is of equal size to the base. The stem is usually pubescent as is also the surface of the pileus; but not too much stress must be laid on this character since it is not unusual for other species of Galera to develop pubescence on cap and stem when growing on dung in shaded, moist situations. The stem also varies considerably as to the striations; these are normally well-marked but may be entirely lacking.

524. Galera sp.

Plate XCVII of this Report.

PILEUS 12-16 mm. broad, campanulate, *not striatulate,* watery-cinnamon-brown when moist, hygrophanous, pale whitish-ochraceous and atomate when dry; FLESH submembranous, concolor. GILLS adnate-seceding, ascending, *rather broad, ventricose,* close to subdistant, ferruginous at maturity. STEM about 5 cm. long, 1-1.5 mm. thick, *equal,* not bulbillate, fibrous-rigid, hollow, even, glabrous or pruinate, white at first, then pallid or pale ochraceous. SPORES large, broadly elliptical, obtuse, smooth, ferruginous in mass, 15-18 x 9-10 micr. CYSTIDIA none. STERILE CELLS on edge of gills, capitate.

On cow-dung in pine woods. New Richmond. September.

Differing from the preceding two, in the large spores, broad and ventricose gills and paler colors. It was distinguished only once and no name is as yet applied to it. It is included merely for comparison. It may prove to be a form of *G. pygmaea-affinis* Fr.

525. Galera tenera Fr.

Syst. Myc., 1821.

Illustrations: Cooke, Ill., Pl. 461.
    Hard, Mushrooms, Fig. 223, p. 276, 1908.
    Murrill, Mycologia, Vol. 3, Pl. 40, Fig. 6.

PILEUS 8-16 mm. broad, *obtusely conic-campanulate,* hygrophanous, pale ferruginous and striatulate when moist, *whitish to creamy-white and even when dry,* glabrous, atomate when dry; FLESH submembranous. GILLS ascending-adnate, close to subdistant, rather narrow, uniform in width, cinnamon when mature. STEM 3-7 cm. long, 1-1.5 mm. thick, equal or subequal, straight, slender, *fragile,* subshining, hollow, concolor (moist and dry), pruinose at apex, even or faintly striatulate. SPORES variable in size, 11-16 x 6-9 micr., elliptical, smooth, obtuse. CYSTIDIA none. STERILE CELLS on edge of gills capitate.

Gregarious or scattered. Especially on lawns in our cities everywhere; also among grass by road-sides, in fields, pastures, etc., sometimes on dung-hills. May to September. Throughout the State. Very common.

This must not be confused with *Bolbitius tener* Berk., which is much more delicate and collapses quickly at maturity. When growing in the same place the two are easily distinguished. *Bolbitius tener* is rather rare, but may appear in similar situations. There seem to be some discrepancies in the spore-measurements of *G. tenera* as given by different authors, a fact easily explained by their variability. The gills, too, are usually said to be "broad," while in most individuals they are relatively somewhat narrow.

526. Galera crispa Longyear

Bot. Gazette, 1899, p. 272.

Illustration: Hard, Mushrooms, Fig. 226, p. 278, 1908.

PILEUS 1.5-3 cm. broad, *persistently conic-campanulate,* subacute, rivulose-striate, sometimes rugulose, *brownish-ochraceous at apex when moist,* whitish-buff elsewhere, glabrous, atomate when dry; FLESH membranous. GILLS adnexed, close to subdistant, rather narrow, *crisped and interveined,* at first white then ferruginous-brown. STEM 5-9 cm. long, 1-2 mm. thick, slender, base slightly bulbous, hollow, *fragile, pure white or tinged ochraceous,* sometimes faintly striatulate. SPORES very *variable in size and shape,* elliptical, ovate or elliptic oval in some individuals, varying 15 x 13 or 12 x 8, etc., (11-16 x 8-14 micr.), smooth. CYSTIDIA none. STERILE CELLS on edge of gills, capitate.

On lawns, pastures, etc., among grass. June-July. Ann Arbor, Lansing, etc. Infrequent.

This species was described by Longyear from our State. The peculiar, crisped appearance of the gills, and the slight development of the hygrophanous character in the pileus distinguishes it from *G. tenera.* Hard gives an excellent photograph of it.

527. Galera teneroides Pk.

N. Y. State Mus. Rep. 29, p. 39, 1878.

PILEUS 5-20 mm. broad, conic-ovate at the very first, then *campanulate-expanded, soft, very fragile,* sublubricous, hygrophanous, *brownish-cinnamon* and striatulate when moist, paler when dry, glabrous. FLESH membranous. GILLS narrowly-adnate, *narrow,* close, pale brown then ochraceous-cinnamon or watery-brown. STEM slender, 3-6 cm. long, 1-1.5 mm. thick, elastic, straight then flexuous, equal, *slightly toughish,* subpubescent, glabrescent and shining, often striatulate. SPORES elliptical, small, 7-8.5 x 5 micr., smooth, obtuse, pale ochraceous-brown. BASIDIA 18 x 8 micr., inflated above, narrowed-stipitate, 4-spored. STERILE CELLS on edge of gills capitate.

On horse-dung and ground or decayed debris in woods. Ann Arbor, New Richmond. August-September.

Remarkable for the soft, fragile pileus and somewhat toughish, persistent stem; the latter separates from the rather watery flesh of the pileus and is found in good condition after the pileus has collapsed. It has affinities with Bolbitius but the gills are Galera-like. The small spores separate it from related species on dung. It seems close to *G. spartea* Fr., but that species is said to prefer mossy or burned-over places in woods. Furthermore, Massee says the gills of *G. spartea* are broadly adnate, while Ricken says they are narrowly-attached, so that a clear idea of that species is hard to obtain.

528. Galera capillaripes Pk.

Torr. Bot. Club. Bull, No. 26, p. 66, 1899.

PILEUS 8-12 mm. broad, obtusely campanulate, hygrophanous, *pale ferruginous* and faintly striatulate when moist, paler and atomate when dry. FLESH membranous. GILLS ascending adnate, *rather broad, subdistant,* pale, ferruginous. STEM filiform, 2-5 cm. long, *flexuous, tough,* glabrous, concolor, persistently rufous-shining, apex pruinate. SPORES 9-11.5 x 5-6.5 micr., elliptical, smooth, obtuse, epispore ferruginous under microscope. CYSTIDIA none. STERILE CELLS on edge of gills capitate, about 20 x 7-8 micr. ODOR none.

Among grass, near woods. Ann Arbor. September. Infrequent.

Similar to *G. tenera,* but with different spores, smaller size and tough stem. It was originally described by Peck from specimens growing on lawns and grassy places in Ohio.

Section II. Bryogeni. Pileus campanulate-convex, always striatulate; gills scarcely ascending, provided on the edge with filiform, awl-shaped or lanceolate sterile cells. Habitat on mosses, sedges, etc.

529. Galera cyanopes sp. nov.

PILEUS 8-12 mm. broad, convex-campanulate, hygrophanous, pale watery cinnamon and striatulate when moist, whitish-buff and almost even when dry, atomate; FLESH membranous. GILLS adnate, narrow, sublinear, close to subdistant, pale cinnamon-ochraceous, edge minutely flocculose. STEM 5-7 cm. long, 1-1.5 mm. thick, filiform, *pale greenish-gray to bluish,* equal or minutely bulbillate at base, elastic, hollow, pruinose at apex, glabrous elsewhere, concolor within. SPORES broadly elliptical, smooth. 8-9.5 x 6.5-7 micr., ochraceous. CYSTIDIA none. STERILE CELLS on edge of gills. ODOR and TASTE none.

On Polytrichum, a species of moss, in a poplar swamp. Ann Arbor. July. Rare.

A beautiful little Galera, well-marked by the blue-gray stem, habit on Polytrichum and its striatulate pileus when moist. In the light from a kerosene lamp the greenish-blue color is intensified. *G. mniophila* Lasch. is said to grow on moss and has an olive-yellow stem, but the spores are larger, according to Ricken 10-12 x 5-6 micr., and according to Massee, 14 x 6 micr.

530. Galera plicatella Pk.

N. Y. State Mus. Rep. 26, p. 59, 1874 (as *Galera coprinoides* Pk.).

PILEUS 10-12 mm. broad, convex-expanded, *plicate-sulcate* to the small even disk, often split on margin, yellowish or ochraceous when moist, straw-whitish when dry, glabrous. FLESH membranaceous. GILLS adnexed, moderately broad, ventricose, close to subdistant, distinct, pale rusty-ochraceous. STEM 2-3 cm. long, 1 mm. thick, slender, equal, flexuous or straight, hollow, minutely pruinose, *white* to pallid. SPORES elliptical, smooth, 6-7.5 x 5 micr., rusty-ochraceous. BASIDIA 15 x 6-7 micr., 4-spored.

On the grass, lawns, roadsides. August-October. Ann Arbor. Rare.

The pileus imitates small species of Coprinus in its plicate margin. The trama of the gills is composed of large, vesicular subhymenial cells, between which runs a narrow layer of axillary, slender parallel hyphae.

531. Galera hypnorum Fr.

Sys. Myc., 1821.

Illustrations: Patouillard, Tab. Analyt., No. 230.
Cooke, Ill., Plate 465.
Gillet, Champignons de France, No. 295 (var. *bryorum*).
Ricken, Die Blätterpilze, Plate 60, Fig. 8.

PILEUS 4-12 mm. broad, campanulate, *cinnamon-yellowish* or yellowish-ochraceous and *striate when moist*, glabrous, yellowish-white or buff and even when dry. FLESH membranaceous; GILLS adnate, *broad, not ascending,* subdistant, fulvous-cinnamon, edge minutely flocculose. STEM short, 3-4 cm. long, 1-2 mm. thick, equal, slender, hollow, flexuous, glabrous, apex pruinose, concolor, often darker toward base. SPORES elliptic-ovate, subinequilateral, 8-10 x 5-6 micr., smooth, ochraceous. CYSTIDIA none. STERILE CELLS on edge of gills *fusiform-lanceolate.*

Gregarious on mosses. Throughout the State. May-October. Common.

This is our commonest little Galera with a moss habitat. Doubtless closely related species are confused with it and a microscopic study may be necessary to distinguish them. A number of varieties have been described, but an account of them here would only confuse the student. Sometimes the pileus is provided with a little umbo, sometimes the plants attain a larger size than that given. A form growing on sphagnum is especially large.

Bolbitius Fr.

(From the Greek, *bolbiton*, cow's-dung.)

Ochre-brown to rusty-ochraceous-spored. Gills *dissolving somewhat* in wet weather, narrowly attached. Margin of pileus at first straight; flesh very thin. Stem fragile and slender. Partial veil very evanescent or none.

Putrescent, delicate, dung-inhabiting fungi, with hollow, elongated stems, with gills which dissolve more or less into a soft mass in age and very thin caps which usually split on the margin. They approach the genus Coprinus in habit and in the structure of the hymenium, differing in the rusty-ochraceous spores. They have something of the appearance of Galera, but their gills are clearly different. Only three species are included below. Some consider *Pluteolus reticulatus* to be a better species of Bolbitius. The genus Pluteolus, in fact, differs only in degree from Bolbitius. Species with free gills and the stem separable from the pileus are referable to Pluteolus; species with gills more or less narrowly attached and with a tendency of the gills to become soft, belonging to Bolbitius. But apparently these characters vary or intermediate forms may occur. The gills of *Pluteolus reticulatus* are sometimes narrowly adnate and those of some species of Bolbitius are free in occasional specimens. The texture of the stem in both genera is different from that of the pileus and the stem is more or less separable. The pileus is viscid or slightly so in nearly all species of both genera. In spite of these facts, the nature of the gills of Bolbitius remains a real distinguishing character and the genus Pluteolus will be retained in its proper place.

Key to the Species
(See Pluteolus)

532. Bolbitius tener Berk.

Outlines, 1860.

Illustrations, Ibid, Pl. 12, Fig. 2.
    Cooke, Ill., Pl. 691.
    Fries, Icones, Pl. 139, Fig. 4.
    Gillet, Champignons de France, No. 46.

PILEUS conical, 1-1.5 cm. high, finally expanded, obtuse, *dull white*, apex creamy-yellow, sometimes slightly subviscid, *even or scarcely striatulate*, glabrous, atomate when dry. FLESH very thin, delicate. GILLS free or nearly so, narrow, close, *dissolving quickly* and becoming brownish-ochraceous. STEM *slender*, 6-12 cm. or more in length, 1-2 mm. thick, equal, *flaccid*, glabrous, hollow, *bulbillate at base, pure white*. SPORES broadly elliptical, smooth, 13-16 x 9-10 micr., rounded-obtuse, ochraceous.

Gregarious or scattered. Among grass on lawns, parks, golf-links.

Marquette, Ann Arbor, Ypsilanti, etc. July-August. After heavy rains. Rare.

This plant must not be confused with *Galera lateritia* which has a larger pileus, a rigid-fragile stem and slightly smaller spores and gills which do not dissolve. This little Bolbitius seldom appears, according to my experience, and only during sultry, rainy weather. It develops overnight and in early morning stands up on its slender stem without difficulty, but soon after the sun strikes it the stems bend over, the gills dissolve and the cap collapses into soft masses which cling to the apex of the flaccid stem. On cloudy days the cap may expand and persist longer but usually it is seen as shown in Cooke's figure. It is described with salmon-colored gills, but in our plants the gills were brownish ochraceous.

533. Bolbitius fragilis Fr.

Epicrisis, 1836-38.

Illustrations: Cooke, Ill., Pl. 720, A.
    Swanton, Fungi, Pl. 40, Fig. 2.

PILEUS 2-5 cm. broad, conical-expanded, subumbonate, more or less viscid, light yellow, fading, umbo slightly deeper yellow, thin, almost pellucid, glabrous, *striate on the margin*. FLESH membranaceous. GILLS narrowly adnate, attenuate behind, sometimes free, *yellow,* then sordid pale cinnamon, moist and *somewhat dissolving.* STEM 7-9 cm. long, 2-3 mm. thick, fragile, hollow, slightly attenuated upwards, *glabrous,* naked at apex, yellow. SPORES elliptical, smooth, 11-13 x 6-7 micr., rusty-ochraceous.

Solitary or gregarious. In cultivated fields. Ann Arbor. May-July. Infrequent.

This is rather difficult of separation from *B. vitellinus.* It differs apparently in its less plicate pileus and the naked, more yellow* stem; but these characters are variable in this genus and intermediate forms seem to be quite frequent.

534. Boibitius vitellinus Fr.

Syst. Myc., 1821.

Illustrations: Cooke, Ill., Pl. 923.
              Gillet, Champignons de France, No. 47.
              Ricken, Blätterpilze, Pl. 23, Fig. 9.

PILEUS 2-5 cm. broad, at first oval, obtuse and *egg-yellow,* at length campanulate-expanded, cinereous toward margin, *sulcate-striate or plicate up to the egg-yellow obtuse umbo,* viscid, glabrous, margin at first straight. FLESH very thin. GILLS narrowly adnate, close, subdistant at full expansion of pileus, narrow, soft, *ochraceous-clay-color and with white edge when young,* rusty-ochraceous in age, *scarcely dissolving in wet weather,* crisped in dry weather. STEM 6-12 cm. long, 2-4 mm. thick, equal or slightly tapering upward, slender, fragile, *pruinose-scaly at apex* or throughout, *white* or slightly sulphur-yellow-tinged, often pellucid-shining, even or innately fibrillose. SPORES elliptical, smooth, 10-12.5 x 6-7.5 micr., rusty-ochraceous. *Hymenium* with large, inflated, sterile cells intermingled with basidia and of the same length as the basidia but much broader. ODOR and TASTE none.

On dung, especially cow dung, in fields, woods, etc., where cows are pastured. Ann Arbor, New Richmond, probably throughout the State. May-July. Rather frequent.

To be looked for in early June. It is a rather variable plant, changing in color as it develops, and again as it ages. Some specimens have white stems, others have stems tinged with sulphur-yellow. The distinctive character is the egg-yellow umbo on the center of the pileus, and before expansion the whole pileus is yellow. In the very young unexpanded stage, the surface of the pileus is provided with a delicate, thin, viscid pellicle, composed of glistening particles; this membrane disappears as the pileus expands. The species is not uncommon in Sweden, where I was able to verify the identity of our plant. The flesh of the stem is sometimes pale yellow. It should be carefully compared with *Pluteolus expansus*.

Pluteolus Fr.

(Diminutive of *Pluteus*.)

Ochre-brown to rusty-ochraceous spored. Gills *free*, not dissolving in wet weather. Stem *distinct from the pileus*, subcartilaginous. Pileus *viscid*, margin at first straight. Veil none.

Putrescent, thin-capped, slender-stemmed fungi, whose distinguishing characters are the spore-color, free gills, separable stem and viscid pileus. Bolbitius differs by the greater or less degree of the softness of the gills which tend to dissolve in wet weather. In Galera the gills are attached, the stem not truly separable and the cap not viscid. In Naucoria the margin of the pileus is at first incurved. Pluteolus corresponds to Pluteus of the pink-spored group in its free gills. The gills are, however, not always free, but may be attached slightly by the upper corner; this is true in *P. expansus* and *P. reticulatus*, which are somewhat intermediate between Pluteolus and Bolbitius. Ricken has discarded this genus, referring the European species to Bolbitius. A consideration of the extremes as shown by *Bolbitius tener* and *Pluteolus coprophilus* will make it evident that a real basis exists for these two genera. For purposes of identification, however, it seems helpful to include the species of both genera in one key.

Key to the Species

(a) On decaying wood; pileus deep violet-gray, fading. 538. *P. reticulatus* Fr.

(aa) On dung, straw piles, grassy places or ground in woods.

   (b) Gills dissolving quickly; pileus conical, 1-1.5 cm., dull white. (See 532. *Bolbitius tener* Berk.)

   (bb) Gills dissolving slowly or not at all.

      (c) Spores large, 12-16 micr. long, pileus rose-gray, striatulate. 535. *P. coprophilus* Pk.

      (cc) Spores 9-13 micr. long.

         (d) Pileus drab-color to grayish-brown; on the ground in woods. 536. *P. aleuriatus gracilis* Pk.

         (dd) Pileus yellow when young.

            (e) Pileus umbonate, umbo yellow.

               (f) Stem yellow, glabrous; pileus striate on margin. (See 533. *Bolbitius fragile* Fr.)

    (ff) Stem white, rarely tinged yellow; pruinose-scaly at
          apex; pileus sulcate-plicate. (See 534. *Bolbitius
          vitellinus* Fr.)
   (ee) Pileus sulcate-plicate, not umbonate; stem citron-yellow.
          537. *P. expansus* Pk.

535. Pluteolus coprophilus Pk.

N. Y. State Mus. Rep. 46, 1893.

PILEUS 2-4 cm. broad, fragile, conical-campanulate then expanded, depressed on disk, *viscid* when moist, striatulate on margin,
whitish at first, *soon rosy-gray or pinkish-cinnamon.* FLESH thin,
submembranaceous. GILLS *free,* narrow, crowded or close, pale
rusty-cinnamon, dotted by the spores. STEM 6-11 cm. long, 2-4 mm.
thick, straight or flexuous, *slender,* hollow, *pure white,* rarely tinged
with pink, glabrous or obscurely squamulose, equal or attenuated
at base. SPORES oval-elliptical, smooth, variable in size, 12-16 x
7-10 micr., bright-cinnamon in mass.

Caespitose or gregarious. On decaying straw piles, on compost
heaps or on dung, especially on lawns, fields, around trees, etc.,
where coarse manure was used. Ann Arbor. Probably throughout
the State. May-June. Infrequent.

During continued wet and sultry weather it is often very abundant
on manure mixed with straw. In June of one year specimens appeared around every tree on the campus of the University of Michigan where such manure had been deposited. Some think *Bolbitius
radians* Morg. is identical with it.

536. Pluteolus aleuriatus gracilis Pk.

Syst. Myc., 1821 (as *P. aleuriatus* Fr.).
N. Y. State Mus. Rep. 54, 1901.

PILEUS 1-2 cm. broad, fragile, soon expanded-plane, *viscid,*
striate-sulcate on margin, hygrophanous, *drab color to grayish-
brown,* paler on depressed disk, glabrous. FLESH thin. GILLS
free or nearly so, narrow, close, whitish at first then pale rusty-cinnamon. STEM 2.5-3.5 cm. long, 1.5-3 mm. thick, equal or narrowed
upwards, glabrous or minutely pulverulent, hollow, white, or pallid.
SPORES elliptical, smooth, 9-12 x 4-6 micr., pale ferruginous.

On the ground among decaying leaves in mixed woods. Houghton, Bay View. July. Rare.

This species does not seem to be very well known. Only a few specimens were found which are here considered to be identical with Peck's variety.

537. Pluteolus expansus Pk.

N. Y. State Rep. 26, 1874 (as *Galera expansus*).

Illustration: Plate XCVIII of this Report.

PILEUS 3-6 cm. broad, *fragile,* oval at first, then expanded-plane, *not umbonate,* slightly depressed in centre, *viscid* when moist, *cinereous-ochraceous* tinged with brownish or greenish hues, margin at first sulphur-yellow, *striate-sulcate or plicatulate.* FLESH thin, submembranaceous. GILLS free or slightly and narrowly adnexed, narrow, close to crowded, at first white, soon ochraceous-cinnamon, edge minutely flocculose. STEM 5-10 cm. long, 2-6 mm. thick, fragile, equal or slightly tapering upward, hollow, sometimes compressed, splitting longitudinally, pruinose or floccose, *citron-yellow,* yellow within except the evanescent pith. SPORES elliptical, smooth, 10-12 x 7.5 micr., ochraceous-cinnamon under microscope. *Hymenium* composed of large, inflated subglobose sterile cells intermingled with basidia which are narrow below, inflated above and 4-spored.

Gregarious or solitary. On rich manured lawns, fields, etc., sometimes on dung; sometimes in woods. Ann Arbor, Houghton, etc. Throughout the State. May-July. Infrequent.

This species seems to differ from *Bolbitius vitellinus* mainly in the absence of the yellow umbo or a yellow centre in the expanded pileus, in the constant yellow stem and the somewhat different distribution of color on the cap. It was first described by Peck from specimens on decaying wood, but later he reported it from "rich ground." The microscopic structure is very similar to that of *Bolbitius vitellinus.* The gills, although rather soft, do not dissolve as in a typical Bolbitius, but are fairly persistent. Var. *terrestris* Pk. is here made an integral part of the species.

538. Pluteolus reticulatus Fr.

Syst. Myc., 1821.

Illustrations: Cooke, Ill., Pl. 495.
  Gillet, Champignons de France, No. 546.
  Berkeley, Outlines, Pl. 9, Fig. 5.
  Ricken, Blätterpilze, Pl. 23, Fig. 10.
  Plate CXIX of this Report.

PILEUS 2-5 cm. broad, campanulate-expanded, obtuse, some-times slightly depressed, *glutinous when fresh,* the gluten drying so as to form *reticulate veins,* radiately-rugose on disk, *violaceous-gray* when fresh, livid to blackish on disk, margin obscurely striate, very pale in age.   FLESH rather thin.   GILLS almost free or narrowly adnate, rounded behind, *seceding,* crowded, ventricose, moderately broad, whitish at first, then rusty-cinnamon, edge white-fimbriate. STEM 3-6 cm. long, 2-6 mm. thick, equal or slightly tapering upwards, elastic, toughish, *white,* minutely floccose-scaly, fibrillose-striatulate, hollow, straight or curved. SPORES ellip-tical, smooth, 9-11 x 5-6 micr., rusty-brownish. ODOR none.

Caespitose or subcaespitose. Around the base of stumps and standing trees, on decayed wood. Ann Arbor. October. Rare.

When fresh the plants are markedly tricolored; pileus deep gray with violet tinge, gills rusty-cinnamon and stem white. Later the color of the pileus fades somewhat as in the plates referred to above, all of which show the cap much decolorized. The gills of our specimens depart somewhat from the character of the genus in being narrowly adnate; on this account it was at first referred by the writer to Naucoria. Ricken places it under Bolbitius because of the structure of the gills. In our plants the gills showed no sign of dissolving or becoming soft under the weather conditions in which they were collected.

Naucoria Fr.

(From the Latin, *Naucum,* a nut-shell, referring to the shape of the pileus.)

Ochre-brown or rusty-brown-spored. Stem *subcartilaginous,* hol-low or stuffed. Partial veil none or fugacious. Pileus slightly fleshy, convex, *its margin at first incurved.* Spores smooth.

Putrescent, terrestrial or lignicolous, usually small, sometimes minute, growing on grassy ground, mosses, sticks, decayed wood, or on the ground in various places. They correspond to the genus Collybia of the white-spored group in the nature of the stem, the incurved margin of the young pileus and in habit and habitat. They differ from Pholiota in lacking an annulus; from Flammula in the subcartilaginous stem, and from Galera in the more convex pileus and darker spore-mass. They are usually devoid of any special odor, but may have a slightly disagreeable taste. Their edibility is mostly uninvestigated, and their small size gives them no special value as edible mushrooms.

The PILEUS is slightly more fleshy in many species than in Galera; others have very thin flesh. It may be hemispherical and convex, even conical in a few species, but then it tends to expand and become plane or depressed. It is often somewhat viscid, sometimes hygrophanous, frequently dry. It is rarely striate on the margin. The color is usually ochraceous or of dark shades of fuscous, brown, etc. The surface is glabrous in two sections, (Gymnolae and Phaeotae), flocculose, scaly or silky in the other (Lepidotae). The GILLS are adnate or adnexed, never decurrent, often broad or ventricose. Most of them have differentiated sterile cells on the edge, which gives a paler or white distinctness. A more careful study of the color in the young stage may make it possible to separate species with greater ease. The STEM is often toughish, when dry somewhat cartilaginous. It is short as compared with the species of Galera, except in a few forms growing on sphagnum or dung. The CORTINA is entirely lacking in the first section, slightly developed in the second and third. It is probable that a universal veil is present in some of the species of the third group.

The species of Naucoria are rather numerous and seem to occur over the whole world. Only a comparatively small number are here described, and a careful study needs to be made of many others found in the State. Fries includes 48 species from Europe in his Hymen. Europ. Peck has described 19 from this country. These species all need microscopic study.

Key to the Species

(A) Growing in grassy places or pastures.
  (a) Pileus dark watery brown when moist; hygrophanous. 548. *N. tabacina* Fr.
  (aa) Pileus yellowish or ochraceous.
    (b) Pileus dry, slightly tomentose or silky on margin. 547. *N. pediades* Fr.
    (bb) Pileus more or less viscid.

   (c)   Stem compressed; gills yellowish at first, some spores angular.
         546. *N. platysperma* Pk.
   (cc) Stem terete; gills pallid at first; spores never angular. 545.
         N. semiorbicularis Fr.
 (AA) Growing in the woods and thickets, on ground, mosses, decayed
       wood, etc.
   (a)   Pileus scaly, dark reddish-brown. 549. *N. siparia* Fr.
   (aa) Pileus glabrous; on wood.
     (b)   Pileus 2-4 cm. broad, dark-fuscous, with a separable pellicle.
           539. *N. nimbosa* Fr. var.
     (bb) Pileus not over 2.5 cm., without a pellicle.
       (c)   Pileus with marked olivaceous tints. 540. *N. centuncula* **Fr.**
       (cc) Pileus without olivaceous tints.
         (d)   Pileus with a conical umbo, minute.
           (e)   Pileus hygrophanous, watery-cinnamon (moist); gills
                 narrow. 543. *N. lignicola* Pk.   '₊
           (ee) Pileus dark reddish-brown; gills ventricose. 542. *N.*
                 triscopoda **Fr.**
         (dd) Pileus hemispherical or convex.
           (e)   Pileus cinnamon-brown; gills broad; stem short. 541. *N.*
                 horizontalis Fr.
           (ee) Pileus and stem reddish-fulvous or darker, gills yellow;
                 spores minute. 544. *N. bellula* Pk.

Section I. Gymnotae. Pileus; veil none. Spores rusty in mass.
(The following species grow on decayed wood.)

*Pileus with a separable pellicle.

539. Naucoria nimbosa Fr. var.

Hymen. Europ., 1885.

PILEUS 2-4 cm. broad, *convex,* firm, obtuse or subumbonate, even,
dark-fuscous with a rufescent center, almost blackish-fuscous, wood-
brown when dry, *with a subgelatinous separable pellicle,* not viscid,
glabrous, subpruinate when dry, veil none. FLESH concolor,
pallid when dry, rather thin but compact. GILLS rounded behind,
narrowly adnate, medium broad, *crowded,* thickish, fuscous-brown,
edge white-fimbriate. STEM 2-4 cm. long, 3-4 mm. thick, stuffed
then hollow, equal, straight or curved, *densely white-flocculose*
above, fibrillose or fibrillose scaly below, striate, *pallid to fuscous-*
brown, dark brown within, *rigid-elastic,* white-mycelioid at base.
SPORES 6-7 x 3.5-4.5 micr., elliptical, smooth, rusty-brown. CYS-
TIDIA scattered on sides of gills, abundant on edge, 35-45 x 10-12
micr., obtuse, ventricose, stout. ODOR none. TASTE sometimes
unpleasant, astringent.

   On decaying logs or debris in hemlock woods; gregarious. Bay
View, New Richmond. September. Infrequent.

This species seems to be intermediate between *N. nimbosa* and *N. cidaris* Fr. It differs from the latter in its flocculose stem and from both in its habitat. The plant is quite well marked by its dark colors, the separable pellicle, firm texture and flocculose stem. The pellicle is composed of erect, clavate cells with fuscous-brown content, and gives to the surface of the cap a gelatinous feel, but is scarcely at all viscid in wet weather. The spores are not genuinely rusty as in the other forms of this section.

**Pileus without a separable pellicle.*

540. Naucoria centuncula Fr.

Syst. Myc., 1821.

Illustration: Cooke, Ill., Pl. 601.

"PILEUS 1.5-2.5 cm. broad, convex-expanded, then plane, obtuse, subundulate, hygrophanous, *sooty-olive to brown-olive and delicately striate when moist,* fading to yellowish, dull, silky under lens, margin at first with sulphur-yellow dust. FLESH submembranaceous, concolor. GILLS rounded behind, adnate, *thickish, broad,* crowded, yellow-gray to olive-brown, *edge crenulate with yellowish-green flecks.* Stem 2-3 cm. long, 2-3 mm. thick, often eccentric, equal, *curved,* hollow, sometimes compressed, paler olive, white-mealy above, white-mycelioid at base. SPORES almost kidney-shaped, 6-7 x 4 micr., smooth, rusty-brown. CYSTIDIA 30-36 x 4-6 micr. ODOR mild."

On decayed wood, in frondose woods. Ann Arbor, New Richmond. July-September.

Usually small and known from all others by the olivaceous coloring of the pileus and gills. The description is adapted from Ricken.

541. Naucoria horizontalis Fr.

Epicrisis, 1836-38.

Illustration: Cooke, Ill., Pl. 601.

"PILEUS .5-1 cm. broad, *hemispherical,* at length depressed, dry, *cinnamon-brown,* even or wrinkled. FLESH relatively thick. GILLS adnexed, *thickish, broad,* close to subdistant, cinnamon-brown, edge white-fimbriate. STEM short and curved, 1 cm. long,

1 mm. thick, brown, naked, base white-mycelioid. Spores somewhat almond-shaped, 14-18 x 6-7 micr., smooth. CYSTIDIA on edge of gills, fusiform, 50-60 x 8-10 mm.

On bark of standing trees (like *Mycena corticola*). Not found with certainty in the State. The description is adapted from Ricken.

542. Naucoria triscopoda Fr.

Monographia, 1863.

Illustrations: Fries, Icones, Pl. 124, Fig. 3.
    Cooke, Ill., Pl. 458.

PILEUS 3-10 mm. broad, small, *at first conical,* then campanulate *with a marked acute umbo,* striatulate to the umbo, *chestnut-brown to rufous-brown,* glabrous. FLESH *submembranaceous.* GILLS adnate, ascending, thickish, ventricose, close, ochraceous-cinnamon then darker, edge white-fimbriate. STEM 2-3 cm. long, 1 mm. thick, *slender, reddish-brown,* darker below, glabrous, hollow, apex pruinose, innately silky. SPORES minute, 6-7 x 3-4 micr., rusty-brown, smooth. CYSTIDIA none. STERILE CELLS on edge of gills, slender, subcylindrical, about 35 micr. long.

On much decayed wood in mixed forests of beech and hemlock. Bay View, New Richmond. September. Infrequent.

A dainty little plant, well-marked by its shape and color. The descriptions omit the striations of the pileus, but they are well shown in Fries' excellent figures. Ricken has referred it to the genus Galera but without explanation. This is the plant referred to in the list of the 8th Rep. Mich. Acad. Sci., p. 35, under *N. cuspidata* Pk. (in ed.) which Peck never published. It is clearly Fries' species.

543. Naucoria lignicola Pk.

N. Y. State Mus. Rep. 23, 1872.

PILEUS 5-20 mm. broad, convex-campanulate, markedly umbonate when young, at length expanded and depressed around the small umbo, *hygrophanous, watery-cinnamon* and *striatulate* when moist, dull ochraceous when dry, glabrous. FLESH thin. GILLS adnate, seceding, plane, close to subdistant, *narrow,* cinnamon-brown, edge concolor. STEM 2-4 cm. long, 1 mm. thick, slender, toughish, equal, subfistulose, curved, glabrous or obscurely pruinate-fibrillose.

SPORES elliptic-ovate, inequilateral, 7-8 x 3-4 micr., smooth, rusty-brown. ODOR none. TASTE slightly farinaceous.

On decayed wood. Ann Arbor. July.

Differs from *N. triscopoda* by its hygrophanous, paler pileus and slightly longer spores.

544. Naucoria bellula Pk.

N. Y. State Mus. Rep. 26, 1874.

PILEUS 1-2.5 cm. broad, firm, moist, convex, obtuse, minutely flocculose or glabrous, even, *bright watery-cinnamon to rusty-fulvous,* pliant. FLESH rather thin, yellowish. GILLS adnate-seceding, sometimes emarginate with tooth, rather narrow, close to crowded, *yellow then rusty-yellow and spotted.* STEM 2-2.5 cm. long, 1-2 mm. thick, slender, equal, short, toughish-elastic, straight or curved, *reddish-brown to rusty-bay,* darker below, stuffed then hollow, fibrillose-scurfy at apex, sometimes scurfy throughout. SPORES *minute,* oval, 5-5.5 x 3 micr., smooth, ferruginous, staining the gills. CYSTIDIA none. TASTE *bitter.* VEIL none.

On decayed coniferous wood in hemlock and pine woods, sub-caespitose or gregarious. September. Bay View, New Richmond.

A distinct plant of the conifer regions of the State. The whole plant has a tendency towards a fulvous-rusty more or less red color. The stem and gills become darker colored with age. The identification was made by Peck. It must not be confused with *Flammula limulata* Fr.

Section II. Phaeotae. Pileus glabrous. Spores and gills dull-colored, fuscous, cinnamon or ochraceous. Veil scarcely noticeable. (The following species grow on cultivated ground.)

545. Naucoria semiorbicularis Fr.

Epicrisis, 1836-38.

Illustrations: Cooke, Ill., Pl. 493.
    Gillet, Champignons de France, No. 489.
    Berkeley, Outlines, Pl. 9, Fig. 4.
    Plate XCIX of this Report.

PILEUS 1-3 cm. broad, *hemispherical-convex,* obtuse, somewhat viscid when moist, *fulvous-yellow,* darker on disk, ochraceous in age, *glabrous,* sometimes rimose, even, veil none. FLESH thin or thickish on disk, pallid. GILLS adnate, often seceding, *broad,* close, *pallid or alutaceous at first,* then rusty-brown, edge white-fimbriate. STEM 4-6 cm. long, 1-3 mm. thick, equal or slightly thickened toward base or apex, subrigid, toughish, *terete,* somewhat silky-shining, stuffed by a white pith, *ochraceous,* darker in age. SPORES elliptical-óval, 12-15 x 8-9 micr., smooth, rusty-brown in mass. CYSTIDIA on edge of gills ventricose flask-shaped, sometimes capitate, 25-35 x 9 micr. ODOR none. TASTE slightly disagreeable.

Gregarious or scattered. On lawns, roadsides and grassy pastures. Throughout the State. May-September. Common.

This species occurs on lawns with *Psilocybe foenisecii* and *Pholiota praecox,* during the warm and rainy weather in May and June, although it may be found throughout the season. Its hemispherical cap and rusty-brown spores distinguish it from similar species of the purple-brown-spored group. Its spores and size separate it from nearby species of Naucoria. *N. verracti* Fr. has been reported from Ohio. According to Ricken, this has spores measuring 12-17 x 8-12 micr. Its stem is said to be rough-fibrillose.

546. Naucoria platysperma Pk.

Torr. Bot. Club, Bull. 25, p. 324, 1898.

PILEUS 2-4.5 cm. broad, *convex* then subexpanded, slightly viscid when moist, *ochraceous,* somewhat darker when young, glabrous, fading, even, veil slight. FLESH white, thick on disk. GILLS adnate, broader behind, close, thin, *yellowish-ochre at first* then fuscous-cinnamon, edge pallid-fimbriate. STEM 3-5 cm. long, 2-4 mm. thick, tough, *hollow and usually compressed,* equal or tapering below, *ochraceous,* often striate above, slightly flocculose with whitish floccules. SPORES 13-15 x 7-10, elliptical, or *sometimes of various shapes, triangular, heart-shaped, lobed, etc.,* fuscous-brown in mass. STERILE CELLS on edge of gills fusiform.

Gregarious. On dung-hills, pastured woods and grassy places. Bay View, Ann Arbor, New Richmond. May, June and September. Frequent during some seasons.

Characterized by the flattened or irregular spores which are present in each mount, although in small numbers. The size of the plant and its compressed stem are often good marks for its identification. Peck gives a greater width for the spores, but this is rare in our plants, which were referred to him and verified. The original description was made from California specimens.

547. Naucoria pediades Fr.

Syst. Myc., 1821.

Illustrations: Cooke, Ill., Pl. 492.

    Gillet, Champignons de France, No. 488.

    Patouillard, Tab. Analyt., No. 346.

    Hard, Mushrooms, Fig. 228, p. 282, 1908.

"PILEUS 2.5-6 cm. broad, campanulate-hemispherical, at length plane, obtuse, *dry, not shining,* fulvous-ochraceous then isabelline-yellow, *delicately tomentulose toward margin,* margin silky-floccose. FLESH pallid, slightly fleshy. GILLS broadly adnate, rounded behind, rather broad, close to subdistant, ventricose, *brownish-pallid at first,* at length sordid-brown. STEM 4-7 (or more) cm. long, 2-3 (or more) mm. thick, often twisted, unequal, *stuffed,* silky-fulvous, concolor or yellowish, *granular-flocculose.* SPORES oval, 10-12 x 6-7 micr., argillaceous-brown in mass. CYSTIDIA (on edge) ventricose-fusiform, 45-50 x 8-10 micr. ODOR subfarinaceous. TASTE sometimes nauseous."

    Reported as common on lawns and roadsides by Longyear. Description adapted from Ricken.

548. Naucoria tabacina Fr.

Epicrisis, 1836-38.

Illustration: Cooke, Ill., Pl. 493.

PILEUS 6-18 mm. broad, convex, obtuse, *then almost plane,* glabrous, *hygrophanous,* even, *watery bay-fuscous* (moist), dull ochraceous-cinnamon (dry). FLESH concolor, thin. GILLS adnate-seceding, narrowed in front, rather broad behind, close, at length horizontal, alutaceous-brownish, edge white-flocculose. STEM 2-3 cm. long, 1-3 mm. thick, *tapering downward,* straight or curved, stuffed then hollow, toughish, *brownish-umber, fibrillose-floccose.* SPORES elliptic-ovate, 6-8 x 4-4.5 micr., smooth, fuscous-brown in mass. ODOR none. TASTE bitterish.

    Caespitose or subcaespitose, on the ground in a cornfield, etc. Ann Arbor. June. Infrequent. Known by its dark colors and small spores. The gills often run down the stem by a line.

Section II. Lepidotae. Pileus flocculose or scaly. Veil manifest (universal). Spores rust-colored.

549. Naucoria siparia Fr.

Syst. Myc., 1821.

Illustrations: Cooke, Ill., Pl. 480.

Patouillard, Tab. Analyt., No. 642.

PILEUS 5-15 mm. broad, broadly convex to plane, obtuse, moist, at first densely tomentose, *breaking up into thick scales of fascicled tufts,* especially on disk, *dark reddish-brown.* FLESH soft, brownish-ochraceous, thin. GILLS adnate, *broad,* close to subdistant, ventricose, brownish-clay-color, edge white-flocculose. STEM 1-2 cm. long, 1-1.5 mm. thick, short, equal, stuffed, lower two-thirds *loosely floccose-fibrillose and reddish-brown,* apex glabrous and whitish. SPORES very variable in size and shape, 9-13 (few 15) x 5-6 (few 7) micr., inequilateral-elliptical, smooth, rusty-brown in mass. CYSTIDIA none. STERILE CELLS on edge of gills numerous, subcylindrical or narrowly clavate, about 40 x 8-9 micr. BASIDIA 4-spored, 27 x 6 micr. ODOR none.

Gregarious, on soil or moss in frondose woods, among debris. Ann Arbor. August.

Although this plant is said to usually inhabit the stalks of ferns, our specimens agree so closely with the descriptions that scarcely a doubt can be raised concerning their identity.

Crepidotus Fr.

(From the Greek, *krepis,* a slipper and *ous,* an ear.)

Ochre-brown to rusty-spored. Stem lateral, eccentric or none. Pileus dimidiate, eccentric or lateral, often at first resupinate. Veil lacking. SPORES sphoeroid or elliptical.

Putrescent, shelving or resupinate mushrooms, from 1 to 5 cm. broad, growing on decaying wood. They correspond to those Pleuroti of the white-spored group which have no veil.

The PILEUS is usually of a soft consistency and soon collapses; in some species it is firmer or tougher and a few have a gelatinous surface layer. The surface of some forms is tomentose or hairy, of others glabrous; when hygrophanous, they often become pruinose when dry. The hygrophanous species are usually striatulate on the margin of the pileus when moist, but become even when dry. The color of most species is white, dingy-white or yellowish, but *C. cinnabarinus* has a deep scarlet-red color. The GILLS radiate from the point of attachment of the pileus, where they either run down to a point or are abruptly rounded behind. They are often broad and soft and collapse when mature, but sometimes are very narrow and crowded; in age they become stained or spotted by the copious spores. The short STEM or tubercle-like point of attachment is usually somewhat tomentose or villose even in otherwise glabrous plants. The SPORES are an important means of diagnosis of the species of this genus, since a number of species have a very similar general appearance. Peck points out that European mycologists have neglected to give us careful measurements for the spores of their species. I have used the spore character in the keys, since it is the only reliable method of studying the group, and as the species are not as a rule used for food, the mycophagist will not need much attention. The spores in different species vary from brown to ferruginous and often stain the pilei when the latter grow in an imbricate fashion.

Fifteen species are reported from Michigan; all but two I have collected.

Key to the Species

(A) Spores elliptical or oval.
  (a) Pileus scarlet-red, substipitate. 555. *C. cinnabarinus* Pk.
  (aa) Pileus not red.
    (b) Pileus viscid, hygrophanous, sessile, white when dry. 550. *C. haerens* Pk.
    (bb) Pileus not viscid.
      (c) Pileus with a subgelatinous surface, sessile, glabrous. 551. *C. mollis* Fr.
      (cc) Pileus not gelatinous.
        (d) Pileus distinctly stipitate, minutely scaly, 4-8 mm. broad, tawny, tinged gray. 556. *C. sepiarius* Pk.
        (dd) Pileus sessile.
          (e) Pileus glabrous, whitish, resupinate. 552. *C. albidus* E. & E.
          (ee) Pileus not glabrous.
            (f) Pileus covered by a white villosity or tomentum.
              (g) Pileus 4-10 mm. broad; spores 7.5 micr. long. 553. *C. herbarum* Pk.
              (gg) Pileus 8-20 mm. broad; spores 9-10 micr. long. 554. *C. versutus* Pk.
            (ff) Pileus covered by a dense dark-colored tomentum when young.
              (g) Spores 8-10 x 5-6; pileus with a thin tawny tomentum, hygrophanous. 557. *C. fulvotomentosus* Pk.
              (gg) Spores 5-6 x 4-4.5; pileus with a rufous-brown tomentum, not hygrophanous. 558. *C. calolepis* Fr.
(AA) Spores spherical.
  (a) Pileus white or whitish.
    (b) Pileus subtomentose, densely villose at base; gills broad; spores 6-7 micr. 559. *C. putrigenus* B. & C.
    (bb) Pileus glabrous except at attachment.
      (c) Stipitate, stem 2-4 mm. long; pileus usually marginate behind. Spores 5-5.5 micr. 562. *C. stipitatus* sp. nov.

(cc) Not stipitate, i. e., pileus sessile.
   (d) Gills narrow and decurrent; spores 4-5.5 micr. 561. *C.*
            applanatus Fr.
   (dd) Gills broad, rounded behind; spores 5.5-7 micr. 560. *C.*
            malachius B. & C.
(aa) Pileus not white.
   (b) Pileus flabelliform, narrowed to the base, ochraceous; gills con-
            color. Spores 4.5-5.5 micr., with a cavity on one side. 563.
            C. crocophyllus Berk.
   (bb) Pileus dimidiate or subreniform, reddish-yellow, tomentose-
            scaly; spores 6 micr. 564. *C. dorsalis* Pk.

(*C. distans* Pk. has an *eccentric* stem; pileus small, 4-8 mm.,
sulcate-striate, pubescent and *tawny,* spores elliptical, 10-12 x
6-7.5 micr.; the gills are very distant. *C. latifolius* Pk. came from
Ohio; pileus is sessile, 3-6 mm. broad, *hygrophanous,* white, almost
glabrous; gills *very broad;* spores globose, 5-6 micr. *C. croceotinctus*
Pk. has a pileus 1.5-2.5 cm. broad, *glabrous,* sessile, yellowish;
gills whitish *becoming dull saffron-yellow;* spores short elliptical,
5-6 micr. long.)

550.   Crepidotus hærens Pk.

N. Y. State Mus. Rep. 35, 1884.

PILEUS 1-5 cm. broad, rarely broader, sessile, flattened-convex,
dimidiate, reniform, broadly cuneate, etc., *hygrophanous, viscid*
from the thin but tough, gelatinous, separable cuticle, glabrous or
slightly floccose-squamulose, obscurely striatulate when moist,
watery-brown or tinged gray (moist) white or whitish (dry), white-
villose at the base, margin at first inrolled. FLESH thin. GILLS
close, narrow, radiating, whitish then brownish. SPORES broadly
ovate-elliptical, obtusely pointed at ends, smooth, 7-9 x 5-6 micr.,
pale rusty-cinnamon in mass.

On decaying woods of deciduous trees. In Washtenaw County it
was found in several localities, but not detected elsewhere. June-
September. Infrequent.

This is our only truly viscid Crepidotus; *C. mollis* may become
slightly so in very wet weather. Our plants average larger than
those described by Peck, and the spores are slightly longer.

551. Crepidotus mollis Fr.

Syst. Mycol., 1821.

Illustrations: Swanton, Fungi, Pl. 40, Fig. 10-12, 1909.
Gillet, Champignons de France, No. 262.
Ricken, Blätterpilze, Plate 61, Fig. 1.
Cooke's Ill., Pl. 498.

PILEUS 1-5 cm. broad, rarely broader, sessile or subsessile, *soft,* obovate to reniform, soon plane *with a gelatinous cuticle* which ·gives it a gelatinous feel, sometimes subviscid, flaccid, *glabrous,* substriate on the margin, livid (moist) becoming ochraceous-whitish (dry). FLESH thin. GILLS *narrow, crowded,* decurrent, radiating, whitish then cinnamon. SPORES elliptical-ovate, sub-acute at one end, rounded at the other, smooth, 7-8.5 x 4-5 micr. ODOR and TASTE not noticeable.

Often imbricated, on decaying logs and limbs. New Richmond. September. Rare.

C. mollis differs from *C. hacrens* in that the gills are more crowded and narrow, the spores are slightly smaller and the surface is not viscid as a rule, even when moist and fresh.

552. Crepidotus albidus E. & E.

Proceedings Amer. Acad. of Phila., 1894.

"PILEUS sessile, *resupinate at first,* whitish, *glabrous,* dry, margin incurved. GILLS thin, rather broad, pallid then yellowish-brown, radiating from a point. SPORES unequally elliptical, yellowish-brown, 5 x 3.5 micr. On bark of tilia, Ann Arbor."

This species has not been recognized, apparently, since it was described. It is included as a basis for further observation. It approaches *C. latifolius* but the spores are not spherical and the pileus is not hygrophanous. Specimens of the type material are in the University of Michigan herbarium. It is very close to the following.

553. Crepidotus herbarum Pk.

N. Y. State Mus. Rep. 26, 1874.

"PILEUS 3-10 mm. broad, sessile, resupinate, suborbicular, *clothed with a white, downy villosity,* incurved on the margin when young, sometimes becoming reflexed. GILLS rather narrow, sub-distant, radiating from a naked lateral or eccentric point, white, then subferruginous. SPORES elliptical, 6-7.5 x 3-4 micr."

On dead stems of herbs, decaying wood, etc., in woods. Through-out the State. June to November. Frequent.

This little species grades into the next, but the spores seem to be constant. The pileus is often only villose toward the base.

554. Crepidotus versutus Pk.

N. Y. State Mus. Rep. 30, 1878.

Illustrations: Atkinson, Mushrooms, Fig. 150, p. 160, 1900.
Hard, Mushrooms, Fig. 227, p. 280, 1908.

"PILEUS 8-20 mm. broad, at first resupinate, then reflexed, reniform or dimidiate, sessile, white, *clothed with a soft, downy or tomentose villosity,* incurved on the margin. GILLS rather broad, subdistant, rounded behind, radiating from a lateral or eccentric point, whitish then ferruginous. SPORES subelliptical, 9-10 x 6-7.5 micr."

On logs, decaying wood, etc., in woods. Throughout the State. June to October. Frequent.

The larger spores and size of pileus distinguish *C. versutus* from *C. herbarum.*

555. Crepidotus cinnabarinus Pk.

Torr. Bot. Club, Bull. 22, 1895.

PILEUS 5-10 mm. broad, subsessile to slightly stipitate, soon reflexed lateral, *scarlet* to cinnabar-red, villose-tomentose, glabre-scent, even on the margin. GILLS rather broad, subdistant, sinuate behind, *scarlet on edge,* which is minutely fimbriate-crenulate. STEM short, 1-2 mm. long, or almost lacking, lateral, minutely red-dish-tomentose, continuous with the base of the pileus on the upper side. SPORES elliptical-oval, 7-9 x 4.5-5.5 micr., smooth, pointed at one end, slightly tinged reddish. BASIDIA 20-25 micr. long by 7-9 wide, with 1, 2 or 4 sterigmata.

On decaying bass-wood log, etc., in low moist woods, southeast of Ann Arbor. September-November. Rare.

This brilliant red but small species was rediscovered by the writer years after it was first collected, when it was sent to Peck from Ann

Arbor by L. M. Johnson, then instructor in Botany in the University. All efforts to get a definite spore print failed, as my plants were collected November 12 and the spores matured slowly in the cold atmosphere. Under the microscope they had a slight tinge of red like that of the edge of the gills and pileus, and some uncertainty remains as to whether the form should not be referred to Claudopus. Quite a number of the spores were abnormal, and in one case one spore grew from the side of another which was the only one attached to that basidium. The *trama of the gills* is composed of narrow, parallel hyphae, 3 micr. thick, hyaline towards the pileus but filled with a red homogeneous substance toward the edge of the gills, where the hyphae terminate in inflated, *sterile,* oval or elliptical *large cells;* this coloring matter gradually breaks up into refractive red globules. The *trama of the pileus* is hyaline toward the gills, composed of interwoven narrow, long hyphae, about 6 micr. thick, which become narrower toward the surface of the pileus and are filled with the red coloring matter, finally ending in tufts or fibrils which stand out from the surface and are intensely scarlet-red.

556. Crepidotus sepiarius Pk.

Torr. Bot. Club, Bull. 25, 1898.

"PILEUS 4-8 mm. long, convex, subumbilicate, even, very minutely scaly, *grayish-tawny.* GILLS adnexed, minutely crenulate on edge, tawny. STEM short, 2-4 mm. long, curved, *generally eccentric,* rarely central, brownish, sometimes mealy or pulverulent. SPORES broadly elliptical, 9-10 x 6 micr., nucleate.

On oak rails. Michigan Agricultural College grounds. Leg. Prof. W. J. Beal. January.

The grayish tint of the pileus is due to the minute, grayish floccose squammules." When central-stemmed the species might be mistaken for a Naucoria. I have not collected it.

557. Crepidotus fulvotomentosus Pk.

N. Y. State Mus. Rep. 26, 1874.

PILEUS 1-5 cm. broad, scattered or gregarious, suborbicular at first then reniform or dimidiate, sessile or attached by a short, villose tubercle, *hygrophanous,* densely tawny tomentose when young, *tomentum breaking up into small, tawny scales as pileus expands,* i. e., variegated, ochraceous beneath the tomentum, margin at first incurved. FLESH firm, thin. GILLS medium close, broad, subventricose, radiating from the tubercle, rusty-tan color, *white-fimbriate on edge.* SPORES elliptical-ovate, inequilateral or with a depression on one side, 8-10 x 5-6 micr., rusty-ochraceous.

Gregarious. On decaying wood, logs, etc., of frondose trees. Throughout the State. Recorded from June 9 to October 12. Common.

This differs from *C. calolepis,* if my motion is correct, by its spores and the tinge of red in the color of the pileus. It is very close to *C. calolepis,* but if the spores are constant must be kept separate. Both are distinguished from other species by the dense tomentum when young, which breaks up into separate but small hairy scales. Both are rather persistent and may remain on logs in a dry condition for quite a time. Peck says the cuticle of *C. fulvotomentosus* is separable. It sometimes forms large colonies with pilei of all sizes.

558. Crepidotus calolepis Fr.

Vet. Ak. Förhandl., 1873 (Hymen. Europ. 1874).

Illustrations: Fries, Icones, Pl. 129, Fig. 4.
    Cooke, Ill., Pl. 499.

PILEUS 1-2 cm. broad, suborbicular when young, convex, twice as wide as long, sessile or attached by a white villose tubercle, reniform or dimidiate, *not hygrophanous nor gelatinous,* covered by a dense *reddish-brown* tomentum when young, breaking up into rufous scales on expanding, margin at first incurved. FLESH firm, thin. GILLS radiating from the obsolete stem, those in the center not always reaching the inner point of the radius, medium close, *broad,* rusty ochraceous at length, edge minutely, white villose. SPORES *oval,* 5-6 x 4-5 micr., smooth, fuscous-brown in mass.

On dead branches of basswood. Houghton. July. Infrequent or rare.

Differs from the preceding in the character of the tomentum, scales and spores. It was at first considered undescribed, as no spore-measurements were found in European descriptions. The spores of this and the preceding species are certainly distinct and they must be kept separate. The plants found were smaller than is usual for *C. fulvotomentosus.*

559. Crepidotus putrigenus B. & C.

Annals Nat. Hist., 1859.

PILEUS 3-9 cm. broad, sessile, dimidiate or subreniform, convex to conchate or subexpanded, *densely short villose-tomentose,* lustre *dull, whitish or yellowish-white,* moist or watery, even on margin when dry, margin incurved. FLESH thickish behind, white (dry) under the somewhat separable pellicle. GILLS *close, broad* (width 4-5 times the thickness of the flesh), radiating from the villose basal tubercle, narrowed in front, rounded-adnate behind, becoming crisped on drying, *edge entire.* SPORES *spherical,* smooth, about 6 micr. diam., rusty-fuscous. BASIDIA 4-spored. CYSTIDIA none. ODOR rather disagreeable. TASTE tardily somewhat nauseous.

Gregarious or imbricate on decaying logs, stumps, etc., of mixed woods. South Haven and New Richmond. July to September. Infrequent.

Whether this species is a mere form of *C. malachius* is hard to determine. The spores are alike, but in our plants the pileus averaged a large size (for a Crepidotus) and its surface was villose throughout, the villosity becoming denser at the base; this may be the result of luxuriant development. All my collections of *C. malachius* average smaller, and the pileus is glabrous except the base. The gills are somewhat closer than in *C. malachius,* and I am not certain that the pileus is truly hygrophanous. It would seem that the villose, non-hygrophanous, large pileus with margin not striate (dry) and the closer gills separate it.

560. Crepidotus malachius B. & C.

Annals Nat. Hist., 1859.

Illustrations: Peck, N. Y. State Mus. Bull. 122, Report for 1907, Pl. 112, Fig. 1-4.
Conn. Survey, Bull. 3, Pl. 22, p. 43.

PILEUS 1-4 cm. broad, convex to plane, varying subreniform, cuneiform or flabelliform, often depressed behind, *sessile or with a very short, white, tomentose stem,* hygrophanous, watery in wet weather, *glabrous* except above attachment, watery-white, *grayish-white or hoary, striatulate on margin* (dry) as well as at first, sur-

face with a slight gelatinous feel. FLESH firm at first, becoming
soft. GILLS almost close, *broad, rounded or abruptly narrowed
behind* but reaching the stem-like base, ventricose, thin, whitish
then tinged flesh color, finally rusty-brown. SPORES spherical,
smooth, 6-7 micr. diam., rusty-brown.

Var. *plicatilis* Pk. has a deeply striate pileus. Found at Bay
View.

On decaying wood of frondose trees. Throughout the State.
June to November. Common.

The smaller size, presence of striations on the margin of the
pileus even when dried, the glabrous surface of the pileus and its
tinge of gray, for the most part distinguish this species from the
preceding. From *C. applanatus* it is easily separated by the gills,
which in the latter species are very narrow toward the base and run
together almost in lines.

561. Crepidotus applanatus Fr.

Epicrisis, 1836.

PILEUS 1-3 cm. broad, variable in shape, suborbicular, reniform, cuneiform or spatulate, convex, soon plane, often depressed
behind, sessile or with a short, compressed, white, tomentose base,
glabrous, hygrophanous, watery-white and striatulate on the margin when moist, white when dry. GILLS *very narrow, decurrent,
crowded,* white then cinnamon. SPORES globose, 5-6 micr. diam.,
smooth.

Gregarious on decayed wood, logs, stumps, etc. Ann Arbor, New
Richmond. September. Infrequently found.

Known from the other species by its crowded, narrow gills which
taper almost to lines where they reach the stem. The pileus becomes convolute on drying and often retains its striations on the
thin margin. It has not been found in the State very often, but is
probably widely distributed. Ricken interprets it differently, assigning to it elliptical spores.

562. Crepidotus stipitatus sp. nov.

PILEUS 1-3 cm. broad, *convex,* suborbicular to reniform, *hygrophanous, glabrous,* watery-white to white, *stipitate,* faintly striatulate on the margin when moist, silky when dry, margin decurved.
FLESH white, firm, rather thick behind, thin in front. GILLS

somewhat close, rather broad, broadest behind, narrow in front, white then pale ochraceous-brown, edge entire. STEM distinct, 2-4 mm. long, *eccentric to nearly lateral,* 1-1.5 mm. thick, equal, white, pruinose, villose at base, somewhat prolonged to the gills. SPORES spherical, 5-6 micr. diam., smooth, pale ochraceous-brown. ODOR and TASTE not noticeable.

Gregarious, on very rotten wood. Low swampy woods. Ann Arbor. September. Found but once.

The texture is rather firm; the stipitate character separates it from *C. malachius,* and the globose spores from *C. sepiarius.* The pileus is marginate behind and with a minute, floccose tuft on the side of the stem. *C. tiliophila* Pk. and *C. haustellaris* Fr. are also said to have a short stem, but the pilei of these are brown or alutaceous and their spores are elliptical.

563.   Crepidotus crocophyllus Berk.

Dec. Hooker's Jour., 1856.

PILEUS 1-3 cm. broad, reniform to flabelliform, *convex,* slightly lobed, narrowed into a stem-like base, delicately hairy or glabrous in front, *basal half covered with a dense cottony white tomentum,* watery-ochraceous when moist, *becoming pale chrome when drying,* even on margin. GILLS rather broad, close, thickish, converging at the very base, ochraceous-buff, becoming rusty-ochraceous from the spores. SPORES spherical, 4.5-5.5 micr., *with a depression or cavity on one side,* ochraceous under the microscope.

Scattered on decaying beech log. Bay View. September. Rare.

Originally collected at Waynesville, Ohio, in 1844 by Thomas G. Lea, and named by Berkeley, along with a list of other fungi sent to him by the same collector. (See Cinn. Soc. of Nat. Hist., Vol. 5, 1882, p. 199.)

Our plant was at first referred to *C. ralfsii* B. & Br., but it is much more like Lea's plant. The ground color of the pileus and gills is yellow to ochraceous, and the peculiar spores add a definite distinguishing character. It is close to *C. dorsalis.*

564.   Crepidotus dorsalis Pk.

N. Y. State Mus. Rep. 24, 1872.

PILEUS 1-3 cm. broad, convex, sessile, at first suborbicular, then reniform or dimidiate, *reddish-yellow to tawny-yellow when fresh,* fading to grayish-brown, *adorned with small, tawny, fibrillose scales,* scarcely striate on the margin, which is decurved. FLESH pliant, thin. GILLS close, rather broad, slightly ventricose, rounded behind, *yellow at first,* becoming ochraceous-fuscous then rusty, radiating from the villose point at the attachment of the pileus. SPORES spherical, 6 micr. diam., smooth, nucleate.

On decaying logs and rotten wood, in low swamps. Ann Arbor, New Richmond. July to September. Infrequent.

The color of the pileus varies from a strong tinge of red in some specimens to no red in others. At times the species may be easily taken for small forms of *Claudopus nidulans,* as the coloring is somewhat similar. The young growing specimens are entirely tomentose-squamulose, forming a variegated surface when the pileus is expanded. The perfectly globular spores as well as the absence of a white tomentum on the basal part of the pileus separate it from *C. crocophyllus.* It is probably found throughout the State.

RHODOSPOREAE

Volvaria Fr.

(From the Latin, *Volva,* a wrapper.)

Pink-spored. Stem provided at its base with a *volva* which is formed from a discrete *universal veil; without an annulus;* stem *separable* from the pileus. Gills *free,* ventricose, rounded behind.

Terrestrial or lignicolous. With the exception of *V. bombycina* and *V. speciosa,* the species are small and rather rare. They correspond to Amanitopsis of the white-spored group, and differ from all the pink-spored, except Chamaeota, in the free gills, the volva, and the separable stem. *V. bombycina* is known to be edible; the others are mostly poisonous.

The PILEUS is soft in texture, corresponding in this respect with the Amanitas. Its surface may be glabrous or beautifully silky, in a few species viscid, margin even or striate. Most of them have a whitish pileus, but a few vary to grayish or brown. The GILLS are broad, ventricose, do not reach the stem, and are soft as in Amanita. The STEM is glabrous, silky or villose, some covered with minute spreading hairs; there is no distinct cortex, but a few species are said to be partly hollow. We need more accurate information concerning the interior stem-structure of the rarer species.

The VOLVA is membranous and persists at the base of the stem; in all our species, except one, it splits apically and leaves no shreds on the pileus, showing the splitting in the form of lobes which are often quite constant for a particular species. There is *never* any ANNULUS. The SPORES are rounded, i. e., not angular, smooth, rose-colored, sometimes nucleate. CYSTIDIA are present in *V. volvacea* Fr., *V. pusilla* Fr., *V. murinella* Quel. and *V. speciosa* Fr. I have followed Patouillard's idea of the species of Europe.

Key to the Species

(a) On tree trunks, large; pileus very silky, white; volva large, firm, tough; spores 6-7 x 5 micr. 565. *V. bombycina* Fr.

(aa) On the ground, among grass, herbs, etc., in woods, on dung or manured places.

  (b) Pileus viscid, grayish-white or smoky-gray; odor disagreeable; rather large.

    (c) Pileus striate on margin, smoky-gray; gills flesh color, without cystidia. 567. *V. gloiocephala* D. C.

    (cc) Pileus even on margin; gills rosy, cystidia present. 566. *V. speciosa* Fr.

  (bb) Pileus only slightly viscid, or not at all.

    (c) Pileus umbonate, striate; stem glabrous and solid. 568. *V. umbonata* Pk.

    (cc) Pileus not markedly umbonate.

      (d) Pileus 5-8 cm. broad, grayish-brown, blackish-brown on disk, streaked with black fibrils; spores small, elliptic-ovoid. *V. volvacea* Fr.

      (dd) Pileus less than 5 cm. broad, whitish.

        (e) Stem densely villose with minute spreading hairs; growing in woods. 569. *V. pubescentipes* Pk.; *V. plumulosus* Quel.

        (ee) Stem glabrous, except at the very base.

          (f) Pileus at length striate or rimulose on margin, white, dry.

            (g) Spores subglobose, 7.5 micr. long; stem rather long, 3-4 cm., gills narrow. *V. striatula* Pk.

            (gg) Spores truly elliptical, 6-8 x 4-5.5 micr.; stem 1-2 cm.; gills medium broad. 571. *V. pusilla* Fr.

          (ff) Pileus not striate, 1-3 cm. broad, conico-campanulate, dry, silky, white or ashy-tinged; stem solid, pubescent; volva bilobed. 570. *V. hypopithys* Fr.

565. Volvaria bombycina Fr. (EDIBLE)

Syst. Mycol., 1821.

Illustrations: Atkinson, Mushrooms, Fig. 134, p. 141, 1900.
    Hard, Mushrooms, Pl. 29, Fig. 191-3, 1908.
    McIlvaine, American Fungi, Pl. 59, 1900.
    Michael, Führer f. Pilzfreunde, Vol. III, No. 102.
    Plate C of this Report.

PILEUS 5-20 cm. broad, globose-ovate at first, then campanulate or convex-expanded, obtuse, *white, very silky,* in age somewhat squamulose, even on margin, edge floccose. FLESH rather thin, white, soft. GILLS free, *remote,* broad, very *ventricose, crowded,* flesh color, edge eroded. STEM 8-20 cm. long, 1-1.5 cm. thick, solid, glabrous, tapering upward, usually curved, white, deeply inserted at the base into the *large, thick, loose* VOLVA, which splits at apex, and persists as an ample bag-like or cup-like sheath, sometimes entire, sometimes torn. SPORES oval to broadly elliptical, 6-8 x 5.5 micr., smooth, rosy in mass.

Solitary or few together on trunks of living trees or decayed wood, of maple, beech, elm, horse-chestnut, etc.; usually from a crack or wound. Throughout the State. July-September. Infrequent.

A noble mushroom, often ensconced on a tree trunk out of reach, its perfect shape and silky dress evoking admiration from everyone. In the egg-stage it reminds one of the large Phalloids. Brought into the house at this stage, and placed in a drinking-glass with a moist cloth about its base, it will expand in all its perfection. It has not been shown as yet that it lives parasitically on the trees from which it grows. Once located, it may be looked for each succeeding year on the same spot. A maple tree on the campus of the University of Michigan is the home of one which fruits regularly every summer. It attains a considerable size. The species occurs throughout the world.

566. Volvaria speciosa Fr. (Poisonous)

Syst. Mycol., 1821.

Illustrations: Patouillard, Tab. Analyt., No. 640.
Ricken, Blätterpilze, Pl. 70, Fig. 1.
Cooke, Ill., Pl. 297.
Bresadola, Fungh. mang. e. vel., Pl. 44.
Gillet, Champignons de France, No. 714.

PILEUS 5-10 cm. or more broad, globose-ovate at first, then expanded to plane, subumbonate, *very viscid, glabrous, white* or tinged gray, margin *not striate.* FLESH thin, soft, putrescent. GILLS free, crowded, rather broad, *ventricose,* deep flesh-color or rosy. STEM 10-20 cm. long, 1-2 cm. thick, equal or nearly so, *at first villose,* glabrescent, base tomentose, white. VOLVA large, splitting apically, close-fitting, flaccid, edge torn. SPORES large, broadly-elliptical, smooth, variable in size, 12-18 x 8-10 micr. CYSTIDIA clavate, obtuse. ODOR strong and disagreeable at times, especially when old.

Solitary or gregarious. On manured ground, dung, rich leaf-mould in woods; often in rich cultivated fields. So far found in the southern half of the State only. May, June and July. Infrequent. Atkinson says plants from Lansing, found in a potato patch, had the odor of rotting potatoes. Sometimes the *odor* is not evident, *especially when the plant is young.* Solitary specimens occur in low woods and are somewhat smaller, but in all cases the large, broad spores are characteristic and separate it from the next species. It is considered poisonous in Europe, but McClatchie, in California, reports it perfectly safe. Bresadola warns against confusing it with *Lepiota naucina* and *Palliota campestris.*

567. Volvaria gloiocephala Fr. (Poisonous)

Syst. Mycol,, 1821.

Illustration: Patouillard, Tab. Analyt., No. 224.
Bresadola, Fúng. mang. e. vel., Pl. 45.
Gillett, Champignons de France, No. 711.
Ricken, Blätterpilze, Pl. 70, Fig. 2.
Cooke, Ill., Pl. 298.

PILEUS 5-10 cm. broad, ovate at first then campanulate-expanded to plane, obtuse, sometimes umbonate, glabrous, viscid to glutinous when moist, *smoky-gray to pearl-gray,* with a metallic luster when dry, margin striate. FLESH thin, fragile, white. GILLS free, rather close, broad toward front, narrowed behind, subventricose, edge concolor. STEM 8-15 cm. or more long, 1-2 cm. thick, tapering upward, solid, even, glabrous above, somewhat villose toward base. VOLVA thin, splitting apically or circularly, sometimes three-lobed, sometimes regular or lacerated on edge, adherent, externally tomentose. SPORES 11-13 x 6-7.5 micr., elliptical, smooth, flesh color. CYSTIDIA none. ODOR and TASTE disagreeable, quite strong.

Solitary. On decaying vegetation, old leaves, rotten wood, in low woods. August. Ann Arbor. Rare.

Except for the darker colors, smaller spores, striations on the pileus and lack of cystidia, this seems close to the preceding, and might perhaps be considered as a variety of it. The spores and colors in these two species are very variable and no doubt intermediate forms occur. Striations are never very satisfactory characters to separate species, although they are useful. The species is con-

sidered *very poisonous,* and if so, is easily confused with *V. speciosa.*
The authors note that the volva breaks in a circular manner, sometimes leaving shreds on the pileus like some Amanitas. Atkinson
has shown that in Amanita the volva of the same species may under-
go the two different modes of breaking, and the same holds true of
this form. Our plants did not show any shreds on the pileus, and
the volva was angularly lobed. The pileus was not truly umbonate.
It must not be confused with the gray form of *Amanitopsis vaginata.*

568. Volvaria umbonata Pk.

Torr. Bot. Club, Bull. 26, 1899.

"PILEUS 2-3 cm. broad, conico-campanulate or campanulate, then
expanded and *furnished with a prominent umbo, white,* slightly
viscid when moist, *silky when dry, strongly striate.* FLESH thin.
GILLS free, remote, medium close, pale flesh color. STEM 5-6 cm.
long, 4 mm. thick, *solid,* glabrous, white, slightly thickened below.
VOLVA white, membranous, persistent, irregularly split into seg-
ments, forming a shallow cap. SPORES variable in size, broadly
elliptical, nucleate, smooth, 5-7 x 4-5 micr.
"On lawns and grassy places."
The above is taken from Peck's and Lloyd's descriptions. Lloyd
finds it in Ohio. It is probably to be found in our State if careful
search be made.

569. Volvaria pubescentipes Pk.

N. Y. State Mus. Rep. 29, 1878 (*V. pubipes* in Sylloge).

Illustrations: Ibid., Pl. I, Fig. 1-3.

PILEUS 1-2 cm. broad, *dry, white,* obtuse, covered with adpressed,
silky squamules, *not striate on margin.* GILLS free, remote, close,
not very broad, white then flesh color, *edge persistently white-fimbriate.* STEM 2-4 cm. long, 1-2 mm. thick, usually slender, equal
or subequal, *densely minutely villose* with spreading hairs, even,
white. VOLVA white, membranous, subappressed, sometimes 3-
lobed. SPORES suboval to broadly elliptical, smooth, 5-7 x 4-5 micr.,
pale flesh color.
(Dried: Buff to pale ochraceous-brown.)
Scattered. On the ground, among debris in hemlock and cedar
swamps of northern Michigan, sparingly in frondose woods of the
southern part. Marquette, Houghton, Bay View, New Richmond,
Ann Arbor, etc. July-September. Frequent locally.

Slender, pure white, with minute hairs all over the stem. Its habitat in woods is a distinguishing character. Patouillard's figure of *V. plumulosus* Quel. of Europe (No. 333, Tab. Analyt.) is somewhat illustrative of our plant. I find the stem of *V. pubescentipes* of the woods always rather long and slender, and the cap and gills more narrow than in Patouillard's figure.

570. Volvaria hypopithys Fr.

Hymen. Europ., 1874.

PILEUS *conico*-campanulate, 6-15 mm. high, dry, *silky,* whitish, *even on margin.* FLESH thin. GILLS free, ascending, rather narrow, close, white then flesh-color, edge minutely crenulate. STEM 2-3 cm. long, 2-3 mm. thick, *solid,* equal, adpressed-silky, whitish. VOLVA vaginate, bilobed, tomentose externally, whitish. SPORES 5-7.5 x 3-4 micr., smooth, elliptical.

I have referred here a collection made by Messrs. Hill and Fischer of the Detroit Mycological Club, and given the description of their plant. It appears to lack the pubescent stem of the typical description, but its conical-shaped cap even at maturity seems to require its reference to this species or to a closely related one. The finders referred it to *V. murinella* because of the gray tinge of the pileus. Patouillard's figure, however, shows the pileus of that species expanded-plane and the plant smaller. Peck (in N. Y. State Bull. 54) reports *V. hypopithys* for New York, but without any notes. Our plant differs from *V. umbonata* Pk. in its pileus being even, not at all viscid, although the spores are the same. Further collections are necessary to determine its true place.

571. Volvaria pusilla Fr.

Syst. Myc., 1821.

Illustrations: Patouillard, Tab. Analyt., No. 332 (as *V. parvula*).
    Ricken, Blätterpilze, Pl. 70, Fig. 3.
    Gillett, Champignons de France, No. 713 (as *V. parvula*).
    Hard, Mushrooms, Fig. 195, p. 243, 1900.
    Clements, Minn. Mushrooms, Fig. 31, p. 57, 1910.
    Plate CI of this Report.

PILEUS 5-12 mm. broad, at first ovate then campanulate-convex, finally plane, *white,* silky-fibrillose, *dry,* even then rimose or striatulate on margin, obtuse or slightly depressed, rarely mammillate. FLESH thickish on disk only, white. GILLS free, close to sub-distant, moderately broad, white then bright flesh color. STEM 1-2 cm. long, 1-3 mm. thick, white, equal, *glabrous, solid,* even. VOLVA split into 3 or 4 nearly equal lobes, firm, loose, white becoming sordid. SPORES elliptic-ovate, 6-8.5 x 4-5.5 micr., smooth, nucleate, incarnate in mass. CYSTIDIA scattered on sides and edge of gills, ventricose, very obtuse, 35-40 x 9-18 micr. ODOR none.

Solitary or scattered, under herbs in moist ground. Detroit, Ann Arbor. July-August. Rarely found.

This species is distinguished by its small size, white color, the regular, three to four-lobed volva and by its cystidia and spores. Dr. Fischer collected the Detroit specimens, from which Hard's figure was obtained; Dr. E. B. Mains found the Ann Arbor speci-mens of our photograph. It seems to be the same plant described by C. G. Lloyd in Mycological Notes, Vol. I, p. 9. Whether it is the true *V. pusilla* of Persoon remains an open question. Fries, in the Systema, does not mention the striations of the pileus, and in his later works includes the form under *V. parvula,* which he al-ways describes with a dry cap. Ricken (Blätterpilze), however, says the cap is at first viscid, soon dry. Berkeley (Outlines) also speaks of the cap of *V. pusilla* as viscid and not striate. The stem is said to be somewhat stuffed to hollow, and hence our plant departs from Berkeley's also in this respect.

From the remarks of various authors it would seem that the spe-cies referred to *V. pusilla* by some and to *V. parvula* by others is an unusually variable plant, inasmuch as the pileus may be somewhat viscid or dry, even on the margin or striatulate, umbonate or plane, and the stem is either solid or with a narrow tubule. Careful study of the caps of our plants failed to reveal more than mere rudiments of a cuticle which could scarcely become viscid in wet weather. The stem was solid and practically homogeneous. There were no signs of striations on the pileus, although the expanded margin became slightly rivulose in age. The trama of the gills was convergent, com-posed of large, inflated cells. It remains for those who are lucky enough to find it often, to note to what extent it may vary as to the contested points.

Chamæota Smith, W. G.

(From the Greek, *chamai*, on the ground. The old generic name . Annularia is pre-occupied.)

Pink-spored. Stem *fleshy, separable* from the pileus, with a persistent or evanescent *annulus.* Gills free. Spores rounded. Terrestrial or lignicolus. Fleshy, putrescent, *rare* mushrooms, corresponding to Lepiota of the white-spored group. They differ from Volvaria in having an annulus but no volva. The annulus is derived from an *inner veil,* which is thin. The annulus is usually movable. About a dozen species are known throughout the world. The two following species seem to be the only ones known in the United States, and their discovery is due to the careful and acute observations of Mr. Bronson Barlow of Greenville, and Dr. O. E. Fischer of the Detroit Mycological Club.

572.   Chamæota mammillata (Longyear)   Murrill

Mich. Acad. of Sci. Rep. 3, 1902.   (As Annularia.)

Illustration: Ibid, Pl. I, Fig. 4.

PILEUS 1-2 cm. broad, plane at maturity *with a prominent mammiform umbo at the center,* whitish, umbo lemon-yellow, surface minutely rough. FLESH very thin, soft. GILLS free, ventricose, broad, thin, close, 3 mm. broad, pale flesh color. STEM 3.5 cm. long, 1.5 mm. thick at apex, gradually enlarging toward base, glabrous above and silky below the ring. ANNULUS membranous, persistent, white. SPORES subglobose, smooth, 5-6 micr. diam., pale flesh color. CYSTIDIA fusiform, inflated in the middle, 50 x 20 micr.

Solitary. On decaying logs in woods. Greenville. July. Rare. Reported by Longyear, collected by Mr. Barlow.

The type material is in the herbarium of Michigan Agricultural College, East Lansing.

573. Chamæota sphærospora (Pk.)

Torr. Bot. Club, Bull. 33, p. 216, 1906. (As Annularia.)

Illustrations: Plates VI, CII of this Report.

PILEUS 3-6 cm. broad, conic or subcampanulate, becoming ex-panded, umbonate, silky-fibrillose, yellow, fading to whitish in part, *umbo brownish.* FLESH thin. GILLS free, close, thin, whit-ish or cream-colored when young, flesh-color when mature, moder-ately broad, *edge white-fimbriate;* trama of parallel hyphae. STEM 3-8 cm. long, 4-8 mm. thick, equal or tapering upward, *solid,* fibrous, substriate, whitish. ANNULUS white, median or below the mid-dle. SPORES globose or subglobose, 5-6 micr. diam., smooth, non-apiculate, dull flesh-color. BASIDIA 4-spored, at maturity pro-jecting beyond the younger hymenium, about 25 x 8-9 micr. CYS-TIDIA none, except on edge, which is densely covered by slender stalked long cells, enlarged at apex.

Subcaespitose. On rotten wood of elm trunk. Detroit. Col-lected by Dr. Fischer. August. Rare. Cotype in the University of Michigan herbarium.

Described by Dr. Peck from material collected near Detroit by O. E. Fischer. It has been suggested that it is identical with *C. fenzlii* Fr., illustrated as follows:

> Kalchbrenner and Schulzer, Icones, Hymen Hung.; Pl. 10, Fig. 1.
>
> Gillet, Champignons de France, No. 30.
>
> Engler and Prantl. I, 1** Fig. 121. B. p. 258.

In some respects it certainly has similar characters, but Gillet, who gives a full description, says the spores are "large" and his figures confirm this if we compare them with those in which he shows small spores of other species. Unfortunately neither Gillet nor any one else appears to have recorded the spore-measurements of *C. fenzlii.* Furthermore, the latter species is described as smaller, the annulus and stem yellow, or yellowish, the former evanescent. Gillet says the stem of *C. fenzlii* is at first solid then hollow. Further information concerning the variation of our plant is necessary before it can be reduced to synonymy. It seems to be a very rare plant and is only recorded from the one locality.

Pluteus Fr.

(From the Latin, *Pluteus*, a protective military covering.)

Pink-spored. *Without volva or annulus.* Stem *fleshy to fibrous,* not cartilaginous, separable from the pileus. Gills *free,* rounded behind, soft. Spores rounded, rarely angular. Hymenium *provided with cystidia.*

Small, soft mushrooms (except *P. cervinus* Fr. which is rather large), *lignicolous* for the most part, i. e., growing on wood, on logs, stumps, decayed wood, forest debris, or sawdust, rarely on manure. The smaller forms are found in very moist situations. *P. cervinus* is common; the others tend to be rare or infrequent.

The PILEUS may be glabrous, silky, velvety, minutely scaly or torn, fibrillose or granular; its surface is even, striate on the margin or varying to quite rugulose. The upper layer of hyphae is sometimes differentiated into a separable, somewhat viscid pellicle, or it is composed of loose, rounded cells of a different color; the shape, size and color of these surface hyphae or cells under the microscope provide a helpful means of definitely determining some of the species. The color of the pileus varies white, yellow, brown, blackish, or rarely orange to red. The GILLS are soft, not attached to the stem but rounded behind and often remote. Usually they are white, in a few cases yellowish, and all become tinged by the flesh-colored or rosy spores. They are coherent, i. e., collapsing on each other as in Coprinus, and often become moist and nearly deliquescent in wet weather. They are provided with large cells projecting beyond the basidia, either on their edge or sides or both, called CYSTIDIA; the shape and structure of the cystidia vary, and can be used with the spores to separate the otherwise often similar species. They are called STERILE CELLS when they occur on the edge of the gills, where they are sometimes arranged in clusters. The STEM is central, fleshy, often with a fibrous cuticle, not cartilaginous except under dry weather conditions; it is solid except in a few species, as e. g., *P. admirabilis* Pk. and *P. salicinus* Fr.; it is usually slender and fragile, equal, rarely subbulbous, glabrous or velvety, etc., like the pileus. The SPORES of the different species are very much alike, minute, subglobose or short-oblong, white and smooth, not angular in our species. They include a number of *edible* forms according to McIlvaine, although the older authors considered them with suspicion. Not all the species have been tested, and all, except perhaps the edible *P. cervinus,* are too small to consider from a food-value standpoint.

The species can for the most part only be identified with the aid of a microscope, since the character of the cystidia must be known before certainty can prevail. Hence the following key is based on the only certain method which can be followed in this genus. Of the species not yet found in the State, *P. stercorarius* Pk. grows on manure heaps, and its spores are exceptionally large, measuring 12-15 micr. long; *P. sterilomarginatus* Pk. has angular spores. It is possible that *Pleurotus subpalmatus* Fr. which as it occurs with us is well illustrated by Cooke under *Pluteus phlebophorus,* Plate 422, B., has been reported as a Pluteus; its adnate gills, however, should prevent confusion.

Fries divided the genus into three sections, given below.

Key to the Species

(A) Pileus white or whitish. [See also (AA) and (AAA).]
  (a) Cystidia with 2-4 horns at apex; pileus subglabrous to fibrillose or rimose, 5-15 cm. broad. 574. *P. cervinus* Fr. var. *albus* Pk.
  (aa) Apex of cystidia without horns; pileus villose-tomentose, 2-7 cm. broad. 578. *P. tomentosulus* Pk.
  (aaa) Cystidia rare, not pronged; pileus glabrous, 2-3 cm. broad. 579. *P. roscocandidus* Atk.
(AA) Pileus yellow, orange or red.
  (a) Pileus orange to vermillion; spores short-oblong. 582. *P. caloceps* Atk.
  (aa) Pileus yellow, sometimes smoky tinged.
    (b) Pileus rugose-reticulate on disk.
      (c) Stem stuffed to hollow, yellow; pileus glabrous, umbonate. 584. *P. admirabilis* Pk.
      (cc) Stem solid, pinkish-white; pileus 4-5 cm. broad, smoky velvety on disk. *P. flavofuligineus* Atk.
    (bb) Pileus not rugose on disk, striate on margin; stem pellucid-white. 585. *P. leoninus* Fr.
(AAA) Pileus brown, fuscous, umber, blackish, etc.
  (a) Cystidia with 2-4 horns at apex; pileus not striate on margin; stem fibrillose.
    (b) Gills with their edges smoky-brown. 575. *P. umbrosus* Fr.
    (bb) Gills unicolorous.
      (c) Pileus usually rather large, 3-15 cm. broad; color dingy pale brown, but variable; common. 574. *P. cervinus* Fr.
      (cc) Pileus small to medium; pileus and base of stem tinged bluish or with a distinct olivaceous tinge; cystidia longer than in the preceding; rare. 576. *P. salicinus* Fr.
  (aa) Cystidia without horns at apex.
    (b) Pileus not truly striate on the margin.
      (c) Stem glabrous, pellucid, innately striatulate.
        (d) Stem and gills white at first. 581. *P. nanus* Fr.
        (dd) Stem and sometimes the gills, yellowish. 581. *P. nanus* var. *lutescens* Fr.
      (cc) Stem velvety to squamulose, brownish, etc.
        (d) Edge of gills of same color, cystidia hyaline. 580. *P. granularis* Pk.
        (dd) Edge of gills with yellowish cystidia. 580. *P. granularis* Pk. var. *umbrosellus* Atk.

(ccc) Stem silky, whitish or tinged fuscous; spores oblong, 6-6.5 x 3 micr. 577. *P. ephebius* Fr. var.
(bb) Pileus short- or long-striatulate on margin.
(c) Pileus slightly striate on margin, glabrous, cinnamon-brown. *P. chrysophaeus* Fr.
(cc) Pileus long-striate on margin, minutely velvety or obscurely granulose.
(d) Pileus 1-3 cm. broad; stem fibrous-striate, glabrous, white or brownish. (See 617. *Leptonia seticeps* Atk.)
(dd) Pileus 2.5-5 cm. broad; stem innately striatulate, glabrous. 583. *P. longistriatus* Pk.

Section I. Surface of the pileus at length fibrillose or floccose, by the breaking up of the horizontal layer of the fibrils of the cuticle.

574. Pluteus cervinus Fr. (EDIBLE)

Epicrisis, 1836.

Illustrations: Cooke, Ill., Pl. 301.
Patouillard, Tab. Analyt., No. 335.
Ricken, Blätterpilze, Pl. 71, Fig. 1.
Atkinson, Mushrooms, Fig. 132, p. 138, 1900.
Hard, Mushrooms, Fig. 188, 189, p. 235, 1908.
Marshall, Mushroom Book, op. p. 87, 1905.
N. Y. State Mus. Rep. 54, Pl. 74, 1901.
McIlvaine, American Mushrooms, Pl. LXI, p. 243.
Plate CIII of this Report.

PILEUS 5-10 cm. broad, rarely smaller, campanulate, then broad- ly convex to expanded, *varying glabrous to fibrillose,* fibrils darker, disk sometimes scaly, even on margin, white, dingy-tan, grayish brown or darker, provided with a somewhat separable, sometimes subviscid, pellicle; FLESH white. GILLS close, free, broad, rounded behind, white then flesh-colored from the spores. STEM equal or slightly tapering upward, 5-15 cm. long, 6-18 mm. thick, firm, solid, dingy white to brownish-tan, glabrous or somewhat fibrillose. · SPORES inconstant in size and shape, *short-oblong, oval,* broadly elliptical, 5-8 x 4-5 micr., sometimes longer or broader, more rarely globular, often nucleate, smooth, flesh-colored in mass. CYSTIDIA abundant, fusoid, stout, terminating in 2-4 short, blunt horns. ODOR and TASTE somewhat disagreeable.

Solitary, scattered, or when growing on sawdust, etc., often caespitose. On stumps, logs, from underground roots or wood, on boards, sawdust, etc. Throughout the State, mostly in broad-leaved woods. June to October (earliest record is May 28; latest, October 4). Very common. Edible.

Like *Armillaria mellea* its frequent fruiting makes it possible to find a great•amount of variation, and many varieties have been named. Var. *alba*. Pk. is whitish, often caespitose and frequents sawdust piles. Var. *viscosus* Lloyd is described as very viscid on the cap, and with narrow gills. Var. *petasatus* Fr. has the cap striate to the middle. It is probable that all of these forms intergrade with the typical plant which along with the varieties varies into many shades of color. Slender forms occur in low woods, on debris, with the stature of *P. leoninus,* but the pileus is almost white.

This species can be distinguished from Entoloma by its free gills and its lignicolous habitat, although of similar appearance otherwise. As Entoloma contains poisonous species, this is important. In Europe, *P. cervinus* has been marked as "suspected"; in this country, however, it is highly praised by mycophagists, since the disagreeable odor and taste disappear on cooking. It has a characteristic relation to the stump on which it is often found, in being so attached that it is difficult to get a piece of the wood and mushroom together, since its stem grows in the vertical cracks of the stump. With us it is found on wood, rarely on soil, although the condition of the woody substratum varies exceedingly. Small plants imitate some of the other species and can only be separated with certainty by the use of the microscope. The pronged cystidia are usually the decisive character. Patouillard says that the flesh has yellowish lactiferous hyphae scattered throughout it.

575. Pluteus umbrosus Fr.

Sys. Mycol., 1821.

Illustrations: Bresadola, Fung. Trid., Vol. 2, Pl. 116.
Ricken, Blätterpilze, Pl. 70, Fig. 4.

PILEUS 5-10 cm. broad, campanulate then convex-expanded, broadly umbonate, *smoky umber* or blackish brown, *rugose-reticulate and floccose-scaly on disk,* even and fibrillose on margin. FLESH white. Gills free, close, broad, ventricose, whitish then flesh-colored from the spores, *edge fimbriate and smoky brown* from the dark cystidia. STEM 3-8 cm. long, 4-8 mm. thick, solid, firm, equal or slightly tapering upward, dingy white to brownish, covered with smoky-brown fibrills. SPORES oval-elliptical, 5-7 x 3-4 micr., smooth, flesh color in mass. CYSTIDIA fusoid, 75-85 x 15-20 micr., apex with 2-4 horns. ODOR and TASTE slightly disagreeable.

Solitary or scattered on rotten wood, in conifer woods, usually on hemlock or pine. Huron Mountains, Houghton, New Richmond. August and September. Infrequent except locally.

Distinguished at once by the smoky-brown edge of the gills. It tends to be smaller than *P. cervinus* and darker in color. *P. granularis* var. *umbrosellus* has yellowish edged gills, and its cystidia are not horned. There seem to be a number of varieties connecting *P. cervinus* and *P. umbrosus*. McIlvaine pronounces it edible.

576. Pluteus salicinus Fr. var.

Syst. Mycol., 1821 (as *Leptonia salicinus*).

Illustration: Cooke, Ill., Pl. 1169.

PILEUS 2-5 cm. broad, convex to expanded, broadly umbonate, smoky-umber, pruinose-velvety, disk flocculose, margin even. GILLS free, close, not broad, reaching margin of cap, *edge concolor,* white then flesh-colored from the spores. STEM equal, 2-4 cm. long, 2-4 mm. thick, base bulbillose, curved, shining, silky-fibrillose, stuffed, whitish but covered with smoky fibrils, *base smoky-olive.* SPORES broadly elliptical, 7.5-8.5 x 5-6 micr., smooth, flesh color. CYSTIDIA 2-4 pronged at apex, 75-90 x 15-17 micr., fuscoid, stout.

Solitary. On rotten wood, in willow and alder swamp. July-August. Ann Arbor. Rare.

The green tinge is not very marked on the pileus but is quite marked at the base of the stem. It agrees best with Massee's description (British Fungus Flora). The typical bluish form has not been seen by me in the State, although collected elsewhere. The horned cystidia separate it from other smoky-umber species, and the white edge of the gills distinguishes it from *P. umbrosus.*

577. Pluteus ephebius Fr. var.

Syst. Mycol., 1821.

Illustration: Cooke, Ill., Pl. 517.

PILEUS 2.5 cm. broad, convex-expanded, *delicately silky-fibrillose,* shining, becoming somewhat fibrillose-scaly, not at all granular, *mouse-gray,* unicolorous, even on margin. GILLS free, rather remote, not broad, pruinose, white then bright pink from spores, edge concolor. STEM about 2 cm. long, equal, curved, silky, white or tinged fuscous, *striate*. SPORES *oblong,* 6-6.5 x 3 micr., smooth, pink. CYSTIDIA about 50 micr. long, slender, sometimes curved and rounded at the apex, abundant on sides and edge of gills.

Solitary. On rotten logs, in woods. New Richmond. Rare.

The fibrillose pileus allies this form with this section. The oblong spores, characteristic of the species according to Massee, induced me to place it here although the absence of "bluish down" which Fries italicises may indicate that it is a different or undescribed species. It seems to be close to var. *drepanophyllus* Schultz, the status of which is uncertain.

578.   Pluteus tomentosulus Pk.

N. Y. State Mus. Rep. 32, 1879.

Illustration: Atkinson, Mushrooms, Fig. 133, p. 139, 1900.

PILEUS 3-7 cm. broad, thin, soon expanded, obtuse, umbonate, *floccose-tomentose,* more densely so on disk, *white* or tinged with pink, especially on the margin, margin even. FLESH thin, white. GILLS free, rather remote, crowded, *broad,* white then rose-colored from the spores, edge fimbriate. STEM 5-10 cm. long, 4-8 mm. thick, equal, solid, fibrillose-*striate,* subbulbous at base, slightly tomentulose, bulb tomentose, white. SPORES subglobose, or broadly short elliptical, 5-7 x 4.5-5.5 micr., smooth, rose-flesh color in mass. CYSTIDIA stout, 85-95 x 22-25 micr., not horned, bottle-shaped on a rather slender stalk, scattered, more numerous on edge of gills.

Solitary or scattered. On rotten logs or prostrate trunks, especially in hemlock, tamarack or cedar swamps. Throughout the State: Marquette, Houghton, Sault Ste. Marie, New Richmond, Ann Arbor. July, August, September. Frequent in the northern part of State.

This is a beautiful species but prefers deep swamps. In Europe *P. pellitus* Fr., a more glabrous species, takes its place. According to Peck, the pileus often has a pink tinge.

579. Pluteus roseocandidus Atk.

Ann. Mycol., Vol. VII, p. 373, 1909.

PILEUS 2-3 cm. broad, *fragile,* convex thén expanded, glabrous, dry, *pure white,* sometimes tinged rose or brownish-buff in wet weather, *striatulate on the thin margin,* with a dull lustre. FLESH thin, white. GILLS free, reaching the stem, elliptical, close, rounded behind, moderately broad, hyphae of trama converging, white at first then pink. STEM 3-4 cm. long, 2.5-4 mm. thick, equal, even, hollow, glabrous, slightly mealy at apex, *fragile,* terete or compressed, subbulbillate, innately fibrillose, *pure white.* SPORES globose, smooth, 6-8 micr., pale diam., flesh color under microscope. CYSTIDIA few or lacking on sides of gills. *Sterile cells* on edge, globose or ventricose-inflated, obtuse, 50-80 x 20-35 micr. *Basidia* 30 x 8-9 micr., 14-spored. ODOR none.

Gregarious. On grassy ground in woods near tamarack swamp. Ann Arbor. October. Rare.

This white species is said to have a two-layered trama in the pileus, the inner floccose, the outer forming a cuticle two to three cells thick of pyriform to subglobose cells. I have found it but once.

Section II. Surface of pileus granulose, pruinate or pulverulent, composed of enlarged globular pyriform or fusoid-elongated, colored cells.

580. Pluteus granularis Pk.

Buffalo Soc. Nat. Sci., Bull. 1, 1873.

Illustration: Hard, Mushrooms, Fig. 190, p. 237.

PILEUS 2-5 cm. broad, convex to plane, subumbonate, *rugose-wrinkled,* yellowish-brown to umber, or chestnut color, *granulose* or *villose-granulose* like plush. GILLS free, crowded, rather broad, ventricose, white then flesh-colored from spores, *edge concolor.* STEM 3-7 cm. long, 2-4 mm. thick, slender, equal, solid, pallid, *velvety pubescent* or covered with brown scales towards base. SPORES globose, 4-5 micr. diam., apiculate, nucleate, smooth, flesh color. CYSTIDIA globose-obovate, about 35-25 micr., infrequent, hyaline.

Solitary or scattered. On rotten logs, etc., in conifer and frondose woods.

Throughout the State: Houghton, Huron Mountains, Marquette,
Bay View, Ann Arbor. July-September. More frequent in mixed
hemlock woods; never common.

The villosity and granulosity 'on the cap, when present, is due
to globular or elongated-fusoid cells, filled with coloring matter.
These cells correspond to the fibrils of such species as *P. umbrosus,*
from which this species is separated by the spherical spores and
cystidia without prongs at the apex. Peck describes the spores in
the 26th report as spherical, later, in the 38th report, he says
"broadly elliptical, 6-7.5 x 5-6 micr." Our plants, like Lloyd's
(Mycol. Notes, 2), have spherical spores.

Var. *umbrosellus* Atk. nov. var. is distinguished by the 'more
villose pileus and the tinge of *yellow on the edge of the gills.*
The villosity is caused by long, yellowish brown cells, 200-
300 micr. long, 20-30 micr. wide, often crowded into erect, pointed
scales, arranged in sooty, radiating or reticulate, velvety ridges.
The edges of the gills are provided with sterile cells filled with a
pale yellow coloring matter. The cystidia are scattered, globose or
pyriform, not pronged. The spores are 4-5 x 3-4 micr., longer than
broad, subglobose, similar to those of *P. umbrosus;* the cystidia,
however, separate it from the latter.

Var. *intermedius* nov. var. approaches *Leptonia seticeps* in size
of spores, and white-fimbriate edge of gills; but the stem is stuffed,
then hollow, and 4-5 cm. long, 4-5 mm. thick. The cap is ruglose-
villose and 2-5 cm. broad.

Solitary or scattered. On rotten wood. Detroit, etc. Infrequent.

581. Pluteus nanus Fr.

Syst. Mycol., 1821.

Illustrations: Patouillard, Tab. Analyt., No. 334.
　　　　Ricken, Blätterpilze, Pl. 70, Fig. 6.

PILEUS 2-3 cm. broad, convex then expanded, obtuse, *radiately
rugose on disk,* margin even or nearly so, *velvety-pruinose,* granulose or *pulverulent, brownish ashy,* umber or darker when young.
GILLS free, close, ventricose, narrowed toward ends, white then
flesh color from spores, edge fimbriate. STEM 2-3 cm. long, 2-3
mm. thick, *solid,.* equal, rigid often curved, *glabrous,* pellucid-white,

striatulate or 'innately fibrillose. SPORES *subglobose,* 4-5.5 micr. diam., smooth, flesh color. CYSTIDIA fusiform bottle-shaped, sometimes tapering to a point at apex, not horned, *vaculoate,* 75-80 micr. long, on the sides and edge of the gills.

Solitary or scattered. On decaying logs, sticks, etc., in low woods and swamps. June to October. Throughout the State: Huron Mountains, New Richmond, Ann Arbor. Infrequent.

The velvety character of the pileus is only apparent since the surface under a lens is granulose or pulverulent; this is due to globular or fusoid cells which compose the surface layer and give it the brown appearance. It is separated from a number of others by the glabrous stem, small size and subglobose spores. It may appear quite early. There is sometimes a smoky tinge on the cap.

Var. *lutescens* Fr. *Stem* and sometimes the *gills* are *yellow.* The spores seem to be more truly spherical in the variety; stem *solid,* striate.

Habitat, etc., as in the type: New Richmond, Ann Arbor. Infrequent.

582. Pluteus caloceps Atk.

Ann. Mycol., 1909.

"PILEUS 2.5-4.5 cm. broad, convex, umbonate, orpiment-orange to vermillion, orange-vermillion on center, glabrous or slightly granular by separation of the cells, or somewhat rimose on margin; trama two-layered, outer layer composed of globose cells. FLESH white. GILLS free, rounded behind, broadly elliptical to subventricose, pale dull flesh color, edge flocculose, tramal hyphae converging. STEM 3-6 cm. long, 3-5 mm. thick, pallid, fibrous-striate. SPORES suboblong, 5-8 x 4-6 micr. CYSTIDIA ventricose on sides of gills, clavate to subfusoid on edge, 60-75 x 12-20 micr."

Solitary. On rotten wood and on the ground. Ann Arbor. Rare.

583. Pluteus longistriatus Pk.

N. Y. State Mus. Rep. 30, 1878.

Illustration: Plate CIV of this Report.

PILEUS 2-5 cm. broad, very thin, convex then expanded, pale brownish-gray to *brownish-ashy,* minutely scaly on disk and cuticle at length breaking into minute granules, *long-striate or subsulcate when old.* GILLS free, close, *rather broad,* width almost uniform, rounded behind, white then pale flesh color from spores, edge pulverulent. STEM 3-5 cm. long, 2-3.5 mm. thick, equal, *solid,* fibrous, innately striatulate, *white,* pulverulent. SPORES sub-globose, 6-7 x 5 micr., slightly longer than wide, granular within, smooth, *pale* flesh color. CYSTIDIA ventricose, cylindrical in upper part, 75-90 micr. long, not horned, apex broadly obtuse to pointed.

Solitary. On rotten wood in moist places. Ann Arbor, South Haven. June-July. Infrequent.

Peck describes the stem glabrous; our plants had a distinctly pulverulent stem when fresh. The spores also did not seem to be dented on one side as indicated by Peck. Nevertheless, the description fits closely in other respects. It differs from *P. chrysophaeus* in the long striations of the pileus and the fibrous-solid stem; the color, also, is not cinnamon. In age, the longitudinal fibres within the stem loosen, so that it appears falsely fistulose. The larger size and truly free gills separate it from *Leptonia seticeps,* which is long-striatulate on cap.

Section III. Surface of pileus glabrous; moist or hygrophanous.

584. Pluteus admirabilis Pk.

N. Y. State Mus. Rep. 24, 1872.

PILEUS 1-2 cm. broad, thin, convex-campanulate then expanded, usually umbonate, *glabrous,* hygrophanous, *rugose-reticulate, ochre-yellow to luteous,* brownish when young, striatulate on margin when moist, subeven when dry. GILLS free, rounded behind, moderately broad, ventricose, close, whitish or yellowish then rosy-flesh color from the spores. STEM 3-5 cm. long, 1-2 mm. thick, slender, equal, subrigid, glabrous, *stuffed then hollow, yellow,* white-myceloid at base. SPORES subglobose, 5.5-7 x 5-6 micr., smooth, rosy flesh color in mass. CYSTIDIA ventricose, cylindrical in upper part, rounded at apex, 55-65 x 18 micr., scattered; more abundant in the interspaces, more ovoid on the edge of the gills.

Scattered or subgregarious. On logs and decayed wood, in mixed conifer or frondose woods. Houghton, Munising, Marquette, New Richmond, Ann Arbor. July, August and September. More fre-quent in hemlock woods of the northern part of the State.

The surface of the pileus is composed of spheroid stalked cells containing the yellow coloring matter; these are 30-35 x 20-25 micr. in diam. The hyphae of the gill-trama converge and are long and cylindrical. From *P. leoninus* this form is separated by its yellow stem and rugulose pileus; the rugosity, however, may be almost lacking at times. Variations occur approaching other species, like *P. chrysophaeus, P. flavafuligineus* and *P. leoninus,* and such are often difficult to place. I have never seen *P. chrysophaeus* Fr. but include it in the key, as it has been reported by Longyear.

585. Pluteus leoninus Fr.

Syst. Myc., 1821.

Illustrations: Patouillard, Tab. Analyt., No. 639.
Ricken, Blätterpilze, Pl. 71, Fig. 5.
Gillett, Champignons de France.

PILEUS 2-5 cm. broad, campanulate-convex, subumbonate, *not rugulose,* glabrous, moist, *yellow,* striate on margin, GILLS free, moderately broad, close, white then deep flesh color. STEM 5-7 cm. long, 2-5 mm. thick, equal or enlarged below, striatulate, glabrous, *solid,* pellucid-white or whitish. SPORES subglobose to oval elliptical, 6-7 x 5 micr., smooth, dull *rose-colored.* CYSTIDIA about 60 micr. long, fusiform, subacuminate above, not abundant, not horned.

Solitary. On rotten wood. Infrequent in the hemlock forests of the north. Negaunee, etc.

A form was found with the surface of the pileus minutely velvety. Patouillard says the surface is glabrous, composed of long slender hyphae. In this respect the form differs markedly from *P. admirabilis* Pk.

Entoloma Fr.

(From the Greek, *entos,* inside; and *loma,* the border of a robe.)

Pink-spored. Without volva or annulus. Stem *fleshy or fibrous,* not cartilaginous, soft, *confluent with the pileus.* Gills *adnate or adnexed, emarginate* or sinuate. Spores *angular,* rarely rounded. Cystidia rarely present in a few species.

Mostly large, soft, putrescent mushrooms; *terrestrial,* frequent in rainy weather; some of the species are *poisonous.* A difficult genus to study.

The PILEUS may be glabrous, pruinose, silky or fibrillose, hardly ever strongly scaly; it is either hygrophanous, viscid or dry, in the last case fibrillose or somewhat scaly. The cuticle varies in structure, the viscid species being provided with a pellicle composed of gelatinous hyphae while in many cases the surface has a gelatinous feel but is not truly differentiated and does not become viscid except in very prolonged wet weather. In one section the surface is distinctly fibrillose, the fibrils sometimes forming definite scales on the disk. In only a few species is the margin striate or striatulate. Many become water-soaked in rainy weather, and it is then often difficult to determine whether they are hygrophanous. The colors vary from white, watery-whitish, grayish, grayish-brown to dark brown; more rarely tinged violet, reddish or yellowish and always with only the soft shades of these colors. The colors are hard to describe in terms which are sufficiently clear, and this has caused considerable confusion; hence other characters must be used as much as possible. Nearly all the species are somewhat fragile, but may become tougher in dry weather.

The GILLS are adnate-sinuate as in Tricholoma, sometimes adnexed, often seceding from the stem in age. It is important to note their color before they become pink from the spores; this is either *white, yellowish* or *ashy.* They are rather broad, even in the small species rarely narrow. In distinction from Pluteus, there are no cystidia except in a very few species, the edge is therefore usually entire. The STEM is central, fleshy or with the outer rind fibrous and spongy within, sometimes loosely stuffed and then hollow, not cartilaginous except under peculiar weather conditions. In the larger species the stem is stout as in Tricholoma. It is intimately connected with the pileus, the trama of the stem extending unaltered into that of the pileus as in all the genera with adnate gills; it is therefore not separable as in Pluteus and Volvaria.

The SPORES are *irregularly-angular,* the general outline varying from spherical to elliptical, often with a prominent, oblique apiculus at the angle where it was attached to the basidium; a few species have rounded spores, i. e., not angled. Their color in mass varies from pale to deep flesh color, to rosy or salmon. *Tricholoma personatum* Fr., *Tricholoma nudum* Fr. and *Tricholoma panoeolum* var. *caespitosa* Bres. have flesh-colored spores in mass and will be looked for here.

A number of the species are known to be very *poisonous; E. lividum* Fr. has been proved so by both Romell and Worthington Smith; *E. grande* Pk. is suspected by its author. The species are difficult for the amateur and even for the expert, and hence it is necessary to proceed with extreme caution when collecting for the table. *It is best not to eat Entolomas at all* because of the danger of confusing the species. The common saying, "only the mushroom which is pink underneath the cap is sure to be safe," illustrates another error in so-called "rules to know mushrooms," since here we have a whole genus which the unsuspecting amateur who is told the above, would be likely to take for *Agaricus compestris*.

This genus corresponds, by its sinuate-adnate gills, its fleshy-fibrous stem, and lack of volva and annulus, to *Tricholoma* of the white-spored group and to *Hebeloma* of the pink-spored group. Peck reports 23 species in New York; we have been able to identify 18 species of those that have been found in Michigan. Others have been collected within our limits but need further study. Some occur seldom; others are more common, especially in showery weather. To what extent certain species are limited to the conifer regions of the State has not yet been determined.

Fries divided the genus into three sections: Genuini, Leptonidei and Nolandei. To these Peck has added a fourth section of Ameri- can species, which he calls Conoidei.

Key to the Species

(A) Pileus scaly, scabrous, flocculose or superficially silky-fibrillose.
    (a) Pileus white, 5-15 mm. broad, silky, spores 9-12 x 7-8 micr. 588. *E. sericellum* Fr.
    (aa) Pileus not white, 1-5 cm. broad.
      (b) Pileus scabrous, dark brown, 1-3 cm. broad; stem slender. 587. *E. scabrinellum* Pk.
      (bb) Pileus not scabrous.
        (c) Pileus and stem tinged purplish or wine color; stem solid. 589. *E. cyaneum* Pk. (cf. also *E. jubatum* Fr.)
        (cc) Pileus and stem not tinged purplish.
          (d) Gills ashy or smoky at first; pileus mouse-gray; stem hollow. 590. *E. jubatum* Fr.
          (dd) Gills white at first; pileus ashy or ashy-brown. 601. *E. peckianum* Burt.
(AA) Pileus glabrous, moist, hygrophanous or viscid.
    (a) Pileus pelliculose or the surface viscid, gelatinous.
      (b) Pileus 2-5 cm., gelatinous above, flesh color, coarsely reticulate; stem eccentric; rare. (See 699. *Pleurotus subpalmatus*.)
      (bb) Pileus not reticulated.
        (c) Stem loosely stuffed then hollow, stout; pileus livid-brownish (moist), 7-10 cm. broad. 586. *E. lividum* Fr.
        (cc) Stem longer, solid; pileus viscid, smaller, grayish. *E. prunuloides* Fr.
    (aa) Pileus not viscid.
      (b) Pileus hygrophanous.
        (c) Odor and taste farinaceous, at least when plants are fresh and crushed.
          (d) Gills gray at first; pileus dark brown, 2-5 cm. broad, striatulate (moist). 596. *E. sericeum* Fr.
          (dd) Gills white or pallid at first.

    (e) Pileus conic-campanulate or umbonate, streaked with darker fibrils; stem short. 591. *E. clypeatum* Fr.

  (ee) Pileus convex or finally plane, subumbonate, grayish-brown (moist).

    (f) Stem at length tinged gray; pileus scarcely fading, with a delicate, separable pellicle. 595. *E. griseum* Pk.

   (ff) Stem white; pileus fading to whitish; gills narrow. 594. *E. sericatum* Britz.

  (cc) Odor and taste not farinaceous.

    (d) Odor of fresh plant nitrous. 593. *E. nidorosum* Fr.

   (dd) Odor not nitrous.

    (e) Pileus umber, fuscous or cinnamon (moist).

    (f) Pileus conic-campanulate or umbonate; stem twisted; spores elongated-angular. 597. *E. strictius* Pk.

   (ff) Pileus at length plane; stem pure white; gills rather broad; spores globose-angular. 592. *E. rhodopolium* Fr.

  (ee) Pileus whitish or yellow-tinged (moist).

    (f) Stout and firm, pileus watery, whitish or tinged yellowish, 5-12 cm. broad; stem 10-20 mm. thick. 598. *E. grayanum* Pk.

   (ff) Rather slender and fragile, pileus whitish, 2-6 cm. broad; stem 3-8 mm. thick. 599. *E. speculum* Fr.

  (bb) Pileus neither viscid nor hygrophanous.

    (c) Pileus conic or campanulate, usually unexpanded, 1-5 cm. broad; among moss, especially sphagnum.

    (d) Color of pileus changing darker in age, from pale yellow to reddish-brown. *E. variabile* Pk.

   (dd) Pileus fading or scarcely changing.

    (e) Spores quadrate, 4-angled.

    (f) Pileus strongly cuspidate at apex, pale yellow. 602. *E. cuspidatum* Pk.

   (ff) Pileus not cuspidate.

    (g) Pileus yellow, smoky-yellow, or greenish-yellow. *E. luteum* Pk.

   (gg) Pileus salmon-colored, subacute at apex. 600. *E. salmoneum* Pk.

  (ee) Spores 5-6 sided, irregular, longer than wide; pileus gray to smoky-brown, umbonate. 601. *E. peckianum* Bert.

  (cc) Pileus convex-expanded, large, yellowish-white or tinged brownish; gills broad; stem solid; spores angular-sphoeroid, 8-10 micr. *E. grande* Pk.

Section I. Genuini. Pileus fleshy, glabrous, moist or viscid; not hygrophanous.

586. Entoloma lividum Fr. (Poisonous)

Epicrisis, 1836.

Illustrations: Cooke, Ill., Pl. 311.
    Ricken, Blätterpilze, Pl. 72, Fig. 2.
    Gillet, Champignons de France, No. 271.

PILEUS 7-10 cm. broad, campanulate then expanded, *glabrous, pelliculose,* the cuticle composed of subgelatinous hyphae about 6 micr. diam., splitting into fibrillose parts on drying, viscid in very wet weather, *pale livid-tan* faded when dry, repand, wrinkled-rugose, margin striate. GILLS *adnexed,* abruptly rounded behind, broad, subventricose, subdistant at stem, pallid then bright flesh color. Stem 6-8 cm. long, 1.5-2.5 cm. thick, stout, *white, glabrous,* apex subpruinose, even, subequal, *stuffed then hollow.* SPORES sphoeroid-angular, 8-10 micr. diam., *bright flesh color in mass,* apiculus prominent, 5-6 angled. CYSTIDIA none or very few, fusoid. ODOR faint. TASTE strongly farinaceous.

Gregarious. On the ground in white pine and beech woods of western Michigan. New Richmond. September. Rare. *Poisonous.*

This rare Entoloma is a rather stout plant. Its pileus is viscid in wet weather, although the descriptions merely call it "pelliculose," so that it is identified with difficulty when one follows the European authors. A specimen from Sweden, which was referred to *E. lividum* by Romell, agrees with our specimens in having subgelatinous thick hyphae in the cuticle, and when dried has the appearance of a surface once viscid or subviscid like that of our plant. Furthermore *E. lividum* is described with a stuffed to hollow stem, while its near relatives *E. sinuatum* and *E. prunuloides* have solid stems. If Gillet's and Cooke's figures of the latter are correct, then I have never collected such Entolomas with a viscid cuticle on the pileus. Romell told me he tested the edibility of *E. lividum* with serious consequences, and hence he ought to know the plant. It seems to be rare and will on that account cause little damage. The gills are often tinged yellowish and the pileus may have a livid-brown color. *E. prunuloides* Fr. is said to have an umbonate ashy cap, sometimes tinged yellowish, considerably smaller according to Cooke's, Gillet's and Patouillard's figures, and the stem is slightly striate and solid. It is said to be viscid.

Section II. Leptonidei. Pileus campanulate-expanded or convex-plane, dry, flocculose or subsquamose; not hygrophanous.

587. Entoloma scabrinellum Pk.

N. Y. State Mus. Rep. 33, 1880.

PILEUS 1-3 cm. broad, broadly convex, expanded and subumbonate, dry, scabrous, densely covered by minute, erect, spine-like scales, *dark mouse-brown or smoky-brown,* the thin incurved margin slightly surpassing the gills. FLESH thin, pallid or tinged brown. GILLS adnexed, rounded behind, becoming deeply emarginate, *broad,* ventricose, at first grayish-white, becoming pink, edge white-flocculose. STEM 3-8 cm. long, 2-3 mm. thick, tapering upward, thicker at base, stuffed then hollow, fibrillose, glabrescent, scurfy-pruinose at apex, white-mycelioid at base, pallid or tinged brownish. SPORES coarsely tuberculate-angular, elliptic in outline, 7-10 x 5.5-6.5 micr., flesh-pink. CYSTIDIA none. *Sterile cells* on edge of gills, capitate, nine-pin shaped. BASIDIA 40 x 9 micr., 4-spored. ODOR none.

Gregarious. On the ground, low mossy woods of pine, beech, etc. New Richmond. September. Rare.

It seems to be nearest to *E. scabrosa* Fr., but it does not possess an umbilicate pileus, the apex of the stem is not black-punctate and the gills are not segmentoid. Our plants were somewhat larger and darker than those found by Peck.

588. Entoloma sericellum Fr.

Syst. Mycol., 1821.

Illustrations: Fries, Icones, Pl. 95, Fig. 3.
　　　　　　　Ricken, Blätterpilze, Pl. 73, Fig. 4 (as *Leptonia sericellum*).
　　　　　　　Cooke, Ill., Pl. 307.

PILEUS 5-15 mm. broad, convex then plane, small, pure *shining* white, or pellucid-white, *silky* or minutely squamulose, even on margin which is incurved at first. GILLS broadly adnate, becoming sinuate, slightly decurrent by a tooth, rather *distant and broad,* white then bright flesh color from the spores. STEM 2-5 cm. long, 1-2 mm. thick, *slender,* pellucid shining white, stuffed then hollow, equal, even, pruinose at apex, glabrous, soft, or slightly toughish and fibrous. SPORES elongated, angular-tuberculate, 9-13 x 6-8 micr., variable in size, apiculus prominent, bright flesh color in mass.

(Dried: Stem pale rufous; pileus pale brownish-buff, tinged rufous.)

Scattered. On debris or humus in low frondose woods, cedar or hemlock swamps, etc. August-September. Throughout the State, Ann Arbor, Bay View, Marquette, Houghton. Frequent.

The color sometimes varies to a creamy tint. The pileus may be obtuse or depressed. It has the stature of an Eccilia, and the depressed pileus and subcartilaginous stem remind one of a Leptonia. It is smaller than *E. speculum* and has very different spores.

589. Entoloma cyaneum Pk.

Buffalo Soc. Nat. Sci., Bull. 1, 1873.

PILEUS 2-3.5 cm. broad, *umbonate,* convex-campanulate, dry, *fibrillose-squamulose,* dark vinaceous-murinus (Sacc.), paler at length, margin even. FLESH white, thin except disk. GILLS *adnate,* later seceding, close, rather broad, at first white-tinged vinaceous then flesh color tinged ashy, *edge white-fimbriate.* STEM 3-6 cm. long, 2-4 mm. thick, equal or subequal, *solid,* fibrillose-striate, *furfuraceous-squamulose* especially upwards, twisted at times, vinaceous above, pallid below, white and fibrous-fleshy within, cuticle subcartilaginous. SPORES angular-tuberculate, subelliptical in outline, 7-9 x 4.5-6 micr., flesh color in mass. CYSTIDIA few on sides of gills, ventricose; sterile cells numerous on the edge and nine-pin shaped.

(Dried: Pileus dark amber-brown.)

Solitary or scattered. Sandy soil and humus, in birch and hemlock swamps of our coniferous regions. August and September. Marquette, Negaunee, New Richmond. Infrequent or rare.

It has the habit of a Leptonia, and might be mistaken for one. Peck describes the stem as hollow; our specimens invariably had the interior filled with a solid fibrous-fleshy substance; this sometimes loosens longitudinally so as to give a false "hollow" interior. It has much the appearance of *E. jubatum* Fr. as illustrated by Cooke, and of *E. griseo-cyaneum* Fr. as figured by Fries (Icones, Plate 94, Fig. 1). It differs from both these in its solid stem and in the color of the pileus. It is said to occur sometimes on decaying wood or mossy logs.

590. Entoloma jubatum Fr.

Syst. Mycol., 1821.

Illustrations: Atkinson, Mushrooms, Fig. 136, 1900.
    Cooke, Ill., Pl. 317.
    Fries, Icones, Pl. 92, Fig. 1.

"PILEUS 2-5 cm. broad, *mouse color,* dry, campanulate then expanded umbonate, *villose-scaly or fibrillose.* GILLS *slightly ad-*

nexed, seceding, ventricose, *crowded, at first dark fuligineous*, then *purple fuligineous*. STEM 5-8 cm. long, 4-6 mm. thick, fleshy-fibrous, rigid, fragile, *hollow*, equal, becoming fuscous and clothed with fuligineous fibrils. SPORES extremely irregular, 9-12 x 6-7 micr., (Ricken). Inodorous."

In woods. East Lansing. Reported by Longyear.

The description is taken from Fries' Hymenomycetes Europei and Stevenson's British Fungi. Atkinson has described a form with a dull heliotrope-purple pileus and stem, with spores 7-11 x 6-7 micr., irregularly oval, coarsely angular, nucleate and 5-7 angled. This species differs from *E. cyaneum* in the hollow stem, adnexed, almost free gills and larger spores. It is rare in Michigan.

Section III. Nolanidei. Pileus thin, *hygrophanous*, somewhat silky when dry, often wavy and irregular.

591. Entoloma clypeatum Fr. (EDIBLE)

Epicrisis, 1836.

Illustrations; Cooke, Ill., Pl. 319.
    Gillet, Champignons de France, No. 270.
    Ricken, Blätterpilze, Pl. 73, Fig. 1.
    Peck, N. Y. State Mus. Rep. 53, Plate D. (As *E. strictius* var. *irregulare.*)

PILEUS 3-10 cm. broad, *campanulate,* with an obtusely conic umbo, hygrophanous, lurid-brown (moist), *brownish-ashy* (dry), often *virgate* with darker lines, glabrous, margin even, often wavy. FLESH thin, white. GILLS adnexed, *rounded behind,* seceding, sometimes emarginate with decurrent tooth, moderately broad, sub-distant to close, whitish then sordid rose-colored, *edge serrate-eroded.* STEM 4-6 cm. long, 6-12 mm. thick, often rather stout, and short, stuffed or hollow, sometimes compressed, fragile, silky-fibril-lose, white or whitish, apex subpruinose, often rivulose. SPORES subglobose, angular, 7-9.5 x 6-7.5 micr., rosy in mass. Taste and odor *farinaceous.*

(Dried: Pileus ashy-brown, gills rose-colored.)

Gregarious to subcaespitose. On the ground in low woods, maple, elm, beech, etc., sometimes in grassy places near woods. Ann Arbor, New Richmond. July to September. Infrequent.

Usually known when dry by the grayish-brown pileus streaked

with darker fibrils, by the rosy gills at maturity and by the whitish stem. When moist the color varies considerably. Sometimes it becomes almost white on drying. *E. clypeatum* has had the reputation in Europe of being *poisonous,* but is eaten with impunity by some who claim it is harmless. Even if its edibility is established, the amateur may have some difficulty in being certain of the species. The pileus is often persistently campanulate with an obtuse apex which separates it from forms having grayish caps.

592. Entoloma rhodopolium Fr. (SUSPECTED)

Syst. Mycol., 1821.

Illustrations: Patouillard, Tab. Analyt., No. 338.
Murrill, Mycologia, Pl. 92, Fig. 4 (as *E. grayanum*)
Gillet, Champignons de France, No. 275.
Plate CV of this Report.

PILEUS 4-8 cm. broad, *campanulate* then expanded-plane, *firm,* hygrophanous, *umber to fuscous.* (moist), pale livid-gray and silky shining (dry), *glabrous,* cuticle slightly differentiated with subcartilaginous hyphae, with a gelatinous feel but not viscid, undulate and even on the margin. FLESH watery then white, scissile. GILLS *adnate,* becoming emarginate, somewhat *subdistant,* sometimes veined, moderately *broad,* whitish then *deep rose color,* edge minutely eroded. STEM 4-10 cm. long, 6-12 mm. thick, *pure white,* subequal, tapering up or down, sometimes curved, *glabrous,* apex furfuraceous, white, spongy-stuffed then hollow, with a thickish, fibrous, subcartilaginous cuticle, readily splitting longitudinally on drying. SPORES subglobose, 5-6 angled, 6-9 micr. in diameter, (with a few larger ones), deep rose color in mass. CYSTIDIA none. ODOR and TASTE *none.*

Solitary or subcaespitose. On the ground, mixed or frondose woods. August-September. New Richmond, Ann Arbor.

The deep rosy spores, pure white stem, the toughish subcartilaginous pileus and colors are characteristic for our plants. The species may have an odor at times. Fries says it has scarcely any odor; others report a farinaceous odor. Our plants differ from the typical description in the toughish cuticle on the pileus and stem although collected in moist weather. The pileus is often dusted on top by the rosy spores as in *Clitopilus abortivus.* It differs fundamentally from *E. griseum* Pk. in the deep rose-colored gills and the glabrous and shining-white stem, but agrees with it in being firm, and in the structure of the cuticle of pileus and stem. *E. griseum* has a farinaceous odor and taste.

593. Entoloma nidorosum Fr. var. (Suspected)

Epicrisis, 1836.

Illustrations: Fries, Icones, Pl. 94, Fig. 3.
Swanton, Fungi, Pl. 42, Fig. 17.

PILEUS 2-5 cm. broad, convex, obtuse, grayish-*brown* (moist), hygrophanous, edge incurved, minutely tomentose-silky. FLESH thin, white, *fragile*. GILLS adnexed, *broad, subdistant,* flexuose, pale flesh color. STEM 4-7 cm. long, 4-8 mm. thick, equal or sub-equal, stuffed soon *hollow,* pruinose at apex, slightly fibrillose, whitish. SPORES angular, ovate, angles not definite except the very marked angle at the oblique prominent apiculus, 8-10 micr. long (with apiculus), 6-7 micr. wide; flesh color. ODOR *strongly acid* or alkaline.

Solitary. On mosses, in a sphagnum bog. Ann Arbor. September. Rare.

Differs from the type in the obtuse to subumbonate cap, less slender habit and by not being entirely glabrous. The European plant is said to have an umbilicate or depressed pileus and slender stem.

594. Entolomá sericatum Britz.

PILEUS 3-8 cm. broad, campanulate then plane, subumbonate, grayish-brown (moist), *fading,* paler to creamy-buff or whitish (dry), *umbo darker while drying,* hygrophanous, margin faintly striatulate (moist) elsewhere· even, glabrous, silky-shining (dry), surface scarcely differentiated, margin at length splitting or re-curved. FLESH thin, concolor, scissile. GILLS *narrow,* narrow-ed to a point in front, moderately close, thin, *adnexed* becoming. emarginate, white at first, maturing slowly, at length *pale flesh color,* edge rather eroded. STEM *long and somewhat slender,* 5-10 cm. long, 5-10 mm. thick, *pure shining white,* variously curved, ob-scurely undulate, innately silky-striatulate but *glabrous,* equal or somewhat attenuated below, white-fibrous-stuffed within then some-what hollow, splitting longitudinally (dry), apex pruinose. SPORES angular-tuberculate, slightly longer than wide, 8-10 x 6-8.5 micr., apiculus prominently oblique, flesh color in mass. CYS-TIDIA none. TASTE and ODOR farinaceous.

Gregarious or subcaespitose. On the ground among leaves and debris in conifer and frondose woods. Ann Arbor, New Richmond. September. Frequent, abundant locally.

The fading colors of the pileus, the pure white, glabrous, long stem, the narrow gills and pale spores distinguish this species. Britzelmayr gives no description except the color of the pileus and the size of the spores, and hence I have used his name to avoid a new one. It has the stature and the colors of *E. rhodopolium*, but differs in its farinaceous odor, the spores, narrow gills and the striate margin of the pileus.

595. Entoloma griseum Pk.

N. Y. State Mus. Bull. 75, 1904.

PILEUS 3-7 cm. broad, campanulate-convex, obtuse, *firm,* then fragile, glabrous, *margin even* and often wavy at length, subhygrophanous, *grayish-brown,* sometimes pale umber (moist), scarcely fading, innately silky (dry), *cuticle somewhat differentiated forming a thin, separable pellicle,* margin decurved. FLESH hygrophanous, *very scissile,* moderately thin. GILLS adnexed, becoming emarginate, moderately broad, close or slightly subdistant, whitish-grayish, slowly flesh color, sometimes veined. STEM 3-8 cm. long, 4-10 mm. thick, subrigid, equal or attenuated either upwards or downwards, silky-fibrillose, *whitish or tinged gray,* stuffed to hollow, sometimes solid below, subshining. SPORES tuberculate-angular, 7-9 x 6.5-8 micr., *sphoeroid,* apiculus prominent, pale flesh color in mass. ODOR and TASTE farinaceous, at least when flesh is crushed, rarely lacking this odor.

Gregarious or solitary. On the ground in low woods, both coniferous and frondose. Throughout the State, Marquette, New Richmond, Ann Arbor. May-October. Frequent but scattered.

This species is similar at times to *E. sericeum* Fr.; it is a stouter plant, usually without an umbo on the pileus, and the colors are paler. The margin of the cap is not striate in typical plants, but this character is sometimes obscure. Specimens which lack the mealy odor are not infrequent in spring. The flesh is rather firm but shot through with watery lines and is scissile. The stem is often abruptly attenuated below and its interior is composed of a fibrous pith at first which disappears in places leaving cavities. The cuticle of the pileus has a slight gelatinous feel but is never viscid. The gills are not always noticeably grayish but merely pallid. Forms which seem otherwise to belong here have a slight alkaline odor. Solitary specimens appear as early as May around Ann Arbor. I have found this species in the Adirondack Mountains, and it agrees in all respects with our plants except that the spores are slightly smaller, 6-7.5 x 6-7 micr., the size assigned to them by Peck.

596. Entoloma sericeum Fr.

Epicrisis, 1836-38.

Illustrations: Cooke, Ill., Pl. 320.
Gillet, Champignons de France, No. 276.
Ricken, Blätterpilze, Pl. 72, Fig. 5.
Plate CVI of this Report.

PILEUS 2-6 cm. broad, convex expanded, *more or less* umbonate, glabrous, hygrophanous, *umber-brown* (*moist*), umbo darker, fading to grayish-brown and silky-shining (dry), striatulate on margin when moist, margin at first regular then wavy. FLESH thin, concolor, moist. GILLS adnexed-emarginate or broadest behind and rounded-adnate, moderately *broad*, close to subdistant, gray or grayish-white at first, edge entire. STEM 2-6 cm. long, 3-5 mm. thick, stuffed then hollow, equal or tapering upward, sometimes compressed or twisted, *grayish-brown or tinged with gray*, innately silky-fibrillose. SPORES sphoeroid, tuberculate-angular, 8-9.5 (incl. apiculus) x 6-7 micr., apiculus prominent, deep flesh color in mass. ODOR and TASTE farinaceous.

Gregarious. On the ground, in open woods among grass or fallen leaves. Ann Arbor. June-July. Infrequent.

This species is characterized by its medium to small size, dark brown cap, the presence of an umbo, the grayish gills and the mealy odor. The umbo almost disappears. In Europe it is said to be abundant and to grow in grassy pastures or meadows. I have not found it in such a habitat. The surface of the cap has a sheen almost velvety as shown in our illustration. *E. griseum* differs in the truly convex cap without an umbo, and is usually larger. The spores of these two species are alike, and there is some question whether they do not run into each other.

597. Entoloma strictius Pk. (SUSPECTED)

N. Y. State Mus. Rep. 23, 1872.

Illustrations: Ibid, Pl. 2, Figs. 6-9.
Atkinson, Mushrooms, Fig. 138, p. 146, 1900.
Plate CVII of this Report.

PILEUS 2.5-6 cm. broad, rigid-fragile, obtusely conic-campanulate to broadly campanulate, then expanded and often *strongly umbonate,* glabrous, hygrophanous, umber to watery cinnamon (moist), pearl-gray and silky-shining (dry), margin even or pellucid-striatulate when moist, somewhat wavy, thin and at length splitting. FLESH quite thin, concolor, scissile. GILLS adnexed, then emarginate or sinuate, *ventricose, broad,* narrowed in front, close to subdistant, white or pallid then rosy-incarnate, edge minutely eroded. STEM 6-10 cm. long, 3-7 mm. thick, *slender, cylindrical* or tapering slightly upward, sometimes obscurely bulbous, *strict,* stuffed then hollow, rigid-fragile, twisted, fibrillose-striate, pallid to pale grayish-white. SPORES elongated-angular, curved toward apiculus, 10-12 x 6-8 micr., nucleate, cinnamon-rose color in mass. BASIDIA about 40 x 8-9 micr., 4-spored. CYSTIDIA none. ODOR and TASTE none.

Subcaespitose. In swampy or low woods or near sphagnum swamps, near or on much-decayed stumps, etc. July-August. Ann Arbor, New Richmond, East Lansing. Infrequent.

Very distinct. The pileus is usually markedly campanulate, with a strikingly mammate umbo, very hygrophanous becoming silvery shining when dry, and the thin flesh is at length split on the margin. The stem is very straight and easily splits longitudinally. The spore-mass is peculiarly colored; when deposited thickly on white paper it has a deep rufous or cinnamon-rose color. The width of the spores are given too large by Peck. The striations on the margin of the cap soon disappear or are lacking. The smaller specimens have the appearance of a Nolanea.

598. Entoloma grayanum Pk.

N. Y. State Mus. Rep. 24, 1872.

Illustrations: Atkinson, Mushrooms, Fig. 157, p. 145, 1900. Plate CVIII of this Report.

PILEUS 4-12 cm. broad, campanulate-convex, then expanded and obtuse or broadly umbonate, *firm, glabrous, hygrophanous,* watery-white, *whitish or yellowish-white* (moist), shining and whitish (dry), not striate, sometimes wrinkled on disk. FLESH *relatively thin,* whitish or tinged yellowish, *scissile,* not compact. GILLS adnexed, becoming emarginate, at first rounded behind, *broad,* ventricose, rather close, thickish, white then deep flesh color, edge entire or eroded-crisped. STEM 5-12 cm. long, 10-20 mm. thick, equal or subequal, firm, *stout,* variously thickened, fibrous-stuffed, solid at base, straight or curved, glabrous, silky-shining, watery-white or tinged faintly with yellowish. SPORES sphoeroid, angular, 5-6 angled, 8-10 (incl. apiculus) x 7-9 micr., bright flesh color in mass. CYSTIDIA and STERILE CELLS none. BASIDIA clavate, 45 x 12 micr., 4-spored. ODOR and TASTE *none* or rarely subfarinaceous to slightly pungent.

(Dried: Pileus fuscous; stem sordid; gills dingy flesh-color.)

Solitary or subcaespitose-gregarious. On the ground in woods. August-October. Ann Arbor, Negaunee.

Distinguished by its whitish or yellowish-white pileus which has a watery cast, the hygrophanous hence scissile flesh, and the spores. It is often a noble plant and our forms surpass considerably the sizes given by Peck. In fact its characters are in some respects so near those of *E. grande* Pk., that only its hygrophanous flesh and thinner pileus seem to separate it. The spores are sharply angled and the apiculus usually stands out straight instead of obliquely as in many others. Atkinson (1900) describes a form with a drab-colored pileus. In dry weather the yellowish hues may be altogether lacking.

599. Entoloma speculum Fr.

Epicrisis, 1836.

Illustrations: Fries, Icones, Pl. 95, Fig. 2.
Cooke, Ill., Pl. 308.
Plate CIX of this Report.

PILEUS 2-6 cm. broad, convex-expanded then expanded-plane or slightly depressed around the umbo, margin somewhat wavy, *hygrophanous, pinkish-white* (moist), white and silky-shining (dry), the *umbo* obtuse and when moist whiter than *the rest of the pileus,* margin even or obscurely striatulate (moist). FLESH thin, fragile, white. GILLS emarginate, broad behind, *subdistant,* sometimes veined, *white at first* then *deep rose-colored,* edge suberoded. STEM 3-9 cm. long x 3-8 mm. thick, *equal,* stuffed by loose pith then hollow, sometimes compressed, *fragile, shining-white,* silky-fibrillose or striatulate, pruinose at apex. SPORES sphoeroid-angular, or slightly longer in one direction, 7-9 (including apiculus) x 6-7.5 micr., apiculus suboblique, nucleate. CYSTIDIA none. ODOR and TASTE *none.*

(Dried: Pileus dark rufous-brown or fuscous-brown, stem brownish.)

Solitary or subcaespitose. In grassy places in woods or on debris. Ann Arbor, New Richmond. Infrequent.

The persistently white umbo, deep color of the gills, fragile texture and the silvery shining-white pileus when dry, characterize the species. The size varies in different collections, normally rather small, but in favorable situations becoming larger than figured in the plates. The stem tends to elongate and is very fragile. The color is not retained on drying. The spores are a little large in some specimens but do not agree with the large size given by Saccardo and Massee, each of whom must have dealt with a different species. The surface of the pileus lacks any kind of differentiated cuticle. The trama of the gills is parallel and the margin of the cap is at first incurved.

Section IV. *Conoidei.* Pileus conic or campanulate, not expanded, moist; stem slender, long and hollow; on mosses, especially sphagnum.

600. Entoloma salmoneum Pk. (Suspected)

N. Y. State Mus. Rep. 24, 1872.

Illustrations: N. Y. State Mus. Rep. 24, Pl. 4, 1872. ·
Hard, Mushrooms, Fig. 199, p. 247, 1908.

PILEUS 10-25 mm. broad, often longer than wide, thin, *conical* or campanulate, *papillate* or subacute, subhygrophanous or moist, *deep salmon color* or tinged with orange, margin even or nearly so. GILLS adnexed, *broad,* subdistant, ascending, ventricose, salmon-yellow or salmon-colored. STEM 5-12 cm. long, 2-4 mm. thick, slender, equal, glabrous, pruinose at apex, *hollow,* salmon-colored, innately silky-striatulate, becoming subcartilaginous. SPORES quadrate-nodulose, measuring 10-12.5 micr. diagonally, about 9 micr. wide from side to side, apiculus prominent, rosy-salmon in mass. CYSTIDIA few or none.

(Dried: Reddish-cinnamon to chestnut color.)

Gregarious or scattered. On the ground in conifer woods, in moist places, usually among mosses. August and September. In northern Michigan, Bay View, Negaunee, Detroit. Infrequent and local.

A beautiful little Entoloma, easily mistaken for a Nolanea. The spores are unique for the most part; under the microscope they appear like 4-sided crystals, but with the sides less straight. Simon Davis reports that the stem and sometimes the pileus may be tinged greenish.

601. Entoloma peckianum Burt. var.

N. Y. State Mus. Rep. 54, 1901.

Illustration: Ibid, Pl. F., Figs. 9-16.

PILEUS 3-5 cm. broad, campanulate or convex-expanded, *brownish-ashy* to grayish, *streaked with brown-gray fibrils,* *umbonate,* glabrescent, even on margin. FLESH white, thin. GILLS adnate, becoming emarginate-sinuate, rather broad, white then bright flesh color. STEM 5-7 cm. long, 4-6 mm. thick, *whitish,* sometimes ashy-tinged, equal or tapering downward, straight or flexuous, stuffed then hollow, white-mycelioid at base, glabrous, sometimes fibrillose-striatulate, *flocculose-pruinose* at apex, subshining and subcartilaginous when dry. SPORES angular, slightly longer than wide, 5-6 angled, 8-9.5 x 6-7.5 micr., apiculus prominent, nucleate. CYSTIDIA none.

Subcaespitose or solitary. Low grounds and swamps of frondose trees. July, August and September. Ann Arbor, New Richmond, Marquette and Houghton. Infrequent.

This Entoloma seems to have characters of both *E. peckianum* and *E. murinum* Pk. It differs from the former in its smaller spores, color and size, as these are given in Peck's description. Our plants were referred to *E. peckianum* by Peck. This species differs from *E. murinum* in the smaller spores and size and in the even margin of the cap. From both it would seem to differ in its lack of a conical pileus and in its stouter habit, so that it may turn out to be a distinct species belonging to the section Leptonidei. In his remarks on *E. murinum,* Peck indicates that it is smaller than *E. peckianum,* although he gives the same size in the published descriptions. Our plants always have spores of the size given.

602. Entoloma cuspidatum Pk. (Suspected)

N. Y. State Mus. Rep. 24, 1872.

Illustrations: Ibid, Pl. 2, Fig. 14-18.
Plate CX of this Report.

PILEUS 1.5-5 cm. broad, conical or persistently *conical-campanulate,* 1-3 cm. high, glabrous, silky-shining, *pale yellow,* even or at length rimulose, *bearing an elongated papilla at the apex,* margin at first straight, at length irregular. FLESH thin. GILLS ascending, narrowly adnate, broad in middle, subdistant, *pale yellow at first,* then bright flesh color, edge uneven. Stem 4-12 cm. long, 2-3 mm. thick, equal, hollow, strict, sometimes twisted, glabrous, *pale yellow,* fibrous or with a subcartilaginous cuticle. SPORES subquadrate, coarsely angular, nucleate, apiculus prominent, 9-12 micr. diam., bright flesh color. CYSTIDIA none; STERILE CELLS lacking on edge of gills. Trama of gills parallel. ODOR and TASTE mild.

Gregarious. On mosses, sphagnum, leucobryum, etc., in swamps and bogs.

Eloise, near Detroit. August. Rare.

A unique plant, collected by Mrs. T. A. Cahn of the Detroit

Mycological Club near Eloise. It does not seem to have been reported outside of New York. The pileus and stem fade on losing moisture, but it is not hygrophanous. It is a close relative of *E. salmoneum,* but with different colors and marked by the prominent cusp at the apex of the cap.

Clitopilus Fr.

(From the Greek, *klitos,* a slope, and *pilos,* a felt-cap.)

Pink-spored, without volva or annulus. Stem *fleshy or fibrous,* not cartilaginous, confluent with the pileus whose margin is at first involute. Gills *decurrent or adnate* but *not becoming sinuate nor seceding.* Pileus usually depressed or umbilicate.

Terrestrial plants, often with a farinaceous odor or taste; none are known to be poisonous. The decurrent gills ally them with the genus Clitocybe of the white-spored group.

The PILEUS is glabrous or pruinose in most species; in *C. abortivus* a delicate silky tomentum covers the surface; in a number it is hygrophanous, and in *C. orcella* it is slightly viscid. The larger species are of a firm consistency; the smaller, membranous or fragile. The colors are usually dull or pale, whitish, grayish or brownish. The GILLS furnish the characteristic mark of the genus. Although usually decurrent, they are sometimes broadly adnate as in Entoloma and Leptonia, but in that case do not become sinuate-emarginate in age, nor readily separate from the stem. When decurrent, they are usually narrowed behind and end in a point on the stem as in many Clitocybes. When mature the gills of the different species present the same variation of color as those of Entoloma. Some are pale flesh-colored or deep rose; Peck grouped them into three groups with this difference in color as a basis. At first the gills are usually white or whitish, but in *C. micropus, C. albogriseus, C. abortivus* and *C. novaboracensis* they are pale gray or ashy at first. The STEM is fleshy-fibrous but may become rather rigid in the smaller forms. It is solid in all the larger forms and in this respect differs markedly from most Entolomas. There is no cartilaginous cuticle as in Eccilia. The SPORES are angular in some species like those of Entoloma, rounded in others as in Clitocybe, varying in intensity of color as shown by the mature gills or spore-prints. Ricken has moved all those with non-angular spores to other genera and omits the genus Clitopilus entirely. CYSTIDIA are absent as far as known. The

TASTE is often farinaceous, sometimes quite strong; that of *C. novaboracensis* is bitter; in others it is mild or insipid.

Fries divided the European species into two sections: one with deeply decurrent gills and the margin of the pileus at first flocculose; the other with adnate or subdecurrent gills and the margin of the pileus naked. Peck suggested the use of the different shades of pink of the mature gills as a basis for the sections. It seems to me that the character of the spores is more fundamental than any of these, since the angular spores simulate those of Entoloma, the rounded ones those of Clitocybe. In this sense, there would be two sections; the Angulosporae and the Globosporae. The genus is not well represented in Michigan.

Key to the Species

(A) Spores angular.
  (a) Pileus hygrophanous, 1-3 cm. broad, fragile.
    (b) Odor and taste farinaceous; pileus grayish-brown (moist). 605. *C. subvilis* Pk.
    (bb) Not farinaceous; pileus pinkish-white (moist). Spores smaller than in the preceding. 604. *C. woodianus* Pk.
  (aa) Pileus not hygrophanous.
    (b) Pileus 5-10 cm. broad, grayish-brown, often abortive. 603. *C. abortivus* B. and C.
    (bb) Pileus less than 5 cm. broad, whitish to grayish or smoky-cinereous.
      (c) Odor none.
        (d) Gills white then somewhat rosy; stem stuffed to hollow. 609. *C. subplanus* Pk.
        (dd) Gills dark ashy; stem solid or fibrous. 606. *C. undatus* Fr.
      (cc) Odor farinaceous; gills gray at first.
        (d) Stem slender, 3-6 cm. long, solid; pileus glabrous. 608. *C. albogriseus* Pk.
        (dd) Stem short, 1-2 cm. long, solid; pileus silky. 607. *C. micropus* Pk.
(AA) Spores not angular. (Slightly in *C. novaboracensis*.)
  (a) Pileus somewhat viscid (moist), white or whitish, 3-7 cm. broad. 611. *C. orcella* Fr.
  (aa) Pileus not viscid.
    (b) Taste bitter; pileus concentrically-cracked, brownish-gray; gills deeply decurrent. 612. *C. novaboracensis* Pk.
    (bb) Taste not bitter.
      (c) Plants very caespitose, fragile, pileus 5-15 cm. broad, whitish, moist. 613. *C. caespitosus* Pk.
      (cc) Plants gregarious, firm; pileus 3-10 cm. broad, white or tinged gray. 610. *C. prunulus* Fr.

Section I. Angulosporae. Spores angular or tuberculate.

603. Clitopilus abortivus B. & C. (Edible)

Ann. Nat. Hist., 1859.

Illustrations: Hard, Mushrooms, Fig. 202, p. 250, 1908.
(Abortive form) Ibid, Fig. 203.
(Abortive form) Minnesota Mushrooms, Fig. 33, p. 57, 1910.
N. Y. State Mus. Bull. 54, Pl. 78, 1902.
Plate CXI of this Report.

PILEUS 5-10 cm. broad, firm, convex then plane to subdepressed, dry, at first covered with a delicate silky tomentum, glabrescent, *grayish-brown, dull, becoming isabelline,* margin even. FLESH *white.* GILLS decurrent, varying to merely adnate with a tooth, thin, close, *pale gray at first,* then *rosy to salmon color,* rather narrow. STEM 3-9 cm. long, 6-12 mm. thick, solid, fibrous, subequal, minutely flocculose, sometimes striate, pale grayish-brown to isabelline. SPORES elongated angular, irregular, 8-10 x 5-6 micr., nucleate, *pale rose color* or almost salmon color *in mass.* CYSTIDIA none. ODOR and TASTE somewhat farinaceous.

(Dried: Pileus brownish-gray, stem sordid white, gills dingy deep flesh color).

Subcaespitose, gregarious, occasionally solitary. Habitat varies: found frequently in low woods of elm, maple, etc., on wooded hillsides, ravines, of frondose or mixed woods; sometimes on rotten wood. Late August to middle October. Common in southern Michigan.

Often some of the individuals of one patch are attacked—apparently by some other fungus—and do not develop the cap and gills, but remain as *abortive,* whitish masses, with the appearance of puff-balls; the interior however retains its whitish color, and does not become brown, olive or purple as in puff-balls. Their shape varies from globular to depressed, often umbilicate above. Sometimes all of the specimens are found in this condition, but careful searching of the locality usually brings to light normal individuals. McIlvaine says the abortive ones are fair eating.

604. Clitopilus woodianus Pk.

N. Y. State Mus. Rep. 24, 1872.

PILEUS 2-5 cm. broad, convex, then plane, obtuse or slightly depressed, sometimes umbonate, fragile, *hygrophanous, brownish-*

buff or watery-white (moist), white or tinged slightly yellowish or brownish and silky shining (dry), glabrous, margin *striatulate* (moist). FLESH thin, white. GILLS *broadly adnate to subdecurrent,* not sinuate, moderately close, rather broad, thickish, whitish then *deep flesh-colored.* STEM 4-6 cm. long, 2-5 mm. thick, equal or tapering upward, glabrous, stuffed with a firm pith, cuticle subcartilaginous, innately silky-striatulate, somewhat pellucid-white, elastic. SPORES sphoeroid-angular, 7 micr. diameter, nucleate, deep flesh color in mass. TASTE and ODOR none.

Solitary. On the ground or on rotten logs in frondose or cedar woods. Ann Arbor, Marquette. September. Rare.

This differs from *C. subvilis* in its small spores, whitish color, close gills and lack of odor. The stem is rather elastic for the genus and inclines to that of Nolanea. The pileus is depressed around the low umbo and tinged brownish there. It has a stouter stem and smaller spores than *Entoloma sericellum,* and is hygrophanous.

605. Clitopilus subvilis Pk. (EDIBLE)

N. Y. State Mus. Rep. 40, 1887.

PILEUS 1.5-3 cm. broad, fragile, convex-campanulate, depressed to umbilicate, *hygrophanous, brown or watery grayish-brown* (moist), paler and silky-shining when dry, margin decurved and somewhat wavy, slightly striatulate (moist), glabrous. FLESH thin, moist. GILLS broadly adnate or subdecurrent, *subdistant,* rather broad, whitish then flesh-colored, edge uneven. STEM 2-5 cm. long, 2-3 mm. thick, fleshy-fibrous, stuffed then hollow, equal or subequal, glabrous, tinged brownish, silky-shining. SPORES strongly 4-6 angled, subquadrate to subrectangular in focus, sides straight or concave, apiculus oblique, 8-10 x 7-9 micr., nucleate. CYSTIDIA none. ODOR and TASTE *farinaceous.*

(Dried: Dark brown to umber.)

Solitary. Ground in hemlock woods. Houghton. July-August. Infrequent.

It differs from *C. woodianus* in the color, subdistant gills and spores. From similar species in other pink-spored genera, it differs by its fleshy-fibrous stem and its adnate, not seceding gills.

606. Clitopilus undatus Fr.
(Sense of Patouillard.)

Epicrisis, 1836-38.

Illustrations: Fries, Icones, Pl. 96, Fig. 4.
    Patouillard, Tab. Analyt., No. 428.
    Cooke, Ill., Pl. 486.

PILEUS 1.5-3.5 cm. broad, *fragile,* deeply umbilicate to subinfundibuliform, *dark smoky-gray* (moist), fading, opaque, silky when
dry, splitting radially in age, sometimes obscurely zonate, *margin
wavy,* fleshy, concolor. GILLS *decurrent,* broad in the middle,
thin, close, *dark cinereous,* at length tinged by the spores,
edge entire. STEM short, 1.5-2 cm. long, 1.5-3 mm. thick, equal,
terete, solid, even, tough-elastic, glabrous, *brownish-ashy to pale
brown.* SPORES irregularly subglobose-oval, angular, 7-9 x 6-6.5
micr., nucleate, reddish-flesh color in mass. CYSTIDIA none.
ODOR none.

On mossy ground or much decayed wood, in open frondose woods.
Ann Arbor. August. Infrequent.

Known by its dark gray gills, lack of odor and angular spores.
Ricken refers it to Paxillus and assigns to it smooth spores, in which
he differs from other authors. Our plants had a solid stem while
Fries describes the stem with a cavity. In all other respects it
agrees well with the Friesian description. Patouillard reports the
stem either solid or hollow and doubtless he had our species.

607. Clitopilus micropus Pk.

N. Y. State Mus. Rep. 31, 1879.

Illustration: N. Y. State Mus. Bull. 54, Pl. 78, 1902.

PILEUS small, 1-2 cm. broad, *fragile,* convex then depressed, *umbilicate, silky, gray,* usually slightly zoned on margin, margin decurved. GILLS adnato-decurrent, *narrow,* narrowed in front and
behind to a point, close, gray then *salmon-colored.* STEM *short,*
1-2 cm. long, 2-3 mm. thick, solid or with a slight cavity, *pruinose,*
gray, white-mycelioid at base. SPORES elongated angular-tuberculate, 9-10 x 5-6 micr., nucleate, pale salmon color. ODOR and
TASTE *farinaceous.*

(Dried: Dark gray.)

Gregarious or subcaespitose. On the ground, grassy places, sandy fields or thin woods. July-September. Throughout the State. Ann Arbor, Detroit, New Richmond, Marquette. Frequent. Sometimes it occurs in abundance in one place. There is a pale variety, almost white, which is widely distributed. The short stem, umbilicate and subzonate pileus distinguish it from *C. albogriseus*. It is rarely if ever found in deep woods. It differs from *C. subplanus* in its fragile cap.

608. Clitopilus albogriseus Pk. (EDIBLE)

N. Y. State Mus. Rep. 31, 1879.

PILEUS 1-3 cm. broad, convex, *firm,* then plane, depressed or umbilicate, glabrous, pale gray, margin even. GILLS adnato-decurrent, close, *rather broad,* grayish then flesh color. STEM 3-6 cm. long, 2-5 mm. thick, solid, subequal, glabrous, pale gray. SPORES elongated-angular, 10-12 x 6-7 micr., apiculus oblique and prominent. ODOR and TASTE *farinaceous.*

Gregarious or solitary. Ground, in conifer or frondose woods. Ann Arbor, Marquette, Houghton. July-September. Not infrequent in northern Michigan.

The large spores and longer stem separate it from *C. micropus;* the solid stem and the spores from *C. subplanus.* These three are closely related.

609. Clitopilus subplanus Pk.

N. Y. Mus. Bull. 122, 1908.

PILEUS 2-3 cm. broad, convex-expanded, somewhat plane, depressed or umbilicate, glabrous, innately silky, *grayish-white* or whitish. GILLS adnato-decurrent, close, moderately broad, *white then flesh color.* STEMS 2-4 cm. long, 2-4 mm. thick, *toughish,* terete or subcompressed, subsilky, cuticle subcartilaginous, even. SPORES angular, 9-11 x 6-7 micr., flesh-colored in mass; no cystidia.

Scattered. On decaying leaves, etc., in mixed woods. New Richmond, Bay View. July-September. Frequent locally.

This species differs from the two preceding in its white gills when young and its stuffed to hollow stem. The whole plant is rather tough and its taste and odor are not farinaceous.

Section II.   Globosporae.   Spores rounded, neither angled nor tubercular.

610.   Clitopilus prunulus Fr.   (EDIBLE)

Syst. Mycol., 1821.

Illustrations: Atkinson, Mushrooms, Fig. 135, p. 142, 1900.
   Hard, Mushrooms, Fig. 200, p. 248, 1908.
   N. Y. State Mus. Rep. 48, Pl. 14, 1896, Bot. ed.
   Swanton, Fungi, Pl. 42, p. 131, 1909.
   Ricken, Blätterpilze, Pl. 27, Fig. 5 (as *Paxillus prunulus*).
   Clements, Minn. Mushrooms, Fig. 34, p. 58, 1910.
   Cooke, Ill., Pl. 322.

"PILEUS 5-10 cm. broad, at first obtuse, convex then nearly plane, *firm, dry, pruinate,* white to dark-gray, often eccentric, margin even and often wavy. FLESH white. GILLS deeply decurrent, *subdistant, narrow,* white then flesh-colored. STEM 3-8 cm. long, 5-15 mm. thick, solid, naked, *striate,* subequal or tapering, sometimes ventricose. SPORES subfusiform to subelliptical, pointed at ends, 10-12 x 5-7 micr., smooth, with three deep longitudinal furrows, tinged salmon. ODOR and TASTE *farinaceous.*"

Ground in open woods.   July-September.   Ann Arbor, Lansing. Infrequent.

The general appearance is that of *C. orcella* but its cap is firm and not viscid and the stem is glabrous.   Massee and Hard give the spores too small.   Only Hennings, in Engler and Prantl, and Ricken mention the characteristic furrows of the spores.   It has not been seen by me in abundance and is apparently rather rare in the State. Its edible qualities are highly praised.   In France it is called the "Mousseron" by the peasants.   An abortive form is described by McIlvaine.

611. Clitopilus orcella Fr. (EDIBLE)

Syst. Mycol, 1821.

Illustrations: N. Y. Mus. Rep. 48, Pl. 14, 1896, Bot. ed.
    Hard, Mushrooms, Fig. 201, p. 249, 1908.
    Cooke, Ill., Pl. 323.
    Gillet, Champignons de France, No. 145.
    Patouillard, Tab. Analyt., No. 427.

PILEUS 3-9 cm. broad, convex at first, soon expanded, plane then
depressed, *soft, somewhat viscid,* silky, white to whitish or tinged
yellowish, margin often undulate-lobed, even.   FLESH white.
GILLS deeply decurrent, *close,* narrow, edge entire, white, then
pale salmon-colored from spores. STEM 3-5 cm. long, 4-10 mm.
thick, rather short, solid, soft, *flocculose,* sometimes eccentric, subequal to subventricose. SPORES 9-11 x 4-6 micr., fusiform to oval-
elongated, narrowed toward apiculus, nucleate, pale salmon color
in mass, furrowed, smooth. ODOR and TASTE *farinaceous.*

(Dried: Pileus and stem dull-white; gills salmon-colored.)

Solitary or gregarious. On the ground or on moss, in low oak
and maple woods, grassy places, etc. July-September. Ann Arbor,
Detroit, Jackson. Frequent in southern Michigan.

This apparently differs from *C. prunulus* in its viscid pileus when
moist, in its closer gills and the soft texture. It is more abundant
than that species. Its edibility is the same and for that purpose
need not be distinguished from the preceding. I have not found it
in conifer regions. It is often considered identical with *C. prunulus,*
but is at least a variety.

612. Clitopilus novaboracensis Pk.

N. Y. State Cab. Rep. 23, 1872.

Illustrations: Hard, Mushrooms, Fig. 204, p. 251, 1908.
    Compare illustrations of *C. popinalis* Fr.
    Fries, Icones, Pl. 96, Fig. 1.
    Cooke, Ill., Pl. 485.

PILEUS 3-6 cm. broad, convex, plane or umbilicato-depressed,
concentrically rivulose, glabrous, obscurely zonate toward margin,
which is inrolled at first and often wavy, dingy-white, tinged ashy.
FLESH thin, white, flaccid.   GILLS deeply decurrent, crowded,

narrow, brownish-ashy to pallid with a slight flesh color, becoming ashy-stained, edge entire. STEM 3-6 cm. long, 2-5 mm. thick, rather slender, *flexible,* stuffed then hollow, *pruinose or tomentose,* white-mycelioid at base, subequal, concolor or paler than pileus. SPORES oval, obscurely or not at all angular, 5-6 x 4-4.5 micr., apiculate, pale flesh color in mass. ODOR farinaceous. Taste bitterish or very bitter.

(Dried: Pileus and gills brownish-gray.)

Subcaespitose or solitary. On the ground in hemlock woods. Ann Arbor, Bay View. August. Infrequent.

Var. *brévis* Pk. is reported by Longyear in frondose woods, East Lansing. This variety is pure white, with gills merely subdecurrent and stem short. The species is referred by some to *C. popinalis* Fr. The spores of the American plant appear rounded under ordinary magnification, but when magnified about 1500 diameters, it is seen that they are slightly angled. The angles are not sharply marked and the spores never appear tubercular-angled as figured by Cooke for *C. popinalis;* some appear to be altogether rounded. The dark plants may be mistaken for *Clitocybe cyathiforme,* but the pileus of the latter is not rivulose-cracked. Some Tricholomas have a pileus of the same color and markings. The plants often turn ashy where bruised.

613. Clitopilus caespitosus Pk.

N. Y. State Mus. Rep. 41, 1888.

Illustrations: Plates CXII, CXIII of this Report.

PILEUS 5-15 cm. broad, at first convex, soon expanded and plane to depressed, somewhat firm but brittle, *very fragile* when moist or water-soaked, glabrous, whitish to gray-tinged when young, watery-dingy-white (moist), *dull whitish to pale tan* and silky-shining (dry), even, margin at first inrolled, often recurved and split in age. FLESH pallid to white, thin, subhygrophanous, somewhat scissile. GILLS very *crowded* and *narrow,* adnate-decurrent, thin, dingy *pale* flesh color, edge sometimes minutely crenulate. STEM 3-7 cm. long, 5-12 mm. thick, *equal or tapering downward,* silky-fibrillose, scurfy at apex, stuffed, fragile in age, pallid, easily splitting. SPORES short-oblong, 4-5 x 2.5-3 micr., smooth, sordid-white with a pink tinge in mass. ODOR slightly fragrant. TASTE none.

(Dried: Pileus and stem dingy-white tinged tan color; gills brownish-flesh color.)

Very caespitose, sometimes singly. On the ground in open oak and maple woods of southern Michigan; in mixed woods of maple and pine in the north. August-October. Throughout the State. Infrequent.

This is easily mistaken for a Clitocybe. The spores have a dingy flesh tinge in mass, like *Tricholoma personatum* and *Tricholoma panoeolum* var. *caespitosum*. In rainy weather it is water-soaked and appears as if hygrophanous. Its fragile flesh and its usually large size separate it from other Clitopili. It seems to be much more closely related to the genus Clitocybe than to Clitopilus.

Leptonia Fr.

(From the Greek, *lepidion*, a small scale.)

Pink-spored. Pileus at length *subexpanded and depressed in center*, umbilicus minutely squamulose, margin at first *incurved*. Stem *cartilaginous*, confluent with the pileus, stuffed, soon hollow. Gills adnexed or adnate, seceding. Spores *angular*.

Terrestrial, lignicolous or sphagnicolous. Rather small, slender-stemmed plants of low wet places in woods or swamps. They correspond to Collybia of the white-spored group. From Nolanea they are distinguished by the more expanded, subumbilicate pileus whose margin is at first incurved instead of straight on the stem.

The PILEUS is often minutely scaly or fibrillose, sometimes glabrous; hygrophanous or merely moist; even or striate on the margin. The colors are often bright, rosy, violet, yellowish, greenish or blue-black. As in Collybia, the pileus tends to expand rather fully, because of the position of the margin when young. The peculiar lustre is due, according to Patouillard, to the presence of air between the hyphae of the surface layer. The GILLS secede from the stem at maturity as in Nolanea; at first they are either adnexed or adnate. The color when young is to be noted, as it varies in different species, at first it may be gray, bluish, or whitish, at length the gills are colored by the spores. The STEM, as in Nolanea and Eccilia, is cartilaginous, hollow (sometimes stuffed), confluent with the pileus but of a different texture; it is composed of parallel hyphae, with long cells, which are regularly cylindrical. It is usually glabrous and polished, but some species are dotted with colored squamules. It is often compressed and furrowed longitudinally. The SPORES vary from flesh color to bright rose and are often prominently angled, sometimes tuberculate. CYSTIDIA are usually lacking except in *L. seticeps*.

The species of this genus are rather difficult to diagnose. In some cases the color is rather striking, as for example, of *L. formosa* and *L. rosea;* in others the color varies considerably in different specimens of the same species, e. g., *L. asprella,* so that a microscopic study must be the final resort. Not much is known concerning their edibility, although several species appear quite frequently. Some of the species are rarely found and this accounts for the smaller number of species for the State. All species likely to occur in the State are included in the key.

Key to the Species

(a)   Stem and pileus rose-tinged; on sphagum.   616.   *L. rosea* Long-year.

(aa)   Stem and pileus white, becoming blackish on drying; pileus striate; gills adnexed; spores 10-12.5 x 7-9 micr.   *L. transformata* Pk.

(aaa) Stem and pileus waxy-yellowish; pileus scaly to fibrillose.   618. *L. formosa* Fr.

(aaaa) Stem and pileus neither rosy, white nor yellowish.

  (b)   Pileus, stem and gills green (aeruginous).

    (c)   Odor strongly of mice.   *L. incana* Fr.

    (cc)   Odor not mentioned.   *L. aeruginosa* Pk.

  (bb)   Pileus and stem grayish-brown to fuscous, dark brown, or light-leather color.

    (c)   Pileus hygrophanous, striatulate.

      (d)   On rotten wood; gills rounded behind, nearly free, whitish; spores 10 x 7.5 micr.   *L. undulatella* Pk.

      (dd)   On the ground; gills adnate-seceding, tinged gray; spores elongate, 10 x 6-8 micr.   621.   *L. asprella* Fr. var.

    (cc)   Pileus not hygrophanous.

      (d)   On rotten wood; pileus walnut-brown; gills slightly adnexed. Spores subglobose.   617.   *L. seticeps* Atk.

      (dd)   On the ground; pileus paler.

        (e)   Pileus innately silky and substriatulate; gills whitish, broad, adnexed; stem glabrous; spores quadrate, 9-11 x 9-10 micr.   *L. solsticiales* Fr.   (Sense of Ricken.)

        (ee)   Gills, stem and pileus gray, gills broad; spores sphoeroid, 8-10 micr.   *L. grisea* Pk.

  (bbb) Pileus and stem violet, bluish-black, smoky or steel-blue.

    (c)   Stem dotted with dark squamules, at least at apex.

      (d)   Gills with a black serrulate edge; on the ground.   619.   *L. serrulata* Fr.

      (dd)   Gills with edge concolor; pileus fuscous, squamulose; stem tinged lavender, squamulose; on rotten wood.   614. *L. placida* Fr.

    (c)   Stem glabrous or with few evanescent squamules.

      (d)   Gills with a black serrulate edge; pileus grayish-white, umbilicus darker and scaly.   *L. subserrulata* Pk.

      (dd)   Gills unicolorous.

        (e)   Pileus hygrophanous, striate (moist), squamulose to glabrous; gills grayish, adnate; spores 11-14 x 6-8 micr.   621. *L. asprella* Fr.

(e) Pileus not hygrophanous, not striate.
(f) Pileus at first bluish-black, then smoky-fuscous; gills adnate, ventricose, stem concolor; spores 9-12 x 6-7 micr.; on the ground. 615. *L. lampropoda* Fr.
(ff) Pileus, gills and stem rather dark violet; squamulose-fibrillose on pileus; spores subsphoeroid, 8-10 x 7-8 micr.; on wood, sawdust, etc. 620. *L. euchroa* Fr.

Section I. Nonhygrophanae. The species of this section are not truly hygrophanous nor markedly striate on the pileus but in wet weather they may appear somewhat hygrophanous, and a few species are faintly or finely striate on the pileus.

*Gills white or whitish at first.

614. Leptonia placida Fr.

Syst. Mycol., 1821.

Illustrations: Fries, Icones, Pl. 97.
Cooke, Ill., Pl. 330.
Plate CXIV of this Report.

PILEUS 3-5 cm. broad, campanulate, then convex, obtuse, rarely depressed, ground color *pale fuscous, covered with brown to blackish silky scales which are denser and darker on disk,* often with an obscure tinge of violet, *not striate.* FLESH pallid, with a pinkish tinge, thin. GILLS *broad behind* but abruptly narrowed and *adnexed,* sometimes subarcuate and subdecurrent, narrowed in front, crowded, thickish, whitish then flesh color from spores, edge concolor, often eroded-crenate. STEM 2-5 cm. long, *rather thick, 3-8* mm., cartilaginous, stuffed then hollow, often compressed and grooved, sometimes twisted or variously curved, *loosely dotted by lavender or dark blue to blackish squamules above,* squamules rosy or violet below, apex usually thickened, base white mycelioid, sometimes glabrous except at apex. SPORES tuberculate-angular, oblong, 8-10.5 x 5-6 micr., apiculus oblique. CYSTIDIA none.
(Dried: Dark fuscous throughout.)
Gregarious. On rotten wood, stumps and logs, in low woods of elm, maple, etc. June to October. Ann Arbor, Detroit. Frequent at times.
A beautiful plant, with a stouter and more curved stem than the terrestrial Leptonias. The shades of lavender and blue vary considerably in different collections, but the peculiar dark scales on the pileus and stem are unmistakable. The gills of our plants always have a decurrent tooth.

615.   Leptonia lampropoda Fr.

Syst. Mycol., 1821.

Illustrations: Cooke, Ill., Pl. 331.
Gillet, Champignons de France, No. 434.
Ricken, Blätterpilze, Pl. 73, Fig. 7.
Swanton, Pl. 42, Figs. 3-5, 1909.

PILEUS 1-3 cm. broad, convex then plane, umbilicate or depressed, *bluish-black to jet-black when young,* becoming smoky-
fuscous when old, *becoming minutely squamulose* by the breaking
up of the cuticle, innately-fibrillose at first, squamules dense in
center, *never striate,* not papillate, sometimes rimose, margin decurved then raised.   FLESH at first bluish-black, then gray to
white, subhygrophanous, thin.   GILLS adnate-seceding, moderately
broad, subdistant, *ventricose,* white at first *then rose-colored,* edge
entire and concolor.   STEM 2.5-5 cm. long, 1-3 mm. thick, equal or
tapering upward, stuffed then hollow, often compressed and
grooved, straight or curved, *glabrous,* even, firm, elastic, *bluish-
black at first, becoming fuscous,* white mycelioid at base, apex not
punctate.   SPORES variable in size, tuberculate, angular, 9-13 x 6-7
micr., *rosy in mass.*   CYSTIDIA none.   ODOR and TASTE none.

Gregarious.   On the ground, wet places in mixed hemlock and
maple woods.   Bay View, New Richmond, Marquette.   July-September.   Frequent in conifer regions.

Easily known by its bluish-black color when young, the lack of
striations on the pileus and the rather firm stem.   It approaches
L. asprella, and I at first referred it to that species, but the margin
of the pileus is never striate and the gills are not gray.   It has the
colors of *L. serrulata* but the edge of the gills does not become black-
dotted.   The figures of European authors do not illustrate our
plant well; this is not surprising, since it is always reported as
growing "among grass."   In fact, the majority of species in England
are reported from grassy places, while with us the high winds and
dryer conditions seldom favor their appearance in fields or meadows,
and the forest forms are slightly different in appearance.   It agrees
well with the description of Fries given in his Monographia.   Ricken
gives broader spores; those of our plants agree with the size given
by Saccardo.

616. Leptonia rosea Longyear

Mich. Acad. of Sci. Rep. 3, 1902.

Illustrations: Ibid, Plate I, Fig. 5.
Plate CXIV of this Report.

PILEUS 1.5-3.5 cm. broad, convex, then expanded, depressed or subumbilicate at center, *not striate, rose color when young,* fading to isabelline with reddish umbilicus, minutely fibrillose-scaly, especially at center. FLESH thin, white. GILLS adnate with slight tooth, close, moderately broad, ventricose, broadest behind, *white then flesh color.* STEM 5-8 cm. long, *slender,* scarcely 1.5 mm. thick, *equal,* cartilaginous, glabrous, *stuffed,* appearing solid, *pale roseate,* white-mycelioid at base, subpellucid-striatulate. SPORES angular, 10-12 x 7-8 micr., flesh color in mass.

Scattered. On sphagnum, in cedar and tamarack swamp (35 specimens). Bay View. "Burnt ground on a sandy hillside, Kent County. Longyear." July-September. Rarely seen.

The difference in habitat of the two localities where this has been found is remarkable. My own collection was made entirely on thick sphagnum, but Longyear found the two type specimens on burnt-over sandy soil. Its pretty colors are attractive and it is not easily mistaken. Gillet's figure of *Nolanea rufocarnea* Berk. reminds one somewhat of *L. rosea,* but our species is a true Leptonia with a non-striate pileus, without the bitter taste of *N. rufocarnea* and with a different color.

617. Leptonia seticeps Atk.

Jour. of Mycol., Vol. 8, 1902.

PILEUS 1-3 cm. broad, convex to expanded, umber to brownish-gray, darker on disk, *faintly and finely long-striate,* minutely granulose under a lens, margin somewhat incurved at first. FLESH whitish, very thin, composed of two layers, surface layer of oval or clavate long-pediceled cells mixed with longer, lanceolate to fusoid cells, all with smoky content. GILLS *slightly adnexed* or free, subdistant to close, broad, elliptical, white then flesh color, edge eroded; the trama composed of converging hyphae. STEM short, 1-2 cm. long, 2-3 mm. thick, glabrous or sometimes villose-dotted, whitish or brownish, subcartilaginous, solid, fibrous-striate, equal or bulbilose, straight or curved, sometimes slightly eccentric.

SPORES broadly-elliptical to subglobose, *not angular*, minute, 6-7 x 5-6 micr. in diameter, pale flesh color in mass. CYSTIDIA more or less numerous on the edge of the gills, clavate to elliptical, sometimes hair-pointed, hyaline, 50-60 x 10-15 micr. ODOR and TASTE not marked. Scattered. On rotten logs. Bay View, Houghton, Ann Arbor. July-September. Frequent in hemlock or tamarack woods, mixed with maple or birch.

This little Leptonia is partial to rotten wood. Its finely striate, granulose pileus reminds one of some of the small species of Pluteus and it approaches that genus also in its smooth spores and clavate cystidia. The gills are slightly adnexed or, in expanded specimens, they may be free, and the stem is subcartilaginous. It seems to form a connecting link between Leptonia and Pluteus.

**Gills yellowish-tinged.

618. Leptonia formosa Fr.

Syst. Mycol., 1821.

Illustration: Fries, Icones, Pl. 98.

PILEUS 1-3 cm. broad, convex then plane and umbilicate, *yellow-wax color*, covered with minute fuscous squamules,· *margin striate.* FLESH thin, yellow, toughish, membranaceous. GILLS adnate, with a tooth, *rather broad,* subdistant, *tinged yellow* then flesh color, edge entire, concolor. STEM 4-5 cm. long, 1.5-2 mm. thick, strict, equal, cartilaginous, stuffed then hollow, *yellow,* glabrous, shining, *striatulate.* SPORES tuberculate-angular, rather rectangular in outline, 10-12 x 6-7 micr., apiculus oblique, flesh color. CYSTIDIA none. ODOR and TASTE mild.

Scattered. In low, swampy woods of hemlock, etc., in northern Michigan, in maple and elm woods in southern Michigan. July-September. Throughout the State. Frequent locally.

Easily recognized by the yellow cast to the whole plant and the striate and squamulose pileus. Fries says "scarcely different from *L. asprella* except in color." This is borne out by the fact that it is subhygrophanous, which makes it difficult to place not only this but other swamp species in the non-hygrophanous section.

***Gills bluish or blackish at first.*

619. Leptonia serrulata Fr.

Syst. Mycol., 1821.

Illustrations: Hard, Mushrooms, Fig. 207, p. 254, 1908.
Gillet, Champignons de France, No. 437.

PILEUS 1-3 cm. broad, convex then plane, umbilicate-depressed, *not striate, at first bluish-black,* then smoky-umber or fuscous squamulose, especially in the umbilicus. FLESH thin, not hygrophanous, whitish. GILLS adnate, white, tinged bluish-gray, *edge black-serrulate,* ventricose. STEM 2-5 cm. long, 1-2 mm. thick, cartilaginous, *·blackish to steel-blue,* stuffed then hollow, rigid, equal, *glabrous, except the black-dotted apex,* white-mycelioid at base. SPORES 11-4 x 7-8 micr., tuberculate-angular, elongated. *Sterile cells* on the edge of the gills, filled with blackish coloring matter.

Scattered or gregarious. In low wet places, of mixed hemlock woods in the north; ash, elm and maple woods of southern Michigan. Throughout the State. July-September. Frequent locally.

This species and *Eccilia atrides* appear to run into each other. Both are characterized by the black-serrulate edge of the gills. In Eccilia they run down the stem by a broad tooth. The colors remind one much of *L. lampropoda,* which differs mainly in that it has not black-edged gills and is not black-dotted at the apex of the stem. Varieties and related species have been described, indicating that these two species run into each other. Var. *expallens* Fr. is *paler;* var. *laevipes* Maire has no black dots on the stem; var. *berkeleyi* Maire has entire gills.

620. Leptonia euchroa Fr.

Syst. Mycol., 1821.

Illustration: Cooke, Ill., Pl. 334.

PILEUS 1-2 cm. broad, convex then plane, not umbonate nor truly umbilicate, *covered with fibrillose squamules, violaceous to wine-color,* not striate, margin fibrillose-scaly. GILLS subdistant, *very ventricose,* narrowed at both ends, narrowly adnate, sometimes pseudo-decurrent when pileus is expanded, *violet at first then pallid.* STEM slender, equal, 2-3 cm. long, 2 mm. thick, stuffed then hollow, toughish, *glabrous* or very delicately fibrillose with *purple fibrils on a dark violet ground.* SPORES tuberculate-angular, elongated, 10-12 x 6-7 micr. (occasionally wider), angles obtuse. CYSTIDIA none.

Subcaespitose. On sawdust, rotten wood, etc. Bay View. July-August. Rare.

This beautiful little plant is a wood-inhabiting species like *L. placida* but much more slender. The spores of our plants are longer than the measurements given by the English mycologists and their coarse obtuse angles make them somewhat unique. When old, the translucent margin of the pileus shows the lines of the gills so as to appear striate, a condition often found in other non-striate species when old.

Section II. Hygrophanae. Pileus hygrophanous, margin striate when fresh and moist.

621. Leptonia asprella Fr.

Syst. Mycol., 1821.

Illustration: Atkinson, Mushrooms, Fig. 139, p. 147, 1900.

PILEUS 2-4 cm. broad, convex, becoming somewhat expanded, umbilicate-depressed, *glabrous or fibrillose, striatulate when moist,* umbilicus villose or scaly, *hygrophanous,* silky-shining when dry, from pale umber to grayish-brown, variable in color, margin becoming split. FLESH watery to whitish, thin, rather fragile. GILLS adnexed to adnate seceding, *subdistant, rather broad, narrowed in front,* whitish to grayish, then rosy from the spores, edge concolor, entire. STEM 3-8 cm. long, 2-3 mm. thick, slender and usually straight, rigid and elastic but fragile, *glabrous,* livid-fuscous to pale, stuffed then hollow, sometimes twisted, white-mycelioid at base, apex pruinose. SPORES angular, angles sharp, 9-13 x 6-8 micr., broadly elliptic-elongate in outline. CYSTIDIA none. ODOR and TASTE mild.

Solitary or gregarious. On the ground in woods. Bay View, New Richmond, Ann Arbor. Infrequent. August-September.

This species varies considerably, and there seems to be no settled notion of its exact limitations. Cooke figures a plant quite different in color and size from that of the above description. The striations are not always definitely present, especially in the dry plant. The spores are variable in size, even in the same plant. One variety occurs in low, mossy or sphagnous places. Its pileus is pale isabelline or pale brownish-gray when moist, slightly virgate with fibrils, scarcely or not at all striatulate. The gills are white at first. The stem is of the same color or is slightly paler than the pileus, so that the whole plant has a uniform color when fresh and mature. The cap is apt to be truncate at the apex and campanulate; in all other respects it agrees with the species. *L. asprella* is found in coniferous regions, e. g., Bay View, New Richmond. See Ricken's figure of *L. anatina*, Pl. 73, Fig. 9. That species, however, has markedly narrow gills.

Nolanea Fr.

(From Latin, *Nola*, a little bell.)

Pink-spored. Stem *hollow* and cartilaginous or tough, usually slender. Gills adnate, adnexed or almost free, seceding, not decurrent. Pileus thin, *campanulate,* usually *papillate,* margin at first straight and applied to the stem. Spores *angular.*

Terrestrial, small, slender plants, corresponding to Mycena of the white-spored group, approaching the smaller Entolomas, and separated from Leptonia by the unexpanded bell-shaped pileus. It is a small genus.

The PILEUS is glabrous, silky or scurfy, dry or hygrophanous; and its campanulate shape which is rather persistent and is due to the position of the straight margin on the stem when young, is quite characteristic. It is usually fragile. The color is some shade of brown in our species except in *N. caelestina.* The GILLS are often broad or ventricose, and generally secede (i. e. separate) from the attachment at the stem, in which respect they differ from those of Clitopilus. The STEM is central, tubular and elastic or fragile in most species; in some, however, it is toughish-cartilaginous like that of certain Mycenas. It has a tendency to become compressed or longitudinally furrowed because of its hollow interior. It is usually glabrous or minutely flocculose; in *N. dysthales* (Pk.) it is densely floccose-hairy. There is *no annulus, nor volva,* and the flesh is confluent with that of the pileus. The SPORES are angular, often irregularly tuberculate-angular. CYSTIDIA are usually absent; in *N. babingtonii* and *N. dysthales* they may be found on the edge of the gills. A few species have a slight ODOR; that of *N. mammosa* is similar to rancid meal. The Nolaneas are difficult to identify to the species, and a microscope is essential to any final decision.

Key to the Species

(a) Pileus and stem lavender to violaceous. 630. *N. caelestina* var. *violacea* Kauff.
(aa) Pileus and stem some other color.
  (b) Spores quadrate or cruciate-four-angled; pileus umber or smoky-umber. 623. *N. pascua* Fr.
  (bb) Spores not distinctly four-angled.
    (c) Pileus with greenish tint, fuscous-brownish, livid or smoky, very shining. 624. *N. versatilis* Fr.
    (cc) Pileus without greenish or olivaceous tints.
      (d) Stem and pileus hairy, fibrillose-scaly or flocculose; gills subdistant.
        (e) Spores 14-20 x 8-9 micr.; whole plant smoky-brown. 622. *N. dysthales* (Pk.) Atk.
        (ee) Spores subglobose, 8-9 micr.; pileus small, covered with loose brown fibrils. 625. *N. babingtonia* Berk.
      (dd) Stem and pileus glabrous, silky and shining.
        (e) Gills white or whitish at first; pileus hygrophanous.
          (f) Pileus conical, cinnamon-brown then pale and shining; gills narrow. 628. *N. conica* Pk.
          (ff) Pileus campanulate, grayish-brown; gills medium broad. 629. *N. fuscogrisella* Pk.
        (ee) Gills grayish at first; odor somewhat rancid-farinaceous. 626. *N. mammosa* Fr. 627. *N. papillata* Bres.

Gills at first gray, brown or fuscous.

622. Nolanea dysthales (Pk.) Atk.

N. Y. State Mus. Report. 32, 1879 (as *Entoloma dysthales*).
Jour. of Mycol., Vol. 8, p. 114, 1902 (as *Nolanea nodospora* Atk.).

PILEUS 6-18 mm. broad, rarely larger, thin, campanulate-convex, obtuse, densely floccose-hairy, sometimes furfuraceous and striate, more often even, the hairy tufts sometimes squarrose, *smoky-umber or dark fuscous*, margin at first straight. FLESH submembranous. GILLS adnate, ascending, *broad*, ventricose, subdistant to distant, thickish, dark fuscous-gray or smoky, tinged flesh color at maturity, edge flocculose. STEM 1-4 cm. long, 1.5-4 mm. thick, equal, more or less densely *floccose-tomentose, dark fuscous* or seal-brown, becoming smoky, toughish-cartilaginous, stuffed then hollow, concolor within. SPORES large, variable, *elongated tuberculate-angular*, 14-20 x 8-9 micr., deep flesh color in mass, faintly colored under the microscope. CYSTIDIA only on edge of gills, *variable*, sometimes elliptical to ventricose and obtuse, sometimes ventricose-lanceolate and pointed, 60-70 x 20-25 micr. ODOR and TASTE mild.

Solitary or scattered. On low, wet, mossy or swampy ground, on leaf mold, etc., in hemlock regions. Bay View, South Haven, New Richmond. July-September. Infrequent.

This species is known by the covering of the cap and stem, its color and the very large tuberculate spores. It is very variable and was considered an Entoloma by Peck, who first described the form with the thin, striate pileus whose surface is only granular-furfuraceous or mixed with the characteristic hairs. Later Atkinson described the form in which the hairy covering is more highly developed, often as if matted, as *Nolanea nodospora*. I have found the two forms in different parts of the state and consider them variations of the same plant. The trama of the pileus is two-layered, the layers being separated by a dark line of narrow hyphae. A form occurs in frondose woods, of which the hair-like fibrils of the stem are almost ferruginous. The gills of *N. dysthales* remain dark grayish-brown a long time and hence it is easily mistaken for an Inocybe; at length, however, they are somewhat colored by the rather bright spores. It seems that in very moist situations the cap is less hairy-scaly and then striate, especially when more fully expanded. The size of the basidia varies as the plant slowly matures and the cystidia seem to take on a different shape in age.

623. Nolanea pascua Fr.

Syst. Myc., 1821.

Illustrations: Cooke, Ill., Pl. 376.
    Gillet, Champignons de France, No. 493.
    Ricken, Blätterpilze, Pl. 74, Fig. 3.
    Swanton, Fungi, Pl. 42, Fig. 10-12.

PILEUS 2-4 cm. broad, *fragile, conico-campanulate,* obtuse or umbonate, hygrophanous, umber-brown and striatulate (moist), fading and even (dry), glabrous, silky-shining. FLESH thin, concolor. GILLS rounded behind, adnexed, rather broad, *ventricose,* grayish, then gray-flesh color, seceding, close. STEM 4-10 cm. long, 2-4 mm. thick, pallid grayish-brown, cartilaginous, hollow, equal, often twisted, *fragile,* splitting longitudinally, fibrillose-striate. SPORES *subquadrate or almost cruciform,* 8-11 micr. diam., deep flesh color in mass. CYSTIDIA none; sterile cells absent on edge of gills.

Gregarious. On low mossy ground in open woods by lakes. Ann Arbor. September. Infrequent.

This species is said to be very common in Europe. I have only one record and the specimens are lost. It was most sharply marked by the quadrate, 4-angled spores. This is a character given by nearly all authors and by the figures. Our plants approached closely *N. staurospora* Bres. (Fung. Trid., Vol. I, p. 18), and this species and *N. pascua* (sense of Ricken) seem to be very similar. It certainly is not a common species with us and I did not observe any olive tints, such as occur in our *N. versatilis.*

624. Nolanea versatilis Fr.

Monographia, 1863.

Illustrations: Fries, Icones, Pl. 98, Fig. 5.
Ricken, Blätterpilze, Pl. 74, Fig. 7.
Plate CXV of this Report.

PILEUS 1-3 cm. broad, at first conic or elongated-oval, then campanulate, fragile, obtuse, at length expanded and subumbonate, silky-shining, sometimes *silky-fibrillose, almost glittering,* color variable, livid-fuscous, olivaceous-brown, smoky-tinged, subhygrophanous. FLESH thin, submembranous, grayish. GILLS narrowly adnexed, almost free, ventricose and *broad in front,* subdistant, *gray,* becoming smoky-flesh color, edge minutely fimbriate. STEM 3-6 cm. long, 1-4 mm. thick, equal, hollow, *often twisted or compressed,* splitting longitudinally, fibrillose-striate, *shining,* glabrous or flocculose, pallid then pale fuliginous or fuscous. SPORES tuberculate-angular, longer than wide, 9-11 x 6-7.5 micr. (few longer), flesh color in mass. CYSTIDIA numerous on edge of gills, few elsewhere, ventricose, often acuminate-pointed, 45-65 x 12-16 micr. ODOR and TASTE slight or none.

Gregarious. Among grass in low moist woods. Ann Arbor, New Richmond. July-August. Infrequent.

This species was abundant in a single wood-lot during one season; elsewhere it occurred as few individuals. It varies in size and shape (within limits); often it has the shape and size of Cooke's figures of *N. pascua,* at other times the caps may be narrow and stem slender and longer, all in the same patch. The cap is beautifully silky and shining and usually has a somewhat olive or greenish hue which suggests the glitter of metal. The shape of the young plant is often like that of *Hygrophorus conicus* or of an Inocybe. In our specimens the stem was frequently somewhat flocculose.

Except for the spores it approaches *N. pascua* quite closely in color and shape. It is here conceived in the sense of Ricken.

625. Nolanea babingtonii Berk.

Outlines of British Fungology, 1860.

Illustrations: Patouillard, Tab. Analyt., No. 429.
Cooke, Ill., Pl. 377.

"Pileus 6-12 mm. broad, conico-campanulate, pale gray, *covered with dark brown fasciculate fibrils free at one end,* silky-shining, disk subsquamulose. FLESH very thin. GILLS adnate, *distant,* gray, ventricose, edge minutely flocculose. STEM 2-3 cm. long, 2 mm. thick, equal, *covered with dark-brown down,* hollow, slightly undulate. SPORES angular-nodulose, subglobose or slightly oblong, 7-8 micr., apiculate."

Lewiston. On moss, in wet places. Rare. Reported by Longyear.

The description is taken from Massee's British Fungus Flora, and the spore-measurements were doubtless made from the type specimen. Patouillard gives spore size as 9-10 x 5-6 micr. It is a delicate little plant, characterized by the loose fibrils which stand out from its pileus and stem. There is some doubt of this determination.

626. Nolanea mammosa Fr. (Sense of Bresadola.)

Epicrisis, 1836.

Illustrations: Bresadola, Fung. Trid., Vol. I, Tab. 82, 1881.
Gillet, Champignons de France, No. 491.

PILEUS 2-4 cm. broad, conic to broadly campanulate, margin decurved, *mammilately umbonate,* faintly striate, umber (moist), soon grayish-brown or fuscous, innately fibrillose and shining when dry. FLESH dingy, brownish near surface, thin, subscissile. GILLS rather broad, rounded behind, usually narrowly adnate but seceding, *subdistant,* thickish, *pale gray at first* then tinged flesh color by spores, edge often uneven. STEM 5-9 cm. long, elongated, 2-5 mm. thick, tubular, terete or compressed, *tinged fuscous,* not white, cartilaginous, slightly fibrillose-striate, *white-pruinose at apex,* otherwise glabrous. SPORES tuberculate-angular, elongate, distinctly longer than broad, 9-11 x 6-7 micr., deep flesh color, nucleate. CYSTIDIA none. ODOR and TASTE of rancid meal.

(Dried: Gills pale brown.)

Gregarious. On the ground in woods, copses, etc., sometimes in grassy places. Throughout the State. July-October. Frequent.

This is our commonest Nolanea. It may be known by its elongated stem which is often furrowed longitudinally, by its gray gills and by the spores; the latter are distinctly longer than broad, and the angles are not as clearly and sharply marked as in other species. It is somewhat hygrophanous. The gills are often broadly adnate. There are short sterile cells on the edge of the gills.

627. Nolanea papillata Bres.

Fungi Tridentini, Vol. I, 1881.

Illustrations: Ibid, Pl. 82.
> Fries, Icones, Pl. 98, Fig. 4 (as *Nolanea mammosa* var. *minor* Fr.).

PILEUS 2-3 cm. broad, campanulate, *then expanded, papillate,* umber to watery-brown and striate (moist), paler when dry, glabrous. FLESH thin, scissile, subhygrophanous, fragile. GILLS sinuate-adnate, seceding, broader toward front, subdistant to close, subventricose, livid-whitish then somewhat salmon-colored from spores. STEM *slender,* 3-5 cm. long, 1-2 mm. thick, tubular, pale grayish-brown, glabrous, slightly pruinose at apex, white-mycelioid at base, straight or curved, cartilaginous, sometimes striatulate. SPORES angular, 9-11 x 6-7 micr., nucleate, salmon-colored in mass. ODOR none or slightly of rancid meal. CYSTIDIA none.

Scattered. Low places in moist frondose woods. Ann Arbor, Bay View, New Richmond. September. Infrequent.

Differs mainly from *N. mammosa* in its more slender habit, smaller size and closer gills.

**Gills white at first.*

628. Nolanea conica Pk.

N. Y. State Mus. Rep. 24, 1872.

PILEUS 5-15 mm. broad, *conical,* then expanded and papillate, *hygrophanous,* watery-cinnamon and striatulate (moist), paler, silky-shining and subzonate (dry). FLESH thin. GILLS nearly free, close, moderately broad, narrowed behind, white at first, *bright flesh color* from spores. STEM slender, 2-5 cm. long, 1-2 mm. thick, equal, straight, tubular, cartilaginous, elastic, white-mycelioid at base, tinged ashy-brown. SPORES tuberculate-angular, 7-9 (including apiculus) x 5-6 micr., longer than broad, *apiculus prominent.* CYSTIDIA none.

Solitary or scattered. On moss or low places in swamps or wet conifer or mixed woods. Northern Michigan. July-September. Infrequent.

The conical, shining, hygrophanous pileus and small spores distinguish it. The length of spores rarely passes 8 microns unless apiculus is included.

629. Nolanea fuscogrisella Pk.

N. Y. State Mus. Rep. 39, 1886.

PILEUS 1-2.5 cm. broad, campanulate, more or less palillate, *hygrophanous,* glabrous, grayish-brown and striatulate (moist), paler and silky-shining (dry), papilla darker. GILLS rather broad, narrowed behind, adnexed, almost subdistant, whitish then bright flesh-colored. STEM 5-7 cm. long, 2-4 mm. thick, glabrous, white-mycelioid toward base, apex pruinose, *brownish,* often darker than pileus, tubular, cartilaginous. SPORES 7-9 x 5-6 micr. (incl. apiculus), angular, apiculus prominent.

Gregarious. On moss, etc., of low mixed woods. Sault Ste. Marie. July. Infrequent.

This differs from the preceding in its stouter stem, and less conic pileus. The spores are very similar. The gills are broader. In our specimens the stem was invariably darker than the pileus, and hoary at base and above by the white mycelium. The spores are slightly shorter than the measurements given by Peck.

630. Nolanea caelestina var. violacea Kauff.

Mich. Acad. Sci. Rep. 10, 1908.

PILEUS 8-10 mm. broad, *conico-campanulate, lavender,* acutely papillate, innately silky-fibrillose, margin even. GILLS adnexed, rather narrow, *subdistant,* white then flesh color, not reaching to the margin of pileus. STEM slender, 5 cm. long, 1 mm. thick, even, glabrous, pruinose at apex, equal, lavender, darker than cap. SPORES tuberculate-elliptical, 9-11 x 6-7 micr. CYSTIDIA none. ODOR none.

Solitary. In low elm swamp. Ann Arbor. Rare.

A beautiful little plant, usually hidden among the debris of the woods. The stem is flexible, subcartilaginous and does not turn reddish when bruised. It differs from the descriptions of the type in the narrow gills. It appears close also to *N. cruenta* Quel. except in color.

Eccilia Fr.

(From the Greek, *ekkoilo,* I hollow out.)

Pink-spored. Stem *cartilaginous,* hollow or stuffed, slender. Gills *decurrent,* either attenuated behind or broadly adnato-decurrent. Pileus *umbilicate* or depressed, its margin at first incurved. Spores *angular.*

Terrestrial or lignicolous. Small, slender plants, corresponding to Omphalia of the white-spored group; differing from the small Clitopili in the cartilaginous stem. A very small genus composed of rather rare species.

The PILEUS is glabrous, silky, or somewhat squamulose in the umbilicus; dry or hygrophanous. It is usually expanded and then the center is depressed to strongly umbilicate. Its margin is at first incurved and this character may persist until maturity. The color varies from white to grayish and brown. The GILLS are attached in two ways, either attenuate-long-decurrent or broadly adnate and then slightly decurrent, remaining attached, i. e., not seceding as a rule. They are often quite distant as in *E. rhodocylia* Fr. or crowded as in *E. atrides Fr.* and *E. polita Fr.* They vary from narrow in some species to broadly triangular in others. In *E. apiculata* Fr., *E. vilis* Fr. and *E. rhodcylicioides* Atk. they are distinctly gray; in others, white or dingy white, finally colored by the spores. Some species possess cystidia, giving the edge a minutely fimbriate appearance. The STEM is usually enlarged somewhat at the apex where it expands into the membranaceous pileus. It is truly cartilaginous, slender, and soon hollow or tubular within. Some species have been described as solid, but it remains to be seen whether these are not really only stuffed at first by a differentiated pith. The color is often that of the pileus or paler. The angular SPORES correspond to those of Leptonia, Nolanea, Pluteus and one of the sections of Clitopilus. CYSTIDIA usually absent; in *E. pirinoides, E. rhodcylicioides* Atk. and *E. roseoalbocitrina* Atk. cystidia-like cells are present on the edge of gills.

The group is difficult, and the rarity of specimens makes it hard to learn much concerning their variability. A microscopic study is essential to determine the species with any satisfaction, as the size of spores and basidia, the structure of the trama, and the presence or absence of cystidia must often determine the final judgment.

Because of their rare occurrence, it seems best to include in the key all forms which may possibly be found in the State. *E. polita* and *E. carneo-grisea* have been reported from the neighboring States.

Key to the Species

(a) Gills crowded or close.
  (b) Edge of gills black-dotted. 631. *E. atrides* Fr.
  (bb) Edge of gills concolor, not black dotted.
    (c) Pileus 2-4 cm. broad, hygrophanous, livid (moist); gills very crowded, broad. *E. polita* Fr.
    (cc) Pileus 5-20 mm. broad, not hygrophanous, mouse-gray; gills close, broad; spores 5-angled, 8-10 micr. 634. *E. pentagonospora* Atk. var.
(aa) Gills subdistant to distant.
  (b) Pileus 2-5 cm. broad, hygrophanous, tough, sordid-brown; stem tough, concolor; taste tardily pungent; gills close to subdistant; on the ground. 635. *E. mordax* Atk.
  (bb) Pileus smaller (rarely as large in *E. carneo-grisea*).
    (c) On wood; pileus deeply umbilicate, 1-1.5 cm., hygrophanous; gills very distant, broad, long-decurrent. *E. rhodocylix* Fr.
    (cc) Not on logs, stumps or wood.
      (d) On sphagnum; pileus umbonate, small, dark-brown; gills long-decurrent, distant, broad. Spores 10-12.5 x 6-7.5 micr. *E. sphagnicola* Pk.
      (dd) On lawns, fields, or in woods on humus, etc.
        (e) Pileus white, 1-2.5 cm., silky; gills adnato-decurrent, subdistant; stem long, white. Spores elongate, 9-11 x 6-9 micr. *E. roseoalbocitrina* Atk.
        (ee) Pileus grayish-brown to fuscous.
          (f) Pileus hygrophanous; gills without cystidia.
            (g) Edge of gills darker, crisped; pileus gray flesh color, margin micaceous; gills distant, spores 6-7 x 4-5 micr. *E. carneo-grisea* B. & Br.
            (gg) Edge of gills concolor; pileus brownish-gray (moist); gills subdistant, broad. 632. *E. grisco-rubella* Fr.
          (ff) Pileus not hygrophanous; gills with cystidia.
            (g) Gills adnato-decurrent, broad behind, distant; spores sphoeroid, angles not sharply marked. 633. *E. pirinoides* sp. nov.
            (gg) Gills arcuate, distant, decurrent; spores prominently angled, quadrate. *E. rhodocyliciodes* Atk.

Illustrations:

E. vilis Fr.: Ricken, Blätterpilze, Pl. 73, Fig. 10.

E. carneo-grisea Fr.: Hard, Mushrooms, Fig. 205, 1908.

E. parkensis Fr.: Icones, Pl. 100, Fig. 5.

E. polita Fr.: Atkinson, Mushrooms, Fig. 140, 1900.

Fries, Icones, Pl. 100, Fig. 3. Hard, Mushrooms, Fog. 206, 1908.

E. rusticoides Gill.: Ricken, Blätterpilze, Pl. 73, Fig. 11.

E. rhodocaylix Fr.: Swanton, Fungi, Pl. 42, 1909.   Fries, Icones, Pl. 100. Fig. 6.

E. sphagnicola Pk.: N. Y. Mus. Rep. 54, Pl. 1, 1900.

631. Eccilia atrides Fr.

Epicrisis, 1836.

PILEUS 1-2 cm. broad, deeply umbilicate, dark *umber,* umbilicus darker, striate to umbilicus, somewhat virgate, pruinose. FLESH thin. GILLS decurrent, narrowed behind, close, pallid, *edge black.* STEM 2-3 cm. long, 1-2 mm. thick, brownish, apex paler and floccose-dotted, dots sometimes black, sometimes pallid, hollow, glabrous below, equal and slender. SPORES tuberculate-angular, elongated, 11-13 x 6-7 micr. (incl. apiculus), bright flesh color in mass.

Solitary or gregarious. On very rotten wood. Houghton, Bay View. July-August. Infrequent in maple and hemlock woods of northern Michigan.

This species approaches *Leptonia serrulata* Fr. which also has black-edged gills. At times this character is almost or entirely absent except in old plants. Our plants had truly decurrent gills, but not extending far down the stem. It is usually found on debris or on very rotten logs in forests. Ricken considers it identical with *L. serrulata.*

632.   Eccilia griseo-rubella Fr.

Epicrisis, 1836.

Illustrations: Fries, Icones, Pl. 100, Fig. 4.
  Gillet, Champignons de France, No. 568.
  Cooke, Ill., Pl. 613.

PILEUS 1-2.5 cm. broad, campanulate, umbilicate, hygrophanous, striate and brownish-ashy (moist), umbilicus darker, minutely squamulose, *elsewhere with innate white fibrils.* FLESH concolor, thin. GILLS *broadly adnate,* slightly decurrent, broad, subdistant, pallid then flesh color, edge even. STEM 2-4 cm. long, 1-2 mm. thick, pallid to buff, *glabrous,* equal, even, cartilaginous, hollow. SPORES tuberculate-angular, elongated, 8-9 x 5-6 micr.

Solitary or scattered. On the ground in cedar swamps. Bay View. September. Infrequent.

Our plant has rather broad gills as is shown in Fries' Icones. The other authors figure narrower gills. The pileus becomes hygrophanous-streaked on drying.

633. Eccilia pirinoides sp. nov.

PILEUS 1-2 cm. broad, campanulate, then subexpanded, margin decurved, depressed-umbilicate, grayish-brown to fuscous, moist, silky shining when dry, *with dense appressed small squamules on disk*, appressed-fibrillose elsewhere. GILLS adnato-decurrent, *broad behind, subdistant,* thin, whitish then rosy-tinged to bright flesh color. STEM 4-6 cm. long, 1-2.5 mm. thick, distinctly cartilaginous, white, slightly fuscescent, pruinate, equal, even, stuffed with a white pith, finally hollow. SPORES sphoeroid-subangular, angles not prominent, 8-10 micr. diam. (without apiculus), *abruptly narrowed to an apiculus which is 2-3 micr. long,* obscurely 5-6 sided. CYSTIDIA not numerous, slender, acuminate, about 75 micr. long. BASIDIA 4-spored, clavate, 45-50 micr. long. ODOR none.

Gregarious. On the ground, among forest debris, hemlock, oak and maple woods; clay ravine. September. New Richmond.

Except for its lack of a strong malic odor, it agrees with all the descriptions which we have of *E. pirina* B. & C. It also approaches *E. rhodocylicioides* Atk.; but it differs from the latter in its bright colored spores, even pileus and broadly adnate, white gills; the shape of the spores is also different. It has so far been found only in one locality.

634. Eccilia pentagonospora Atk. var.

Jour. of Mycol., Vol. 8, p. 113, 1902.

PILEUS 5-20 mm. broad, fragile, convex-plane, umbilicate, hygrophanous, *at first blackish-gray, fading to steel-gray and shining,* even, at first minutely tomentose-flocculose over the entire surface, later appressed scurfy. FLESH thin, membranous. GILLS broad behind and *adnate-subdecurrent,* at first grayish then dark flesh color, close to subdistant, thickish, somewhat crisped, edge concolor. STEM 1-2.5 cm. long, 1-1.5 mm. thick, equal, hollow, entirely *glabrous,* cartilaginous, *metallic gray,* whitish-mycelioid at base. SPORES tuberculate-angular, mostly 5-angled, angles obtuse, 7-9.5 micr. (incl. apiculus), deep flesh color in mass. CYSTIDIA none. BASIDIA about 30 x 9-10 micr.

Gregarious. On moist soil in frondose woods. Ann Arbor. August.

This collection departs from Atkinson's description in the more flocculose, hygrophanous pileus and the hollow stem. The microscopic characters seem to be the same.

635. Eccilia mordax Atk.

Jour. of Mycol., Vol. 8, p. 113, 1902.

PILEUS 2-5 cm. broad, convex, *tough,* umbilicate, hygrophanous, glabrous, *dull-reddish-brown to pale chestnut or cinnamon (moist),* sordid isabelline (dry), even, margin inrolled. FLESH dirty white, thin. GILLS adnate to subdecurrent, close, *dingy brown at first* then tinged flesh color, narrow. STEM 3-6 cm. long, 3-5 mm. thick, *tough,* equal, fibrous-cartilaginous, fistulose, often compressed, *concolor,* glabrous or pruinose, white mycelioid at base. SPORES oval, 6-7 x 4-5 micr., smooth, pale flesh color. CYSTIDIA none. BASIDIA clavate, 25-30 x 6-8 micr., 4-spored. TASTE at first mild, after 15-20 minutes pungent in the throat and causes nausea.

Gregarious. On the ground, springy sides of ravines. Ann Arbor. August. Infrequent.

This species approaches *Clitocybe cyathiforme* in external appearance, but differs by its flesh-colored spores, its umbilicate pileus and the habitat on the ground. It seems to be our largest Eccilia and is probably somewhat poisonous.

Claudopus Smith.

(From the Latin, *claudus,* defective, and *pes,* foot.)

Pink-spored. Stem *eccentric, lateral or wanting.* Pileus dimidiate or resupinate, irregular. Gills not seceding nor anastomosing, radiating from an eccentric or lateral point. Spores angular or rounded.

On rotten wood or humus. Corresponding to the genus Pleurotus of the white-spored group. With the exception of *C. nidulans,* they are small, insignificant, soft plants, often growing in small hollows of decayed wood or on humus at the base of stumps, etc. The small forms are white, grayish or brown; *C. nidulans* is *yellow to buff.* All except one of the small species are at first resupinate, i. e., applied to the substratum with gills uppermost, but finally becoming reflexed with gills in the usual position. The stem is entirely lacking or is small and inconspicuous, usually tomentose or villose at the point of attachment of the stem or pileus. Only a few species are known in our flora.

Key to the Species

(a) Pileus medium to large, yellowish; gills orange yellow. 636. *C. nidulans* Fr.
(aa) Pileus small, 3 cm. or less in diam.; not yellow.
  (b) Pileus white or whitish, at first resupinate.
    (c) Spores angular; pileus silky to villose-floccose. 637. *C. depluens* Fr.
    (cc) Spores not angular; pileus tomentose. *C. variabilis* Fr.
  (bb) Pileus gray to brown.
    (c) Pileus hygrophanous, striatulate (moist); gills scarcely reaching stem. *C. griegensis* Pk.
    (cc) Pileus not hygrophanous, subdecurrent. 638. *C. byssisedus* Fr.

636. Claudopus nidulans Fr.

Syst. Mycol., 1821. (As Pleurotus.)

Illustrations: Atkinson, Mushrooms, Pl. 41, Fig. 141, p. 149, 1900.

Hard, Mushrooms, Fig. 208, p. 256, 1908.

Clements, Minn. Mushrooms, Fig. 35, p. 59, 1910.

Plate CXV of this Report.

PILEUS 1-7 cm. broad, shelving, sessile or narrowed behind into a short stem-like base, nearly orbicular, dimidiate or reniform, *coarsely hairy or tomentose on the surface,* rich yellow or buff, margin at first involute, even. FLESH soft, rather tough. GILLS *orange-yellow,* medium broad, close to subdistant, adnate, rarely subdecurrent. STEM or attached base tomentose next to the gills beneath. SPORES elongated, slightly curved, 6-8 x 3-4 micr., smooth, *pink in mass.* ODOR *very disagreeable* when fresh. TASTE becomes rather mild at length; not desirable for the table.

Gregarious or imbricately caespitose. On decaying logs, etc., of frondose trees. Throughout the State; Marquette, Houghton, Ann Arbor, etc. July-October. Infrequent.

Panus dorsalis Bosc. is now agreed to be the same. The toughish consistency of *C. nidulans* approaches that of the genus Panus. In general appearance it looks like a Pleurotus and was so called by Fries, and as its spore-color is not a very bright pink it would seem to fit that genus as well as *Pleurotus subpalmatus* does. The latter, in my opinion, might equally well be made a species of the pink-spored group. The beginner will be apt to refer *C. nidulans* to the ochre-spored group in Crepidotus if he neglects to make a spore-print. This all emphasizes the fact that nature takes no account of the convenience of the student and probably no system can ever be devised in which some plants will not be found half-way between the groups. This is the largest of the genus, and is not easily confused with other mushrooms except *Crepidotus dorsalis* which resembles it in colors but is smaller and has globose, ochre-brown spores. The pileus is more often dimidiate or kidney-shaped rather than the shape given in Atkinson's illustration.

637. Claudopus depluens Fr.

Syst. Mycol., 1821.

Illustrations: Patouillard, Tab. Analyt., No. 431.
    Cooke, Ill., Pl. 344.

PILEUS 1-5 mm. broad, *white,* resupinate at first then reflexed, suborbicular, subreniform, conchate, etc., *variable in form, floccose,* almost sessile or attached by a *short,* white, villose STEM. FLESH membranous, very thin. GILLS radiating from the stem, *broad,* subdistant to distant, rose-colored at maturity. SPORES *angular,* somewhat longer than broad, sphoeroid-angular from the end-view, 7-10 x 6-7.5 micr., distinctly rose-colored in mass, nucleate.

On very decaying wood or black humus, in hemlock and birch mixed woods, in springy places. New Richmond. September. Rarely found.

Massee gives the spores as sphoeroid; Patouillard and Peck give them slightly longer. It may be that varieties occur which might explain the difference. There was no tinge of red or gray present in our plants, as described by Fries. They are small and insignificant plants. *C. variabilis* is similar, but has non-angular spores. Ricken reports the above species under Crepidotus and with smooth spores.

638. Claudopus byssisedus Fr.

Syst. Mycol., 1821.

Illustrations: Patouillard, Tab. Analyt., No. 432.
    Cooke, Ill., Pl. 344.

"PILEUS 5-20 cm. broad, at first resupinate, then reflexed, nearly plane, reniform, covered with a fine pruinosity, gray tinged with pink, or grayish-brown, *striate on the margin.* FLESH thin, membranous. GILLS subdecurrent, grayish, rosy from the spores. STEM short, eccentric, or lateral, incurved, villose, *white fibrils radiating from the base* forming an interlaced membrane." SPORES elongate-angular, 9-11 x 6-7 micr., rosy in mass.

On very rotten wood. Swamps of frondose or conifer trees. Throughout the State. Summer. Infrequently found.

The description is taken from Fries and Patouillard. As in the preceding species, there is a difference in the spore-measurements given. Our plants have spores agreeing with those of Peck, while in Europe they seem to be smaller. Patouillard and Massee, give them 7-8 x 6 micr. The American form must, therefore, be considered as a variety. It is scarcely distinct from *C. griegensis* Pk.

LEUCOSPORAE

Amanita Fr.

(From the Greek *Amanos,* the name of a mountain in Asia Minor, which doubtless abounded in edible fungi, for the Roman physician Galen used the term Amanites to refer to *Agaricus campestris.* Persoon first applied it to this genus, using *Amanita caesarea* as the type.)

White-spored; stem provided with an *annulus* and a *volva,* and separable from the pileus. The gills are *free* or attached by a line, *white,* cut off squarely at anterior extremity. The volva is formed from a *universal veil* which covers the whole plant in the egg-stage and is *discrete* from the cuticle of the pileus. The hyphae of the trama of the gills are *divergent.*

Soft-fleshy, terrestrial, mostly *poisonous* mushrooms, usually of rather large size; never truly caespitose; mostly in forests or on the border of woods and thickets; sometimes, however, in fields or on lawns.

The PILEUS is soft, entirely enveloped at the beginning, along with the stem, by a differentiated layer of tissue called the universal veil. When this splits above the pileus during the enlargement of the plant, it is pulled off from the pileus and leaves the surface of the pileus glabrous; when it splits circularly around the edge of the pileus (circumscissile) the loose layer left on top ceases to grow and as the pileus expands and enlarges, this covering is broken into patches or warts, sometimes called scales; if the universal veil is of a powdery or loose consistency, it tends to disappear on the surface, or remains as floccose or mealy granules either irregularly disposed over the pileus or only on the margin; all intermediate arrangements occur when affected by the weather, as when rains wash off the scales, etc., or dry weather causes slow expansion and corresponding irregularities. The margin is markedly striate in some species like *A. caesarea* and *A. russuloides,* or striations may be entirely lacking as in *A. phalloides.* The shape of the pileus varies in the young stage, usually ovoid or spherical, sometimes campanulate or somewhat conical. Many species have the surface of the pileus, under the scales, provided with a delicate *viscid* pellicle, which causes fresh specimens when wrapped in tissue paper to adhere to the paper, and indicates one of the ways of recognition. The color of different species varies from pure snowy white to smoky brown, yellow, orange or bright red; bright green or blue colors do not occur in our species of this genus, olive, ashy to lead-color or livid-purplish being the only shades in this connection.

The GILLS are white or whitish, in some species tinged yellow. They are free from the stem, sometimes remote leaving an open space around its apex, sometimes reaching it by the narrowed point which may run down the stem as a line. Their shape varies, sometimes ventricose, often broader in front, sometimes almost equal in width except at stem; the anterior end is more or less sharply truncate, and this can be used to distinguish this genus and Amanitopsis from other Agarics even after cooking. Shorter gills alternate with those of full length. The trama of the gills is composed of hyphae which in this genus diverge toward the hymenium, instead of being noticeably parallel; in this respect it agrees with the genera Armillaria and Hygrophorus.

The STEM is usually soft; the interior is *stuffed by a pith* which is sometimes weblike and evanescent, sometimes forming a spongy column in the stem, and only disappearing at full maturity; in both cases the stem may become hollow. In *A. strobiliformis, A. solitaria* and *A. chlorinosma* the pith approaches the condition of solid stems, but all Amanitas have practically a form of stuffed stem. The texture of the stem is not homogeneous with that of the pileus and the apex separates rather easily from the pileus leaving a socket. It is cylindrical or tapers upward, the base enlarged in most cases into a bulb, but occasionally cylindrical throughout as in *A. spreta.* The base is enveloped in the volva which is found in various degrees of development or persistency and which can be grouped under three heads: (1) The VOLVA is the remains of the whole universal veil which has split above the pileus and has formed a true cup or sheath at the base of the stem, the margin usually extends above the bulb or base. (2) The VOLVA in this case is only the lower half of the universal veil and adheres closely around the bulb, sometimes forming circular rolls or scaly rings on the lower part of the stem. (3) The VOLVA is very incomplete and fragmentary, floccose, mealy or minutely warty; this is due to the loose, friable texture of the universal veil, the remnants of which disappear easily when the stem is pulled from the soil. Thus the presence of a *volva* is not a safe or positive characteristic in case persons depend on the "death-cup" for their identification of the poisonous Amanitas. Besides the volva, the stem is provided with an ANNULUS. The annulus is sometimes formed from an outer layer of the stem. In the young, "button" stage the gills lie with their edges closely against and adnate to the stem, and during elongation of stem and expansion of pileus, this thin outer layer is pulled loose from the stem by the fact that it adheres more closely to the gills than to the stem. If it begins to tear off from the stem in the early stage of elongation, it peels the entire stem upwards and after loosening from margin of pileus. it drops down on the lower part and forms an "inferior" annulus. When it is not loosened from the gills or margin of pileus until the stem is nearly elongated, it peels off only from the apex of the stem and later from the gills and margin of pileus and forms a "superior" annulus. The latter is much the commonest method, and the layer of tissue which in this case holds on to the gills for a time and conceals them is called the "inner veil." Sometimes this inner veil separates at the stem instead of at the margin of the pileus and so hangs in shreds or in pieces from the margin of the pileus. In fact conditions of weather, etc., may cause all sorts of variations from the above two most common methods. The surface of the stem where the outer layer has been peeled off to form the annulus, usually becomes roughly floccose. Sometimes also the outer rind is split and broken in various ways by drying, as shown in our figures of *A. rubescens;* at other times the stem is glabrous.

Properties. This is usually called the "poisonous genus," as some of the species are sure to cause death. Poisonous species occur also in many other genera, but the poisons are not as deadly. Some Amanitas are known to be edible, as for example, *A. caesarea* and *A. rubescens.* But one who has not a thorough knowledge of most of the mushrooms, including their microscopic characters, would be unwise to eat any of the species of Amanita, since the poisonous species sometimes approach the edible ones quite closely in general appearance. And to serve them to others under ordinary circumstances is worse than criminal. For further discussion see "Chapter on Mushroom Poisons," and remarks on individual species.

Identification of Amanitas is not always easy. Even those who know all the genera and their characters will proceed cautiously. The stems with their volvas are often deep in the ground and one must get the whole plant if amateurs are to be asked to pass upon them, else they may not take account of this danger-signal—the presence of a volva "death cup". The species with a powdery volva often lose the remnants by the time they are fully expanded, and might be referred to Lepiota by mistake. *When both volva and annulus are present on a plant with white gills or white spores, an Amanita is certain.* Young undeveloped "buttons" are the more dangerous, since they then imitate to an extent the common widely used, edible mushroom *Agaricus campestris* in its button stage. Of course, an experienced mycologist would "feel" the difference when picking it up, but amateurs and those who collect only the "pink gilled" mushroom, may in this way easily make a sad mistake. The prudent collector of mushrooms for the table, no matter where they grow, or how many he has examined, will always look on the under side of the cap for the white gills, and at the bottom of the stem for the remains of the volva.

The SPORES vary from spherical to elliptical. They are rather large, smooth, granular or nucleate, and white, and their size and shape are most important in diagnosing closely related species.

The TASTE of fresh Amanitas varies. The deadly *A. phalloides* has a bitter taste due to its poisonous content. The edible *A. caesarea* is considered in Europe one of the finest flavored mushrooms, and is highly prized. The ODOR is sometimes strong, as in *A. chlorinosma* Pk. In this species it resembles chloride of lime. In many species the odor is not marked, and cannot be used to recognize species.

HABITAT. Amanitas prefer the woods or borders of woods and thickets. Rarely, however, they are found on lawns, or in fields, especially in towns which have groves or whose outlying residences are situated among the original forest trees. Some species prefer conifer forests, others hardwoods, while others are partial to particular soils. *A. spreta, A. russuloides* and *A. peckiana* have been found in Michigan only in the sandy regions. *A. phalloides* prefers the deep moist forest humus. *A. verna* is partial to the edge of groves, although widely found elsewhere. I have occasionally found it growing from the very rotten cavities of stumps or logs. There is no rule which we can be sure that they may not break in their selection of a place to grow.

The genus is with difficulty divided into natural sections. Those mycologists who laid the foundations of classification, like Fries and Quelet, divided the genus by the different ways in which the universal veil forms a volva. Prof. Atkinson has shown that a single species, *A. phalloides,* may act, under different weather and growth conditions, so that some specimens can be placed under one section, other specimens under another section. Monsieur Bondier (Bull. Soc. Myc. France, 18, 1902) has pointed out that although this is true, we can still tell them apart if we take account of the differences in the structure of the universal veil. For example, in the "Phalloides" section the universal veil is membranous and composed of narrow-celled hyphae, and the veil when it does tear in a circumscissle manner, leaves thin shreds on the cap, never in the form of elevated warty-scales; while in the "Muscaria" section the universal veil is composed of large, rounded cells which do not cohere well, and hence the veil breaks in a circumscissle manner, and leaves thick floccose warts on the cap. We will therefore follow the old divisions and group them in sections with reference to the texture and dehiscence of the universal veil. Twenty-two species have been so far found in the State. Since the genus Amanita, by virtue of its species with poisonous properties, is of great interest, and its species need to be known as widely as possible, it has seemed best to include in the following synoptical key all of the species of the northeastern part of the United States that one might be likely to find in Michigan.

Key to the Species

(A) Base of stem, or bulb, provided with a distinct, membranous, loose cup-like sheath, or rarely with a shallow cup.
  (a) Pileus orange-red, yellow or straw-colored.
    (b) Volva entire, large; pileus deep yellow to orange, striate on margin, glabrous. 639. *A. caesarea* Fr.
    (bb) Volva saucer-shaped; pileus straw-yellow, usually with floccose warts, margin even. 649. *A. mappa* Fr. (form B).
  (aa) Pileus white with delicate pinkish or cream-colored appressed, fibrillose scales; inner veil evanescent; volva large; stem faintly rubescent. 645. *A. peckiana* Kauff.
  (aaa) Pileus pure white; bulb rounded below.
    (b) Pileus conical at first; inner veil adhering to gills or edge of pileus. 643. *A. virosa* Fr.
    (bb) Pileus convex to subcampanulate; stem with a well-formed annulus.

  (c)   Plant rather stout; basidia 4-spored; volva large. 641. *A. verna* Fr.

  (cc)   Plant slender; basidia 2-spored; otherwise like preceding. 642. *A. bisporigera* Atk.

(aaaa)   Pileus brown, umber, gray, drab or shades of these.

  (b)   Base of stem cylindrical, not bulbous; pileus pale brown to umber. 646. *A. spreta* Pk.

  (bb)   Base of stem bulbous, bulb rounded.

    (c)   Pileus viscid, pale smoky olive, umber, or smoky white, often with shreds of veil on top; annulus apical, white. 640. *A. phalloides* Fr.

    (cc)   Pileus scarcely viscid or dry; stem slender.

      (d)   Spores elliptical, 11-13 x 7-9 micr.; pileus brown or grayish-brown; disk with white patch-like scales. 648. *A. recutita* Fr.

      (dd)   Spores globose.

        (e)   Pileus scarcely viscid, fuscous to pale brown, glabrous; annulus distant, brownish; bulb rather small. 644. *A. porphyria* Fr.

        (ee)   Pileus with numerous ash-colored appressed scales; ash-colored pulverulence on stem. 647. *A. tomentella* Kromb.

(AA)   Base of stem or bulb without a cup-like, free-margined volva.

  (a)   Pileus orange, yellow or straw colored.

  (b)   Margin of pileus markedly tubercular-striate, yellowish to straw color; annulus evanescent; volva usually evanescent or a few scales on bulb. 656. *A. russuloides* Pk.

  (bb)   Margin even or only slightly striate; pileus orange to bright yellow; annulus persistent.

    (c)   Flesh of stem changing to reddish when bruised or in age. 658. *A. flavorubescens* Atk.

    (cc)   Flesh not reddish.

      (d)   Pileus large, more than 7 cm. broad; stem stout, provided with prominent, concentric scales or rings on or above bulb. 650. *A. muscaria* Fr.

      (dd)   Pileus less than 7 cm. broad.

        (e)   Bulb with an adherent, inrolled, collar-like ring on its upper margin; spores spherical. 651. *A. frostiana* Pk.

        (ee)   Bulb and pileus with a few, flocculent masses of the friable, yellow volva; spores oval; common. 659. *A. flavoconia* Atk.

(aa)   Pileus not yellow nor yellowish.

  (b)   Odor strong of chlorine or chloride of lime; stem bulbous-napiform, more or less deeply rooting; plant entirely white and very densely floccose-scaly. 655. *A. chlorinosma* Pk.

  (bb)   Odor not penetrating like chlorine.

    (c)   Base of stem more or less deeply rooting below an enlarged or concentrically furrowed bulb.

      (d)   Pileus white to grayish; plants large and stout, densely floccose scaly. 654. *A. solitaria* Fr. *A. strobiliformis* Fr.

      (dd)   Pileus or its scales grayish-brown to umber-brown; plants slender, covered with a loose pulverulence; spores 8-12 x 4-6 micr. *A. cinereoconia* Atk.

    (cc)   Base of stem rounded, or at most short conical below.

      (d)   Flesh of stem or of whole plant turning to reddish where bruised or in age.

        (e)   Pileus decorated with yellow powdery masses; flesh changing to red only toward base of stem. 658. *A. flavorubescens* Atk.

        (ee)   Pileus decorated with grayish or reddish-stained, floccose warts; whole plant becoming reddish, never yellow. 657. *A. rubescens* Fr.

(dd) Flesh not turning red when bruised.
  (e) Pileus, etc. white or whitish.
    (f) Bulb at base of stem provided with a concentrically
        grooved close-fitting inrolled sheath; annulus superior.
        652. *A. cothurnata* Atk.
    (ff) Bulb with remnants of volva variously disposed.
      (g) Stem floccose-scaly or torn, below with an ovate bulb,
          which is concentrically scaly.
        (h) Annulus adorned with yellow floccules, ample, dis-
            tant; stem stuffed by pith, soon hollow; pileus
            covered with dense, white, floccose patches. 653.
            A. chrysoblema Atk. sp. nov.
        (hh) Annulus white, ample, apical; stem solid-stuffed;
            pileus with angular or pyramidal warts. *A. cau-
            dida* Pk.
      (gg) Stem slender, glabrous or pulverulent, bulb naked or
          with remains of friable volva.
        (h) Entirely white; pileus 5-10 cm. broad, with angular,
            erect warts; bulb subglobose, abrupt; annulus per-
            sistent. *A. abrupta* Pk.
        (hh) Pileus grayish-white or yellow-tinged, 2-5 cm. broad,
            adorned with flocculent scales; annulus evanescent,
            slight; edge of gills crenulate-floccose. *A. crenu-
            lata* Pk.
  (ee) Pileus brown-gray, smoky brown to umber.
    (f) Annulus inferior, broadly pendant; pileus rich hair-
        brown to umber-brown; bulb ring-margined above. *A.
        velatipes* Atk.
    (ff) Annulus superior.
      (g) Margin striate; upper margin of bulb with appressed
          ochreate volva, sometimes with rings above it. *A.
          pantherina* Fr.
      (gg) Margin not striate; pileus with grayish scales.
        (h) Volva friable; pileus with mealy scales; gills ad-
            nexed by decurrent lines; bulb oval or globose.
            Spores 8-9 x 5-6 micr. 660. *A. spissa* Fr.
        (hh) Volva friable-floccose; gills free; bulb marginate-
            rounded, concentrically grooved. Spores 11-13 x
            6-8 micr. (Boudier). *A. excelsa* Fr.

Section I. Universal veil splitting at apex; volva *persistent* on
bulb or base of stem, usually *forming a true cup,* its upper part
free from stem or merely collapsing on it, *membranous;* surface of
pileus bare (except occasionally in *A. phalloides* and *A. spreta* in
which thin membranous shreds or patches remain on pileus).

639. Amanita cæsarea Fr. (EDIBLE)

Syst. Myc., 1821.

Illustrations: Michael, Vol. II, No. 97.
    Bresadola, Fungh, mang. e. vel., Pl. 1.
    Atkinson, Mushrooms, Plate 18 and 19, 1900.
    Hard, Mushrooms, Fig. 28 and 29, 1908.
    Marshall, Mushroom Book, Pl. 4. op. p. 50, 1905.
    Peck, N. Y. State Mus. Rep. 48, Pl. 15, 1897.

Not yet reported in Michigan. It is occasionally found farther south. The present known range seems to be as far north as latitude 43°. This would bring it into southern Michigan where no doubt it will yet be found. Its name indicates that it is the emperor of its genus, and its large, showy, orange to red cap and perfect volva fully justify the name. *The pileus is striate and glabrous; gills and stem are yellow.* "The thick volva, before splitting is about the size of a hen's egg and of like shape and color." It is edible, and was served to the Caesars of Rome as a delicacy long ago. It approaches the deadly *A. muscaria* in color, except that the gills of the latter are white. Avoid eating it unless intimately acquainted with both species. It often forms large fairy rings.

640. Amanita phalloides Fr. (DEADLY POISONOUS)

Syst. Myc., 1821.

Illustrations: Gillet, Champignons de France, No. 3 (as *A. bulbosa,* the green variety).
    Bresadola, Fungh. mang. e. vel., Pl. 2, (green variety).
    Cooke, Illustrations, Plate 2, (yellow variety).
    Ricken, Blätterpilze, Pl. 75, Fig. 2.
    Fries, Sverig. ätl. u. gift. Svamp., Pl. 2.
    Farlow, Bull. No. 15, U. S. Dept. Agr., Plate XXIII, 1898.
    (See also Hard, Mushrooms, Fig. 11, p. 21, 1908, for same figure.)
    Atkinson, Mushrooms, Plate 14, Fig. 56, 57 (umber to olive variety).
    Marshall, Mushroom Book, p. 48, 1905.

PILEUS 5-12 cm. broad, at first ovate or rounded, then subcampanulate to expanded, quite *viscid* when moist, *umber-brown* to *smoky olive,* sometimes virgate, often paler or whitish on margin, glabrous or with few remnants of the universal veil in the form of thin shreds or patches, *margin even.* GILLS free or adnexed by a line, medium broad, close, white. STEM 8-20 cm. long, 6-12 mm. thick, cylindrical above bulb, varying stout to slender, *glabrous* to subsquamulose, stuffed by fibrils then hollow, white or tinged by color of pileus. ANNULUS superior, *white,* ample, pendant, membranous. VOLVA mostly buried in the ground, forming a loose or appressed cup, sometimes entire and lobed, often irregularly torn, formed by the *universal veil dehiscent or tearing in shreds at the apex,* not truly circumscissile, *its texture membranous,* not floccose. SPORES spherical-ovate, the ovate-pointed side ending in a rather stout apiculus, 9-12 (with apiculus) to 8-9 micr., granular within, white, smooth. ODOR rather nauseous.

Scattered or gregarious. In conifer or frondose woods, borders of woods, thickets, rarely on lawns, etc. Common throughout the State. July to September (earliest record July 9, latest September 24).

The form with circumscissile universal veil belongs under *A. mappa.* The typical form with dark cap described above is rather common and recognizable by the umber to olive-brown colors or paler shades of these colors, the even margin, the rather ample volva which may be reduced in size by the shreds it sometimes leaves on the cap, by the subglabrous stem and spherical-ovate spores. It is distinguished from *A. mappa,* form (*A*) by the membranous texture of its universal veil which does not split in a truly circumscissile manner, by the more ample volva, and by the shreds which when present on the cap are membranous, not floccose-warty. In this separation, I have followed Boudier, the eminent French mycologist. This is one of our most deadly mushrooms, no antidote having yet been discovered for its poison. The amateur need not attempt to keep *A. phalloides* and *A. mappa,* form (*A*) apart, as they are equally poisonous. The autumnal yellow form is more easily distinguished but is also a deadly species. See Chapter on Poisons. In Europe, the green variety is very common; their yellow variety (*A. bulbosa*) is referred by Ricken to *A. mappa.* We do not seem to have these color forms here.

641. **Amanita verna** Fr. (Deadly Poisonous)

Epicrisis, 1836-38.

Illustrations: Cooke, Ill., Plate 3 (bulb imitates that of *A. mappa*).
Gillet, Champignons de France, (as *A. bulbosa* var. *alba*).
Bresadola, Fungh. mang. e. vel., Pl. 4.
Atkinson, Mushrooms, Fig. 59, and 60; also Fig. 55 (as *A. phalloides* var. *alba*), 1900.
Marshall, Mushroom Book, p. 48 (probably *A. verna,* given as *A. phalloides*), 1905.
Murrill, Mycologia, Vol. 5, Pl. 87, Fig. 1. (As *A. phalloides.*)
Hard, Mushrooms, Fig. 16, p. 27, 1908.
Plate CXVI of this Report.

PILEUS 5-12 cm. broad, elongated ovate then *convex* to subcampanulate, finally expanded, *pure white,* viscid when moist, *glabrous,* without patches from the veil, *even* on margin. GILLS free or adnexed by a line, not broad, subventricose, crowded, *white,* edge floccose or pulverulent. STEM pure white, 8-20 cm. long, *rather stout,* 8-15 mm. thick, cylindrical above bulb, or tapering upward, *stuffed,* then somewhat hollow, glabrous or floccose-scaly, bulb oval or orbicular, not as wide as in *A. mappa, sunk in the ground.* ANNULUS ample, superior, pendant, white, membranous, not disappearing normally. VOLVA firm, thick below, thinning out toward lobed margin, derived from the entire universal veil, which dehisces at its apex, membranous, white, forming a genuine cup the ample free margin of which is at first rigid then appressed to stem. SPORES spherical-ovate, the ovate-pointed end terminating in a rather stout apiculus, granular within, white, 9-12 (with apiculus) x 8-9 micr., immature spores smaller. BASIDIA 4-spored. ODOR nauseous or slightly so.

Solitary or scattered gregarious. In conifer, mixed or frondose woods or thickets, rarely on lawns, often in clearings. Very common throughout the State. July-October (latest record October 11.)

This beautiful, pure white, stately and deadly poisonous Amanita is called the "destroying angel." In the egg-stage it is easily confused by the inexperienced with *Agaricus campestris.* *The hidden volva must be looked for in every white mushroom gathered for the table so as to avoid it.* *A. verna* has spores like *A. phalloides;* and spores which are larger and less truly spherical than in *A. mappa*. From the next species it is separated by its four spores to each basidium and by its stouter habit. But to the amateur, *A. verna*, *A. bisporigera* and *A. virosa* will look alike, and as they are equally poisonous, he need not separate them. They are only kept distinct for scientific reasons. The bulb, as well as the adjustment of the volva on it varies considerably so that unless it can be shown that the microscopic characters differ, the so-called *"alba"* var. of *A. phalloides* and *A. verna* proper are here combined into one. It seems to have no soil preference with us, although Boudier says it is partial to limestone land. I have found it on clay and sandy soil in southern Michigan, and on the rocky foundations of the Lake Superior region. See Chapter on Poisons.

642. Amanita bisporiger Atk. (DEADLY POISONOUS)

Botanical Gazette, Vol. 41, 1906.

Illustration: Atkinson, Mushrooms, Fig. 61, 1900 (as *A. verna*).

Like *A. verna,* except in its more slender habit, and the *2-spored basidia.* Pileus 4-7 cm. broad. Stem 8-12 cm. long, 5-8 cm. thick above the bulb which varies from 2-4 cm. in thickness. Whole plant is pure white, and only separable from *A. verna* in the field after some experience. I have examined the 2-spored character frequently and it seems to be constant.

Usually solitary. Throughout the State, in hemlock or frondose woods. One specimen was found growing from a rotten hemlock trunk near its base, in the Huron Mountains. July to September. Frequent. Poisonous.

643. Amanita virosa Fr. (DEADLY POISONOUS)

Hymen. Europ., 1874.

Illustrations: Fries, Sverig. ätlig. u. gift. Svamp., Pl. 84.
Cooke, Ill., Pl. 1.
Gillet, Champignons de France, No. 6.
Atkinson, Mushrooms, Fig. 62, p. 62, 1900.

Like *A. verna,* except that it has a conical pileus when young; the annulus is rarely formed, because the inner veil remains attached to gills and edge of pileus and becomes torn into parts or shreds; the stem has a tendency to be eccentric, and is usually floccose or squamulose, and the spores are slightly smaller, spherical-ovate, 8-9 (with apiculus) x 7-8 micr., white. It seems to be partial to sandy soil in this State. Ann Arbor, New Richmond. September. Infrequent. Poisonous.

644. Amanita porphyria Fr. (SUSPECTED)

Syst. Myc., 1821.

Illustrations: Gillet, Champignons de France, No. 5.
Plate CXVII of this Report.

PILEUS 3-6 cm. broad, at first campanulate then expanded, *glabrous, pale brown,* disk smoky-brown, moist or subviscid, silky and obscurely virgate when dry, *margin even.* Flesh thin, white. GILLS white, slightly *adnexed,* close, medium in width, subventricose, thin. STEM rather slender, 7-12 cm. long, 4-6 mm. thick, subequal, soft, even, glabrous, stuffed then hollow, whitish to pale brown, *with a small bulb.* ANNULUS superior but distant, thin, membranous, white *becoming brown-tinged, pendant.* VOLVA white, thin, flaccid, membranous, forming a thin cup, imbedded with the bulb in the soil, somewhat evanescent. SPORES spherical, 7-9 micr. diameter, granular within, smooth, white. BASIDIA 4-spored.

In low, swampy ground, among poplars and willows. July. Ann Arbor. Rare.

Distinguished from *A. tomentella,* by its sheathing cup and glabrous pileus. Our plants did not have the purplish tinge reported as frequent in European plants. Gillet gives a good figure. The annulus becomes brownish and is thin and drapes the stem at some distance from the apex. In this and other respects it differs from small forms of *A. phalloides.* This appears to correspond with Ricken's *"forma volvata."* (Blätterpilze, Pl. 75, Fig. 3.)

645. Amanita peckiana Kauff. (SUSPECTED)

Mycologia, Vol. V, p. 67, 1913.

PILEUS 5-9 cm. broad, at first ovate, becoming broadly convex or nearly plane, white, glabrous at first, *then fibrillose or somewhat scurfy with numerous minute pinkish or cream-colored squam-*

ules, not striate, margin at first incurved and bordered by the thickish union of the universal and partial veil, at length crenate-fringed or lacerate-appendiculate. FLESH firm, thickish, white. GILLS free or attached by a line, reaching the stem, moderately broad, much broader in front, subellipsoid, pure white, flocculose on edge, trama divergent. STEM 5-9 cm. long (rarely up to 13 cm., 1-2 cm. thick, stout, tapering slightly upward, stuffed by loose pith, then hollow, white, *at first bulbous,* the bulb covered by a thick, firm, loose VOLVA which is margined with ovate lobes, the flesh often pinkish or salmon-colored, especially toward base. AN-NULUS evanescent, but in the young plants the gills are concealed by the very thin inner veil. SPORES elongate-oblong or sub-cylindrical, obtuse, 13-16 x 5-7 micr., sometimes slightly narrower toward one end, white in mass. BASIDIA 46-50 x 9 micr., elongate-clavate, 4-spored. STERILE CELLS on edge of gills, inflated, pyriform, variable in size. ODOR none or very slightly of radish.

Gregarious. On sandy ground under white pine in open groves. New Richmond. September. Infrequent.

Known by the fringed margin of the pileus, the large, two-layered volva, the thin, evanescent inner veil, the peculiar delicate innate, fibrillose scales on the cap and stem and the large subcylindric spores. The volva is entirely immersed in the sand; it splits usually at the top of the young cap into ovate lobes and at length seems spuriously two-layered below by the separation of a thick layer of the bulb so that finally the stem is removable and appears subcylindrical at base. Rarely the volva breaks so as to leave a large thick piece on top of the cap as in *A. coccola* Scop. In some respects it approaches *A. spreta* Pk., but differs distinctly in color and spores. Sometimes the surface of the cap is beautifully dotted by the pale salmon-colored, delicate scales. The volva may reach a large size, 4 to 5 cm. high and 3 to 4 cm. across. The inner veil is very thin and often remains adnate to the stem at first, and appears to be absent; in the mature plant it is rarely to be made out. This species is close to if not identical with *A. coccola* Scop. (sense of Boudier, Soc. Myc. d. France, Bull. 18, p. 253 and Pl. 13). The shape and size of the spores are figured and described like those of our species. The margin of the pileus. however, is said to be always striate, Saccardo says "sulcate." On the other hand, the inner veil of *A. coccola* is said to be very thin and evane-scent, and the figures, showing the volva, are very suggestive of our plant. Furthermore, Ricken (Blätterpilze, under *A. ovoidea*) quotes Quelet as authority for the statement that the flesh of *A.*

coccola assumes a reddish hue. Some consider the latter species a form of *A. ovoidea* Fr. to which our plant cannot be referred, but to which it may be related.

646. Amanita spreta Pk. (DEADLY POISONOUS)

N. Y. State Mus., Rep. 32, 1879.

Illustrations: Atkinson, Mushrooms, Fig. 71, p. 69, 1900. Plate CXVIII of this Report.

PILEUS 7-12 cm. broad, ovate at first, then broadly convex-expanded, *pale brown to umber-colored,* often unicolorous, *glabrous* or with a few large patches of the white universal veil, slightly viscid, *margin even* or obscurely striatulate. FLESH white, soft, thick, abruptly thin at margin. GILLS crowded, *reaching the stem* and adnexed by a decurrent line, rather broad, narrowed behind, subventricose, pure white, edge fimbriate-serrulate, its trama with diverging hyphae. STEM 10-15 cm. long, *stout,* 10-20 mm. thick, equal or tapering slightly upward, stuffed then hollow, striate and mealy above the annulus, subglabrous or subfibrillose below, *whitish, not bulbous,* inserted at base into the *rather large, thickish, persistent, membranous, sheathing, white* VOLVA. ANNULUS white above, tinged umber beneath, thin, membranous, superior. SPORES elliptical, 11-12 x 6-7 micr., *nucleate* at maturity, smooth, white. No cystidia. Basidia 4-spored.

Solitary or gregarious. On *sandy soil,* in the pine plains of western Michigan now covered with scrub-oak, etc., where it is frequent. September. New Richmond, along the Kalamazoo River.

Known by the sheathing volva and the bulbless stem, which are both deeply immersed in the sandy soil and imitate *Amanitopsis vaginata* in this respect. The color of the pileus is uniformly darker than it is given by Peck. It prefers sandy soil. Its stout habit and its spores, as well as the base of the stem, are strikingly different from *A. porphyria. A. cinerea* Bres. of Europe also lacks the bulb but is a much smaller plant.

Section II. Universal veil splitting in a circular line between bulb and pileus (*circumscissile*), the upper half adhering *on the pileus* in the form of *floccose scales, warts, or pyramids,* the lower half adhering to the bulb or the base of the stem and forming abrupt inrolled sheaths, or several imperfect rings. The universal veil is composed of globose, inflated cells, at least in the upper part.

*Annulus median or inferior.

647. Amanita tomentella Kromb. (SUSPECTED)

Naturgetreue Abbildungen, 1831.

Illustrations: Krombholtz, ibid.
Ricken, Blätterpilze, Pl. 76, Fig. 1. (As *A. porphyria.*)

PILEUS 4-9 cm. broad, convex then expanded, umber-brown or paler, with a tinge of violaceous (ecru-drab, Ridg.), almost dry, *radiately-silky,* shining, covered by numerous, delicate, pulverulent-floccose, appressed, ash-colored scales, *margin even* and decurved. FLESH white or tinged ashy under the separable pellicle. GILLS white, rather narrow, of equal width, close, free or decurrent by a line, *edge minutely fimbriate and sometimes ashy-tinged.* STEM 7-9 cm. long, tapering upward from the thick, ovoid bulb, stuffed then hollow, often *with an ashy pulverulence both above and below the distant annulus,* innately scaly below, whitish. VOLVA thick, circumscissile, covered with tomentose pulverulence, its margin thick, short and somewhat angled. ANNULUS median, usually ample, membranous, thin, persistent, ashy-colored on under side, somewhat striate above. SPORES *spherical,* 8-9.5 micr. in diam., smooth, white with minute apiculus.

(Dried : Cap shining, chestnut, scales paler ; gills pale alutaceous.)

Solitary. In conifer and mixed woods of northern Michigan. Isle Royale, Houghton, Munising. August-October. Infrequent.

I have restored Krombholtz's name in order properly to limit our plant. According to Boudier *A. recutita* has oval spores, 11-12 x 7-9 micr. in size. Except for this discrepancy, this form would be referred to that species. It differs from *A. porphyria* in belonging to this section, by reason of its circumscissile universal veil and the floccose structure of the scales on the cap, which are numerous; the spores, however, are the same. No doubt our plant is one of three different species, which are closely related. It is easily known by the ashy-colored pulverulence on cap and stem, and the median, pendant annulus. The main color of the pileus varies from umber-brown to drab, with an obscure tinge of lilac or purplish. It is an autumnal Amanita of the conifer forests.

648. Amanita recutita Fr. var. (Suspected)

Epicrisis, 1836-38.

Illustration: Michael, Führer f. Pilzfreunde, Vol. 3, No. 124.

PILEUS 5-8 cm. broad, convex-plane, dry, grayish, *brown on disk,* disk dotted with patch-like whitish scales, striate on margin. FLESH rather thin, white. GILLS free but with decurrent line, *rather narrow,* close, white or whitish, trama divergent. STEM 8-9 cm. long, *slender,* 7-10 mm. thick, *silky,* white, equal above the small rounded bulb. ANNULUS membranous, thin, subpersistent, distant ,narrow, whitish. VOLVA sheathing but short, truncate, thickish, extending above bulb, whitish. SPORES broadly elliptical, oval to subpyriform, 11-13 x 7-9 micr., variable in shape, smooth, white. BASIDIA 40-45 x 10 micr., attenuated downward, 4-spored. ODOR none.

On sandy soil, coniferous region, under thickets. New Richmond. September. Rare.

This species is distinct from *A. porphyria* and *A. tomentella,* which it imitates in size and coloring, and by its large spores. It differs also from *A. porphyria* in the mode of breaking of the universal veil, the greater part of which remains at the base of the stem in the form of a thimble. The spores agree with the species as known to Boudier. (Soc. Myc. d. France, Bull. 18, p. 259.) The striations of our plants extend halfway to the center of the cap and this seems to be an aberrant feature, although the descriptions by European authors are not very full.

Annulus superior.

649. Amanita mappa Fr. (DEADLY POISONOUS)

Hymen. Europ., 1874.

Illustrations: Cooke, Ill., Pl. 4 (shape, etc., but not with the
colors of the American plant).
Bresadola, Fungh. mang. e. vel., Pl. 5.
Rolland, Bull. de la soc. Myc. de France, Pl. IV, Fig. 1.
Ricken, Blätterpilze, Pl. 77, Fig. 2.
Atkinson, Mushrooms, Fig. 58, p. 58 (as *A. phalloides*), 1900.
Hard, Mushrooms, Fig. 24, p. 35, 1908.

PILEUS 4-8 cm. broad, convex then expanded, usually very
regular, *margin even.* FLESH white, not very thick. GILLS *free*
or adnexed by a line, close, medium broad, *white.* STEM subcylindrical above the *very broad, abrupt, subdepressed bulb,* stuffed then
hollow.

There are two forms·with us: (A) PILEUS *smoky-umber varying to dark olive,* sometimes almost white, often paler in color or
umber color only present on disk, the rest being whitish covered with
floccose soft scales, the upper part of the universal veil. STEM
with a very abrupt, depressed, margined bulb above the edge of which
the margin of the circumscissile volva may project slightly, bulb
rounded below, surface of stem glabrous or nearly so, white or
tinged smoky brown. SPORES globular, 8-9 micr., apiculate. AN-
NULUS superior, white, membranous. VOLVA evanescent on bulb,
but remaining on cap. This form is usually confused with *A. phalloides.*

(B) PILEUS *yellowish-white to straw-color,* rarely approaching
sulphur·yellow, covered with more or less persistent, *floccose,* sordid-
white or pale brownish scales. GILLS with edge floccose-crenulate,
due to globose-pyriform sterile cells, its trama with divergent
hyphae. STEM with *depressed saucer-shaped* wide bulb, up to 3 cm.
diameter, cylindrical above, 10-15 mm. thick, pallid, or tinged very
slightly with drab, almost glabrous, 6-9 cm. long. ANNULUS
superior, *straw-colored* as a rule, membranous, rather ample.
VOLVA appressed on the bulb, its short, thick, cup-margin free from
stem and leaving a space between it and the stem, rarely obtusely
short-lobed. SPORES *perfectly globular,* with an abrupt apiculus,
7-9 micr. diameter, or smaller when immature, granular within,
white.

Form (B) is autumnal, rarely appearing before September, when it is common throughout the State. September to November (earliest record August 25th, latest November 2). It seems to prefer sandy soil, but also occurs in sandy-clay soil. Boudier says it seems to be lacking in clay soil in France; he also gives spores slightly larger. Found in white pine or hemlock forests, as well as in oak, maple, etc. Both forms have a circumscissile volva, the upper part of which is floccose in structure, the lower membranous. It is therefore intermediate between the first and second sections. The European form is said to have a nauseous odor. It is *poisonous* like *A. phalloides*. The spores of the yellow form are entirely spherical and the apiculus is abrupt and very slender and short; in this it differs from *A. phalloides,* which has spores with the spherical shape but on the side of the apiculus becomes somewhat ovate-pointed, the point ending in a rather stout apiculus; this diameter is therefore a few microns longer, sometimes 10-12 micr. long to 9 broad.

650. **Amanita muscaria** Fr. (DEADLY POISONOUS)

Syst. Myc., 1821.

Illustrations: Gibson, Our Edible Toadstools and Mushrooms, Pl. IV (colored), 1895.
    Farlow, Bull. No. 16, U. S. Dept. Agr., Pl. 22, copied by Hard, Mushrooms, Fig. 13, 1908.
    Atkinson, Mushrooms, Frontispiece (colored), also Pl. 12-13, Figs. 52, 53 and 54, 1900.
    Marshall, Mushroom Book, Pl. III (colored), 1905.
    Murrill, Mycologia, Vol. 5, Pl. 85 and Pl. 87, Fig. 3.
    McIlvaine, Amer. Mushrooms, Pl. IX, 1900.

PILEUS 8-20 cm. broad, at first ovate or hemispherical, then broadly convex to plane, viscid when young and moist, *yellow,* sometimes orange or orange-red, rarely whitish, *covered with numerous, whitish or pale yellowish warts,* margin at maturity *slightly striate.* FLESH white, or yellowish under the separable pellicle. GILLS reaching the stem, but free or decurrent by a line, crowded, broadest toward front, *white.* STEM 10-20 cm. high, equal or tapering upward, loosely stuffed then hollow, ovate-bulbous below, *white* or tinged yellow, with a white annulus above, the lower half floccose-scaly or somewhat lacerate, and near the bulb *provided with prominent concentric scales or rings,* which are the remains of the broken *veil.* ANNULUS large, thick, superior, white. VOLVA is much torn and surrounds the bulb and the stem just above the bulb in the form of scales or rings. SPORES broadly oval, 9-10.5 x 6-7.5 micr., smooth, usually with a large oil-globule nearly filling the spore, obliquely apiculate, white. ODOR and TASTE usually insipid in the fresh condition of the mushroom; its poison when extracted is, however, extremely bitter.

(Dried: More or less ochraceous to alutaceous throughout, the scales on pileus always paler.)

Gregarious or closely massed, often in large fairy rings. In thickets of poplar, wood-lots of oak and maple, forests of pine or hemlock, cemeteries, roadsides, etc., widely distributed *throughout the State.* Sometimes on poor, gravely soil, sometimes in swampy poplar woods, usually on denuded or pastured ground if found under conifers. July-October. Frequent.

One of the most showy and attractive mushrooms of the State. Known by its size, its yellow caps ornamented with whitish patches, its white gills and scaly bulb. *A. frostiana* and *A. flavoconia* have similar colors, but are much smaller. In Europe, the colors are bright scarlet and very striking. With us this form does not occur. Our species is really a color-variety of the European plant, much like that which European mycologists name var. *formoso,* except that our plant has white scales on its pileus. *A. flavorubescens* has soft yellow scales but is otherwise much different from var. *formosa* as described, with which it must not be confused. I have no record of the European var. *formosa,* and am not sure that it exists in this country. The color of *A. muscaria* varies somewhat, and in deep shaded places may be white; this is var. *alba.* The stately var. *regalis* with a pale liver colored cap has not been found in the State, although I have seen it in Sweden; it is very large. In wet situations the veil may split as in the preceding section and leave the cap bare; this is var. *puellaris* and is usually smaller.

The deadly *A. muscaria has few uses.* Its poison may yet be found to be of medicinal value, and the early settlers used an infusion of it to make "fly paper," which was an effective remedy for the troublesome house-fly—sometimes, but which caused disaster if small children partook of it. It is a delightful object for the artistic eye of the nature lover but in all other respects a menace.

651. Amanita frostiana Pk. (Not Poisonous)

N. Y. State Mus. Rep. 33, 1880.

Illustration: Atkinson, Mushrooms, Frontispiece, Fig. 2 (colored), 1900.

PILEUS 3-6 cm. broad, convex or expanded, bright orange or yellow, only slightly viscid, decorated with yellowish scales or warty patches, which are sometimes lacking, striate on margin. GILLS free, white or slightly tinged with yellow, close, broadest toward front. STEM 5-8 cm. long, 4-5 mm. thick, white or yellowish, *stuffed,* bearing a slight, sometimes evanescent annulus, *with a distinct bulb which is margined above with a collar-like ring.* ANNULUS superior, thin, fragile. VOLVA floccose-membranous, adhering on bulb in concentric scales or prominent rings as in *A. muscaria,* but less marked. SPORES globose, 7.5-10 micr., smooth, white, granular within.

Solitary or few. On very rotten hemlock logs and debris, in hemlock and mixed woods of the northern part of the State. Huron Mountains, Marquette. August-September. Infrequent.

This species is doubtless most often confused with *A. flavoconia* which is sometimes of similar size but has a universal veil composed of a powdery yellow substance, and whose bulb has therefore a different appearance. *A. frostiana* appears more like a small form of *A. muscaria* and prefers shady conifer woods, while *A. flavoconia* is more common in the southern part of the State in frondose woods, even in the open. McIlvaine says it becomes reddish-orange to scarlet farther south and imitates *A. caesarea* in color; but no confusion should be possible between the two since they have different volvas. *A. frostiana* has globose spores; *A. muscaria* has oval spores; besides the spores, the size seems the only important difference. Ford and Sherrick found it contained no deadly poison.

652. Amanita cothurnata Atk. (Suspected)

Studies of Amer. Fungi, Mushrooms, etc., 1900.

Illustrations, Ibid, Figs. 68, 69, 70, pp. 67-68.
Hard, Mushrooms, Fig. 26, p. 37.
Pl. CXIX of this Report.

PILEUS 3-8 cm. broad, at first globose to hemispherical, then convex-expanded, viscid, especially when moist, *white,* sometimes slightly tinged on centre with yellow or tawny-olive, *covered with numerous, white floccose scales,* margin finely striate when mature. GILLS free, remote, rounded behind, crowded, white, broader in front, edge floccose. STEM 6-12 cm., cylindrical, even, white, *hollow,* minutely floccose-scaly, with a large oval bulb below. ANNULUS superior, white, rather persistent. VOLVA forming a close-fitting covering for bulb and ending above the bulb by a circular roll which is often abrupt. SPORES globose, 8-9 micr., smooth, white, almost filled by a large oil globule.

Gregarious. In oak and maple woods. Ann Arbor, Detroit. July-August. Infrequent.

Have seen only the pure white form in Michigan. This species approaches *A. pantherina,* common in Europe. The latter has a brown to fawn-colored pileus which is long-striate and has whitish warts; its annulus is median, and there are usually several oblique rings of the volva a little above the bulb. Murrill's figure in Mycologia, Vol. 5, Pl. 87, is not of a typical plant. *A. cothurnata* has the bulb abruptly terminated by a close-fitting roll; its cap may have a slight tinge of umber or yellow on the disk. Quelet and Battaile give the spores of *A. pantherina* as oval-elongate, 10-12 micr. long; Karsten and Smith give them 8-9 x 4-5 micr.

653. Amanita chrysoblema Atk. sp. nov. (PROBABLY DEADLY POISONOUS)

Illustration: Plate CXX of this Report.

PILEUS 8-10 cm. broad, convex-expanded, *pure white,* densely covered with white floccose patches or scales, *viscid,* margin finely striate. GILLS free, somewhat remote, *narrow,* close, *white,* plane, heterophyllous. STEM stout, 10-14 cm. long, 1 cm. thick above, *tapering from the clavate-bulbous base,* 2 cm. thick, stuffed by a pith then hollow, very torn-scaly below annulus, floccose above, white, bulb and lower part of stem somewhat adorned by narrow thick rings, the remains of the volva. ANNULUS superior, rather ample, thin, pendant, somewhat distant, *white except a sprinkling of yellow flocules on upper side.* VOLVA floccose, rather fragile, white, in broken rings on bulb and lower stem. SPORES broadly-elliptical, 9-10 x 6-7 micr., smooth, white, granular within.

Solitary. On the ground, in the edge of a sphagnum swamp. September-October. Ann Arbor. **Rare.**

Differs from *A. cothurnata* in its bulb and annulus characters, and in its elliptical spores. The scales of the stem are due to its torn surface and point upward. The floccose structure of the universal veil and its manner of breaking separates it from *A. verna, A. phalloides* and *A. virosa*. The yellow floccules on the annulus are a character peculiar to this species. *A. crenulata* differs from *A. chrysoblema* in its very evanescent volva, in its gills which reach the stem and have a strongly floccose edge, the floccules of which are sometimes yellow, and in its nucleate spores.

654. Amanita solitaria Fr. (EDIBLE, BUT USE CAUTION)

Syst. Myc., 1821.

Illustrations: Atkinson, Mushrooms, Pl. 21 and 22, 1900.
   Gillet, Champignons de France, No. 16 (as *A. pellita*), No. 8 (as *A. echinocephala*).
   Cooke, Ill., Pl. 939.
   Var. (A) (*A. strobiliformis*) ?

PILEUS 10-15 cm. broad, globose-hemispherical at first, finally expanded-plane, *at an early stage covered by large, firmly adhering, pyramidal warts,* when expanded dotted with floccose, rather soft, brownish warts, not striate, whitish. FLESH white. GILLS free or almost so, crowded, narrow, white or tinged cream-color, *edge entire.* STEM 10-15 cm. or more in length, solid, *rooting napiform-bulbous at first,* then elongated and 1-2 cm. thick, the thick bulb at the first concentrically corrugated by thick, pointed warts, when full grown oval ending below in a large, tapering "root" which penetrates the soil deeply, the bulb then covered with smaller, scattered warts, becoming almost glabrous upward to the ring, whitish. ANNULUS pendant, apical, white then dingy yellowish and disappearing. SPORES variable in shape, 9-12 x 6-7.5 micr., elliptical, smooth, white. ODOR none at any stage.

Solitary on the ground in low woods of maple, oak, etc. Ann Arbor. August. Infrequent.

The spore-measurements agree with the spore-measurements by Bresadola, but not at all with his figure (Fungh. Mang. et. vel., Pl. 8), which shows the surface of the stem torn-scaly like the surface of an open pine cone. It is more like the forms photographed by Atkinson (Mushrooms, Pl. 21, 1900), except for the more napiform bulb and larger spores. Authors disagree widely as to the characters of *A. solitaria* and *A. strobiliformis*. Boudier (Soc. Myc. de France, Bull. 18, 1902) differentiates *A. solitaria* by its larger spores, 13-15 x 8-10 micr., by its floccose, thinner warts, by the thin, fragile and the cream-colored annulus; and his *A. strobiliformis* has spores 10-13 x 6-8 micr., a turbinate, napiform bulb, and grayish cap covered with very large, thick, adnate angular scales. Ricken (Blätterpilze) reverses the spore size and also considers them smaller: 9-10 x 5-6 micr. for *A. solitaria;* 12-14 x 8-9 for *A. strobiliformis;* at the same time his other characters agree pretty well with those of Boudier's description of the two species. Both Bresadola and Atkinson consider the two species identical under *A. solitaria*, assuming that great variations occur in the nature of the scales on the cap and stem, and in the shape of bulb and stem. That weather conditions cause great variation in these plants, whether a single or composite species, is quite certain. But with such data as those given above, as to size of spores, it becomes necessary to explain by further studies the discrepancies reported by these eminent mycologists.

All European mycologists agree in omitting any mention of an odor of chloride of lime. Hard and McIlvaine report both *A. solitaria* and *A. strobiliformis* with such an odor. I infer from this that American plants which have often been referred here, belong to *A. chlorinosma* Pk. or one of its varieties.

655. Amanita chlorinosma Pk. (EDIBLE, BUT USE CAUTION)

Torr. Bot. Club. Bull., Vol. 6, 1878.
Bot. Gazette, Vol. IV, 1879.

Illustration: Hard, Mushrooms, Pl. 3, Fig. 22, 1908. (As *A. strobiliformis.*)

PILEUS 8-15 cm. or more broad, subglobose at first then convex to expanded, *white* or tinged dingy cream-color, surface with a very variable covering of *dense white floccose scales* or *warts,* sometimes mealy-floccose, sometimes as rounded masses, sometimes pyramidal pointed warts, *always floccose in structure,* except in age they may become hard and adherent, sometimes few and large then again smaller and numerous, margin appendiculate with shreds of veil. FLESH thick, compact, pure white, thinner on margin. GILLS free or adnexed by a point, relatively narrow, subventricose, broader in front, white tinged cream-color, *edge minutely flocculose.* STEM 6-15 cm. long, rooting, root up to 10 cm. long, ventricose varying to napiform and then very thick, up to 3 cm. at bulb, equal upwards, firm and hard, solid below; spongy-stuffed within the hard outer rind, sometimes becoming cavernous, *floccose-torn* from bulb to annulus, often concentrically floccose near bulb, white. ANNULUS fragile, lacerated, sometimes remaining as a ring with margin quite torn, sometimes adhering to gills or margin of pileus. VOLVA densely floccose, white, mostly left on pileus, sometimes attached to bulb or stem as floccose, irregular concentric, soft scales. SPORES *not large,* 8-12 x 5-7 micr., varying in both dimensions. Young immature spores are spherical then ovate, *elliptical at maturity,* granular within. ODOR *strong of chlorine or chloride of lime, disagreeable.*

(Dried: Dingy-white.)

Solitary or gregarious. In woods on the ground, often on hard, gravelly soil. Lansing, Detroit. Infrequent.

The original description, copied by McIlvaine, was made by Peck from a single specimen. Austin the finder, also published a description at the same time. Since the plant is very variable, in the manner so fully described for *A. solitaria* by Atkinson in his mushroom book, the original description must naturally have many short-comings. Hence I will assume, until we have further data, that all our plants with the strong chlorine odor belong under this species.

Like *A. solitaria, A. chlorinosma* is a large and striking species, usually pure white, becoming dingy cream color; the surface of the whole plant is sometimes thick with a mass of cottony scales. The spores have been found variable and add to the confusion of species. Under the microscope the young and matured spores are shown detached. The young spores naturally measure much less than the mature spores. *A. radicata* Pk. (Bull. Torr. Bot. Club, Vol. 27, p. 609) is described as having large and firm scales; the odor, the spores and the rooting stem are the same as in *A. chlorinosma.* It seems to bear the same relation to *A. chlorinosma* as *A. strobili-formis* bears to *A. solitaria.*

656. Amanita russuloides Pk. (SUSPECTED)

N. Y. State Mus. Rep. 25, 1873.

PILEUS 5-12 cm. or more broad, ovate at first, then convex-expanded, *pale yellow or straw-color,* paler on margin, surface viscid, covered with whitish, floccose warts which are often lacking entirely or in part, *margin* markedly *tuberculate-striate, striae* 1 to 3 cm. long. GILLS *white,* free or at first reaching the stem, crowded, rather narrow, broadest in front and tapering to stem. STEM 8-15 cm. long, *tapering upward* from bulb, varying in thickness 5-10 mm. at apex to 8-20 mm. above bulb, bulb 1.5 to 2.5 cm. thick, stuffed by webby pith then hollow or cavernous, *white,* glabrous or fibrillose-floccose, the cortex sometimes squarrose-torn. ANNULUS superior, thin, *mostly evanescent,* sometimes loosened and near the bulb, edge sometimes floccose. VOLVA circumscissile, *thin,* fragile, *often disappearing* or forming at first a few subconcentric delicate rings on bulb. SPORES 9-10 x 5-6 micr., elliptical, *nucleate* when mature, smooth, white, apiculate.

Gregarious, rarely subcaespitose, often in large circular patches. *On the sand plains* along the Kalamazoo River, originally white pine forest, now scrub oak, etc. New Richmond. Abundant locally. September.

Known by its peculiar long tuberculate-striae on the margin of the pileus and its thin evanescent volva. The annulus separates and breaks early, and often clings to the apex of the bulb, simulating the species with close-fitting inrolled volva. It was found in great abundance all over the oak-barrens about New Richmond during September, 1910, and is partial to sandy soil which clings to its caps.

This species cannot be *A. junquillea* Quel., as some authors intimate. The spores are larger, the colors paler and the long striations are markedly tuberculate.

Section III. Universal veil *friable* and pulverulent-floccose, circumscissile, *fugacious.* Pileus with soft floccose masses or warts, rarely bare. Bulb of stem bare or with flocculent masses which soon vanish.

657. Amanita rubescens Fr. (EDIBLE, BUT USE CAUTION)

Syst. Myc., 1821.

Illustrations: Fries, Sverig. ätlig. u. gift. Svamp., Pl. 74.
  Cooke, Ill., Plate 1163.
  Bresadola, Fungh. mang. e vel., Pl. 9.
  Gillet, Champignons de France, No. 16.
  Patouillard, Tab. Analyt., No. 303.

Ricken, Blätterpilze, Pl. 80, Fig. 1.
Atkinson, Mushrooms, Plates 19, 20, and Fig. 73, 1900.
Hard, Mushrooms, Fig. 27, 1908.
Plate CXXI of this Report.

PILEUS 5-12 cm. broad, oval at first, then broadly convex or campanulate, sometimes expanded, *obtuse,* subviscid when moist, *pale brownish-buff to sordid reddish-brown,* covered with floccose masses or soft warts which are whitish, grayish or reddish-stained, margin even or obscurely striatulate. FLESH soft, thin, whitish, *becoming reddish-stained* when bruised or in age. GILLS narrowed toward stem and free, moderately broad in front, close, *white or whitish,* edge pulverulent under lens. STEM 10-20 cm. long, 8-15 mm. thick, subcylindrical above, clavate-bulbous to rounded-bulbous below, *stuffed,* subglabrous, even or the apex slightly striate and mealy, pink-tinged within and without, dull red where bruised. ANNULUS *broad,* superior, membranous, fragile, often striate on the upper side. VOLVA mostly lacking, *evanescent,* grayish. SPORES elliptical, 7-9 x 6 micr., when mature (immature plants shedding smaller spores), smooth, white.

Solitary or scattered. In oak and maple woods of southern Michigan, mixed woods of conifer regions; it seems to prefer clay soil. Especially common in open or pastured woods. Throughout the State. July to September, far more common in July. Edible.

The color is quite variable, soon tinged with the reddish stains which separate this species from all others except *A. flavorubescens.* When fresh the flesh turns red rapidly where bruised. The stem has a rather hard cortex in dry weather which cracks across and peels in part. Sometimes there are minute, reddish or tawny scales on the stem. The spores are 1 to 2 micr. shorter than in the European plant as shown in specimens I have from Sweden, and by the measurements given by Boudier. Cooke in the Illustrations refers to shorter spores, so that they were probably immature. It is easy to find expanded specimens whose spores are not fully developed. The annulus is usually large and pendant. It is edible, but one must be extremely careful.

658. Amanita flavorubescens Atk. (Suspected)

Jour. of Mycology, Vol. 8, 1902.

Illustrations: Murrill, Mycologia, Vol. 5, Pl. 87, Figs. 4 and 7. Plate CXXII of this Report.

PILEUS 10 cm. broad, convex to expanded, *covered with floc-cose or powdery chrome-yellow patches or masses,* which are easily rubbed off, beneath which the surface is lemon-yellow to brownish on disk, margin even or faintly striatulate. FLESH thin, *yellow-ish.* GILLS *white,* long-elliptical, rather narrow, free or adnexed by a line, close. STEM 8-13 cm. long, 6-12 mm. thick, white, cover-ed above with fine floccose yellow scales, below with reddish scales, its base ending in an oval bulb, stuffed then hollow; its flesh turn-ing slowly reddish when bruised. ANNULUS superior, distant, thin, membranous, fragile, yellow below, white above. VOLVA yellow, powdery, evanescent. SPORES oboval, 8-10 x 6-8 micr., smooth, granular within; basidia 4-spored.

Solitary or gregarious. In frondose woods mixed with Larix. Ann Arbor. Rare. July.

The bright yellow volva, annulus and margin of pileus, and the reddening of the flesh of the stem are its chief distinguishing char-acters. The pileus may be entirely yellow at first, becoming red-dish or sordid brown in age.

659. Amanita flavoconia Atk. (Probably Poisonous)

Jour. of Mycology, Vol. 8, 1902.

Illustrations: Hard, Mushrooms, Fig. 15 (as *A. frostiana*). Plate CXXIII of this Report.

PILEUS 3-8 cm. broad, convex then expanded, obtuse, viscid, chrome yellow to orange yellow, *covered with numerous, yellow, flocculent masses of the universal veil,* which are easily rubbed off, sometimes bare, margin even. FLESH thin, white. GILLS free, close, medium broad to narrow, *white,* edge minutely fimbriate, trama with divergent hyphae. STEM 6-10 cm. long, 5-10 mm. thick, stuffed then hollow, straight or flexuous, subequal, covered with flocculent scales which are sometimes tinged sulphur-yellow, yellow-pulverulent above annulus, bulbous. ANNULUS superior, membranous, sulphur-yellow to chrome-yellow. VOLVA evanescent, yellow-pulverulent at first adhering to bulb as small, chrome-yellow, pulverulent masses. SPORES oval, 6-9 x 4-5 micr., white, smooth.

Solitary or scattered. In low, conifer or frondose woods, among decayed debris, on mosses, etc. Throughout the State: Ann Arbor, Detroit, Palmyra, New Richmond, Bay View, Munising, Marquette, Houghton. July-September. Common.

In the even margin of the pileus and the powdery volva it differs from *A. frostiana* which it resembles most, and from small forms of *A. muscaria*. It is about the same size as *A. frostiana*, sometimes larger, and is often erroneously referred to it. With us, *A. frostiana* occurs only in the conifer regions of the State. *A. flavoconia* occurs annually on a bed of *Polytrichum commune* bordering a small lake north of Ann Arbor. It is our commonest, small yellow Amanita and like *A. muscaria*, is widely distributed. The bulb does not become reddish when bruised as in *A. flavorubescens*.

660. Amanita spissa Fr. (Deadly Poisonous)

Epicrisis, 2836-38.

Illustrations: Cooke, Ill., Pl. 69.
    Gillet, Champignons de France, No. 3 (as *A. ampla*) and No. 19.
    Bresadola, Fungh. mang. e. vel., Pl. 7.
    Ricken, Blätterpilze, Pl. 80, Fig. 2.
    Plate CXXIV of this Report.

PILEUS 6-10 cm. broad, convex then campanulate-expanded, obtuse, subviscid when moïst, shining when dry, *gray with brown or sooty-brown disk,* covered by small, angular, *floccose or pulverulent,* soft grayish scales or warts, glabrescent, margin *not striate.* FLESH rather thin, white. GILLS free but reaching the stem and decurrent by a line, medium broad, crowded, *shining white,* obscurely flocculose on edge. STEM 8-12 cm. long, 1 cm. or more thick, stuffed by a pith, firm, tapering upward, white or grayish, pruinose above, the ring, the clavate or globose bulb, and sometimes the stem above the bulb, covered at first by loose, gray floccose masses. ANNULUS membranous, apical, pendant, entire, white or tinged gray below. VOLVA pulverulent, floccose, evanescent, gray. SPORES broadly elliptical, obtuse, 7-9 x 6 micr., smooth, white. STERILE CELLS on edge of gills inflated-pyriform or globose on a slender stalk. ODOR mild.

Gregarious or scattered. On the ground in frondose woods of oak, maple, etc. Ann Arbor. July. Infrequent.

This species has usually been considered of doubtful occurrence in this country. It has been one of the last of the Amanitas mentioned in this report that I have collected. It is certainly distinct and usually agrees thoroughly with the descriptions, but seems to be rare. Its gray to smoky-brown cap, the pulverulent-floccose, friable, gray universal veil, the non-striate pileus and spores characterize it well. Only the little gray masses on the lower part of the stem and on the surface of the cap, indicate the presence of an outer veil. The annulus is distinct, far up on the stem and sometimes with gray particles on the lower side. After rains there may be no remnants of the veil either on the cap or stem.

Amanitopsis Roze

(From the Greek, *opsis,* appearance of, and *Amanita.*)

White-spored. Stem inserted at base into a volva formed as in Amanita; *partial veil and annulus are lacking;* otherwise like Amanita.

Soft, fleshy, terrestrial, long or slender-stemmed, non-caespitose mushrooms, growing mostly in forest humus, rarely in fields or lawns.

The characters, except the absence of an annulus, imitate so closely the species of Amanita, that the reader is referred to the discussion of that genus. None are definitely known to be poisonous, but the ease with which they can be confused with Amanitas should make everybody extremely cautious. The poisonous *Amanita spreta* Pk. imitates some of the species of Amanitopsis closely, because of its thin, close-appressed annulus. Other Amanitas sometimes lose their annulus, and might be taken for Amanitopsis. Only three species have been collected in the State; about twelve species have been reported from the United States. The following species, not yet found, but included in the key, may be looked for: *A. albocreata* Atk. (this is considered the same as the one described by Peck in the 33d N. Y. State Rep. under *A. nivalis*); *A. farinosa* (Schw.) Atk. which has, however, a somewhat southern and eastern distribution and is one of the smallest Amanitopses; *A. adnata* (Smith) Sacc. reported from the Chicago region, departs from the demands of the genus in having adnate gills. *A. pusilla* Pk. is another small species, its pileus hardly 3 cm. broad. *A. par-*

civolvata Pk. has a brilliant orange pileus shading to whitish on the margin; it has been found from New Jersey to North Carolina. (See colored plate, Marshall, Mushroom Book, Frontispiece, 1905.)

Key to the Species

(A) Volva membranous, cup-shaped or sheathing the base of the stem.
  (a) Pileus small, 2-3 cm. broad, pale brown; stem bulbous, slender; spores elliptical, 5-6 x 4 micr. *A. pusilla* Pk.
  (aa) Pileus larger; spores 8 micr. or more in the longest diameter.
    (b) Gills adnate; pileus even on the margin, yellowish-buff; volva close-fitting, white. *A. adnata* Smith.
    (bb) Gills free; pileus more or less striate on margin.
      (c) Pileus hairy-squammulose; volva large, firm, cup-shaped. 661. *A. volvata* Pk.
      (cc) Pileus glabrous except for occasional patches of the universal veil; volva sheathing, flabby.
        (d) White. 662. *A. vaginata* Fr. var. *alba* Sacc.
        (dd) Tawny-yellowish. 662. *A. vaginata* Fr. var. *fulva* Sacc.
        (ddd) Gray to mouse-colored. 662. *A. vaginata* Fr. var. *livida* Pk.
(AA) Volva friable, floccose, etc., not membranous.
  (a) Pileus orange to yellow, plicate-striate on margin; stem and gills pale yellow; volva thin and evanescent. *A. parcivolvata* Pk.
  (aa) Pileus some other color.
    (b) Pileus small, 2-3 cm. broad, pulverulent, striate, grayish to mouse-colored. *A. farinosa* Schw.
    (bb) Pileus larger, with floccose patches or warts on its surface.
      (c) Pileus white to pale yellowish, finely striate on the margin; volva ocreate, as in *Amanita pantherina. A. albocreata* Atk.
      (cc) Pileus grayish-brown, sulcate striate, covered with mouse-colored warts; volva breaking up into sub-annular fragments on stem. 663. *A. strangulata.* Fr.

Section I. Universal veil membranous, splitting at the apex; the volva vaginate or cup-shaped at the base of the stem, entire.

661. Amanitoposis volvata Pk. (Poisonous)

N. Y. State Mus. Rep. 24, 1872.

Illustrations: Murrill, Mycologia, Vol. 5, Pls. 86 and 87, Fig. 2.

PILEUS 5-7 cm. broad, convex then plane, even or slightly striate on margin, *covered with fibrillose or floccose scales, whitish to brownish.* GILLS free, close, white. STEM 5-10 cm. long, 5-10 mm. thick, white to brownish-gray, equal or tapering slightly upward, stuffed, densely pulverulent-floccose or shaggy above the volva, *with a very large, persistent, membranous, firm, brown volva* sheathing the base. SPORES elliptic-oblong, 9-11 x 6-7 micr., smooth, white, granular within.

In open frondose woods, solitary. August-September. Detroit. Rare.

This is easily separated from *A. vaginata* by its oblong spores and floccose-scaly pileus. The volva is also more firm and ample. It is said to be identical with *A. agglutinata* B. & C. Our specimens were brownish throughout on cap and stem. The gills become dull-brown on drying. According to Peck the volva sometimes leaves patches on the pileus.

662. Amanitopsis vaginata Fr. (EDIBLE)

Var. *alba* Sacc.
Var. *fulva* Sacc.
Var. *livida* Pk.
Syst. Myc., 1821. (As Amanita.)

Illustrations: N. Y. State Mus. Rep. 48, 1896, Bot. ed.
    Atkinson, Mushrooms, Plate 23, p. 75, 1900.
    Marshall, Mushroom Book, op. p. 54, 1905.
    Hard, Mushrooms, Figs. 30 and 31, p. 44, 1908.
    Bresadola, Fungh. mang. e. vel., Pl. 12.
    Ricken, Blätterpilze, Pl. 75, Fig. 1.
    Minn. Mushrooms, Fig. 5, p. 11, 1910.
    Plates CXXV, CXXVI of this Report.

A composite species; according to the present custom including a number of *color forms,* here called varieties. The constancy of these varieties indicates that they could, with entire propriety, be referred to under species names, e. g., *Amanitopsis alba, Amanitopsis fulva,* and *Amanitopsis livida.* The description, however, applies equally well to all forms except as to color.

PILEUS 5-10 cm. broad, ovate to campanulate at first, then convex to plane, *glabrous* or rarely with fragments of the universal veil, slightly viscid when young or moist, *sulcate-striate* on the thin margin, *white, fulvous,* or *grayish-mouse color* in the corresponding varieties. FLESH white. GILLS free, white or whitish, close, broad, broadest in front, narrowed behind. STEM 8-18 cm. long, 4-8 mm. thick, rather slender, fragile, glabrous or mealy-squamulose, stuffed then hollow, subcylindrical, *base without a bulb* and inserted deep into the ground with the elongated, sheathing, flabby, white VOLVA. SPORES spherical, 8-10 micr. diam., nucleate by a large oil-globule, smooth, white.

Solitary or scattered. In conifer or frondose forests; in open, low woods; in copses, sometimes on much decayed wood. July, August and September, rarely earlier or later. Throughout the State. Very common. *Edible.*

In some localities the white and tawny forms prevail, as at Ann Arbor; in others, especially in conifer regions, the tawny and livid forms are found more commonly. The pileus and stem are rather fragile, and the volva is apt to break and adhere to the soil so that the extracted stem appears to be without a volva. The variation in size and color seems to be greater in Europe than with us; Secretan differentiated ten forms and raised them to the rank of species. The spores of our plants, at least of the fulvous form, are always spherical, with an obscure angle on the apiculus side. Saccardo gives them ovate and 10-15 micr. long, and Patouillard figures them ovoid. Quelet and Battaile agree with us, calling them spherical and 10 micr. diam. The gray form must not be confused with *Amanita spreta* Pk. which is also without a bulbous stem. The beauty and symmetry of the different forms are a constant delight to the field botanist.

Section II. Universal veil breaking into floccose or powdery scales or fragments, which cover the pileus and base of stem.

663. Amanitopsis strangulata Fr. (EDIBLE)

Epicrisis, 1836-38.

Illustrations: Marshall, Mushroom Book, p. 53, 1905.
 N. Y. State Mus. Rep. 51, Plate 50, 1898.
 N. Y. State Mus. Mem. 4, Plate 44, 1900.
 Fries, Icones, Pl. II.
 Gillet, Champignons de France, No. 11. (As *A. inaurata.*)
 Patouillard, Tab. Analyt., No. 401.
 Cooke's Ill., Plate 13.

PILEUS 5-10 cm. broad, ovate to campanulate at first, then convex to plane, slightly viscid when young or moist, *sulcate-striate* on margin, pale umber colored, *decorated with floccose, cinereous to mouse-gray scales or warts,* the remnants of the veil. GILLS free, close, white or ashy-tinged, broader in front. STEM 8-15 cm.

long, 5-12 mm. thick, equal or tapering upward, stuffed then hollow, subglabrous, or furfuraceous, white above, darker to pale umber *below where it is somewhat decorated by the fragments of the mouse-gray volva.* SPORES spherical, 9-12.5 micr., granular within.

Solitary or scattered. In mixed forests of hemlock, maple and yellow birch, of the northern part of the State. Bay View, Marquette, Houghton. July-September. Not infrequent at times. Edible.

It is remarkable that this species does not occur in the southern part of the State; at least I have never seen it there. Peck and McIlvaine say it occurs "in open grassy places, in wheat-stubble, etc." as well as in the woods, in Pennsylvania, New Jersey and West Virginia. So far I have seen it three different summers in the Northern Peninsula, always in hemlock woods.

The SPORES are not in entire agreement with the European measurements. With us they are spherical or nearly so. Saccardo is evidently in error when he says they measure 9-15 micr. and are ovate; Stevenson quotes Smith's measurements as 16 x 8 micr., and Boudier gives them as 12-13 micr. Peck considers it clearly distinct from *A. vaginata* and in the 51st Report has given an excellent account of the plant.

Lepiota Fr.

(From the Greek *lepis,* a scale.)

White-spored (except *L. morgani*); stem *fleshy, separable* from the pileus, provided with a persistent or evanescent *annulus;* gills *free* (except in some of the "granulosi" section).

Fleshy, firm or soft mushrooms, growing on the ground, on debris, or on more or less rotten wood in forests; large and small.

The PILEUS is scaly from the breaking up of the cuticle, rarely smooth, most often white, but also tinged yellow, brown or red; there are a few species with a viscid pileus. The STEM is stuffed or hollow, firm or soft, fleshy and different in texture from the trama of the pileus, and easily separable from it. The GILLS are white, but may change color in age or when bruised; (in *L. morgani* they become sordid-green from the greenish spores). They are usually free, but a small group has adnate or adnexed gills, although otherwise like the genus; e. g., *L. granosa, L. amianthina,* etc.

The VEIL is theoretically double, as in Amanita, but the outer

or "universal veil" is concrete with the pileus and does not split
or break to form a volva on the stem or to form superficial patches
on the cap. Sometimes it breaks away early at the base of the
stem and is pulled up on the stem as the latter elongates, like a
movable ring, as in *L. procera;* then again it breaks away only
from the margin of the pileus, leaving a sheath on the stem terminated above by a flaring margin, as in *L. rugosa.* The inner veil
is quite variable in texture, membranous to fibrillose, floccose or
granulose; sometimes the delicate structure soon disappears or is
washed away by the rain. The TASTE is mild, and all the large
species except the green-spored *L. morgani* can be eaten with safety.
Some of the smaller species, like *L. clypeolaria* Fr., *L. helvola*
Bres. and *L. charcarias* are suspected. The SPORES are white in
mass (except one species) and varying in shape, usually longish,
sometimes subfusiform, often minute and then elliptical or ovate,
in a few cases somewhat angled; they often mature slowly, so that
measurements must be made with care.

The genus can be divided into three natural groups with reference to the character of the cuticle of the pileus or of the veil;
these groups can be further subdivided into sections, as follows:

A.   Cuticle of pileus glutinous or viscid; trama of gills divergent (= Limacella Earle) :

I.   Lubricae

II.   Viscidae

B.   Cuticle dry; annulus terminating a sheath or such other
remnants of the veil as remain on the stem:

III.   Clypeolariae

IV.   Asperae

V.   Granulosae

C.   Cuticle dry; annulus independent, often movable; stem without any other remains of the veil:

VI.   Subclypeolariae

VII.   Procerae

Key to the Species

(A)   Pileus viscid.
  (a)   Pileus small, 2-5 cm. broad, stem slender.
    (b)   Stem and pileus both very viscid or glutinous, white. 664. *L.
      illinita* **Fr.**
    (bb)   Stem not viscid; pileus with a subviscid, thin separable pelli-
      cle, tinged pink. 667. *L. delicata* Fr. var.
  (aa)   Pileus larger, 5-10 cm., and stem stout.
    (b)   Pileus whitish to pinkish-tan, slightly viscid; stem fibrillose-
      glabrescent. 666. *L. fischeri* sp. nov.
    (bb)   Pileus reddish-bay, viscid; stem scaly. 665. *L. glioderma*
      Fr.

(AA) Pileus not viscid.
 (a) Growing in fields, pastures, gardens, lawns, and on decomposing vegetable matter (rarely in open woods) ; large to medium-sized.
  (b) Annulus movable; plant very large.
   (c) Plant taller than broad; spores white, 14-18 x 9-11 micr. 686. *L. procera* Fr.
   (cc) Plant as broad or broader than tall; spores greenish, 10-13 x 7-8 micr. 687. *L. morgani* Pk.
  (bb) Annulus not freely movable (except sometimes in *L. americana*).
   (c) Plant assumes a dull reddish color when bruised or on drying; annulus rather large; spores 8-10 x 5-8 micr. 688. *L. americana* Pk.
   (cc) Plant not changing as above.
    (d) Stem thickened toward base like the seed-stalks of onions, densely caespitose. 680. *L. cepaestipes* Fr.
    (dd) Stem not of the above shape.
     (e) Gills becoming pink in age; pileus firm, medium large, white; stem with persistent annulus. 689. *L. naucina* Fr. (syn. *L. naucinoides* Pk.).
     (ee) Gills remaining whitish; pileus *small*, rugulose, widely striate, whitish. *L. rugulosa* Pk.
 (aa) Growing in forests, open woods, under copses, bushes, etc. (rarely on lawns) ; medium to·small.
  (b) With some shade of blue or purple, either when fresh or on drying; small.
   (c) Gills, stem, flesh etc. changing to blue when drying; annulus membranous, persistent; pileus brownish-scaly. *L. caerulescens* Pk.
   (cc) Gills, etc., not changing to blue when drying; annulus powdery, evanescent.
    (d) Odor foetid; pileus lavender; stem dark brown to blackish below. *L. ecitodora* Atk.
    (dd) Odor not foetid; plants small.
     (e) Pileus whitish, covered with a heliotrope-purple, powdery substance; flesh tinged yellow. *L. purpureoconia* Atk.
     (ee) Pileus whitish, tinged with blue around margin; flesh turning brownish where bruised. *L. cyanozonata* Longyear.
  (bb) Without shades of blue or purple.
   (c) Stem clothed with a floccose, squamose or filamentous sheath; pileus not granular nor mealy.
    (d) Spores 12 micr. or more in length.
     (e) Pileus and lower stem brown; spores truncate at base, with oblique apiculus. *L. geniculospora* Atk.
     (ee) Pileus ochraceous or yellowish-white, sometimes reddish-tinged; spores subfusiform, 13-18 x 4-6 micr. 668. *L. clypeolaria* Fr. (*L. metulaespora* B. & Br.)
    (dd) Spores less than 12 micr. long.
     (e) Growing on rotten wood, small; pileus pale tawny to subalutaceous, floccose-scaly; spores 8-11 micr. long. 673. *L. acerina* Pk.
     (ee) Growing on the ground, or among debris; spores usually smaller.
      (f) Pileus medium size, with erect, tomentose or floccose wart-like scales; veil copious.
       (g) Spores 7-9 micr. long.
        (h) Gills crowded, much forked. 671. *L. friesii* Lasch.
        (hh) Gills crowded, not forked. 670. *L. acutaesquamosa* Wein.
       (gg) Spores 4-5 micr. long. 672. *L. asperula* Atk.
      (ff) Pileus with *appressed*, tomentose, spot-like or patch-like scales.

(g) Annulus persistent; stem slender, about 1 mm. thick, blackish-brown. *L. gracilis* Pk.
(gg) Annulus evanescent or obscure.
(h) Pileus 4-8 cm. broad, patches tawny-olive; stem stout; spores attached at basal angle. *L. caloceps* Atk.
(hh) Pileus dark-brown, usually less than 4 cm. broad.
  (i) Spores minute, 4 x 2 micr.; veil forming a dense, brown tomentum on stem. *L. eriophora* Pk.
  (ii) Spores larger, 6-8 x 4-5 micr.; veil of more delicate and loose floccose filaments. 669. *L. felina* Fr.
(cc) Stem without evident sheath, but provided either with an evanescent or a persistent annulus. (See ccc.)
(d) Spores 9 micr. or more in length.
  (e) Pileus moderately large, with red appressed scales; annulus persistent. 681. *L. rubrotincta* Pk.
  (ee) Pileus small, minutely squamulose; annulus evanescent; base of stem mycelioid, forming a "sand-bulb." *L. arenicola* Pk.
(dd) Spores less than 9 micr. long.
  (e) Pileus rather small, 1.5-4 cm. broad, with reddish-brown scales on a white surface; spores attached at basal angle; with a marked odor. 682. *L. cristata* Fr.
  (ee) Pileus white, small, minutely fibrillose-squamulose; spores minute; annulus thin and fragile. 684. *L. miamensis* Morg.
  (eee) Pileus with minute pale-yellow hairy scales. 683. *L. alluviinus* Pk.
(ccc) Stem clothed or peronate with squamulose, granular, furfuraceous, or minutely warty scales; pileus granular, warty or furfuraceous.
(d) Gills adnate.
  (e) Pileus distinctly rugose on disk.
    (f) Plant growing on rotten logs, stumps, etc., large; the sheath membranous-margined above. 674. *L. granosa* Morg.
    (ff) Plant growing on the ground or on leaf-mould, small; the floccose-scaly sheath not margined above. 675. *L. rugoso-reticulata* Lorin.
  (ee) Pileus not rugose.
    (f) Stem long, slender; pileus often umbonate. *L. amianthina* Fr.
    (ff) Stem short, stouter; pileus not umbonate. 676. *L. adnatifolia* Pk.
(dd) Gills adnexed or emarginate.
  (e) Growing on rotten wood; color whitish to pale tawny. 678. *L. pulveracea* Pk.
  (ee) On the ground; color rusty-yellowish. 677. *L. granulosa* Fr.
  (eee) Like preceding but whitish throughout. 677. *L. granulosa* var. *albida.*
(ddd) Gills free; plants quite small; soft, fragile.
  (e) Pileus dingy-white, or brownish. 679. *L. pusillomyces* Pk.
  (ee) Pileus white, disk pinkish. 685. *L. cristatatellus* Pk.

Section I. Lubricae. The young plant enclosed in a universal glutinous veil. The trama of the gills divergent.

664. Lepiota illinita Fr.

Syst. Myc., 1821.

Illustrations: Fries, Icones, Pl. 16, Fig. 1.
Patouillard Tab. Analyt., fasc. VII, No. 609.
Gillet, Champignons de France, No. 425.

PILEUS 2-6 cm. broad, thin, soft, ovate then campanulate-expanded, subumbonate, *glutinous* (moist), *glabrous, white,* or whitish, even or substriate on margin. GILLS free, close, moderately broad, white, soft, trama divergent. STEM 5-8 cm. x 3-6 mm., white, glutinous, equal, stuffed to hollow, not scaly. FLESH white, soft, thin. SPORES 4-6 x 3-4 micr., subglobose to ovoid, smooth, white. TASTE and ODOR none. ANNULUS obsolete, glutinous.

Singly or gregarious. Ground, white birch woods near Marquette. Elm and maple woods, southern Michigan. September.

Known by its glutinous and slimy cap and stem. The European plants are a little larger.

Section II. Viscidae. Surface of pileus provided with a continuous gelatinous, separable pellicle; stem dry. Trama of gills divergent (except in *L. delicata*).

665. Lepiota glioderma Fr.

Monographia, 1857.

Illustration: Cooke, Ill., Pl. 118 A.

PILEUS 2-5 cm. broad, obtusely convex, *viscid, reddish-bay* fading to dull ferruginous, glabrous, even, cuticle separable. FLESH thin, white or tinged rufous. GILLS close, *broad,* subventricose, white, free but reaching apex of stem by a point, edge very even, trama divergent. STEM 5-7 cm. long, 4-6 mm. thick, *dry,* covered with *reddish-floccose scales* up to the slight ANNULUS, equal or attenuated downwards, solid, fibrous. SPORES globose, 4-5 micr.

diam., smooth; basidia 4-spored; no cystidia.   TASTE farinaceous.
ODOR none.

(Dried: Cap and gills brownish-tan to fuscous.)

Singly or few.   Debris on ground, in hemlock, maple or birch woods.   Marquette, Houghton, Bay View and New Richmond, apparently limited to conifer territory.   August and September.   Infrequent.

This Lepiota approaches the genus Armillaria in appearance, but the gills are not attached to the stem. The annulus is sometimes well-developed and flaring.

666.   Lepiota fischeri sp. nov.

Illustration: Plate CXXVII in this Report.

PILEUS 4-9 cm. broad, convex-campanulate, obtuse, even, *subviscid,*-cuticle separable and continuous, fleshy, rather soft, *white to pale alutaceous.* FLESH white, thick, rather soft. GILLS crowded, rather narrow, free and somewhat remote, plane, white, edge entire. STEM 4-10 cm. long, 4-10 mm. thick, subbulbous, somewhat curved, *striate,* fibrillose, *solid, firm,* fibrous-fleshy, separable from pileus. ANNULUS superior, large, membranous, at length pendulous, white, subpersistent, fragile. SPORES minute, 3-4 x 2-3 micr., smooth, oval; *basidia* small, with 1 to 2 long sterigmata, (5-7 micr. long), rarely 3 or 4, rarely also a forked sterigma, tramal hyphae of gills divergent. TASTE slight; odor becoming strong on drying, like that of *Tricholoma sulfureum.*

(Dried plants: Pale alutaceous, gills brownish.)

Gregarious.   On ground in low frondose woods.   Near Detroit. September and October.   Infrequent.

Related to *L. lenticularis (Amanita lenticularis* Fr.), and is perhaps its American counterpart.   Our plants differ in lacking the dark green drops oozing from apex of stem and annulus, (see Quelet and Battaile, Flora Monographic des Amanites et des Lepiotes, 1902), and in character of stem which is said to be stuffed or hollow and floccose-scaly in the European plant. Quelet, Ricken and Battaile give the spores 6 to 8 micr. It also differs from *L. persoonii* Fr. in stem and gill characters.   I have dedicated it to the energetic student of mushrooms, Dr. O. E. Fischer of Detroit, who found it.

667. Lepiota delicata Fr. var.

Syst. Myc., 1821.

Illustration: Fries, Icones, Pl. 15, Fig. 2.

PILEUS 2-4 cm. broad, thin, subumbonate, campanulate-expanded, with a continuous, separable, *subviscid cuticle,* delicately *pink-colored,* sometimes shading to white on margin, even, radiately innately silky. FLESH pure white, *unchanged* when bruised, thin, fragile. GILLS narrow, close, free, somewhat remote, pure white. STEM 5-9 cm. long, 3-5 mm. thick, tapering upwards from a subclavate bulb, dry, *glabrous,* curved or straight, soft, stuffed. ANNULUS membranous, thin, subpersistent, white, median, at length pendant. SPORES 5-6.5 x 3-4 micr., elliptical, subacute at ends, white, smooth. CYSTIDIA on edge of gills subcylindrical, clustered, numerous, 7 x 4.5 micr., none on sides of gills; basidia 4-spored. ODOR and TASTE none.

(Dried: Annulus *snow-white,* stem and gills pale alutaceous, cap pink with brownish umbo.)

Gregarious. On the ground in swampy woods of elm, etc., also under hemlock in ravines. New Richmond. September. Infrequent.

L. oblita Pk. differs in its viscid stem and more tawny pileus; the spores are similar. It is apparently much like *L. incarnata* Clem. and *L. rufescens* Morg. The presence of a separable gelatinous cuticle, the unchangeable flesh, and the cystidia distinguish it from these. A hot-house variety is said to occur in Europe.

Section III. Clypeolariae. Stem clothed at first by a floccose or filamentous sheath. Pileus pruinose, floccose or appressed scaly, the cuticle at first continuous.

668. Lepiota clypeolaria Fr. (SUSPECTED)

Sys. Mycol., 1821.

Illustrations: Fries, Icones, Pl. 14, Fig. 2.
    N. Y. State Mus. Rep't. 54, Pl. 76, 1901.
    Gillet, Champignons de France, No. 416.
    Ricken, Blätterpilze, Pl. 85, Fig. 2.
    Plate CXXVIII of this Report.

PILEUS 2-5 cm. broad, campanulate-convex to expanded, obtuse or umbonate, floccose-scaly, even or striate beneath the scales on margin when old, color of scales variable: white, yellowish, rufous-ochraceous or ochre, the disk often darker, brown or reddish-brown, white beneath scales, margin often appendiculate from remnants of the veil. FLESH white, thin, *flaccid.* GILLS free, close, white, narrower in front, edge minutely flocculose. STEM slender, 3-10 cm. long, 3-5 mm. thick, equal or tapering upward, sheathed up to the evanescent, floccose annulus, by soft, loose, floccóse, white or yellowish scales or tomentum, hollow, fragile, whitish under scales and at apex. SPORES very variable in size, even in the same specimen, 10-16 x 4-6 micr., subfusiform, elongated-elliptical, broader at the distal end or symmetrical, etc., smooth, white.

(Dried: Pileus pale ochraceous or rufous-tan; stem covered by a *white* floccose sheath.)

Scattered. Ground or debris in woods. Marquette, Bay View, Ann Arbor, New Richmond; throughout the State. July to October. Frequent.

There is much uncertainty among all mycologists concerning the limits of this species. *L. metulaespora* is said to be a very similar plant. Studies so far made, both of the European and American plant, seem to have increased the confusion. Some (Morgan, Mycol., Vol. 12) give the spores of *L. clypeolaria* 15-20 x 5-6 micr., and *L. metulaespora* 9-12 x 4-4 micr. Others (Beardslee, Jour. Mycol., Vol 13, p. 26, 1907) reverse this. The spore-sizes of the Michigan specimens overlap both. I have so far found none with spores 18-20 micr. long, but, of course, shorter, immature spores are always present. Most European authors omit the spore-size of *L. clypeolaria* Massee (Massee, European Fungus Flora Agaric-aceæ, 1902) gives 15-16 micr. for *L. metulaespora,* which is close to ours; for *L. clypeolaria,* he gives 6 micr. Peck (Peck, N. Y. State Mus. Rep. 54, 1901, p. 173) has come to the conclusion that there is no essential difference except the striatious on the cap of *L. metulaespora;* this is hardly a specific distinction. A number of varieties have been split from these species, (Quelet & Battaille, Flore des Amanitos et des Lepiotes, 1902, p. 66) and they are evidently very variable in color, and this may be true of the spores within certain limits. For the present we will use one name for all the forms.

669. Lepiota felina Fr.

Hym. Europ., 1874.

Illustrations: Pat., Tab. Analyt., No. 505.
Ricken, Blätterpilze, Pl. 86, Fig. 3.

PILEUS 3-5 cm. broad, campanulate-convex, subumbonate, whitish under the numerous subtomentose or floccose *blackish scales.* FLESH white, thin. GILLS free, close, rather narrow, white. STEM slender, equal or tapering upward, base with slight bulb, hollow, whitish, clothed below by floccose, brown or blackish scales. ANNULUS slight, evanescent, inferior or median, sometimes tinged black on edge. SPORES 6-8.5 x 4-5 micr., elliptic-ovoid, white; basidia 4-spored.

On the ground, hemlock woods. Bay View. August-September. Infrequent or rare.

Distinguished from *L. clypeolaria* by its spores, from *L. cristata* by the blackish scales and floccose stem. SPORES 8-10 x 3-4 micr., as given by Ricken. The Michigan plant may be *L. fuscosquamea* Pk.

Section IV. Asperae. Pileus fibrillose-scaly at first, then with pointed, or pyramidal or fasciculate, erect or squarrose scales or warts; stem variously sheathed or glabrescent.

670. Lepiota acutæsquamosa Fr.

Epicrisis, 1836-38.

Illustrations: Hard's Mushrooms, Fig. 38, p. 55 (from Michigan plants).
Gillet, Champignons de France, No. 409.
Michael, Führer f. Pilzfreunde, III, No. 122.
Ricken, Blätterpilze, Pl. 86, Fig. 1 (as *L. friesii*).

PILEUS 5-15 cm. broad, soft, at first subhemispherical then convex-expanded, obtuse, even, at first covered by a soft tawny or pale umber tomentum which usually breaks up into brown or rufous-brown, *pointed, pyramidal, erect scales or warts,* the tips of which become blackish, are crowded and darker on disk, the cracks showing the white flesh beneath, margin extending beyond gills. FLESH white, moderately thick. GILLS *crowded,* free, rather narrow, thin, not forked, white becoming dingy, edge serratulate. STEM 6-12 cm. long, 6-12 mm. thick above, tapering upward from a bulbous base, sometimes equal and subbulbous, stuffed to hollow, soft, whitish, at first covered by the fibrils of the veil, with scattered brown squamules, terminating in a floccose-fibrillose, often oblique and broken, rather evanescent ANNULUS. SPORES elongated oblong, smooth, white, 7-9 x 2.5-3 micr. ODOR and TASTE not marked.

(Dried: Cap, gills and stem alutaceous to wood-brown.)

Gregarious. On the ground or on very rotten wood in forests, on flowerbeds, conservatories, etc. Ann Arbor, Bay View, New Richmond. September. Frequent.

Much the appearance of the next two species; separable with certainty from *L. friesii* by its entire gills, from *L. asperula* by the spores. The veil is composed of silky filaments woven into a membrane which is at length lacerated vertically so as to appear like a "cortina" of the genus Cortinarius.

671. Lepiota friesii Lasch.

Epicrisis, 1836-1838.

Illustrations: See Hard's Fig. of *L. acutaesquamosa,* which it imitates in appearance.
Marshall, Mushroom Book, 1902, op. p. 65.

The description of the preceding species is sufficient for all the characters except the following: GILLS very narrow, *abundantly forked,* very crowded. SPORES 6-9 x 2 micr., narrowed at one end, smooth, white, elongated-oblong to subfusiform. Sterile cells on edge of gills as in the preceding species. Habitat, etc., same as in *L. acutaesquamosa.*

Ann Arbor, Houghton, Munising, New Richmond.

The spores in our plants are narrower than in *L. acutaesquamosa,* which may be a constant character. The forking of the crowded gills is very marked. The pointed warts are crowded on the disk, or may be scattered over the entire surface of the pileus, and easily rubbed off.

672. Lepiota asperula Atk.

Atkinson, Mushrooms, p. 82, 1900.

Illustration: Ibid, Pl. 26, Fig. 84, p. 82.

PILEUS 1-4.5 cm. broad, campanulate-convex to expanded, obtuse, "hair-brown to olive-brown" or ochraceous-brown, cuticle breaking up into erect, rather pointed, blackish-brown warts, more numerous on disk, sometimes *subconcentrically rimose,* not striate. FLESH white, thickish, scissile, rather fragile. GILLS free, rather narrow to medium width, crowded, white becoming dingy, not forked, edge minutely eroded. STEM 2-6 cm. long, 4-6 mm. thick, *cylindrical* above the bulbous base, stuffed by fibrils, then hollow, covered at first by the loose, silky or fibrillose veil which collapses at the pileus and terminates on the stem by an evanescent ANNULUS, glabrous or fibrillose above annulus, below annulus sometimes minutely brown-squamulose. SPORES *minute,* 4-5 x 2-3.5 micr., oblong, smooth, white. Basidia 4-spored; sterigmata slender. No cystidia. ODOR and TASTE not marked.

(Dried: Like *L. acutaesquamosa* and *L. friesii.*)

Gregarious. Hemlock or mixed woods, on the ground among debris. Bay View, New Richmond. August-September. Infrequent.

Differs from *L. acutaesquamosa* in minute spores, and smaller size. Probably often confused with that species and difficult of separation from it. The veil is sometimes quite copious and cobwebby.

673. Lepiota acerina Pk.

N. Y. Mus. Rep. 51, p. 283, 1898.

PILEUS 1-2.5 cm. broad, convex then expanded, covered with tawny or pale rufous-brown, appressed, fibrillose or floccose scales, darker and erect and pointed on the disk, margin even. FLESH thin, white. GILLS free, close, thin, rather broad, white or whitish, edge minutely fimbriate. STEM 2-4 cm. long, 1.5-4 mm. thick, stuffed to hollow, equal or slightly bulbous, covered up to the obsolete ANNULUS by small, dark, fibrillose scales colored like those of pileus. SPORES 8-11 micr. long, 3-4 micr. wide, obliquely apiculate and truncate at one end, narrowed toward other end, smooth, white; sterile cells on edge of gills clavate.

(Dried: Pileus and gills umber or fuscous-brown.)

Gregarious. On very decayed wood, in woods of maple, birch, hemlock, etc. Houghton, Munising, Bay View, New Richmond. July, August and September. Infrequent.

Shape of spores like those of *L. boudieri* Bres. (see Tab. XLVI, Fungi Trid.), but different in other respects. *L. cristata* has similar spores.

Section V. Granulosae. Pileus and stem granular, furfuraceous, pulverulent or minutely warty.

674.   Lepiota granosa Morg.

Jour. Cincinnati Soc. Nat. Hist., 1883.

Illustrations: Marshall, Mushroom Book, Pl. 12, op. p. 63, 1905.
  Hards, Mushrooms, Pl. VIII, Fig. 36, p. 52.
  Plate CXXIX of this Report.

PILEUS 5-9 cm. diam., ovate then convex-expanded, umbonate or obtuse, ochraceous to fulvous, *furfuraceous-granulose, rugose-wrinkled* to almost even, margin regular or undulate. FLESH thick, whitish or tinged ochraceous. GILLS narrow, *crowded, adnate,* sometimes subarcuate, whitish to ochraceous. STEM 5-10 cm. long, 8-15 mm. thick, equal or tapering upward from the clavate base, straight or curved, fibrous-stuffed to hollow, *peronate* by furfuraceous or floccose scales, colored like the pileus and terminating above in a *rather large, flaring or reflexed, membranous, persistent* ANNULUS, yellowish within, pallid or brownish above the annulus. SPORES smooth, white, 4-5 x 3 micr.

Gregarious or subcaespitose. On rotten wood; maple, birch and beech woods. Marquette, Bay View. September. Infrequent.

In size, it stands at the head of this group. It is easily known by its large, persistent annulus. It differs from *L. amianthina* in size and the character of sheath and annulus.

675.   Lepiota rugoso-reticulata Lorin.

Oest. Bot. Zeitschrift, 1879.

PILEUS 1-4 cm. broad, convex, *rugose-reticulate,* covered with dense, glistening granules, pale cinnamon-brown, *tinged reddish,*

mostly unicolorous, margin appendiculate. FLESH thick, *white.*
GILLS adnate, sometimes subdecurrent, crowded, rather narrow,
whitish, edge entire. STEM 4-7 cm. long, 3-4 mm. thick, equal or
tapering upward, *solid,* peronate with cinnamon- or reddish-brown
floccose scales, terminating in an *incomplete or obsolete* ANNULUS,
pallid above, white-mycelioid at base. SPORES 4-5.5 x 3 micr.,
smooth, ovoid, apiculate. ODOR not noticed.

(Dried: Pileus pale brick-red, gills alutaceous, stem white-mycelioid at base.)

Gregarious. On mosses, low woods of white birch in northern
Michigan, elm, etc., in south. Ann Arbor, Marquette. August-
September. Infrequent.

This species resembles *L. granulosa* in color, etc., but differs in
its slender stem and rugose pileus; it approaches *L. granosa* in
pileus characters but is small and the annulus is rarely persistent.
It differs from *L. amianthina* in its lack of an umbo, and its small
spores.

676. Lepiota adnatifolia Pk.

N. Y. State Mus. Bull. 54, p. 947, 1902.

PILEUS 2.5 cm. broad, broadly convex, granulose to warty or
scaly on disk, dark *ferruginous-red,* not umbonate, even, margin appendiculate. FLESH white. GILLS *adnate,* close, narrow, thin,
whitish, edge entire. STEM 2-4 'cm. long, 4-6 mm. thick above,
tapering upward from a clavate base, solid, peronate by reddish or
whitish squamules, and terminating in an evanescent *annulus,*
apex white or tinged pink. SPORES minute, 5-5.5 x 2.5-3 micr.,
oval-oblong, slightly curved in one view. CYSTIDIA very slender,
hyaline, about 50 micr. long, 3 micr. thick, subcylindrical, apex
capped by conical covering, sometimes infrequent or entirely lacking, on edge and sides of gills. ODOR slight.

On debris or decayed logs in woods of hemlock, maple, etc. New
Richmond, Ann Arbor. September-October. Rare.

Differs from *L. amianthina* and *L. granulosa* in the presence of
cystidia and lack of an umbo, and by its color. The spores are
smaller than given by Peck. The main part of the cap is covered
closely with appressed, flat, tomentose warts.

677. Lepiota granulosa Fr.

Syst. Myc., 1821.

Illustrations: Patouillard, Tab. Analyt., No. 611.
Ricken, Blätterpilze, Pl. 81, Fig. 3.
Cooke, Ill., Pl. 18, Vol. I.

PILEUS 3-6 cm. broad, ovate then convex-expanded, obtuse or subumbonate, *furfuraceous-granular,* often radiately wrinkled, ochraceous *tinged brick-red,* but varying to buff or dark-rufous with a hoary lustre. FLESH thin, white, rufescent. GILLS *adnexed, rounded behind,* close, medium width, white. STEM short, 2-5 cm. long, 4-8 mm. thick, stuffed to hollow, equal or tapering upward, granulose to floccose-scaly and pale reddish up to the *slight* evanescent annulus, whitish at apex. SPORES minute, 4-5 x 3-3.5 micr., ovate, smooth; cystidia none.

(Dried: Cap and scales of stem rufous-ochraceous, gills ochraceous-alutaceous.)

Gregarious to subcaespitose. On leaf-mould, mosses, etc., in open woods of maple, oak, hemlock, etc. Ann Arbor, Marquette, New Richmond. August-October. Local but frequent.

The spores are smaller than given by Patouillard (Tab. Analyt.) and Quelet and Battaille (Flore des Am. et des. Lep.). Hennings in Engler & Prantl, however, gives the size as found in American plants. Also our plants are usually shorter and thicker stemmed than the figures of Patouillard and Cooke would indicate, i. e., the plant is more squat, except possibly when it grows in low, wet situations. It approaches other species, like *L. charcharias* and *L. amianthina,* which were formerly called varieties of it. There is a hoary sheen to the granularity on the cap, by which one may know it. The way the gills are attached distinguishes it from the three preceding species.

678. Lepiota pulveracea Pk.

N. Y. Mus. Rep. 54, p. 144, 1900.

"PILEUS 1-2.5 cm. broad, hemispheric then convex-expanded, *pulverulent* or minutely granulose and squamulose, even, tawny or paler. GILLS *adnexed,* close, thin, narrow, yellowish-white. STEM equal, hollow, sheathed with *delicate* brownish, small granulose scales terminating in the obsolete ANNULUS, pruinose and whitish at apex." SPORES minute, oblong-elliptical, obscurely curved, smooth, white, 4-5.5 x 3 micr.

(Dried: Cap pale fulvous, stem paler with scattered floccose-squamules.) Gregarious. On *moss* growing over an old hemlock log. Marquette. September. Rare.

The spores are not ovate as in *L. granulosa,* and the adnexed gills and color, etc., separate it from *L. rugoso-reticulata.* The dried specimens lack the rich tints of the others of this group.

679. Lepiota pusillomyces Pk.

N. Y. Mus. Rep. 28, p. 48, 1876.

Illustration: Ibid, Plate I, Figs. 1-3.

PILEUS 4-8 mm. broad, thin, convex, obtuse, furfuraceous or *covered with minute granular floccules,* white or nearly so, remains of veil clinging in granular flocs to edge of pileus. TRAMA of pileus composed of vesicular cells, pulverulence on surface also of thin-walled globular cells. GILLS *broad,* free, ventricose, moderately close, white. STEM 1-3 cm. long, 1-2 mm. thick, slender, equal, stuffed with fibrils, rufescent beneath the *white mealiness* which terminates at the obsolete ANNULUS. SPORES elliptic-oblong, 4-5 x 2.5-3 micr., smooth, white.

Single and scattered. On rich soil in woods. Ann Arbor, Bay View. August. Infrequent.

This is close to *L. seminuda* of Europe, and may be the same, unless the microscopic characters are shown to be different. Patouillard figures the spores of *L. seminuda* more ovate then elliptical, but other authors give the latter shape. This is a delicate Lepiota and approaches *L. cristatatellus* Pk. which is distinguished by the pinkish tinge usually present on the pileus, and the glabrous stem.

Section VI. Subclypeolariae. Pileus thin, minutely scaly, pruinose or pulverulent. Annulus membranous, persistent or evanescent. STEM for the most part glabrous or denuded.

680. Lepiota cepæstipes Fr. (EDIBLE)

Epicrisis, 1836-38.

Illustrations: N. Y. State Mus. Bull. 94, Pl. 87, 1905.
Hard's Mushrooms, Fig. 37, p. 54.
Gillet, Champignons de France, No. 414.
Michael, Führer f. Pilzfreunde, Vol. III, No. 94.
Plate CXXX of this Report.

PILEUS 2-8 cm. broad, thin, oval then campanulate-expanded,
obtuse, soft, at length umbonate, *striate-plicate* and splitting on the
margin, covered with minute, numerous, *mealy* or wart-like scales,
which are often brown, elsewhere white. FLESH white. GILLS
narrow, free, close, white then dingy, thin, edge pruinose. STEM
4-12 cm. long, 4-6 mm. thick at apex, tapering upward or
often *somewhat ventricose,* flexuous, glabrous or occasionally with floccose particles, hollow, white. ANNULUS thin, membranaceous, subpersistent, white. SPORES oval-elliptical, smooth,
white, 9-10 x 5-7 micr., nucleate. ODOR and TASTE mild.

Caespitose. On rich soil of gardens, conservatories, etc., decaying straw-piles, sawdust, stumps, or decomposing vegetable matter
of any kind. Ann Arbor, Bay View, New Richmond. June-September. Not common. Edible.

Often in dense clusters. Sometimes the pileus is yellow-tinged.
The name refers to the shape of the stem which often resembles the
enlargement on the seed-stalk of the onion. The plants soon droop
and collapse in the wind. Hennings (in Engler and Prantl) says
this mushroom was introduced into Europe from Brazil and also
states that at first there is a small *sclerotium.*

681. Lepiota rubrotincta Pk.

N. Y. State Mus. Rep. 35, p. 155.

PILEUS 2-6 cm. broad, ovoid then convex-expanded, obtuse or subumbonate, the unbroken cuticle at first even, and innately fibrillose
and *uniform reddish-pink,* darker or reddish-brown on disk, *at*

length breaking up into appressed red scales and rimose. FLESH white, thin. GILLS free, narrow, tapering toward stem, crowded at first, less so after expansion, white, edge minutely flocculose. STEM 4-9 cm. long, 3-8 mm. thick, tapering slightly upward or clavate at base, stuffed then hollow, even, *easily splitting lengthwise,* silky-fibrillose or glabrous. ANNULUS *well-developed,* membranous, persistent, edge.thickish and often tinged red. SPORES 9 x 5 micr., but variable, often larger, narrow-elliptical, apiculate; CYSTIDIA on edge of gills about 36 x 6 micr.

(Dried: Color of cap red, gills dingy white, stem pale fuscous.) Scattered or singly. On the ground among decaying leaves, mixed or hardwood forests. Ann Arbor, Detroit, New Richmond. August-September. Infrequent.

682. Lepiota cristata Fr. (EDIBLE)

Syst. Myc., 1821.

Illustrations: Atkinson, Mushrooms, Fig. 83, p. 81, 1900.
Gillet, Champignons de France, No. 417.
Patouillard, Tab. Analyt., No. 504.
Ricken, Blätterpilze, Pl. 84, Fig. 3.
Cooke, Ill., 29.
Plate CXXXI of this Report.

PILEUS 1.5-4 cm. broad, thin, ovate then campanulate-convex or expanded, obtuse or umbonate, cuticle at first continuous, and entirely dull reddish or reddish-brown, then *broken into small concentric reddish-brown scales* except the darker umbo, the cracks white, margin often denuded of cuticle. FLESH white, thin. GILLS free, rather close, narrow to subventricose, white, edge minutely crenulate. STEM 3-5 cm. long, 2-5 mm. thick, slender, equal, hollow or stuffed with loose pith, glabrous or silky-fibrillose below ring, whitish or tinged dingy lavender, pinkish within. ANNULUS white, small, soon broken and deciduous. SPORES somewhat wedge-shaped, or angular, sometimes irregularly fusiform to oblong, depending on the view, white, 6-7 x 3-4 micr. ODOR rather disagreeable.

(Dried: Stem rufescent, pileus brownish to alutaceous.) Gregarious. In grassy places or on the ground in low woods, etc., often on lawns. Marquette, Ann Arbor, Detroit, Houghton, New Richmond, etc. July-October. Common.

An effort was made by Morgan (Jour. of Mycol., Vol. 12, p. 244, 1906), to separate this into two species, *C. cristata* Fr. and *C. angustana* Britz. The separation was based on the spores and odor. Our plants sometimes have angular spores and no odor, and the spores vary, even in the same plant. Atkinson (Mushrooms, 1900, p. 92) has already pointed out that they are identical. The odor seems to be strong, weak or absent under different conditions. The pileus may be as much as 5 cm. across.

683.   Lepiota alluviinus Pk.

N. Y. State Mus. Rep. 35, p. 157, 1884.

"PILEUS 1-3 cm. broad, thin, convex or plane, sometimes reflexed on margin, *white, adorned with minute pale-yellow hairy or fibrillose scales.* GILLS free, thin, close, white or yellowish. STEM 2-4 cm. long, 2-3 mm. thick, slender, fibrillose, whitish or pallid, slightly thickened at the base. ANNULUS slight, subpersistent, often near the middle of the stem. SPORES elliptical, 6-7.5 x 4-5 micr."

Alluvial soil among weeds and shrubs. East Lansing. August. Reported by Longyear.

"In drying the whole plant assumes a rich yellow hue."

684.   Lepiota miamensis Morg.

Jour. Cincinnati Soc. Nat. Hist., 1883.

PILEUS 2-4 cm. broad, soft, convex-expanded, subumbonate, even, *fibrillose-scaly* except disk, *white,* disk sometimes brownish. FLESH white, very thin, fragile. GILLS free, *rather broad,* rounded behind, ventricose, *white.* STEM 3-5 cm. long, 2-4 mm. thick, slender, hollow, subequal, glabrous or pruinose at apex, often compressed, *white.* ANNULUS thin, fragile, subpersistent, *median.* SPORES oblong-oval, 5-6 x 3-3.5 micr., white.

(Dried: Pileus whitish, with brownish center, gills dingy-white, stem pallid.)

Singly or few. On the ground in rich woods among leaves. Ann Arbor. September. Rarely found.

Apparently similar to *L. alluviinus,* differing in lack of yellow color, especially on drying, and rather broad gills.

685. Lepiota cristatatellus Pk.

N. Y. State Mus. Rep. 31, p. 31, 1879.

PILEUS 5-8 mm. broad, soft, oval then convex, covered by minute granular-mealiness, *at first tinged pink all over,* then white with pinkish disk, margin mealy. GILLS free, white, medium broad, rounded behind, subventricose, *subdistant.* STEM 2-3 cm. long, 1 mm. thick, slender, equal, hollow or stuffed with fibrils, whitish, subglabrous below the *evanescent* ANNULUS, pruinose above. SPORES minute, subelliptical, 4-5 x 3 micr., smooth, white. Scattered. In low, moist woods, on mosses, etc. Ann Arbor, Bay View, New Richmond. September. Frequent.

A small Lepiota, near *L. pusillomyces,* from which the pink of the cap and the white stem seem to distinguish it so that the two are quite easily recognized in the field. *L. cristatellus* is also said to have narrower gills, and its stem is usually glabrous, while *L. pusillomyces* has broad gills and a mealy stem below the annulus.

Section VII. Procerae. Pileus thick and fleshy, the cuticle commonly broken into large scales (continuous in *L. naucina* in most cases) ; annulus thick, mostly movable.

686. Lepiota procera Fr. (EDIBLE)

Syst. Myc., 1821.

Illustrations : Atkinson, Mushrooms, Pl. 25, Fig. 81, p. 79.
  Peck, N. Y. State Mus. Rep. 48, Pl. 18, 1896.
  Hard, Mushrooms, Pl. VI, Fig. 32, p. 46.
  Freeman, Minn. Plant Diseases, Fig. 18, p. 39, 1905.
  McIlvaine, Amer. Fungi, Pl. XIII, p. 34.
  Fries, Sverig. ätl. u. gift. Svamp., Pl. 3.
  Michael, Führer f. Pilzfreunde, No. 53.
  Gillet, Champignons de France, No. 429.
  Ricken, Blätterpilze, Pl. 83, Fig. 1.
  Plate CXXXII of this Report.

PILEUS 8-15 cm. broad, elliptic-ovate before opening, then campanulate-convex to subexpanded, *umbonate,* at first covered with a reddish-brown or umber-brown *cuticle, which breaks up into large brown scales or patches* during expansion of pileus, with smaller floccose scales between and exposing the white flesh beneath, cuticle

on umbo often continuous. FLESH thick, white. GILLS free,
remote from stem, *broad anteriorly,* narrowed behind, thin, close,
white or tinged pink, brownish in age, edge flocculose. STEM *15-
30 cm. long,* cylindrical or tapering upward from a bulb, 6-12 mm.
thick above, apex sunk deep into the flesh of the pileus as into a
socket, hollow or stuffed with delicate long fibrils, *surface layer
breaking up into small brownish scales,* or furfuraceous so as to appear variegated, white beneath and within. ANNULUS *movable,*
thick, formed of the firm, membranous veil which breaks away early,
its outer and lower surface covered with small brown scales, repre-
senting a continuation of the cuticle of the pileus at a very early
state. SPORES 14-18 x 9-12 micr., elliptical, smooth, white; no
cystidia found. Sterile cells on edge of gills, numerous, 35-45 x 10-
15 micr., subcylindrical.

(Dried: Pileus buff with fuscous scales, stem pale fuscous, gills
dingy-buff.)

Solitary or gregarious. On the ground, in meadows, pastures,
open woods, or preferably in pastured clearings. August, September, October. Throughout the State. Edible.

Its long stem, movable annulus and *shaggy, spotted cap,* distinguish it from all others. Its height is often surprising, sometimes
reaching a foot and a half, with a cap six to ten inches broad. Its
cap is delicious, when after removing the scales, it is fried in butter.
Its distribution is world-wide.

687. Lepiota morgani Pk. (Poisonous)

Botanical Gazette, Vol. 4, 1879.

Illustrations: Hard, Mushrooms, 1908, Pl. VII, Fig. 35, p. 50.
McIlvaine, Amer. Mushrooms, 1900, Pl. XIV, p. 36.
Plates CXXXIII and CXXXIV of this Report.

PILEUS 10-20 cm. broad, at first globose then convex and expanded, cuticle at first continuous, buff to pale umber, soon *broken
up* except on disk, *into irregular scales or patches,* which are
drawn apart and disappear in part. FLESH thick, firm, white.
GILLS free, remote (4-5 mm.) from stem, close, rather broad,
ventricose, *at first white then changing to dull green.* STEM *stout,*
10-20 cm. long, 1-2 cm. thick above, 2-4 cm. at base, tapering upward
from a clavate base, stuffed with fibrils, *hard and firm,* glabrous,
whitish or grayish-white to pale umber. ANNULUS thick, *mov-*

able, superior, toughish but soft. SPORES bright to dull *green in mass,* subelliptical, obliquely apiculate, 9-12 x 6-8 micr., nucleate.

Gregarious, often in large fairy rings. In meadows, pastures and open woods. In southern Michigan, Ann Arbor. Frequent but local.

Unsafe. Eaten with impunity by some persons, but others suffer vomiting, etc. This is our largest-capped meadow mushroom known; it attains a diameter of 14 inches. Its *large size, movable ring* and *greenish spores and gills* distinguish it. The underside of the ring next to the stem is at first covered by the remains of the cuticle which was continuous with the pileus. All the cuticle of the pileus except the center may disappear. The young margin of the cap is beautifully torn-serrate and floccose at first. Reports have come in that the whole plant is sometimes green or greenish.

688.   Lepiota americana Pk.   (EDIBLE)

N. Y. State Cab. Rep. 23, p. 71, 1872.

Illustrations: N. Y. State Rep. 49, Pl. 44, 1896.
Atkinson, Mushrooms, Fig. 82, p. 80, 1900.
Hard, Mushrooms, Fig. 34, p. 49, 1908.
Murrill, Mycologia, Vol. 3, Pl. 49, Fig. 6.
McIlvaine, Amer. Mushrooms, Pl. XV, p. 48, 1900.

PILEUS 3-10 cm. broad, ovate then convex-expanded, umbonate or subumbonate, cuticle at first reddish-brown and continuous, *then broken up* except on umbo into large, scattered, *reddish or bay-brown scales,* elsewhere white when young and fresh but *becoming dingy-red in age,* more or less striate on margin. FLESH thin, white, *reddening when bruised or in age.* GILLS free, close, rather broad in front, narrowed behind, white. STEM 7-12 cm. long, 4-6 mm. thick at apex, *tapering upward from a clavate base,* sometimes fusiform, stuffed then hollow, glabrous, white becoming reddish where handled. ANNULUS rather large, membranous, flaccid, sometimes movable, sometimes evanescent. SPORES elliptic-ovate, 8-10 x 5-7 micr., nucleate, white. ODOR and TASTE mild.

(Dried: Whole plant tinged dull red or smoky-red.)

Solitary to caespitose. On rich soil in grassy places, in fields or around old stumps. Ann Arbor and Ludington. August. Apparently rare in Michigan. Edible.

Bresadola (Tab. Analyt., Vol. 2, p. 83) suggests that our plant is

the same as the European *L. haematosperma* (*Agaricus haematosperma* of Hymen. Europ.), as well as *L. badhami* Berk. In these
also the flesh changes to reddish in age or on drying. The French
mycologists (Quel. and Battaile, Aman. et Lep., 1902, p. 73) have
taken exception to this view, claiming that *L. haematosperma* actually has reddish or purplish spores when mature, while *L. badhami* has white spores. Hence the American name must be retained. Our plants can be distinguished from our other Lepiotas by
this character of the flesh. The shape of the stem imitates at times
that of *L. cepaestipes,* being enlarged just above the base, sometimes,
however, it merely tapers from the very bottom; in the former case
the base is sometimes short-pointed. The pileus is sometimes
almost entirely white when fresh. The gills and flesh may assume
a yellow tinge at first.

689. Lepiota naucina Fr.   (EDIBLE)

Epicrisis, 1836-38.

Illustrations: N. Y. State Mus. Rep. 48, Plate 19, 1896.
    Gillet, Champignons de France, No. 428.
    Atkinson, Mushrooms, Figs. 79-80, p. 76-78.
    Bresadola, Fungh. mang. e. vel., Pl. 15.
    McIlvaine, Amer. Mushrooms, Plate XV, p. 44.
    Ricken, Blätterpilze, Pl. 84, Fig. 2.
    Plates CXXXV, CXXXVI of this Report.

PILEUS 4-8 cm. broad, at first subglobose to ovoid, then convex
to subexpanded, obtuse, soft, *glabrous,* rarely broken into scales on
the surface, white or smoky-white. FLESH white, thick, rather
firm, abruptly thin on margin. GILLS free, not remote, close,
moderately broad, narrowed behind, white at first, *slowly changing
to pinkish then dingy-brown,* edge minutely flocculose. STEM 5-10
cm. long, 6-12 mm. thick above, tapering upward from a thickened
base, sometimes subequal, stuffed then hollow, glabrous or silky
below the ring, pruinose above, *white within and without.* AN-
NULUS formed from the membranous veil and outer layer of stem;
the latter is shown peeled off up to the ring in the section of the
young plant in our illustration. It is white, rolled together in the
form of a collar, persistent and superior, in age it often becomes
movable. SPORES elliptic-oval, 7-9 x 5-6 micr., but variable, some
longer, occasionally abnormal and then spherical, nucleate, smooth,
white. ODOR and TASTE mild.

Gregarious. Grassy ground, in pastures, fields, roadsides, and parks. Ann Arbor, Marquette, New Richmond, etc. September-November. Common throughout the State. *Edible.*

(Dried: Gills pale cinnamon-brown to umber, pileus smoky-buff, stem buff tinged umber or fuscous-brown.)

It seems to be agreed that there is an European plant like ours with elliptical spores. (Beardslee, Jour. Mycs., Vol. 13, p. 27, 1907.) Whether there is also one in Europe with uniformly globular spores is as yet uncertain. (Morgan, Jour. Mycs., Vol. 13, p. 10.) Our species will probably be known henceforth as *L. naucina* instead of *L. naucinoides* Pk., a name it has held so long. The spores vary remarkably in some individuals, while in others they are quite constant. All our specimens had mostly elliptical-oval spores; in some cases a few spheroid spores were present, but such occur in other mushrooms, and must be considered abnormal. This is one of the best mushrooms for the table. Its white gills and veil when young might lead the novice to think it to be an Amanita. The stem is firmer and lacks remnants of a volva, and the gills turn brown when heated or toasted, while in Amanita they remain white" (McIlvaine). It is not infested by larvae, and some method of cultivation is awaited eagerly by mushroom gardners. *Lepiota excoriata* Fr., as figured by Bresadola, has the same general appearance, but differs in the torn surface of the cap near its margin, in the bulblet at the base of the stem and in the much larger spores, which measure 15-17 x 9 micr.

Armillaria Fr.

(From the Latin, *armilla,* a ring.)

White-spored.. Stem continuous with the hymenophore, provided with an *annulus.* Volva none. Gills adnexed, adnate or decurrent, partly with a diverging trama.

Fleshy, often compact, firm mushrooms; either terrestrial or on wood; mostly autumnal.

The PILEUS is either viscid or dry, glabrous or scaly, often provided with a separable pellicle; the surface sometimes cracked in dry weather. Most of the rarer species are large and stout, the pileus of dull shades of color: whitish, yellowish, brownish or reddish. The margin is often incurved. The scales on the pilei of some species represent the broken cuticle which is continuous with the veil but concrete. The GILLS are variously attached, and

Fries used this character to subdivide the genus into three groups,
e. g., Tricholomata, with sinuate-adnexed gills; Clitocybae, with
gills attenuated behind and subdecurrent; Collybiae, with gills
equal. No examples of the Collybiae are known from the State.
The stems of these three groups are normally central. With Patouillard (Les. Hymen. Eur., p. 95) it seems to me desirable to include
here a fourth group: the Pleurotoidae, with eccentric or lateral
stem, to include the species *Armillaria dryina* and *Armillaria corticata.* The gills are usually white but may turn yellowish or become stained in age, depending on the species. Some species possess
a gill-trama with diverging hyphae, but in other species the hyphae
are parallel. The relationships shown by this character in this
genus are not yet very clear. The STEM is usually stout; in *A.
bulbigera* it is marginate-bulbous as in some Cartinarii. Usually
it is solid, and often peronate by a more or less persistent
sheath when young, later scaly-spotted by the breaking up
of this sheath. The VEIL is probably double in such species as
A. caligata and *A. aurantia,* the outer veil being continuous with
the cuticle of the pileus, the inner veil closely adherent to it between
the margin of the pileus and the underside of the young gills. It
is mostly membranous, but inclines to a cobwebby or fibrillose texture in *A. bulbigera* and when it sheathes the stem it breaks away
from the margin of the pileus to form the spreading annulus. Sometimes it is lacerated at the junction of cap and stem and parts of
it may remain on the margin of the pileus so that the pileus becomes appendiculate. In *A. mellea* the veil is extremely variable;
it is usually membranous, but sometimes floccose-fibrillose or very
thin and webby so that no annulus is formed on the stem. In other
characters also *A. mellea* is quite variable. The SPORES are white,
varying much in shape and size; in most species they are small
and almost spherical; in some, as in *A. macrospora* Pk. from
Colorado, they are elliptical and measure 10-15 x 6-8 micr. Several
species have a distinct ODOR; that of *A. nardosmia* Ell. is said to
resemble oil of almonds; that of *A. viscidipes* Pk. is strong and penetrating, somewhat alkaline. Nearly all the species are said to have
a slight odor of some kind by which they can be distinguished.
A. mellea Fr. is very common and plentiful in its season; the other
species of Armillaria are infrequent and can be considered rare
during any series of years. So far only five of the latter class
have been found in the State, although doubtless our northern
hemlock and pine forests hide others. It has seemed best, therefore, to include in the key such species as may occur within our

area. About 18 species of Armillaria have been mentioned in the literature as having been observed in the United States; only about half of these were reported east of the Mississippi River. Ricken, (Blätterpilze), refers all Armillarias to the genus Tricholoma. Some species of Clitocybe, Tricholoma, and Pleurotus will be looked for here.

Key to the Species

(A) Stem lateral or eccentric; pileus white. 694. *A. dryina* Fr. 695. (*A. corticata* Fr.)

(AA) Stem usually central.

  (a) Pileus or stem viscid.

    (b) Lignicolous, growing on tree-trunks, etc., pileus glutinous. *A. mucida* Fr.

    (bb) Terrestrial.

      (c) Only the stem viscid; pileus large, whitish, or yellow-tinged; odor penetrating, alkaline. *A. viscidipes* Pk.

      (cc) Stem not viscid; pileus with a slightly viscid pellicle.

        (d) Pileus and stem covered with tawny-orange to ochraceous-rufous scales. 691. *A. aurantia* Fr.

        (dd) Pileus glabrous, pale-brick red; stem covered with pink-red floccose scales. 692. *A. focalis* Fr. var.

  (aa) Pileus and stem not viscid.

    (b) In caespitose clusters about stumps, trunks, etc., honey-yellow, becoming rusty-stained; gills adnate to subdecurrent. 693. *A. mellea* Fr.

    (bb) Not caespitose; gills emarginate or rounded behind, not decurrent.

      (c) Veil cortina-like, white, fugaceous; stem marginate-bulbous; pileus glabrous, gray, brownish or rufescent; spores 7-10 x 5 micr. *A. bulbigera* Fr.

      (cc) Veil membranous; stem not marginate-bulbous.

        (d) Pileus white or whitish.

          (e) Stem sheathed by the subviscid, persistent veil; pileus large, 10-15 cm. broad, white or yellowish, glabrous. Spores globose, 4 micr. diameter. *A. magnivelaris* Pk. *A. ponderosa* Pk.

          (ee) Stem not sheathed; veil fibrillose—membranous, not viscid; pileus 5-10 cm. broad, whitish to rusty-tinged; spores subelliptical, 7.5 x 5 micr. *A. appendiculata* Pk.

        (dd) Pileus or scales dark brown, reddish-brown or grayish brown.

          (e) Pileus glabrous, hard and compact; veil ample, gills broad; spores 7 micr., ovoid-globose. *A. robusta* Fr.

          (ee) Pileus with brown or reddish-brown scales; gills narrow.

            (f) Odor strong, of spikenard or oil of almonds; pileus whitish, except the brown scales; spores 6 micr., globose. *A. nardosmia* Ell. (See *A. caligata*.)

            (ff) Odor none, scales reddish-brown to chestnut-brown; spores globose-ovate, nucleate, 6-7.5 x 5 micr. 690. *A. caligata* Fr.

A. TRICHOLOMATA. Gills sinuate-adnexed; stem fleshy, similar in substance to the pileus.

690. Armillaria caligata Vitt.-Bres.

Hymen. Europ., 1874.

Illustrations: Bresadola, Fungh. mang. e. vel., Pl. 17.
Gillet, Champignons de France, No. 33.
Barla, Champignons de Nice, Pl. 10, Fig. 4-7.
Patouillard, Tab. Analyt., No. 306.
Hard, Mushrooms, Fig. 42, p. 59 (as *A. nardosmia* Ell).
Van Hook, Ind. Acad. Sci. Proc., 1911, Fig. 1, p. 348 (as *A. nardosmia*).
Plate CXXXVII of this Report.

PILEUS 6-10 cm. broad, firm, convex then expanded and depressed, *spotted by appressed, rufous-brown* or dark brown, elongated *fibrillose scales,* elsewhere silky, white between scales or brunescent, margin at first incurved and margined by remnants of the veil. FLESH white, thick, compact. GILLS sinuate-adnate, at length with decurrent tooth, medium *broad* (5-8 mm.), heterophyllous, white, crowded, edge entire, trama of parallel hyphae. STEM *stout,* 4-7 cm. long, 2-3 cm. thick, subequal or tapering down, solid, sheathed at first to the middle or above it by *the veil* which *terminates above by an ample, flaring, thickish, membranous* ANNULUS, later breaking below into subconcentric, *rufous-brown* scales, white and rough-scurfy above the ring, then glabrous and shining, white within. SPORES spherical-ovoid to short elliptical, 6-7.5 x 5 micr., smooth, white in mass. BASIDIA 38-40 x 7-8 micr., 4-spored. ODOR none. TASTE of nuts or slightly bitterish-acrid.

Solitary or in caespitose pairs. On the ground, oak hillside bordering a tamarack bog. Ann Arbor. October. Rare.

Our plants agree so well with Bresadola's description and figure of *A. caligata* that I have no hesitancy in referring them there. There is a slight discrepancy as to odor. Bresadola describes the European plant with an agreeable, fruit-like odor. On this point our specimens also differ from the description of *A. nardosmia* Ell. Several correspondents from the eastern part of the United States inform me that their specimens of *A. nardosmia* often or always lack the odor of almonds attributed to it. Peck (Rep. 33) first referred the New York species to *A. rhagadisma* Fr., but in the

43d Report assigned it to *A. nardosmia.* I am inclined to think the New York species all belong to *A. caligata.* I have collected the same but smaller plant in New York, and it seems usually to be smaller farther south and east. Whether any microscopic characters accompany the almond odor remains to be seen. As in *A. aurantia,* the parallel hyphae of the gill-trama are an exception for this genus.

691. Armillaria aurantia Fr.

Syst. Myc., 1821. (As *Tricholoma aurantia.*)

Illustrations: Fries, Icones, Pl. 27.
Gillet, Champignons de France, No. 31 (too pale).
Bresadola, Fungh. mang. c. vel., Pl. 18.
Michael, Führer f. Pilzfreunde, Vol. III, No. 121.
Atkinson, Mushrooms, Fig. 86, p. 85, 1900.
Ricken, Blätterpilze, Pl. 87, Fig. 2. (As Tricholoma.)

PILEUS 5-7 cm. broad, convex then expanded, subumbonate, viscid in wet weather, *ochraceous-fulvous to tawny-orange-red,* with a pellicle which soon breaks up into numerous, crowded, appressed, concolorus scales, *margin at first inrolled and glutinous-floccose.* FLESH white, thick, abruptly thin on margin. GILLS rounded behind, slightly adnexed, rather narrow, close, *white,* rusty-brown-spotted in age, a few forked, edge entire, trama of parallel hyphae. STEM 4-7 cm. long, 8-15 mm. thick, equal or narrowed downwards, *covered by concolorous subconcentric scales* up to the obscure annulus, white at apex and between scales, solid. SPORES minute, globose-oval, variable, 4-5 x 3-4 micr., smooth, nucleate, white. CYSTIDIA and sterile cells none. BASIDIA 25-28 x 4-5 micr., 4-spored. ODOR strongly farinaceous, somewhat disagreeable.

Scattered. On sandy ground under hemlock trees. New Richmond. September. Infrequent.

This is *Tricholoma peckii* Howe. The quite young plant has an ovate obtuse pileus with an inrolled margin, and an external, colored layer which breaks up into appressed floccose patches or scales, but scarcely ever leaves an annulus. That it is a better Tricholoma, where Fries at first placed it, is shown by the structure of the gill-trama whose hyphae lie in a parallel position. The tawny-orange red color of the scales is a distinguishing character. Cooke's figure (Ill., Pl. 33) evidently illustrates a different species. Bresadola says it has the odor of stale olives, while Maire (Soc. Myc. France, Bull. 27, p. 404) reports a slight dextrine odor.

692.   Armillaria focalis Fr. var.

Epicrisis, 1836-38.

Illustration: Cooke, Ill., Pl. 245.

PILEUS 3-6 cm. broad, campanulate-convex, *soft-fleshy,* obtuse, even, *glabrous,* provided with a thin, separable, *viscid* cuticle, *bright brick-red.* FLESH thin, tinged pink. GILLS *sinuate-adnexed,* rather broad, about 5 mm., ventricose, soft, close, white or tinged brick-red, edge thin. STEM 4-11 cm. long, 5-8 mm. thick, rather slender, subequal, attenuated below, soft, solid, fragile, *covered by brick-red, floccose scales up to the evanescent, median annulus,* whitish and silky-shining above.   SPORES globose, 3-4.5 micr., white, smooth; basidia 4-spored, slender, about 24 micr. long. CELLS of the gill-trama large, 75-125 micr. long, about 12 micr. wide, *divergent.* Cells of the cuticle of pileus long, narrow, 5-6 micr. wide, gelatinous. ODOR and TASTE farinaceous.

Gregarious or solitary, on the ground, in mixed hemlock and maple woods, clay ravines. New Richmond. September. Rare.

This plant seems to be intermediate between *A. focalis* and *A. aurantia.* Its pileus is somewhat viscid and in this respect differs from *A. focalis* and is related to *A. aurantia.* Its spores also approach those of *A. aurantia.* In stature, texture of the flesh, character of pileus, etc., it is, however, quite different from *A. aurantia.* The soft texture is given as an important character of *A. focalis,* and Cooke's illustration gives a good idea of the coloring and the appearance of the stem of our plants, except that the stem is much more elongated and attenuated downward. No critical studies of *A. focalis* Fr. could be found, and it is possible that its cap may be provided with a viscid pellicle in wet weather.

B. *CLITOCYBAE*. Gills attenuated behind, more or less decurrent; stem solid.

693. Armillaria mellea Fr. (EDIBLE)

Syst. Myc., 1821.

Illustrations: Cooke, Ill., Pl. 32.
  Atkinson, Mushrooms, 1900, Pl. 27, p. 84.
  Hard, Mushrooms, 1908, Figs. 39, 40, p. 56, 57.
  Marshall, Mushroom Book, p. 61.
  Murrill, Mycologia, Vol. 1, Pl. 1, Fig. 2.
  Conn. Nat. Hist. Survey, Bull. No. 3, Pl. IV.
  Plates CXXXVIII, CXXXIX, CXL of this Report.

PILEUS 3-10 cm. and more broad, oval to subhemispherical at first, then convex to almost plane, obtuse, normally honey-colored, varying to yellowish-brown, rusty-brown, or quite pale, adorned with dark-brown or blackish pointed tufts or scales, sometimes glabrescent, striate on margin in age. FLESH whitish. GILLS *adnate* or decurrent, subdistant, whitish or dingy yellowish, becoming rusty-stained in age, not broad, at length powdered by the white spores. STEM variable in length, 5-15 cm. long, 6-20 mm. thick, *equal,* stuffed then hollow, often spongy within, fibrous without, elastic, floccose-scaly, glabrescent, glabrous or striate and mealy at apex, whitish above, dingy yellowish, brownish or rusty-stained below. The VEIL is usually well-developed, membranous, and at first conceals the gills, at length collapsing to form a superior *annulus;* sometimes both veil and annulus are almost or entirely lacking; they are white or whitish, sometimes stained like cap and stem. SPORES elliptical-ovate, 8-9.5 x 5-6.5 micr., white, smooth, nucleate; basidia 4-spored; trama of gills composed of divergent hyphae. TASTE somewhat disagreeable or acrid.

Caespitose. At base of living tree-trunks, around stumps, decaying roots, etc., of all sorts of trees, both conifer and broad-leaved. Throughout the State. July-November (earliest record July 13, latest November 2). Very common. Parasitic and saprophytic.

In an abundant species like this, the variations are much more easily observed than in a rare plant, so that about ten varieties have been named and described. The most important of these is var. *exannulata* Pk. This is an ecological form, doubtless, whose dense, caespitose clusters, stem attenuated below, undeveloped an-

nulus and small glabrous pilei, are the result of unfavorable conditions. Other varieties, like *obscura, flava, glabra, radicata, bulbosa,* etc., differ from the normal condition in the characters indicated by their respective names. An abortive form occurs, doubtless parasitized like *Clitopilus abortivus,* by some other fungus
whose identity is unknown. This form consists of irregular round-
ish white masses composed of fungus mycelium. For a fuller account see N. Y. State Mus. Rep. 48, page 262.

Armillaria mellea is of considerable economic importance.. At
times it grows from living roots to which it is connected by black,
twine-like strands called Rhizomorphs.   These are often found
even where no fruit-bodies are present, and before their connection
with this species was known, the strands were referred to an independent fungus and called *Rhizomorpha subcorticalis.*   These
strands extend under the bark of living roots and eventually injure
or kill the trees. The American *A. mellea* is safely edible. Large
quantities are collected by the foreign-born population of some
localities—Detroit and the mining regions of the Northern Peninsula; they are dried, and used for the table during the winter. The
taste is somewhat disagreeable, and many people do not think them
particularly palatable.

Clitocybe monodelpha Morg. has been considered by some as a
variety of this species. It is, however, clearly separated by the character of the hyphae in the gills, which do not diverge as in the
genus Armillaria, but lie parallel between the subhymenial layers.

C. PLEUROTOIDAE.   Stem eccentric or lateral; gills decurrent.

694.   Armillaria dryina Fr.-Pat.

Syst. Myc., 1821.

Illustrations: Cooke, Ill., Pl. 226. (As Pleurotus.)
      Patouillard, Tab. Analyt., No. 517.
      Atkinson, Mushrooms, Pl. 32, Fig. 106, 1900. (As Pleurotus.)

PILEUS 4-8 cm. broad, firm, convex-plane, *floccose-tomentose at
first,* in dry situations *becoming scaly* from the breaking up of the
floccose covering, *white,* scales darker in age, margin at first involute. GILLS decurrent, subdistant, attenuated at ends, broadish
in the middle, white, not anastomosing behind. STEM eccentric or
lateral, 2-4 cm. long, 1-1.5 cm. thick, subequal, sometimes stouter

at first, covered by a more or less dense tomentum, especially toward base, above with a somewhat temporary *annulus* from the thin, membranous veil, which is quickly lacerated and disappears as pileus expands. SPORES oblong, 9-10 x 4-4.5 micr., smooth, white. ODOR very strongly of oil of bitter almonds (benzaldehyde).

From base of stumps, on trunks, etc. Marquette. August. Infrequent.

The plants described above were growing near the ground and in a moist situation and this may account for the unusual tomentosity on the stem. The size of the spores, which appeared to be mature, would seem to be one basis of separation from the next species. When the stem is lateral or nearly so, the pileus is usually subreniform.

695. Armillaria corticata Fr.-Pat.

Syst. Myc., 1821.

Illustration: Atkinson, Mushrooms, Pl. 33, Fig. 107. (Small forms as Pleurotus.)

PILEUS 6-15 cm. or more broad, convex-expanded, obtuse or depressed, *firm, dull white or becoming brownish* tinged, finely floccose at first, then the *cuticle breaks up into scale-like areas,* margin at first involute and appendiculate. FLESH thick, white. GILLS decurrent, moderately close, *rather broad,* narrowed behind, white becoming yellowish, *anastomosing on the stem,* edge entire. STEM 4-10 cm. long, eccentric or almost lateral, sometimes stout and short, solid, firm to rigid, subtomentose or floccose, reticulate in large specimens, equal or tapering down. VEIL attached near apex, leaving a thin, white floccose-membranous evanescent ring, or sometimes remnants on the margin of the pileus. SPORES *cylindrical-elongated, large,* 13-17 x 4-5 micr., smooth, white. BASIDIA 4-spored. ODOR slightly acid-aromatic to foetid.

Solitary or caespitose, on wood, especially on living trunks of hickory, maple, etc. Ann Arbor, Marquette. September-November. Infrequent.

This is considered by Atkinson (Mushrooms, p. 106, 1900) as merely a form of *A. dryina,* and as far as the variation of stem-length and size of plant are concerned, such a conclusion is well supported. The difference in the size of the spores in our collections has, however, opened up the question again, and further study seems necessary. Schroeter gives 13-15 x 4-5 micr. as the size of the spores of *A. corticata,* a measurement nearly equal to the spore length of our form. The size of the spores of *A. dryina* is not mentioned by most authors; Massee says they are 10 x 4 micr. Large specimens of this species when the veil has disappeared, might be mistaken for *Pleurotus ulmarius* or *Panus strigosus;* but *P. ulmarius* has sinuate-adnexed gills and *P. strigosus* has a nap of strigose-villose hairs on cap and stem and is much larger.

Pleurotus Fr.

(From the Greek, *pleuron,* a side, and *ous,* an ear.)

White-spored, (except *P. sapidus* and *P. subpalmatus*). Stem fleshy, *eccentric, lateral or lacking,* continuous with the pileus. Gills adnate, adnexed or decurrent. Veil *none.*

Putrescent, (except *P. atrocaeruleus P. atropellitus, P. niger,* and *P. striatulus*), *lignicolous,* medium to large, or often small and then resupinate. Intergrading with the genera.Clitocybe and Armillaria. They correspond to the genera Claudopus and Crepidotus of the pink-spored and ochre-brown-spored groups respectively. All are believed to be *edible,* and are considered by many people the most delicious of our mushrooms when properly prepared.

The PILEUS varies from quite large in those attached laterally or with a stem, to quite small when it is resupinate. *P. ulmarius* and *P. ostreatus* and their near relatives have a thick, fleshy pileus and ample gills, thus providing a large amount of food for the mushroom enthusiast. The small species are rather thin, often membranous; four of the species revive on moistening. Our large species are nearly all white when fresh, becoming tan-colored or darker when old, and are always firm and even tough in age. The medium-sized species are ashy, greenish, yellowish or reddish in color. The small forms are white, gray or blackish. Several are hygrophanous. Several have a gelatinous or viscid upper layer, of which the thick-fleshed *P. serotinus* is the most note-worthy. The GILLS are fastened to the stem, but their mode of attachment is so different in the various species as to have given some authors ground for making distinct genera out of the sections. In some they are deeply decurrent as in Clitocybe, in others, sinuate-adnexed as in Tricoloma, and in the resupinate and lateral species they radiate from the point of attachment of the pileus as in Crepidotus of the ochre-brown-spored group. In the large species they are usually very broad. Among the medium-sized forms there are cases where the gills are very narrow and very crowded, reaching the base almost as lines; examples of this class are *P. petaloides, P. borealis,* and *P. porrigens.* The small, resupinate forms expose the gills on the upper side while the pileus is closely applied to the substratum; later the pileus becomes reflexed so that the gills project downward, giving the older a different appearance than the younger plant. This genus is often separated from Clitocybe with difficulty, especially in the cases where the stems are only slightly eccentric, so that different authors have placed the same plant under the two genera. The STEM is occasionally almost central in the large-stemmed species, which may then be mistaken for Tricholomas; the latter, however, grow practically always on the ground. Otherwise, the stem is lateral, eccentric or entirely wanting. The interior of the stem is fleshy-fibrous in most species, but several, have a stuffed to hollow axis, with a tough exterior, as in *P. lignatilis.*

The SPORES are white except in the aberrant species *P. sapidus, P. euosmus* and *P. subpalmatus* in which the spores have a slight flesh color or lilac tint. *P. sapidus* and *P. euosmus* resemble *P. ostreatus* so closely in other respects, that placing them among the pink-spored agarics would not improve matters. *P. subpalmatus* seems to me nearer Entoloma as its stem is sometimes central; its reticulate, toughish, gelatinous pileus is rather unique, and reminds one of the genus Heliomyces. The spores of the Pleuroti are smooth, mostly spherical and then minute, or oblong; in a few species, elliptical. CYSTIDIA are known to be present in *P. serotinus, P. stratosus, P. petaloides* and *P. mastrucatus. P. ostreatus* is said to produce scattered conidia on top of its pileus, which represent another kind of spore. The ODOR is often fragrant and agreeable, and the flavor of most of the species makes them very desirable for the table.

The genus may be divided into three sections:
Section I. Eccentrici.
Section II. Dimidiati.
Section III. Resupinati.

The subdivision which was used by Fries and others for those forms with an inner veil is omitted here, since our two species *P. corticatus* and *P. dryinus* have been transferred to the genus Armillaria, where it seems to me they more properly belong, and for which they have often been mistaken. A few species not yet found in the State have been included in the key.

Key to the Species

(A) Stem eccentric; pileus entire or at least marginate behind; plants of medium size to very large.
  (a) Pileus brown or blackish brown, umbonate, 2-7 cm.; gills subdistant, broad; spores 5-6 x 4-5 micr. *P. umbonatus* Pk.
  (aa) Pileus yellow, yellowish or reddish. [See also (aaa).]
    (b) Pileus glabrous, gelatinous on top, coarsely-reticulate, pinkish or flesh color; spores globose, echinulate. 699. *P. subpalmatus* Fr.
    (bb) Pileus strigose hairy, scaly or fibrillose.
      (c) Very large; pileus lateral, cream-color then yellowish, strigose hairy; gills very broad; stem short. (See 12a. *Panus strigosus* B. & C.)
      (cc) Medium-size; stem medium long and not very eccentric.
        (d) Pileus and stem densely dotted with brown or blackish scales; spores globose, minute. (See 760. *Clitocybe decora* Fr.)
        (dd) Pileus unicolorous, silky-fibrillose, umbonate; spores elliptical, 7-9 x 5-6 micr. 698. *P. sulfuroides* Pk.
  (aaa) Pileus white when young or fresh.
    (b) Plant large, on standing elms, etc., stem rather long and stout; gills emarginate or sinuate, rounded behind, broad. 696. *P. ulmarius* Fr. 697. *P. elongatipes* Pk.
    (bb) Gills adnate, adnate-decurrent or long-decurrent.
      (c) Spore print pale dingy lilac; pileus thinner and more flaccid than *P. ostreatus*. 702. *P. sapidus* Fr.
      (cc) Spore print white.
        (d) Stem stout, usually quite short.
          (e) Gills running down the stem in lines and anastomosing; plant rather stout. 700. *P. ostreatus* Fr.
          (ee) Gills not anastomosing on stem, but strongly decurrent. Spores longer than in the preceding two, 12-15 x 5 micr. 701. *P. subareolatus* Pk.
        (dd) Stem slender, 2-5 mm. thick; gills narrow and crowded.
          (e) Pileus hygrophanous, hyaline-white, thin; stem solid, pruinose-floccose. 705. *P. fimbriatus* var. *regularis* var. nov.
          (ee) Pileus not hygrophanous, tough, medium size to small.
            (f) Dingy-white; pileus irregular; stem curved, subvillose, odor farinaceous-oily. 703. *P. lignatilis* Fr.
            (ff) Entirely white; pileus regular, orbicular; stem straight, glabrous; odor faint. 704. *P. circinatus* Fr.
(AA) Stem none or very short; pileus sessile or continuous with the stem.
  (a) Pileus at first resupinate.
    (b) Upper layer of pileus gelatinous, forming a pellicle.
      (c) Pileus 2-5 cm. broad, more or less reniform to obovate.
        (d) Pileus gray or blackish-brown, margin paler, villose, gills not very broad, whitish. 714. *P. atrocaeruleus* Fr. var. *griseus* Pk.
        (dd) Pileus rich brown, covered with squarrose or erect scales; gills broad, grayish-white. 713. *P. mastrucatus* Fr.
      (cc) Pileus minute, in the shape of a pendulous, reversed vase or cup, pale gray; on herbaceous stems. *P. cyphellaeformis* Berk.
    (bb) Pileus without a gelatinous pellicle.
      (c) Pileus pure white, rarely varying to pale tan.
        (d) Pileus 3-7 cm. long, flabelliform, obovate or cuneate; gills narrow, crowded, forked.
          (e) Pileus tomentose; spores spherical; gills scarcely forked. 713. *P. albolanatus* Pk.
          (ee) Pileus glabrous, margin involute; spores longer than broad; gills forked. 710. *P. porrigens* Fr.

(dd) Pileus minute, 3-10 mm. broad, plane; gills rather broad, subdistant. 711. *P. septicus* Fr.

(cc) Pileus gray to blackish, minute.

(d) Pileus glabrous, striate; gills few, distant. *P. striatulus* Fr.

(dd) Pileus not glabrous.

(e) Spores elliptical; pileus 7-16 mm. broad; gills close, blackish. 716. *P. atropellitus* Pk.

(ee) Spores globose; gills broad, thick.

(f) Pileus dark cinereous, subpruinate, margin striatulate. 715. *P. applicatus* Fr.

(ff) Pileus black, plicate on margin, pulveraceous; gills close. *P. niger* Schw.

(aa) Pileus never resupinate, sessile nor attached by a short lateral stem, but pileus not marginate behind.

(b) Upper layer of pileus gelatinous or viscid.

(c) Pileus smoky yellowish green, dimidiate; flesh thick; spores oblong, 4.5 x 1.5 micr. 706. *P. serotinus* Fr. (Syn. *P. serotinoides* Pk.)

(cc) Pileus whitish or tinged alutaceous coreaceous-fleshy, cuneate, spathulate or fan-shaped, spores minute, globose; cystidia abundant. (See 16. *Panus angustatus* Berk.)

(bb) Without a gelatinous surface layer.

(c) Pileus hygrophanous, grayish-brown; gills rather distant, narrow, stem lateral. *P. tremulus* Fr.

(cc) Pileus not hygrophanous.

(d) Pileus sessile, pure white, small, flattened, radiately rugose; gills subdistant, broad. 709. *P. candidissimus* B. & C.

(dd) Pileus not pure white, 1-2 cm. broad, cuneate, or spathulate.

(e) Spores elliptical, 7.5 x 4-5 micr. 708. *P. spathulatus* Fr.

(ee) Spores globose, 3-4 micr. diam. 707. *P. petaloides* Fr.

(Morgan, Cinn. Soc. Nat. History, Vol. 6, p. 78) reports *P. craspedius* Fr. a rather large, brown, stipitate species, margin of pileus crenate or lobed, gills close, narrow and white, spores globose, 5-6 micr.)

Section I. Eccentrici. Pileus entire or at least marginate behind; stem eccentric.

*Gills sinuate emarginate, or obtusely adnate.

696. Pleurotus ulmarius Fr. (EDIBLE)

Syst. Myc., 1821.

Illustrations: Atkinson, Mushrooms, Fig. 102-3, p. 102, 1900.
Hard, Mushrooms, Fig. 119, p. 156, 1908.
Clements, Minnesota Mushrooms, Fig. 19, p. 32, 1910.
Chicago Nat. Hist. Surv. Bull. VII, Part I, Plate V, 1909.
N. Y. State Mus. Rep. 48, Plate 26, Fig. 1-4, 1906, Bot. ed.
Freeman, Minnesota Plant Diseases, Frontispiece, 1905.
Plate CXLI of this Report.

PILEUS 5-15 cm. or more broad, compact, firm, convex then expanded, obtuse, moist, *glabrous* or somewhat tomentose, *white or whitish*, becoming dull leather color in age, sometimes with yellowish or brownish shades, even on margin but often cracked in age. FLESH white, thick. GILLS *sinuate-adnexed* becoming emarginate or rounded behind, broad, close to subdistant, *white or whitish*. STEM 3-7 cm. long, variable, 1-2 cm. thick, *stout, solid,* firm, eccentric, straight or curved, glabrous, sometimes slightly or densely tomentose, whitish. SPORES spherical, 5-7 micr. diam., smooth, *white in mass.* ODOR and TASTE pleasant.

(Dried: Brownish-tan throughout.)

Solitary or caespitose. On decayed or living wood of elm, hickory, maple trunks, etc.; often from a crack or wound of the living tree. Throughout the State. September-November. Rather infrequent except locally.

This Pleurotus apparently occurs only on frondose trees, especially on the elm—whence its name. It is not known whether it is parasitic on the living trees or not. Shade-trees in cities are frequently its home. It is one of our best edible mushrooms when young, but in age it becomes somewhat leathery. Once located on a tree, it may often be found fruiting in successive seasons. It often appears on the pruned ends of branches, and may be found far up on the tree. This species is largely free from grubs, especially in the late fall, and often persists or dries in place. It forms a good article of diet in winter, if it is collected when young and the caps are dried. Some of its characters are quite variable. It may appear in dense clusters, or only as a single individual. When growing from the side of a trunk, the stems often grow downward and the cap develops horizontally. Others grow erect, especially when they appear on top of the branch. When the plant grows to considerable size, it is usually quite tomentose on the pileus and stem, which normally are glabrous. The color is often quite deceptive. Early, fast-growing individuals are pure white, but late, slow growing ones become brownish or tan-colored; all of them tend to become darker in age. The stems are mostly eccentric, but erect plants may have central stems. The mode of attachment of the gills is the most important distinction between this species and *P. ostreatus* and *P. sapidus;* for although the latter have short and lateral stems, *P. ulmarius* also may have stunted stems growing far to one side. As all of them are equally edible, this point is only of diagnostic importance. Several varieties have been described, based on the variations mentioned above.

697. Pleurotus elongatipes Pk. (EDIBLE)

Jour. of Mycology, Vol. 14, 1908.

PILEUS 5-10 cm. broad, convex or nearly plane, glabrous, white, even on the margin. FLESH *rather thin,* white. GILLS *adnexed then emarginate,* rounded behind, close, moderately broad, thin, white. STEM very long, 5-15 cm., 6-10 mm. thick, *stuffed then hollow,* variously curved or flexuous, usually eccentric, glabrous above, more or less tomentose toward base, white. SPORES minute, sphoeroid, 4-5 micr. in diam., smooth.

(Dried: Pileus and gills ochraceous-tan, stem dingy buff.)

Subcaespitose or solitary. On prostrate trunks or decaying logs. Whitmore Lake, Washtenaw County and Stevens Lake, Wayne County. October. Rare?

This species seems most closely related to *P. ulmarius,* and is no doubt often confused with it. Peck, who described it from the Wayne County specimens sent him by Dr. O. E. Fischer, considers it most closely related to *P. lignatilis.* It differs from *P. lignatilis* in its much stouter habit, and adnexed-emarginate gills. From *P. ulmarius* it seems separable by its stuffed to hollow stem. All of the cotype specimens in my possession have a rather large hollow stem when dried. Those in another collection have the habit and appearance of *P. ulmarius,* but with the characteristic hollow stem in the dried condition. Dr. Peck's acuteness has thus, I believe, found that our common *Pleurotus ulmarius* is composed, at least in this region, of two distinct species. It is no doubt edible and the separation is only of scientific interest. The stems of the type specimens were very long, but it is likely that those were plants of an extreme form.

698. Pleurotus sulfuroides Pk.

N. Y. State Mus. Rep. 23, 1872.

Illustration: Atkinson, Mushrooms, Fig. 108, p. 107.

PILEUS 2-7 cm. broad, convex, *umbonate,* subexpanded, silky-fibrillose or minutely scaly, glabrescent, pale yellow, variegated when moist. FLESH thin, soft. GILLS slightly decurrent at first, *soon emarginate* and rounded behind, close, rather broad, *sulfur-yellow to yellowish,* white-floccose on edge when young.

STEM 3-8 cm. long, 5-7 mm. thick, *eccentric,* rigid-elastic, variously curved, equal, fibrillose, *pale yellow, stuffed then hollow,* apex floccose, even. SPORES oval to short elliptical, 6-9 x 5-6 micr., granular within, smooth, white. CYSTIDIA none.

(Dried: Bay-brown throughout.)

Gregarious or subcaespitose. On decaying logs, hemlock or mixed woods. Bay View, New Richmond. September. Rare.

This species is usually rather long-stemmed, but it also occurs with a short, firm stem. Sometimes it is rather soft in texture but in dry weather it becomes firm. It is easily distinguished by the pale yellow color of the whole plant. In one collection the color was more truly sulfur-yellow. When it is dried, it assumes a bay-brown or dingy chestnut color.

699. Pleurotus subpalmatus Fr.

Epicrisis, 1836-38.

Illustrations: Lloyd, Mycological Notes, Vol. I, Fig. 23, p. 51.
Cooke, Ill., Pl. 255. (This has not the appearance of our plant.)

PILEUS 3-5 cm. broad, fleshy, convex-plane, obtuse, *the cuticle gelatinous, coarsely reticulated* and separable, *brick-red to flesh color,* glabrous. FLESH rufescent, thick except at margin. GILLS *adnate,* moderately broad, subventricose, close, thin, a few forked at times or interspaces venose, *becoming salmon color.* STEM coricaceous-fleshy, confluent with pileus, 2-3 cm. long, 5-6 mm. thick, equal, *somewhat eccentric,* curved, fibrillose, fibrous-stuffed, reddish within and without. SPORES globose, *echinulate,* whitish, *flesh color in mass.*

On prostrate maple trunk, cut timber, etc. Houghton, Detroit (Grosse Isle). August-September. Rare.

This rare species has been collected in this country in a small number of widely separated localities. Morgan and Lloyd both report it from Ohio. It seems to have been collected in Kansas and Minnesota. We have it from the northern and southern sections of our State. It departs so widely from the genus Pleurotus in its echinulate spores, which are flesh-colored, and the peculiar raised net-work of reticulations on the upper surface of the pileus, that it might be considered well marked as an independent genus. It is just as properly an Entoloma as a Pleurotus; and why not a

Heliomyces? Its flesh becomes tough at maturity, at least in dry weather. Lloyd's figure is an excellent illustration of the plant as I found it at Houghton.

**Gills adnate-decurrent or deeply decurrent, narrowed to a point or line on the stem.*

700. Pleurotus ostreatus Fr. (EDIBLE)

Syst. Myc., 1821.

Illustrations: Atkinson, Mushrooms, Pl. 30, Fig. 104, 1900.
Hard, Mushrooms, Pl. 18, Fig. 117, 1908.
McIlvaine, Amer. Mushrooms, Plates 35 and 35a, 1900.
Marshall, Mushroom Book, Pl. 9, 58, 1905.
Michael, Führer f. Pilzfreunde, Vol. II, No. 79 (dark form).
Plate CXLII of this Report.

PILEUS 5-20 cm. or more broad, firm, ascending or shelving, *conchate,* subdimidiate to elongated, convex or depressed, white or whitish becoming darker or brownish-ashy, moist, glabrous, margin thin and even, sometimes subrimose. FLESH thick, somewhat soft. GILLS, close to subdistant, *decurrent and running down the stem in raised lines which anastomose,* broad in the middle, narrowed at ends, white or whitish. STEM *lateral, short or almost lacking,* stout, solid, firm, often tomentose or strigose-hairy at base, whitish. SPORES oblong, 7-10 x 4 micr., smooth, *white in mass.* ODOR and TASTE agreeable.

Caespitosely imbricated, often in large shelving clusters on standing dead trunks of poplar, maple, elm, birch, willow, etc.; rarely on hemlock or pine; often on sawed logs scarcely decayed. Throughout the State. May to November. Common.

Distinguished from *P. sapidus* and *P. ulmarius* by the peculiar cross-connections of the decurrent gills on the stem. It has usually stouter and thicker pilei than *P. sapidus* and has white spores. *P. ostreatus* is apparently more common in southern Michigan, while *P. sapidus* is the usual form in the north, although both are found in the same region. It varies in color from dirty-white to smoky-white, becoming brownish-tan in age like the two related species. In luxuriant specimens the gills are very broad, but taper at the ends. It is called the "Oyster Mushroom" because of its conchate pileus. Authors differ as to whether it is of first or

second quality for the table the difference in quality is probably
due to the manner of cooking. Dr. Cooke says it may be spoiled
by improper preparation. Hard says they must be carefully and
thoroughly cooked, and this is an important fact. My own preference is the method used in frying oysters, only it is better to cut
the cap *into small pieces* since they do not cook as quickly as an
oyster. The caps should be collected within a few days of their
appearance, as they become infested with small beetles; these, however, usually hide only between the gills, and can be shaken out,
leaving the plants still fit to eat. At the first signs of decay they
are no longer desirable.

701. Pleurotus subareolatus Pk. var.

N. Y. State Mus. Rep. 30, 1878.

PILEUS 3-8 cm. broad, almost as long, firm, convex, spatulate,
cuneate or flabelliform, lateral but marginate behind, *white then
dingy,* tomentose behind, silky tomentose in front, obscurely areolate, margin at first involute. FLESH thick, surpassing width of
gills, rather soft. GILLS decurrent, scarcely or not at all anastomosing on stem, *rather broad,* attenuate at ends, *subdistant,*
white, at length brownish, edge entire. STEM short, almost lateral,
ascending, 2-3 cm. long, about 1 cm. thick, firm, solid, sometimes
spongy within, equal, even, white then dingy or subrufescent, tomentose. SPORES *long, subcylindrical,* 12-15 x 4-5 micr., smooth, white.
CYSTIDIA none. BASIDIA about 45 x 7 micr., attenuated downward, 4-spored. ODOR and TASTE mild or slightly nauseous.

Solitary or few in cluster. On living trunks of maple, basswood,
etc. Ann Arbor, New Richmond. September-October. Infrequent.

This species is referred here with some hesitancy. Peck described his plants from a single collection, and emphasizes the areolate
character of the surface of the cap. He does not give the shape
of the pileus, but the stem is said to be eccentric, so that the pileus
was probably much more regular than in our plants. The spores,
gills and most of the other essential characters agree. It is probable that if we had accounts of the spore-size of some of the European species, our plant could be easily placed. The margin remains involute a long time, and Peck, in a note (Rep. 54, p. 164)
states that his species had a small, white membranous veil in the
young condition, showing its relation to Armillaria. No such veil
was observed in my plants.

702. Pleurotus sapidus Kalch. (EDIBLE)

Hymen. Hungariae, 1873.

Illustrations: Atkinson, Mushrooms, Plate 31, Fig. 105, 1900.
Hard, Mushrooms, Pl. 20, Fig. 123, 1908.
N. Y. State Mus. Rep. 48, Pl. 27, 1896, Bot. ed.
Cooke, Ill., Pl. 954.

PILEUS 5-10 cm. or more broad, firm, ascending or shelving, subdimidiate or elongated, convex to subexpanded, depressed behind, *glabrous*, often irregular and with wavy margin, white or whitish, often tinged tan, yellowish, gray or brownish, margin thin and even. FLESH white, moderately thick. GILLS close to subdistant, decurrent, *rarely anastomosing*, broad, white or whitish. STEM short or almost lacking, strongly eccentric or lateral, solid, firm, glabrous or slightly tomentose at base. SPORES narrowly oblong, 7-11 x 3-4.5 micr., smooth, *tinged lilac in mass* on white paper. ODOR and TASTE agreeable.

Caespitosely imbricated, habit variable, as in *P. ostreatus*. On dead tree-trunks and firm logs, of maple, elm, beech, oak, birch, willow, etc. Throughout the State. May to November. Very common.

Like *P. ostreatus* in general appearance and in practically all of its characters except the lilac tinged spores. The gills anastomose only at times, and the flesh is on an average thinner in Michigan plants. Our plant is mostly shelving and lateral-stemmed as shown in Atkinson's figure. Only occasionally does one find suberect, eccentric or almost central-stemmed plants like those figured by Peck and Cooke. The lilac tinge of the spores is aberrant within the white-spored group, and yet the plant is so close to *P. ostreatus* in other respects that it would be a stranger in the pink-spored group; this species illustrates again that no grouping can be made perfect. Its edible qualities are just like those of the oyster mushroom, and the remarks made under that species apply equally here. Both of these species are much sought in Europe, and the peasants there often water the trunks of the trees where they occur, and in this way obtain a new crop of the mushrooms. Both are apt to appear, after the spring or autumn rains, in the same logs and trunks, so that one may visit the same place year after year and obtain a supply.

703. Pleurotus lignatilis Fr. (EDIBLE)

Syst. Myc., 1821.

Illustrations: Cooke, Ill., Pl. 257.
  Hard, Mushrooms, Fig. 126, p. 163 (as *P. abscondens*).
  Gillet, Champignons de France, No. 538.
  Plate CXLIII of this Report.

PILEUS 2-5 cm. broad, tough, *irregular,* convex, sometimes depressed or umbilicate, flocculose-pruinose, then glabrous, *whitish.*
GILLS adnato-decurrent, *crowded, narrow,* white. STEM 2-4 cm.
long, 2-4 mm. thick, slender, *stuffed then hollow,* equal, irregular-
curved, eccentric, somewhat villose. 'SPORES minute, oval, 3-5 x
2-3 micr., smooth, white. ODOR markedly *farinaceous.*

Gregarious on logs, etc. Bay View. August-September. Infrequent.

Var. *abscondens* Pk. has gills truly adnate becoming emarginate;
spores elliptical, 4-5 micr. long.

The plants referred here agree with the figures of European authors in having the gills acuminate-adnate on the stem, so that as
the pileus expands they appear subdecurrent. This is also true
of the following two species. On account of this characteristic,
it seems to me these three species had better be grouped under our
second section than with *P. ulmarius,* where Fries and all others
have placed them. *P. lignatilis* and *P. circinatus* and *P. fimbriatus*
var. are very much alike in general appearance. To distinguish
the species one has to rely on the farinaceous odor of *P. lignatilis,*
on the subsolid stem and peculiarly hygrophanous pileus of *P.
fimbriatus* var., and on the very regular cap of *P. circinatus.* The
spores in all three are minute and somewhat alike. The pileus of
P. lignatilis often tends to be subinfundibuliform.

704. Pleurotus circinatus Fr. (EDIBLE)

Epicrisis, 1836-38.

Illustrations: Fries, Icones, Plate 88.
  Cooke, Ill., Pl. 257.

PILEUS 2-5 cm. broad, or less, *regular, tough,* convex, then plane
and slightly depressed, *white or whitish, silky pruinate.* FLESH

thickish, white. GILLS adnato-decurrent, *crowded, narrow,* white. STEM 2-5 cm. long, *stuffed then hollow,* equal, eccentric, slightly curved or straight, *glabrous,* mycelioid at base. SPORES minute, elliptical, 4-5 x 2-3 micr., smooth, white. ODOR slight, *not farinaceous.*

(Dried: Gills yellowish-ochraceous; pileus and stem ochraceous-tan.)

Gregarious. On logs in hemlock woods of northern Michigan; frondose woods in the south. Bay View, Detroit (Grosse Isle). August-September. Infrequent.

The plant is white at first but becomes dingy-tan when old. It is toughish and the flesh is rather thick as in *P. lignatilis.* Both lack the thin, hygrophanous appearance of the next species. The stem is usually longer than the width of the pileus. It lacks the distinct farinaceous odor of *P. lignatilis.*

705. Pleurotus fimbriatus Fr. var. regularis var. nov.

Sys. Myc., 1821. (As *Clitocybe fimbriatus.*)

Illustration: Plate CXLIV of this Report.

PILEUS 2-5 cm. broad, broadly convex, then plane, obtuse, depressed or subinfundibuliform, *pseudohygrophanous, hyaline-white,* then opaque-pruinose, wavy, irregularly lobed or almost regular, glabrous, even on margin. FLESH thin, slightly tough, white. GILLS acuminately adnato-decurrent, *narrow, crowded,* thin, whitish becoming yellowish in age. STEM 1-3 cm. long, 2-5 mm. thick, slender, curved, toughish, equal, *solid* except a narrow tubule, floccose at apex, pruinose or silky fibrillose, pallid. SPORES minute, ovate, 4 x 3 micr., smooth, white. CYSTIDIA none; sterile cells on edge of gills, slender. ODOR somewhat *farinaceous* to oily. TASTE slightly bitterish-astringent.

On hemlock, elm, etc., logs in woods. Bay View, Ann Arbor. June-September. Infrequent.

The pileus when moist has the appearance of a delicate, translucent, immature egg-shell; its margin is sometimes concentrically rivulose. The stem is at first firmly stuffed then tubular. For comparisons see notes on the preceding two species.

Section II. Dimidiati. Pileus lateral, not marginate behind, not at first resupinate, sessile or continuous with the stem-like base.

706. Pleurotus serotinus Fr. (EDIBLE)

Syst. Myc., 1821.

Illustrations: Hard, Mushrooms, Fig. 24, p. 161, 1908 (as *P. serotinoides* Pk.).
> Cooke, Ill., Pl. 258. (Without the olive tints, etc.)
> Patouillard, Tab. Analyt., No. 629.

PILEUS 3-8 cm. broad, campact, convex or nearly plane, lateral, orbicular, dimidiate or reniform, *with a gelatinous pellicle* which becomes viscid when moist, *olivaceous-umber* but varying to yellowish greenish or brown, surface often covered with a short, dense tomentum. FLESH white, thick, firm. GILLS abruptly subdecurrent, thin, broad, narrow in front, close, whitish or tinged ochraceous or tan. STEM *very short*, lateral, continued above with the pileus, stout, 5-20 mm. long, 8-10 mm. thick, *yellowish beneath,* subtomentose or dotted with brown or blackish scales, solid. SPORES minute, linear-oblong, slightly curved, 4-6 x 1-1.5 micr., smooth, white in mass. CYSTIDIA fusiform, yellowish, about 25 micr. long. BASIDIA 4-spored. ODOR and TASTE none.

(Dried: Colors similar to those of fresh condition.)

Caespitose, imbricated, often laterally connate, sometimes solitary. On fallen elm trunks, or dead branches of various frondose trees. Southern Michigan; probably throughout the State. August-November. Frequent locally.

The mode of growth is similar to that of *Claudopus nidulans,* but lacks the odor of the latter and is usually more compact and the colors are dingy. The spores usually found deposited on the lower pilei from those above are white. The tomentum on the pileus often breaks up into punctate scales. The short stem, seen only below, has a yellow-tomentose covering. It may appear in considerable quantity on a single tree trunk.

707. Pleurotus petaloides Fr.

Syst. Myc., 1821.

Illustrations: Atkinson, Mushrooms, Fig. 109-10, p. 108, 1900. Cooke, Ill., Pl. 259.

PILEUS 1-5 cm. broad, elongated in a *wedge-shaped to spathulate* manner, 2-10 cm. long, tapering to a stem-like base, *glabrous* except sometimes tomentose toward base, *whitish to brown, tan or reddish-brown,* margin at first inrolled and finely striate when moist. FLESH rather thin, white, homogeneous. GILLS decurrent, very narrow, crowded, whitish or yellowish, *edge fimbriate.* STEM not apparent from above, on the underside it is somewhat distinguishable as a compressed, short, somewhat villose portion on which the gills descend. SPORES *globose,* minute, 3-4 micr. in diameter, white in mass. CYSTIDIA abundant.

Caespitose on decaying wood, logs, stumps, from underground portions of wood, etc. July to September. Marquette. Infrequent.

Close to *P. spathulatus,* which has oval-elliptical spores. The European authors as a rule give the spores under the description of this species as oval-elliptical, so that if Peck's conception is correct their measurements were taken from a form like Peck's *P. spathulatus.* Fries and apparently most others have considered *P. spathulatus* as a variety with a more broadly expanded and lobed pileus. Our species is distinguished from *P. porrigens* and *P. albolantus* by the presence of cystidia, as well as by the non-resupinate pileus in the young stage.

708. Pleurotus spathulatus (Fr.) Pk.

N. Y. State Mus. Rep. 39, 1886.

Illustration: Hard, Mushrooms, Fig. 120, p. 108, 1908. (As *P. petaloides.*)

"PILEUS 1-5 cm. broad, ascending, spathulate," petaloid, subflabelliform, "tapering behind into the stem, glabrous, convex or depressed on the disk and there sometimes pubescent, *alutaceous or brownish tinged with gray, red or yellow.* FLESH rather thin. GILLS decurrent, crowded, linear, whitish or yellowish. STEM compressed, sometimes channeled above, grayish-tomentose. SPORES *elliptical,* 7.5 x 4-5 micr. ODOR and TASTE *farinaceous.*"

This description was taken from Peck's Report. It is submitted, so that more data may be obtained on the relation of this and the preceding species. Patouillard's figure of *P. petaloides* var. *lobatus* (Tab. Analyt., No. 421) may be this species, as he figures the spores elliptical-ovate. Hard gives the spore measurements elliptical, although he says "globose." His figure could be either species. Galtfelter (Trans. St. Louis Acad. of Sci., Vol. XVI, No. 4, p. 44) gives the spores of *P. petaloides* as 3-4 micr., and globose. There is thus considerable discrepancy between European and American notices of *P. petaloides,* so that Peck appears justified in separating the one with globose spores from the one with elliptical spores. It is more than likely, however, that American authors have confused *Panus angustatus* Berk. with *P. petaloides* in which case *P. spathulatus* would revert to *P. petaloides* as a variety, just as Fries placed it, and the elliptical spores would belong to *P. petaloides* as in Europe. All these species are doubtless edible so that the mycophagist is unaffected by the situation. Both *Panus angustatus* and *Pleurotus petaloides* have abundant cystidia, and both have been found in northern Michigan.

709.   Pleurotus candidissimus B. & C.

Ann. Nat. History, 1859.

PILEUS 2-18 mm. broad, flaccid, reniform or dimidiate, soft-membranous, ascending, convex then plane, attached laterally, *never resupinate,* subsessile i. e. stem very short, sometimes sessile, *pure white, pulverulent,* with a chalky lustre, villose at point of attachment, *margin sulcate,* varying to rugose-striate. GILLS radiating, decurrent, *subdistant to distant,* broader in front, narrowed to the villose base, thin, white. SPORES *globose,* 4-6 micr. diam., smooth.

Gregarious, on rotten wood. Mixed hemlock, maple and beech woods. Houghton, Bay View, New Richmond. July to September. Infrequent.

This little species is easily mistaken for *P. septicus* from which it differs in its globose spores and its sulcate and non-resupinate pileus. The pileus may become resupinate on drying or when old. It varies from sulcate to obscurely striate or lacunose-rugose, but vigorous specimens show this character well. Other Friesian species differ as follows: *P. mitis* has an even pileus; *P. limpidus* is hygrophanous and the gills are crowded and linear; and *P. acerosus* has crowded gills. Our plant seems to be overlooked usually, as it is delicate and soon shrivels.

Section III. Resupinati. Pileus at first resupinate, then reflexed, sessile.

*Pileus fleshy, rather thick; trama homogeneous.

710. Pleurotus porrigens Fr.

Syst. Myc., 1821.

Illustrations: Michael, Führer f. Pilzfreunde, Vol. III, No. 100.
Cooke, Ill., Pl. 259.

PILEUS 2-4 cm. broad, elongated ear-shaped, obovate or fan-shaped, 3-8 cm. long, *at first resupinate* and suborbicular *with persistently inrolled margin,* then reflexed and prolonged, ascending or horizontal, *pure white, sessile, glabrous* except the base which is villose-tomentose, margin regular or lobed. FLESH thin, rather brittle. GILLS radiating, *narrow, crowded,* linear, thin, *much forked* or even anastomosing at base, at length creamy-yellowish. SPORES slightly longer than wide, oval, or subglobose, 6-7 x 5-6 micr., smooth. CYSTIDIA none.

Caespitosely imbricated. On decayed wood of conifers. In the hemlock and pine regions of the State. August-September.

Easily confused with *Panus angustatus* and *Pleurotus albotomentosus.* It differs from these in the absence of a gelatinous layer in the pileus. From *P. petaloides* it is distinguished by its white color and absence of cystidia on the gills. Its home is usually on very rotten wood of hemlock or pine. *P. nephretus* Ell. is said to be the same thing.

711. Pleurotus septicus Fr.

Syst. Myc., 1821.

Illustrations: Patouillard, Tab. Analyt., No. 627.
Cooke, Ill., Pl. 259.

PILEUS 5-20 mm. broad, *resupinate at first,* then reflexed, convex then plane, *short-stipitate, white, pubescent, even on margin.* FLESH thin, not truly membranous. GILLS *subdistant, rather broad,* radiating, white. STEM slender, short, incurved, *pubescent,* disappearing, surrounded at the base by a webby zone of filaments, white. SPORES elliptic-ovate, pointed-apiculate, *8-10 x 6 micr.,* white in mass. CYSTIDIA none.

On decaying wood, etc., in woods. Probably throughout the State. July-September. Infrequently found.

Often confused with *Claudopus variabilis* when the latter is young and white-gilled. It has no doubt also been mistaken for *P. candidissimus* which however is not resupinate at first and has globose spores. Probably several other small white species occur, but have not been distinguished.

***Pileus fleshy, with a gelatinous layer on or just beneath the surface.*

712. Pleurotus albolanatus Pk., sp. nov.

Illustration: Plate CXLV of this Report.

PILEUS 5-10 cm. or more broad, *resupinate at first,* fleshy, lateral, sessile, becoming obovate, reniform or flabelliform, convex to subexpanded, trama slightly differentiated into several layers, *upper part subgelatinous,* surface *pulverulent-tomentose,* margin involute at first. FLESH rather thin, white, scissile, *becoming brittle.* GILLS decurrent on stem-like base, *very crowded, narrow,* white to yellowish, somewhat forked, thin. SPORES *spherical,* 4-6 micr. diam., smooth, white in mass. CYSTIDIA *none.*

Caespitosely imbricated. On decaying logs of beech, hemlock, etc., of northern Michigan. Bay View, Marquette, Houghton. August-October. Frequent.

This species approaches *Panus angustatus,* but differs consistently in the lack of cystidia, in its larger spores, and perhaps in its resupinate pileus. No record seems to be on hand that *P. angustatus* is at first resupinate. The pileus has a gelatinous feel and is composed of several layers, but in some specimens these are hard to distinguish. Specimens referred to Peck, were labelled by him *P. porrigens* var. *albolanatus.* The spherical spores, which are constant, and the ˙subgelatinous layer in the upper part of the pileus warrant me in using Peck's varietal name for a distinct species. Luxuriant specimens become lobed as in the related species, and measure up to 14 cm. in width. The flesh becomes brittle on drying and is rather thin throughout. The tomentosity extends usually over the whole pileus but sometimes the margin is glabrous. There are no striations. Sometimes the base arises from a white, mycelioid subiculum.

713. Pleurotus mastrucatus Fr.

Syst. Mycol., 1821.

Illustration: Cooke, Ill., Pl. 243.

"PILEUS 2.5-10 cm. broad, *at first resupinate* then reflexed and expanded, sessile, subdimidiate, obovate, sometimes lobed, flaccid, *trama with an upper gelatinous layer,* mouse-gray, *rough-squamulose with blackish* hairs and rigid points intermixed, margin involute at first. GILLS converging to the base of pileus, (without a rudimentary stem), broad, subdistant, whitish-gray. SPORES oblong, oblique, 8-9 x 4-5 micr., white.

"Caespitosely imbricated. On logs or decaying wood. September-November."

This species has been found in surrounding States and no doubt occurs with us, though I have not found it. Reported in the Chicago Nat. Hist. Surv. Report, and in Morgan's Flora of the Miami Valley, Ohio. It is rare.

714. Pleurotus atrocaeruleus Fr. var. griseus Pk.

N. Y. Mus. Rep. 44, 1891. (Syst. Myc., 1821.)

PILEUS 2-5 cm. broad, *at first resupinate,* then reflexed and horizontal, obovate or reniform, *upper layer of trama gelatinous and tough,* dark grayish-brown shaded with bluish or blackish tints, *coarsely villose* toward the base, glabrous on margin, even or slightly wrinkled, margin often lobed. FLESH stratose, gelatinous above, composed of floccose-hyphae below, the lower layer varying in thickness, thinner in front. GILLS radiating, decurrent to the region of the attachment of pileus or to the hairy stem-like base, moderately broad, somewhat close, whitish or yellowish, edge minutely fimbriate. SPORES elliptic-oblong, narrower toward one end, 6-7.5 x 3-4 micr., smooth, white in mass. CYSTIDIA slender, acuminate and scattered on the sides of gills and then about 45 micr. long; more numerous but shorter, about 30 micr., on the edge of the gills, often capped with coarse granules.

(Dried: Pileus blackish, gills ochraceous-tan.)

Caespitose, subimbricate, on the bark of various trees, in woods, lawns, etc. On mountain ash on a lawn at Marquette. July-September. Throughout the State. Infrequent.

The plants, like the plants of the genus Marasmius, revive when moistened. Mounted in water under the microscope, a section through the pileus shows a gelatinous upper layer of uniform thickness, bounded by dark hyphae on both sides of this layer, the upper hyphae forming the villosity on the pileus, the lower forming an opaque line next to the white flesh beneath. In front the flesh is thinner than the pellicle, behind it is several times thicker. Whether the variety is entirely distinct from the European species, cannot be decided from data at hand. The cystidia are thick-walled, slender, penetrate deep into the subhymenium, and do not project far above the hymenium.

715. Pleurotus applicatus Fr.

Syst. Myc., 1821.

Illustrations: Atkinson, Mushrooms, Fig. 111, p. 109, 1900.
Hard, Mushrooms, Fig. 125, p. 162, 1908.
Cooke, Ill., Pl. 244.
Patouillard, Tab. Analyt., No. 519.

PILEUS 3-6 mm. broad, *minute,* arising from an orbicular re-supinate tubercle, soon horizontal but *cupulate,* convex, submembranous, *trama mainly gelatinous,* surface pruinate to villose behind, obscurely striatulate, *dark gray to blackish,* tinged blue, sessile or with a villose, base-like tubercle. GILLS *subdistant,* relatively broad, radiating, whitish at first, soon gray or even darker than the pileus. SPORES spherical, minute, 4-5 micr. diam., smooth, white in mass. CYSTIDIA none.

Gregarious, on rotten wood, often on old stems of grape vines, in moist woods. Probably throughout the State; Ann Arbor, etc. June-September. Infrequently collected.

The dark color of this little Pleurotus causes it ordinarily to escape detection, but persistent examination of the lower side of moist logs or brush-heaps is likely to disclose it. It revives on moistening, and so simulates a Panus. It differs from *P. atropellitus* in its globose spores and gelatinous trama. A large portion of the thin pileus is composed of gelatinizing hyphae, on the top of which are dark floccose threads which form the villose surface of a part of the pileus. The gills are subdistant with alternating shorter gills, which often develop poorly so that the main gills appear quite distant. When growing from the underside of wood the pileus is attached at its center.

***Pileus membranous, trama homogenous, not gelatinous.*

716. Pleurotus atropellitus Pk.

N. Y. State Mus. Rep. 39, 1886.

PILEUS 5-15 mm. broad, small, *resupinate at first*, very thin, membranous, toughish, suborbicular, then obovate or reniform, convex to nearly plane, *villose-tomentulose*, glabrescent in front, sessile by a villose tubercle, ashy-gray to blackish, *widely-striate to subsulcate on margin* when moist. FLESH homogeneous, with dark hyphae on the surface of pileus. GILLS close to subdistant, relatively broad, short ones often narrow, concolor, radiating from the stem-like villose base. SPORES *elliptical-oval*, 7-9 x 4-5 micr., smooth, white in mass. CYSTIDIA none.

On decayed wood, low woods. New Richmond, Ann Arbor. March (21, 1909), September, etc. Infrequent.

This is similar to *P. applicatus*, but more flaccid, more definitely striate on the pileus, and with broadly elliptical spores. Our plants were paler than those described by Peck. The closeness of the gills varies in these small plants and makes a poor character to emphasize. It revives poorly when moistened as compared with *P. applicatus*. Another small species, related to these two, is *P. niger* Schw. This has subglobose spores and is plicate on the margin of the pileus. *P. striatulus* Fr. has very distant gills, subglobose spores and a pendulous, obconic, striate brown or ashy pileus. I have not found these two in the state.

Tricholoma Fr.

(From the Greek *thrix*, genitive *trichos*, a hair; and *loma*, a fringe, referring to the remnants of the cortina in some species.)

White-spored. Stem continuous with the pileus, *without an annulus, spongy-fleshy to fibrous*, central; partial veil in the form of a slight fibrillose or floccose cortina, or lacking. Volva none. Gills

adnate or truncate-adnexed, *becoming emarginate*. Pileus viscid
or dry.

Putrescent, *terrestrial,* fleshy, firm and rather large mushrooms.
A large genus, approaching Clitocybe and Pleurotus, being separated from the former by the non-decurrent gills, from the latter
by the central stem. Collybia is distinguished by its cartilaginous
stem, and by the absence of a cortina, and more often grows on
wood or decayed leaves, etc. The trama of the gills is composed
of parallel hyphae which distinguishes them from those Hygrophori
which are similar in appearance. The genus corresponds to Hebeloma, Entoloma and Hypholoma of the ochre, pink and purple-
spored groups. Many of them are edible, and their thick flesh furnishes considerable substance; on the other hand several species
are known to be poisonous and must be avoided.

The PILEUS may be glabrous, silky or in some species scaly;
viscid, dry or hygrophanous. Accordingly they are placed under
corresponding sections of the genus. The colors are seldom bright,
although several are sulfur-yellow and others purplish or lavender.
Many of them are dull whitish to gray or tan, sometimes umber or
blackish. The character of the *margin of the pileus* is used exten-
sively to determine to which sub-genus they belong. It is, therefore, important to observe carefully the presence or absence of
silky fibrils or flocci on the margin, as their presence indicates a
slight *cortina* in the very young stage and suggests the sub-genus
Cortinellus. The viscidity indicates the subgenus Limacina, although species of other sections sometimes become slightly viscid
or gelatinous in very wet weather. The GILLS are used to separate
this genus from Clitocybe. Theoretically, they are always *emarginate* behind, but this condition varies considerably. It is true, that
in the mature plant, when the pileus is fully expanded, they become
either sinuate or emarginate in most cases, although a single specimen may not always be normal in this respect. When young, however, they often do not show this character clearly, but are then
adnexed, rounded-adnate, or adnate in such a way that they are
merely a little less broad at the attached portion than they are
a few millimeters away from the stem, and this short distance is
often marked by a straight edge rather than by a rounded edge.
Such a condition may be referred to as *truncately-adnate,* rather
than as adnexed. In old stages the gills may even become spuriously decurrent, and their Tricholoma nature is then evident only
by a slight sinuate portion near the stem, since in Clitocybe the

edge is uniformly continuous or straight. Fayod (Ann. d. Sci. Nat., 7 Ser., Vol. 9, p. 346), says that in the very young button stage they are truly decurrent but his observations were limited to few species. The *color of the gills* changes at maturity or in age in some species, and this character is used to separate the species under each section into two groups. The color changes to reddish-spotted, flesh-color, ashy or even black in age or when bruised, and hence it is often impossible to locate a species properly until it has been kept several hours after picking. In some species the gills are very narrow; in others, very broad, and this is a reliable character when well-developed plants are at hand; poorly-developed or stunted specimens often produce narrow gills in broad-gilled species. The gills of some species are easily separable from the trama of the pileus, and such species have been referred by some authors to a separate genus: Lepista. There is, however, not sufficient data at hand to know with certainty what species have this character and why, and hence in this report they are included under Tricholoma. The STEM varies from fibrous-fleshy to fibrous-spongy; more often quite firm, compact and stout. It lacks the cartilaginous rind of the stem of Collybia, although in dry weather forms a rind is sometimes simulated. *T. albiflavidum* Pk. often has a distinct cartilaginous stem and is grouped under Collybia. There is no annulus, the cortina being evanescent when present at all, or in a few extreme cases leaving only slight fibrillose remnants on its surface, as in *T. vaccinum* Fr. and *T. imbricatum* Fr. It is nearly always dry, and scarcely ever sharply bulbous. The SPORES are white except in a small aberrant group including *T. personatum, T. nudum* and *T. panoeolum,* where they are tinged pale dingy-flesh color in mass. They vary from elliptical to oval or spherical, and are usually medium to small or minute in size. The epispore is rarely rough, e. g., in some of the species under the subgenus Melanoleuca. CYSTIDIA are lacking in this genus; *sterile cells* are seldom present on the edge of the gills; they have been noted in *T. rutilans* and *T. acre.* The ODOR is quite characteristic of many species; many have a farinaceous odor, while some are distinguishable by a heavy disagreeable odor. When it is not otherwise noticeable, the odor may often be obtained by crushing a piece of the cap between the fingers. The TASTE varies also. In those species with the farinaceous odor, there is a corresponding taste. Some species have an acrid taste. The Tricholomas usually have a terrestrial *habitat.* They are most common in open woods, mossy places and thick forests. Some grow in meadows or grassy places, but these are rare in the vicinity of Ann Arbor. *T. rutilans* grows on wood, and *T. ustale* is partial to the remains of very rotten logs, etc. Their EDIBILITY varies. Some of them, like *T. resplendens* and *T. personatum* are among our very best mushrooms for the table. Others like *T. equestre, T. transmutans, T. sejunctum* and *T. terreum* are fairly good when properly cooked. Some, such as *T. laterarium*, are very bitter, or have various kinds of disagreeable flavors which, however, almost disappear in cooking. In serving those mushrooms of disagreeable flavor it is safer to discard the liquid in which they were prepared, as this contains the objectionable constituents. In several species, of which *T. sulfureum* is an example, the disagreeable flavor cannot be removed, and such should not be eaten. In all cases, except those species which are well-known, it is necessary to exercise extreme caution, since the genus includes several *poisonous* species. *T. venenatum* for example, has a mild taste and odor, and is yet known to cause severe sickness. Many of those with a farinaceous taste and odor, on the other hand, are known to be edible. One must therefore be able to discriminate in order to be on the safe side.

The grouping of this large genus is fraught with considerable difficulties. The separate species are often closely related, and some of them approach other genera in such a way as to cause disagreement among authors as to their generic position. I have attempted an arrangement along conservative lines until our data are more complete. The species included in this report do not, I am sure, represent more than half the species occurring within the State. It has been impossible to make a search for Tricholomas in the northern part of the State in the late fall, so that doubtless that region is poorly represented. Hence, also, it was impossible to study the genus in such a way as to form a definite opinion as to the value of various arrangements which have been proposed. Some have segregated it into four or more genera. Others have separated those species with rough spores under the genus Melanoleuca, while still others have placed those species in which the gills separate easily from the trama of the pileus under Lepista Fr. The most natural arrangement with the data at hand, seems to be a division into subgenera, based on (1) the viscid pileus: Limacina; (2) the dry pileus, with a fibrillose cortina when young: Cortinellus; and (3) the moist or hygrophanous pileus: Melanoleuca. I am inclined also to consider those with separable **gills** as a distinct subgenus, but have avoided that arrangement in this report for lack of data.

The key to the species includes a number which have not yet been found in Michigan but which occur in neighboring States.

Key to the Species

(A) Pileus viscid, medium to large. [See also (AA) and (AAA).]
  (a) Pileus pure white. 721. *T. resplendens* Fr.
  (aa) Pileus not pure white.
    (b) Gills sulfur-yellow; pileus not virgate. 717. *T. equestre* **Fr.**
    (bb) Gills not sulfur-yellow.
      (c) Gills becoming discolored in age, often spotted with brownish-red.
        (d) Flesh and gills yellowish; stem at first viscid; pileus **brown.** *T. flavobrunneum* Fr.
        (dd) Flesh and gills white at first.
          (e) Pileus pale pink to rosy-red, margin at first involute. (See 163. *Hygrophorus russula* Fr.)
          (ee) Pileus reddish-brown to bay-brown.
            (f) Odor distinctly farinaceous when flesh is crushed; **taste** of surface of pileus bitter. 722. *T. transmutans* Pk.
            (ff) Odor not farinaceous; stem mostly rooting. 723. *T. ustale* Fr.
      (cc) Gills not discolored, not rufescent.
        (d) Pileus streaked with innate blackish fibrils.
          (e) Taste bitterish or nauseous; pileus whitish to **yellowish.** 718. *T. sejunctum* Fr.
          (ee) Taste mild; pileus gray, smoky, lurid. 719. *T. portentosum* Fr.
        (dd) Pileus not streaked.
          (e) Stem floccose-fibrillose; pileus alutaceous. 720. *T. terriferum* Pk.
          (ee) Stem glabrous.
            (f) Pileus slightly viscid, greenish-yellow; stem white. *T. intermedium* Pk.
            (ff) Pileus glutinous, yellow-tawny, disk reddish-brown; **base** of stem brown. *T. viscosum* Pk.
(AA) Pileus hygrophanous (water-soaked plants of the (AAA) group sometimes have an hygrophanous appearance).
  (a) Stem sulcate or coarsely striate; pileus reddish or reddish-fawn color (moist), 5-10 cm. broad. *T. grammopodium* Fr.
  (aa) Stem not sulcate; pileus usually less than 6 cm. broad.
    (b) Gills violaceous (young), then smoky; often in greenhouses, **gar-** dens, etc. 754. *T. sordidum* Fr.
    (bb) Gills not at first violaceous.
      (c) Pileus 1-3 cm. broad, stem hollow.
        (d) Pileus olive-gray (moist); odor of rancid meal. *T. putidum* Fr.
        (dd) Pileus watery-brown (moist); odor farinaceous. *T. rimosum* Pk.
      (cc) Pileus 3-7 cm. broad.
        (d) Odor strongly farinaceous; pileus grayish-brown or **brown** (moist); gills whitish. 753. *T. leucocephaloides* Pk.
        (dd) Odor not farinaceous.
          (e) Stem brown within and without, short; pileus ashy, **gray-** ish-brown, darker on disk. *T. brevipes* Fr.
          (ee) Stem whitish within; in fields, gardens, open ground, **etc.**

    (f)   Stem streaked with blackish fibrils, elastic; pileus smoky-brown. 752. *T. melaleucum* Fr.

    (ff) Stem covered with a cinereous pulverulence, soft; pileus gray. *T. humile* Fr.

(AAA)   Pileus neither viscid nor hygrophanous.

  (a)   Pileus white or whitish at first, disk often with tints of other colors.

    (b)   Taste acrid, bitter or unpleasant (often tardily).

      (c)   Gills becoming dingy flesh color. 751. *T. panoeolum* var *caespitosum* Bres.

      (cc) Gills white or whitish, not becoming dingy incarnate in age.

        (d)   Stem stuffed or hollow; pileus with grayish-brown disk; taste and odor strong, unpleasant. *T. terreolens* Pk.

        (dd) Stem solid.

          (e)   Gills broad; pileus minutely scaly; taste slowly acrid or unpleasant.

          (f)   Pileus with ochraceous, drop-like scales on disk. 726. *T. nobile* Pk. (*T. serratifolium* Pk.) (See also *T. venenatum* Atk.)

         (ee) Gills not broad; pileus glabrous.

          (f)   Taste very bitter; gills narrow and crowded. 743. *T. acerbum* Fr.

          (ff) Taste tardily acrid; gills medium broad and close. 742. *T. album* Fr.

    (bb) Taste mild or farinaceous.

      (c)   Stems connately joined at base or several growing from a thick fleshy mass.

        (d)   Pileus mottled with reddish scaly spots. *T. albellum* Fr.

        (dd) Pileus mottled with watery spots. 741. *T. unifactum* Pk. var.

      (cc) Stems simple or subcaespitose.

        (d)   Pileus small; gills broad; stem solid; taste farinaceous. *T. silvaticum* Pk.

        (dd) Pileus usually more than 2-3 cm. broad.

          (e)   Odor and taste farinaceous.

          (f)   Pileus large, 8-12 cm., scaly with brownish scales; spores 9-11 x 6 micr. *T. grande* Pk.

          (ff) Pileus 3-6 cm., glabrous; spores 6-8 x 3-4 micr. 745. *T. leucocephalum* Fr.

         (ee) Odor and taste mild.

          (f)   Stem rooting and tomentose at base. *T. lascivum* Fr.

          (ff) Stem not rooting. (*Clitocybe candida* Bres. may be sought here.)

            (g)   Margin of pileus with short, radiating ridges; gills narrow and crowded. 744. *T. laterarium* Pk.

            (gg) Margin even.

               (h)   Gills rather broad.

                 (i)   Plant pure shining white, but without a separate pellicle. 727. *T. columbetta* Fr.

                 (ii) Plant dingy whitish, pileus fibrillose-scaly. 725. *T. venenata* Atk.

                 (iii) Plant whitish, caespitose. (See 774. *Clitocybe multiceps.*)

             (hh) Gills narrow and crowded, pileus not pure white; stem striate. (See 813. *Collybia albiflavidum* Pk.)

(aa) Pileus yellow, yellowish or smoky-yellowish. [See also (aaa).]

  (b)   Growing on wood; edge of gills flocculose.

    (c)   Pileus yellow beneath the dark reddish scales. 724. *T. rutilans* Fr.

    (cc) Pileus pale yellow, slightly silky. *T. flavescens* Pk.

  (bb) Growing on the ground.

    (c)   Odor strong of coal tar, etc., disagreeable or farinaceous.

(d) Plant sulfur-yellow to olivaceous-yellow; odor disagreeable, strong. 737. *T. sulfureum* Fr.

(dd) Plant pale yellow or smoky-yellow.

  (e) Stem solid; gills yellowish, taste farinaceous. 738. *T. chrysenteroides* Pk.

  (ee) Stem stuffed or hollow; gills rather broad.

    (f) Pileus smoky-yellowish; taste and odor farinaceous; gills white. 746. *T. fumosiluteum* Pk.

    (ff) Pileus pale yellow; gills whitish tinged pink; odor rather strong. 739. *T. odorum* Pk.

(cc) Odor none or slight.

  (d) Pileus large, 4-10 cm.

    (e) Pileus very fragile, bright yellow, variegated with other hues; gills broad, white. *T. davisiae* Pk.

    (ee) Pileus firm, yellow, umbonate; gills white; stem solid, white within; spores globose. *T. subluteum* Pk.

  (dd) Pileus small, 1-3 cm., dull saffron; gills yellow. *T. fallax* Pk. (See also *T. cerinum* Fr.)

(aaa) Pileus neither white, whitish, yellow nor yellowish.

(b) Pileus violet, lilac or purplish.

  (c) Pileus 6-12 cm. broad; stem stout, lavender or lilac; common. 747. *T. personatum* Fr.

  (cc) Pileus smaller; stem more slender.

    (d) Pileus at first conic-campanulate and flocculose on the margin; gills whitish. *T. ionides* Fr.

    (dd) Pileus at first convex and naked on margin, gills bluish to lavender. 748. *T. nudum* Fr.

(bb) Pileus not violet, lilac or purplish.

  (c) On wood or rotten logs.

    (d) Pileus covered with dense, minute, blackish or brownish scales; flesh yellow. (See 760. *Clitocybe decora* Fr.)

    (dd) Pileus covered with reddish tomentum or scales, flesh yellow. 724. *T. rutilans* Fr.

  (cc) On the ground.

    (d) Pileus cinereous, grayish-brown, smoky or blackish. [See (dd).]

      (e) Gills becoming blackish or bluish-black when bruised. Pileus 2-7 cm. broad.

        (f) Gills narrow, crowded. 733. *T. fumescens* Pk.

        (ff) Gills moderately broad, close to subdistant. 734. *T. fuligineum* Pk.

      (ee) Gills not becoming black when bruised; some changing to ashy, yellowish or flesh color in age.

        (f) Taste acrid, peppery or disagreeable.

          (g) Stem rooting; gills white; pileus grayish-brown, taste disagreeable. *T. radicatum* Pk.

          (gg) Stem not markedly rooting.

            (h) Pileus virgate with gray or blackish fibrils.

              (i) Pileus acutely and prominently umbonate; gills and stem white. *T. subacutum* Pk. (cf. *T. virgatum* Fr.)

              (ii) Pileus obtuse; gills at length pale cinerascent. 731. *T. acre* Pk.

            (hh) Pileus not virgate.

              (i) Pileus buff, grayish-brown or dingy-tan, large, caespitose; gills crowded, narrow, soon flesh color. 571. *T. panoeolum* var. *caespitosum* Bres.

              (ii) Not caespitose; pileus livid-brown; flesh of stem becoming reddish. 735. *T. saponaceum* Fr.

        (ff) Taste mild or farinaceous.

          (g) Very large; pileus 10-20 cm. broad, grayish-tawny; stem rooting. *T. grave* Pk.

    (gg)   Moderate size.

      (h)   Pileus 2-6 cm. broad, innately fibrillose or fibrillose-scaly. 732. *T. terreum* Fr.

     (hh)   Pileus 5-10 cm. broad.

        (i)   Pileus smoky-umber to blackish; gills broad, cinerascent. 736. *T. laticeps* sp. nov.

       (ii)   Pileus grayish or grayish-brown.

         (k)   Gills broad, subdistant.

           (1)   Streaked with darker fibrils; gills white. (See 816. *Collybia platyphylla* Fr.)

          (ll)   Pileus usually water-spotted not streaked; gills slightly cinerascent; autumnal. 749. *T. tumidum* Fr.

        (kk)   Gills close or crowded.

           (1)   Gills easily separable from flesh of pileus, becoming dingy-yellowish in age; stem stuffed. 751. *T. cinerascens* Fr.

          (ll)   Gills not separable, veined on the sides. *T. patulum* Fr.

  (dd)   Pileus reddish, tawny, tan, fuscous-livid, etc.

   (e)   Growing on wood; pileus and stem covered with tawny, tomentose scales. *T. decorosum* Pk.

   (ee)   Not on wood.

     (f)   Flesh of pileus or stem changing to reddish when bruised or in age; pileus red-brown.

      (g)   Stem hollow. 729. *T. vaccinum* Fr.

     (gg)   Stem solid. 728. · *T. imbricatum* Fr.

    (ff)   Flesh not turning reddish.

      (g)   Becoming ferruginous-stained when handled; pileus whitish to brownish. *T. submaculatum* Pk.

     (gg)   Not becoming rusty-stained.

      (h)   In pastures, etc., in the spring; pileus pale tan, watery-spotted; odor farinaceous. *T. gambosum* Fr.

     (hh)   In the woods.

       (i)   Pileus pale alutaceous to russet; gills pale yellow; stem white. 730. *T. tricolor* Pk.

      (ii)   Pileus flesh color, 1-2 cm. broad. 740. *T. carneum* Fr.

SUBGENUS I. LIMACINA. Pileus provided with a gelatinous pellicle, viscid, not hygrophanous. Cortina none.

*Gills not at length brown or rufescent-spotted.

717. Tricholoma equestre Fr. (EDIBLE)

Epicrisis, 1836.

Illustrations: Cooke, Ill., Pl. 72.

     Berkeley, Outlines, Pl. 4, Fig. 2.

     Gillet, Champignons de France, Pl. 672.

     Ricken, Blätterpilze, Pl. 90, Fig. 3.

PILEUS 5-10 cm. broad, compact, convex-expanded, obtuse, pale yellow, variegated with reddish or smoky-reddish especially on disk, *viscid,* somewhat scaly on broad disk, not virgate, margin even and naked. FLESH white or tinged yellow under cuticle, thin on margin. GILLS slightly adnexed or nearly free, rounded-truncate behind, *sulfur-yellow,* close, rather broad, ventricose, edge entire or suberoded. STEM stout, 3-6 cm. long, 1-2 cm. thick, equal or sub-bulbous, solid rarely cavernous, pale yellow or white, *white within,* even, minutely scaly or glabrescent. SPORES elliptical-oval, 6-7 x 4 micr., smooth, white. CYSTIDIA and *sterile cells* none. ODOR slight or none; TASTE subfarinaceous, tardily disagreeable.

Gregarious or subcaespitose. On the ground among or under leaves in conifer and frondose woods. Ann Arbor, Detroit, Jackson, Houghton, Marquette. August-October. (Earliest record July 28.) Infrequent.

This is usually a large and noble species, but late in the fall it is often found with smaller dimensions. The color of the stem is pale yellow or even white, but in Europe it is said to be sulfur-yellow, as is also the flesh. The scales on the pileus are not always developed. The margin of the cap is at first incurved and irregularly wavy. It differs from *T. sejunctum* by lacking the radiating sooty lines which characterize the pileus of that species, and by its yellow gills. It is found sparingly, and rather late in the fall. When covered with leaves the yellow color of the cap is more highly developed.

718. Tricholoma sejunctum Fr. (EDIBLE)

Syst. Myc., 1821.

Illustrations: Atkinson, Mushrooms, Fig. 89, p. 88, 1900.
    Hard, Mushrooms, Fig. 60, p. 82, 1908.
    Cooke, Ill., Pl. 53.
    Gillet, Champignons de France, No. 700.
    Fries, Icones, Pl. 23 (luxuriant form).
    Ricken, Blätterpilze, Pl. 89, Fig. 2.

PILEUS 4-8 cm. broad, convex-expanded, obtuse or umbonate, *subviscid,* whitish to yellowish, *streaked with innate blackish fibrils,* often gibbous or irregular. FLESH white or slightly yellowish, fragile. GILLS emarginate, *white,* usually broad, subdistant to close, edge entire. STEM elongated, 5-8 cm. long, 1-1.5 cm. thick, subequal or *variously thickened and flexuous,* solid, sometimes cavernous, subglabrous, even, white or tinged yellowish. SPORES oval to subspherical, 6-7 x 4-5.5 micr., white. CYSTIDIA none. ODOR slight; TASTE bitterish to nauseous.

Gregarious or subcaespitose. On the ground in oak and maple woods. Ann Arbor, New Richmond. September-November.

Frequent around Ann Arbor in the late fall. Usually this species is more slender than *T. equestre.* Its virgate pileus and white gills distinguish it from that species. The color is quite variable; sometimes the pileus is a dull white with a few yellow stains, while the other extreme, with the pileus almost entirely smoky-brown or blackish on disk, is equally common. The disk of the pileus sometimes develops blackish fibrillose scales while normally it is glabrous. In any case there is usually some sign of the streaked condition. Specimens have been found in which slight yellowish stains appeared on the edge of the gills in the older specimens, but these could not be referred to *T. coryphaeum* Fr. which species is said to have yellow-edged gills. Peck remarks that the taste is scarcely bitter. In our plants a bitterish-nauseous taste was nearly always present. *Tricholoma intermedium* Pk. is said to be halfway between *T. equestre* and *T. sejunctum,* and is distinguished by its crowded gills. It should be considered as a variety, since it is doubtless an example of the extreme variation of *T. sejunctum.*

719. Tricholoma portentosum Fr. (EDIBLE)

Syst. Myc., 1821.

Illustrations: Hard, Mushrooms, Fig. 63, p. 87, 1908.
Michael, Führer f. Pilzfreunde, Vol. II, No. 93.
Peck, N. Y. State Mus. Mem. 4, Pl. 45, Figs. 1-5, 1900
(var. *centrale* Pk.)
Cooke, Ill., Pl. 54.
Gillet, Champignons de France, Pl. 692.
Fries, Icones, Pl. 24.
Ricken, Blätterpilze, Pl. 89, Fig. 3.

"PILEUS 6-12 cm. broad, convex-expanded, subumbonate, sometimes irregular and repand, *viscid,* even, glabrous, generally *fuliginous,* sometimes violet-tinged, *lurid,* virgate with innate black fibrils, margin always naked and thin. FLESH white, obsoletely lutescent, fragile. GILLS rounded behind, slightly adnexed, *broad* (up to 2 cm.), *distant* when mature, whitish at first, *finally yellow-*

ish or grayish-tinged. STEM 6-8 cm. long, 1-2 cm. thick, *stout,* firm, solid, subequal, *innately fibrillose-striate, whitish.* SPORES 6-7 x 3-4 micr., elliptical. ODOR none; TASTE *mild.*"

Said to occur in conifer woods. Perhaps in the northern part of the State.

It has not been found with certainty in America, but is reported by some American authors. The figures of European authors vary considerably as to color of cap. Schroeter says it is gray or rusty-brown; Gillet figures it pale gray with black lines radiating from center. In Michael and Fries' Icones, the gray color is mixed with a dark lurid hue. It is in the sense of the last author that the description taken from the Icones applies. The spore measurement is Schroeter's; the English authors give smaller measurements. According to Fries' Icones, and others (see Louis Maire, Bull. d. 1. Soc. Myc. France, Vol. 26, p. 251) the lack of odor and taste separate it from *T. sejunctum.*

Var. *centrale* Pk. is said to have the sooty-brown color on disk only; elsewhere it is yellow or greenish-yellow. The gills are moderately broad and close, white or yellowish. The flesh is white and the taste is mild. Spores 7.5 x 5 micr. It has not been identified within our territory.

720. Tricholoma terriferum Pk.

N. Y. State Rep. 41, 1888.

PILEUS 6-12 cm. broad, convex-plane, irregular or wavy on margin, glabrous, *viscid, alutaceous,* even, margin at first incurved. FLESH white, thick on disk, thin on margin. GILLS adnexed, emarginate, *crowded,* thin, narrow, whitish, *not becoming rufescent.* STEM 2-3 cm. long, 1-2 cm. thick, equal or subequal, solid, *floccose-scaly at apex,* floccose-fibrillose elsewhere, white. SPORES *minute,* subglobose, 3 x 2 micr., white. CYSTIDIA none. BASIDIA 20-24 x 4-5 micr., 2 to 3-spored. TASTE and ODOR not marked.

Solitary or gregarious. Frondose woods. Detroit. October. Apparently rare.

Our specimens had a subhygrophanous character and the flesh was scissile. The minute spores separate it from related species. More data are needed to place this species on a firm footing.

721.　Tricholoma resplendens Fr.　(Edible)

Hymen. Europ., 1874.

Illustrations:　Fries, Icones, Pl. 29.
　　Hard, Mushrooms, Fig. 504, p. 600, 1908.
　　Cooke, Ill., Pl. 55.
　　Gillet, Champignons de France, 695.

PILEUS 4-10 cm. broad, convex-plane, *viscid,* glabrous, *white, shining* when dry, even, margin naked and at first straight. FLESH white, rather soft, thin on margin. GILLS narrowly adnexed, emarginate, *close,* medium broad, ventricose, scarcely thickish, white, sometimes intervenose, edge entire. STEM 4-8 cm. long, 7-15 mm. thick, subequal or tapering downward, often subbulbous at base, *solid,* rarely with tubule or cavernous, glabrous, *dry,* even, white. SPORES 6-7.5 x 4 micr., short elliptical, smooth, white. CYSTIDIA and *sterile cells* none. ODOR and TASTE mild.

Gregarious or scattered. On the ground, in conifer or frondose woods. September-November (earliest record August 9). Marquette, Bay View, New Richmond, Detroit. Common in the vicinity of Ann Arbor.

The viscid pileus distinguishes this from other white Tricholomas of this size which have a mild taste and odor. Slender forms imitate *Hygrophorus eberneus,* but that has a glutinous or viscid stem. Stout forms approach *Hygrophorus sordidus* Pk. which, however, has more distant gills, a stouter stem and waxy decurrent gills. When dry, it imitates *Tricholoma columbetta,* but the pileus of the latter is said to become silky-fibrillose and the margin is at first involute and subsquamulose. The pileus is sometimes yellowish or hyaline-spotted on the disk. The stem tends to be variously curved toward base. The plant varies considerably and several *forms* have been found.　(A) Pileus conical-ovate when young, then expanded and subacutely umbonate; stem fibrillose striate. Entirely white. In woods of white pine, beech, etc., at New Richmond.　(B) Stem blue-spotted toward base, with a narrow tubule. Entirely white elsewhere, stature smaller than type. After frosts in the late fall. In oak, etc., woods, at Ann Arbor. This would seem to correspond to the blue-spotted form of *T. columbetta* mentioned by various authors; in our plant the pileus was distinctly viscid, and the stem dry. They grew under the fallen leaves during November. The spores of both these forms were typical.

**Gills becoming rufescent or reddish-spotted in age.

722. Tricholoma transmutans Pk. (EDIBLE)

N. Y. State Mus. Rep. 29, 1878.

Illustrations: Peck, N. Y. State Mus. Rep. 48, Pl. 21, Fig. 1-5, 1896.

PILEUS 4-10 cm. broad, convex-expanded, obtuse, *surface of pellicle bitter,* brownish, *reddish-brown* or tawny-red, *viscid,* glabrous or nearly so. FLESH white, rufescent in age, thin on margin. GILLS adnexed, emarginate, narrow, close, whitish or pale-yellowish, *at length rufescent or reddish-spotted,* finally sordid-blackish. STEM 6-8 cm. long, 6-12 mm. thick, equal or subequal, dry, glabrous or subfibrillose, *whitish or rufescent, solid,* sometimes cavernous above. SPORES oval-globose, 5 x 4 micr., sometimes nucleate. CYSTIDIA none. ODOR and TASTE of flesh distinctly *farinaceous,* pellicle of cap bitter.

Gregarious, scattered or subcaespitose. On the ground in frondose woods, sometimes *forming mycorhiza on the roots of the black oak.* Ann Arbor, Jackson, Detroit, New Richmond. September-October (earliest record August 9). Common in southern Michigan.

It is related to the European species *T. flavobrunneum* Fr. and *T. frumentaceum* Fr. which possess a farinaceous odor. The former has a viscid stem at first and the flesh is usually yellow. As to *T. frumentaceum,* there seems to be some uncertainty. The English authors say the spores are elliptical, and Cooke figures it as an Entoloma (Ill., Plate 470). That cannot be our plant. On the other hand, continental authors are silent as to the size of spores, although Barla mentions a variety with spherical spores. The stem of *T. transmutans* is usually solid, but often tunnelled by grubs in warm weather. When growing in the open, in pastures, etc., it is usually tufted and the pileus is irregular. It is said to be excellent eating.

723.   Tricholoma ustale Fr.

Syst. Myc., 1821.

Illustrations: Fries, Icones, Pl. 26.
  Cooke, Ill., Pl. 88.
  Michael, Führer f. Pilzfreunde, Vol. III, No. 115.
  Ricken, Blätterpilze, Pl. 88, Fig. 3 (represents form B.).
  Plate CXLVI of this Report.

PILEUS 4-10 cm., broadly convex, obtuse or subumbonate, sub-gibbous, *reddish-bay to dark chestnut,* sometimes paler, viscid, *naked, even,* not virgate nor scaly, margin persistently incurved. FLESH *white,* thickish, firm, rufescent. GILLS adnate-seceding or emarginate, moderately broad, *crowded, pure white at first* then rufescent or *reddish-brown when bruised,* edge eroded. STEM 5-8 cm. long, 8-15 mm. thick, subequal or irregularly compressed, *often rooting, stuffed,* sometimes hollow, white, becoming reddish down-wards, *floccose-pruinose,* sometimes twisted. SPORES elliptical-ovate, 6-8 x 4-5 micr., white. CYSTIDIA and *sterile cells* none. ODOR *none;* TASTE *bitter.*

Solitary or subcaespitose. On very decayed wood or leaf-debris in conifer or frondose woods. Ann Arbor, New Richmond. September-October. Rare.

This is allied to the European species *T. flavobrunneum* and *T. pessundatum* which are said to possess a distinct farinaceous odor, while in *T. ustale* this odor is lacking. From *T. transmutans* it is separable by the spores and the rooting stem. Two forms—already mentioned by Fries (Icones)—have been found in the State. (A) Large, with the base of the stem ending in a root-like prolongation which is 2-5 cm. long, and occurs in conifer woods (white pine). (B) Smaller, with a narrowed, short subrooting base, growing in frondose woods. Form (A) is illustrated by Plate CXLVI, and is rather well represented by Cooke's figure of *T. flavobrunneum* (Ill., Plate 58), which may be the same plant. There was no yellow present in our specimens.

SUBGENUS II. CORTINELLUS. Pileus *dry,* not absorbing water, nor hygrophanous; silky, fibrillose or somewhat scaly, sometimes subglabrous. Margin of pileus slightly fibrillose or floccose with remains of an evanescent cortina, except in species of "Rigida."

Cortinellus has been raised to the rank of an independent genus by some authors, e. g. Roze, (Bull. de la Soc. bot. de France, 1876), Schroeter, (Die Pilze Schlesians, Vol. 1, 1885), and Earle, (Bull. N. Y. Bot. Garden, Vol. V., 1908). The first two authors include only species whose cortina is sufficiently developed to leave a slight ring on the stem. Earle extended it as above. It seems better to keep the species which belong here subordinate on account of their close relation to the genus Tricholoma as a whole. Some of its species need further study to determine their exact position. The following sections are taken in the sense of Fries.

Section I. Genuina. Pellicle of pileus torn into fibrillose or floccose scales, its margin at first involute.

**Gills not becoming rufescent, cinereous nor blackish.*

724.   Tricholoma rutilans Fr.

Syst. Myc., 1821.

Illustrations: Cooke, Ill., Pl. 89.
    Gillet, Champignons de France, No. 697.
    Michael, Führer f. Pilzfreunde, Vol. I, No. 54.
    Ricken, Blätterpilze, Pl. 91, Fig. 1.

PILEUS 4-8 cm. broad, campanulate-expanded, dry, at first covered with a purplish-red tomentum, *soon tomentose-scaly with dark reddish scales* on the yellowish surface beneath, margin at first involute. FLESH yellow, moderately thick. GILLS rounded-adnate then emarginate, *crowded,* rather narrow, *yellow or golden-yellow,* thickish, *edge flocculose.* STEM 5-10 cm. long, curved, equal, stuffed then hollow, yellow or yellowish within and without or *variegated with minute reddish tomentose scales,* even. SPORES oblong, 6-7 x 3-4 micr., white. CYSTIDIA none; *sterile cells* on edge of gills numerous, large, clavate-inflated, narrowed toward base, 65-100 micr. long, 15-20 micr. thick above. ODOR and TASTE mild.

Solitary or caespitose on decaying wood of pine, balsam and hemlock. Isle Royale, Bay View, Houghton, New Richmond. July-October. Infrequent.

This is one of the few species of Tricholoma inhabiting wood It also departs from the other Tricholomas in having well-developed sterile cells on the edge of the gills, a modification which causes the fine floccosity and is sometimes abnormally developed. The fine tomentum of the pileus is seen under the microscope to be composed of long, intertwined fibrils filled with reddish-yellow substance. This covering of pileus and stem in well-developed specimens is quite marked and represents a sort of universal veil. This species must not be confused with *Clitocybe decora* Fr., in which the gills do not become emarginate, and the scales are blackish-brown and fibrillose.

Var. *variegatus* (*T. variegatus* Fr.). Differs in smaller size, gills white or whitish, scarcely tinged yellowish, and without sterile cells. Flesh white or yellowish-white. New Richmond. Infrequent. In both the color varies somewhat, and the reddish scales are sometimes practically lacking on the stem.

725. Tricholoma venenata Atk. (POISONOUS)

Botanical Gazette, Vol. 46, 1908.

"PILEUS 4-7 cm. broad, convex-expanded, subumbonate, center fleshy, moist, not viscid, *pale buff to clay-color,* minutely scaly with fibrous scales, with a subtomentose area over the center, the scales possessing the darker color, under the lens some of them appear nearly black. FLESH white with a dull clay-colored tinge and stain. GILLS adnexed, broadly sinuate, subdistant, whitish, thin, *dull clay color where bruised.* STEM subbulbous, with a bulb like that of *Lepiota lenticularis* (see *L. fisheri*), fibrous-striate, solid, sordid white, becoming *dull-clay color* in age or when handled. SPORES oval to broadly elliptical, smooth, 5-7 x 3.5-5 micr., white. CYSTIDIA none. ODOR and TASTE mild."

Gregarious. On the ground in frondose woods. Rochester, Oakland County. September.

This *poisonous* Tricholoma caused severe illness of a family at Rochester, Michigan, who were advised that it was harmless because of its mild taste and odor. The species was not known to the persons to whom it was referred but it was thought to be a Tricholoma and hence, since mushroom amateurs usually think that the species of that genus when mild are perfectly safe, they felt safe in its use. It is only another case in favor of the argument that it is necessary to know mushrooms by their specific distinctions, and to use only those whose identity is known to the user. Better learn a few species well than take chances. The description is adapted from that of Atkinson, and was made from some of the specimens growing in the same place as those which caused the sickness. It does not have very striking characteristics, but can be distinguished by the tendency of the plant to assume an ochraceous or dull clay color in age or when bruised. Specimens which were doubtless the same species were collected at Ann Arbor, September, 1907, and August, 1909, and were at first thought to be *T. nobilis;* the spores, however, were found to be elliptical and the plants could not be placed until after the publication of Atkinson's species. The spores of our plants were up to 8.5 micr. long, the gills rather broad, and the pileus covered with delicate ochraceous, fibrillose scales except toward the margin which was silky-fibrillose to silky-tomentose. There was no odor at first, but a slight, disagreeable odor developed. The species seems closely related to the following, and apparently imitates it in its general appearance. Hence both species should be let alone.

726. Tricholoma nobile Pk. (SUSPECTED)

N. Y. State Mus. Rep. 42, 1889.

Illustration: Plate CXLVII of this Report.

PILEUS 5-10 cm. broad, convex-expanded, subplane, obtuse, dry, whitish, *dotted by minute, drop-like grayish-ochraceous scales,* at least on disk, even, margin irregularly-wavy at maturity. FLESH pure white, thick on disk, brittle, thin on margin. GILLS truncate-adnate, varying emarginate-adnexed to spuriously decurrent, *broad,* close to subdistant, white becoming dingy yellowish in age, edge entire. STEM 4-7 cm. long, 8-16 mm. thick, *stout,* equal, sometimes slightly tapering downward, *solid,* subglabrous, innately fibrillose-striate, white becoming dingy in age. SPORES minute, spherical, smooth, subnucleate, 5-6 micr., white. CYSTIDIA and *sterile cells* none. BASIDIA 35 x 5-6 micr. ODOR slight or lacking; TASTE at first slight, slowly *unpleasant or burning.*

Gregarious. On the ground, on a lawn which was recently a grove. Ann Arbor. October. Infrequent.

This species has superficial resemblances to *T. album,* both in stature and color, but differs in its slightly scaly cap and in spores. In moist weather the pileus appears watery-stained and this indicates an affinity to the section Guttata, but the presence of scales on the pileus and its rather dry flesh point to the position here given it. It is easily confused with *T. venenata* when the spores are not examined, and hence should not be eaten. It is also likely that both *T. nobile* and *T. venenata* have been referred to *T. columbetta,* in the absence of available information on these plants, as both these species when young and fresh are rather white. The description of *T. serratifolium* Pk. very closely approximates this of *T. nobile.* It is entirely distinct from *Clitocybe piceina.*

727. Tricholoma columbetta Fr. (EDIBLE)

Syst. Myc., 1821.

Illustrations: Fries, Icones, Pl. 29.
      Bresadola, Fungh. mang. e. vel., Pl. 23.
      Gillet, Champignons de France, Pl. 671.
      Cooke, Ill., Pl. 48.

"PILEUS 5-10 cm. broad, convex-plane, obtuse, dry, rigid, *pure white, satiny-shining,* at first glabrous, then silky-fibrillose or minutely scaly, *often with stain-like, carmine, yellow, or blue spots,* margin at first incurved and minutely tomentose. FLESH white. GILLS emarginate, almost free, close, rather broad, white, not changing color, edge uneven. STEM 5-9 cm. long, 1-1.5 cm. thick, equal or unequal, *not bulbous, solid, white,* shining, fibrillose-striate. SPORES 6-7 x 4-5 micr. ODOR none. TASTE mild."

In beech and birch woods, on the ground. The silky-shining and dry, white cap and stem, mild taste and elliptical spores distinguish this species from our other white plants of the genus. It must not be confused with *T. album* Fr. which has a bitter taste, nor with *T. nobile* which has a slight burning taste; both of these lack the pure white color of *T. columbetta.* The name refers to the satiny sheen of white pigeons. Several varieties, based on the different habit and various color-stains, have been described. It has not been found with certainty in the State; see remarks under *T. resplendens.*

***Gills becoming rufescent, cinereous or blackish.*

728. Tricholoma imbricatum Fr. (EDIBLE)

Sys. Myc., 1821.

Illustrations: Hard, Mushrooms, Fig. 53, p. 73, 1908.
N. Y. State Mus. Rep. 48, Pl. 21, Fig. 6-11, 1896.
Fries, Icones, Pl. 30.
Cooke, Ill., Plates 60 and 199.
Gillet, Champignons de France, No. 676.
Ricken, Blätterpilze, Pl. 90, Fig. 1.

PILEUS 5-8 cm. broad, convex-plane, obtuse or subumbonate, *dry,* brownish-red to pale reddish-umber, *innately fibrillose-scaly,* disk lacerate-scaly, margin thin, at first incurved and pubescent. FLESH compact, firm, white, *changing to light red when bruised.* GILLS slightly adnexed, sinuate, close, moderately broad, altogether white at first, changing to reddish in age or rufescent-spotted. STEM 5-9 cm. long, 1-1.5 cm. thick, *solid,* firm, equal or subequal, white, reddish-brown at base, *apex white-mealy,* elsewhere fibrillose. SPORES broadly elliptical, 5-6.5 x 4 micr. CYSTIDIA and *sterile cells* none. BASIDIA 24-28 x 5 micr., 2-4-spored. ODOR and TASTE mild or slightly farinaceous.

Gregarious or subcaespitose. On the ground in coniferous and mixed woods.

Frequent in the north. Rare in southern Michigan. Detroit. October.

It must not be confused with *T. transmutans,* which has a viscid cap, whose surface is bitter to the tongue. The stem is solid or hollowed by grubs. *T. vaccinum* Fr. differs mainly from this in the stuffed to hollow stem and the more scaly cap; it occurs also in conifer woods.

729. Tricholoma vaccinum Fr. (SUSPECTED)

Syst. Myc., 1821.

Illustrations: Gillet, Champignons de France, No. 707.
Ricken, Blätterpilze, Pl. 90, Fig. 4.

PILEUS 4-7 cm. broad, subhemispherical to campanulate, then expanded, obtuse or subumbonate, dry, cinnamon-rufous to dark *reddish-brown,* not striate, rimose in wet weather, *at first densely scaly,* becoming fibrillose-scaly, *margin at first involute and tomentose.* FLESH rather thin except disk, white at first, becoming tinted with rufous hues. GILLS subadnate then sinuate, moderately broad, broader than the thickness of the flesh, close, pallid then *rufescent in age* or when bruised. STEM 5-7 cm. long, 10-15 mm. thick, subequal, somewhat irregular, *hollow,* fibrillose or lacerated-fibrillose, fibrils reddish-brown, pallid elsewhere but rufescent. SPORES sphoeroid, 5 x 4 micr., smooth, white. TASTE somewhat disagreeable, subastringent. ODOR similar.

Gregarious-subcaespitose. On the ground under conifers. In the northern portion of the State. August-September.

The stuffed then hollow stem and the dense fibrillose scales of the reddish-brown cap distinguish it. The color of the cap in large specimens approaches umber, but the rufous shades are always present. The margin of the pileus is distinctly tomentose.

730. Tricholoma tricolor Pk.

N. Y. State Mus. Rep. 41, 1888.

"PILEUS 5-10 cm. broad, broadly convex or nearly plane, sometimes slightly depressed in the center, firm, dry, obscurely striate on the margin, *pale alutaceous, inclining to russet.* FLESH white. GILLS adnexed, thin, narrow, close, *pale yellow,* becoming brown or purplish-brown in drying. STEM stout, 5-7 cm. long, 1-2 cm. thick, short, firm, tapering upward from the thickened or subbulbous base, *white.* SPORES broadly elliptical or subglobose, 7 micr. long."

Reported by Longyear from Chatham in the north, and from Lansing. I have not found it. The peculiar hue of the dried gills is said to characterize it.

731. Tricholoma acre Pk. (Suspected)

Bull. Torr. Bot. Club, Vol. 24, 1897.

Illustration: Plate CXLVIII of this Report.

PILEUS 4-9 cm. broad, campanulate at first, then subexpanded, plane to obtuse, virgate, *dry, pale silvery-gray or mouse-gray with innate silky fibrils,* or fibrillose-scaly on disk, sometimes whitish, even. FLESH rather thin, *firm,* white, at length tinged ashy. GILLS adnexed, emarginate, rather broad, ventricose, close, white, at length pale cinereous, edge minutely fimbriate. STEM 3-6 cm. long, 7-15 mm. thick, equal or subequal, sometimes subbulbous or tapering downward, short, *stuffed then hollow, white* or slightly cinereous, innately silky-fibrillose, shining, apex flocculose. SPORES broadly elliptical, 6-7 x 4-5 micr., smooth, with a clear cavity on one side. CYSTIDIA none; *sterile cells* on edge of gills, 30-35 x 9 micr., subclavate. ODOR none. TASTE *acrid,* sometimes tardily so.

Gregarious or subcaespitose. On the ground in frondose woods, especially oak and maple. Detroit, Ann Arbor, Jackson. September-November. Rather frequent.

The acrid Tricholoma is probably the American form of *T. muri-naceum* Bull., in the sense of Berkeley and Gillet, but digers in the closer gills and glabrous, not scaly, stem. The figures of Cooke (Ill., Plate 49) and Gillet, (Champignons de France, No. 683), are very suggestive of our plant, except in the character of the stem. *T. murinaceum* in the sense of Fries has a disagreeable, strong odor, and was originally referred by him to Hygrophorus, now *H. nitratus* Fr. Gillet's figure of *T. portentosum* is a fairly good picture of some of our plants when the gills and stem are white. *T. acre* is quite variable in size and in the shade of gray of the cap. Normally the radiating fibrils of the pileus are pale gray or silvery-gray, but in luxuriant individuals are much darker gray or blackish, and in such examples the stem may be streaked with dark fibrils. Sometimes the cap is almost entirely white or buff and then silky or obscurely virgate, sometimes somewhat fibrillose-scaly on disk. The plant is closely related to *T. terreum,* from which it differs in its acrid taste, its firmer flesh, larger size, presence of cystidia and flocculose, edge of gills and broader spores.

732.   Tricholoma terreum Fr.   (EDIBLE)

Epicrisis, 1836.

Illustrations: Hard, Mushrooms, Fig. 55, p. 76, 1908.
Swanton, Fungi, Pl. 8, Fig. 9.
Michael, Führer f. Pilzfreunde, Vol. II, No. 92.
Bresadola, Fungh. mang. e. vel., Pl. 24.
Patouillard, Tab. Analyt., No. 307.
Ricken, Blätterpilze, Pl. 92, Fig. 4.
Gillet, Champignons de France, No. 704.
Cooke, Ill., Pl. 50.
Peck, N. Y. State Mus. Mem. 4, Pl. 45, 1900 (as var. *fragrans*).
Plate CXLIX of this Report.

PILEUS 2.5-6 cm. broad, *thin,* convex-campanulate or nearly plane, dry, subumbonate, *gray,* grayish-brown or mouse-color, *innately fibrillose to fibrillose-floccose and at length scaly,* not striate. FLESH white, cinerascent or gray near surface of pileus, thin. GILLS adnate, then emarginate and uncinate, close but distinct, white, pale ashy or cinerascent, sometimes yellowish-stained, medium broad, edge entire.   STEM 2.5-4 cm. long, 4-8 mm. thick, equal, straight or slightly curved, *solid or persistently fibrous-stuffed, readily splitting lengthwise,* white, whitish or cinerascent, subrigid, *fragile.*   SPORES *minute, nucleate,* narrowly oblong-ovate, 5-6 x 3, smooth.   CYSTIDIA *none, sterile cells* short or lacking.   ODOR and TASTE *farinaceous,* especially when plant is crushed.

Gregarious or subcaespitose. On the ground in grassy places in frondose woods, thickets, etc. Ann Arbor, Detroit, New Richmond. August-November. Rather frequent about Ann Arbor.

After reading the descriptions and remarks of a dozen writers concerning this species and related ones such as *T. scalpturatum* Fr. and *T. squarrulosum* Bres., and adding one's own observations, it becomes clear that we have here a series of many forms which run so close into each other that the amateur will hardly be able to diagnose them satisfactorily in most cases. This fact is already recognized by the number of varieties which have been described both under *T. terreum* and *T. scalpturatum.* The above description applies to the plants which have been found in frondose woods of southern Michigan. Variations will be found in which the pileus is more densely scaly with almost blackish scales on center, and others where the color is pale silvery-gray. The color of flesh and gills may remain almost white, or there may be an ashy tinge in all parts of the plant. Several characters seem to be constant in our plants, viz. the fragility, the nucleated narrow spores, and the fibrous nature of the interior of the stem. By these characters and the taste it is separable from *T. acre.* Authors give various shapes and sizes for the spores, which fact indicates that there are several independent species at present not separated. Bresadola has segregated a dark, scaly species whose spores measure 7-9 x 4-5 micr., as *T. squarrulosum. T. scalpturatum* (Fr.) Bres. has a well-developed but evanescent cortina at first; this approaches our form, and has the same spores, but lacks the distinct farinaceous odor. Our typical plants had no sterile cells on the edge of the gills. A form found at New Richmond had short cystidia and gills whose edges were minutely flocculose and spotted with drab-color, darker than the rest of the gills. Peck has named our form with the farinaceous odor var. *fragans.* The farinaceous odor seems to be the most common character of the American form of *T. terreum.*

733.   Tricholoma fumescens Pk.

N. Y. State Rep. 31, 1879.

Illustration: Hard, Mushrooms, Fig. 54, p. 75.

PILEUS 2-6 cm. broad, convex-plane, regular at first, then undulate, obtuse, dry, *covered with a minute, appressed tomentum,* whitish to pale grayish-brown, darker where handled, even, margin at first incurved. FLESH rather thin. GILLS rounded behind at first, then acuminate adnexed, narrow, *very crowded,* whitish, *changing to bluish-black in age or when bruised,* easily separable from trama of pileus. STEM 2-6 cm. long, 5-10 mm. thick, short, rather stout, *whitish then brownish,* solid, becoming cavernous and splitting, pruinose at apex. SPORES narrow, subfusiform-elliptical, 5-6.5 x 3 micr.; *sterigmata* prominent, 3-4 micr. long. ODOR and TASTE slightly farinaceous.

Gregarious or subcaespitose. On the ground, in low, frondose woods. Jackson, Ann Arbor. September-October. Infrequent.

Recognizable by the narrow, crowded gills, which become bluish-black in fresh specimens if bruised; in age or when dried they are almost as black as old gills of *Agaricus campestris.* The pileus and stem do not change as much, inclining to brownish, and in this differ markedly from *T. fuligineum.* The latter also possesses subdistant and broader gills. Our plant is not frequent, having been collected only thrice. The separable gills ally it to those species which W. G. Smith placed under the genus Lepista.

734. Tricholoma fuligineum Pk.

N. Y. State Rep. 41, 1888.

Illustration: Plate CXLIX of this Report.

PILEUS 3-7 cm. broad, convex, then expanded-subdepressed, or obtuse, often irregular, sometimes with sinus on one side, *sooty-brown to dark grayish-brown,* becoming blackish on handling, dry, minutely innately scaly or fibrillose, even. FLESH white at first, cinerascent, scissile. GILLS adnate or adnexed, then emarginate, *subarid,* very tough when dry, *close to subdistant,* moderately broad, whitish or cinereous, *becoming black when bruised.* STEM 3-6 cm. long, 6-10 mm. thick, short, rarely elongated, solid or spongy-stuffed, equal or subequal, innately fibrillose, pruinose at apex, whitish or cinereous, *blackish when handled.* SPORES narrow, elliptical-fusiform, 7-9 x 4-5 micr., smooth, white. CYSTIDIA and *sterile cells* lacking. BASIDIA about 30 x 6-7 micr. ODOR and TASTE more or less farinaceous.

Gregarious or caespitose. On the ground among mosses, leaves, etc., frondose woods of oak and maple. Jackson, Detroit, Ann Arbor. September-October. Infrequent.

Somewhat variable in size and shape, etc., under different conditions of weather and situation. It differs from *T. fumescens* in that the entire plant becomes sooty when dried, and it has larger spores and gills. The gills often assume a reddish hue when bruised, then become black, as in *Russula nigricans.* The stem is sometimes slightly floccose at first, as if frosted, and occasionally becomes cavernous. Small forms of *T. cinerascens* have a more watery pileus and the gills do not turn sooty-black. Dr. O. E. Fisher reports that it has appeared abundantly in his back yard on discarded mushroom beds.

Section II. Rigida. Pellicle of the pileus rigid, with a tendency to crack into small smooth scales, sometimes punctate-granulose; neither viscid, floccose-scaly nor fibrillose. Flesh of pileus rigid, somewhat cartilaginous.

*Gills not becoming reddish nor cinereous, nor yellow-stained.

735. Tricholoma saponaceum Fr. (UNPALATABLE)

Epicrisis, 1836.

Illustrations: Hard, Mushrooms, Fig. 56, p. 77, 1908.
Michael, Führer f. Pilzfreunde, Vol. II, No. 90.
Ricken, Blätterpilze, Pl. 93, Fig. 1.
Cooke, Ill., Plates 91 and 216.
Gillet, Champignons de France, No. 698.
Fries, Icones, Pl. 32.

PILEUS 4-8 cm. broad, convex-expanded, firm, glabrous or becoming cracked to form small scales, not virgate, pale *livid-brown to lead-gray* but variable in color, often olive tinged, margin at first naked and incurved. FLESH white, *becoming pinkish,* thick, firm. GILLS adnato-emarginate then uncinate, subdistant, *distinct,* rather broad, *whitish, not cinerascent,* edge entire. STEM 5-8 cm. long, 1.5-2 cm. thick, rather stout, *ventricose, attenuated or subradicating below,* solid, fibrous-fleshy, apex flocculose, *becoming pink within,* white without, glabrous varying to floccose or minutely dark-scaly. SPORES minute, elliptical-ovate, smooth, 5 x 3-3.5 micr. ODOR and TASTE strongly oily-farinaceous (soapy), distasteful.

Solitary or gregarious. In frondose woods, on the ground. September-October. Ann Arbor, New Richmond, Detroit. Infrequent. The colors of the pileus vary and are difficult to describe, sometimes varying from whitish to grayish-brown or smoky-brown. The gills are said to become greenish or rufescent at times. The odor, color of the flesh and minute spores distinguish it. Where bruised the flesh of the stem retains the pink tinge in a persistent manner, and this character is quite marked. It is unfit for food on account of its taste. The odor and taste are sometimes very slight. *T. pallidum* Pk. is probably a variation of this species.

***Gills becoming stained or changing to ashy or reddish in age.*

736. Tricholoma laticeps sp. nov.

Illustration: Plate CL of this Report.

PILEUS 3-10 cm. broad, *rigid,* broadly convex, obtuse, *smoky-umber to blackish,* moist, even, *glabrous, or punctate-granulose on disk,* margin at first strongly decurved, then spreading naked. FLESH firm, brittle, *thick,* thinner at margin, *cinerascent, scissile.* GILLS broadly adnexed, emarginate, close to subdistant, *broad,* white, at last cinereous, edge sometimes eroded. STEM *short,* rigid, spongy-solid, 1-3 cm. long, 7-16 mm. thick, equal or subequal, white or pallid, cinerascent within, innately silky. SPORES short and broadly elliptical to subglobose, smooth, 6-7 x 5-6 micr., white. BASIDIA 30 x 6-7 micr. CYSTIDIA and *sterile cells* none. ODOR and TASTE mild.

Gregarious to caespitose. On the bare ground or among mosses or in grassy places, in conifer or frondose woods or groves. Ann Arbor, Detroit, New Richmond. September-November. Infrequent.

Distinguished by its very short stem and relatively broad pileus which hugs the ground so as to hide the stem. The pileus is often broader in one diameter. It seems to be related to *Tricholoma cartilagineum,* but the gills are broad and subdistant in well-developed specimens, and the pellicle is rarely granular-punctate and then only on the disk. The pellicle is rather adnate and composed of long, narrow, horizontal cells. It cannot be referred to *T. lugubre* Pk. since that species is described as having narrow and close gills; nor to *T. tumidum* Fr. whose stem is longer, and whose gills have a rufescent tinge. The scissile flesh indicates a hygrophanous condition, but this is not marked. Its edibility was not tested.

Section III. Sericella. Pileus without a distinct pellicle, silky or glabrous, very dry; neither moist, viscid, hygrophanous, nor distinctly scaly. Pileus opaque, rather thin.

737. Tricholoma sulphureum Fr. (Unpalatable)

Syst. Myc., 1821. (As Clitocybe.)

Illustrations: Cooke, Ill., Pl. 62.
Gillet, Champignons de France, No. 703.
Bresadola, Fungh. mang. e. vel., Pl. 27.
Patouillard, Tab. Analyt., No. 507.
Berkeley, Outlines, Pl. 4, Fig. 4.
Swanton, Fungi, Pl. 44, Fig. 1.
Hard, Mushrooms, Fig. 46, p. 65.

PILEUS 2-8 cm. broad, convex-expanded, mostly *umbonate,* at first silky, soon glabrous, *sulphur-yellow to olivaceous-yellow,* usually tinged brown on disk, subgibbous, even, margin decurved. FLESH yellow or yellowish, thick on disk. GILLS adnexed with tooth, emarginate at length, *subdistant, yellow,* moderately broad, thick, firm. STEM 4-8 cm. long, 5-10 mm. thick, equal or variously enlarged, sometimes curved, fleshy-fibrous, innately fibrillose, stuffed, sometimes compressed, yellow to olivaceous-yellow, yellowish within. SPORES elliptical-oval, 8-10 x 5-6 micr., smooth. ODOR strong, foetid or of coal-tar; TASTE disagreeable.

Gregarious. On the ground in frondose woods of maple, birch, oak, etc. Houghton, Ann Arbor. July-September. Infrequent.

Our plant is well illustrated by Cooke, but it is usually a less deep yellow, and often tinged with olive or reddish-brown on the cap. It is well marked by the disagreeable, coal-tar odor and taste, by the subdistant gills and by the spores. Bresadola (Funghi mang. et. vel.) gives the spores as warty; this cannot be our plant. In Stevenson the spores are given too small, being nearer those of *T. sulphurescens* Bres., which also has the odor and color of *T. sulphureum* but whose gills are said to be crowded and whitish. Unler a lens the dry pileus is often seen with micaceous-shining spots. It differs from *T. chrysenteroides* Pk. in its disagreeable odor, subdistant gills and stuffed to hollow stem.

738. Tricholoma chrysenteroides Pk.

N. Y. Mus. Rep. 24, 1872.

"PILEUS 2.5-5 cm. broad, convex or plane, *not umbonate,* firm, dry, slightly silky or glabrous, *pale yellow or buff,* becoming dingy with age. FLESH pale yellow. GILLS *close*, emarginate, yellowish, dingy or pallid in age, marked with transverse veinlets along the upper edge, intervenose. STEM 5-7 cm. long, 6-8 mm. thick, firm, equal, *solid*, glabrous, fibrillose-striate, yellowish within and without. SPORES elliptical, 7-10 x 5-6 micr. ODOR and TASTE *farinaceous.*"

Gregarious. On the ground in woods.

This species has not with certainty been collected within the State. The description is adopted from Peck, and included for the sake of comparison.

739. Tricholoma odorum Pk.

Torrey Bot. Club. Bull., Vol. 25, 1898.

PILEUS 2-5 cm. broad, convex-expanded, obtuse, glabrous, "soft like kid," shining when young, *waxy yellow to pale tan,* even. FLESH thick, concolor. GILLS adnexed, emarginate, *rather broad,* subdistant, thick, *whitish, tinged flesh-pink,* edge entire. STEM 3-7 cm. long, 4-10 mm. thick, equal or subbulbous, *stuffed then hollow,* subflexuous, silky-fibrillose, yellowish white, darker yellow at base and within, pruinose at apex. SPORES broadly elliptic-ovate, smooth, 7-9 x 5-6 micr., variable, white. CYSTIDIA and *sterile cells* none. ODOR rather strong, reminding one of that of *T. sulfureum;* TASTE farinaceous.

Gregarious. On the ground in beech and pine woods. New Richmond. September. Rare.

This seems to approach *T. sulfureum* and is probably a variation of it. Further data are necessary to establish it fully. The incarnate tinge to the whitish gills, and the peculiar odor are characters which distinguish it.

740. Tricholoma carneum Fr.

Syst. Myc., 1821.

Illustrations: Fries, Icones, Pl. 40, Fig. 3.
        Cooke, Ill., Pl. 96.
        Patouillard, Tab. Analyt., No. 614.

PILEUS 1.5-2 cm. broad, convex-plane, obtuse, sometimes umbonate, even, glabrous or *subpruinose,* testaceous when young, then *flesh color* to whitish tan, margin thin and at length spreading or recurved. FLESH thickish on disk, white, soft, rather fragile. GILLS sinuate-adnexed, uncinate, at length subdecurrent, *crowded,* rather narrow, *pure white,* edge mostly even. STEM 1.5-2.5 cm. long, 2-3 mm. thick, equal, *fibrous,* hollow, sometimes compressed, *tinged flesh color,* pruinose above, subtomentose below. SPORES minute, oblong, 4-5 x 2.5 micr. smooth, white. ODOR and TASTE none or subfarinaceous.

Gregarious or subcaespitose. On the ground among leaves and debris in frondose woods. Ann Arbor. August-September. Infrequent.

This small species of Tricholoma is well-marked by the incarnate color of cap and stem which contrasts with the pure white of the gills. Fries has described a species near it, *T. paeonium,* which is said to differ in the "ruber"-red color of cap which does not fade as in our plants; the latter species also has a softer stem than ours.

SUBGENUS III. MELANOLEUCA. Pileus glabrous, either watery-spotted, moist or hygrophanous; not viscid (except when very water-soaked), nor silky, scaly nor granular. FLESH soft, spongy, or very thin, moist, watery or hygrophanous.

Section I. Guttata. Pileus fleshy, fragile, watery-spotted or rivulose. Usually caespitose.

741. Tricholoma unifactum Pk. var.

N. Y. State Mus., Bull. 105, 1906.

Illustration: Ibid.

PILEUS 3-8 cm. broad, *convex,* dull white *mottled with watery spots,* subpruinose, even, creamy-buff in age. FLESH thick on disk, thin elsewhere, white, fragile. GILLS adnexed, becoming emarginate, narrow, narrowed anteriorly, crowded, whitish, edge entire. STEM 5-10 cm. long, prolonged by insertion into a crack in the log, 8-15 mm. broad, equal or tapering upward, curved, solid, even, floccose-pruinose, tomentose at base. SPORES subglobose, minute, 3-4.5 x 3.5 micr., smooth, white. CYSTIDIA and *sterile cells* none. ODOR and TASTE slight.

Caespitose. On decayed charred log, probably hemlock, in mixed woods of ravines. New Richmond. September. Rare.

The plants from which Peck derived his description grew on the ground under hemlock trees and in that situation formed a thick fleshy mass from which the stems arose. Although our plants were caespitosely united only at the base, and grew from a woody substratum, I have scarcely any doubt that they are the same. When dried, the cap, gills and base of stem are ochraceous. In some ways it approaches *Pleurotus elongatipes* Pk. but the stem is solid and scarcely eccentric, and the pileus is spotted with watery marks. *T. conglobatus* Fr. (Eddelbuttel, Ann. Mycol., Vol. 9, p. 512) differs in its brownish-gray pileus and spores 6-7 x 5 micr., although Schroeter (Die Pilze Schlesiens, p. 660) says the cap of that species is often whitish. Our plants are very close to *T. boreale* Fr., whose spores, according to Massee (European fungus Flora) are the same, but whose pileus is at first bright flesh color, then fades to whitish.

Section II. Spongiosa. Pileus fleshy, compact, becoming spongy, obtuse, even, glabrous, moist. Neither hygrophanous nor viscid. (Water soaked specimens sometimes become subgelatinous; the pileus in all cases absorbs water in wet weather.)

742. Tricholoma album Fr.   (Sense of Fries)   (UNPALATABLE)

Syst. Myc., 1821.

Illustrations: Fries, Icones, Pl. 43.
        Cooke, Ill., Pl. 65.
        Berkeley, Outlines, Pl. 4, Fig. 6.
        Patouillard, Tab. Analyt., No. 615.

"PILEUS 6-10 cm. broad, convex then plane and depressed, not umbonate, *glabrous,* dry, even, margin at first involute at length repand, *sometimes entirely white, sometimes yellowish especially on the disk.* FLESH tough, moderately thick, but not compact. GILLS more or less emarginate, close, up to 8 mm. broad, white, unchanging. STEM 6-10 cm. long, 8-12 mm. thick, attenuated upwards, *solid, elastic,* externally fibrous, glabrous, obsoletely pruinose at apex under lens, concolor. ODOR none; TASTE acrid, unpleasant." SPORES (Massee, Stevenson, Winter) elliptical, 5-6 x 2.5-3; (Romell) 6-7 x 4-4½; (Ricken) lanceolate, 7-8 x 3-3.5 micr.

This species has not yet been found with certainty in the State. The description is adopted from that of Fries in Icones *T. venenata* Atk. and *T. nobile* Pk. approach it by their external characters, but if the spore-measurements given by the English authors actually belong to this species, then *T. nobile* is quite distinct by its spherical spores, and *T. venenata* by its larger spores. It is easy to confuse *T. album* with *T. panoeolum* in some of its forms when young and white, but later the changing gills of the latter species mark it sufficiently. The pileus is said to be entirely glabrous, and this also separates *T. album* from *T. venenata* and *T. nobile*. The taste is given by Fries as "acrid" in Icones, and "bitter" in Hymen. Europ. In Lindblad's Svampbok the pileus is said to become sordid-stained an hour after being bruised, the odor is said to be strongly radishy; and the plant is said to have a sharp burning taste after being chewed awhile. Some authors consider it *poisonous,* and it is evidently not edible, and must be regarded close to *T. venenata* in this respect. It appears that this species needs further study, and it is desirable that continental authors give us exact data concerning the spores of their plants.

743. Tricholoma acerbum Fr. (Unpalatable)

Syst. Mycol., 1821.

Illustrations: Gillet, Champignons de France, No. 662.
Plate CLI of this Report.

PILEUS 7-10 cm. broad, firm, convex-expanded, *obtuse,* dry, sub-pruinose, soft to the touch, *dull buff to yellowish-white, or whitish with a flesh color tinge,* margin at first inrolled and *obscurely ridged.* FLESH white, thick on disk, thin on margin. GILLS emarginate with decurrent tooth, *narrow, crowded,* whitish becoming creamy-white or slightly rufescent, edge entire. STEM 4-6 cm. long, 1-2 cm. at apex, 2-2.5 cm. below, sometimes abruptly short-rooting, *solid,* firm, at first bulbous then *tapering upward,* at first covered by a thin satiny tomentum or pruinosity, becoming fibrillose, whitish becoming dingy where handled. SPORES minute, spherical, nucleate, 4-5 micr., white. CYSTIDIA none. BASIDIA about 30 x 5-6 micr. TASTE *very bitter;* ODOR scarcely agreeable, somewhat aromatic-farinaceous.

Gregarious to subcaespitose. On the ground in frondose woods. Ann Arbor, Detroit, New Richmond, Bay View. June-October (earliest record, June 11). Frequent.

The bitter taste and changing gills and stem distinguish *T. acerbum* from *T. laterarium* Pk. with which it is easily confused. Both species are marked by the narrow, crowded gills, spherical spores, the whitish to pale yellowish-tan cap, and the slight ridges which are found on the margin of the cap. The gills are sometimes spuriously decurrent, when it might be confused with small forms of *Clitocybe candida,* but the latter has a mild taste and its pileus becomes concave. Superficially it approaches *T. panoeolum* var. *caespitosum* also. Bresadola (Fungh. mang.) assigns to it obovate spores, measuring 6-7 x 3-3.5 micr., while others give them globose.

744. Tricholoma laterarium Pk. (EDIBLE)

N. Y. State Mus. Rep. 26, 1874 (Buffalo Soc. Nat. Hist., 1873).

Illustration: Hard, Mushrooms, Fig. 47, p. 66, 1908.

"PILEUS 5-10 cm. broad, convex-expanded, sometimes slightly depressed in center, pruinose, whitish, *disk often tinged with brick-red or brown,* the thin margin marked with slight, subdistant, short, radiating ridges. FLESH white. GILLS emarginate, decurrent in slight lines, *narrow, crowded, white.* STEM 5-7 cm. long, nearly equal, solid, white. SPORES globose, 4-5 micr. diameter."
Gregarious. On the ground in conifer woods. Probably in the northern part of the State.

I have no notes on this species, hence have given Peck's description. No data are at hand as to its taste and odor. It is close to *T. acerbum,* apparently only distinguishable by its mild taste and white gills, and may prove to be identical with that species.

745. Tricholoma leucocephalum Fr.

Epicrisis, 1836.

Illustrations: Fries, Icones, Pl. 43.
Cooke, Ill., Pl. 78.

PILEUS 3-6 cm. broad, *thin,* convex then plane, obtuse, even, moist, glabrous, the slight silkiness disappearing, *white.* FLESH compact, *white, watery in wet weather.* GILLS rounded behind, *free,* thin, crowded, *pure white,* edge very entire. STEM 5-7 cm. long, 4-8 mm. thick, subcartilaginous to fibrous, *hollow, solid at the narrowed, rooting base, glabrous,* white. SPORES 6-8 x 3-4 micr.

(perhaps longer when fully mature), elliptic-ovate, apiculate. ODOR and TASTE distinctly *farinaceous.*
Gregarious. On the ground in conifer woods. Marquette. September. Rare.
The description is adapted from the Icones of Fries. The figures cited represent a plant like that of form (B) of *T. resplendens* (which see), whose stem was minutely hollow, but whose cap was distinctly viscid. *T. leucocephalum* has been found but once, and is apparently rare. It has been confused, according to Fries, with *T. columbetta* and *T. album;* "the former is mild and edible, the latter bitter and very poisonous, while *T. leucocephalum* has a strong odor of fresh meal."

746. Tricholoma fumosiluteum Pk.

N. Y. State Mus. Rep. 27, 1875.

"PILEUS 3-7 cm. broad, convex-expanded, *moist, glabrous,* smoky-*yellow.* FLESH white or yellowish under the subseparable cuticle. GILLS rounded behind, deeply emarginate at length, *broad,* close, white. STEM 6-10 cm. long, *rather elongated,* 6-10 mm. thick, glabrous, *hollow,* white. SPORES globose, 4.5-6 micr. diameter. ODOR and TASTE farinaceous when flesh is crushed."
Gregarious to subcaespitose. On the ground in frondose woods. Ann Arbor. October. Rare.
The description is adapted from that of Peck. "The disk of the pileus is often darker, and sometimes spotted." My specimens show a tendency for the stem to become elongated relative to the width of the pileus.

747. Tricholoma personatum Fr. (EDIBLE)

Syst. Myc., 1821.

Illustrations: Atkinson, Mushrooms, Fig. 87 and 88, 1900.
  Murrill, Mycologia, Vol. 2, Pl. 19, Fig. 1.
  Hard, Mushrooms, Fig. 61 and 62, p. 84, 1908.
  Marshall, Mushroom Book, Pl. 21, p. 72, 1905.
  Ricken, Blätterpilze, Pl. 95, Fig. 3.
  Michael, Führer f. Pilzfreunde, Vol. II, No. 89 (as *T. bicolor*), and Vol. III, No. 113.
  Peck, N. Y. Mus. Rep. 48, Pl. 22, 1896.
  See also Cooke, Gillet, Berkeley, etc.

PILEUS 5-12 cm. broad, convex-expanded to plane, obtuse, glabrous, moist or water-soaked, *variable in color,* grayish to brownish,
tinged with lilac, lavender or purplish hues, fading in age to pale
livid or sordid-white, even, *margin at first involute and villose-
pruinose,* at length spreading, naked and undulate. FLESH laven-
der-tinged when fresh, fading to whitish, often water-soaked in wet
weather. GILLS slightly truncate-adnate to almost free, rather
broad, crowded, *at first blue, then lavender, grayish-rufescent, etc.,*
separable from pileus, edge entire. STEM 3-7 cm. long, 1-2 cm.
thick, rather short, stout, at first bulbous, becoming clavate or
tapering upwards or sometimes equal, *solid, at first blue then persistently lavender or lilac,* sometimes fading to pale livid, etc.,
frosted by minute, furfuraceous-squamules, glabrescent, pale grayish within. SPORES narrowly elliptical, smooth, non-nucleate, 7-8
x 4-5 micr. (rarely longer), *pale flesh color in mass.* CYSTIDIA
and *sterile cells* none. BASIDIA 28-30 x 6-7   micr., 2-4-spored.
ODOR and TASTE mild.

Gregarious or subcaespitose. On the ground among decaying
leaves or brush piles, in mixed or frondose, open or thin woods.
Throughout the State. September-November. (Earliest record
August 25.) Common.

This is a favorite for the table. It is easily known among the
large Tricholomas by its bluish or lavender colors when fresh, and
in this respect imitates some of the Cortinarii, but such confusion
will not lead to trouble, as the latter are equally safe. *Cortinarius
michiganensis* and *Cortinarius albatus* have similar colors, but are
distinguished by the cortina when young, and the darker gills when
old. It is not easily confused with *Cortinarius violaceous,* as some
have stated, since that species is long-stemmed, has a much darker
color and the cap is minutely scaly. *T. nudum* is a more slender
plant, and differs mainly in its deeper blue or purplish colors on
cap and stem, and the naked margin when young. All are edible.
Our plant loves to grow among heavy masses of fallen or decaying
leaves which often completely hide it in the late autumn. It varies
in color, so that several varieties have been named; these varieties
are mostly the result of weather conditions, of habitat or of late
growth. After having been soaked by rains it is less palatable. The
color of the spores shows it to be intermediate between Tricholoma
and Entoloma, and induced W. G. Smith and others to call it
Lepista personata.

748. Tricholoma nudum Fr. (EDIBLE)

Syst. Myc., 1821.

Illustrations: N. Y. State Mus. Bull. 116, Pl. 104, Fig. 1-9, 1907.
  Cooke, Ill., Pl. 67 (too faded).
  Gillet, Champignons de France, No. 685.
  Bresadola, I. Funghi mang. e. vel., Pl. 30.
  Ricken, Blätterpilze, Pl. 95, Fig. 4.

PILEUS *3-8 cm. broad, thin,* convex-expanded to plane, obtuse, sometimes depressed, glabrous, even, soft to the touch, moist, *purplish-violaceous to lavender,* fading to pale violaceous-brown or dingy rose-color, *margin at first incurved and naked.* FLESH tinged violet, at length whitish, thin, rather firm. GILLS truncate-adnate then subdecurrent and slightly sinuate, crowded, narrow, violaceous at first. STEM 3-7 cm. long, 4-10 mm. thick, *slender or moderately stout,* solid, equal or slightly enlarged at base, silky-pruinose, glabrescent, purplish-violaceous then grayish-brown. SPORES 6-7 x 4-5 micr., elliptical, sordid flesh color in mass. ODOR and TASTE mild or slightly acid.

Gregarious or subcaespitose. On the ground in woods. Ann Arbor. September.

This is intermediate in size between *T. personatum* and *T. ionides,* and all three have similar colors. *T. ionides,* which has been reported from the state by Longyear, is known by its conic-campanulate pileus, which is at first flocculose on the margin, its stuffed to hollow stem, and whitish gills and spores; its cap is 2-5 cm. broad. Huyot (Soc. Myc. de France, Vol. 16, p. 95) states that it can always be distinguished, since the flesh of the stem is uniformly *blue,* while that of *T. personatum* is pallid or grayish. Peck says the stem of his plants was stuffed or hollow, while European authors describe it as solid. The spores, as in *T. personatum,* are pale flesh color, and show the relation of these plants to the rosy-spored group; but as it is now pretty well admitted that the sum of the other characters of a plant are of more generic importance than the spore-color, especially where it is not very marked, it would seem best to keep them in this genus.

749.   Tricholoma tumidum Fr.

Syst. Mycol., 1821.

Illustrations: Cooke, Ill., Pl. 93.
    Michael, Führer f. Pilzfreunde, Vol. III, No. 111.
    Plate CLII of this Report.

PILEUS 6-10 cm. broad, firm, convex-expanded, then plane or broadly depressed, *moist,* regular at length wavy, glabrous, sometimes watery-spotted, clouded with *gray to brownish-gray especially on disk,* whitish on margin, even, margin thin and *at first tomentulose.* FLESH white, slightly and slowly cinerascent, thin on margin, rather brittle. GILLS adnexed, then deeply sinuate, *broad, subdistant,* ventricose, at first shining white then slightly cinerascent, brittle, scarcely intervenose, edge entire. STEM 5-7 cm. long, 1.5-2 cm. thick, *stout, solid,* compact spongy within, subequal or subbulbous, sometimes abruptly subradicating, *glabrous,* slightly scurfy at apex, white then slightly cinerascent. SPORES minute, subfusiform-elliptic, smooth, 5-6 x 3 micr., white. CYSTIDIA and *sterile cells* none. ODOR and TASTE mild.

Scattered or singly. On the ground among fallen leaves, etc., in frondose woods. October. Ann Arbor. Infrequent.

A rather noble plant when fresh, rather firm at first, becoming brittle. It was placed by Fries in section Rigida, but is placed here because of its similarity to *T. cinerascens.* The pileus has a slightly raised circular ridge a short distance from the margin as indicated in Cooke's figure. In some individuals the pileus was marked by watery spots toward the margin (like those on the stem of *Lactarius scrobiculatus*) and sometimes it was slightly ochraceousstained. The thin margin at length becomes subplicate-crenate. The stems are not ventricose nor is the cap as dark, but otherwise it seems to have all the marks of the species figured by Cooke and Michael. It differs from *T. cinerascens* which it approaches closely in color, by its more rigid habit and by its subdistant gills which do not separate easily from the trama of the pileus.

750. Tricholoma cinerascens Fr. (EDIBLE)

Monographia, 1863.

Illustration: Ibid, Pl. 153.
Ricken, Blätterpilze, Pl. 97, Fig. 2.
Plate CLIII of this Report.

PILEUS 5-10 cm. broad, convex then expanded, obtuse, obscurely floccose-tomentose or glabrous, *white or buff, then gray,* sub-unicolorous, *moist,* even, margin thin, naked. FLESH white, thick on disk. GILLS adnexed, slightly emarginate, *close, medium broad,* dingy white, becoming yellowish, *easily separable from pileus,* edge entire. STEM 5-7 cm. long, 1-1.5 cm. thick, equal, except spongy-thickened base, which is often mycelioid-tomentose, *spongy-stuffed to hollow,* sometimes curved, white, then cinerascent, subglabrous, pruinose at apex. SPORES minute, elliptical, 5 x 3 micr. (rarely longer). TASTE when crushed, farinaceous. ODOR subfarinaceous.

Gregarious to caespitose. On the ground among decaying leaves in frondose woods. October. Ann Arbor. Infrequent.

The pileus is more spongy and less firm than in *T. tumidum,* the gills are close and become more or less dingy yellowish. The pileus feels glabrous, although there is an innate floccosity to it. The gills separate from the trama of the pileus as in the genera Lepista, Paxillus and Gomphidius, etc. It belies its name, since the fresh plant may become only slightly cinereous.

751. Tricholoma panoeolum var. caespitosum Bres.

Fungi Trid., Vol. 2, 1892.

Illustration: Ibid, Pl. 153.

PILEUS 5-12 cm. (sometimes up to 20 cm.) broad, convex-expanded, then irregular or sinuate-lobed, sometimes eccentric, *whitish, buff, grayish-brown or dingy tan,* sometimes *shining white,* glabrous or obscurely flocculose on disk, *cuticle subcartilaginous, margin persistently incurved.* FLESH rather firm, very moist in wet weather or water-soaked and then fragile. GILLS *very crowded, narrow, easily separable from the pileus, varying subdecurrent or truncate adnate or slightly sinuate,* white at first, *soon dingy-flesh color.* STEM 3-8 cm. long, 8-15 mm. thick, subequal, solid or spongy within, at first covered with white frostiness, then fibrillose, apex scurfy, pallid-whitish. SPORES elliptic-ovate, minute, smooth, 5-6 x 3-3.5 micr., whitish or pale dingy flesh color in mass. ODOR slight or of rancid meal. TASTE slowly peppery or disagreeable, remaining in the mouth a long time.

Caespitose, rarely solitary. On the ground in frondose or conifer woods. Ann Arbor, Detroit, Bay View, Marquette and New Richmond. September-November. Frequent.

This is one of the most difficult species of Agarics to place properly. Its gills which are often subdecurrent tend to throw it into the genus Clitocybe; and the ease with which they separate from the trama of the pileus is characteristic of the genus Paxillus. The attachment of the gills varies furthermore, sometimes becoming sinuate, sometimes not at all decurrent. In other respects the gills form the very best means of recognizing this species, as indicated in the description. The plants also vary in size and color; clusters composed of several very large specimens are sometimes found, which simulate *Clitocybe gigantea* and *Clitocybe candida,* but differ from both in that the gills become flesh color, and in the tardily peppery taste. After being exposed to rains, the plants become water-soaked, take on a flesh-tint throughout and are quite fragile. It is probable that *T. rancidulum* Banning is the same plant.

Section III. Hygrophana. Pileus thin, hygrophanous. Flesh at first compact, then soft, moist and hygrophanous.

The color of the pileus changes as the moisture escapes, usually becoming much paler. Patouillard (Les Hymenomycetes d'Europe, p. 36, 1887) has separated certain species, e. g., *T. melaleuca,* from this section on the basis of their echinulate spores, spongy consistency and grayish or blackish tinge, and erected the genus Melaleuca for them. Fayod (Ann. d. Sci. Nat., 7 ser., vol. 9, p. 348) did the same, including *T. brevipes, T. nudum, T. grammopodium, T. personatum* and *T. sordidum* in that genus, and using mainly the irregular hyphae of the gill-trama as the separation character. It has seemed best however, to keep the Friesian arrangement of this section until the data are more complete. Only a few species of this section have so far been identified.

752. Tricholoma melaleucum Fr.

Syst. Mycol., 1821.

Illustrations: Fries, Icones, Pl. 44.
Ricken, Blätterpilze, Pl. 96, Fig. 5.
Gillet, Champignons de France, No. 682.
Cooke, Ill., Pl. 119.
Hard, Mushrooms, Fig. 50, p. 69, 1908.
Michael, Führer f. Pilzfreunde, Vol. III, No. 112.
Murrill, Mycologia, Vol. 3, Pl. 49, Fig. 4.

PILEUS 3-7 cm. broad, thin, *convex-plane,* regular or wavy, obscurely umbonate, glabrous, moist, hygrophanous with a somewhat separable cuticle, *smoky-brown or fuliginous* (*moist*), ochraceous-tan, buff or paler (dry), umbo darker. FLESH scissile, grayish, or grayish-white. GILLS adnexed, emarginate, narrow to moderately broad, subventricose, rather close, thickish, pure white at first becoming dingy. STEM 3-8 cm. long, 3-6 mm. thick, *strict,* elastic, equal or thickened at base, whitish, *streaked with smoky fibrils,* persistently stuffed. SPORES 6-8 x 4-5 micr., minutely rough, elliptical-oval, white.

Scattered or growing singly. On the ground or among grass in cultivated fields, gardens, lawns, etc., rarely in woods. Spring and autumn, June, September-October. Ann Arbor, New Richmond, Marquette. Frequent.

This is usually an open ground Tricholoma. The somewhat rigid, subcartilaginous stem reminds one more of Collybia than of Tricholoma. The pileus is sometimes quite blackish and the stem streaked with black fibrils. It was formerly (Mich. Acad. Sci.) referred to *Collybia stridula* because of the spores. The measurements given by Massee for *T. melaleucum* are 10 x 4-5 micr. Schroeter and Ricken, however, find spore measurements the same as in our plants, and hence, as it agrees well otherwise, it is referred to *T. melaleuca.* The gills vary from linear to subventricose. The stem is sometimes smoky, covered with white fibrils.

753. Tricholoma leucocephaloides Pk.

N. Y. State Mus. Rep. 49, 1896.

PILEUS 3-6 cm. broad, convex, obtuse, undulate or irregular, *hygrophanous,* brown or grayish-brown (moist), whitish or whitish-tan (dry), subviscid in wet weather, even. FLESH becoming white, thin. GILLS adnate to subdecurrent, slightly emarginate, close to subdistant, moderately broad, whitish. STEM 3-6 cm. long, 5-8 mm. thick, equal, curved, spongy-stuffed, apex floccose, elsewhere glabrescent, whitish (dry). SPORES minute, elliptical, smooth, 5-6 x 3-4 micr. ODOR and TASTE *strongly farinaceous.*

Gregarious. On the ground, frondose woods. Ann Arbor. October. Rare.

754. Tricholoma sordidum Fr.

Syst. Myc., 1821.

Illustrations: Fries, Icones, Pl. 45.
    Cooke, Ill., Pl. 100.
    Hard, Mushrooms, Fig. 44, p. 63, 1908.
    Ricken, Blätterpilze, Pl. 95, Fig. 5.

PILEUS 2-6 cm. broad, convex then expanded and depressed, with or without an obscure umbo, hygrophanous, *flesh color* to *avellanus* (Ridg.) when young, wood-brown in age, fading, glabrous, even or substriatulate on the naked and incurved margin. FLESH thin, except disk, toughish, drab color when young or moist, pallid in age. GILLS adnate, at length emarginate-sinuate, *vinaceous-drab* to subviolaceous, close, thin, moderately broad, edge entire. STEM *short,* 2-4 cm. long, 4-8 mm. thick, equal, solid, toughish-fibrous, *fibrillose,* naked at apex, whitish or sordid, curved, base mycelioid or subrooting. SPORES elliptic-oblong, 6-7.5 x 3-4 micr., smooth, white. *Trama of gills* parallel. CYSTIDIA none. BASIDIA clavate, 30-32 x 4-5 micr. ODOR and TASTE mild.

Caespitose or gregarious-subcaespitose. On decaying vegetable matter, straw-heaps, etc., in fields and gardens. August-October. Ann Arbor. Infrequent.

Known by the caespitose habit, by the dingy flesh-colored or subviolaceous pileus and gills and by the place of growth. Usually it appears only after abundant rains. The stem is said to be sometimes eccentric. It must not be confused with *T. nudum.*

Clitocybe Fr.

(From the Greek, *clitos,* sloping, and *cybe,* head.)

White-spored; stem *spongy-fleshy to fibrous,* elastic, its fibers continuous with the trama of pileus, hence not separable. Gills *decurrent* or acutely adnate, often separable from the pileus, *not emarginate* nor sinuate, margin of pileus at first involute. No annulus.

Fleshy, firm or soft mushrooms, growing mostly on the ground or decaying leaves, sometimes on wood, in fields, road-sides or forest. Mostly medium to large size.

The PILEUS is mostly glabrous or silky fibrillose, scaly in a few species, sometimes with rather thick flesh, often quite thin and flexible. Many are hygrophanous and change color during dry weather and have scissile thin flesh, others are merely moist and have thicker unchanging flesh. The surface is never viscid. The shape of the pileus varies greatly, convex to plane, obtuse, depressed in the center, umbilicate or infundibuliform; very regular, irregular or compressed when clustered, or often merely wavy in outline. The color of the pileus is generally white to tan, gray, dull reddish or brownish, although a few bright-colored species like *C. illudens* and *C. anisearia* are quite common. The STEM lacks the true cartilaginous rind of the genus Collybia; its outer layer being fibrous or sometimes soft-fleshy, (though it may become hard and cartilaginous-like in dry weather). Within it may be fibrous throughout, i. e., solid, or spongy-stuffed and becoming more or less hollow. The fibrous structure is length-wise and is continued into the trama of the pileus and gives the stem considerable elasticity. The color of the stem is usually like that of the pileus. The GILLS are mostly white, some are ashy-brown, or become ashy-colored in age; in the subgenus Laccaria, they are colored reddish, violet or yellow. They are always attached to the stem, sometimes deeply decurrent, sometimes adnate at first and later pseudo-decurrent when the expanding pileus is elevated anteriorly; whatever the mode of attachment, the gills are narrowed to a point where they terminate on the stem. In one species, *C. laccata,* the gills are aberrant, being emarginate-adnate as in Tricholoma. The gills, when decurrent, are often unequally so, some extending farther down the stem than others, especially when the pileus is irregular. In many species the gills are of different texture from the trama of the pileus and can be peeled off from it, in this character approaching the genus Paxillus as set up by Fries. It has seemed best, however, to follow Peck, by referring white-spored species with decurrent and separable gills, even if they anastomose on the stem, to the genus Clitocybe instead of Paxillus. The VEIL is poorly developed or entirely lacking in this genus. Where it becomes evident, as in *C. praecox* sp. nov. we have a transition to the genus Armillaria. But no species in which the veil forms an annulus can be included here. The SPORES are white, mostly small, elliptical and smooth in the larger number of species, globose and echinulate in others. As seen below, this character with others will be used to separate the two subgenera. The spores of *Clitopilus caespitosa* are only slightly tinged with flesh color, so that it is easily mistaken for a Clitocybe. The TASTE is mild in nearly all the species; sometimes it is farinaceous; in *C. piccina* and a few others it is disagreeable. Two species are known to be poisonous, viz. *C. illudens* and *C. morbifera;* as far as known, the others are safe, and become tender and palatable when properly cooked. *C. sudorifica* Pk. (N. Y. State Mus. Bull. 157) causes profuse perspiration and should be avoided.

The genus is large, and may be divided into two subgenera: Clitocybe (propria), and Laccaria.

The former is again divided into sections and groups as follows:

SUBGENUS CLITOCYBE.

Section   I.   Paxilloideae.

Section   II.   Squamulosae.

Section III.   Siccae.

Section   IV.   Hygrophanae.

SUBGENUS LACCARIA.

Key to the Species

(A) Pileus hygrophanous, changing color from wet to dry weather; flesh usually scissile.
  (a) Pileus becoming furfuraceous-squamulose; spores spherical, markedly echinulate; gills adnate.
    (b) Plant large; stem 8 mm. or more thick; gills purplish. 796. *C. ochropurpurea* Berk.

(bb)   Plants rather small; gills flesh color, pallid or violaceous.
   (c))   Stem 3-7 cm. long; spores 8-9 micr. diam., very common. 794.
       C. laccata Fr.
   (cc)   Stem 1-2 cm. long; spores 12-14 micr. diam., rare. 795. *C.*
       tortilis Fr.
(aa)   Pileus glabrous or dotted with dark points.
  (b)   Pileus thin, funnel-form, cup-shaped or deeply umbilicate at
     maturity.
   (c)   Gills distant or subdistant.
    (d)   Growing on lichens; pileus grayish-brown (moist), very
       small. 790. *C. peltigerina* Pk.
    (dd)   Growing on wood, sometimes on the debris of forests.
     (e)   Pileus virgate, with black scaly points; gills yellowish.
       783. *C. ectypoides* Pk.
     (ee)   Pileus, stem and gills smoky to ashy-brown (moist), pileus
       glabrous. 782. *C. cyathiforme* Fr.
   (cc)   Gills crowded or close.
    (d)   Pileus grayish-brown when moist at least in the center;
      gills close.
     (e)   Caespitose; pileus infundibuliform; gills long-decurrent.
       787. *C. caespitosa* Pk.
     (ee)   Not truly caespitose; pileus umbilicate; gills subdecur-
       rent. 786. *C. albidula* Pk.
    (dd)   Pileus white or whitish-tan, gills very crowded.
     (e)   Stem attached by long white strands to decayed wood or
       debris, often eccentric; gills decurrent. 785. *C. eccen-*
       trica Pk.
     (ee)   Stem without such strands; gills long decurrent. 784.
       C. adirondackensis Pk.
 (bb)   Pileus obtuse to convex-depressed; plants rather small.
  (c)   Gills, pileus and stem ashy-colored or brownish-gray.
   (d)   Taste farinaceous. 789. *C. ditopoda* Fr.
   (dd)   Taste mild. 788. *C. metachroa* Fr.
  (cc)   Gills, pileus and stem white or tinged tan color.
   (d)   Pileus shining-white when dry. 793. *C. angustissima* Fr.
   (dd)   Pileus not shining-white.
    (e)   On lawns, etc., among grass. 791. *C. morbifera* Pk.
    (ee)   In woods, among leaves. 792. *C. compressipes* Pk.
(AA)   Pileus not hygrophanous.
  (a)   Stem 2-6 cm. thick; pileus very large, ochraceous tan, obtuse; gills
     soon dingy yellowish. 758. *C. maxima* Fr.
  (aa)   Stem not as stout.
   (b)   Caespitose, often in large clusters; plants large.
    (c)   Gills extending down the stem in lines or ridges; pileus dull-
      white or pale tan. 757. *C. piceina* Pk.
    (cc)   Gills rarely decurrent in lines.
     (d)   Pileus becoming deep funnel-shaped or depressed-concave;
      very large.
      (e)   Margin of pileus sulcate; gills anastomosing on stem. 755.
        C. gigantea Fr.
      (ee)   Margin of pileus even; gills rounded behind at first. 756.
        C. candida Bres.
     (dd)   Pileus obtuse, umbonate or only slightly depressed.
      (e)   Pileus becoming scaly, reddish-tawny to honey-colored.
       759. *C. monodelpha* Morg.
      (ee)   Pileus glabrous.
       (f)   Whole plant saffron or dingy golden-yellow. 773. *C.*
        illudens Schw.
       (ff)   Plants not at all yellow.
        (g)   Pileus with a cartilaginous cuticle, smoky-tan or
         paler. 775. *C. cartilagineus* Bres.

       (gg)   Pileus without cartilaginous cuticle; whole plant whitish. 774. *C. multiceps* Pk.

(bb)   Singly, gregarious or subcaespitose; plants small to medium size; stems seldom over 8 mm. thick.

  (c)   Pileus yellow, covered with dark brown scales; on wood. 760. *C. decora* Fr.

  (cc)   Pileus not like the preceding.

    (d)   Pileus greenish, bluish or yellowish, not scaly.

      (e)   Whole plant yellowish, soft; spores globose, minutely echinulate. 781. *C. pulcherrima* Pk.

      (ee)   Tinged green or blue.

        (f)   Stem solid.

          (g)   Pileus green or tinged green. 767. *C. odora* var. *viridis* Fr.

          (gg)   Pileus tinged blue. 771. *C. connexa* Pk.

        (ff)   Stem stuffed then hollow; pileus greenish.

          (g)   Gills narrow, crowded. 767. *C. odora* var. *anisearia* Pk.

          (gg)   Gills rather broad, close. 767. *C. odora* Fr.

   (dd)   Pileus not green, blue nor yellow.

    (e)   Pileus funnel-form or deeply concave at maturity.

      (f)   Pileus buff-white. 776. *C. catina* Fr.

      (ff)   Pileus reddish-tan fading to dingy white. 777. *C. infundibuliformis* Fr.

    (ee)   Pileus obtuse, umbilicate or slightly depressed.

      (f)   Pileus smoky-brown, ashy brown or clouded with gray.

        (g)   Gills deeply decurrent.

          (h)   Pileus obtuse, 3-7 cm. broad; gills white or tinged yellowish, subdistant; stem clavate, stout. 763. *C. clavipes* Fr.

          (hh)   Pileus more or less depressed, 1-3 cm. broad; gills dingy white, close; stem equal, slender. 779. *C. parilis* Fr.

        (gg)   Gills short-decurrent.

          (h)   Stem slender, 1-3 mm. thick; pileus depressed; gills tinged ashy. 766. *C. vilescens* Pk.

          (hh)   Stem stout, 8-16 mm. thick; pileus obtuse to umbonate.

            (i)   Gills rather crowded. 762. *C. nebularis* Fr.

            (ii)   Gills subdistant; stem subequal.

              (k)   Gills entire. 764. *C. media* Pk.

              (kk)   Gills forked. 765. *C. carnosior* Pk.

      (ff)   Pileus rufous-brown to brick red; 2-5 cm. broad.

        (g)   Gills very crowded; flesh thin; pileus umbilicate. 780. *C. sinopica* Fr.

        (gg)   Gills hardly close; flesh thick on disk; pileus obtuse. 761. *C. praecox* Kauff.

      (fff)   Pileus whitish to shining white.

        (g)   Growing on wood; gills narrow and crowded. 772. *C. truncicola* Pk.

        (gg)   On the ground among leaves, or in grassy places.

          (h)   Pileus dingy-white to pale tan, umbilicate; on pine needles on the ground. 778. *C. pinophila* Pk.

          (hh)   Pileus shining-white when dry.

            (i)   Pileus 3-8 cm. broad; stem solid; spores minutely echinulate. 770. *C. albissima* Pk.

            (ii)   Pileus smaller, 1-4 cm. broad; stem stuffed to hollow; spores smooth.

              (k)   Stem cartilaginous; pileus regular; in woods. 768. *C. candicans* Fr.

              (kk)   Stem fibrous-tough; pileus wavy on margin; usually in fields and pastures. 769. *C. dealbata* Fr.

SUBGENUS CLITOCYBE (propria). Spores elliptical to ovate, when spherical not spinulose (see *C. pulcherrium*).

Section I. Paxilloideae. Pileus firm; flesh thickish, not hygrophanous. Gills separable from trama of pileus, more or less anastomosing on the stem. Plants medium to very large.

755. Clitocybe gigantea Fr. (EDIBLE)

Sys. Mycol., 1821.

Illustrations: Gillet, Champignons de France, Pl. 100.
Cooke, Ill., Pl. 106.

PILEUS *large,* 15-25 cm. broad, relatively thin, soon expanded, plane *then infundibuliform,* soft, glabrous, *white* or tinged tan, slightly flocculose when dry, *margin* involute, then spreading, at length *coarsely sulcate.* Flesh thin, white. GILLS subdecurrent, *very crowded,* rather *broad,* (2-3 times thickness of pileus), some forked, *anastomosing on the stem.* STEM short and *stout,* 2-6 cm. long, 2-3 cm. thick, *solid,* glabrous, even, whitish. SPORES 5 x 3 micr., elliptical, apiculate, white. ODOR and TASTE mild.

(Dried: Pileus rufous-brown in patches, dingy whitish elsewhere. Gills cinnamon brown.)

Caespitose. Ground, in rich woods of maple, oak, basswood, etc. Ann Arbor. September-October. Infrequent. Edible.

Certain remarks found in fungi books indicate that this species needs further study in its relation to *C. maxima* and *C. candida.* Massee says the gills are not separable from the hymenophore, although Fries does not mention the matter in Hymen. Europ., Epicrisis and Systema. The lengthy quotations of McIlvaine do not meet the difficulties in deciding between the three mentioned. This is one of our largest fungi, often a foot across the cap, and a caespitose cluster of them is a marked feature of the forest. It differs, according to our diagnosis, from *C. maxima* by the anastomosing gills, the sulcate-ridged margin of the pileus, lack of any umbo and smooth stem; and from *C. candida* in the character of the gills and the sulcate margin of the pileus. Large fresh clusters of *Tricholoma panoeolum* var. *caespitosum* have all the appearance of this plant, but in that species the gills turn slowly flesh color and the spores are smaller. The illustrations of *C. gigantea* fail to show its size and caespitose character.

756. Clitocybe candida Bres.

Fungi Tridentini, 1881.

Illustrations: Ibid, Pl. XVIII, Vol. I.
Atkinson, Mushrooms, p. 89, 90, Plates 28, 29, Figs. 90, 91.

PILEUS 10-20 cm. broad, convexo-plane, *then depressed and infundibuliform,* relatively thin, glabrous to obscurely scaly on disk, *white,* somewhat shining, *even* or obscurely striate on margin, not umbonate. FLESH white, unchanging, very *scissile.* GILLS subdecurrent, rounded at point of attachment, not emarginate, *very crowded, narrowly linear,* few forked, many shorter, edge entire. STEM 5-9 cm. long, stout, about 2 cm. thick, subequal, spongy-stuffed, white, fibrillose, mycelioid-tomentose at base. ODOR and TASTE mild. SPORES 6-7 x 3-4 micr., elliptical, apiculate, white.

(Dried: Pileus whitish-tan, gills pale fuscous-cinnamon.)

Caespitose. On the ground, under balsam-fir, in conifer forest. Marquette. August. Infrequent.

Differs from preceding in even pileus, in narrow gills which do not anastomose; from *C. maxima* in lack of umbo, gills not long decurrent and pileus not squamulose. Atkinson says gills are broad; in our plants they are narrow as shown in Bresadola's figure. It is made a variety of *C. gigantea* by Quelet, and present information seems to show that the two forms run into each other.

757. Clitocybe piceina Pk.

Torr. Bot. Club. Bull., Vol. 31, p. 178, 1904.

Illustrations: Chicago Nat. Hist. Surv. Bull. VII, Part I, Pl. 2, Fig. 2.
Plate CLIV of this Report.

PILEUS 5-20 cm. broad, rarely more, firm, convex-expanded to *plane,* dull white or tinged ochraceous to tan, dry, obscurely silky, tomentose, margin *even, involute.* FLESH white, rather thick, not scissile. GILLS close, rather narrow, thin, whitish or tinged yellowish, *decurrent* especially *by lines or ridges* running down the stem and *anastomosing,* separable from hymenophore, transversely split in age, edge entire. STEM 5-8 cm. long, 1-3 cm. thick, short and *stout,* solid, firm, sometimes spongy, subequal to subbulbous, whitish, *minutely tomentose,* often curved at base, *rigid at apex.*

SPORES broadly elliptical, 6-7 x 4-5 micr., apiculate, with a large oil-drop nearly filling the interior, white. ODOR strong, somewhat aromatic to disagreeable. TASTE unpleasant, bitter.

(Dried: Cap and gills dingy ochre to ochraceous-buff.)

Single or subcaespitose. On very rotten wood, or on debris under hemlock trees in northern Michigan; under maple, etc;, in the southern part of the State. Ann Arbor, New Richmond, Detroit, Houghton, Huron Mountains, Marquette. Infrequent. Edibility not tested.

This is one of the large Clitocybes, one of my specimens measuring 25 cm. across the cap. It is easily known by the peculiar gills and the narrow ridges at the apex of the stem. The change to yellow on drying is very marked, and distinguishes this species from *C. gigantea* and *C. candida*. Small to medium plants are apparently more common than those of full size. The oil-drop in the spores is large and simulates a globular spore. The white mycelium gives a white, mouldy appearance to the neighboring leaves, etc. It appears to be the same as *Paxillus extenuatus* Fr., in the sense of Ricken.

758. Clitocybe maxima Fr. (EDIBLE)

Epicrisis, 1836-38.

Illustrations: Barla, Champignons des Alpes-maritimes, Pl. 50. Plate CLV of this Report. (Much reduced.)

PILEUS 10-30 cm. or more broad, thick-fleshy, firm, *at first broadly convex with broad umbo, then plane,* scarcely subinfundibuliform in age but obtuse or broadly umbonate, always dry, with a thin, interwoven, silky-tomentosity on surface, slightly floccose-scaly in age, at first pallid, *soon ochraceous-tan to rusty alutaceous,* margin at first involute and pubescent-tomentulose, then spreading and *even* or only obscurely short-striate. FLESH *thick and compact on disk,* abruptly thin toward margin, later attenuated, whitish becoming dingy. GILLS at first submarginate becoming decurrent to long-decurrent in fully expanded plants, relatively narrow (4-10 mm.), acuminate at both ends, *close,* not ventricose, whitish at first, *soon dingy yellowish,* pale tan in age, separable from pileus, edge entire. STEM *stout* and usually *short,* 6-12 cm. long, inflated-bulbous to clavate-bulbous, 2-5 cm thick above, 3-8 cm. at bulb, *spongy-solid, covered by a thin,* continuous, appressed white *tomentum,* often ferruginous-stained, white or whitish, bulb at length color of pileus. SPORES elliptic-oval, 7-7.5 x 5-5.5 micr., obscurely echinulate, nucleate, white. CYSTIDIA none; *sterile cells* on edge of gills acicular. ODOR *rather strong,* oily-farinaceous. TASTE mild.

Gregarious or subcaespitose. On the ground in frondose woods. Ann Arbor, Detroit. August-September. Infrequent.

In America this huge and massive mushroom is distinguished by its exceedingly stout stem, by the compact flesh of the half-grown plant, by the gills which soon become deep straw-yellow and by the odor. When developing slowly the pileus remains compact and thick on the central portion, but under favorable growth-conditions it expands more fully, the flesh becomes thinner throughout and it tends to become infundibuliform. The majority of plants found, although many of them very large, had a plane or obtuse pileus, sometimes with a very broad umbo. Solitary, relatively small specimens approach the appearance of the figures given for *C. geotropa* Fr. and such specimens being the only ones seen the first time the species was found, I referred them to *C. geotropa* Fr.; later collections showed me the error. The gills in the young plants are merely sinuate-emarginate, but when the pileus expands they become decurrent. The decurrent character of the gills is not as strongly marked as the European descriptions indicate, and our plant departs from European forms in several particulars. Fries (Monographia) says the gills are whitish, not changing, whereas the yellowish to tan color which the gills soon assume in our plants is one of the most marked characteristics, becoming more noticeable after the specimens are picked. The thin tomentose coating on the stem, its bulbous tendency and the rusty-tan color of the old plants is also not mentioned. Clearly we have a distinct American form. The relation between *C. maxima* and *C. gigantea* does not seem to be clear to most European authors. The two are very distinct as Fries has pointed out. The American *C. gigantea* has a whitish, thinner, much more infundibuliform pileus and its gills are more crowded and anastomose on the stem, and the margin of the pileus is strongly marked by sulcate-ridges. The attachment of the gills relates this to the genus Tricholoma. But in all other respects it is a Clitocybe of the Paxilloideae group.

Section II. Squamulosae. Surface of pileus broken up into scales, dry; flesh rather thick, stem scaly or fibrillose.

759. Clitocybe monadelpha Morg. (EDIBLE)

Jour. Cinn. Soc. of Nat. Hist., Vol. VI, 1883.

Illustrations: Ibid, Pl. 4.
N. Y. State Mus. Memoir, Vol. III, No. 4, Pl. 46, 1900.
Hard, Mushrooms, p. 103, Pl. XXI, Fig. 75, 1908.
McIlvaine, Amer. Mushrooms, p. 88, Pl. XXVII.

PILEUS 3-10 cm. broad, size very variable in a cluster, convex then plane, obtuse, depressed in age, entire surface dry, *becoming innately fibrillose-scaly,* scales floccose and more dense on disk, *rufous-tawny* to chestnut on disk, honey-colored beneath scales, margin recurved and splitting in age. FLESH white or tinged ochraceous-brown, very thick on disk. GILLS subdecurrent, subdistant, rather broad in the middle, tapering to both ends, intervenose, *pallid then dull flesh color* and often stained with brown spots, edge entire. STEM *elongated,* 7-20 cm. long, tapering downward and *attenuated at the caespitose and crowded bases,* fibrous-stuffed, at length hollow, densely fibrillose or fibrillose-scurfy, glabrescent, twisted, pallid then fuscous-brown, darker to blackish-brown at base, brownish within. SPORES broadly elliptical, 6-7.5 x 5-5.5 micr., smooth, white. ODOR and TASTE mild, or slightly bitter.

(Dried: Umber-brown.)

Very caespitose. On the ground in woods, usually attached to old roots or rotten wood. New Richmond. September. Rare.

This is apparently the American form of *C. tabescens* Bres. of Europe. In the few collections examined, the spores of the native plant rarely measured over 7 micr. long, while Bresadola gives 8-10 x 5-7 micr. for his species. When young this species simulates *Armillaria mellea,* but without a veil, later it is not easily confused with it. The scales on the cap are often well-developed.

760.   Clitocybe decora Fr.

(= *Tricholoma multipunctum* Pk.)

Syst. Mycol., 1821.   (N. Y. State Mus. Rep. 25, 1873.)

Illustration: Fries, Icones Select, Vol. I, Pl. 60.

PILEUS 3-6 cm. broad, convex, rather thin, depressed in center or plane, yellow (luteous) or tinged brown or olivaceous, covered with dense, innate, fibrillose, minute, blackish or brownish scales, disk darker. FLESH yellowish. GILLS *obtusely adnate,* crowded, seceding, yellow, rather narrow. STEM 3-6 cm. long, 4-10 mm. thick, subequal, stuffed then hollow, yellow, dotted with minute scales, central or eccentric. SPORES variable, broadly-ovate to subelliptical, 6-7 x 4.5-5.5 micr., mixed with a large per cent of young globose spores 4-5 micr. diameter.

Single or subcaespitose. On rotten logs, in hemlock and spruce swamp. Sault Ste. Marie. July-September.

The generic position of this species is unsettled. Fries first placed it under Clitocybe, then Pleurotus. Gillet referred it to Clitocybe; Quelet to Tricholoma; Saccardo to Pleurotus. Peck name it anew *Tricholoma multipunctum,* then referred it back to *Clitocybe decora,* where it is to be hoped it will remain. It is an aberrant Clitocybe, like *C. laccata,* in departing from the manner in which in this genus the gills are attached.

761.   Clitocybe praecox sp. nov.

Illustration: Plate CLVI of this Report.

PILEUS 2-5 cm. broad, fleshy, *dry,* convex, then plane or obtuse, somewhat irregular, or deformed, sometimes lobed, *flocculose or covered with minute rufous-brown scales,* umber-brown or paler when young; margin incurved at first, obscurely fibrillose, even. FLESH whitish, thick on disk. GILLS acutely subdecurrent, close to subdistant, not broad, narrowed toward both ends, whitish or ward, obscurely bulbous, curved, *solid,* fibrous, dotted below with venose. STEM 3-4 cm. long, 6-8 mm. thick, equal or tapering downward, obscurely bulbous, curved, *solid;* fibrous, dotted below with delicate floccose scales from the veil, mealy at apex, at length silky-fibrillose throughout, pallid to brownish, white within, outer rind subcartilaginous. VEIL thin, fibrillose, whitish, evanescent. SPORES broadly elliptical, 7-9.5 x 5-6 micr., smooth, obtuse, white; basidia 4-spored. CYSTIDIA none. ODOR and TASTE strong, farinaceous.

Singly or subcaespitose. On lawns, parks, etc. Ann Arbor. April 20-June 1. Edibility not tested.

First found on the Campus of the University of Michigan among moss and grass through which it pushed and which probably caused its deformed appearance. The earliest specimens mature slowly. The collapsing veil at first leaves remnants on the stems in the form of obscure, transverse, delicate rings or scales, which soon disappear. Its scaly cap and veil indicate that it is related to the Friesian section "Versiformis" but the flesh is not hygrophanous. It has some affinities with *C. incilis* Fr.

Section III. Siccae. Pileus not scaly nor hygrophanous; flesh not watery nor scissile.

Subsection I. Disciformis. Pileus convex, then plane or depressed, obtuse, *regular;* gills equally decurrent. Stem *simple* or somewhat subcaespitose.

**Pileus cinereous or fuscous.*

762. Clitocybe nebularis Fr. (EDIBLE)

Syst. Mycol., 1821.

Illustrations: N. Y. State Mus. Rep. 48, Pl. 23, 1896.
　　Fries, Sverig. ätl. u. gift. Svamp., Pl. 45.
　　Gillet, Champignons d. France, Pl. 115.
　　Bresadola, Fungh. mang. e. vel., Pl. 33.
　　Cooke, Ill., Pl. 79.
　　Michael, Führer f. Pilzfreunde, Vol. II, No. 84.

PILEUS 5-9 cm. broad, convex, then plane, obtuse, rarely depressed, margin often wavy, even, *subpruinose,* glabrescent, *smoky-brown to grayish-buff,* margin pliant and soft. FLESH pure white, thick on disk, thin on margin. GILLS subdecurrent finally decurrent, *crowded,* attenuate at both ends, narrow, white then dingy or tinged gray, edge entire. STEM stout, 5-7 cm. long, 1-2.5 cm. thick, sub-clavate at base, or subventricose, *fibrous-spongy and solid, pruinose, smoky-buff,* concolor, even. SPORES minute, 5-6 x 3-4 micr., elliptical-ovate, smooth, white. ODOR and TASTE mild or very slightly acrid.

(Dried: Cap grayish-brown to smoky-isabelline; gills ochraceous-buff.)

Subcaespitose. Ground in woods of oak, maple, etc. Ludington, Ann Arbor. September. Infrequent.

This is called the "Clouded Clitocybe," because of the smoky hue of cap and stem. The spores of the American plant seem to be smaller than those of the European species, since Bresadola gives them 9 x 6-7 micr. Some specimens have a bit of acridity to the taste, a fact also recorded by Barla in Europe. McIlvaine, Bresadola, Cooke, Badham, Quelet and Michael report it as edible. Older authors in Europe have reported it as unsafe, e. g. Cordier, Paulet and Barla. The American plant has no evidence against it. It is sometimes attacked by another mushroom, *Volvaria loveianus,* which forms fruit-bodies on its cap. (See Fig. 7, Pl. XI, Swanson, Fungi.)

763. Clitocybe clavipes Fr. (Edible)

Syst. Mycol., 1821.

Illustrations: N. Y. State Mus. Mem., Vol. III, No. 4, Pl. 46, 1900.
> Fries, Icon., Vol. I, Pl. 47.
> Gillet, Champignons de France, Pl. 117.
> Cooke, Ill., Pl. 80.
> Hard, Mushrooms, p. 94, Fig. 69.

PILEUS 2-7 cm. broad, soft, convex then plane, almost obconic, rarely umbonate, obtuse, even, *glabrous, sooty-brown,* fuscous-cinereous to brown, sometimes paler. FLESH white, thick on disk. GILLS deeply *decurrent, subdistant,* rather broad in middle, narrowed toward both ends, flaccid, white or tinged yellowish, edge entire. STEM 2-6 cm. long, 6-8 mm. thick at apex, clavate at base, tapering upwards, sometimes bulbous, concolor, spongy-solid, white within, fibrillose. SPORES 6-7.5 x 4-5 micr., subelliptical, smooth, white. ODOR and TASTE agreeable.

(Dried: Pileus fuscous-cinnamon; gills sordid gilvous.)

Scattered or tufted. On the ground, mostly reported in conifer woods, but also in southern Michigan, under maple, oak, etc. September-October. Infrequent. Edible.

Water-soaked in wet weather. Differs from *C. nebularis* in its subdistant, decurrent gills, and slightly larger spores.

764. Clitocybe media Pk. (EDIBLE)

N. Y. State Mus. Rep. 42, 1899.

Illustrations: Ibid, Pl. 1, Figs. 9-12.
N. Y. State Mus. Rep. 48, Pl. XXIII, Fig. 1-7, 1896.
Hard, Mushrooms, p. 88, Fig. 64, 1908.

This is a variety of the preceding, recognizable by the subequal, not bulbous stem, broader and more distant gills, varying decurrent. The spores are 7.5-8 x 5 micr. TASTE mild. Edible.
On the ground, in oak, maple or birch woods. Marquette, Ann Arbor.

765. Clitocybe carnosior Pk.

N. Y. State Cab. Rep. 23, p. 76, 1872.

This may be considered as another *variety* of *C. clavipes,* distinguished by the forked gills. The pileus is brown to grayish-brown. TASTE pleasant. Habit, etc., of the type. Marquette. August.

766. Clitocybe vilescens Pk.

N. Y. State Mus. Rep. 33, 1880.

PILEUS *small,* 1-3 cm. broad, convex then plane and obtuse or slightly umbilicato-depressed, fragile, glabrous, even, pale-ashy to brownish-ashy, sometimes subpapillate, slightly pruinose at first on the involute margin. FLESH whitish, soft, thickish. GILLS subdecurrent, whitish tinged ashy, close, moderately narrow, occasionally veined. STEM *slender,* 2-5 cm. long, 1.5-4 mm. thick, concolor or paler, solid, glabrous, equal, straight or curved, white-mycelioid at base. SPORES short and subglobose or broadly elliptical, 5-6 x 3-5 micr., smooth, white. ODOR and TASTE mild.
(Dried: Cap grayish, gills dingy pale tan.)
In frondose or mixed woods. July-August. Marquette, Ann Arbor. Infrequent.

****Pileus greenish.*

767.   Clitocybe odora Fr.   (Edible)

Syst. Myc., 1821.

Illustrations: Michael, Führer f. Pilzfreunde, No. 86.
  Fries, Sverig. ätlig. u. gift Svamp., Pl. 85.
  Gillet, Champignons de France, No. 113.
  Marshall, Mushroom Book, p. 71, Pl. XV.   (As *Clitocybe*
    or *virens.*)
  Conn. Nat. Hist. Surv. Bull. 3, Pl. XVII.

PILEUS 3-8 cm. broad, rather thin, convex then expanded-plane, subrepand, even, glabrous, margin incurved and pliant, sometimes substriate, *pale dingy-green to bluish-green* varying to whitish. FLESH white, *rather tough.* GILLS *rather broad,* close, adnate-decurrent, white then yellowish or tinged green. STEM 3 to 8 cm. long, 4-6 mm. thick, equal or thickened below, pruinose at apex, stuffed then hollow, white mycelioid or often soft-spongy at base, white or tinged green. SPORES 6-8 x 4-5 micr., broadly elliptical, smooth, white. ODOR *fragant,* sometimes evanescent. "Flavor, when cooked, rather strong, but not unpleasant." (McIlvaine.)

(Dried: Green color disappears; pileus grayish-tan to dark fuscous; the deep green colored pileus darkest when dried, those merely tinged green, paler; gills alutaceous.)

Subcaespitose, base of stem often deeply sunk in leaves and forest-mould. In conifer and broad-leaved forest. Marquette, Houghton, Ann Arbor. August-September. This typical form is rare.

This species runs into two varieties, *C. anisearia* Pk. and *C. viridis* Fr., of which the first variety is by far the commonest of the three in Michigan. The odor is usually strongly fragrant, but is variable, so that a normal green plant may be almost inodorous in age, further, the color varies to white with no sign of green, in which case the odor may be very marked. The color may therefore be white, or tinged a delicate green, dull uniformly green, grayish-green to bluish-green. The variability of the plant has caused some uncertainty as to whether our form is the same as the European plant. Our commonest form or variety has *narrow, crowded* gills, and is given below as *C. anisearia* Pk. Fries and others describe *C. odora* with *broad* gills, not crowded; and *C. viridis* with *crowded, white* gills and *solid* stem. I believe that all these characters are variants of one species, and have been unduly emphasized. The European plants as well as ours are *edible,* though strong-flavored when alone.

Var. *anisearia* (*Clitocybe anisearia* Pk.) (EDIBLE.)

N. Y. State Mus. Rep. 32, 1879.

Like the preceding, of which it may be considered a variety. -It differs in the *narrow, crowded* gills, and perhaps in the stronger development of the fibrillose cuticle of the cap. The gills are white then cream-color. SPORES, etc., the same. Habitat the same.

Houghton, Marquette, Ann Arbor, Detroit, New Richmond, etc. Common throughout the State. August-October. Edible.

Var. viridis (*Clitocybe virdis* Fr.)

Syst. Myc., 1821.

This variety, with the *solid* stem, has not been found in Michigan. Fries separated it because of information he obtained from others. He never saw it. Cooke and others consider it identical with *C. odora.* Under certain conditions of growth, the interior "stuffed" center of stems of mushrooms often appears as if composed of the same substance and texture as the rest of the stem, i. e., as if "solid," and care must be taken to distinguish between such appearances.

***Pileus white or whitish.*

768. Clitocybe candicans Fr.

Syst. Myc. Fr., 1821.

Illustrations: Fries, Icones, Pl. 51, Fig. 3.
    Cooke, Ill., Pl. 82.
    Gillet, Champignons de France, Pl. 110.

"PILEUS 2-3 cm. broad, thin, dry, convex then plane or depressed, *shining white* in dry weather, with a superficial micaceous silkiness, dull white when moist, even, *margin decurved, regular.* FLESH white, thin. GILLS adnate then decurrent, crowded, very thin, narrow, white, edge entire. STEM 2-5 cm. long, 2-4 mm. thick, even, equal, *waxy-shining, cartilaginous, glabrous,* stuffed then hollow, curved and villose at base, somewhat rooting among the leaves, etc., to which it is attached. SPORES *broadly-elliptical* to subglobose, 5.5-6 x 4 micr., smooth, white. ODOR and TASTE mild."

Subcaespitose. Among leaves, etc., in woods. Reported by Longyear.

The cartilaginous stem and broader spores separate it from *C. dealbata* and the other Clitocybes. In the character of the stem it approaches the genus Omphalia.

769. Clitocybe dealbata Fr.

Syst. Myc., 1821.

Illustrations: Cooke, Ill., Pl. 104.
Gillet, Champignons de France, Pl. 111.

PILEUS 1-4 cm. broad, convex then expanded, depressed in center, or umbilicate, glabrous, even, dry, *shining-white,* margin *undulate and becoming recurved* or ascending, very thin. FLESH white, thin. GILLS adnate then subdecurrent, persistently white, rather narrow, *crowded,* thin, edge entire or minutely erose. STEM 2-3 cm. long, 2-5 mm. thick, rather slender, stuffed then hollow and often compressed, white to pallid, *tough* and fibrous, straight, glabrous, even, equal, base oblique and villose, apex subprúinose. SPORES narrowly elliptical-oval, 4-5.5 x 2.5-3 micr., apiculate, nucleate, smooth, white; basidia 4-spored. ODOR and TASTE mild.

(Dried: Cap buff-white, gills whitish, stem sordid.)

Subcaespitose, usually in *twos* as figured by Cooke. Attached to decaying leaves in pastured woods of deciduous trees; also on lawns and pastures. Ann Arbor, etc. September-November. Frequent.

This species is known by its persistently white cap and gills, small size, etc. The tendency of mycologists to describe new varieties of it, shows that it varies considerably. Peck has named a variety growing in mushroom beds var. *deformata.* The above description applies to the Ann Arbor form. It is very probable that there are intermediate grades between this species and *C. candicans.* Our plants were thin, and hence more like *C. candicans.* The two differ from such species as *C. albissima* Pk. and *C. phyllophila* Fr. in the entire absence of a yellowish color in cap or gills when old or dried. The stem is toughish-fibrous instead of cartilaginous as in *C. candicans;* the other points of difference are italicised, but may all vary. Some say the caps of both species are sometimes mamillate. Our plants grow in the woods among leaves, in twos or singly, and might be taken for *C. candicans* if one failed to examine the stem structure and the spores. The minute spores are only slightly different in the two species, but can be used as a good diagnostic character, since those of *C. candicans* are broader and shorter.

770. Clitocybe albissima Pk.

N. Y. State Mus. Rep. 26, 1874.

PILEUS 3-8 cm. broad, *medium large,* convex to expanded, dry, *thin and flexible, pure shining white;* not changed by weather, very regular, margin subzonate. FLESH white. GILLS close, short decurrent, narrow, whitish. STEM 5-8 cm. long, 5-10 mm. thick, subequal or tapering upward, *solid* or sometimes with cavity at one place, glabrous above, subtomentose towards spongy base. SPORES 6-8 x 4-5 micr., broadly elliptical, thin-walled, *minutely spinulose.* ODOR sometimes slightly of radish. TASTE slightly bitter or mild.

(Dried: Cap soft and white; gills yellowish.)

Gregarious, sometimes in fairy-rings.

In conifer woods of northern Michigan, Marquette, Greenville. August-September. Infrequent.

The snowy-white cap and size distinguish *C. albissima* from *C. candicans* and *C. dealbata.* In our specimens, which were identified by Peck, the gills become yellowish in dried specimens, while the cap, as in *C. dealbata,* retains its whiteness. The spores are unique in being very minutely echinulate, like those of *C. pulcherrima.* It is said to be close to *C. cerussata* Fr. of Europe, which has globose spores. Our specimens reported as *C. cerussata* in 12th Report, Michigan Academy of Science, were found to belong here.

771. Clitocybe connexa Pk.

N. Y. State Mus. Rep. 26, 1874.

"PILEUS 5-7 cm. broad, convex, then expanded, subumbonate, minutely silky, *white, sometimes faintly tinged blue,* especially on margin. GILLS crowded, narrow, decurrent, whitish. STEM 5-7 cm. long, 4 mm. thick, equal or tapering upwards, *solid,* whitish. SPORES ovoid, 7 x 5 micr."

Reported by Longyear, Jackson County. Apparently rare.

Morgan says the pileus is sometimes quite bluish. The gills are said to be rounded behind and to imitate the genus Tricholoma. The odor is weak but aromatic.

772. Clitocybe truncicola Pk.

N. Y. State Mus. Rep. 26, 1874.

"PILEUS 2-5 cm. broad, thin, firm, expanded and slightly depressed, glabrous, dry, white. GILLS narrow, thin, crowded, adnato-decurrent, white. STEM equal, stuffed then hollow, glabrous, often eccentric and curved. SPORES oval, 4-5 x 3-4 micr."

On logs and branches of maple. Our specimens were found on old roots of maple. September. Detroit.

A few other species of Clitocybe are partial to wood, e. g., *C. cyathiforme* Fr., *C. leptoloma* Pk., *C. ectypoides* Pk., and *C. decora* Fr.

Subsection II. Difformis. Pileus thick on disk, convex to plane, obtuse or umbonate, *irregular.* Gills unequally decurrent or variable in this respect, some rounded behind as in Tricholoma. Stem *caespitose,* stout in our species.

773. Clitocybe illudens Schw. (Poisonous)

Synopsis Fung. Carolina, 1822.

Illustrations: McIlvaine, Amer. Fungi, Pl. 29 a, p. 96, 1900.
    Marshall, Mushroom Book, p. 70, 1904.
    Hard, Mushrooms, Pl. 10, Fig. 67, p. 92, 1908.
    Conn. Nat. Hist. Surv. Bull. 3, Pl. 18, 1905.
    Rep. 32, Geol. and Nat. Resources Ind., p. 1231, Fig. 8, 1907.
    N. Y. State Mus. Mem. 4, Pl. 68, 1900.

PILEUS 8-20 cm. broad, thick, convex to expanded, plane or depressed, glabrous, often umbonate, bright *golden or saffron yellow, irregular,* or lobed, margin elevated in age but often decurved. FLESH white to yellowish. GILLS unequally long decurrent, close, *yellow,* becoming discolored, narrowed to both ends, sometimes forked. STEM *long,* 7-20 cm. long, 1-1.5 cm. thick, *firm,* solid, glabrous, *irregularly and variously curved or twisted, narrowed at base, concolor,* becoming darker at base. SPORES globose, 4-5 micr. diameter, white, copious. ODOR and TASTE strong and disagreeable.

Caespitose. On and around old stumps or decaying roots, forming large clusters often of 25-50 individuals. August-October. Frequent. Unsafe.

An attractive-looking mushroom, forming large golden-yellow masses, which catch the eye from a distance. It has poisonous properties, however, which affect most people with nausea and vomiting. When fresh clusters are brought into a dark room, it is shown to be strongly phosphorescent. This phenomenon is accompanied by a liberation of heat. The species is not found in Europe, and was first discovered by Louis de Schweinitz in North Carolina. Most of the photographs mentioned above look like *Armillaria mellea* without rings. I have seen it but occasionally about Ann Arbor, though Longyear marks it "common."

774. Clitocybe multiceps Pk. (Edible)

N. Y. State Mus. Rep. 43, 1890.

Illustrations: N. Y. State Mus. Bull. 139, Pl. 117, 1910.
    Clark & Kantor, Mycologia, Vol. 3, Pl. 52.
    Atkinson, Mushrooms, 2d ed.
    McIlvaine, Amer. Mushrooms, Pl. 27 a, p. 94, 1900.
    Plate CLVII of this Report.

PILEUS 3-8 cm. broad, thick on disk, *firm*, convex, *white or whitish*, sometimes tinged gray or yellowish-gray, even, moist, glabrous, regular or irregular. FLESH pure white. GILLS *close*, *adnate to slightly decurrent*, sometimes sinuate, whitish, medium broad. STEM 5-10 cm. long, 6-12 mm. thick, *stout, solid*, equal or slightly thickened at base, glabrous or pruinose at apex, white or whitish. SPORES globose, 5-8 micr. in diameter, smooth, white. TASTE slightly unpleasant.

(Dried: Caps grayish-fawn color, gills pale cinnamon.)

Very caespitose. Pastures, fields, grassy roadsides, open woods usually of broad leaved trees. Ann Arbor, Bay View, Marquette, New Richmond, etc. June to October. Frequent. Edible but not of the best variety for culinary purposes.

Except in color and in the nature of the cuticle of the cap, this species approaches *C. cartilaginea* Bres. The variations in the attachment of the gills shade into the genus Tricholoma. *C. multi-ceps* appears after prolonged rainy weather, and when developed rapidly it is quite tender and sweet. The clusters are often densely crowded and may usually be recognized by their firmness and dull white color.

775. Clitocybe cartilaginea Bres.

Fungi Tridentini, 1892.

Illustration: Ibid, Pl. 111.

PILEUS 4-8 cm. broad, convex, obtuse, dry, *provided with a cartilaginous cuticle, smoky-tan or whitish-tan,* tinged with gray or brown, glabrous, even, margin splitting. FLESH white, *thick.* GILLS *crowded,* attenuate subdecurrent, sometimes adnate and becoming sinuate or almost free when old, *narrow,* tough, sub-cartilaginous, attenuate at both ends, sordid white to *pale straw color.* STEM 5-7 cm. long, tapering upwards or subequal, 1-2 cm. thick at apex, stout, paler than pileus, somewhat spongy-clavate at base, cuticle toughish, solid, pruinose above, subfibrillose, bases somewhat connate. SPORES globose, 5-7 micr., nucleate, smooth, white. CYSTIDIA none; basidia 30-32 x 6-7 micr. ODOR and taste mild.

Caespitose. In woods. June, etc.

Sent in from outside the southern boundary of the State, and apt to occur within the State. The darker colors of the cap, and the straw-colored, truly crowded gills seem to be the only characters besides the cartilaginous cuticle of the pileus, by which to separate pale forms of *C. cartilaginea* from *C. multiceps.* Superficially, the habit, etc., of the two species are much the same. It was placed among the Tricholomas by Fries as *T. loricatum.* When quite young the color of the pileus is smoky-black.

Subsection III. Infundibuliformis. Pileus at length infundibuliform or deeply umbilicately depressed. Gills deeply and equally decurrent from the first. Color of pileus often fading but not hygrophanous.

776. Clitocybe catina Fr.

Epicrisis, 1836-38.

Illustration: Fries, Icones, Pl. 51, Fig. 4.

PILEUS 3-5 cm. broad, pliant, convex-infundibuliform, *regular, glabrous,* with a gelatinous feel when moist, not striate on margin (moist or dry), buff-white, after repeated rains pale dingy brownish, moist, not hygrophanous, never becoming shining-white, margin decurved. FLESH thin, *white, toughish.* GILLS decurrent, *crowded,* narrow, *dull whitish,* never yellowish nor cinereous, simple, edge entire. STEM 3-4.5 cm. long, 3-5 mm. thick, equal, terete, *straight,* stuffed then hollow, *tough,* white becoming sordid, pruinose above, tomentose toward base. SPORES ovate, 4-5.5 x 3 micr., smooth, white. CYSTIDIA none. ODOR farinaceous.

Gregarious or scattered, on the ground among leaves and pine needles in woods of beach and white pine. New Richmond. September-October. Abundant locally.

This seems to be merely a form of *C. catina,* from which it varies slightly. The gills are more crowded and after rains no incarnate tint is noticeable. It agrees very well in other respects with the figures and descriptions of Fries. The plants have the size and much the shape of *C. infundibuliformis,* but the latter has a reddish-tan colored cap when young, fading in age. *C. catina* is watery-whitish when fresh and the surface of the pileus becomes perfectly smooth and almost slippery, but is not truly hygrophanous. The shape of the cap is that of a regular vase or deep bowl and this character gives it·the name. The pileus is more regular and smaller than *C. phyllophila* although the two species may apparently be easily confused.

777.   Clitocybe infundibuliformis Fr.   (EDIBLE)

Elenchus Fungorum, 1828.

Illustrations: Cooke, Ill., Pl. 107.
    Bresadola, Fungh. mang. e. vel., Pl. 38.
    Gillet, Champignons de France, Pl. 107.
    Hard, Mushrooms, p. 89, Pl. 9, 1908.
    Conn. Geol. and Nat. Hist. Surv. Bull. 3, Pl. 19, 1905.
    Plate CLVIII of this Report.

PILEUS 5-7 cm. broad, at first convex and *subumbonate* then
depressed and finally entirely *infundibuliform*, dry, flaccid, coated
with a delicate silkiness, *reddish to pale tan color,* fading with age,
margin even and thin.   FLESH white, thickish on disk.   GILLS
deeply decurrent, close, *thin,* white or whitish, narrow, acuminate
at both ends, edge rather serratulate.   STEM 4-8 cm. long, 5-10
mm. thick, tapering slightly upward, glabrous, spongy within, externally firm, rather elastic, pale reddish or pallid, white-mycelioid
at base where attached to leaves, etc.   SPORES ovate to subpyriform, obliquely sharp-pointed and apiculate, 5-8 x 3-4 micr.
when mature, smaller when immature; basidia 4-spored.   ODOR
pleasant, TASTE mild.

(Dried: Cap reddish-tan, gills alutaceous to tan.)

Single or somewhat caespitose.   Attached to decaying leaves and
debris in both conifer and non-coniferous woods.   Throughout the
State as far as Isle Royale.   July-October.   My first record is July
8, the last October 20.   Very common.

This is one of the first species to appear after the July rains set in.
It becomes very robust at times, simulating *C. geotropa,* but the
spores are longer than in that species.   (See Patouillard, Tab.
Analyt.)   The color of the cap changes in a definite direction;
when young and fresh the red color is predominant, when old the
whitish hues appear.   *C. flaccida* Fr. is said to differ in the tawny
to rust-colored pileus which does not fade in age; I have been un-
able to recognize it in this State.   The gills become yellowish.   Its
shape and habit are like *C. infundibuliformis,* and are therefore
well shown in the illustrations of the latter.   Both are edible and
not likely to be confused with any injurious mushrooms.

778. Clitocybe pinophila Pk.

N. Y. State Mus. Rep. 31, 1879.

PILEUS 2-3 cm. broad, convex, then plane and slightly umbilicate, subinfundibuliform in age, moist, glabrous to minutely squamulose, *tan-color* to dingy-white, even on margin. FLESH whitish. GILLS subdecurrent, close, *narrow,* intervenose, whitish. STEM short, 1.5-2 cm. long, 2 mm. thick, equal, even, *solid,* fibrillose to pruinose, concolor. SPORES elliptical-ovate, narrowed to the apiculus, 5-6 x 4 micr., smooth, white. CYSTIDIA none; basidia 4-spored. ODOR farinaceous. TASTE farinaceous slowly becoming biting to the tongue.

Gregarious. On beds of pine needles, under white pine. New Richmond. September. Infrequent.

The plants do not agree in every respect with Peck's description. The stem is solid when fresh and young. It seems to approach two other species, *C. gallinacea* Fr. and *C. pithyophila* Fr. From *C. gallinacea, C. pinophila* differs in color and habitat and in the tendency to become infundibuliform; from *C. pithyophila, C. pinophila* differs in its small size, color and solid stem, etc. The acridity is slight. We need more microscopic data on these three species.

779. Clitocybe parilis Fr.

Syst. Myc., 1821.

Illustrations: Fries, Icones, Vol. I, Pl. 48.
Cooke, Ill., Pl. 281.

PILEUS 2-3 cm. broad, convexo-plane, obtuse, depressed or cupshaped, dry, *minutely flocculose-scaly, brownish-ashy,* margin even, decurved and flexible, splitting when old. FLESH thin, white, soft. GILLS close to subdistant, long decurrent, arcuate, narrow, becoming dingy-white, *at first slightly cinereous,* few forked. STEM 3 cm. long, 2 mm. thick, equal or subequal, even, pruinose, glabrescent, terete, toughish, stuffed, pale ashy to pallid, base white mycelioid. SPORES 6 x 3.5 micr., elliptic-ovate, smooth, white. TASTE slightly but tardily disagreeable. ODOR somewhat farinaceous.

Singly or gregarious. On the ground in frondose and mixed woods. Ann Arbor. New Richmond. October. Infrequent.

Our specimens had close gills, whereas the European plant is said to have crowded gills. Otherwise it seems to belong here. Barla says the odor is like that of *Armillaria caligata,* or of *jasmine,* at first agreeable then nauseous.

780. Clitocybe sinopica Fr.

Syst. Myc., 1821.

Illustrations: Cooke, Ill., Pl. 647.
       Fries, Icones, Pl. 55, Fig. 2.
       Gillet, Champignons de France, No. 105.

"PILEUS 2-3 cm. broad, thin, soon plane and depressed, *umbilicate,* dry, at first glabrous then flocculose, brick-red then becoming pale. FLESH white, elastic. GILLS decurrent, *very crowded, rather broad,* white becoming yellowish. STEM 2-4 cm. long, 3-8 mm. thick, stuffed, *equal,* subfibrillose, concolor or yellowish. SPORES 6-8 x 4-5 micr. ODOR and TASTE strong, farinaceous."
    Woods. Spring and summer. Infrequent. Reported by Longyear. *C. praecox* might be mistaken for it, but that species has a stouter habit, is quite fleshy on the disk, and the gills are not at all crowded.

781. Clitocybe pulcherrima Pk.

Jour. of Mycology, Vol. 14, 1908.

PILEUS 3-7 cm. broad, convex, then umbilicate-depressed, *citronyellow to cream-color* (Sacc.), fading, opaque, moist, not hygrophanous, *soft,* slightly silky-tomentose on disk, margin even. FLESH white or sometimes tinged cream color, thin on margin. GILLS equally decurrent, *narrow,* subdistant, *ochraceous-yellow,* few forked, edge entire. STEM 4-8 in. long, equal or subequal, spongy at base, stuffed then hollow, at first silky-tomentose then fibrillose with loose longitudinal fibrils, even. SPORES globose, 4-5.5 micr. diameter, *minutely echinulate,* white. ODOR and TASTE mild.
    On decaying leaves or wood. Detroit, New Richmond. September-October. Infrequent.
    The above description was made from fresh co-type material, at the time the type was sent to Peck. The spores have an obscure angularity, and are very minutely spinulose. In this character

they approach *C. spinulosa* Smith, a British species, whose spinulose spores are said to be larger, as much as 8-9 micr. The type was found near Detroit by members of the Detroit Mycological Society. I found it again in the western part of the State. It seems to be rather rare. Its yellow color is unusual in this genus. *C. sulphurea* Pk. has a streaked yellow pileus and stem, adnate gills and larger spores.

Section IV. Hygrophanae. Pileus thin, hygrophanous, not scaly. Flesh soft, watery, scissile.

Subsection I. Cyathiformis. Pileus depressed then cup-shaped: flesh scissile, thin.

*Gills cinereous.

782. Clitocybe cyathiforme Fr.

Syst. Myc., 1821.

Illustrations: Cooke, Ill., Pl. 113.
Plate CLIX of this Report.

PILEUS 2-7 cm. broad, thin, convex, soon plane and umbilicate-depressed, or *cup-shaped,* hygrophanous, fuliginous-brown when young and moist, becoming brownish-gray, glabrous or innately fibrillose, opaque, margin involute and even. FLESH watery, concolor, scissile. GILLS becoming acuminate-decurrent, narrow, *subdistant,* intervenose, varying to close or distant, grayish-brown, edge entire. STEM 4-7 cm. long, 3-6 mm. thick, tapering upwards, *spongy-stuffed, elastic, brownish to cinereous,* fibrillose when fresh, the fibrils forming reticulations, tomentose at base. SPORES 7-9.5 x 5-6 micr., occasionally some larger, elliptical-ovate, with an oblique apiculus, smooth, white; sterigmata stout; basidia 4-spored. ODOR slightly aromatic or none, TASTE mild.

(Dried: Pileus smoky-fuscous to smoky cinnamon; gills brownish-gray.)

Scattered, *on rotten wood,* logs, etc. Ann Arbor, Bay View, Marquette, New Richmond. In coniferous, mixed or frondose woods. September-October. Infrequent.

This is an autumnal species, and with us always occurs on rotten wood. The gills are said to be distant in the European plants.

The gills of our plants are never separated to such extent; they are either truly subdistant or rather close. *C. expallens* Fr. is a species with close gills, but European mycologists seem to consider that this is an ecological variant of *C. cyathiforme*. Excepting the gills all the characters of our specimens are those of the European *C. cyathiforme,* and I am inclined to think that variations with close gills will also have to be included under *C. cyathiforme.* The spores of our collections are all alike, although quite variable in single plants. Barla says the odor is that of hay. Although the gills are ashy-brown, the spores are white. Peck has described two related species, *C. subcyathiforme* and *C. subconcava.* *C. subcyathiforme* is watery-white on the cap when moist, and the gills are white, but the stem is fibrillose-reticulate as in *C. cyathiforme,* the spores slightly smaller; *C. subconcava* has a brownish to reddish-brown cap, its gills are close and subcinereous, but the spores are only 5-6 x 3-4 micr. I have not seen them.

**Gills yellowish.

783.   Clitocybe ectypoides Pk.

N. Y. State Mus. Rep. 24, 1872.

PILEUS 2-5 cm. broad, thin, broadly umbilicate to infundibuliform, finely *virgate* with close-pressed blackish fibrils, *squamulosepunctate, the black points seated on the radiations,* hygrophanous, watery-gray to dull watery-yellow, margin spreading and even. FLESH with an aqueous juice, concolor. GILLS long decurrent, narrow, sometimes forked, *subdistant* or nearly so, *yellowish.* STEM 2-5 cm. long, 2-4 mm. thick, equal, firm, *solid,* concolor or paler, white-mycelioid at base. SPORES elliptical, 8-9 x 4-5 micr., smooth, white.

Scattered, on rotten logs in conifer or mixed woods of northern Michigan. Bay View, Marquette, Huron Mountains. August-September. Frequent locally.

The pileus is sometimes irregular, and the stem may be eccentric. In our plants the gills are always more nearly subdistant than close.

***Gills whitish.*

784. Clitocybe adirondackensis Pk. (EDIBLE)

N. Y. State Cab. Rep. 23, 1872.

Illustrations: N. Y. State Mus. Rep. 54, Pl. 69, 1901.
Hard, Mushrooms, Fig. 71, p. 97, 1908.

PILEUS 2-5 cm. broad, thin, convex then plane and *umbilicato-depressed* to infundibuliform, glabrous, hygrophanous, *white or tinged tan-color,* margin at first decurved, then elevated, even, *with a narrow zone near the edge when moist.* FLESH white, thin. GILLS long decurrent, *crowded, very narrow,* thin, white. STEM 3-7 cm. long, 2-4 mm. thick, cylindrical, *glabrous, stuffed then hollow,* even, white or whitish, mycelioid-thickened at the base. SPORES minute, elliptical-ovate, smooth, 4-5.5 x 3-3.5 micr. TASTE "like that of the common mushroom," Peck.

(Dried: Cap and gills ochraceous-tan, stem paler.)

Gregarious or subcaespitose among leaves, etc., in frondose and mixed woods. Ann Arbor, Marquette, Detroit. Frequent. August-October.

The characters are well shown in Dr. Fischer's photograph in Hard's book. The crowded narrow gills, the dingy white color of the cap varying into a circular zone near the edge, and the stuffed stem distinguish the plant. It seems to be quite common on wooded hillsides of southern Michigan. It approaches *C. eccentrica.*

785. Clitocybe eccentrica Pk.

Bull. Torr. Bot. Club, Vol. 25, p. 321, 1898.

PILEUS 2-5 cm. broad, convexo-plane, umbilicate then infundibuliform and turbinate, glabrous, subhygrophanous, *watery-white and shining when moist,* sometimes tinged ochraceous, buff whitish when dry, the thin surface layer slightly differentiated into long subgelatinous cells, the thin margin even, often lobed, split and finally recurved. FLESH thin, whitish. GILLS *short-decurrent* from beginning, *very crowded, narrow,* somewhat forked, *dingy-white.* STEM 2-4 cm. long, 2-4 mm. thick, slender, equal, stuffed, fibrous, elastic, whitish, pruinose above, *base inserted by a tuft of strigose hairs and continued into the substratum by long white strings or rhizomorphs,* often eccentric. SPORES very minute, 4-5 x 2-3 micr., elliptical-ovate, smooth, white. ODOR mild, TASTE sometimes slightly bitter.

(Dried: Cap and gills pale rufous-tan.)

Caespitose or scattered. On very rotten wood in mixed and frondose woods. Ann Arbor, Bay View, Houghton, etc. July-September. Frequent throughout the State.

This species approaches *C. adirondackensis,* from which the short decurrent gills, the different lustre of the cap and the rhizomorphs at the hairy base of the stem separate it; the spores too, average half a micron smaller. These differences may be merely an expression of habitat, since the one grows mainly on rotten wood, the other among leaves and humus. Another species of Peck, said to grow on rotten wood, is *C. leptoloma.* Here also, the strigose base of the stem and the rhizomorphs are about the only characters of *C. eccentrica* which separate it. It is likely that these three species are variations of one of them.

786. Clitocybe albidula Pk.

N. Y. State Mus. Rep. 46, 1893.

Illustrations: N. Y. State Mus. Rep. 53, Pl. C, Figs. 16-20.

PILEUS 1-4 cm. broad, thin, convex-plane, umbilicate, subhygrophanous, *pale grayish-brown* to whitish, the *umbilicus always darker and brown,* glabrous, margin faintly striatulate. GILLS subdecurrent, crowded, narrow, thin, sometimes forked, intervenose, whitish. STEM 2-5 cm. long, 2-4 mm. thick, equal, stuffed then hollow, concolor, fibrous-toughish, even, white-mycelioid at base. SPORES 5-6 x 3-4 micr., elliptic, smooth, white. ODOR and TASTE farinaceous.

Gregarious, in woods of hemlock and cedar. Bay View. September. Infrequent.

A form occurs with creamy-white pileus and brown umbilicus with spores the same. This form has only a faint odor, but no doubt belongs here. The brown umbilicus and slightly larger spores, along with the grayish tinge in the color, separate this species from the preceding two. It never becomes truly cyathiform nor infundibuliform.

787. Clitocybe caespitosa Pk.

N. Y. State Mus. Bull. 41, 1888.

"PILEUS 2-4 cm. broad, convex-plane then infundibuliform, *often irregular,* slightly silky, hygrophanous, *grayish-brown when moist,* subcinereous or argillaceous when dry. GILLS decurrent, narrow, close, somewhat forked, white. STEM 2-3 cm. long, 4-6 mm. thick, equal, stuffed then hollow, silky, white. SPORES minute, subelliptical, 3-4 micr. long."

In woods. Caespitose, the caps deformed and made irregular by mutual pressure. Reported by Longyear.

Subsection II. Orbiformis. Pileus convex then plane or slightly depressed, often obtuse, polished, not squamulose nor mealy.

****Gills grayish.*

788. Clitocybe metachroa Fr.

Syst. Myc., 1821.

Illustrations: Cooke, Ill., Pl. 115.
　　Patouillard, Tab. Analyt., No. 308.

PILEUS 1-4 cm. broad, thin, convex then plane and depressed, *at first dark-fuscous* then brownish-gray or livid (moist), dull grayish-white (dry), hygrophanous, glabrous, margin even, substriate (dry). FLESH thin, concolor. GILLS adnate to slightly subdecurrent, sometimes by lines, *crowded,* narrow, dark fuscous when young, *then whitish-ashy,* thin, at length flaccid, edge entire. STEM 3-4 cm. long, 2-4 mm. thick, subequal, even, at first *dark fuscous and pruinose-silky,* then grayish and glabrescent, stuffed then hollow, often compressed, toughish. SPORES minute, ovate, 5 x 2.5 micr., smooth, white. CYSTIDIA none. ODOR none or faintly farinaceous after crushing the flesh. TASTE mild.

Gregarious or scattered. On the ground in frondose and conifer woods. Ann Arbor, Marquette. September-November. Infrequent.

The color of the whole plant changes remarkably from the young stage to maturity and in age. *C. ditopoda* Fr. is similarly colored, differing mainly in its strong farinaceous odor and probably in the spore characters. It should not be confused with *C. cyathiforme,* which is larger, has larger spores and usually grows on wood.

789.   Clitocybe ditopoda Fr.

Syst. Myc., 1821.

Illustration: Cooke, Ill., Pl. 116.

PILEUS 2-5 cm. broad, convex then subexpanded and *umbilicate-depressed,* pliant, glabrous, even, hygrophanous, *cinereous or gray-ish-brown* (moist), dull white (dry), margin somewhat irregular. FLESH thin.   GILLS adnate or scarcely subdecurrent, *crowded,* rather narrow, pallid at first, soon *cinerascent* and smoky-gray, edge entire. STEM 2-3 cm. long, 3 mm. thick, terete or more *often compressed,* irregular, *pale cinereous,* stuffed soon hollow, pruinose downwards. SPORES elliptic-ovate, 5-6 x 3-4 micr., smooth, white. CYSTIDIA none.   ODOR and TASTE farinaceous.

Gregarious or subcaespitose. On the ground, among needles and debris of tamarack trees in wet swamp.

Ann Arbor.   October-November.   Infrequent.

This species was abundant in this one locality. It has much in common with *C. metachroa,* but differs from it in the farinaceous odor and in the different color changes in passing from the young to the old stage. The plants also do not have the stiff appearance of *C. metachroa.*

790.   Clitocybe peltigerina Pk.

N. Y. Mus. Rep. 30, 1878.

PILEUS 4-10 mm. broad, *small,* subexpanded, umbilicate, hygrophanous, *grayish-brown and striatulate when moist,* whitish to pale gray when dry, glabrous. GILLS decurrent, *distant,* narrow, somewhat forked and intervenose, *grayish-brown,* thickish, pruinose. STEM 1-2 cm. long, 1.5 mm. thick, equal, solid, elastic, pallid or tinged grayish-brown, pruinose below, base minutely tomentose. SPORES elliptical-ovate, pointed-apiculate, 8-10 x 4-5.5 micr., smooth, white; basidia 4-spored; cystidia none. ODOR and taste none.

Singly or subcaespitose. On Peltigera, one of the lichens. Ann Arbor.   May 5.   Rarely found.

Remarkable for its habitat. It is small and imitates the color of its substratum and is easily overlooked.

**Gills whitish.*

791. Clitocybe morbifera Pk. (Poisonous)

Bull. Torr. Bot. Club, Vol. 25, p. 321, 1893.

Illustration: Plate CLIX of this Report.

PILEUS 1.5-4 cm. broad, convex then plane, sometimes slightly depressed or obtuse, hygrophanous, or at least moist, glabrous, grayish-brown to grayish-buff when moist, *white to alutaceous when dry,* somewhat reviving, margin even and incurved. FLESH thin, whitish. GILLS adnate-decurrent, moderately close, slightly broad in middle, narrowed to a point at both ends, whitish, becoming pale tan in age, thin, edge entire. STEM 2-3.5 cm. long, 2-4 mm. thick, subequal, *solid* and *spongy-fibrous within, pruinose,* slightly fibrillose, *tough,* colored like pileus or paler, straight or curved, not slender.

Microscopic: SPORES oval, minute, about 5 x 3 micr., white, smooth, usually poorly developed; basidia about 20 micr. long; trama of gills of parallel hyphae, 4 micr. in diameter; trama of pileus only slightly wider, all of the trama being composed of compact, narrow, long hyphae; the cuticle is not noticeably differentiated. Cystidia none. ODOR none. TASTE varies, sometimes slight, when fresh it is slightly astringent.

(Dried: Entirely dirty white or grayish-white.)

Singly or subcaespitose among grass *on lawns,* roadsides, etc. Specimens from Adrian found under a syringa bush and elsewhere. October. Adrian, Ann Arbor, and Detroit. Frequency not yet certain, as it is probably often overlooked. *Poisonous.*

This is apparently a dangerous plant. In the case of *C. illudens,* there is no uncertainty in its recognition, as it is more brightly and differently colored than any related mushrooms; but *C. morbifera* has many near relatives which, like *C. dealbata,* are sometimes difficult of separation. Fortunately, no one except beginners, or extreme mycophagists, collect these small species. Still the fact that it grows on lawns where only edible species are normally found, makes this a troublesome intruder. Several families in different parts of the country are now known to have been made sick from eating it. Peck reports a case from Washington, D. C., from which source came the material for his description. Our specimens were sent by E. D. Smith from Adrian, Michigan. Several persons in

Adrian ate *C. morbifera* with a mess of *L. naucina*. The victims suffered blindness, swollen throat, etc. Our specimens did not have the marked taste described by Peck, nor a truly "hollow" stem. It is doubtless the same species however.

792. Clitocybe compressipes Pk.

N. Y. State Mus. Rep. 33, 1880.

PILEUS 2-5 cm. broad, convex then plane and depressed or sub-umbilicate, hygrophanous, thin, glabrous, *pale watery-brown and even when moist,* whitish or tinged tan when dry, edge of margin persistently incurved. FLESH rather thin, concolor, upper layer of trama differentiated and composed of delicate, long, subgelatinous cells. GILLS subdecurrent, close, rather narrow, *pale watery-ochraceous or brownish when moist,* whitish when dry, intervenose. STEM short, 2-3 cm. long, 2-3 mm. thick, soon hollow and compressed, equal, even, glabrous or subvillose, grayish-brown to pallid, attached by tomemtum to leaves, etc. SPORES 4-5.5 x 2.5-3.5 micr., elliptical-ovate, smooth, white. ODOR and TASTE mild.

(Dried: Cap pale tan to dingy white, gills sordid white.)

Scattered or subcaespitose. Among leaves in frondose woods. Ann Arbor. September-October. Infrequent.

These plants do not have the farinaceous odor which is present in *C. albidula* of conifer woods.

793. Clitocybe angustissima Fr.

Epicrisis, 1836-38.

Illustrations: Fries, Icones, Pl. 59, Fig. 2.
    Gillet, Champignons de France, No. 111.
    Cooke, Ill., Pl. 125.

PILEUS 2-5 cm. broad, convex-expanded, *obtuse or subdepressed,* subhygrophanous, glabrous, *watery-white, candicans,* even (moist), slightly striatulate (dry), margin spreading, at length recurved. FLESH thin, whitish. GILLS slightly *subdecurrent,* very narrow, *very crowded,* thin, whitish, edge entire. STEM 3-5 cm. long, slender, 2-5 mm. thick, whitish, flexuous or curved at base, equal or tapering downward, *apex naked,* pubescent at base. SPORES short elliptical, 5-7 x 3-4 micr., smooth. CYSTIDIA none. BASIDIA about 27 x 6 micr., 4-spored. ODOR none or faint.

Scattered, on the ground among leaves in low frondose woods. September. New Richmond. Infrequent.

This is one of a number of similar species, in this case well-marked by the very crowded and narrow whitish gills, the watery-white color and the lack of odor. *C. albidula* Pk. differs mainly in its farinaceous odor. *C. compressipes* Pk. can probably be differentiated by its close rather than very crowded gills and by the compressed stem; both of Peck's species are said to have the caps tinged brownish when moist, and not shining-white (candicans) as in *C. angustissima.*

SUBGENUS LACCARIA. Spores globose, echinulate; pileus usually minutely scaly or floccose.

794. Clitocybe laccata Fr. (EDIBLE)

(*Laccaria laccata*)

Syst. Myc., 1821.

Illustrations: N. Y. State Mus. Rep. 48, Pl. 25, 1896.
    Murrill, Mycologia, Vol. 3, Pl. 40, Fig. 4.
    Hard, Mushrooms, Fig. 76, 77, p. 105, 1908.
    Cooke, Ill., Pl. 139.
    Patouillard, Tab. Analyt., No. 104.
    Gillet, Champignons de France, No. 99.

PILEUS 2-5 cm. broad, thin, convex then plane, subumbilicate, variable in shape, hygrophanous, glabrous at first, then scurfy-scaly, pale red to flesh-red when moist, pale ochraceous-whitish when dry. FLESH thin, moist. GILLS broad, *distant,* broadly emarginate, tinged flesh color, white-pruinose. STEM 2-7 cm. long, 2-6 mm. thick, slender, equal, *fibrous and tough,* stuffed, *pale flesh-red,* sometimes striate. SPORES globose, 8-10 micr., echinulate, spines 1 mm. long, white. ODOR agreeable. TASTE fungoid.

Scattered everywhere in woods, groves, swamps or grassy places, on naked soil, mosses, or leaves, etc. Throughout the season; my earliest record is May 5, the last November 8. Everywhere in the State, in coniferous or frondose woods. Very abundant in wet weather. It is edible, but not particularly well-flavored.

Varieties occur, and the common form shades gradually into var. *striatula* Pk., var. *amethystina* Bolt and var. *pallidifolius.* Var.

striatula Pk. has a very thin cap which is radially striate from near the umbilicate center; spores 9-11 micr. diam., globose, echinulate, the spines about 1 micron long. Var. *amethystina* Bolt. has a darker cap, and beautiful deep-violaceous gills, which are broadly adnate-decurrent. The spores of our specimens of var. *amethystina* are like those of the normal form. Var. *pallidifolia* Pk. is like the common form except that the gills are pallid. This species and its varieties are sometimes confused with *Lactarius subdulcis.*

795.   Clitocybe tortilis Fr.

(*Laccaria tortilis*)

Hymen. Europ., 1874.

Illustration: Patouillard, Tab. Analyt., No. 105.

PILEUS 5-12 mm. broad, submembranaceous, convex then expanded and depressed on disk, *distantly radiately striatulate from the center* when moist, hygrophanous, pale reddish or salmon color, pruinose, disk whitish-scurfy, margin sometimes plicate or splitting, often deformed or irregular. GILLS *distant,* rather narrow, *adnate-subdecurrent,* thick, not forked nor veined, salmon-colored, edge concolor. STEM 1-2 cm. long, 1 mm. thick, slender, equal, *fibrous-toughish, stuffed with a white pith,* pellucid flesh color, glabrous, base white-mycelioid. SPORES *large, globose,* long-echinulate, white, 12-14 micr. diam.; basidia 2-spored.

On the ground, in wet places, sometimes on moss. Marquette. August-September.

This is a distinct species and must not be confounded with *C. laccata* nor its varieties. The spores are nearly twice as large as in that species. It is easily mistaken for a species of the rosy-spored genus Eccila. It has sometimes been referred to as a variety of *C. laccata.*

796.   Clitocybe ochropurpurea Berk.   (EDIBLE)

(*Laccaria ochropurpurea*)

Illustrations: N. Y. State Mus. Bull. 116, Pl. 106, 1907.
   Hard, Mushrooms, p. 98, Pl. XI, Fig. 72, 1908.
   Chicago Nat. Hist. Surv., Bull. VII, Fig. 2, 1909.

PILEUS 5-20 cm. broad, sometimes large, *subhemispherical,* then convex with a decurved margin or nearly plane or depressed, *compact,* rather thick, hygrophanous, purplish-brown when moist, pale grayish-alutaceous when dry, unpolished, margin regular or wavy, upturned in age. FLESH *tough,* concolor or pallid. GILLS *distant, thick,* broad, *adnato-decurrent, purple.* STEM 5-20 cm. long, 1-2 cm. thick, varying much in length and shape, subequal to fusiform or cylindrical, fibrous, often rigid and hard, solid, concolor or paler, sometimes curved or twisted. SPORES globose, short-echinulate, 8-9.5 micr., white, or tinged in mass with a lilac hue. TASTE rather disagreeable.

(Dried: Cap and stem grayish-white to sordid-white, gills smoky-fuscous.)

Scattered or subcaespitose. On bare ground or open grassy places, preferring a hard soil, often in woods, conifer, mixed or frondose. From Isle Royale to the southern limit of the State, everywhere. July-October.

Not as common as *C. laccata.* In its colors and shape it appears somewhat like a purple-gilled Cortinarius, but its texture is different and it lacks a veil. It becomes tender and of agreeable flavor when cooked.

Collybia Fr.

(From the Greek, *kollybos,* a small coin; probably because of the regularity of the disk-like pileus.)

White-spored. Stem *cartilaginous* or with a cartilaginous cuticle. Pileus *soon expanded,* not very fleshy, *its margin at first involute.* Gills adnate, adnexed or almost free, *not decurrent.* Spores mostly small or minute, smooth. Volva and annulus lacking.

Putrescent, thin capped, mostly lignicolous mushrooms, of slow growth, not reviving when moistened except in the section Marasmioideae, and, with few exceptions, of medium or small size. They are mostly attached to decayed wood, like stumps, logs, old buried roots, twigs, leaves, etc.; a few species even occur on decayed mushrooms, while others seem to grow on naked soil. The genus is most closely allied to Marasmius, but the plants differ in not reviving after drying up; from Mycena, the involute margin of the pileus, with its resultant expansion at maturity, is the main distinction. As this is only clearly seen in the very young stage, it is often difficult in mature plants to decide whether one has a Collybia or

Mycena. In the majority of Collybias, however, the pileus is expanded at maturity, but in Mycena the pileus usually remains
campanulate.

The PILEUS is rarely brightly colored. The color may be brown,
ashy, blackish, tan, yellowish, white, or shades of these colors. A
few have a viscid cap, and in one section the cap is hygrophanous;
it is glabrous except in *C. longipes,* and some of the Marasmioideae.
In several of the hygrophanous species the margin is striatulate
when moist. The GILLS are submembranous and soft, and continuous with the trama of the pileus. They are usually white, yellowish,
rufescent or ashy. In one species they are lilac. Some mycologists
have divided the sections by the difference in the width of the gills,
ome species have quite broad gills, others narrow gills. The mode
of attachment separates the genus from Omphalia and Clitocybe,
since they are never decurrent. The STEM is primarily cartilaginous, as in Mycena, Omphalia and many Marasmii. This character
is not always easily recognized, and in some large species like *C.
platyphylla,* the otherwise soft stem may mislead one. Furthermore, the stems of plants belonging to the fleshy-stemmed genera
may, on drying in the wind, become somewhat cartilaginous in
texture, so as to be mistaken for true cartilaginous forms. The
base of the stem is usually rooting, sometimes remarkably so, as
in *C. radicata,* and *C. longipes.* Some species have glabrous stems,
while one section is composed of species with hairy, floccose, or
pruinose stems. The presence of deep or at least evident striations
running up and down the stem is used to set off another section.
A few small species form a small sclerotium from which the fruit-
body develops.

No poisonous species of Collybia are known, although the smaller
species have probably never been tested. Many of the large species
are of good flavor and much sought.

It is probable that some forty-five species occur within the State,
but so far only thirty-four have been identified. The species have
been grouped in various ways by different authors. In the main,
the Friesian arrangement is retained, although somewhat modified.
It seemed that relationships could be better shown by using the
color of the gills to divide the main sections, rather than divide the
whole genus into two main groups having white and cinereous
gills respectively as Fries had done. A new section has been established to contain those species which approach the genus Marasmius. This is called the Marasmioideae and serves as a bridge to
that genus. The genus is therefore composed of the five sections:

I. Tephrophanae.
II. Laevipedes.
III. Striaepedes.
IV. Vestipedes.
V. Marasmioidae.

Key to the Species

(A) Not reviving when moistened. [See also (AA).]
  (a) Stem velvety, tomentose, floccose or pruinose. [For *C. myria-dophylla* with lilac gills, see (aa).]
    (b) Stem with a dense, tawny-brown to blackish, velvety covering.
      (c) Pileus with a viscid, even, separable pellicle; mostly caespitose. 818. *C. velutipes* Fr.
      (cc) Pileus not viscid, striatulate; growing scattered. *C. amabilipes* Pk.
    (bb) Stem not densely velvety.
      (c) Flesh changing to purplish-black where cut or bruised; stem fuliginous, pubescent. 820. *C. succosa* Pk.
      (cc) Flesh not changing black; gills white or whitish.
        (d) Pileus 2.5-5 cm. broad.
          (e) Stem very long, deeply rooted; pileus velvety, brown. 819. *C. longipes* Fr.
          (ee) Stem 3-4 cm. long covered with a close white tomentum, not rooting; pileus glabrous, whitish to pale reddish on disk. 825. *C. hariolorum* Fr.
        (dd) Pileus less than 2 cm. broad; stems slender. (Mycena-like plants.)
          (e) Stem arising from a small tuber, on decaying mushrooms or rich mold; pileus small, 1 cm. or less, whitish. 823. *C. tuberosa* Fr.
          (ee) Stem not arising from tuber-like sclerotia.
            (f) Growing on pine cones, needles, etc.
              (g) Pileus 1-3 cm. broad, fuscous; stem elongated by a tomentose "root." *C. conigena* Fr.
              (gg) Pileus 2-10 mm. broad, creamy-white to pale brownish, minutely pubescent. 822. *C. conigenoides* Ell.
            (ff) Growing on the ground, humus, etc.
              (g) Pileus whitish, faintly reddish-tinged: stem white-pulverulent. 824. *C. cirrhata* Fr.
              (gg) Pileus grayish-brown to smoky brown; stem white, under lens with minute dark points. 821. *C. floccipes* Fr.
(aa) Stem glabrous (often tomentose-hairy at base and pruinose at apex).
  (b) Stem deeply rooting.
    (c) Pileus viscid, radiately wrinkled, grayish, brown, or almost white; gills pure white; very common. 815. *C. radicata* Fr.
    (cc) Pileus not viscid, hygrophanous, rufous-tan, smaller; gills dingy flesh color. 806. *C. hygrophoroides* Pk.
  (bb) Stem without a long, root-like prolongation.
    (c) Pileus large, 6-12 cm. broad.
      (d) Gills broad, subdistant; pileus grayish-brown, etc., streaked with darker fibrils. 816. *C. platyphylla* Fr.
      (dd) Gills narrow, crowded.
        (e) Stem equal, subbulbous at base; pileus whitish, tinged creamy-yellow. 812. *C. albiflavidum* Pk. (*Tricholoma albiflavidum*).

    (ee)   Stem narrowed toward base, short-rooting.
       (f)   Gills yellow or yellowish; pileus ochraceous, not stained.
           817.   *C. scorzonerea* Fr.
      (ff)   Gills white or whitish; pileus stained ferruginous in
           spots. 817.   *C. maculata* A. & S.
(cc)   Pileus less than 6 cm. broad.
  (d)   Pileus white, small, 4-10 mm. broad.
    (e)   Gills narrow; spores narrowly-elliptical, 10 x 4-5 micr.
        C. delicatella Pk.
    (ee)   Gills broad, ventricose; spores subglobose, 4-5 x 3-4 micr.
        C. alba Pk.
  (dd)   Pileus not truly white.
    (e)   Gills lilac-color, narrow, very crowded; pileus 1-2.5 cm.
        broad. 807.   *C. myriadophylla* Pk.
    (ee)   Gills some other color.
      (f)   Gills white or whitish.
        (g)   Gills rather broad, ventricose.
          (h)   Odor alkaline when crushed; pileus grayish-umber,
              hygrophanous, striatulate. 801.   *C. alcalinolens*
              Pk.
         (hh)   Odor not alkaline.
          (i)   Taste bitter; pileus pale yellowish-brown, umbili-
              cate. *C. esculentoides* Pk.
          (ii)   Taste farinaceous; pileus and stem dark rufous-
              brown, obtuse. 814.   *C. succinea* Fr.
       (gg)   Gills rather narrow.
         (h)   Caespitose or densely gregarious on decaying logs;
             pileus grayish-brown to buff.
          (i)   Pileus subumbilicate, not hygrophanous; gills ad-
              nate. 813.   *C. abundans* Pk.
          (ii)   Pileus obtuse, hygrophanous; gills nearly free.
              802.   *C. familia* Pk.
          (iii)   See also *C. dryophila.*
        (hh)   Solitary, gregarious or subcaespitose.
          (i)   Pileus smoky-brown; not hygrophanous; stem 4-6
              mm. thick, brown. *C. fuliginella* Pk.
          (ii)   Pileus pale, chestnut, reddish-brown, yellowish
              brown, waxy-yellow or tan.
            (k)   Stem striate; pileus umbonate; gills crenu-
                late on edge. 797.   *C. butyracea* Fr.
            (kk)   Stem not striate.
             (l)   Stem reddish-brown or yellowish, pileus pale
                reddish-brown, yellowish, tan, etc. 798.   *C.*
                dryophila Fr.
            (ll)   Stem white or whitish.
             (m)   Pileus yellowish-white tinged rufous,
                slightly rugose; stem strict. 800.   *C.*
                strictipes Pk.
             (mm)   Pileus reddish-brown to chestnut
                (moist); gills serrate on edge. 799.   *C.*
                lentinoides Pk.
  (ff)   Gills not at length white or whitish.
    (g)   Gills yellow or yellowish.
      (h)   On decaying wood, scattered; pileus yellow; gills
          brownish-red on drying. 804.   *C. colorea* Pk.
      (hh)   On the ground, caespitose; pileus watery-rufous-
          brown at first, then honey-yellow. 803.   *C. aquosa*
          Fr. var.
    (gg)   Gills soon rufescent or cinerascent or darker.
      (h)   Pileus pale tan or flesh-reddish (moist); gills tinged
          flesh color. 805.   *C. acervata* Fr.

      (hh)   Pileus hygrophanous, blackish or smoky-brown at first; gills cinerascent or dark brown.
       (i)   Odor and taste farinaceous; pileus striatulate (moist). 811. *C. expallens* Pk. var.
      (ii)   Odor none or slight; pileus even.
         (k)   Stem 2-3 cm. long, pileus umbilicate, pitch-black (moist); on burnt ground. 808. *C. atrata* Fr.
       (kk)   Stem longer; pileus blackish - chestnut (moist), obtuse; on mossy ground. 809. *C. plexipes* Fr. var.
     (kkk)   Stem 2-3 cm. long; pileus grayish-brown; gills fuscous; on wood. 810. *C. atratoides* Pk.
(AA)   More or less reviving when moistened.
  (a)   Pileus umbilicate, fibrillose-hairy.
    (b)   Pileus 1-2.5 cm. broad, zonate, dark tawny. 827. *C. zonata* Pk.
   (bb)   Pileus 0.5-1 cm. broad, umbilicus papillate. 828. *C. stipitaria* Fr.
  (aa)   Pileus not umbilicate.
    (b)   Pileus and stem sulphur-yellow, tough, sub-rigid. 830. *C. lacunosa* Pk.
   (bb)   Not yellow.
    (c)   Pileus 2-5 cm. broad, convex-plane, hygrophanous; stem densely whitish-pubescent; on the ground. 826. *C. confluens* Fr.
   (cc)   Pileus 5-8 mm. broad, conical-campanulate; stem instititious, on twigs of arbor vitae. 829. *C. campanella* Pk.

Section I. Tephrophanae. Pileus more or less hygrophanous; at least watery.

**Gills white or whitish.*

797. Collybia butyracea Fr. (EDIBLE)

Syst. Myc., 1821.

Illustrations: Michael, Führer f. Pilzfreunde, Vol. III, No. 104.
Cooke, Ill., Pl. 143 (faded).
White, Conn. State Geol. and Nat. Hist. Surv. Bull. 15, Pl. VIII, 1910.
Gillet, Champignons de France, No. 149 (faded).

PILEUS 3-7 cm. broad, convex-expanded, *umbonate* to subumbonate, even, glabrous, reddish-brown, darker when young, fading with age, surface *with a fatty lustre when moist,* subhygrophanous, or watery and soft in wet weather. FLESH becoming white, thickish on disk. GILLS adnexed, almost free, crowded, thin, rather narrow, *white,* edge *crenulate.* STEM 3-7 cm. long, conico-attenuated upwards, 4-6 mm. thick above, at length subequal and sub-bulbous, *striate,* glabrous or slightly downy toward base, cuticle rigid-cartilaginous, base mycelioid. SPORES 5-7 x 3-3.5 micr., narrowly ovate, pointed-apiculate, smooth, white; CYSTIDIA none. ODOR and TASTE mild.

Solitary or gregarious. Very common in woods of white pine, New Richmond; infrequent in frondose woods, Detroit, Ann Arbor and Marquette. July-October.

The "buttery Collybia" is often hard to separate from *C. dryophila* by descriptions, and there are probably intermediate forms. The typical plant seems to be limited to *coniferous woods*. The striate stem influenced Fries to refer it tb the Striaepedes; but it seems to belong more naturally to this group, from its general appearance and the somewhat hygrophanous flesh. The umbo often disappears somewhat in age, but the crenulate gills, and striate stem seem quite consistent for the typical plants of conifer woods. The spores of this species and several of those following are practically the same. It is probable that the form in frondose woods is an ecological variety, as it rarely possesses a distinct umbo.

798.   Collybia dryophila Fr.   (EDIBLE)

Syst. Myc., 1821.

Illustrations: Cooke, Ill., Pl. 204.
  Gillet, Champignons de France, No. 156.
  Michael, Führer f. Pilzfreunde, Vol. III, No. 103.
  Patouillard, Tab. Analyt., No. 315.
  Murrill, Mycologia, Vol. 3, Pl. 40, Fig. 8.
  N. Y. State Mus. Bull. 122, Pl. 111, 1908 (coloring poor).
  Plate CLX of this Report.

PILEUS 3-5 cm. broad, convex-expanded, obtuse or depressed, often irregular, even, glabrous, subhygrophanous, color variable, *tan, with reddish or yellowish shades,* disk darker, sometimes bay-brown, often faded. FLESH white, rather thin and pliant, somewhat watery. GILLS adnexed or narrowly adnate, *narrow, crowded, whitish* or pallid (yellowish in variety), edge entire or minutely crenulate. STEM 3-6 cm. long, 2-4 mm. thick, equal or tapering upward, *reddish-brown* or yellowish-tinged, usually concolor, glabrous, hollow, cuticle cartilaginous, white-mycelioid at base. SPORES 5-7 x 3.5 micr., smooth, narrowly ovate, white, CYSTIDIA none. ODOR and TASTE mild.

Gregarious or subcaespitose. Typical form in hard-wood forests, groves, etc. June to October. (Earliest record, May 28; latest, October 4.) Very common, throughout the State.

This species is the center of a "group," including *C. butyracea, C. lentinoides, C. estensis* Morg., *C. aquosa* and *C. acervata,* which may be called the "dryophila" group. There seem to be a whole series of variations, connecting *C. dryophila* and *C. butyracea* on the one hand, and *C. dryophila* and *C. aquosa* on the other. It is difficult in many cases to refer individual collections in a very strict way to the species mentioned, except by generalizing the descriptions. In this report, it seemed best to select plants which well fit the Friesian descriptions, and draw our descriptions from them, and consider intermediate plants as "forms" or "varieties" of these, leaving such identifications to the students. Secretan, long ago, named a number of these varieties; but such names carry very little meaning, as even the varieties may vary. It is very probable that the varieties occur under different influences of habitat, i. e., grow in different soil, under different moisture conditions, etc. The spore print is white at first, but may become yellowish-tinged with age. The plants appear at their best growing from thick mats of leaves and humus, and are then often caespitose and the stems are covered toward the base with a white down. The caps are delicious when fried with bread-crumbs and egg.

799. Collybia lentinoides Pk.

N. Y. State Rep. 32, 1879.

"PILEUS 1-2.5 cm. broad, convex or nearly plane, obtuse, glabrous, *hygrophanous,* reddish-brown or chestnut color when moist, reddish-tan color when dry. GILLS adnexed, narrow, close, *white,* serrate on edge. STEM 3-5 cm. long, about 2 mm. thick, equal, even or slightly striate, hollow, slightly pruinose at top, *white or whitish.* SPORES 6-7.5 x 4 micr.

"This species bears some resemblance to *C. dryophila,* from which it is differentiated by its hygrophanous pileus, serrated gills and white stem."

Reported by Longyear. Swamps. Summer. Apparently rare.

800. Collybia strictipes Pk. (EDIBLE)

N. Y. State Mus. Rep. 41, 1888.

Illustration: Plate CLXI of this Report.

PILEUS 2.5 to 6.5 cm. broad, convex then plane, margin at

length raised, obtuse to subdepressed, *slightly rugose on disk,* rarely even, glabrous, *subhygrophanous,* yellowish-white, tinged with red, more deeply colored on disk, margin often slightly striate when moist. FLESH thin, watery-white when moist. GILLS adnexed or nearly free, rather crowded, medium width, *white or whitish,* edge minutely fimbriate. STEM 2-5 cm. long, 3-6 mm. thick, strict, *equal,* hollow, terete or subcompressed, sometimes twisted, even, glabrous, pruinose at apex, *white to pellucid,* white-mycelioid or strigose at base. SPORES narrowly elliptic-ovate, 6.5-8 x 3-3.5 micr., pointed at one end, smooth, white in mass. CYSTIDIA none; *sterile cells* on edge of gills short and slender. ODOR and TASTE mild.

Gregarious or scattered. Low, moist, rich frondose woods; on the ground or among mosses. Ann Arbor and New Richmond. Probably throughout the State. September-October. Infrequent.

The straight, pellucid-white stem and rugose cap distinguish it. Luxuriant specimens have rugose lines over the whole surface of the cap. The colors are rather clear compared with those of *C. dryophila* and *C. butyracea.* Peck compares it with *C. maculata,* from which it is easily distinct. *C. estensis* Morg. (Cinn. Soc. of Nat. Hist. Journ., Vol. 6, 1883, Plate 5) is very close, and may be a variety.

801.   Collybia alcalinolens Pk.

N. Y. State Mus. Rep. 49, 1896.

Illustration: Plate CLXII of this Report.

PILEUS 1-2.5 cm. broad, at first ovate with incurved margin, *hygrophanous,* glabrous, grayish-umber (moist), grayish-brown or cinereous (dry), *margin striatulate when moist.* FLESH thin, whitish or grayish-tinged. GILLS sinuate-adnexed or emarginate, rather broad, *subdistant,* subventricose, white then obscurely grayish-tinged, edge entire. STEM 3-5 cm. long, 2-4 mm. thick, rarely thicker, equal, subpruinose, glabrescent, *shining even,* flexuous, stuffed then hollow, cartilaginous, elastic, whitish. SPORES oblong-ovate, narrow, 7-10 x 4 micr., smooth, white. CYSTIDIA and *sterile cells* lacking. BASIDIA about 27 x 5-6 micr., 4-spored. ODOR strong, *alkaline.* TASTE mild.

Gregarious or subcaespitose. On the ground among leaves, rich frondose woods. Ann Arbor. October-November. Frequent locally.

This species is known by its odor, its finally striate pileus and by its shining stem. It has the appearance and size of a Mycena, but the pileus is soon expanded. It reminds one strongly of *Collybia floccipes,* but the latter has numerous cystidia and no odor, although it grows in similar places.

802. Collybia familia Pk. (EDIBLE)

N. Y. State Cab. Rep. 23, 1872.

Illustrations: N. Y. State Mus. Bull. 75, Pl. 84, 1904.
Marshall, The Mushroom Book, Pl. 16, op. p. 67, 1905.
Plate CLXIII of this Report.

PILEUS 1-3.5 cm. broad, *fragile,* convex or hemispherical, then expanded, *obtuse,* glabrous, hygrophanous, even or margin substriatulate when moist, watery-brownish-buff (moist), *creamy-buff to whitish* (dry), margin at length recurved and split radially. FLESH thin, concolor. GILLS adnexed or almost free, crowded, narrow, whitish, edge entire. STEM 4-8 cm. long, 2-3 mm. thick, *slender,* equal, toughish, stuffed then hollow, glabrous, rarely minutely flocculose, subconfluent at base with mycelioid tomentum, whitish. SPORES subglobose to oval, 3-4.5 x 3 micr., few larger, smooth, white. CYSTIDIA and *sterile cells* none. ODOR and TASTE none.

Densely *caespitose.* On decaying trunks and logs of hemlock and tamarack. Huron Mountains, Marquette, Munising, New Richmond, Ann Arbor. August-October. Infrequent.

Because of their edibility, it is fortunate that the abundant clusters of from ten to twenty individuals are rarely attacked by grubs; these clusters often cover a large part of a log. The species has the general habit of *Collybia abundans* from which it is distinguished by the hygrophanous flesh and by the pileus not being umbilicate nor virgate. The European *Collybia lacerata* Fr. has a similar habit and appearance, but its gills are said to be broad and distant. Peck compares it with *C. acervata,* a caespitose species with very different colors. The Ann Arbor specimens were found on tamarack logs.

**Gills yellow or yellowish.*

803. Collybia aquosa Fr. var. (EDIBLE)

Syst. Myc., 1821.

Illustration: Fries, Icones, Pl. 66, Fig. 2.

PILEUS 2-5 cm. broad, convex at first, soon plane or depressed, distinctly *hygrophanous,* watery-brown or rufous-brown *with a yellow cast* (moist), pale tan to buff (dry), obscurely rugulose, *margin striatulate when moist,* even when dry. FLESH thin, subpliant, whitish, soft. GILLS adnexed or almost free, rounded behind, narrow, crowded, *luteous or pallid with sulphur tinge,* becoming erose. STEM 5-7 cm. long, 4-6 mm. thick, *equal or subequal,* hollow, subterete or compressed, minutely flocculose-pubescent, even, cuticle cartilaginous, straight or flexuous, *pallid or tinged sulphur-yellow,* especially above, extreme base slightly inflated-bulbous. SPORES 5-6 x 3 micr., narrowly ovate, smooth, white. CYSTIDIA none. ODOR and TASTE mild.

Caespitose. On the ground, among tamaracks or low frondose woods. Ann Arbor. May 20-June.

This is intermediate between *C. dryophila* and *C. aquosa,* but because of its hygrophanous, watery flesh and finely striatulate pileus it seems closer to *C. aquosa.* The plant has a honey-yellow cap and stem, shading its citron or sulphur when fresh and moist, but soon fading. The gills of *C. aquosa* are said to be pallid, in which respect our plant differs somewhat. It forms tufts among grass in drained tamarack swamps or among leaves in low woods. The base of the stem is slightly enlarged, not truly bulbous nor strigose-hairy. It seems to be somewhat related to *C. acervata.* Whether it has been described is uncertain.

804. Collybia colorea Pk.

N. Y. State Mus. Rep. 26, 1874.

"Pileus 1-3 cm. broad, convex-expanded, subumbilicate, *hygrophanous,* glabrous, "luteous"-yellow, not striate, paler when dry. FLESH rather thin, soft, yellowish. GILLS adnexed, emarginate, close, moderately broad, *luteous* to sordid-ochre, edge entire. STEM 2-4 cm. long, 2-4 mm. thick, *equal,* even, subpruinose, hollow, gla-

brous, colored like pileus. SPORES subglobose or broadly elliptical, 4-5 micr."

Scattered or subcaespitose. On decaying wood, especially of pine.
Negaunee, New Richmond, Greenville (Longyear). June-September. Rare.

An unidentified Michigan plant approaches this rather closely.
It has the same colors, etc., but differs in its fleshy-fibrous, solid
stem and bitterish taste. The spores are white.

***Gills rufescent.

805. Collybia acervata Fr. (EDIBLE)

Syst. Myc., 1821.

Illustrations: Fries, Icones, Pl. 64, Fig. 2.
Gillet, Champignons de France, No. 147.
Cooke, Ill., Pl. 267.
Hard, Mushrooms, Fig. 87, p. 117.
Peck, N. Y. State Mus. Bull. 75, Pl. 84, 1904.

"PILEUS 2-5 cm. broad, convex, becoming expanded or nearly
plane, glabrous, *hygrophanous,* pale tan color or incarnate red and
sometimes obscurely striatulate on the margin when moist, whitish
after the escape of the moisture. GILLS close, rounded behind,
slightly adnexed or free, whitish, or slightly tinged pink. STEM
5-7.5 cm. long, 3-5 mm. thick, equal, hollow, slender, rigid but brittle,
glabrous except the white-tomentose base, *reddish-brown* or purplish-brown. SPORES elliptic, 6-7.5 x 4 micr., white."

Caespitose: On decaying prostrate trunks and leaves, or on half-
buried rotten wood. August-September. Ann Arbor. Infrequent.

The description is obtained from Peck, (N. Y. State Mus. Bull.
75), as my own notes are incomplete. This species may be merely an
ecological variety of *C. dryophila.* Like Hard, I have found it in
localities formerly occupied by saw-mills. The gills become slightly rufescent in age. Our plant does not seem to agree well with
the European descriptions.

806.   Collybia hygrophoroides Pk.

N. Y. State Mus. Rep. 32, 1879.

Illustration: Plate CLXIV of this Report.

PILEUS 2-4 cm. broad, *obtusely conical at first* and reddish-brick color, then campanulate to expanded and almost plane, with or without umbo, rufous-tan (moist), dull-tan or isabelline (dry), hygrophanous, glabrous, even, margin straight at first.   FLESH thin, whitish.   GILLS arcuate-uncinate or deeply emarginate, almost free at times, close, *rather broad,* ventricose, dingy white at first, *then tinged flesh color,* edge becoming eroded.   STEM 5-12 cm. long, 2-5 mm. thick, *tough,* often long and twisted, *longitudinally striate* to sulcate, lower third *rooting* and densely white-to-mentose, upper part pallid to rufescent and pruinose, stuffed then hollow, curved or straight.   SPORES oblong, 5-6.5 x 3-3.5 micr., smooth, white in mass.   CYSTIDIA rather abundant on sides of gills, *slender, acuminate above,* 50-60 x 4-5 micr.

Solitary to subcaespitose or scattered.   On the ground in low, moist, maple and oak woods.   Ann Arbor.   May-July.   Rare and local; rather common in a single locality.

This is apparently a Mycena as shown by the straight margin of the young pileus.   It somewhat resembles Cooke's figure of *M. excisa* (Plate 148), (= *M. berkeleyi* Mass.) which is certainly not the *M. excisa* figured by Fries (Icones).   That species, however, grows on trunks of pine, and the color is different from ours according to Fries' description.   The young, unopened pileus resembles that of *Hygrophorus conicus* in color and shape, as pointed out by Peck.   It seems to have no direct relationship to either Mycena or Collybia.   The lower half or third is usually immersed in the soil which adheres to the tomentum when pulled up; this portion may be attenuated or scarcely so as shown in our plate.   The older plants have rufescent gills and stem, but the spore-print is white.   Our specimens were seen and identified by Peck, who says it is a very rare species.

****Gills lilaceous.*

807. Collybia myriadophylla Pk.

N. Y. State Mus. Rep. 25, 1873.

Illustration: Hard, Mushrooms, Fig. 85, p. 115, 1908.

PILEUS 1.5-2.5 cm. broad, soon plane or depressed, flexible, *hygrophanous,* glabrous, even, sometimes umbilicate or mammilate, *dull umber-brown with lilac tinge* (moist), ochraceous-buff (dry). FLESH very thin. GILLS slightly adnexed, *very crowded, narrow,* linear, thickish, *dark lilac,* edge entire. STEM 2-3 cm. long, 1-1.5 mm. thick, slender, equal, terete or compressed, stuffed by a white pith, then hollow, *dull lilac to reddish-brown,* subglabrous, sometimes densely silky-pruinate. SPORES very minute, 3-4 x 2 micr., elliptic-oval. CYSTIDIA none.

Gregarious. On mossy hemlock or tamarack logs or wood. July to October. Ann Arbor (on tamarack), New Richmond, South Haven, Bay View and Houghton. Infrequent.

A very distinct little Collybia, sometimes lilac-tinged throughout; this color persists longer on the gills than elsewhere. The gills are often glaucous, and on drying become reddish-brown. The stem is sometimes attenuated below and rooting; at times it is entirely white-pruinose with a tuff of lilaceous strigose hairs at the base. The species seems to be limited to coniferous woods.

*****Gills cinerascent or rufescent.*

808. Collybia atrata Fr.

Syst. Myc., 1821.

Illustrations: Fries, Icones, Pl. 70, Fig. 1.
   Cooke, Ill., Pl. 155.
   Gillet, Champignons de France, No. 148.
   Hard, Mushrooms, Fig. 83, p. 113, 1908.

"PILEUS 1-2.5 cm. broad, *tough,* plano-depressed, never papillate, convex toward margin, very glabrous, orbicular, umbilicate, *even,* *pitch-black* and shining (moist), fuscous (dry). FLESH rather thick, firm. GILLS adnate, scarcely decurrent, at first arcuate, then straight, *rather broad, subdistant,* whitish to gray, then fuscous. STEM *short,* 2-3 cm. long, 2-4 mm. thick, tough, equal or subequal, *glabrous,* stuffed then hollow, *cartilaginous, fuscous* within and without." SPORES 5-6 x 4 micr., elliptical (Schroeter, W. G. Smith). ODOR *none.*

Around burned stumps or burned over soil, in exposed places.

The above description is taken from Fries' Icones. The occurrence of the species in Michigan is somewhat uncertain, as my notes are incomplete. June. Ann Arbor. Infrequent to rare.

A Marasmius-like plant in appearance, but it does not revive. When young and fresh, it seems to be firm, but the thin margin is soon flexible. The gills are not ventricose, and a section through them reveals peculiar hyphae forming the central layer, which are dark colored from blackish-brown granules in their interior; they are not truly ashy, but dark cinnamon-brown when fresh and mature. The base of the stem is sometimes strigose-hairy with fuscous-brown hairs, and under high magnification the rest of the stem is seen to be covered with short, intertwined or spreading dark hairs. On drying the pileus becomes rusty-reddish, or occasionally appears scorched. There are some very similar species and the group needs further study. It is said to occur in autumn.

809. Collybia plexipes Fr. var.

Syst. Myc., 1821.

Illustration: Plate CLXV of this Report.

PILEUS 1-2.5 cm. broad, campanulate-expanded, *obtuse,* glabrous, hygrophanous, *blackish-chestnut* (moist), *rufous when drying,* obscurely rugulose-striatulate when moist, not shining. FLESH concolor, very thin on margin. GILLS slightly adnexed, narrow, tapering outward, thickish, close to crowded, plane, *brown, glaucescent,* edge entire. STEM 3-5 cm. long, 1.5-2.5 mm. thick, subequal, opaque, tubular, *subterete or compressed and furrowed,* flexuous, cartilaginous, often curved, tough, subglabrous, black, paler at apex. SPORES minute, elliptic-ovate, 5-7 x 2.5-3 micr., white, smooth. CYSTIDIA none. ODOR and TASTE none.

Caespitose or subcaespitose to solitary. On very rotten wood, among moss, etc., about old stumps and mounds, in frondose woods.

810. Collybia atratoides Pk.

N. Y. State Rep. 32, 1879.

Illustration: Hard, Mushrooms, Fig. 86, p. 116, 1908.

"PILEUS 1-2 cm. broad, convex, subumbilicate, glabrous, hygrophanous, *blackish-brown (moist)*, grayish-brown and shining (dry). FLESH thin. GILLS adnate, *rather broad, subdistant,* intervenose, grayish-white. STEM 2-3 cm. long, 1-2 mm. thick, equal, hollow, glabrous, grayish-brown, with a mycelioid tomentum at base. SPORES nearly globose, about 5 micr. diameter.

"Gregarious or subcaespitose. On decaying wood and mossy sticks in woods."

The description is adapted from Peck. Hard points out that the margin of the pileus is often crenate. It doubtless occurs within the State, and may be confused with Mycena by its shape and size.

811. Collybia expallens Pk. var.

N. Y. State Mus. Rep. 44, 1891.

PILEUS 1-2.5 cm. broad, orbicular, convex-expanded, depressed or subumbilicate on disk, *hygrophanous, at first blackish,* then brown to pale fuscous, *glabrous, striatulate on margin when* moist. FLESH rather thin, brownish then whitish. GILLS adnate, seceding, medium width, close to subdistant, fuscous, edge entire. STEM 1-2 cm. long, 2-4 mm. thick, tapering downward, tough, hollow, sometimes compressed or grooved, cartilaginous, livid-brown, sometimes blackish on handling, pruinose-pubescent.   SPORES subglobose, 5 x 4 micr., smooth, white. CYSTIDIA and STERILE CELLS none. ODOR and TASTE *farinaceous.*

Gregarious among fallen needles of white pine. New Richmond. September. Infrequent.

Differs from *C. atrata* and *C. atratoides* by the presence of a distinct farinaceous odor, and a striate margin to the pileus. It approaches *C. ambusta* except in odor and the lack of a papillate pileus. The stem is pruinose, at least at the apex.

Section II. Laevipedes. Putrescent; not hygrophanous; stem *glabrous, not conspicuously striate.*

812.   Collybia albiflavida (Pk.)   (EDIBLE)

N. Y. State Mus. Rep. 23, 1872 (as *Tricholoma albiflavidum*).

PILEUS 5-12 cm. broad, convex-expanded, then depressed, obtuse or slightly umbonate, umbo subobsolete and darker, moist, *whitish or creamy-yellow*, even, glabrous, margin at first involute.   FLESH white.   GILLS adnexed-emarginate, *narrow, crowded,* thin, white or whitish, edge entire.   STEM 6-18 cm. long, 5-8 mm. thick, equal above the *bulbous base,* solid, fibrous within, *cuticle cartilaginous,* whitish.   SPORES elliptical, smooth, obtuse, 7-10 x 4.5-5.5 micr., white in mass.   CYSTIDIA lanceolate, scattered or infrequent on sides of gills, often crystallate at apex, 55-65 x 10-15 micr.   ODOR and TASTE none.

Solitary, gregarious or subcaespitose.   On the ground in frondose or coniferous woods, among fallen leaves.   Throughout the State. June-September.   Frequent.

This noble plant is found frequently, especially in moist ravines of most kinds of woods.   It was referred by Peck to Tricholoma, where he considered it close to *T. lascivum.*   Collectors nearly always mistake it for a Collybia, and this tendency is given a basis because of the presence of cystidia on the gills, and by the nature of the stem, whose rind is cartilaginous.   The plant presents a stiff appearance due to the straight and rather rigid-elastic stem.   It sometimes attains a much larger size than the original description indicates.   A form occurs in low, wet or swampy places, with similar habit and structure, but smaller and darker in color.   The color is almost smoky-brown, and the general appearance suggests a form of *Tricholoma melaleucum;* its microscopic details, however, agree with the above species; its pileus is 2.5-5 cm. broad.   *T. albiflavidum* has a disagreeable odor at times, but this may disappear, especially after it is picked and left overnight.

813.   Collybia abundans Pk.   (EDIBLE)

N. Y. State Mus. Rep. 29, 1878.

Illustration: Plate CLXVI of this Report.

PILEUS 1-3 cm. broad, convex or nearly plane, *subumbilicate,* whitish or pale grayish-brown, disk darker, *innately fibrillose,* fibrils more dense on disk, the thin margin at length splitting. FLESH thin. GILLS adnate, rather narrow, close, sometimes veiny, white. STEM 3-5 cm. long, 2 mm. thick, rather short, equal, glabrous, hollow, often curved, easily splitting, concolor or whitish. SPORES subglobose, 5-6 micr. ODOR and TASTE mild.

Caespitose. On decaying wood and logs, in frondose and mixed woods, especially in the north. Ann Arbor, Marquette, Houghton. August-October. Infrequent.

The "abundant Collybia" usually grows in great profusion when it occurs. It is very similar in general appearance to *Collybia familia,* but is usually smaller and shorter-stemmed; its pileus has a slight umbilicus; it is not hygrophanous, and when dried usually becomes rufescent,—a special characteristic of the stem.

814. Collybia succinea Fr.

Epicrisis, 1836.

Illustrations: Fries, Icones, Pl. 65, Fig. 3.
　　　　　　　 Cooke, Ill., Pl. 151.

PILEUS 1-3 cm. broad, convex-campanulate, subexpanded, smoky rufous-brown, becoming paler, moist, glabrous, even, firm at first then flexible. FLESH becoming whitish, rather thin. GILLS *adnexed, broad,* close to *subdistant,* thickish, ventricose, whitish, edge minutely serrulate. STEM 2-3 cm. long, 1.5-3 mm. thick, equal, *glabrous,* stuffed then hollow, even, cartilaginous, tough, pruinose at apex, *dark rufous-brown.* SPORES oblong, obtuse, 8-9 x 3-3.5 micr., white. CYSTIDIA ventricose, acuminate-pointed above, 45 x 12 micr., abundant on edge of gills, few elsewhere. TASTE and ODOR farinaceous.

Gregarious. On the ground in hemlock-beech woods. New Richmond. September. Infrequent.

The colors are well represented by the illustrations referred to. The farinaceous odor is not mentioned by the European authors, but in other respects the characters of our plants are apparently the same as of those of Europe.

Section III.   Striaepedes.   Putrescent; not hygrophanous; stem *conspicuously striate,* glabrous.

815.   Collybia radicata Fr.   (EDIBLE)

Syst. Myc., 1821.

Illustrations: Hard, Mushrooms, Fig. 78, p. 107, 1908.
> McIlvaine, One Thousand Amer. Mushrooms, Pl. 29, op. p. 112, 1900.
> White, Conn. State Geol. and Nat. Hist. Surv., Bull. No. 3, Pl. 6, op. p. 27, 1905.
> Cooke, Ill., Pl. 140.
> Gillet, Champignons de France, No. 165.
> Peck, N. Y. State Mus. Mem. 4, Pl. 48, 1900.
> Plate CLXVII of this Report.

PILEUS 3-10 cm. broad, convex to nearly plane, sometimes um-bonate, *viscid,* glabrous, grayish-brown to smoky-brown or umber, sometimes nearly white, even or rugose.   FLESH rather thin, white. GILLS *adnexed, broad,* thick, subdistant, white.   STEM elongated, 5-20 cm. long above the surface of the ground, with a long root-like prolongation penetrating the earth, tapering upward, 4-8 mm. thick, rigid-erect, *glabrous, twisted-striate* to sulcate, white above, usually brownish or smoky-brownish elsewhere, cartilaginous. SPORES broadly elliptical, smooth, 14-17 x 9-11 micr.   CYSTIDIA scattered, on edge and sides of gills, 60-80 x 15-18 micr.   ODOR and TASTE mild.

Gregarious or solitary.   On the ground in woods, groves, clear-ings, etc., throughout the State.   June-October.   (Earliest record June 26, latest October 4.)   Common.

The "rooted Collybia" is closely related to *C. longipes,* whose stem has a similar root-like prolongation at the base.   The viscidity of the pileus is almost absent in dry weather.   The stem is usually thick-ened just above the "root," and as Atkinson has pointed out, this "root" is sometimes attached to dead tree roots deep in the soil. They often grow from much decayed stumps or logs, especially in recent clearings.   The clear white of the gills is quite marked. It is one of the first summer mushrooms with which the beginner becomes acquainted, and the great variation in color and size will often mislead him into thinking he has several kinds, especially if he collects without getting the "root."   Peck has named two varieties: Var. *furfuracea:* (Ill., Peck, N. Y. State Mus. Mem. 4, Plate 48, Fig. 9-11). STEM *minutely scurfy.* This variety, therefore, differs mainly from *C. longipes* in viscid cap and spores. **Var.** *pusilla:* (Ill., Peck, N. Y. State Mus. Mem. 4, Plate 48, Fig. 12-14). Cap 1-3 cm. broad, otherwise like the typical form. All of these are edible.

816. Collybia platyphylla Fr. (Edible)

Syst. Myc., 1821.

Illustrations: Marshall, The Mushroom Book, Pl. 15, op. p. 66, 1905.
Hard, Mushrooms, Fig. 79, p. 109, 1908.
White, Conn. State Survey Bull. 15, Pl. 7, 1910.
Peck, N. Y. State Mus. Mem. 4, Pl. 49, 1900.
Michael, Führer f. Pilzfreunde, Vol. III, No. 106.
Fries, Icones, Pl. 61.
Cooke, Ill., Pl. 128.

PILEUS 6-12 cm. broad, at first ovate-campanulate, then convex-expanded, obtuse or depressed, grayish-brown to whitish-gray, *streaked with darker fibrils* or innate scurfy scales, often wavy on margin. FLESH thin, fragile, scissile, white. GILLS adnexed, deeply emarginate, *broad,* subdistant, often transversely striate and splitting, edge entire or eroded, white. STEM 7-12 cm. long, *stout,* 1-2 cm. thick, *fibrous-fleshy,* cuticle subcartilaginous, equal, fibrous-solid becoming cavernous, *fibrillose-striate,* white or whitish, base blunt or attached to thick strands of mycelium. SPORES broadly elliptical, smooth, 8-10 x 6-7 micr., white. (Immature spores abundant in mounts.) CYSTIDIA none. STERILE CELLS on edge of gills, inflated-rounded, 25 x 13 micr. ODOR mild, slightly of anise. TASTE slightly unpleasant when fresh, disagreeable when old.

Solitary, gregarious or subcaespitose. On decaying wood, stumps, humus, etc., in frondose woods, throughout the State after heavy rains. June-October. (Earliest record June 15, latest October 4.)

This species is our largest Collybia although *C. radicata* sometimes has a cap equal in width. The fleshy, scarcely cartilaginous, consistency of its stem may lead one to refer it to the genus Tricholoma. Peck and others say the stem is stuffed or hollow. I have found the young stem solid-fibrous, later tunneled by grubs, and the interior loosened. Insects attack the plant readily and spoil it for use on the table, but as it does not rank very high in flavor, this is of little consequence. Stevenson has incorrectly given the spore measurements as 19 x 13 micr., and McIlvaine has copied the error.

817. Collybia maculata A. & S. (Edible)

Syst. Myc., 1821.

Illustrations: Marshall, The Mushroom Book, Pl. 15, op. p. 66, 1905.
Hard, Mushrooms, Fig. 82, p. 113, 1908.
Murrill, Mycologia, Vol. 6, Pl. 130.

PILEUS 5-15 cm. broad, *compact,* convex then expanded, obtuse or broadly subumbonate, *glabrous,* even, *white with ferruginous* stains or spots, later becoming rusty-red throughout, margin at first inrolled, then waxy or lobed. FLESH white, firm. GILLS adnexed, or nearly free, *very narrow, crowded,* white or whitish, edge entire. STEM 6-16 cm. long, 6-12 mm. thick, equal or sub-ventricose, *attenuated below* and praemorsely rooting, *firm, carti-laginous, striate* or subsulcate, hollow. SPORES subglobose to short-elliptical, 6 x 3-4 micr., smooth, white. CYSTIDIA none.

Solitary or subcaespitose. On the ground, conifer or mixed woods of northern Michigan. Isle Royale, Marquette, Houghton, Bay View. July-September. Infrequent.

The firm, compact flesh, the narrow crowded gills and stained pileus characterize this plant. The pileus is often narrow com-pared with the long and rather stout stem. With age the stains spread and the whole plant becomes reddish. Specimens were found in frondose woods of southern Michigan which approach *C. szorconerea* Batsch. with cream-colored to ochroleucous gills, and bitterish taste; the spores of this form measured 6 x 3 micr. The pileus was rufous-tinged or darker on disk. *Tricholoma subma-culatum* Pk. has smaller spores and a solid stem; otherwise it seems to approach some of the variations of *Collybia maculata.*

Section IV. Vestipedes. Putrescent; stem *velvety, fibrillose* hairy, *floccose* or *pruinose.*

818. Collybia velutipes Fr. (EDIBLE)

Syst. Myc., 1821.

Illustrations: Hard, Mushrooms, Pl. 15, p. 119, 1908.
   Reddick, Dept. of Geol. & Nat. Resources of Indiana, Rep. 32, 1907, Fig. 10.
   Peck, N. Y. State Mus. Mem. 4, Pl. 47, 1900.
   Cooke, Ill., Pl. 184.
   Gillet, Champignons de France, No. 169.
   Murrill, Mycologia, Vol. 1, Pl. 3, Fig. 6.
   Michael, Führer f. Pilzfreunde, Vol. II, No. 82.
   Plate CLXVIII of this Report.

PILEUS 2-5 cm. broad, convex-expanded, *viscid,* obtuse, glabrous, the viscid pellicle separable, tawny, *reddish-yellow,* usually darker on disk and yellowish on margin, even, margin often irregular. FLESH rather thickish, white or tinged reddish-yellow. GILLS adnexed, emarginate, broad, subdistant to close, whitish or yellowish, edge minutely fimbriate. STEM 2-7 cm. long, 3-6 mm. thick, firm, stuffed, then hollow, *densely velvety with short, tawny or blackish-brown hairs,* yellow at apex, *tough,* short-radicating. SPORES oblong, smooth, 7-9 x 3-4 micr. (rarely longer), white in mass. CYSTIDIA none. STERILE CELLS on edge of gills, slender, awl-shaped. ODOR and TASTE mild.

Caespitose. On decaying stumps, logs, roots, etc., as well as on bark of living trees; throughout the State. Most abundant in autumn, in September to December, occurring, however, occasionally any time during the year. In winter it may be found during warm weather, almost surrounded by ice, seeming *to revive* at each warm period. As soon as the snow is gone fresh specimens, which have developed at the first touch of the warm spring sunshine, may be found.

The viscid, reddish-yellow pileus and dark velvety stem are characters by which it is easily known. It may appear to grow from the ground, but in such cases the "root" is usually attached to dead woody matter below the surface. Specimens which had no pileus, and were composed only of a stem, several feet long, were found in the Calumet mine almost a mile beneath the surface of the ground; the characteristic blackish-brown velvety covering on the lower portion indicated that it was clearly a monstrous form of this species; it was growing on the mine timbers. Whether it is truly parasitic on living trees has not been satisfactorily proven. When preparing it for table use, it is best to peel off the viscous pellicle of the cap.

819. Collybia longipes Fr.

Epicrisis, 1836.

Illustrations: Cooke, Ill., Pl. 201.
     Gillet, Champignons de France, No. 160.

"PILEUS 3-5 cm. broad, convex-expanded, subumbonate, *dry,* radiate-wrinkled, clear brown, disk darker, *densely velvety with short brown hairs.* FLESH thin. GILLS almost free, rather broad, subdistant, ventricose, *pure white,* edge fimbriate. STEM 8-12 cm. long, 4-5 mm. thick, solid, firm, straight, thicker below, the base prolonged into an oblique "root," white within, leather-brown to chestnut-brown, pale above, *covered with spreading, tomentose, brown hairs.* SPORES broadly elliptical, 9-10 x 6-7 micr., smooth, white. CYSTIDIA large, flask-shaped, 55 x 17 micr., scattered on sides and edge of gills."

On decayed wood, stumps and logs.

Not with certainty found within the State. The description is adopted from Schroeter, as my notes are incomplete. The plant has much the appearance of *C. radicata,* but the pileus is dry and velvety. McIlvaine reports it in West Virginia, but his remark that "it is more glutinous" than *C. radicata* eliminates his claim. It is included for purposes of comparison.

820. Collybia succosa Pk.

N. Y. State Mus. Rep. 25, 1873.

PILEUS 1-3 cm. broad, subcartilaginous, campanulate to convex, *cinereous-brown to fuliginous, minutely pubescent,* margin incurved and surpassing the gills. FLESH thickish, white at first, *becoming purplish-black where wounded.* GILLS adnate with a slight decurrent tooth, becoming emarginate, moderately broad, tapering in front, close, whitish, *turning blackish where bruised.* Stem 2-5 cm. long, 2 mm. thick, equal, cartilaginous, compact except the stuffed axis, often curved, *clothed with a fine, fuliginous pubescence,* becoming blackish. SPORES minute, globose-ovoid, 3-4 micr. in diameter, smooth, white. CYSTIDIA none; *sterile cells* on edge of gills, abundant, slender, subfiliform. ODOR and TASTE not marked.

Scattered or caespitose. On decayed wood, logs, etc., mostly on hemlock, in coniferous regions. Marquette, Munising, South Haven, New Richmond. July-September.

Easily distinguished by the change of color when bruised. This change is due to lactiferous tubes containing a juice which turns blackish on exposure to the air. These tubes are specialized hyphae interspersed throughout the trama of the pileus, gills and stem. Under the microscope it may be seen that the pubescence is composed of elongated hyaline cells. The presence of a juice which exudes on wounding the plant is unusual in this genus, and reminds one of a section of the genus Mycena; but the incurved margin of the young pileus indicates its relationship with Collybia.

821. Collybia floccipes Fr.

Epicrisis, 1836.

Illustrations: Cooke, Ill., Pl. 1168.
Plate CLXIX of this Report.

PILEUS small, 5-20 mm. broad, conic-campanulate, subexpanded to almost plane, *papillate, grayish-brown to sooty-brown,* almost blackish on umbo, glabrous, faintly striatulate and shining when moist, margin at first incurved. FLESH thin, whitish except cuticle, which is composed of erect, vesiculose cells. GILLS narrowly adnexed, medium broad, close to subdistant, subventricose, *white,* edge pulverulent-fimbriate. STEM 3-5 cm. (sometimes up to 10 cm.) long, flaccid, filiform, 5-2 mm. thick, often rooting, *toughish,* equal, flexuous, even, hollow, white, *minutely dotted under lens, with subcolorous to blackish points,* base with white spreading fibrils. SPORES subglobose, prominently apiculate, 5-6 x 4-5 micr. (with apiculus 1 micr. longer), smooth, white. CYSTIDIA *abundant,* on edge and sides of gills, narrowly lanceolate, 60-90 x 7-11 micr., subobtuse at apex. ODOR and TASTE *none.*

Gregarious, scattered or subcaespitose. On humus, decayed leaves, very rotten wood, etc., in frondose woods. Ann Arbor. May-June. Frequent locally.

This species has the appearance of a Mycena, but the pileus has an incurved margin. A lens is often necessary to detect the minute brownish points on the stem, at other times they are easily visible. These points are due to short, microscopic, dark, cystidia-like hairs. Otherwise the stem is shining and whitish. When growing on much decayed wood the stem may be long, deeply rooting; when on the ground it is scarcely more than attached by the spreading white hairs and is shorter. In size *C. floccipes* reminds one somewhat of *C. alcalinolens* and it grows in similar places, but it has no odor and is not hygrophanous.

822. Collybia conigenoides Ellis

Torr. Bot. Club Bull., Vol. 6.

PILEUS small, 1-5 mm. broad, *convex* then plane, pellucid-striate, dingy cream-colored or tinged tan, *covered by a minute pubescence* (under a lens). FLESH thin, white. GILLS slightly adnexed or free, close to subdistant, medium broad, whitish, becoming yellowish, edge minutely pubescent. STEM filiform, 2-3 cm. long, delicate, minutely pubescent under a lens, attached at base by small rooting white hairs, white. SPORES minute, oblong, smooth, 4-5 x 2-3 micr., white. CYSTIDIA mostly on edge of gills, lanceolate, 25-35 micr. long.

On half-buried cones of white pine. New Richmond. September. Rare.

Peck has described a similar species growing on cones, which he called *C. albipilata*. It has the same kind of spores and cystidia as our species. It is said to be larger with an 8-12 mm. pileus which is brown. In other respects *C. albipilata* is like *C. conigenoides*. I suspect *C. albipilata* is merely a luxuriant form. Cystidia are apt to vary somewhat in large and small plants. Two European species which grow on pine cones have been critically discussed by Bresadola. They are *C. esculenta* and *C. conigena*. Their spores measure 6-8 x 3-4 micr., and hence our plant cannot be referred to them. Their size is also markedly different, the pilei being 1-3 cm. across. Their stems are long, creeping and rooting, and are covered on the rooting portion with a fibrillose tomentum.

823. Collybia tuberosa Fr.

Syst. Myc., 1821.

Illustrations: Michael, Führer f. Pilzfreunde, Vol. II, No. 80.
Gillett, Champignons de France, No. 168.
Cooke, Ill., Pl. 144.

PILEUS *small,* 5-10 mm. broad, convex or nearly plane, obtuse
or subumbonate, even, glabrous or nearly so, *whitish, often tinged
reddish or yellowish.* FLESH thin, white. GILLS adnate, thin,
close, whitish, edge minutely pubescent. STEM slender, 2-4 mm.
long, 1 mm. thick, flaccid, hollow, whitish or reddish-tinged, covered by a thin white cortinoid pulverulence, often nearly glabrous
above, *arising from a reddish-brown or blackish, small sclerotium.*
SCLEROTIUM 2-5 cm. long, 1-2 mm. wide, variable in shape.
SPORES elliptical, 4-5.5 x 2-3 micr., smooth, white.

Gregarious or crowded. On the remains of decayed Agarics
or damp humus. Throughout the State. July-September. Frequent.

The tuber-bearing Collybia is usually aggregated in numbers
on the blackened remains of some mushroom, in which the small,
tuber-like sclerotia are imbedded. Occasionally, however, it appears to develop on much decayed leaf-humus on the ground.
It resembles *C. cirrata* in color and size.

824. Collybia cirrata Fr.

Epicrisis, 1836.

Illustrations: Cooke, Ill., Pl. 144.
Gillet, Champignons de France, No. 150.

PILEUS 5-12 mm. broad, soon plane or slightly depressed, *at
length umbilicate,* sometimes papillate, *slightly silky,* toughish,
white or tinged reddish. FLESH thin, white. GILLS adnate,
narrow, close, whitish. STEM 2-5 cm. long, filiform, equal, somewhat hollow, flexuous, pallid, *covered by a white pulverulence,* with
a fibrillose, radicating base. SPORES minute, elliptical, smooth,
4-5 x 2-3 micr.

Decaying vegetable matter in woods, throughout the State. July-
September. Infrequent.

This little Collybia is closely related to *C. tuberosa.* Authors
differ with reference to the presence or absence of a sclerotium.

Schroeter (Die Pilze Schliesiens, p. 645) describes a small yellow-ish sclerotium from which the stem arises, and which he says forms abundantly between the gills of decaying fungi, especially *Hypho-loma fasciculare*. Berkeley also notes that it is "often attached to a little, yellowish, nodular schlerotium." Stevenson remarks that "it never has a radical tuber." Fries, Gillet and others do not mention a sclerotium; I have not observed any. Most authors agree that it occurs on decaying mushrooms, as well as humus, etc. It differs from *C. tuberosa* in its umbilicate pileus.

825.   Collybia hariolorum Fr.   (EDIBLE)

Syst. Myc., 1821.

Illustrations: Cooke, Ill., Pl. 150.
    Gillet, Champignons de France, No. 159.

PILEUS 2-5 cm. broad, broadly convex-expanded, thin, flexible, *becoming soft and flabby in moist weather,* even, glabrous, *whitish with a rufescent disk* or altogether rufous-tinged, often fading to pallid-whitish; flesh thin, white, *soft.* GILLS adnexed or almost free, *very narrow, crowded,* hollow, thickish, edge entire, collapsing. STEM 2-5 cm. long, 2-3 mm. thick, equal or tapering slightly up-ward, pallid or tinged rufescent, *covered by a white tomentum* which is thinner towards apex, hollow, elastic, cartilaginous, be-coming soft when wet. SPORES small, 6-7.5 x 3 micr., narrowly oblong-ovate, smooth, white. CYSTIDIA none. ODOR strong and somewhat disagreeable when plants are crushed.

Gregarious, often scattered, sometimes caespitose. Among fallen leaves in frondose woods, probably throughout the State. August-September. Rather frequent.

This Collybia may be known by its soft and somewhat collapsible texture, the white tomentosity of the stem, and the pale rufous-white or whitish cap. It has somewhat the appearance of *C. con-fluens* to which it seems related, but as a rule it has a shorter stem, and in wet weather, instead of reviving becomes soft and fragile. The figure of Cooke illustrates our plant fairly well. The rufous tinge of the pileus is apparently more characteristic of American than of European plants.

Section V. Marasmioidae. Plants partially or wholly reviving (not truly putrescent). Hygrophanous or dry. Stem pulverulent, floccose, fibrillose-hairy or floccose-hairy.

The species placed under this new section have anomalous characters which ally them equally with the genus Marasmius. In fact this section and the section Collybiae under Marasmius contain species which intergrade between the two genera, and hard and fast lines of separation are impracticable. *Marasmius oreades* might be included here, as its flesh is more like Collybia than Marasmius. *C. confluens* is an equally good Marasmius.

826. Collybia confluens Fr. (Edible)

Syst. Myc., 1821.

Illustrations: Hard, Mushrooms, Fig. 84, p. 114, 1908.
Cooke, Ill., Pl. 150.
Gillet, Champignons de France, No. 153.

PILEUS 2-5 cm. broad, tough, flaccid, convex-plane, obtuse, *hygrophanous*, reddish-brown (moist), grayish-flesh-colored to whitish (dry), subumbonate, striatulate when moist. FLESH rather thin toward stem, almost as thick as width of gills, white. GILLS free, *narrow, very crowded,* whitish. STEM 5-10 cm. (or more) long, 2-5 mm. thick, subequal, hollow and often compressed, subcartilaginous, tough, *reddish under the dense, whitish pubescence,* even, sometimes grooved, often joined at base by a floccose myceliod web which spreads among the leaves on which it grows. SPORES minute, narrowly pip-shaped, 4-6 x 3-4 micr., white. CYSTIDIA none. STERILE CELLS on edge of gills small. ODOR and TASTE mild or slightly unpleasant.

Coherent in tufts, or gregarious in troops or part-rings. Among fallen leaves on the ground. Throughout the State. July-October. Common.

The colors of the young and old pilei vary considerably; when young they may be almost bay-red, later becoming reddish-brown to grayish or white. The stem is rather long in proportion to the pileus. The species is most common in frondose woods, where its mycelium forms a whitish mould over and among the fallen leaves.

827. Collybia zonata Pk.

N. Y. State Mus. Rep. 24, 1872.

Illustrations: Hard, Mushrooms, Pl. 14, Fig. 81, p. 111, 1908.
White, Conn. State Surv. Bull. 15, Pl. 9, 1910.
Murrill, Mycologia, Vol. 4, Pl. 56, Fig. 8 (as *Collybidium zonatum*).
Lloyd, Mycological Notes, Vol. I, No. 5, Fig. 17, p. 43.

PILEUS 1-2.5 cm. broad, convex or nearly plane, *umbilicate, covered with coarse, tawny, densely matted hairs, arranged in obscure zones*. GILLS free, close, narrow, white. STEM 2-5 cm. long, about 2 mm. thick, firm, equal, hollow, covered with tawny hairs similar to those of the pileus. SPORES broadly elliptical, smooth, 5 x 4 micr., white.

Solitary or subcaespitose. On decaying wood. New Richmond. August-September. Infrequent or rare.

The dark tawny color, the zones on the pileus and the fibrillose-hairy covering of cap and stem distinguish our plant. It revives after drying. When dry the pileus becomes concentrically grooved. Some think it is a large variety of *C. stipitaria*, but as it is easily distinguished from that species, such a view is speculative. To prove this point, it would be necessary to grow one form from spores or tissue derived from the other. This has not been done.

828. Collybia stipitaria Fr.

Syst. Myc., 1821.

Illustrations: Lloyd, Mycological Notes, Vol. I, No. 5, Fig. 15, p. 42.
Berkeley, Outlines, Pl. 5, Fig. 6.
Cooke, Ill., Pl. 149.

PILEUS *small*, 5-12 mm. broad, convex-expanded to plane, *umbilicate, with a minute blackish papilla* in umbilicus, whitish, grayish or pale grayish-tawny, *minutely and radiately fibrillose-hairy* or strigose-hairy, radiate-rugulose when dry. FLESH thin, submembranous, soft. GILLS adnexed-seceding, subdistant to close, narrow, white. STEM 2-5 cm. long, filiform, .5-1 mm. thick, equal, *reddish-black when moist, whitish when dry*, tough, cartilaginous, tubular, *instititious*, clothed with a grayish-white fibrillose covering when dry, sometimes twisted-striate. SPORES elliptic-ovate, pointed at one end, smooth, white, 6-8 x 3-4 micr. Odor none.

Gregarious. On twigs, wood, acorns, etc., in mixed or frondose woods. Throughout the State. Frequent and abundant. June-October.

The pileus of this fine little plant has a delicate circular ridge around the papillate umbilicus. The color of the stem changes markedly; when thrown into water it becomes reddish to blackish, on drying the fibrillose covering becomes pale gray or whitish. The margin of pileus is often fimbriate from the minute strigose hairs. Peck has named a long-stemmed form var. *setipes*. This was found in northern Michigan on several occasions.

829. Collybia campanella Pk.

N. Y. State Mus. Bull. 116, 1907.

Illustration: Lloyd, Myc. Notes, Vol. I, No. 5, Fig. 16 (probably as *C. stipitaria* var. *robusta*).

"PILEUS 6-8 mm. broad, *conical or campanulate* with a papilla at the apex, covered with coarse appressed or deflexed strigose hairs, dark tawny. GILLS ascending, moderately close, whitish. STEM 2-3 cm. long, 1 mm. thick, *institious,* firm, equal, floccose-hairy, colored like the pileus." Spores elliptic-oval, smooth, 7-8 x 3-4 micr., white.

Gregarious. On dead and dry twigs of arbor vitae. Houghton. August.

My specimens were identified by Peck, whose description is reproduced. The plant has the appearance, like all of this section, of a Marasmius. It differs from *C. stipitaria* in its persistent conic-campanulate cap, a character retained when dried. The dark tawny color also remains uniform on the cap and stem of the dried specimens. The floccose-strigose covering of the stem is thick and concolorous. Its habitat seems to be exclusively on cedar twigs.

830. Collybia lacunosa Pk.

N. Y. State Mus. Rep. 26, 1874 (as Tricholoma).

PILEUS 8-15 mm. broad, convex then expanded, dry, *lacunose,* densely furfuraceous, sometimes sulcate-striate to rugose, *sulphur-yellow to golden-yellow.* GILLS adnate to subdecurrent, rather broad, *distant*, thick, sometimes *intervenose*, white, edge pruinose. STEM 2-5 cm. long, about 2 mm. thick, firm, *tough*, solid, equal, instititious, *floccose-scaly or furfuraceous*, sulphur or pallid-yellow. SPORES broadly-oval, or subglobose, granular-punctate, 8-10 x 6-7 micr. STERILE CELLS on edge of gills, subcylindrical, rounded-subcapitate, about 45-50 x 9 micr.

Solitary or scattered. On fallen branches and decaying wood, in mixed woods of coniferous regions. Marquette, Bay View, New Richmond. August-September.

The attractive color, the tough texture, furfuraceous to floccose covering of cap and stem distinguish this species easily from all other Collybias. The plant has occasionally been wrongly identified as *Lentinus chrysopeplos* B. & C. Its texture is doubtless very similar to Lentinus and Panus, but it lacks the arid gills of those genera. The description of *Omphalia scabriuscula* Pk. also fits our plant rather closely, but if it were that species it would be far removed from *Omphalia umbellifera* to which Peck attached *O. scabriuscula* as a variety. The gills have a tendency to become decurrent, and if referred to the genus Omphalia the plant would become *O. lacunosa*. In many respects it is an anomalous mushroom, half-way between Omphalia, Collybia and Panus.

Mycena Fr.

(From the Greek, *mykes*, a fungus.)

White-spored. Stem *cartilaginous*, slender, hollow. Pileus thin, conic or sub-cylindrical at first, then *campanulate, margin at first straight and applied to stem*. Gills adnexed or adnate, *not decurrent*, sometimes uncinate.

Epiphytal, lignicolous or terrestrial, putrescent, small or minute plants; separated from Collybia by the unexpanded, bell-shaped pileus; from Omphalia by the non-decurrent gills; and from Marasmius by their non-reviving consistency. The genus is a large one. Many species are probably edible, but because of their small size most of them yield very little substance. Peck (N. Y. State Mus. Bull. 167, 1913) reports *M. splendidipes* Pk. as poisonous. They correspond to Nolanea of the pink-spored group, and Galera of the ochre-spored group. The genus is of great interest scientifically.

The PILEUS is either conical at first, or parabolic-cylindrical, or ovate. On opening it usually remains campanulate, except in a comparatively small number of species in which it often develops a marked umbo. In certain species like *M. pelianthina, M. pura, M. cohaerens, M. galericulata,* etc., the mature pileus usually expands like that of Collybia, and the margin may even become recurved; this is more often true of the larger species. The tendency however for the pileus to remain conical or conic-campanulate for quite a time is due to the position of the margin of the young cap on the stem; the growth-tensions in such cases do not easily raise the margin outward, except in the more fleshy and larger caps. The caps may be very fragile or quite tough, usually very thin or membranous in the smaller species. The *trama* of the mature pileus is composed of large, vesiculose cells with a more or less differentiated cuticle of various structures. The color of the caps is often very delicate, red, blue, yellow, brown, gray and white being found in the various shades and tints. The surface is usually glabrous and striatulate on the margin. The GILLS are adnexed or adnate, sometimes running down the stem by a short tooth, and in *M. vulgaris* becoming somewhat decurrent as the pileus expands. In some species they are pure white, in others they become slightly ashy or flesh color in age, and in a few cases, like *M. leajana* and *M. pelianthina,* are brightly colored. There are CYSTIDIA present in a number of species. In one group (Calodontes) these are colored and hence the edges of the gills where they occur have the corresponding color. In others the cystidia are hyaline or colorless. They may be very numerous on both sides and edges as in *M. cohaerens* and *M. leajana,* in which species they give the color to the entire surface of the gills; in *M. atroalboides, M. dissiliens* and *M. polygramna* var. *albidus,* they are hyaline. In some the cystidia are found only on the edge and are then referred to as *sterile cells,* especially if of different shape from the others, e. g., *M. alkalina, M. polygramna* and *M. metatus.* In these species the shape of the cystidia varies considerably—they may be flask-shaped, lanceolate, pear-shaped, sac-shaped, or hair-like. In some species no cystidia, or only a few scattered ones occur; e. g., *M. galericulata, M. pura* and *M. epipterygia.* It is an open question whether the numbers or shapes do not vary to a considerable extent in a species. The STEM in each of the different groups has quite distinct characters, and these are the most convenient means of distinguishing the species. Some stems exude a colored juice, others are viscous; the base is sometimes attached by a disk, and at other times it penetrates the substratum by a hairy, root-like extension. It may be firm, fragile or flaccid. The interior is mostly tubular, and the rind is cartilaginous. The surface may be glabrous, horny and shining, or dull opaque and pruinose or hairy. It is delicate and filiform in the smaller forms. The SPORES with very few exceptions are smooth. It seems to be a marked characteristic of this genus, that the immature spores are easily loosened when sections of the gills are mounted in water. The result is that abundant immature spores are present in a mount, and great care must be taken to get the measurements from mature spores. The immature spores are usually delicately punctate-granular or irregular in shape but practice will soon make the observer properly discriminating. The spores of different species vary from spherical to oval or elliptical, and are white when deposited in a mass. In *M. lasiosperma* the spores are rough with short knobs. The ODOR of some species is alkaline or *nitrous,* sometimes of radish, and when collecting it is well to test the fresh plant, since the odor may disappear. If the plants are kept in a tight box till one gets home, the odor is often very marked on opening the box. Omission to test for the odor may make it difficult to identify the plant correctly.

Mycenas may be found from early spring until the late autumn. They are usually gregarious or caespitose, and the wood-inhabiting species often form dense clusters of individuals. Many are quite small, and are hidden among leaves, sticks and grass. The caps of others reach a size of one or two inches.

The genus was divided by Fries (in Hymen. Europ.) into nine sections, largely with reference to the characters of the stem. These divisions have been found so fundamental and satisfactory that most later mycologists have followed the Friesian arrangement. The nine sections are characterized in the key, and in the text following.

Key to the Species

I.	Stem with a colored or milky juice, (Lactipedes) (A).
I.	Stem without colored juice, II.
II.	Stem viscous, (Glutinipedes) (B).
II.	Stem not viscous, III.
III.	Base of stem dilated into a disk or bulb; pileus white or delicately tinted, 4-10 mm. broad, (Basipedes) (C).
III.	Base of stem not with abrupt bulb or disk, IV.
IV.	Edge of gills darker-colored from colored cystidia, (Calodontes) (D).
IV.	Edge of gills not of a different color, V.
V.	Stem inserted by the naked base on the wood, leaves, etc., from which it grows, (Instititiae) (E).
V.	Stem attached by a villose or fibrilose more or less rooting base, VI.
VI.	Gills remaining clear white; mostly on the ground; pileus rarely above 1 cm. broad, white or brightly colored, (Adonidae) (F).
VI.	Gills tending to ashy, fuscous or flesh tints in age, VII.

VII.   Stem firm, rigid; mostly on wood and usually caespitose, (Rigipedes) (G).

VII.   Stem not markedly firm or rigid, VIII.

VIII. Stem fragile, slender; pileus hygrophanous; plants often odorous, (Fragilipedes) (H).

VIII. Stem flaccid, filiform; pileus not hygrophanous; on the ground, mosses, mossy logs, etc., (Filipedes) (I).

(A) LACTIPEDES

(a) Edge of gills deeply colored, provided with red to dark-purple cystidia; juice dull red. 832. *M. sanguinolenta* A. & S.

(aa) Edge of gills not differently colored. Juice reddish; margin of pileus crenate; pileus and gills soon stained. 831. *M. haematopa* Fr.

(B) GLUTINIPEDES

(a) Pileus and stem both with a more or less viscid thin pellicle.
  (b) Pileus, stem and gills bright orange-yellow; caespitose; pileus 2-4 cm. broad. 833. *M. leajana* Berk.
  (bb) Colored differently, smaller.
    (c) Gills at length decurrent; pileus convex, umbilicate, 4-10 mm. 834. *M. vulgaris* Fr.
    (cc) Gills at most with decurrent tooth; pileus conic-campanulate, obtuse.
      (d) Stem slender, 0.5-1 mm. thick, elongated.
        (e) Stem yellowish; spores 8-10 x 4-5 micr. 835. *M. epipterygia* Fr.
        (ee) Stem brownish; spores broader, 8-9 x 5-6 micr. 835. *M. epipterygia* var. B.
      (dd) Stem yellowish, 1.5-2 mm. thick, not long; spores 9-10 x 6-6.5 micr.
(aa) Pileus without a viscid pellicle; stem viscid, slender.
  (b) Pileus, stem and gills white; spores 7-9 x 5 micr. 836. *M. clavicularis* Fr. var. *alba.*
  (bb) Pileus, stem and gills yellowish; spores 11-12 x 7-8 micr. 836. *M. clavicularis* var. *luteipes.*

(C) BASIPEDES

(a) Base of stem attached by a flat, orbicular disk to fallen leaves, twigs, etc; gills free. 837. *M. stylobates* Fr.

(aa) Base of stem attached by white radiating hairs, forming a floccose bulblet.
  (b) Pileus and stem beset with minute glandular particles; gills close. 838. *M. crystallina* Pk.
  (bb) Pileus glabrous, pellucid-striate; gills distant, thick. 839. *M. echinipes* Fr.

(D) CALODONTES

(a) Pileus 2-6 cm. broad, at length fully expanded; gills violet to brown; stem 3-5 mm. thick. 840. *M. pelianthina* Fr.

(aa) Pileus conic-campanulate, less then 2 cm.; stem fiiliform.
  (b) Pileus and stem violet, rosy or purple-tinged, becoming paler; pileus striatulate.
    (c) Gills tinged flesh color, edge deeper-colored; spores oblong-elliptic. 841. *M. rosella* Fr.
    (cc) Gills white, edge purplish; spores subglobose. 842. *M. purpureofusca* Pk.
  (bb) Pileus livid-gray, grayish-brown or dark-brown; edge of gills purplish-brown.

   (c)   Pileus striate (moist), hygrophanous; stem fragile. *M. capil-*
         laripes Pk.
   (cc) Pileus not striate nor hygrophanous; stem toughish. 843. *M.*
         denticulata Pk.

(E)   INSTITITIAE

(a)   On the bark of living tree trunks; common on shade trees; gills
      broad. 844. *M. corticola* Fr.
(aa) On fallen leaves in woods; stem hairy; gills narrow. 845. *M.*
      setosa Fr.

(F)   ADONIDAE

(a)   Pileus 2-5 cm. broad, thick, rose color to pale lilac; odor of radish.
      846. *M. pura* Fr.
(aa) Pileus usually less than 2 cm. broad. Pileus, stem and gills
      entirely white; small; gills rather broad, subdistant.
   (b)   Stem at first minutely-pulverulent; pileus papillate on disk.
         847. *M. minutula* Pk.
   (bb) Stem glabrous, pellucid; pileus not papillate. 848. *M. immacu-*
         lata Pk.

(G)   RIGIPEDES

(a)   Pileus bluish at first, 5-12 mm. broad; stem grayish-brown. 855.
      M. cyaneobasis Pk.
(aa) Pileus not bluish, larger, 1-4 cm. broad.
   (b)   Gills brown from the brown cystidia; stem horny, shining, dark
         brown. (See 46. *Marasmius cohaerens*).
   (bb) Gills not deep brown.
      (c)   Gills assuming an incarnate tinge in age; stems rufous-brown
            downwards; odor and cystidia lacking. 849. *M. galericulata*
            Fr.
      (cc) Gills usually cinerascent in age.
         (d)   Pileus some shade of gray or almost white.
            (e)   Odor nitrous; cystidia abundant on sides of gills; pileus
                  white to pearl-gray. 853. *M. polygramma* Fr. var. *albida*
                  Kauff.
            (ee) Odor not nitrous.
               (f)   Pileus 1-3 cm. broad, dark ashy to pearl-gray; cystidia
                     few; gills not with decurrent tooth. 852. *M. para-*
                     bolica Fr.
               (ff) Pileus 0.5-2 cm. broad, dark ashy; gills uncinate; spores
                     tubercular-rough. 854. *M. lasiosperma* Bres.
         (dd) Pileus dark fuscous or dark brown, 2-4 cm.
            (e)   Gills subdistant, with cystidia, rather broad but narrowly
                  adnexed. 851. *M. excisa* Fr.
            (ee) Gills crowded, narrow; whole plant brownish-fucescent,
                  dark. 850. *M. inclinata* Fr. var.

(H)   FRAGILIPEDES

(a)   Odor alkaline or nitrous in fresh plants.
   (b)   Stem lubricous; spores symmetrically elliptical; pileus grayish-
         brown to grayish-umber (moist). 856. *M. alcalina* Fr.
   (bb) Stem not lubricous; usually gregarious, not very caespitose.
      (c)   Pileus glaucous-pruinose when dry, soon grayish-white; gills
            not decurrent by tooth. 859. *M. leptocephala* Fr.
      (cc) Pileus not glaucous.
         (d)   Gills adnate with tooth; odor strong; pileus dark fuscous-
               gray (moist). 857. *M. ammoniaca* Fr.

(dd)   Gills not uncinate; odor weak, evanescent; among mosses and grasses in wet places. 858. *M. metata* Fr.

(ddd)   Cystidia abundant on sides of gills. (Not identified).

(aa)   Without nitrous or alkaline odor.

(b)   Cystidia numerous on sides of gills; pileus 5-15 mm. broad.

(c)   Pileus tending to convex, brownish to umber (moist); stem white. 860. *M. dissiliens* Fr. var.

(cc)   Pileus conic-campanulate, fuscous-cinereous; young stem and pileus bluish-blackish-gray. 862. *M. atroalboides* Pk.

(bb)   Cystidia none on sides of gills.

(c)   Pileus 1-2.5 cm., with smoky-fuscous umbo; stem 1.5-2.5 mm. thick, short. 861. *M. atroalba* Fr.

(cc)   Pileus 5-15 mm., conic-campanulate, brown tinged lead color; stem very long, filiform; on sphagnum. 863. *M. praelonga* Pk.

(I)   FILIPEDES

(a)   Plants with bluish, reddish or yellowish tints; small and very slender.

(b)   Base of stem adorned with blue hairs or mycelium threads. 865. *M. cyanothrix* Atk.

(bb)   Without any blue tints.

(c)   Gills somewhat flesh-color, uncinate; pileus rufous-yellowish; on wood. 866. *M. subincarnata* Pk.

(cc)   Gills yellowish, not uncinate.

(d)   Spores 7-9 x 3-4 micr.; pileus orange-red to bright-red, 2-6 mm. broad. 868. *M. acicula* Fr.

(dd)   Spores 7-8 x 5-6 micr.; pileus dull-red to yellow, 5-12 mm. broad. 867. *M. pulcherrima* Pk.

(aa)   Plants without any bright colors.

(b)   Gills attached to a collar at the stem. 864. *M. collariata* Fr.

(bb)   Gills not attached to a collar; small and very slender plants, fuscous.

(c)   Gills free, crowded, white. *M. filopes* Fr.

(cc)   Gills not free.

(d)   Gills broadly adnate, distinct. *M. debilis* Fr.

(dd)   Gills attenuate-adnexed, subdistant; pileus brownish to livid ashy. *M. vitilis* Fr.

Section I. Lactipedes.   Flesh exuding a juice when broken; stem rooting, not viscid.

831.   Mycena haematopa Fr.

Sys. Myc., 1821.

Illustrations: Fries, Icones, Pl. 83, Fig. 1.

Cooke, Ill., Pl. 162.

Gillet, Champignons de France, No. 450.

Atkinson, Mushrooms, Fig. 100, p. 100, 1900.

Hard, Mushrooms, Fig. 90, p. 123, 1908.

Marshall, The Mushroom Book, Pl. 37, op. p. 93.

Conn. State Geol. & Nat. Hist. Surv. Bull., No. 15, Pl. 10, 1910.

PILEUS 1-3 cm. broad, at first narrow elliptical then campanulate, obtuse, at first purplish-maroon then livid-reddish or paler, glabrous, striate, stained darker in age; the sterile *margin extends beyond the gills and is crenate.* FLESH thin, *bleeding when cut.* GILLS narrowly adnate, ascending, narrow, subdistant, whitish *soon reddish-stained,* edge flocculose. STEM 4-8 cm. long, 1.5-3 mm. thick, rigid, fragile, hollow, white-pruinate when young, at length glabrous except the hairy base, even, rufous-tinged, *exuding reddish juice when broken.* SPORES elliptical, 8-10 x 5-6 micr. (few larger), smooth, white. CYSTIDIA none. *Sterile cells* on edge of gills numerous, with swollen-ventricose base and tapering to a narrow acuminate point, about 50 micr. long. ODOR and TASTE mild.

Caespitose or subcaespitose, sometimes confluent, on decaying wood. In frondose and coniferous woods throughout the State. June to September. Rather frequent.

Known by the reddish juice of the flesh, the crenate flaps on the margin of the cap and the caespitose habit. The juice is not always equally abundant depending on weather and vigor of plant. All the parts of the plant become stained darker reddish in age. Fries does not mention the striations on the cap, which are sometimes quite marked.

A variety occurs on hemlock logs whose pileus is often markedly umbonate, at first striate, very rugose striate in age, its margin scarcely crenate. The gills at length secede and remain attached to each other behind by a false collar, often very veiny and staining reddish after being bruised. The stem and cap also become reddish-stained from the watery juice contained in the flesh. The juice itself seems uncolored but causes the bruised parts to assume the reddish stains. The base of the very caespitose stems is imbedded in cracks in the logs and is strigose with white hairs. It was collected during several seasons at New Richmond. It occurs in dense clusters. The spores are like those of *M. haematopa.*

832. Mycena sanguinolenta Fr.

Syst. Myc., 1821.

Illustrations: Fries, Icones, Pl. 83, Fig. 3.
        Cooke, Ill., Pl. 163, Fig. 1.

PILEUS small, 4-6 mm. broad, soft, campanulate, obtuse or sub-umbonate, striate, glabrous, pale reddish then fuscous. FLESH membranaceous. GILLS narrowly adnate, broader in front, subdistant, rufous-tinged, *edge dark purple.* STEM 4-8 cm. long, filiform, fistulose, flaccid, soft, glabrous, mycelioid, pallid or pale rufescent, *exuding reddish juice when broken.* SPORES 8-11 x 4-5 micr., long-elliptical. *Sterile cells* on edge of gills numerous, enlarged below, tapering to a point above, about 30 micr. long.

On the ground among leaves in frondose and mixed woods, sometimes in tamarack swamps. Throughout the State. June-September. Infrequent.

This little Mycena is smaller than *M. haematopa* and lacks the crenate margin of that species. It has a somewhat different habitat, is very soft and slender and when young the cap is dark red. It is readily distinguished from *M. haematopa* by the colored edge of the gills. Stevenson says it is common in Great Britain, but with us it occurs rather seldom, and prefers the northern area.

Section II. Glutinipedes. Stem viscid, without juice; gills at length uncinate.

833. Mycena leajana Berk.

Hooker, London Journal, Vol. IV, p. 300.

Illustrations: Hard, Mushrooms, Fig. 94, p. 127, 1908.
　Conn. State Geol. & Nat. Hist. Bull. No. 15, Pl. 11, 1910.

PILEUS 2-3 cm. broad (rarely larger), convex, subexpanded, umbilicate, *covered by a tough, viscid, orange separable cuticle,* shining when moist, glabrous. FLESH rather thick, livid-whitish. GILLS adnate, becoming sinuate, rather narrow, close, thickish, yellowish to pale orange, *edge reddish to vermillion.* STEM 3-7 cm. long, 2-4 mm. thick, equal, even, hollow, tough-cartilaginous, viscid, at first yellow and covered by orange scurfy-pulverulence, varying below to strigose tomentum at times, attached by an orange-colored mycelium. SPORES elliptic-oblong, 8-9.5 x 5-6 micr., smooth, dented on one side. CYSTIDIA none; *sterile cells* on and near the edge of the gills, numerous, reddish-orange, about 45 micr. long, apiculate.

Caespitose on logs, branches and stumps in frondose and conifer woods. Throughout the State. July-September. Rather frequent, especially in the north.

This is a striking and beautiful species, easily recognized at a distance by the reddish-orange color of the rather dense clusters. The cap often fades to a livid-tan and finally to a whitish color, and then develops striations on the margin. This species does not seem to be closely related to other Mycenas, and its position here is uncertain. It belongs more nearly to Heliomyces.

834. Mycena vulgaris Fr.

Syst. Myc., 1821.

Illustrations: Cooke, Ill., Pl. 191.
    Berkeley, Outlines, Pl. 6, Fig. 4.
    Atkinson, Mushrooms, Fig. 9, p. 97, 1900.

PILEUS 5-15 mm. broad, convex to subexpanded, subviscid when moist, pale grayish-brown to fuscous, *umbilicate,* striatulate to umbilicus, somewhat darker in center, soft, fragile, sometimes papillate on center. FLESH membranaceous, subhygrophanous. GILLS *broad behind and subdecurrent,* subdistant, thin but sometimes thickish, often venose, white then grayish-white. STEM 2-5 cm. long, 1-1.5 mm. thick, cartilaginous, toughish, hollow, glabrous, somewhat rooting, *very viscid when moist,* straight or flexuous, equal, even, pallid brownish or grayish. SPORES broadly elliptical, 6-8 x 4-5 micr., smooth, white. CYSTIDIA and STERILE CELLS none or few. BASIDIA slender, 30 x 5 micr., clavate. ODOR and TASTE none.

Caespitose or gregarious. Attached to pine needles, leaves and sticks in conifer or frondose woods, so far only in the coniferous regions of the State. New Richmond, Marquette. August-September.

Mycena vulgaris, except for its viscidity, would be looked for under the genus Omphalia. Fries describes the pileus as "depressed," but it usually has the umbilicate character in our plants, and is practically an Omphalia with broad, subdecurrent gills. Authors differ widely as to size of spores. Massee and Karsten (Stevenson's British Fungi) give the measurements very small, 4-5 x 2 micr., while Schroeter says they are 9-11 micr. long. This discrepancy shows that these authors were dealing with different species. American authors do not give any spore measurements. When young and moist the pileus is quite viscid, but soon dries. The species is often very abundant under favorable weather conditions in the localities where it occurs.

835. Mycena epipterygia Fr.

Syst. Myc., 1821.

Illustrations: Cooke, Ill., Pl. 208.
  Patouillard, Tab. Analyt., No. 215.
  Gillet, Champignons de France, No. 462.
  Atkinson, Mushrooms, Fig. 96, p. 96, 1900.
  Hard, Mushrooms, Fig. 96, p. 129, 1908.

Var. *A.* PILEUS 1-2 cm. broad, conic-ovate then campanulate or subhemispherical, obtuse, *subviscid* by a thin, separable pellicle, hygrophanous, at first yellowish-gray *then gray to fuscous,* glabrous, striate on the margin which is at first straight. GILLS arcuate-adnexed, uncinate, rather broad, ventricose, subdistant. whitish at first, grayish-rufescent in age, edge entire. STEM 4-5 cm. long, *2 mm. thick,* yellowish or pellucid pale yellow, *tough,* equal, straight or flexuous, tubular, sometimes twisted or compressed, *viscid by a thin, separable pellicle,* rooting. SPORES broadly elliptical, 9-10 x 6-6.5 micr., smooth, obtuse, white. CYSTIDIA none. ODOR none or slightly farinaceous. BASIDIA attenuated downward, clavate, 45 x 6-7 micr., 4-spored.

On the ground in low, elm woods. Detroit. October.

Form *typical.* This is a much more slender-stemmed plant, described and illustrated by Atkinson and Hard. The pileus is elongated-conical at first and the stem filiform. The colors are similar to Var. *A.* I have seen this form rather frequently in northern Michigan, but have no notes on it.

Var. *B.* PILEUS 5-8 mm. broad, obtusely conic-campanulate. glabrous, *with a viscid, separable, thin pellicle,* obscurely striatulate, *grayish-brown.* GILLS adnate-arcuate, uncinate, rather narrow, subventricose, *white,* intervenose. STEM *filiform,* 3-8 cm. long, 0.5 mm. thick, equal, *viscid,* flaccid, shining, glabrous, even, pruinose at apex, *pallid with brown tinge,* rooting and mycelioid at base. SPORES broadly elliptical, 8-9 x 5-6 micr., smooth, obtuse, white. CYSTIDIA none. BASIDIA about 24 micr. long. ODOR none or slightly nitrous. TASTE none.

On decorticated, half-decayed logs. New Richmond. September.

Mycena epipterygia, like the following, is probably a composite species, as Maire has pointed out. (Bull. Soc. Myc. France, Vol. 26, p. 160.) Fries placed a series of previously described species under this one and considered the colors insufficient to differentiate them.

Color, like size, shape and habitat, is very variable, but Fries did not consider any microscopic characters, hence it is likely he has been too conservative in this series, and sooner or later several species will be segregated.   Maire (l. c.) has already separated *M. viscosa* Maire, a plant of the coniferous regions.

836.   Mycena clavicularis Fr.

Syst. Myc., 1821 (var. *alba*, N. Y. State Mus. Rep. 28, 1885).

Illustrations: Fries, Icones, Pl. 84, Fig. 1.
    Cooke, Ill., Pl. 208.

Var. *álba* Pk.   PILEUS 5-7 mm. broad, conico-campanulate, *dull-white*, not changing, sulcate-striate, pruinose, dry (not viscid), without pellicle.   FLESH membranaceous.   GILLS adnate, moderately broad, close, *white*, edge obscurely flocculose.   STEM 5-6 cm. long, *filiform*, .5 mm. thick, *pellucid-whitish, viscid when moist*, glabrous, long-rooting, even, fistulose, flaccid, flexuous, loosely hairy below.   SPORES 7-9 x 5 micr., elliptical, obtuse at ends, smooth, white.   CYSTIDIA none.   *Sterile cells* on edge of gills inflated, rounded-pyriform on narrow stalks, 15-30 micr. in diam.   BASIDIA about 24 micr. long, subclavate, 4-spored.   ODOR none.

Caespitose or singly, attached to fallen leaves by the rooting, hairy stem, in mixed woods.   New Richmond.   September.   Infrequent.

Var. *luteipes* nov. var.   PILEUS 10-15 mm. broad, convex-campanulate, obtuse, striate up to the papilla, silky, not viscid, *sulphur-yellow with olivaceous or green shades*, brownish or grayish in age. GILLS adnate, uncinate or arcuate-subdecurrent, *yellowish, flesh color or rufescent in age*, rather narrow and distant, edge entire. STEM 5-8 cm. long, 1-1.5 mm. thick, slender, equal, hollow, *tough*, pruinose at apex, *viscid*, darker yellow than pileus, rooting at the somewhat attenuated base.   SPORES broadly elliptical, 11-12 x 7-8 micr., smooth, white in mass.

On the ground among debris, mosses, etc.   Bay View, Detroit. Rare.

M. clavicularis Fr. is doubtless a composite species.   Fries, himself, considered it composed of a number of color forms, with caps either whitish, pale yellow or fuscescent.   Peck named three varieties: *alba, cinereus* and *filipes*.   The size of the spores seems to be omitted by authors.   The two varieties described above are probably distinct species but further data on all the supposed varieties are needed. The *M. clavicularis* group differs from the *M. epipterygia* group in the lack of a viscid pellicle on the pileus. Until these two groups have been more fully studied with reference to the microscopic characters, it is better not to segregate new species from them. Fries' figure shows a yellowish plant, somewhat smaller than var. *luteipes*.

Section III. Basipedes. Stem dry, juiceless, not rooting, the base naked and dilated into a disk, or strigose and swollen into a little bulb. Very thin, solitary, becoming flaccid.

837. Mycena stylobates Fr.

Syst. Myc., 1821.

Illustrations: Cooke, Ill., Pl. 249.
Berkeley, Outlines, Pl. 6, Fig. 5.
Patouillard, Tab. Analyt., No. 624.

PILEUS 3-6 mm. broad, *campanulate-convex,* obtuse, dry, glabrous, *white, striate.* FLESH membranaceous. GILLS free, distinct behind, *distant,* ventricose, *white.* STEM, 2-5 cm. long, *filiform,* hollow, *white,* equal, glabrous, dry, seated upon an *orbicular, plane, striate subvillose base.*

Solitary on fallen leaves, in frondose woods. Ann Arbor. October. Rare.

Only two specimens were obtained. The pileus of our plant was glabrous, lacking the scattered pilose hairs attributed to it. Very delicate and fragile.

838. Myccna crystallina Pk.

N. Y. State Mus. Rep. 41, 1888.

PILEUS 4-10 mm. broad, conical then campanulate, subumbonate, *pure white to creamy-white,* obscurely striatulate, *pruinate* under lens, *due to minute, shining, glandular, capitate hairs and particles.* FLESH membranaceous. GILLS *narrow,* narrowly adnate or scarcely adnexed, thin, close, white. STEM 2-5 cm. long, filiform, hollow, white and adorned like pileus, *attached by a white-hairy strigose base.* SPORES narrow, 7-9 x 3 micr., smooth, white. CYSTIDIA none.

On cedar twigs, mosses, etc., in cedar and tamarack swamps.

Bay View and New Richmond. September. Infrequent.

Known by the glandular particles and hairs which cover the surface of cap and stem of the fresh plant. These can scarcely be seen with the lens on account of the minute size. The color varies somewhat as indicated above. This species was referred to the section Basipedes by Peck, but might with equal propriety be placed among the Adonidae. At times the strigose hairy base is not well-developed and it is then easily mistaken for *M. immaculata* Pk., but that species lacks the glandular covering. *Marasmius resinosus* is also glandular-viscid, but is a larger plant.

839. Mycena echinipes Fr.

Epicrisis, 1836 (Lasch, in Linn.).

Illustration: Fries, Icones, Pl. 84, Fig. 5.

PILEUS 2-5 mm. broad, very thin, convex, widely pellucid-striate, *white,* glabrous. FLESH membranaceous. GILLS broadly adnate, thick, distant, subvenose, *white.* STEM 2-3 cm. long, fili-form, glabrous, hollow, white, *attached by a villose, bulbillose base.* SPORES 7-8 x 3 micr., smooth, white.

On decaying leaves in birch and hemlock woods. Bay View. September. Rare.

A minute species, closely related to others of the group.

Section IV. Caldontes. Stem juiceless, dry, base not bulbillate or dilated into a disk; edge of gills provided with cystidia which give it a deeper color than elsewhere.

In the preceding sections, *M. sanguinolenta* and *M. leajana* also have this character of the gills, but differ in other respects.

840. Mycena pelianthina Fr.

Syst. Myc., 1821.

Illustrations: Cooke, Ill., Pl. 156.
    Berkeley, Outlines, Pl. 6, Fig. 1.
    Patouillard, Tab. Analyt., No. 418.

PILEUS 2-5 cm. broad, hemispherical-convex then expanded, ob-tuse, moist, *hygrophanous, varying purplish-livid to sordid brown-ish-violet,* fading to dingy whitish, striate. FLESH somewhat fleshy, white. GILLS adnexed-rounded behind, becoming sinuate, narrow, at first dull violet, becoming brownish, close, *edge purple.* STEM 5-8 cm. long, 2-5 mm. thick, equal, often curved at base, fragile, hollow, even, glabrous, *sordid whitish or streaked with violaceous fibrils.*

Solitary or scattered. Among fallen leaves in frondose woods. Throughout the State. July-September. Frequent.

Has the size of *M. pura,* but differs from it in that the edge of the gills is darker from the colored cystidia, in the more solitary habit and the cylindrical stem. Generally only one or two plants are found in a place. It seems to prefer maple, oak and beech woods. The color of the cap is variable and hard to describe, usually of a dirty color. Fries says it is intermediate between the genera Collybia and Mycena.

841. Mycena rosella Fr.

Syst. Myc., 1821.

Illustration: Cooke, Ill., Pl. 131.

PILEUS 4-15 mm. broad, campanulate-convex then hemispherical to subexpanded, obtusely umbonate, sometimes plane on disk, *sulcate-striate, pale rose color,* paler and tinged ochraceous in age, glabrous. FLESH membranaceous, fleshy at umbo. GILLS broadly adnate, slightly subdecurrent, medium broad, subdistant, *pale rose-colored, edge darker.* STEM 4-5 cm. long, 1 mm. thick, *pellucid-flesh color,* filiform, hollow, cartilaginous, slightly tough, *glabrous,* even, attached at base by white, hairy tomentum. SPORES oblong-elliptical, 8-9 x 4 micr., smooth, white. CYSTIDIA on sides and edge of gills, dense on edge, ventricose, narrowed to acuminate above, 60-70 x 12-15 micr., filled with a rosy to flesh-colored sap when mature. ODOR at first none, becoming nitrous after being picked.

Caespitose, usually of 2 or 3 stems, sometimes connate by the white tomentum, sometimes gregarious. On and among pine needles and other fallen leaves, in woods of white pine and oak.

New Richmond, Marquette. September-October. Common locally.

This pretty little Mycena is well named. It can be easily distinguished by the pale rosy coloring of the cap and gills and by its habitat. The surface of the cap and stem is slightly viscid or lubricous when the plant is fresh, and this is due to a very thin layer of subgelatious hyphae which cover these parts. After drying out somewhat it was found that a nitrous odor developed; this fact does not seem to be mentioned elsewhere. Peck reports the species from New York, but elsewhere it seems to have been overlooked. The attachment of the gills is almost like that of the genus Omphalia, and the color of the gills is apt to lead one to place it among the pink-spored group. *Mycena capillaripes* Pk. (N. Y. State Mus. Rep. 41, 1888) is very close to if not identical with it.

842. Mycena purpureofusca Pk.

N. Y. State Mus. Rep. 38, 1885.

"PILEUS 8-16 mm. broad, *not hygrophanous,* campanulate or convex, obtuse, glabrous, *striate, purplish-brown.* FLESH membranous. GILLS adnate, ascending, lanceolate, subdistant, white or whitish, *purplish-brown* on the edge. STEM 2.5-7.5 cm. long, scarcely 2 mm. thick, *slender,* even, hollow, glabrous, with white hairs at the base, colored like the pileus or a little paler. SPORES subglobose or broadly elliptical, 6-7.5 x 6.5 micr."

On mossy hemlock logs in woods. Bay View. September. Rare.

Peck says it is closely related to *M. rubromarginata* Fr., from which it differs in its darker color and non-hygrophanous striate pileus. Longyear, in the 4th Report of the Michigan Academy of Science, lists *M. rubromarginata* Fr. but he is uncertain of the identification; it is probably Peck's species.

843. Mycena denticulata Pk.

Torr. Bot. Club, Bull. 32, 1905.

PILEUS 8-18 mm. broad, campanulate, toughish, often obtusely subconic, glabrous, *not striate,* grayish-brown, darker on center, margin soon split. FLESH thin, membranous. GILLS adnate with slightly decurrent tooth, often adnexed-emarginate then broader, *medium broad,* ventricose, subdistant, thickish, whitish, *edge dark brown, crenulate,* sometimes venose-connected or a few forked. STEM 3-6 cm. long, 1-1.5 mm. thick, equal, slender, even, hollow, *toughish,* glabrous or subfurfuraceous with minute brown dots, pallid. SPORES sub-globose to elliptic-oval, 7-8 x 5-7 micr., smooth, white. CYSTIDIA none. *Sterile cells* on edge of gills, short, subelliptical-saccate, obtuse, 30-35 x 12-15 micr., filled with brownish substance as shown under microscope.

On rotten wood or humus, in oak and maple woods. Ann Arbor, New Richmond. June-September. Infrequent.

This little Mycena was described by Peck from material sent to him from St. Louis, Mo., by Glatfelter. Peck says the edge is purplish, but there is scarcely any tint of that color in the gills of our specimens; nevertheless the two forms appear to be identical in other respects. In general appearance and habitat it imitates *Collybia floccipes* Fr., but the stem is less purely white, the gills have the brown-dotted edge, cystidia are lacking and the spores are slightly larger.

Section V. Instititiae. Stém inserted (i. e. attached directly to other plant parts without root-like base or tubercle, etc.), dry. Gills adnate, uncinate (not truly decurrent as in Omphalia).

844. Mycena corticola Fr.

Syst. Myc., 1821.

Illustrations: Cooke, Ill., Pl. 164.
    Fries, Icones, Pl. 85, Fig. 2.
    Gillet, Champignons de France, No. 458.
    Hard, Mushrooms, Fig. 93, p. 126, 1908.
    Patouillard, Tab. Analyt., No. 217.

PILEUS 4-8 mm. broad, hemispherical, obtuse or at length sub-umbilicate, distantly *striate,* flocculose-pruinate, blackish (when young), becoming fuscous, cinereous, grayish-ochraceous, etc. FLESH thin, membranaceous. GILLS adnate, uncinate, *distant, broad,* subovate, paler than pileus. STEM 6-12 mm. long, 1 mm. thick, slender, *incurved,* glabrous or minutely furfuraceous, paler than pileus.

On the bark of living trunks of frondose trees; everywhere, especially on shade trees of cities. Probably throughout the State, very common in southern part. July-October.

After rains, in late summer and fall, this little Mycena appears in large numbers, scattered over the trunks of our shade trees, elm, maple, etc. It appears to revive somewhat after succeeding rains, but the texture is that of a Mycena rather than a Marasmius. The color is very variable, especially during development. *M. hiemalis* Fr. is said to be its near relative, and to grow in similar situations, but I have been able to distinguish only *M. corticola* within our area.

845.   Mycena setosa (Sow.) Fr.

Hymen. Europ., 1874.

Illustration: Cooke, Ill., Pl. 193.

PILEUS 1-2 mm. broad, minute, very thin, hemispherical, obtuse, glabrous, *becoming fuscous.* GILLS distant, *narrow,* white. STEM delicately filiform, 10-12 mm. long, *inserted,* capillary, *every-where shaggy with distant spreading hairs.*

On fallen leaves and pine needles, in woods of white pine and beech. New Richmond. September. Rare.

Section VI.   Adonidae.   Stem dry and usually growing from the ground.   Gills of one color, neither darker on edge, nor becoming ashy nor fuscous.

The plants in this section are usually brightly colored or white, not with ashy or fuscous shades on cap and gills. Those of the following sections often have white gills at first but become tinged with cinereous or fuscous color, although this character is in some cases scarcely determinable in fresh specimens.

846.   Mycena pura Fr.

Syst. Myc., 1821.

Illustrations: Cooke, Ill., Pl. 157.
       Gillet, Champignons de France, No. 476.
       Gillet, (var. *alba*) No. 477.
       Gillet, (var. *lutea*) No. 478.
       Bresadola, Fung. Trid., Vol. 2, (var. *multi-color*) Pl. 114.
       Patouillard, Tab. Analyt., No. 313.
       Atkinson, Mushrooms, Fig. 95, p. 95, 1900.
       Hard, Mushrooms, Fig. 95, p. 128, 1908.
       Swanton, Fungi, Pl. 8, Fig. 3 and 4, 1909.

PILEUS 2-4 cm. broad, rarely broader, campanulate to convex, finally expanded, more or less obtusely *umbonate,* sometimes broadly so, moist, striatulate on margin, *bright rosy-red,* sometimes rose-purplish, lilac or violet. FLESH thin, moist. GILLS adnate, sinuate, *broad,* ventricose, subdistant to close, varying rose, violet, white, etc., often veined or with the interspaces veiny. STEM 5-10 cm. long, 2-4 mm. thick, *cylindrical,* sometimes twisted, even, toughish, *glabrous,* hollow, more or less hairy at base, colored like or paler than pileus. SPORES elliptic-oblong, 6-7 x 3-3.5 micr., smooth, white. CYSTIDIA few on sides of gills, clavate-cylindrical, about 40-50 x 12-15 micr. *Sterile cells* not abundant on edge of gills, similar but smaller. ODOR somewhat of radish.

Caespitose or scattered to solitary. On humus, moss or much decayed logs in frondose or mixed woods, or tamarack, balsam and cedar swamps. Throughout the State. June to October. (Earliest record June 14, latest October 4.) Common.

A widely distributed Mycena, beautifully colored and one of the larger species of the genus. Its prevailing color, which often extends into the gills, is a pale rose-purple (Ridgway, new ed.), although it varies, under different conditions, localities or in age, to darker or lighter shades. Peck (23rd Rep.) says the umbo is lacking, but I have seen it often in the form shown by Cooke, Patouillard and Gillet in their illustrations. Schroeter (Die Pilze Schliesiens) says the edges of the gills are densely beset with cystidia. This is shown in Patouillard's figure; these I have usually referred to as "sterile cells." The very young pileus is ovate-subconical, and hoary-pubescent.

847. Mycena minutula Pk.

N. Y. State Mus. Rep. 25, 1873.

PILEUS 2-8 mm. broad, campanulate then expanded, *white, papillate,* glabrous, moist, striatulate to center. GILLS adnate with tooth, subdistant, *rather broad, white,* interspaces venose. STEM 2-4 cm. long, filiform, scarcely .5 mm. thick, *white,* elastic, *covered throughout its length by microscopic, subcylindrical hairs,* about 30 micr. long, 4-6 micr. thick, which give it a mealy appearance. SPORES 6-8 x 3.5-5 micr., elliptical, oval, smooth, white. BASIDIA 4-spored, 18-20 micr. long. CYSTIDIA none. ODOR and TASTE none.

Gregarious or scattered on moss of prostrate trunks, on rotten wood, twigs, etc., of pine, beech and oak woods. New Richmond, Ann Arbor. September-October. Infrequent.

The pruinosity of the stem and the entirely white color of the spores characterize this little species. It must not be confused with *M. crystallina* Pk. and *M. immaculata* Pk.

848.   Mycena immaculata Pk.

N. Y. State Mus. Rep. 38, 1885.

PILEUS 4-8 mm. broad, conical or subhemispherical, *glabrous,* slightly striate on the margin, pure *white.* FLESH membranaceous. GILLS adnate or uncinate-decurrent, moderately broad, *distant,* white. STEM 1.5-3.5 cm. long, scarcely .5 mm. thick, slender, *pellucid-white,* glabrous, generally villose-strigose at the base, slightly thickened at apex. SPORES oblong or cylindrical, 7.5-9 x 3 micr.

On mosses and fallen leaves on the ground. Bay View. August.

This seems to differ sufficiently from *M. lacteus* Fr. which has crowded narrow gills; the latter grows caespitosely on wood according to Stevenson (British Fungi), while Fries (Epicrisis) says it is generally found on the ground. *M. minutula* Pk. and *M. crystallina* Pk. should be compared with it.

Section VII. Rigipedes. Stem firm, rigid, somewhat tough, juiceless, somewhat strigose and rooted at the base. Gills becoming tinged with gray, flesh color, fuscous, etc. Pileus *not hygrophanous.*

Tough, persistent, inodorous, normally *growing on wood and caespitose.*

Fries originally (Syst. Myc., Vol. I, p. 13) included some of the following species under *M. galericulata.* In Epicrisis he divided the latter into a number of species. As Fries did not consider any microscopic characters, some of these species have been much misunderstood, and even today no clear account can be given by which they can, with entire certainty, be separated. I have attempted below, by using such critical studies as others have made with the microscope, and adding my own, to separate those which have been found in my collecting by using the characteristics of the spores and cystidia. As Fries pointed out (Epicrisis, p. 104), the color, especially of the stem, is very deceptive in many of these species, and cannot be relied on to any great extent for their separation.

Pileus and stem usually brown or dark colored, not constantly gray.

849. Mycena galericulata Fr. (EDIBLE)

Syst. Mycol., 1821 (in part).

Illustrations: Fries, Icones, Pl. 80, Fig. 2 (var.).
Cooke, Ill:, Pl. 222 and Pl. 223 (var.).
Gillet, Champignons de France, No. 462.
Patouillard, Tab. Analyt., No. 214 and No. 317.
Hard, Mushrooms, Pl. 16, Fig. 89, p. 121.
Marshall, The Mushroom Book, Pl. 7, op. p. 55.
Michael, Führer f. Pilzfreunde, III, No. 92.
Clements, Minnesota Mushrooms, Fig. 17, p. 30, 1910.
Moffatt, Nat. Hist. Surv. Chicago Acad. of Sci., Bull. 7, Pl. 4.

PILEUS 2-4 cm. broad, campanulate or obtusely conic-campanulate, umbonate, *striate or subsulcate to umbo,* glabrous, *buff on margin, shading to brown or umber on umbo,* ashy white and sub-shining when old, often with brown or blackish-ferruginous stains. FLESH thin, toughish, whitish. GILLS *adnate* or arcuate-adnate, *uncinate,* moderately broad, subdistant, dull white, *usually tinged with flesh color in age,* often stained when old, edge entire or crenulate-eroded, interspaces usually venose. STEM 4-10 cm. long or longer, 1-3 mm. thick, *tough,* very tough in age, *cartilaginous,* hollow, *even* or only innately striatulate, flexuous, sometimes twisted, *from pallid to rufous-brown or ferruginous-stained below,* paler to whitish at apex, glabrous and shining, base often connate with ferruginous or dingy-yellow strigose hairs, and rooting. SPORES 8-9 x 5-6 micr., broadly-elliptical *when mature,* smooth, white, immature spores with large globule simulating globular spores. BASIDIA 4-spored, with long and stout sterigmata. CYSTIDIA *none.* ODOR none or slightly farinaceous.

Very caespitose on rotten wood, old logs, stumps, etc., of all kinds of trees.

Throughout the State. March-November. (Earliest record March 15; latest, November 2.) Very common.

Reported throughout North America, Europe, Tasmania, etc. The weather and locality bring about much variation in this species, especially as to color and texture. The essential characters seem to be the lack of cystidia, the absence of a nitrous odor, the caespitose rufous-brown stems, the sulcate-striate cap, which is often stained in moist weather, the tendency for the white gills to assume a flesh tint and the size of the spores. The stains on cap and gills and base of stem are dingy yellow, purplish-brown or dark ferruginous. At other times, especially in dry places, the pilei become silvery-shining and scarcely stained. In mounting a section of the gills the large mature spores with homogeneous contents sink to the bottom of the water on the slide. The immature spores are subspherical and contain a large globule which is more prominent than the wall of the spore and accounts for the fact that to some observers the spores look spherical. Patouillard reports that a common variety has 2-spored basidia; I have not found it. *M. haematopa,* which becomes stained in the old stage must not be confused with this species. Occasionally the stem is striate but this form differs from *M. polygramma* var. *albida* in the lack of cystidia, and in our territory by the different colors.

Var. *calopus* Fr.

Illustrations: Fries, Icones, Pl. 80, Fig. 2.
          Cooke, Ill., Pl. 223 A.

Like *M. galericulata,* except that the gills are adnexed, the stem striatulate and coherent or proliferous at base, joined together and covered by rusty or brown strigose hairs, elsewhere rufous-bay color and shining. Spores as in *M. galericulata.* No cystidia. The appearance of the stem reminds one of that of *Marasmius cohaerens,* but the pileus, etc., are very different.

Caespitose, on decaying logs in woods. Ann Arbor. May and June. Infrequent.

850.   Mycena inclinata Fr. var.

Epicrisis, 1836-38.

Illustration: Plate CXLIX of this Report.

PILEUS 2-3 cm. broad and high, obtusely conical at first, then persistently conical-campanulate *with a broad oblong strongly marked umbo,* at length with a spreading or recurved margin, often gibbous-cernuous, dry, striate to the middle, *fuscous-brown,* umbo smoky-fuscous, darker colored in age. FLESH thin, concolor or paler. GILLS narrowed behind and sinuate-adnexed, *not uncinate,* narrow, ascending, crowded, soft, whitish or grayish-fuscescent, edge entire. STEM 3-6 cm. long, 2-5 mm. thick, curved, *twisted,* hollow, *often compressed or furrowed,* toughish-fibrous and splitting longitudinally under pressure, subfibrillose, pallid above, fuscous below, *fuscescent or blackish-fuscous throughout in age,* rooting. SPORES broadly elliptical, 8-10 x 5-6 micr., smooth, white. CYSTIDIA none. ODOR fungoid.

Caespitose or subcaespitose on logs in woods of juniper, oak, etc. Ann Arbor. October. Infrequent.

Apparently intermediate between *M. prolifera* and *M. inclinata,* concerning whose microscopic characters little is known. It is allied to the former by its broad and dark umbo and to the latter by the character of the stem, the cernuous pileus which is at first much incurved and the strongly fuscescent colors of cap and stem. The narrow gills are still more narrowed and broadly sinuate behind. The pileus often undulates from umbo to margin, and remains obtusely conic-campanulate. No tendency of the stem to proliferate was observed. It is very distinct from *M. galericulata.* The figure of Gillet does not appear to agree at all with the description of Fries.

851. Mycena excisa Fr.

Epicrisis, 1836.

Illustration: Fries, Icones, Pl. 81, Fig. 1.

PILEUS 1.5-4 cm. broad, *firm,* campanulate, broadly umbonate, gibbous, dark brown, *dark umber or blackish-fuscous, rugulose,* margin at first straight. FLESH concolor or paler. GILLS adnexed by an abruptly much narrower portion, elsewhere *rather broad,* ventricose, *subdistant, thickish,* pallid then tinged brownish. STEM short, 2-3 cm. long, 2-4.5 mm. thick, equal, floccose-fibrillose, glabrescent, stuffed then hollow, *rigid, toughish,* often twisted, sometimes compressed, *fuscous-brownish,* darker in age. SPORES elliptical, 8-10 x 5-6 micr., smooth, apiculate, white. CYSTIDIA moderately abundant, cylindrical above, ventricose above the slender pedicel, obtuse, 75-110 x 15-18 micr. BASIDIA about 40 x 6 micr., 4-spored. ODOR and TASTE none.

Caespitose or subcaespitose to gregarious. On the ground, among grass in oak woods. Ann Arbor. October-November. Infrequent.

Known by its dark brown cap, its short stem which is rigid and rather tough, and the abruptly narrowed and slightly adnexed gills. It has scarcely any tinge of gray to either cap or stem. The stem is sometimes strongly entwined on the grass-stalks or obliquely attached to buried roots, etc. Fries has not adhered to the same description in his different works; our plants agree best with the description in Icones, although in size and build they are more like the figures of *M. dissiliens* of the same work. The cystidia are large and striking.

**Pileus fundamentally gray, or some shade of gray, or white.

852. Mycena parabolica Fr.

Epicrisis, 1836.

Illustrations: Fries, Icones, Pl. 80, Fig. 3.
    Cooke, Ill., Pl. 224.

PILEUS 1-3 cm. broad, campanulate, *margin at length recurved,* umbo obtuse, *striate,* becoming coarsely rugose-striate, *sometimes sulcate,* moist, glabrous, *at first blackish-cinereous,* especially on center, *then gray to pearl-gray* or whitish when dry, disk darker. FLESH thin, *concolor at first.* GILLS narrowly adnate, *not uncinate, narrow,* at first ascending and close, then subdistant, whitish, *then tinged cinereous,* edge entire. STEM 3-10 cm. long, 1.5-2.5 mm. thick, sometimes long and rooting, cartilaginous, hollow, terete or compressed, *even,* glabrous, *cinereous,* fading, the rooting base white-hairy and curved or flexuous. SPORES 8-10 x 5-7 micr., elliptical, ends obtuse, smooth, white. CYSTIDIA few, lanceolate, soon collapsing, sometimes on the edge of the gills; sterile cells none. BASIDIA 4-spored, 27 x 8 micr., with prominent awl-shaped sterigmata, 6 micr. long. ODOR none.

Solitary, gregarious or subcaespitose. On or around decaying logs, stumps in mixed woods of white pine and beech. New Richmond. September.

This gray Mycena is frequent locally. The margin of the cap becomes expanded or recurved and is then coarsely sulcate on account of the thin flesh. The young stage distinctly shows its non-identity with *M. galericulata.* The stem is not as rigid as that of its neighbors and becomes somewhat flaccid in age.

853. Mycena polygramma Fr.

Epicrisis, 1836.

Illustrations: Cooke, Ill., Pl. 223.
Michael, Führer f. Pilzfreunde, III, No. 91.

Var. *albida* Kauff. Mich. Acad. Sci. Rep. 13, p. 219.

PILEUS 2-5 cm. broad, campanulate or conic-campanulate, dry, obtusely subumbonate, *sulcate-striate on margin* in large specimens, *white*, whitish-buff or grayish, glabrous, atomate when dry. FLESH white, thin. GILLS *narrowly adnate, not uncinate,* ascending or arcuate, rather broad in middle, subdistant, white, with a faint flush of pink in the gray forms, edge even. STEM 5-10 cm. long, 2-4 mm. thick, *equal,* cartilaginous, hollow, *striatulate or distinctly striate at apex or throughout,* sometimes twisted, straight or flexuous, firm and rather rigid but fragile, glabrous and *shining,* white or grayish-white, hairy at base. SPORES 8-10 x 5-6 micr., broadly elliptical, ends rounded, smooth, white. CYSTIDIA fusiform-acuminate, *abundant,* 45-75 x 9-15 micr. BASIDIA 4-spored, sterigmata slender. ODOR *nitrous,* varying from slight to strong.

Caespitose, gregarious or solitary on decaying logs of maple, elm, basswood, etc. Ann Arbor. May-June. Frequent locally.

Not to be confounded with *M. alkalina,* which lacks cystidia or possesses but a few of them, and which has pseudo-viscid stems. The typical *M. polygramma* of Europe has not been recognized with certainty and appears to be rare. Atkinson has referred *M. praelonga* Pk. to it, but the latter is kept intact in this report. Our plants, described above, are relatively large, almost pure white and have striate stems and a nitrous odor. It cannot be *M. sudora* Fr. since the cap is not viscid.

854. Mycena lasiosperma Bres.

Fung. Trid., 1881.

Illustration: Ibid, Pl. 37, Fig. 1.

PILEUS 5-20 mm. broad, conic-campanulate then expanded-umbonate, *subviscid,* striatulate to umbo, subhygrophanous, *dark cinereous,* almost black on umbo, paler toward margin. FLESH thin, concolor. GILLS adnexed, with tooth, close, ventricose, whitish then tinged gray, interspaces venose, stem 3-7 cm. long, 1-2 mm. thick, equal or attenuated below, *toughish* and *firm,* flexuous, hollow, white-pulverulent, brownish above, paler below, curved-rooting. SPORES spherical, *covered with blunt, rod-like tubercles,* 6-7 micr. diam., *white.* CYSTIDIA moderately abundant, fusoid, attenuate above, 45-60 x 8-12 micr. ODOR slight or none.

On very rotten wood and debris in beech and maple forest (Quirk's woods, east of Ypsilanti, Michigan). Gregarious or subcaespitose. August. Rare.

An interesting find of a remarkable plant which does not seem to have been noted except by its discoverer. The structure of the spores naturally leads one to suspect an Inocybe, but their color is white (hyaline under the microscope), and the habit of the plants is that of a Mycena. Bresadola describes it as having a strong odor of rancid meal, which our plants seemed to lack. The stems become firmer and tougher on drying and it is placed by Saccardo under the Rigipedes next to *M. raeborrhiza* which is said to have tuberculate spores. The latter is, however, a very different plant both in color and shape, according to the figure of it by Fries. (Icones, Pl. 83, Fig. 4.) Two other species of Mycena have been described with tuberculate spores, *M. bryophila* Vogl. and *M. receptibilis* Britz.

855. Mycena cyaneobasis Pk.

N. Y. State Mus. Rep. 51, 1898.

Illustrations: Ibid, Pl. B, Fig. 1-7.

PILEUS 6-15 mm. broad, tough, firm, elliptic-oval at very first, then conic-campanulate, dark aeruginous-brown at first, at length paler and grayish, especially toward *the bluish margin,* glabrous, papillate or obtuse, striatulate on margin. *Trama* composed of a thick amorphous to subgelatinous upper layer, elsewhere pseudoparenchymatous. GILLS narrowly *adnate,* not uncinate, ascending, rather narrow, close, whitish or tinged grayish, edge minutely fimbriate. STEM 5-8 cm. long, 1-1.5 mm. thick, equal, slender, *flexuous,* terete or composed, tubular, cartilaginous, elastic, *floccose-pruinose at first,* glabrescent, *grayish-brown,* hairy and rooting at base. SPORES subspherical, 7-8 micr. diam., smooth, white. CYSTIDIA none. *Sterile cells* on edge of gills *filiform,* numerous, 40 x 2 micr., hyaline. OROR and TASTE mild or slightly of radish.

Subcaespitose, among leaves and much decayed wood in frondose woods. Ann Arbor. June and October. Infrequent.

This differs but little from *M. cyanothrix* Atk. The pileus and stem are slightly gelatinous when moist. The mycelium has a bluish tinge or is dull white. There is a bluish-green tinge to the young pileus which is sometimes slightly zonate. Peck referred it to the Rigipedes where it is somewhat doubtfully retained. *M. cyanothrix* seems to have a much longer rooting stem, adnexed gills, and the stem is glabrous and differently colored. It may turn out to be identical with *M. cyaneobasis*. In Europe three other small Mycenas with blue tints have been described, *M. marginella* Fr., *M. iris* Berk. and *M. calorhiza* Bres., all closely related. The last, however, has spores very different from either of ours.

Section VIII. Fragilipedes. Stem *fragile,* dry, juiceless, scarcely rooting, neither dilated nor inserted. Pileus *hygrophanous.* Gills white then tinged grayish or fuscous.

Delicate, fragile, often soft, *usually odorous,* normally on the ground, debris, leaves, etc., not densely caespitose on wood (except *M. alkalina*).

This section, like the preceding, needs a revision on a microscopical basis, especially of those species with nitrous or alkaline odor; the latter have been arranged as well as possible in the absence of detailed information from European sources. We have a number of forms with a more or less nitrous odor, some of which have not been included below for lack of data.

856. Mycena alcalina Fr.

Syst. Myc., 1821.

Illustrations: Fries, Icones, Pl. 81, Fig. 3.
Cooke, Ill., Pl. 187.

PILEUS 1-2.5 cm. broad, campanulate (at first narrowly ovate to conic-campanulate), obtusely umbonate or obtuse, glabrous, *hygrophanous,* deeply striate (moist), *grayish-brown to grayish-umber (moist),* fading to grayish when dry, center always darker. FLESH thin, membranous. GILLS narrowly adnate, arcuate ascending, close to subdistant, *whitish then glaucous-gray,* or yellowish in age. STEM 3-7 cm. long, 1-2 mm. thick, rigid, *fragile,* terete or compressed, slippery-subgelatinous, hollow, *even,* glabrous, pallidbrown, sometimes darker at first, fading, the rooting base whitestrigose. SPORES 9-10 x 5-6 micr., broadly elliptical, smooth, obtuse at ends, white. CYSTIDIA none or few, then sublanceolate to subfusiform, 45-65 mm. long. *Sterile cells* ventricose below, obtuse-cylindrical above, abundant, 35-42 micr. long. ODOR strongly *nitrous.*

Caespitose, gregarious or solitary, on decayed logs and debris of tamarack, elm, etc. Ann Arbor, New Richmond. May-June and September-November. Not very common.

Characterized by the odor, by the few cystidia, and the slippery pseudo-viscous stem. The surface of the cap is composed of large, brown, erect, vesiculose cells. There is no separable pellicle, and the stem is not truly viscid, but feels gelatinous when applied to the lips. It differs from *M. ammoniaca* in its slippery stem, lack of a decurrent tooth at the attachment of the gills, and in the differently shaped spores. In *M. alcalina* the spores are symmetrically ellip-tical, in *M. ammoniaca* they are pip-shaped, i. e., narrowed and pointed toward one end. Both may be found on the decayed debris of leaves and wood on the ground and both may occur solitary or gregarious, although *M. ammoniaca* is rarely, if ever, caespitose. Both differ from *M. metata, M. leptocephala* and *M. constans* in the marked excess of brown shades instead of gray.

857. Mycena ammoniaca Fr.

Epicrisis, 1836.

Illustration: Cooke, Ill., Pl. 238.

PILEUS 5-15 mm. broad, conic-campanulate, but obtuse (at first elliptic-ovate), umbonate, hygrophanous, *striatulate* on margin, glabrous, fuscous-blackish to grayish-brown (moist), grayish buff or paler (dry). FLESH membranaceous, concolor. GILLS adnate, *uncinate,* close to subdistant, *narrow* and *linear,* interspaces venose at times, whitish then pale cinereous, often dark cinereous at the very first. STEM 3-5 cm. long, 1-1.5 mm. thick, toughish, equal, *straight, hollow, even, not slippery, whitish to pale brownish-ashy,* white mycelioid at base, scarcely rooting. SPORES 8-10 x 6-7 micr., pip-shaped, or elliptical-ovate, *pointed at one end,* smooth, white. CYSTIDIA none or few, *short, stout,* ventricose and obtuse, 36-40 x 15 micr. BASIDIA about 30 x 6 micr., slender. ODOR strongly *nitrous.*

Gregarious or scattered among leaves, remnants of decayed wood, etc. Ann Arbor, New Richmond. May-June and September-Octo-ber. Infrequent.

Mostly separable from *M. alcalina* by its terrestrial, scattered habit, smaller size and dry stem. *M. metata* has narrower spores, the odor is faint or obsolete, and the shape of the pileus is often more convex. The stem of this species is slightly tough and might on this account be referred to the Filipedes. The trama of the gills is composed of rather large cells, among which globose vesicular cells are conspicuous.

858. Mycena metata Fr.

Syst. Myc., 1821.

Illustration: Cooke, Ill., Pl. 228.

PILEUS 5-20 mm. broad, convex-campanulate, varying to ' *narrowly campanulate, hygrophanous,* umbonate, obtuse, *striate* and *ashy-brown (moist),* pale ashy to brownish-ashy (dry), glabrous. FLESH thin, membranaceous. Gills adnate, ascending, *narrow,* close to subdistant, cinerascent or tinged flesh color, *edge obscurely flocculose.* STEM 4-6 cm. long, 1.5-2.5 mm. thick, equal, fragile, toughish, dry, hollow, even, grayish-brown or paler, flexuous, hairy at base. SPORES 9-11 x 4-5 micr., *narrowly* elliptical, sometimes narrower toward one end, variable, smooth, white. CYSTIDIA none. *Sterile cells* on edge of gills globose-pyriform, about 25-30 x 18 micr., covered above by very short, rod-like protuberances. ODOR weakly alkaline when plants are fresh.

Gregarious or subcaespitose among moss and grass, in tamarack, cedar and hemlock swamps. Ann Arbor, Bay View. September-November. Infrequent locally.

The microscopic characters are the best mark of this species. The color is between grayish brown and ashy (see Chapman), fading to pale ashy or whitish. The shape of the cap varies considerably in the same patch. Fries, in his later works, Epicrisis and Hymen. Europ., does not give the shape. In Systema, however, he says it is campanulate, one-half inch across. Massee (British Fungus Flora) and Stevenson (British Fungi), mislead by speaking of the young cap as hemispherical. It is apparently most abundant in late autumn, in or on the borders of swamps among sphagnum or other moss and grasses, even after heavy frosts. The trama of the gills is composed of large, cylindrical cells. It differs from *M. ammoniaca* in its microscopic characters and its habitat, and by the paler color of its cap.

859. Mycena leptocephala Fr.

Epicrisis, 1836.

Illustration: Cooke, Ill., Pl. 187.

PILEUS 5-20 mm. high and broad, conico-campanulate, *scarcely hygrophanous,* fuscous-ashy (young and moist) *soon grayish-white or buff,* obtuse umbo tinged drab, often unicolorous, *striate to subsulcate when dry* and with a *glaucous* pruinosity, opaque. GILLS ascending, narrowed behind, adnate, *not uncinate,* not broad, ventricose, close to subdistant, whitish, then tinged pale cinereous. STEM 5-10 cm. long, .5-1 mm. thick, *filiform,* cartilaginous, elastic, glabrous, even, hollow, *darker than pileus when dry,* whitish above, subrooting. SPORES 8-9.5 x 5-6 micr. (rarely up to 10 x 7 micr.), elliptic-ovate, apiculate and somewhat pointed at one end, smooth, white. CYSTIDIA and *sterile cells* lacking. BASIDIA short, about 15-18 x 6-7 micr., 4-spored; sterigmata prominent, 6 micr. long. ODOR nitrous, varying weak or strong.

Solitary, scattered or rarely subcaespitose, among fallen leaves, mosses, decayed debris on the ground in woods. Ann Arbor, New Richmond. September-October. Not infrequent.

This is one of the gray Mycenas. It has been placed here because of the glaucous bloom on the cap when dry, referring to the "pruinosity" of Fries' description. No certainty can be reached in placing it because of lack of detailed data of related European species. It cannot be referred to *M. constans* Pk. which is a small plant and has a decurrent tooth to the gills. It might be referred to *M. consimilis* Cke., but that species is figured with shorter stems, and has no odor. Sometimes the cap and stem have a pale drab or faint purplish tint. The stem becomes flaccid in age, allying it to the Filipedes. The odor is often not noticeable until sometime after the plants have been picked, or when crushed.

860. Mycena dissiliens Fr. var.

Epicrisis, 1836.

Illustrations: Fries, Icones, Pl. 81, Fig. 2.
     Cooke, Ill., Pl. 285.

PILEUS 5-15 mm. broad, obtusely convex at first, then campanulate to subexpanded, subumbonate, striatulate and *grayish-brown to umber* (Sacc.) when moist, hygrophanous, fading to whitish, glabrous, substriate or even when dry, *margin at first straight.* FLESH watery brownish then whitish, membranous, not very fragile. GILLS adnate, *with a decurrent tooth,* ascending-arcuate, moderately broad, subventricose, close to subdistant, *white* then tinged with gray. Edge obscurely fimbriate, scarcely venose. STEM 3-4 cm. long, 1-3 mm. thick, often rather thick, *pellucid-white,* shining, glabrous, even, straight, equal, hollow, *fragile, easily split longitudinally.* SPORES 7-9 x 4-4.5 micr., narrowly elliptical, pointed at one end, smooth, white. CYSTIDIA rather abundant, subcylindrical, obtuse, 50-65 x 8-9 micr. on sides and edge of gills. ODOR none.

Scattered-gregarious on the ground among pine needles, moss, leaf mold, in woods of white pine, beech, etc. New Richmond. September. Infrequent.

These plants have been temporarily referred to *M. dissiliens;* they differ in that the pileus is not sulcate and the odor is lacking. The smell of *M. dissiliens* is said to be unpleasant. Our plant has a subgelatinous feel to the cap and stem, but there is no pellicle. The base of stem is scarcely hairy except where the mycelium masses among the decaying leaf mold from which it sometimes grows. The pileus dries to a glistening white, as does that of *M. stannea* Fr. It has the stature of a Collybia, as shown in Fries' figure of his species. It differs from *M. hemispherica* Pk. to which it appears to be related, in the much larger spores. The stem becomes very fragile with age and breaks on picking.

861. Mycena atroalba Fr.

Syst. Myc., 1821.

PILEUS 1-2.5 cm. broad, narrowly elliptical at first, then campanulate to expanded, umbonate, glabrous, hygrophanous, *umbo smoky-fuscous,* elsewhere pale grayish-white, sometimes uniformly fuscous-gray, fading, striate to the umbo when moist, radiately wrinkled or furrowed when dry, opaque. FLESH thin, concolor, rigid-fragile. GILLS narrowly adnexed, uncinate, close to scarcely subdistant, narrow, subventricose, white then pale cinereous, edge entire. STEM 4-6 cm. long, 1.5-2.5 mm. thick, equal, striate, rigid-fragile, subshining, glabrous, shining, even, *whitish above, dark fuscous below,* toughish, sometimes compressed, hollow, mycelioid-hairy and somewhat rooting. SPORES broadly elliptical, 8-9 x

5.5-6 micr., smooth, white. CYSTIDIA *none*. STERILE CELLS on edge of gills short, lanceolate, ventricose below. ODOR and TASTE none.

Gregarious. On the ground, moss and debris under tamarack trees. Ann Arbor. October. Infrequent.

The plants have the habitat of *M. metata,* but differ from it in the lack of odor, the dark-colored umbo and the microscopic characters. The gills are not provided with cystidia as in *M. atroalboides* and the stem is differently colored. Despite the similarity of the descriptions the two species are very distinct. Our plants differ from Fries' description in that the base of the stem lacks any marked "bulbous-tumid" root, therefore they are only provisionally referred to *M. atroalba.*

862. Mycena atroalboides Pk.

N. Y. State Mus. Rep. 27, 1875.

PILEUS 5-15 mm. broad, acorn-shaped at the very first, then conico-campanulate, finally umbonate and margin recurved, striatulate and *blackish-fuscous when moist and young,* hygrophanous, fading to fuscous or cinereous, and then subsulcate. FLESH *very thin,* membranaceous, whitish with a gray tinge. GILLS uncinate-adnexed, *narrow, close,* white, faintly grayish at length, edge entire. STEM *slender,* 4-10 cm. long, 1-1.5 mm. thick, equal or attenuated upwards, glabrous and even above, hollow, wavy, *fragile,* shining, terete or compressed, easily splitting lengthwise, *dark bluish or blackish-gray at apex,* tinged gray or fuscous elsewhere, sometimes connate with cottony fibrils below. SPORES 7-9 x 5-6 micr., broadly elliptical, smooth, white. CYSTIDIA numerous on sides of gills, subcylindrical, slightly ventricose below, obtuse, 75-85 x 7-8 micr. STERILE CELLS none.

Solitary or subcaespitose, on decayed wood and mosses, in woods of hemlock, beech, etc. New Richmond. August-September. Infrequent.

Manifestly related to *M. atrocyaneus* Fr. and *M. atroalbus* Fr. *M. atrocyaneus* is said to have the gills joined to a collar and distant, while the pileus is deeply sulcate. From *M. atroalbus, M. atroalboides* differs in possessing abundant cystidia on the sides of the gills and by its more uniformly colored pileus. A *form* occurs with pileus cylindric when very young and at first dotted with white, scattered, silky fibrils on the surface; its cystidia are thicker,

12-16 micr. in diameter. The young stem has a watery juice which is at first dark-colored. The tint of blackish-blue on young cap and stem is common to both forms.

863. Mycena prælonga Pk.

N. Y. State Cab. Rep. 23, 1872.

Illustration: Atkinson, Mushrooms, Fig. 94, p. 94, 1900. (As *M. polygramma.*)

PILEUS 5-15 mm. broad, at first subcylindrical then conic-campanulate or subexpanded, umbonate, glabrous, striate, *dark brown with a leaden tint.* GILLS adnate, uncinate, arcuate-ascending, *narrow,* close to subdistant, white, at length subcinereous. STEM very long, 10-20 cm. long, .5-1 mm. thick, *filiform,* firm, innately striatulate, glabrous, hollow, tinged rufous-brown, white at apex, rooting in the sphagnum. SPORES 8-9 x 5-6 micr. when mature, subglobose or broadly elliptical, smooth, white. CYSTIDIA only on edge of gills, flask-shaped, with narrow, acuminate neck about 45 x 12-14 micr.

Gregarious. On sphagnum in tamarack swamps; local. Ann Arbor. May-June.

This species has been referred by Atkinson to *M. polygramma* Fr. It is known by its very long slender stem, by the leaden tint of the brown cap, and by the microscopic characters. Many of the bog species develop these long stems, apparently the result of the moisture present.

Section IX. Filipedes. Stem *filiform, flaccid,* somewhat tough, rooting, dry, juiceless. Gills whitish or tinged with the color of the cap. Pileus not hygrophanous.

Stem commonly very long in proportion to pileus; very slender, tense and straight when fresh, collapsing with age because of the flaccid texture; growing on the ground among mosses and grass, singly, i. e., not caespitose. Inodorous. Sometimes not easily distinguished from those of the Fragilipedes which have slender, filiform stems; and from the Adonidae, which differ, however, in the persistently white gills. A few brightly colored species are included here, which might perhaps be as well placed under the Adonidae.

864. Mycena collariata Fr.

Epicrisis, 1821.

Illustrations: Fries, Icones, Pl. 82, Fig. 5.
Cooke, Ill., Pl. 189.

"PILEUS 6-12 mm. broad, campanulate-convex, subumbonate, striate, typically fuscous, but *commonly whitish-gray* and only fuscous on disk, fading, glabrous. FLESH membranaceous. GILLS adnate, *joined in a collar behind,* thin, crowded, distinct, whitish or obsoletely incarnate. STEM filiform, 2-3 cm. long, tough, glabrous, shining, striatulate under a lens. SPORES 8-10 x 4-6 micr. (Sacc. and Berk.)."

Not yet found in the State. I have seen specimens on decayed logs in a neighboring State and it doubtless occurs in Michigan. It has the stature and appearance of *M. vulgaris,* but the cap is not viscid.

865. Mycena cyanothrix Atk.

Mushrooms, Edible, Poisonous, etc., 1900.

Illustrations: Ibid, Fig. 99, p. 99.
Conn. State Geol. and Nat. Hist. Surv., Bull. 3, Pl. 37.

PILEUS 1-2 cm. broad, *ovate to convex,* viscid when young, glabrous, striatulate on margin, *bright blue when young,* becoming pale and whitish in age or fuscous in the center. GILLS free, narrow, close, white then grayish-white, edge minutely fimbriate. STEM 6-9 cm. long, 1-1.8 mm. thick, slender, hollow, faintly purple when young, becoming whitish or flesh color, flexuous or nearly straight, even, rooting. SPORES globose, smooth, 6-9 micr., white or with a delicate bluish tinge.

Gregarious, subcaespitose or solitary, on decayed wood, debris, etc. Marquette, Bay View. Not rare in the north.

A slender, delicately tinted plant, so far found in our northern regions only. It differs from *M. cyaneobasis* in its thinner substance, *free gills and brighter colors.*

866. Mycena subincarnata Pk.

N. Y. State Cab. Rep. 23, 1872.

PILEUS 5-12 mm. broad, hemispherical then campanulate-convex, finally subexpanded, fragile, striatulate, *glabrous, pale, incarnate* or yellowish, usually dull reddish on center. FLESH thin, membranaceous. GILLS adnexed, rounded behind, not broad, ventricose, close, whitish *tinged flesh color.* STEM 2-5 cm. long, filiform, *pruinose,* equal, hollow, even, toughish, *pellucid-white,* base rooting and white-villose. SPORES 6-7 x 4 micr., elliptic-ovate, smooth, white. ODOR none.

Gregarious, on the ground or on mossy logs in hemlock or pine woods. Bay View, New Richmond. September. Infrequent.

Near *M. pulcherrima,* but differing in color, and size of spores. The stem becomes fuscous or darker in age.

867. Mycena pulcherrima Pk.

N. Y. State Cab. Rep. 23, 1872.

PILEUS 5-10 mm. broad, conico-campanulate to subcampanulate, subexpanded, obtuse, faintly striatulate on margin, *dull, yellowish to reddish,* paler toward margin, delicately glaucous, glabrous. FLESH membranaceous. GILLS adnexed, not uncinate, broad in the middle, *ventricose,* close to subdistant, *yellowish* or tinged like pileus. STEM 3-5 cm. long, .5-1 mm. thick, filiform, flaccid, equal, even, flexuous, white-pulverulent when young, glabrescent, *pellucid-white* and shining, white-hairy at base. SPORES 7-8 x 5-6 micr., oval-elliptical, smooth, white. CYSTIDIA none. ODOR none.

Scattered or in twos and threes, on very decayed wood or debris, under hemlock and pine. New Richmond.

A distinct little plant, to be separated from *M. acicula* Fr. by its habitat, larger size and different spores.

868.   Mycena acicula Fr.

Epicrisis, 1836.

Illustrations: Fries, Icones, Pl. 85, Fig. 3.
    Cooke, Ill., Pl. 190.
    Patouillard, Tab. Analyt., No. 108.
    Atkinson, Mushrooms, Fig. 98, p. 98, 1900.

PILEUS 2-4 mm. broad, campanulate-convex, sometimes papillate, glabrous, glaucous, striatulate on margin, *vermillion, reddish-orange or yellowish* with red center. FLESH very thin, membranaceous. GILLS adnexed, ascending, ventricose, rather broad, *subdistant to distant,* yellow, yellowish, creamy white, or white, edge minutely crenulate. STEM 2-5 cm. long, filiform, equal, toughish, hollow, glabrous or minutely pulverulent at first, *pellucid-yellowish or yellow,* more or less rooting. SPORES 7-9 x 2.5-4 micr., *narrow, fusiform or narrowly subovate,* smooth, white. CYSTIDIA none. ODOR none.

Gregarious or scattered.   On rotten wood, or among leaves and grass, in woods, meadows, thickets, etc.   Ann Arbor, Detroit, etc. May-June and September-October.   Frequent.

This is a pretty little Mycena and one of the earliest to appear. It is not by any means limited to the woods or to growing on wood or twigs as most authors remark, but may be found among grass on the ground in low, moist meadows in spring.   The spores are quite characteristic and help not a little in its positive identification.   I suspect, in fact, that it has been reported as *M. adonis* Fr. when occurring on the ground in grassy places, but no spore measurements of that species seem to have been printed.   On decayed wood the stem is rooting and hairy along the root, whereas on the ground it has few hairs and is scarcely at all rooting.   Other minute Mycenas with rosy or red caps have been described by Fries from Europe: *M. stipularis* and *M. juncicola* have non-rooting stems inserted on stipules of fallen leaves; *M. pterigenus* has a bulbillose stem attached to roots and leaves of ferns, etc.

Omphalia Fr.

(From the Greek, *omphalos,* an umbilicus.)

White-spored.   Stem *cartilaginous,* slender, usually hollow or loosely stuffed, widened above with the pileus in trumpet-form.

Gills *decurrent,* or adnate-decurrent. Pileus more or less *membranaceous,* its margin at first either incurved or straight-appressed.

Epiphytal, lignicolous or terrestrial; putrescent plants, with few exceptions small or minute. Very closely related to Collybia when the margin of the pileus is at first incurved; and to Mycena when it is straight; differing from these by the decurrent gills. Toughish, reviving species are referred to Marasmius. They differ from Clitocybe by the cartilaginous character of the stem.

The PILEUS varies conical, hemispherical, convex or campanulate, often quite expanded in the Collybiariae, and usually marked by a distinct umbilicus which becomes widened in some species to infundibuliform; some species show the umbilicate character only in occasional specimens, e. g., *O. gracillima,* while the other specimens are obtuse or somewhat papillate. Its color is often pure white; it may be gray, fuscous, brown, yellow, orange or reddish. It is generally hygrophanous and then striate when moist. The surface is usually glabrous or with a very minute pubescence which is rarely glandular. The GILLS are decurrent, sometimes not strongly so, most often running far down as the cap expands. Their width and spacing are used to separate the species into subdivisions, although this is not always sharply marked. Peck in his monograph of the New York species (Rep. 45, 1892) states that in his opinion this grouping is unsatisfactory, but as no better is offered, it is adhered to in this paper. CYSTIDIA are lacking in most species, and when present are rather few and inconspicuous. The STEM is usually slender to filiform, and when dry its cartilaginous cortex is like that of Mycena. The surface is glabrous, horny and shining, or varying to pruinose or hairy at base. The SPORES are smooth. As in Mycena the immature spores are loosened in a microscopic mount; so the same precaution must be observed as when studying the spores of Mycena in order that one may get the correct measurements of the mature spores. Very few Omphalias have a distinguishing ODOR, and none of the following are nitrous or fragrant. Their EDIBILITY is of no interest because of their thin texture and small size; none are known to be poisonous, but probably few have been tested.

They are found from early spring to late autumn, during wet weather and in low or damp, shaded places. With the exception of *O. campanella* and *O. fibula,* they occur sporadically, few of them are found in quantities, many are but rarely found. A rather large number of species are described, Peck has named about twenty-five.

Key to the Species

(a) Plant wholly white.
  (b) Gills broad.
    (c) Stem tubular; plant snow-white. 879. *O. gracillima* Fr.
    (cc) Stem solid; plant soon dingy-white. 878. *O. albidula* Pk.
  (bb) Gills rather narrow.
    (c) Gills crowded; plant pure white. 869. *O. scyphoides* Fr. •
    (cc) Gills moderately close; plant dull white. 870. *O. scyphiformis* Fr.
(aa) Plant not wholly white.
  (b) Pileus viscid.
    (c) Gills lilac; pileus greenish-yellowish. 872. *O. lilacifolia* Pk.
    (cc) Gills whitish; pileus pale grayish-brown. (See 834. *Mycena vulgaris* Fr.)
  (bb) Pileus not viscid.
    (c) Pileus yellowish, orange or reddish.
      (d) Stem date-brown, horny; on coniferous wood; gills very veiny. 883. *O. campanella* Fr.
      (dd) Stem not date-brown and horny.
        (e) Gills white or cream-colored; on mosses.
          (f) Pileus 10-20 mm. broad; convex. 882. *O. fibuloides* Pk.
          (ff) Pileus 3-8 mm. broad, cucullate. 880. *O. fibula* Fr.
        (ee) Gills not white.
          (f) Pileus brick-red to reddish-brown. 873. *O. pyxidata* Fr.
          (ff) Pileus olivaceous-yellowish; stem dusky yellowish. 871. *O. olivaria* Pk.
    (cc) Pileus with grayish, fuscous or brown shades.
      (d) Pileus 3-7 mm. broad, whitish except the fuscous-brown center. 881. *O. schwartzii* Fr.
      (dd) Pileus usually larger.
        (e) Gills broad, crowded; pileus and stem dark, umber-fuscous to blackish. 884. *O. umbratilis* Fr.
        (ee) Gills rather narrow.
          (f) Pileus dotted with scurfy-blackish points; on sphagnum. 877. *O. gerardiana* Pk.
          (ff) Not with blackish points.
            (g) On decaying wood, logs, stumps, etc.
              (h) Pileus rugose, brown; flesh emitting watery juice when cut. 874. *O. rugosodisca* Pk.
              (hh) Pileus even, ashy to smoky, non-hygrophanous. 875. *O. epichysium* Fr.
            (gg) On the ground, pileus hygrophanous, substriate; gills subdistant. 876. *O. onisca* Fr.

Section I. Collybiariae. Margin of pileus at first incurved.

*Gills narrow; crowded, close or subdistant.

869. Omphalia scyphoides Fr.

Syst. Myc., 1821.

Illustrations: Fries, Icones, Pl. 75, Fig. 2.
      Patouillard, Tab. Analyt., No. 419.

"PILEUS 4-8 mm. broad, umbilicate then infundibuliform, often irregular, *pure white,* even, silky. FLESH submembranaceous. GILLS decurrent, *narrow, crowded, white.* STEM 8-16 mm. long, *short,* stuffed, subvillose, white. SPORES 6 x 2 micr. (Sacc., Massee) ; 6 x 4-5 micr. (Pk.)

"Gregarious, in mossy, grassy places on the ground. (Dead leaves in woods—Longyear.)

"Variable, often flexuous and eccentric, commonly small, not hygrophanous, yellowish on drying, stem woolly at least at base, pileus sometimes often an inch broad."

Reported by Longyear. Greenville. July. Rare.

870. Omphalia scyphiformis Fr.

Epicrisis, 1836.

Illustration: Fries, Icones, Pl. 75, Fig. 3.

PILEUS 5-9 mm. broad, convex, then umbilicate or infundibuliform, glabrous, sometimes silky, *dull white,* margin obsoletely striatulate. FLESH membranaceous. GILLS decurrent, thin, *narrowly triangular,* whitish, close, moderately broad in middle, attenuate at ends, edge entire, trama of interwoven hyphae. STEM 1.5-2.5 cm. long, equal, even, somewhat hollow, whitish, glabrous or loosely pubescent by flexuous longish hairs, base attached to moss by radiating hairs. SPORES 6-7 x 3.5-4 micr., ovate or pip-shaped, pointed at one end, smooth, white. CYSTIDIA none. ODOR none.

Gregarious on mosses or on moist earth. Ann Arbor. August. Rare.

This species is closely related to *O. scyphoides.* It differs in the dull white (albidus) color of the whole plant, whereas *M. scyphoides* is said to be pure white (candidus) ; the gills are not as narrow and crowded as in that species, and probably the spores differ. Our plants approached *M. scyphoides* in the pubescence toward the base of the stem, which Fries says is glabrous. On moss the silky-webby mycelium sometimes spreads some distance.

871. Omphalia olivaria Pk.

N. Y. State Mus. Rep. 25, 1873.

PILEUS 6-15 mm. broad, convex, subclavate, with decurved margin, *deeply umbilicate,* glabrous, *pale yellowish* to olive-green, even or obscurely striatulate. FLESH thin. GILLS long decurrent, subdistant, *rather narrow, yellow* when fresh, edge entire. STEM 2-2.5 cm. long, 1 mm. thick, *tough,* equal, even, tubular, *dusky yellowish,* minutely pubescent, glabrescent. SPORES 6-7 x 5 micr., subglobose or broadly elliptical, smooth, white.

On decayed logs. Ann Arbor. September. Rare.

The plant revives somewhat after being moistened. The pubescence of the stem is white after the escape of the moisture. The trama of the gills is composed of interwoven, narrow hyphae, quite compactly arranged. *O. luteola* Pk. differs in having a brown and solid stem. *O. subclavata* Pk. has yellow gills, but the pileus is grayish-brown and stem white.

872.   Omphalia lilacifolia Pk.

N. Y. State Mus. Rep. 24, 1872 (as *O. lilacina*).
N. Y. State Mus. Rep. 29, 1878.

Illustrations: Peck, N. Y. State Mus. Rep. 24, Pl. 1, Fig. 10-13.

"PILEUS 1-2 cm. broad, convex, deeply umbilicate, *glabrous, viscid,* hygrophanous, dingy yellow with greenish tinge and striatulate when moist, bright sulphur-yellow when dry. GILLS decurrent, arcuate, close, narrow, *pale lilac.* STEM 1-2.5 cm. long, 1-2 mm. thick, equal, glabrous, hollow, *viscid,* yellowish, *with a pale lilac-colored mycelium* at the base. SPORES subelliptical, 5-6 x 3 micr."

Scattered or solitary, rarely subcaespitose, on decaying trunks of hemlock, in the coniferous regions of the State. Munising, Houghton, Huron Mountains, Bay View, New Richmond. July-September. Infrequent.

The colors and viscidity make this an easily recognized species. *O. lilacina* was described from Lapland, and anteceded Peck's first name; it is said to be violaceous except for the yellow gills; its cap is not viscid.

873.   Omphalia pyxidata Fr.

Syst. Myc., 1821.

Illustrations: Cooke, Ill., Pl. 194.
      Patouillard, Tab. Analyt., No. 636.

"PILEUS 1-2 cm. broad, convex, umbilicate to infundibuliform, glabrous, hygrophanous, *brick red or reddish-brown and radiate-striate when moist,* paler and silky when dry. FLESH membranaceous. GILLS decurrent, *narrow, subdistant,* tinged with flesh color then gilvus. STEM 2-3 cm. long, 2 mm. thick, equal, tough, glabrous, even, stuffed or hollow, *pallid rufescent.* SPORES ovoid, smooth, white, 6-8 x 5 micr. (Patouillard.)

"On the ground, roadsides, etc." East Lansing, on the campus. Reported by Longyear.

Evidently rare. Peck says he found it but once. Not much reliance can be placed on the spore-measurements given; Stevenson quotes three different sizes, one of which is followed by Saccardo. The pileus is said by Fries to fade strongly, even to become whitish. Some think that *O. muralis* Fr. and *O. hepatica* Fr. are to be considered as varieties of *O. pyxidata.* (See Barbier, Bull. 1, Soc. Myc. de France, Vol. XX, p. 105, 1904.)

874. Omphalia rugosodisca Pk.

N. Y. State Mus. Rep. 26, 1874.

PILEUS 1-2.5 cm. broad, broadly convex or nearly plane, depressed or umbilicate, sometimes obtuse or slightly umbonate, *rugose,* hygrophanous, *watery cinnamon-brown* and striatulate (moist), paler when dry. FLESH thin. GILLS short-decurrent, *narrow,* close, whitish. STEM 2-3 cm. long, 1-2 mm. thick, glabrous, hollow, cartilaginous, concolor, paler at apex. SPORES elliptical, 6-7 x 4-5 micr., smooth, white.

On decaying prostrate trunks of hemlock. Bay View. July.

Known by the rugose cap, the brown color and the fact that every part of the plant emits a watery juice when cut or bruised. It seems to be limited to decaying wood of coniferous trees. Peck referred this species to Collybia in the 31st New York Museum Report, but later returned it to Omphalia. Saccardo placed it in the genus Mycena without giving any reason for doing so. At times the odor is said to be slightly of radish.

875.   Omphalia epichysium Fr.

Syst. Myc., 1821.

Illustrations: Atkinson, Fig. 101, p. 101, 1900.
    Plate CLXXI of this Report.

PILEUS 1-4 cm. broad, convex then expanded and umbilicate
or umbilicate-infundibuliform, margin arcuate with decurved edge,
striatulate and dark cinereous to smoky-brown (moist), even, silky
and light gray to whitish (dry). FLESH thin, soft. GILLS
acuminate-subdecurrent, ascending-arcuate, *narrow,* close, thin,
whitish-cinereous, edge entire. STEM 1.5-3 cm. long, 1-3 mm. thick,
equal, glabrous, *almost solid* or subfistulose, *smoky-cinereous,* concolor within. SPORES 7.5 x 4 micr., pip-shaped, smooth, white.
CYSTIDIA none.

On decaying logs or remains of decayed wood in frondose or
mixed woods. Throughout the State. Ann Arbor, New Richmond,
Marquette and Houghton. July-September. Infrequent.

The pileus is often fibrillose-floccose on the umbilicate center.
The plants are rather soft and watery and the stem soon shrivels.
O. onisca Fr. differs in the hygrophanous pileus which is entirely
glabrous, the smaller size and large spores; the gills are somewhat
different in shape and spacing.

876.   Omphalia onisca Fr.

Syst. Myc., 1821.

Illustrations: Fries, Icones, Pl. 75, Fig. 3.
    Cooke, Ill., Pl. 209.

PILEUS 5-15 mm. broad, convex, soon plane and cyathiform-
umbilicate, *glabrous,* flaccid, *hygrophanous,* smoky-fuscous or ashy-
brown and striate on margin (moist), pale cinereous and hoary
(dry), the umbilicus darker. FLESH thin, concolor when moist,
pale grayish-white when dry. GILLS *short, decurrent,* broadish
in middle, *subdistant,* thickish, cinereous-fuscous, sometimes forked,
edge entire. STEM short, 1-1.5 cm. long, .5-1 mm. thick, slender,
equal, toughish, firm, solid, *concolor,* glabrous, becoming pale
within. SPORES 9-11 x 5 micr., distinctly *ovate,* apiculus curved,
smooth, white. CYSTIDIA and sterile cells none. BASIDIA

clavate, 30-35 x 4-5 micr., 4-spored, sterigmata slender, 6-7 micr. long. ODOR and TASTE none.

Scattered or gregarious on the ground, in low, wet places in woods. Ann Arbor. May and September. Rare.

Differs from *O. epichysium* by its habitat on the ground, its glabrous, hygrophanous pileus and by its gills and spores. The hymenium occasionally has sterile basidia intermixed, bearing only a single long abortive sterigma. Authors disagree as to the size of the spores. Britzelmayr gives them as 12 x 7-8 micr. and Massee as 6 x 5 micr. It differs from *O. umbratilis* in the rather distant gills and larger spores.

877. Omphalia gerardiana Pk.

N. Y. State Mus. Rep. 26, 1874 (as Clitocybe).

PILEUS 10-20 mm. broad, nearly plane or soon infundibuliform, hygrophanous, fragile, *grayish-brown to brownish-ashy and striatulate* (moist), paler when dry, *the surface is dotted by scurf-like scattered points which become blackish.* FLESH thin, concolor. GILLS decurrent, *narrow*, subdistant, whitish then tinged with ashy or obscure yellowish, sometimes forked. STEM 3-5 cm. long, 1-2 mm. thick, *cartilaginous*, equal, even, hollow by a narrow tubule, glabrous or pruinose-villose toward base, *at length darker than pileus.* SPORES 7-11 x 3.5-4 micr., variable in size, maturing slowly, oblong-ovate, narrow, smooth, white. CYSTIDIA none. ODOR none.

On sphagnum in cedar and tamarack swamps. Ann Arbor, Houghton. May, July. Local.

Differs from *O. sphagnophila* Berk., in color and spores, according to the description. Cooke (Ill., Pl. 289) gives figures which are very like our plants. *O. sphagnophila* is said to have a dingy pale ochre-colored pileus and gills, is tough, and has smaller spores. Peck vacillates in deciding whether this is an Omphalia or Clitocybe; it was originally described as a Clitocybe, then in the 45th Report it was placed among the Omphalias, finally in the list of species described by Peck (N. Y. State Mus. Bull. 131), it was referred back to Clitocybe. My collections indicate that it has mostly a distinctly cartilaginous stem, hence it is placed here. The color varies considerably during its development; in old specimens the whole plant becomes dingy dark brown. The scurfy points on the cap are somewhat as in that of *Clitocybe ectypoides* Pk.

**Gills broad, distant.

878. Omphalia albidula Pk.

N. Y. State Mus. Rep. 49, 1896.

PILEUS 3-8 mm. broad, *convex-hemispherical,* at times papillate, with or without an umbilicus, glabrous, striatulate, at first pûre white, then dingy. FLESH membranaceous. GILLS decurrent, *distant, broad,* white, then dingy. STEM *very slender,* 1-4 cm. long, .5 mm. thick, *toughish,* glabrous above, white, "solid," attached below to leaves, etc., by a very strigose base. SPORES 8-10 x 2-4 micr., elongated-oblong, on slender sterigmata, 4-5 micr. long, smooth, white.

On leaves and bark in frondose or mixed woods. Bay View. July. Rare.

Related to *O. stellata* Fr. which differs mainly in its fragile stem, diaphanous pileus and different spores. *O. papillata* Pk. seems to be very similar, but with a conic or campanulate cap, few gills and different spores; it is said to be pure white.

Section II. Mycenariae. Margin of pileus at first straight, appressed to stem.

879. Omphalia gracillima Fr.

Epicrisis, 1836.

Illustrations: Fries, Icones, Pl. 75, Fig. 5.
    Cooke, Ill., Pl. 252.
    Gillet, Champignons de France, No. 502.
    Plate CLXXI of this Report.

PILEUS 3-10 mm. broad, at first campanulate, becoming *hemispherical,* sometimes *papillate,* sometimes depressed, *snowy-white,* pellucid-striate, soon sulcate, glabrous, subflocculose when dry, fragile. FLESH membranaceous. GILLS decurrent, *triangular, broad,* subdistant to distant, thin, pure white, edge fimbriate. STEM filiform, 2-5 cm. long, .5 mm. thick, equal, tubular, minutely subpruinose, *white* like pileus, toughish, flaccid, attached by floccose base or almost inserted. SPORES 6-8 x 3-4 micr., *oval-lanceolate,* apiculate, smooth, white. CYSTIDIA and *sterile cells* none. BASIDIA 24 x 6 micr., 4-spored.

Gregarious among and on fallen leaves and grass in frondose woods. Ann Arbor, Marquette. Spring and autumn. Infrequent. A very pretty little plant as its snowy-white color shows against a background of leaves or grass in open woods. The sulcate character of the margin of the cap appears as the plant loses moisture; sometimes a slight papilla is present. The gills are quite distant at times, with shorter gills alternating. Under the microscope the stem is seen to be covered with very short hair-like cells which under a hand-lens appear only as a slight pruinosity. The trama of the gills consists of interwoven hyphae. Our plants were not attached by floccose hairs as shown in Cooke's figures, but were almost free of them.

880. Omphalia fibula Fr.

Syst. Myc., 1821 (c. syn.).

Illustrations: Cooke, Ill., Pl. 274.
　　　　　　Gillet, Champignons de France, No. 500.
　　　　　　Patouillard, Tab. Analyt., No. 110.
　　　　　　Hard, Mushrooms, Fig. 99, p. 134, 1908.

PILEUS 3-8 mm. broad, subhemispherical or *cucullate,* often not expanded, *subumbilicate,* obscurely striatulate, nonhygrophanous, *pallid ochraceous-orange,* fading, even when dry, minutely pubescent under lens. FLESH thin, pallid. GILLS arcuate-decurrent, *narrow,* close (or subdistant after expansion of pileus), rarely forked, subpruinose, whitish or creamy-yellowish, edge entire. STEM 2-5 cm. long, *scarcely 1 mm. thick,* equal, flexuous, at length subtubular, toughish, *whitish or with tinge of yellowish* or straw color, scarcely pubescent under a lens, cartilaginous when dry. SPORES elongated oblong, 4-6 x 2 micr., smooth, white. CYSTIDIA scattered on sides and edge of gills, narrowly fusiform-acuminate, sometimes capitate, 3-4.5 x 7-9 micr. ODOR and TASTE none.

On *mosses,* in low woods or moist places. Throughout the State. May-October. Common.

This is our commonest Omphalia, although often only several specimens are found in one place. Its cap is at the very first almost cylindrical, then the margin turns out like the brim of a hat, so that it has much the shape of a man's "high silk hat;" hence it is said to be cucullate. Under the microscope the stem and cap are found covered with hyaline hairs, 50-60 micr. long. The gills are narrow and deeply decurrent, running up the inside of the unexpanded cap and down below it on the stem. The cap often becomes top-shaped instead of cucullate. Stevenson (British Fungi) and Massee (Fungus Flora) say the gills are broad, a statement which is clearly an error.

881. Omphalia schwartzii Fr.

Epicrisis, 1836 (as var. of *O. fibula*).

Illustrations: Patouillard, Tab. Analyt., No. 420.
  Gillet, Champignons de France, No. 504.

PILEUS 4-7 mm. broad, *rather firm,* soon campanulate, obtuse or at first umbonate, at length slightly umbilicate, even or striatulate, subpruinose, *whitish* with a slight fuscous tinge, *disk fuscous-brownish.* FLESH thin, pale fuscous. GILLS adnate-decurrent to strongly decurrent, arcuate, moderately broad, subdistant, whitish. STEM 2-3 cm. long, filiform, hollow, equal, pallid below, *tinged violaceous above,* pruinose, even. SPORES oblong-elliptical, 5-6 x 2.5-3 micr., smooth, white. CYSTIDIA on sides and edge of gills, *scattered,* subventricose, subcapitate at apex, some cylindrical above, 40-45 x 9-12 micr.

Gregarious on moss (Mnium, etc.) in hemlock woods. New Richmond. June. Infrequent.

O. schwartzii is constantly distinct from *O. fibula* to which Fries joined it as a variety. Peck (45th Rep. N. Y. State Mus.) considered it an independent species. Patouillard (Tab. Analyt.) had already pointed out that it was distinct from Bulliard's *O. fibula,* giving figures of spores and cystidia as evidence. It seems to be limited to regions of coniferous forests.

882. Omphalia fibuloides Pk.

N. Y. State Mus. Rep. 24, 1872.

"PILEUS 1-2 cm. broad, convex, deeply umbilicate, glabrous, hygrophanous, *dull orange* and striatulate when moist, paler when dry. FLESH thin. GILLS strongly decurrent, arcuate, rather close, *white,* the *interspaces venose.* STEM 3-5 cm. long, scarcely 2 mm. thick, equal, *glabrous,* hollow, colored nearly like the pileus. SPORES *elliptical,* 7.5 x 5 micr."

On moss. Jackson County. June.

Reported by Longyear. It is unknown to me. It is said to occur on burned, mossy ground like *O. fibula,* "which it resembles in color, but from which it may easily be distinguished by its much larger size, more robust habit and venose interspaces; the spores also are larger than in that species."

883. Omphalia campanella Fr.

Syst. Myc., 1821.

Illustrations: Cooke, Ill., Pl. 273.

Michael, Führer f. Pilzfreunde, Vol. III, No. 67 (as *O. fra-gilis*).

Hard, Mushrooms, Pl. 17, p. 131.

White, Conn. State Geol. & Nat. Hist. Surv., Bull. 3, Pl. 16, p. 36.

Murrill, Mycologia, Vol. 4, Pl. 8, Fig. 10.

Plate CLXXII of this Report.

PILEUS 8-22 mm. broad, convex-campanulate, expanded, *umbilicate,* glabrous, striatulate to the umbilicus, *dull orange-yellow* or tinged reddish, watery when moist, paler when dry. FLESH thin, membranaceous, yellow. GILLS adnate-decurrent to deeply decurrent, arcuate, *thick, very veiny,* narrow, tapering to front, *subdistant to distant,* pruinose. STEM 1-4 cm. long, 1 mm. or less in thickness, *horny-cartilaginous,* minutely tubular, curved or straight, even, *dark rufous-bay to date-brown,* yellowish above, concolor within, glabrous above, pruinose elsewhere and *with fulvous strigose hairs at the slightly thickened base.* SPORES oblong, 6-7.5 x 3-3.5 micr., smooth, white. CYSTIDIA widely scattered on sides of gills, more abundant on the edge, subcylindrical or sublanceolate with obtuse apex, 50-55 micr. long. BASIDIA 30-32 x 4-5 micr. ODOR mild. In dense and spreading clusters on hemlock and pine logs, stumps, etc.; also on tamarack logs, stumps or their remains in the southern part of the State; sometimes on debris on the ground.

Throughout the State; collected from Detroit to Isle Royale in Lake Superior. June-November. (Earliest collection May 6.) Common on coniferous wood.

The Bell-omphalia is a striking and easily recognized plant because of its habit of forming extensive clusters, by its colors, and by its horny stem and veined gills. In the non-coniferous regions it appears on tamarack and perhaps always on remains of wood of coniferous origin. Here it shows a marked variation from the typical plant as it appears on pine and hemlock; the gills are distant, always pruinose, and the stem is also pruinose and often solid. The typical stem of the plant from coniferous regions is usually attenuated below, but in the plant of the non-coniferous regions the stem is equal. The plants of non-coniferous regions are larger and the surface of the cap somewhat rivulose. Hard has illustrated a species (Mushrooms, Figure 98, p. 123, 1900) which he refers to *O. caespitosa* Bolt. It seems probable that this is a var. of *O. campanella,* perhaps var. *terrestris* Quel. Peck says its mycelium is regarded as destructive to the wood of coniferous trees.

884.   Omphalia umbratilis Fr.

Syst. Myc., 1821.

Illustrations : Fries, Icones, Pl. 77, Fig. 3.
      Cooke, Ill., Pl. 274.

"PILEUS 2-2.5 cm. broad, campanulate to convex, then *umbilicate,* glabrous, hygrophanous, *umber-fuscous* (moist), hoary when dry, margin somewhat striate. FLESH submembranaceous. GILLS adnato-decurrent, *broad, crowded,* becoming fuscous. STEM 2-5 cm. long, 2 mm. thick, equal, *tough,* stuffed then tubular, glabrous, *dark fuscous to blackish.* SPORES 6-7 x 4-5 micr." (Britz.)

Reported by Longyear. Chandlers. June. Rare.

Said to be gregarious on the ground, and imitating in color the blackish species of Collybia, like *C. atratus* and *C. ambustus.*

MUSHROOM POISONING

BY O. E. FISCHER, M. D.*

No one who has not followed the development of the study of mycology in its scientific or popular fields during the last twenty years can realize its development and the changes in our views that have taken place. Within this time a number of popular works have appeared, keeping pace with the great volume of general nature literature. Mycological and toadstool clubs have been organized in many cities in order to interest people in this fascinating branch of botany. Such clubs have easily won the interest of people at large because of their appeal on the score of mycophagy, the eating of fungi. In the purely botanical and technical field, colleges, universities and state herbaria have given more and more attention to the scientific and economic aspects of mycological study and have brought about the publication of journals devoted exclusively to studies made in these specialties. For centuries almost every community has had its enthusiastic amateur botanist who has collected and sought to name—to classify—the higher plants of his hunting ground. Now cometh also the humble collector of toadstools and mushrooms who finds that his hobby meets with sympathy and interest. Thus "The Spectator" in Outlook (January 13, 1915) gives a charming account of his initiation into the accuracies and delights of mycology.

It has been the purpose of Dr. Kauffman to supply in these volumes a manual for the use of both the amateur and advanced student of the Agaricaceae or gilled fungi of Michigan. It is similarly the purpose of this chapter on mushroom poisoning to place before layman, mycologist, mycophagist and physician an account of the present state of our knowledge of the subject. Having in mind such a varied class of readers, the author must include matter which will seem hopelessly technical to the one, and matter that may seem superfluously simple to the other. It is not the purpose of the paper to present much that is either new or original but it does

*The author would acknowledge his thanks to the libraries of Parke, Davis & Co., to the University of Michigan and to the Wayne County Medical Society, as well as to Professor Kauffman and to numerous private correspondents and co-workers whose services have aided in the preparation of this paper. Our knowledge of mushroom poisoning is still far from complete and further aid from any source will be welcomed.
Detroit, Michigan, 507 Field Ave., March, 1915.

seem possible, in the light of recent advances, to record more vital information about deleterious and suspected species than is to be found in similar articles in all the text books combined. The strictly technical literature of the subject is very large. A bibliography might easily include one hundred books and papers in French, German and English. Most of these are quite inaccessible to the average student and an attempt is made herein to present part of the matter they contain. No popular handbook covers a tenth of the field. The earliest views, still popularly held, regarded the Agarics as a large group of poisonous plants. Then, under the influence of teaching-mushroom-clubs and the invaluable published results of Peck and of McIlvaine and Macadam, the impression that there were but few deleterious and hundreds of edible species, has led to a reckless mycophagy which resulted in the discovery of new harmful species. These can no longer "be counted on the fingers" (Plowright), nor will Bagnall's "dozen in over a thousand edible" include all the toxic species. The bibliography, On Mushroom Poisoning, will guide the reader to the sources found most useful in the preparation of the paper.

A number of factors give myco-toxicology or mushroom intoxication increasing importance. The daily press endeavors to keep alive the fear of "mistaking a toadstool for a mushroom" in its frequent reports of the disastrous consequences of such a blunder if the toadstool is eaten, but the Sunday paper is not so consistent inasmuch as it prints and reprints irresponsible articles or quotes unreliable and dangerous rules and tests to apply, which, if followed, will lead the man of newspaper education into real danger. The enormous influx of foreigners from southern Europe, accustomed to seeing in the markets and gathering and eating certain species of higher fungi at home, gives us individuals who mistake some American deleterious species for an edible European one which resembles it. These people furnish most of the cases of poisoning which occur in the United States. It is affirmed that nearly all of more than thirty deaths from mushroom poisoning in and near New York City in 1911 occurred among them[39].* Through the growth of nature and mycological clubs, the sale and use of the several excellent popular books and bulletins, and the offering of wild species for sale in our markets, the use of fungi for food is rapidly increasing. This necessarily means that a larger number of poisonings of both major and minor importance will come about, since insufficiently trained, self-constituted "experts" may blunder

---

* For numerical references see bibliography: On Mushroom Poisoning.

or fall into minor error. Some reasons for even the well trained student going a bit wrong will appear in other paragraphs. If he will but report his error in the manner indicated below much, or even all, may be forgiven or even approved.

Mushroom poisoning must have been fairly frequent in early times since it is well known that the Romans employed fungi in great quantity both as delicacies and as daily food. Paulet, in 1793, records their collection in Russia, China, Hungary, Italy and especially in Tuscany, and their public sale in Pekin, Petrograd and Florence. Thus they have numbered among their victims the family of the Greek poet Euripedes, a wife, two sons and a daughter, Pope Clement VII, Emperor Jovian, Emperor Claudius, King Charles VI of France, and Czar Alexsis of Russia[1]. The Princess of Conti nearly lost her life through mistaking *Amanita muscaria* for *A. caesarea*. Definite knowledge of the number of fatalities from mushrooms begins with Paulet who states that from the year 1749 to 1788 there were a hundred deaths in the environs of Paris alone. More recently (1883) Bardy reported 60 cases in 6 years in Les Vosges, and Guillard (1885) estimated 100 deaths annually in southwestern France. Falck collected 53 cases in Germany with 40 deaths and Inoko in Japan reports 481 cases of mushroom intoxication in 8 years (1889). In this country Palmer, of Boston, collected 33 cases with 21 deaths and Forster, of Charlestown, 44 cases with 14 deaths[1]. Bagnall[2] quotes Clark and Smith to the effect that in one ten-day period (September, 1911), 22 deaths occurred in New York City and vicinity, 15 in 1906 and 30 cases with 12 deaths in 1905. In 1913 there were 26 cases of poisoning in Hartford in a few weeks. In 1900 Gillot found over 200 authentic cases of mushroom poisoning mostly in France (123 fatal due to *Amanita phalloides*) and Ford[3] added nearly as many more recorded in the German, English and French literature since 1900. Sartory, in France, records for the summer of 1912, 249 cases of fungus poisoning with 153 deaths. Of these 90% occurred in 15 days[1]. Ford is convinced that the majority of cases do not find their way into medical literature. I do not believe that 10% do. Thus in one summer there were unreported 2 cases (not fatal) in Baltimore, 2 deaths in Cleveland, 9 poisoned in Fostoria, Ohio with several deaths, and 10 in Toronto with 2 deaths. Murrill[7] estimates the annual deaths in the United States as probably 50 or more, as many are not reported. My own records, by no means complete, for southeastern Michigan only, for 10 years show 77 cases with 16 deaths. None reported medically. Most cases undoubtedly escape publicity.

AMANITA PHALLOIDES

(See *A. verna, virosa* and *bisporiger.*)

Amanita phalloides is by long odds the most important of all poisonous mushrooms. It is widely distributed, common through-out most of the season and often exceedingly abundant. It is in-nocent in appearance, of delicious taste and of extreme toxicity. In considering it we may regard *A. verna, A. virosa* and *A. bisporiger* as included under the term "*A. phalloides.*" Bulliard a hundred years ago gave it the common name "Destroying Angel." It is also known as the Death Cup, White or Deadly Amanita. The earlier species, named in Europe, such as *Amanita bulbosa* and its varieties, *alba, citrina, virescens* and *olivacea, Agaricus bulbosus, Amanita viridis, A. venenosa* and a number of others are without doubt identical. In older French literature it is known as *l'orange cigue, l'orange souris, l'orange blanche ou citronee, l'orange cigue jaunâtre* and *l'argaric bulbeux* and in German as *Giftwulstling* and *Knollenblaetterschwamm.*[1] Its identification is comparatively simple even in its disguises and no one who does not know this fungus well should dare to eat wild mushrooms or to recommend a portion of such to his neighbor. The possibility of its presence in a collection intended for the table should always be rigorously excluded. The 153 deaths of 1912, above mentioned, were due chiefly to *A. phalloides.* Gillot's thesis[4] maintains that all fatal cases are due to this Agaric. This is not strictly true. The statement that nine-tenths of all fatal cases are due to it, seems conservative enough. In 1845 Orfia reported 8 ill and 4 dead from its ingestion; Bock Ziemssen, 11 fatal cases; Mautner (1861), 4 cases with one death; Handford (Lancet, 1886), 2 fatal; Palmer, 16 cases, 7 fatal; Tappeiner, 5 cases, 2 fatal; Pfromm, 4 Italians, all died; Plowright, 6 cases, 4 fatal; Bulletin of French Mycological Society, 18 deaths 1900-07; in October, 1884, eleven children died in an orphanage in 5 days. Incomplete records for southeastern Michigan (10 years) show 16 deaths in 44 due to *phalloides* illnesses. In 22 of this 44 the white the Amanita was surely to blame, in 14 probably, in 5 presumably.

Surprisingly small quantities may bring on fatal consequences and there are numerous deaths on record from eating one or two good-sized specimens.[1] Plowright[5] has reported the death of a child of ten years from one-third of the top of a small plant eaten raw; Pfromm, that of two children after taking a bit of juice soaked into bread.

The mortality from *A. phalloides* intoxication is extremely high, varying from 60 to 100 per cent and is dependent largely upon the amount ingested and probably somewhat upon the treatment.[1] Sixty to one hundred percent seems too high for adults, judging from local cases. One-half this would be more nearly correct, unless much is eaten or several children are included in each group. Recovery may be regarded as rare but not impossible. It may follow eight to twenty-one days of extreme suffering. Practically all deaths from mushrooms are attributed to this one species.

The cruelty of the poison and the horrible suffering it causes its victim may be faintly realized from a perusal of the clinical histories of the more fully reported cases. One gets the impression that scarcely another agent bears equal power to torture. A few typical, though varied, cases may be briefly quoted. Thus an Italian family at 6 p. m. on Sunday ate heartily of a cooking of fungi. By midnight vomiting had begun, attended by violent abdominal pain, headache and extreme thrist. A doctor was summoned the next morning. The father was cyanotic and twitching and delirious. The pupils were contracted. He improved slightly for a few hours. Periodical remissions and exacerbations of symptoms continued for eight days when coma and death supervened. The mother presented similar symptoms, with thirst and vomiting more violent, miscarried at five months and also died on the eighth day. Both children died in 58 hours. (Pfromm.[6])

The Deep Valley, Pennsylvania, cases occurring in August, 1907, are of especial interest.[8] About 7 p. m. on Sunday a physician, three others and the man-of-all-work ate one quart of mixed fungi fried in flour and butter. Before 2 a. m. all began to suffer from excessive vomiting and violent diarrhea which continued all day Monday. Atropine, narcotics and an oil purgative were given. The gastrointestinal symptoms continued three days accompanied by subnormal temperature, more or less delirium (no salivation or urinary suppression) and in case of Dr. D., severe muscular cramps of limbs and abdominal muscles. His death occurred on Thursday morning. By Saturday the man-of-all-work was up and about, the three others still abed. In these, vomiting and diarrhea had ceased and an enlarged liver, distended gall bladder and jaundice were appearing. The man who had gathered the fungi conducted the investigator to the place and indicated the varieties gathered and what had constituted most of the lot. These were *Amanita phalloides,* with smaller numbers of Cantharellus, *Amanitopsis vaginata* and a very few *Russula emetica.*

The following group of cases is very typical. In September, 1911, six persons were poisoned, two fatally, in Cleveland. The children, aged four and six, had a little gravy and recovered after nausea, vomiting and diarrhea. Mr. C., aged 67, ate some at supper, felt bad during the night but ate more for breakfast! About noon violent illness began with intense pain in the epigastrium, vomiting and diarrhea with loss of control, clonic spasms and great prostration. Urinary suppression was obstinate and lasted till death, three days after the first meal. Mrs. C., aged 65, ate one forkful at the first meal but did not like the taste. Profuse vomiting and diarrhea with great prostration began one hour after Mr. C.'s symptoms. She recovered rapidly after two days. The daughter-in-law, aged 40, ate at the second meal and, though feeling hot and feverish, ate more at noon! Eight hours later she had exactly the same symptoms as Mr. C. The physician arrived early on the next day. He gave oil, began stimulations with strychnia, nitroglycerin, aromatic spirits of ammonia and, after removal to the hospital, saline solution continuously and oxygen. Some improvement was noted except that the heart action was weak and intermittent and the extremities could not be kept warm. Hiccough for two days, great agony and unconsciousness preceded death on the seventh day. A son, aged 19, ate the second meal—breakfast. Though feeling bad, he worked until 4 p. m. By 9:30 he presented the same symptoms as mother and grand-father. After ten days of apparently as grave illness as theirs under "most terrific stimulation" (nitroglycerin, strychnia, oxygen and salines) he was reported out of danger though "looking like a corpse." "The fungi were gathered from a shady hillside. Some were over six inches across and white inside and out; others were yellow as saffron through and through and about four inches across. Others were white outside and brown under; some were small, white on top and pink under."[9] The brief case histories leave no doubt as to *Amanita phalloides* being the offender. The botanical notes admit of considerable speculation. In every respect this report is pregnant with meaning—and full of food for reflection—for the student of toadstool poisoning.

Grouping the clinical histories from numerous sources the symptomatology of *phalloides* intoxication may be described. When due to the deadly Amanita alone the clinical symptoms are practically always the same and are characteristic. Nevertheless IN EVERY CASE OF POISONING the etiology, i. e., WHAT FUNGUS HAS BEEN EATEN should by all means be determined at the earliest possible moment! Why? Not only for its scientific importance to myco-toxicology but more especially for guidance as to what treatment is indicated and required and very especially what the outlook may be for the patient. If *A. phalloides* can be ruled out the prognosis at once becomes very much better and useless fears may be allayed. The sufferer is entitled to this. Uneaten fungi should be submitted to competent authority, more should be gathered from the sources whence the suspected species were derived, and the opinion of the patient or of some one who gathered them with or for him as to their identity with those eaten, obtained.—Returning to symptomatology: After ingestion there is a prodromal stage of from six to fifteen hours— generally over ten—in which little or no discomfort is felt. Then follows a sudden seizure of extreme abdominal pain, cramp-like in character, accompanied by vomiting and diarrhea of undigested food, with blood and mucus. Discharges soon become cholera-like (serous) or rice-water in character. There is burning, consuming thirst. Anuria is usual; constipation rare. Prostration and sleeplessness, with the great nervous restlessness of weakness and suffering, are conspicuous. Muscular spasms in various groups are frequent, accompanied by cries or screams of pain. Loss of strength is rapid and excessive. Periods of pain and vomiting alternate with remissions and ameliorated symptoms. Haemaglobinuria does not occur. Within a few days jaundice, cyanosis and coldness of the skin and extremities develop followed by profound coma from which the patient does not rally. Ocular symptoms, the pupils varying, and convulsions are rare but may occur. Convulsions are often terminal, and death is due to cardiac failure. The course of the disease requires from four to six days in children and eight to ten in adults but death may occur within 48 hours if large quantities of the fungi have been eaten or they have not been thoroughly cooked. These points should be weighed in considering prognosis. The resemblance of the clinical picture to that of cholera and to acute yellow atrophy of the liver has often been remarked.

Atypical features occur especially in cases where *Amanita phalloides* was not proven to have been the sole etiological factor. Such cases may show dilated pupils, clear cerebration, albuminuria.[2]

Schuerer's six cases—most thoroughly studied and reported[10]—show-ed cramps in calf of leg, arms and other muscles, the left arm es-caping in one. Many days of pains in the legs persisted. Recovery was more or less rapid according to age but the youngest (5) died in thirty-five hours after violent convulsions and coma. If recovery takes place the liver and spleen enlarge about the third day, after which day, according to Maass,[12] the prognosis becomes better. "In clear-cut cases the physician can diagnose the variety of toadstool from the typical symptoms."[10]

Reports on the post mortem findings in man in fatalities due to *A. phalloides* are not overly satisfactory. There is little to be found to account for the violent paroxysms of pain, vomiting and diarrhea. Schuerer found, in a child, colitis, pleural haemorrhages and fatty degeneration of liver, heart and kidneys. Microscopically there were "Very wide-spread and obviously severe lesions of the cell elements of the central nervous system, as heretofore hardly known in this form and to this extent"—regressive changes like those seen in the septic deliria. Harmsen, Maass and Kobert liken the postmortem findings to those of phosphorous poisoning. Thus, the normal liver contains from 8 to 25 per cent of fat, that of phosphorus and of alcohol poisoning 50 to 70 per cent and that of Amanita-toxin (2 cases) 53 and 69 per cent. Death seems to be due to this extreme fatty degeneration of the liver. (Ford, Schuerer.) Medico-legally, such a liver, with the addition of the other findings, makes the postmortem picture pathognomonic of *Amanita phal-loides*.[10]

Treatment of Poisoning by *A. phalloides*

All authorities agree unanimously that therapeutic measures in these grave emergencies are almost useless. Case histories show that often the cause is not recognized, or the gravity of the cases not appreciated. There is no antidotal drug for Amanita-toxin and the treatment is that of poisoning and septic intoxication in general. Competent medical advice should be obtained as soon as possible. Active emetics (ipecac, mustard, apomorphine), assisted perhaps by the stomach-tube, purgatives (castor oil being preferable to the salines) should be administered at once and every effort thereby made to reduce further absorption of the poison to a minimum. By the time symptoms from *A. phalloides* have be-gun, the toxin is already in the circulation. High enemata to empty the lower bowel may be used early. Later normal saline solution should be given thus, or hypodermically, or even intravenously to supply the body's need for fluid and to ease the torturing thirst. Narcotics and anodynes in large doses are necessary to relieve the intense pain and to quiet convulsive movements. Nitroglycerine and strychnia frequently, and up to the limit of tolerance, are of great value. Cyanosis calls for oxygen inhalations. Atropine may be of use as a stimulant and a corrective with morphine *but it has no antidotal value here.* Milk, raw or boiled, may be regarded as a mild natural antidote.[18] Alcohol should probably not be given in any form. Strong coffee is indicated as are hot dry applications to the body. Digitalis may be used but requires from six to ten hours before effects are seen. Camphor[10, 30] in sterile oil given subcutaneously every hour is valuable. Suprarenal extract is mentioned. Large draughts of hot water, flaxseed tea, slippery elm or starch water[14] may be used, as well as tannigen, bismuth subcarbonate and opium to quiet excessive diarrhea and vomiting. Supportive measures and good nursing are of the greatest importance. Transfusion of blood would seem worthy of trial in graver, slower cases.

Ford, finding that protective and curative sera were theoretically possible, worked for three years on the serum-therapy. He was able to immunize animals to the aqueous extract up to five or six times the fatal dose[15] but efforts to manufacture a curative serum have thus far been unsuccessful.

The Fochier treatment by abscess of fixation[53] has been applied by Dr. A. Pic of the University of Lyon in 23 cases of which 9 died. The conclusion that "it is a therapeutic agent of the first order in those terrible intoxications due to *Amanita phalloides*" seems to have made no impression on the medical profession. Judging from Michigan cases—37 illnesses with 16 deaths—this is not a remarkably low mortality, 39 per cent versus 42. Pic and Martin contrast it with "the usual 86.8," based on 38 cases with 33 fatalities in France, 1913.

Poisonous Constituents of *Amanita phalloides*

The first attempt to obtain the active principle or poison of *A. phalloides* is probably that of Letellier, who in 1826 obtained a heat-resistant substance from a number of fungi. This was termed amanitin. Later he found two substances, one of an irritating nature, acting upon the mucous membranes of the alimentary canal and another characterized as a glucosidal alkaloid—the Amanitia. Boudier in 1866 ascribed the poisonous action to an alkaloid which he named bulbosine, but was never able to isolate. In 1877 Oré concluded, on biological grounds alone, that *Amanita phalloides* must contain an alkaloid and this hypothetical poison he named phalloidin. These names are no longer employed. Kobert (1891) established the important fact that extracts of *A. phalloides* contain a substance which lakes or dissolves the red blood corpuscles of many animals and of man. With this "hemolysin" we shall have much to do in the remainder of this paper. Ford and his co-workers have investigated it most satisfactorily in their epoch-making labors which have been fully reported. This hemolysin is not the active principle—for we shall see that it is very easily destroyed by heat, much less than is usually employed in cooking, and that the digestive juices break it up as a rule. Furthermore, individuals dying of *A. phalloides* intoxication do not show symptoms which are to be ascribed to this kind of poison. Kobert gave this blood-dissolving hemolysin the name of phallin, regarded it as the essential poison, and gave it undeserved importance. He placed it in the group of protein-like poisons known as toxalbumins because of its susceptibility to destruction by heat. Beside the hemolysin, and more constantly present, Kobert found later an alcohol-soluble substance which was extremely poisonous to animals. This he regarded (1900) as an alkaloid, soluble in alcohol, which would not produce fatty degenerations. A toxalbumin (near thujon and pulegon), was held responsible for these.

Frey,[16] in 1912, comments, "The whole study of mushroom poisoning still lies very much in the dark. It is on the same plane as thirty years ago." He says that studies on muscarin and phallin show old results and theories to be wrong, but otherwise there is no progress. The publication of results of recent American investigators seems to have been unknown to him, for progress has been made, and a basis for further results established. Murrill[17] comments (1910) that it is remarkable how little is really known, and that the practical importance of the subject is vastly increasing. The important work of recent American investigators began with the proof (Ford[18]) that extracts of *Amanita phalloides* contain the hemolytic material described by Kobert and in addition a heat-resistant body which will reproduce in animals the majority of the lesions described in fatal cases of *A. phalloides* intoxication in man. These two substances were named by him the Amanita-hemolysin and the Amanita-toxin. The further chemical study upon the plant was carried out by Abel and Ford,[19] by Schlesinger and Ford,[20] and Ford and Prouty.[21] In these papers it was shown that the hemolytic agent is not proteid (toxalbumin) but an easily-decomposed glucoside, insoluble in alcohol, extremely sensitive to heat, to small traces of acid, to pepsin and pancreatin, and that it can therefore play no role in poisoning in man when the fungi are cooked. It may be a factor if large quantities are eaten raw or insufficiently cooked, or if through deranged digestive action the hemolysin escapes destruction.[15] It is present in such great amount that under such circumstances the possibility of its having a poisonous action cannot be eliminated. The Amanita-toxin has so little in common with alkaloids that they hesitate to class it with them.[15] Amanita-toxin is the alcohol-soluble active principle, *the essential poison,* resisting the action of heat, of drying and of the digestive juices, and reproduces in animals the lesions found in *phalloides* intoxication in man. Chemically it cannot be characterized definitely, but the purest preparations do not give the reactions of either proteins, glucosides or alkaloids. Rabbits are not affected by various extracts by mouth, both the hemolysin and Amanita-toxin being quite innocuous to them, when one-fortieth of the amount was fatal when given subcutaneously. Dogs and cats are poisoned by the cooked fungus in the same degree as human beings. The raw hemolysin given subcutaneously has pronounced blood-dissolving properties, giving the picture of a hemolytic intoxication with extreme haemaglobinuria and pigmentation of the spleen.[13] [These are the properties assigned to the European *Helvella (Gyromitra) esculenta.*] Even when made from dried specimens of *Amanita phalloides* hemolysin will dissolve the red blood cells of guinea pigs, rabbits, fowls, pigeons, dogs, goats and man. Swine, sheep and beef bloods are not susceptible. The blood of the guinea pig is most susceptible and that of the goat least. When this hemolysin is heated to 140° F. it loses some of its activity, and 150° maintained for one-half hour, suspends it. (Hence the term "thermo-labile.") It may be classed with the bacterial hemolysins. Injection experiments on animals show its extreme toxicity. Within a few hours the fur ruffles and they refuse to eat. There is rapid loss of weight and strength, death occurring within one to three days under great dyspnoea. The heart stops last. In smaller doses a chronic intoxication is produced lasting three, four or six weeks. Convulsions are unusual and there is no salivation or gastro-intestinal disturbance—in contrast to muscarin poisoning.[18] Frequently, even in *A. phalloides,* the hemolysin is present only in small amounts and it may be absent whereas the edible *A. solitaria* and *A. rubescens* contain it in great abundance. "It is probably a food and certainly harm-less,"[3] i. e., when cooked and eaten by man.

The Amanita-toxin is the more active and acutely fatal, pro-ducing approximately the lesions seen in man from the whole cooked plant, ulcers in the stomach and intestine, serious hemor-rhages, and in other organs, especially liver and kidney, cell necrosis and fatty degeneration.[13] It loses potency somewhat but not greatly on boiling. In a later report[31] Ford and Brush say that *Amanita phalloides* var. *citrina* gathered in France corresponds in all particulars to the *A. phalloides* gathered in America, and has identical properties and contains the same poisonous sub-stances.

OTHER AMANITAS

Amanita verna and *A. virosa* have been already mentioned as included in the above section. *A. spreta* is recognized to be deadly poisonous. A group in which Amanita-toxin is present in small quantities includes *A. porphyria, strobiliformis, radicata, chlori-nosma, mappa, morrisii, citrina,* and *crenulata.* The first four of this latter group are devoid of haemolysins but owe their toxicity to small amounts of Amanita-toxin. In *A. spreta* the hemolysin is small. The extract caused both acute and chronic intoxication in guinea pigs but not in rabbits. Poisonous, Boston Mycological Club, and Atkinson.

Ford and Sherrick[41] found in *Amanita mappa* a small amount of thermo-labile hemolysin, a chronic intoxication of guinea pigs closely resembling that of *Amanita phalloides.* No muscarin. Rabe says *A. mappa* has the same poisons as *A. phalloides* but in much smaller amount. It should be classed as perhaps less dangerous than *A. phalloides.* Other Amanitas may be grouped here by Ford's reports.[22] The agglutinin will receive attention in the account of *Amanita muscaria.* The chronic intoxication is shown by a pro-gressive emaciation and death in 18 to 20 days.

Amanita citrina (of Europe) a yellow variety of *A phalloides* (Kobert). No hemolysin or agglutinin. Poisonous to guinea pigs and rabbits by both acute and chronic intoxication. Seldom, if ever, toxic to man.[18] A distinct species from *Amanita phalloides* var. *citrina.*

Amanita crenulata—No hemolysin or agglutinin. Chronic in-toxication in guinea pigs and rabbits. Extract made after one year of drying was fatal by chronic action after an acute. Poison, small in amount, similar to Amanita-toxin. McIlvaine records it as edible.

A. morrisii—Small amount of hemolysin destroyed at 60° C. Poisonous to guinea pigs and rabbits. Should be grouped with the deadly species. Edibility not tested.

A. chlorinosma is probably seriously poisonous. *A. strobili-formis* acts like *phalloides* on frog's heart.

The species of the genus *Amanitopsis* as a whole are regarded as edible. McIlvaine warns against confusing *A. spreta* with these species.

Amanitopsis volvata may be grouped with *phalloides*. No hemolysin or agglutinin, fatal in 7 to 22 days to guinea pigs and rabbits, the intoxication resembling Amanitas. McIlvaine pronounces it edible, but it should be avoided. *Amanitopsis vaginata* is easily learned and is edible.

Amanita junquillea—rare and unimportant—free from poisonous properties.

Amanita solitaria—difficult to recognize. Contains small amount of hemolysin. Edible, McIlvaine. Ford[32] reports it almost free from poisonous action on rabbits and guinea pigs, but large doses produced a salivation in the latter. *Muscarin is more widely distributed in fungi than was originally supposed.*

Amanita rubescens—commonly known as "The Blusher," Red Amanita. Non-toxic to animals and man. Free from Amanita-toxin but has a powerful hemolysin. European authorities differ but our American form is a well-known edible species.

Amanita frostiana—difficult to identify, is closely related *botanically* to *A. muscaria,* of which it has been regarded as a small or depauperate form. It contains a small amount of a thermo-labile hemolysin, but no muscarin. Its extracts have no effect on animals. Not tested but probably edible.[22] CAUTION! lest *A. muscaria* be used.

AMANITA MUSCARIA

Amanita muscaria, the Fly Agaric, is a most interesting fungus. It is also called "the false orange" and "Fliegen Schwamm." It is less common and less toxic than the group of *A. phalloides* but is widely distributed over the world. In importance it ranks next to the white Amanitas. It is subject to great variations in color, size and markings, but is easily learned so that it may be distinguished from the famous edible *Amanita caesarea*. Ford [3, 18] and Michael and others agree that its taste is bitter and unpleasant and this factor may save people from serious accident. Occasionally the bitter taste is absent, more is eaten and quick fatality may result.

Through the publication[23] of Circular No. 13, U. S. Dept. of Agriculture and of Prentiss' account[24] the fatal poisoning of Count de Vecchii in November, 1897, has become classic. He bought from a countryman a quantity of *Amanita muscaria,* picked in Virginia, seven miles from the capital. The Count was familiar with mushrooms and took these to be the Royal Agaric, *Amanita caesarea.* At breakfast, which was finished at 8:30, he ate two dozen and pronounced the taste particularly good. Dr. K. ate one dozen. By 9 a. m. the Count was lying on his bed in a state of collapse, filled with a sense of impending death, and soon lost consciousness. Blindness came on before this, as did rigid spasm of the lower jaw, and difficulty in swallowing. Convulsions were so violent as to break down the bed. Emetics were given and apomorphine and atropine subcutaneously. He became continually worse and died without regaining consciousness on the evening of the next day. Dr. K. went by car to his office. While sitting on a chair, about 9 a. m., he gradually passed into unconsciousness without feeling any premonitory pain or distress, though half-stupid and very restless just before. He noted, about 9:10, uncertain eyesight and double vision, without nausea. A prominent early symptom was sudden jerking back of the head. He remained unconscious for five hours; at one time his life was almost despaired of. He did not suffer the least pain but on the contrary was in a comfortable dreamy state. By 7 p. m. he was out of danger. Cold sweats were a prominent symptom. A total of one-tenth grain of atropine was given in 24 hours. Apomorphine produced no emesis, vomiting not occurring until evening. Castor oil and sweet oil were given about noon.

THE CLINICAL FEATURES of poisoning by *Amanita muscaria* are quite as characteristic and distinctive as those in *Amanita phalloides* intoxication and should enable physicians to distinguish clearly between the two conditions—when either fungus is eaten alone. So often a mixed lot of different varieties is used that the symptoms in patients point to the combined action of different toxic principles. In *A. muscaria* poisoning there is usually a very short interval between ingestion and first symptoms, one-half to one hour or at most three hours. If small amounts are eaten even five or six hours may elapse. This feature is of greatest value in deciding upon the kind of intoxication which the cases present. Severe ones show excessive salivation and perspiration, a flow of tears, a feeling of laryngeal constriction, nausea, retching, vomiting and watery diarrhea. The last named almost always occur. The pulse is usually slow and irregular. There is no fever; pupils are small. Respirations are accelerated and the patients dyspnoeic, the bronchii being filled with mucus. (The action of atropine is the opposite of this, point for point.) Mental symptoms are also present, particularly giddiness with confusion of ideas and rarely hallucinations. All these symptoms may vary in intensity, at some times the gastro-intestinal predominating, and at other times the mental. In light cases only salivation or perspiration may be noticed, with uneasiness in stomach and bowels, for a few hours. In severe cases the vomiting and diarrhea may rapidly rid the alimentary canal of the offending material and the nervous symptoms then become predominant—delirium, violent convulsions and loss of consciousness developing in rapid succession and the patient's sinking into a deep coma. Rarely, consciousness is retained till the end, death resulting from paralysis of the respiration. Finally, in many cases, after the vomiting and diarrhea, the patients sink into a deep sleep, awakening later profoundly prostrated but on the road to recovery. Normal health reappears rapidly—two or three days. There are no late effects in *muscaria* intoxication as in that of *Amanita phalloides* with its degenerative changes in the internal organs. The prognosis is always good if the patient recovers from the preliminary symptoms. When, rarely, the nervous symptoms dominate the alimentary, excitement and hallucinations simulate alcoholic intoxication. (Quoted freely from Ford and Clark.[25]) The delirium is occasionally followed by loss or impairment of memory. The pupils dilate as death approaches. The action of muscarin is almost identical with that of pilocarpin.

Post-mortem examination reveals surprisingly little. The pathology of *Amanita phalloides* is absent, particularly the lesions of the liver. In general the findings point to the action of a profound nerve poison.[3] Medico-legally, remains of fungi in the alimentary canal would be of great importance.

Poisonous Constituents of *Amanita muscaria*

Schmiedeberg and Koppe, in 1869, showed by the most careful work, both chemical and pharmacological, that *Amanita muscaria* contains an active principle which they called muscarin. At first regarded as an alkaloid of the same general nature as strychnine and morphine, later work has shown that it is probably a complex ammonia derivative. Muscarin is an extremely active substance, well known from the attention it has received in all works on toxicology and materia medica and therapeutics. In the latter field it can well be spared on account of its variability and unreliability and because we have better drugs of similar action. Muscarin is near pilocarpin and nicotine in action, exciting smooth muscle and stimulating all glands. At almost every point in its action it is the direct antagonist of atropine (from belladonna) but is far less powerful. It is present in the fungus in but small amounts but is nevertheless able to exert its characteristic effects, frequently with fatal outcome. In producing paralysis of heart and respiration it does so by stimulating the inhibitory nerve endings of the vagus. Atropin has a depressing action upon the same nerves which muscarin stimulates. The muscarin excitement, remarkably, does not pass over into a paraylsis, its curare action (that of arrow-poison) being slight. Muscarin has been synthetically prepared by the oxidation of cholin but does not keep as well as the natural product, and differs materially in its action upon animals.[18]   A ptomaine muscarin is also known.

But poisoning by *Amanita muscaria* and muscarin poisoning are by no means identical (Harmssen[26]). Kobert says the fly-agaric drunk (Fliegenschwamm Rausch) is by no means a pure muscarin "jag" but resembles haschisch (*Cannabis indica*). Harmsen found that he could extract from 100 g. of fresh *muscaria* 16 mg. of a fairly pure muscarin. This was twice as deadly to cats as to frogs. That it is not the sole factor in poisoning is shown from the following: (1) with the lethal dose of muscarin at 0.525 g., it would require 4 kg. (8.8 lbs.) of the fresh fly-fungus to produce a fatal outcome[26];   (2) when the action of the muscarin-part of an entire extract is physiologically neutralized by atropin, the animals nevertheless die; (3) the extract is deadly even when the muscarin is removed. He has also shown[26a] that the entire extracts of *A. muscaria* are twice as toxic, weight for weight, as pure muscarin and contain a poison which produces in animals continued convulsions with fatal outcome, not prevented by atropin. He therefore assumes the presence of at least one other substance which he names "Pilz-toxin." This pilz-toxin must be very unstable since it loses potency on drying, and is sensitive to heat (thermolabile). It does not appear in the urine. (Compare intoxication of the Koraks.) His work casts doubt over the value of atropin as an antidote and is in accord with clinical experience. In 1910 Ford[22] said *Amanita muscaria* acts in all animal experiments as a convulsant and no other agaric shows similar action, not even the closely related *A. frostiana*.

Treatment for *Amanita muscaria* Poisoning

Just as in cases of *A. phalloides* intoxication, it is the important duty of physician and friends to get all the information possible as to the exact nature of the toadstool eaten and the amount ingested. *It will be shown below that a number of species of fungi, mildly toxic or simply deleterious and unwholesome, can produce a more or less typical picture of muscarin intoxication.* Confirmation of the species will therefore be of great value in determining prognosis and in giving a clew to antidotal treatment. The outlook in poisoning by the fly agaric is more hopeful than when the Destroying Angel (*A. phalloides*) has been ingested, the mortality runs much lower, the illness is briefer and the suffering less cruel— though bad enough. We do not have here the chronic and degenerative lesions produced by the white Amanita which defer death or prolong convalescence. The *muscaria* intoxication is acute, comes on soon after eating the fungus, develops rapidly and is amenable to treatment. Recovery often occurs without untoward symptoms. Lachrymation, salivation, contracted pupils, delirium, hallucinations, and coma call for atropin in large doses subcutaneously or intravenously. Even though the vomiting and diarrhea are pronounced, the stomach and bowels should be further emptied by the free use of emetics and purgatives, for parts of the fungus are often found in the canal post-mortem when profuse emptying seemed to have taken place. On account of coma, apomorphine subcutaneously is less apt to work, and other means of emptying the stomach should be begun early (stomach tube, mustard, zinc sulphate, sulphate of copper). In cases with bad heart action, respiratory distress and coma, atropin (intravenously) offers the only hope, though many other measures, as mentioned under *A. phalloides* treatment, should not be neglected. Absolute recumbent rest is enjoined. Sustain the heart. Give nitroglycerin for cold skin and extremities, and dry heat.[24] Atropin is not medically indicated in every case, and good nursing may easily be of greater importance to tide over periods of weakness and depression. Nourishment should be concentrated. Tannic acid is useless; acidulated water bad. Transfusion of blood, oxygen and galvanism, have been suggested.

The fly Amanita possesses interest in several other respects. It

is eaten in the Erzgebirge of Saxony and Bohemia.[11]   Treated and
untreated it has been eaten without bad results. A colored woman
in Washington recited in detail how she was in the habit of cooking it. Rejecting gills and peeling the cap, specimens were boiled
in salt water and then steeped in vinegar, then washed and cooked
and served with steak, the whole process a rational process to
remove poisons (?). Michael[27] worked up to eating a thick medium-
sized cap (cooked) and "properly peeled." It tasted ill but did
no harm. Then he ate a specimen prepared as salad which tasted
worse. On this ground he classes it as "inedible." For reasons
like this we are loath to take any one man's testimony in the
great field of mycophagy. Peck has repeatedly received reports
from various people who eat it.[54] He also records the eating of the
fine variety *formosa* of *A. muscaria* by a sheep, but Ford[22] suggests
that the herbivora are (at least, by mouth) immune to this toxin
as well as to others. There seem to be *seasonable and local variations in the toxicity of Amanita muscaria*[55] *and of other species.*

One-tenth of a raw *A. muscaria* has produced in a man of thirty-
seven years, eleven days of illness, with typical *muscaria* symptoms,
but accompanied by fever.[56]

The use of *Amanita muscaria* simply and purely for producing
drunkenness is well known, but has not been satisfactorily explained. Krasheninnikoff, who travelled in Siberia and Kamchatka for
ten years (1733), reports that the Koraks used the fly Amanita—
three or four for a moderate dose, and ten for a thorough drunk.
Langsdorff (1803) confirms this and Kennan[28] describes it in some
detail in his first Siberian journey. The natives call the fungus
"muk-a-moor." Its sale has been made a penal offense by Russian
law but "prohibition does not prohibit." One fungus may sell for
$20 worth of furs, and supply does not equal demand. The dried
cap is used; a duly flavored decoction is made from them or pieces
are swallowed whole. First effects come on rapidly and make the
candidate cheerful and merry, then drowsy and sleepy for ten
or twelve hours and he awakes in a state of exhaustion. During
the stage of excitement there is a horrible kind of delirium and the
experience of visions of varied character. The intoxication is
prolonged or passed on (among the lowest and most degraded
Koraks) by drinking the renal excretion and thus a spree may be
economically kept up for a week.[24] Evidently the muscarin is ex-
creted unchanged. (See Ziemssen, Fungus Poisoning, Vol. 17.)
Toleration develops, though death from an orgy is not uncommon.
The meat of animals dead of muscarin poisoning has a pronounced

poisonous action if eaten by others (Stellar & Erman). In regard to the use of *Amanita muscaria* as a fly poison, D. R. Sumstine (Penn.) reports that the apparently dead flies revive fully in about two hours. One of our mycologists has seen them recover after two days. Tappeiner[30] states that the fly poison is easily destroyed.

Toxic Principles of Amanitas

Harmsen's "Pilz-toxin" was never confirmed. Ford[22] agrees that *A. muscaria* owes its action to muscarin but in place of the second poison hypothecated by Harmsen it contains also an hemolysin (as in *A. phalloides*) soluble in alcohol and *a constantly-present agglutinin* belonging to the glucosides. Agglutinins are bodies capable of causing groupings, coherence or agglutination of blood corpuscles when brought in contact with them. They act directly on the blood cells. Given subcutaneously the agglutinin of *muscaria* always caused death in typical convulsions. Violent cooking of the plant, deadly without boiling, was shown to destroy both the muscarin and agglutinin. Subsequent studies of other fungi were based upon a search for the actions of the four active agents thus far enumerated. We have seen from the foregoing consideration of two deadly toadstools that *Amanita phalloides* contains two poisons, (1) an hemolysin which is thermolabile and also easily destroyed by the digestive juices and (2) an Amanita-toxin which is the very definite and powerful poison of the species. Now in *Amanita muscaria* we have (1) muscarin, a poison with its characteristic and individual physiological action, (2) hemolysin in small amount and (3) an agglutinin. Agglutinins are not common in plants. Out of ninety-nine examined they were present in four non-poisonous Papillionaceae and in six Daturas. Among 40 fungi they were present in one-quarter, thermolabile in some, in others heat-resistant. They resisted drying of the fungi better than did the hemolysins and were found to last for years in dried *A. muscaria.*[22]

Amanita pantherina, though rare or lacking in America, may be associated with *A. muscaria* since it is said to be used in Japan to produce mushroom drunkenness. Muscarin has been isolated from it as from the Siberian fungus. Delirium, dilated pupils and hallucinations with visions of beautiful red, yellow and brown objects predominate over the gastro-intestinal symptoms. *A. pantherina* is also used as a fly poison. Poisoning from it shows the usual alimentary irritation coming on within a few hours, great excitement, delirium and convulsive seizures. Ocular symptoms, loss of memory and syncope are frequent. Gillot has collected thirty cases with two deaths and Inoko, in Japan, a series of thirty-two with one fatality. Recovery is usually rapid but occasionally convalescence requires fourteen days. Atkinson's *Amanita cothurnata* may be the American representative of *A. pantherina*, hence both of these should be avoided as esculents. *A. cothurnata* will poison flies. *A. pantherina* extracts were without effect on animals but only a few plants were tested.[41]

There has been in recent years a tendency to explain away too many cases of minor poisoning as due to indigestion, decomposition of the abundant proteid of mushrooms, or to the possible insect-infection of good fungi—and to refer too many of the cases to "probably *phalloides* or *muscaria*." Now the rich labors of Ford and his co-workers, both in the field and in the laboratory, and the results of Clark, Smith and Kantor have verified certain clinical experiences and shown us that the list of more or less poisonous species must be considerably extended. *Amanita phalloides* and its few congenors still stand quite alone, head and shoulders above all others, for extreme toxicity. They are, most fortunately, not likely to have any rivals for dangerous qualities. They have retained their place easily at the head of the list of noxious species, but the minor and less poisonous list has been somewhat increased. These nearly all belong, in a way, to a *muscaria* group. It will be the problem of pharmacological and biologic chemistry to show why they cause such a variety of clinical disturbances,—by no means explainable by "indigestion,"—and yet resemble the action of muscarin.

THE GENUS LEPIOTA

In contrast to the genus Amanita with its very dangerous species and its few safe edible forms we have in the equally large genus Lepiota a number of highly prized edibles. Amanita requires close discrimination to distinguish its species; Lepiota, for the mycophogist, principally, that he shall not confuse its *L. naucina* with *Amanita phalloides* and that he shall not mistake the black sheep of the section, *Lepiota morgani* or green-spored Lepiota for *Lepiota procera*, "The Parasol." *L. morgani* is an enticing plant and probably the largest Agaric in the world. It is distinctly American. This fine fungus shows very consistent partiality in selecting its victims for it always poisons certain individuals who try to eat it and never distresses others of the same family. It is credited with at least one death and many serious illnesses. Significant it is that heating destroys the greater part of its toxic properties.

Dr. Blount (Illinois) says[33]: "One day last month the Man of Science of our house came home with a fine specimen of large white mushroom which he took to the library and identified as 'horse mushroom.'" (If you do not care to discriminate between white-spored and purple-brown-spored Agarics, mycophagy is a danger-ous field for you!) "So a few were collected and prepared for dinner. The Man of Science ate a small piece raw at 2 p. m. At 5 p. m., feeling well, he tried another piece, raw, as large as the little finger. At 6 p. m. he felt generally ill and ate no supper. In half an hour he began to have profuse, painless watery bowel movements, but blamed a dentist and his drugs for this." Dr. B. took two small portions each as large as a pea about 6 p. m. The after-taste created loathing. Discomfort was immediate, and consisted of a warm heavy sensation, slight pharyngeal spasm and difficulty of swallowing. By 7 p. m. vomiting had begun, became very violent and continued every five to ten minutes. Diarrhea began and lasted all of the next day. Intense burning pain in the stomach alternated with intervals of lassitude and exhaustion.

At 9 p. m. hypodermic medication (strychnia 1/30, atropine 1/100, morph. sulph. 1/4) and cocaine produced relief and slumber came on at 11 p. m. Pulse was weak and rapid; perspiration free. The Man of Science vomited three times and had diarrhea all night. He felt as usual the next day. He ate most and suffered least. The action of the poison suggests muscarin.

V. K. Chestnut[34] records that the president of the Chicago Mycol-ogical Society mistook *L. morgani* for *L. procera*. Prof. Miller (Terre Haute) eats *L. morgani* and tells of six families that do so. One or two members of each family are made sick, though two families have eaten it repeatedly without trouble resulting. "The meat is simply delicious." Galveston and Milwaukee record seven cases of illness and V. K. Chestnut adds twenty beside. Detroit might add four. The symptoms are as above described, apparently also from cooked specimens. The fatal case was that of a two-year old child who died in convulsions in seventeen hours after eating of a raw plant. Poisoning has resulted after every variety of cooking and after soaking in salt water. Webster[35] tells of a New England my-cophagist who removed to Missouri, identified *L. morgani* as *L. procera* from pictures (!) and paid the penalty within two hours. He draws the moral, *"Eat only what you KNOW!"* McIlvaine[38] (p. 711) reports another case from Wisconsin of violent illness from raw (?) *L. morgani,* mistaken for *L. procera* and eaten in very small amount, presenting all symptoms above recorded but with the addition of temporary blindness. Warren (Port Huron) records that in a family of five who ate it two girls were made ill. Symptoms came on early the next morning—seven hours after eating—and were "almost as bad as from Gyromitra poisoning as it is known in Port Huron."

THE GENUS TRICHOLOMA

In this genus McIlvaine agrees to label *T. saponaceum* and *T. sulfureum* as inedible on account of taste. I had for years regarded the entire genus as safe, but in August, 1908, we had a group of seven cases of rather violent poisoning from an innocent-appearing Tricholoma. Good specimens were at once sent to Atkinson who described them as a new species which he named *Tricholoma venenatum.* This agaric has not been found again nor further tested. Of the lot eaten many were badly infested by insects when examined two days later. The symptoms came on one hour after supper and consisted of vomiting, sometimes bloody, retching and considerable prostration in three individuals. All recovered. Surprises like this will continue to occur as long as fungi are eaten. It may be years after some varieties of poisoning occur before the etiology is satisfactorily settled: whether due to a new deleterious species; a known inedible variety not recognized by the consumer; a personal physiologic sensitiveness of the individual; decayed fungi of good species or some infested by acrid insects; the rare presence of a minor toxin in some generally-esteemed edible variety; or simple acute indigestion—perhaps due to gluttony. The observer should endeavor to fix positively the responsibility on the one real cause.

THE GENUS CLITOCYBE

Like Lepiota, this large genus has for years been credited with but one deleterious species. Within a few years two others have been added. All three show muscarin symptoms in variety.

Clitocybe illudens, known as the "Jack o' Lantern" because of its phosphorescent glow, or the "Deceiving Clitocybe," is mistaken every year, in Detroit, by our foreign residents for *Armillaria mellea* or for the European Chanterelle. And on such annual fall occasions it holds high carnival and breaks into the newspapers. The attending physician has a busy night or a few busy hours—

and is credited in the daily press with having saved lives in toadstool poisoning. The mycological investigators visit the family and
usually find its members up and about their usual occupations.
This is the impression one gets of *Clitocybe illudens* from twenty-
nine Detroit cases. The remnants of the feast are usually found
to be large half-cooked tough masses. McIlvaine reports a sapon-
aceous taste—and the ability to retain the fungus when eaten. It
is possible to make it comparatively harmless by heating it in salt
water for half-hour, then taking it out and frying it in butter.[39]
Farlow[36] reports illness of four persons. They found the fried flavor
excellent. Within two hours all had free vomiting lasting all after-
noon, no depression, no intestinal disturbance. No emetics were
used since the Jack o' Lantern carries this property with it and
may thus ward off more serious results. At a New York state
institution eight teachers and children, after terrible nausea, recovered. No fatalities have been recorded. Diarrhea and prostration may occur. Clark and Smith[37] found that extracts of the plant
would stop a frog's heart which would recover under atropine.
Similar results were obtained on the creature when paralyzed by
the extract. They conclude that *Clitocybe illudens* exerts a characteristic muscarin effect on exposed hearts which effect is completely overcome by atropin. (Not the case in extracts of *Amanita
muscaria*.) Ford finds no hemolysin but the power to produce an
acute intoxication in guinea pigs, fatal in one to seven days or a
chronic intoxication lasting fifteen days. No lesions postmortem.
Rabbits unaffected. After one year of drying boiling for half-hour
destroyed the toxicity.

The characteristic American *Clitocybe illudens* has its phosphorescent and related European correspondent in *Agaricus* (or *Pleurotus*) *olearius,* which, mistaken for the Chanterelle, caused illness of the *illudens* type in France.[44]

Fabre writes, "The soft light of *Agaricus olearius* has confounded
our ideas of optics; it does not reflect, it does not form an image
when passed through a lens, it does not affect ordinary photographic plates." (Fabre, Poet of Science—LeGros.)

Clitocybe dealbata var. *sudorifica* or *Clitocybe sudorifica,* the
sudorific Clitocybe, is an interesting little toxic toadstool recently
added to the black list. It is often found among "fairy rings" (*Marasmius oreades*). I believe it has been picked with the latter and
thus caused trouble, though easily distinguished. The flavor is
good. Minneapolis has a record of two cases of poisoning. Peck
himself tested it, eating eight caps slightly fried, and got the usual

reaction, i. e., some five hours of profuse perspiration beginning on the forehead and spreading over the body. This may be attended by increased nasal and salivary secretion, hiccough and discomfort, though there are no other ill effects.[42] The original lot was tested on animals.[40, 41] In a rabbit the watery extract produces profuse salivation in a few minutes with weakness and sickness, increased renal activity and activity of the bowels, followed by gradual improvement. Fatal to guinea pig in one quarter hour. Even the boiled extract paralyzed the respiration in seven minutes. Autopsy negative. One rabbit died with slightly contracted pupils. In a third guinea pig there was salivation, lachrymation, etc., increased respiration and then respiratory paralysis. Drops in the eye contracted the pupil for four hours. Its action therefore is that of the muscarin-pilocarpin series. The little Clitocybe seemed more poisonous than *muscaria* extract tested side by side with it for it killed rabbits that withstood larger doses of *muscaria* extract. A frog's heart could be stopped for one hour with it and then revived with atropine. *Clitocybe dealbata* should likewise be avoided for *C. sudorifica* has been mistaken for it by a well-trained mycologist.

Clitocybe morbifera is similar in habitat and appearance to the preceding and is closely related to it.[42] In four cases in Middleville, Michigan, which have come to my attention, the symptoms were more severe and serious than those of *C. sudorifica*. There was more discomfort and the attending physician recognized the likeness of the clinical picture to muscarin disturbance and used atropine. Four people ate, and three were made ill. The one that suffered most had over-taxed her digestive powers the day before—a factor that seems to predispose to mushroom poisoning. Symptoms came on two hours after eating and were abdominal pain, vomiting of food including entire specimens of tough "Fairy Ring" fungi, purging, sweating, cold extremities and collapse. In one case there was some blindness. All were fairly well the next day. Animal tests have not been made. These must henceforth be regarded as a necessary part of the record.

Clitocybe nebularis which made Cordier ill, and is reported as poisonous when raw (Bertillon), is legally allowed among the thirty varieties permitted in the markets of Munich.[11] Here legal enactments, duly enforced, have reduced the number of poisoning cases.

THE GENUS HYGROPHORUS

Experimentally in man no Hygrophorus is known to be inedible and there are many fine esculents. *Hygrophorus conicus* used to be forbidden and Demange has attributed a serious outbreak of poisoning to it. It is fatal to guinea pigs by chronic intoxication—as are many perfectly safe fungi. Cooke and McIlvaine say it is all right. *H. pratensis* var. *cinereus* is toxic to guinea pigs.[22] It is edible. Var. *albus* contained a heat-resistant agglutinin and hemolysin: toxic to guinea pigs. Edible. *H. marginatus* similar and edible. See Bibliography, reference 22, for several others. The genus is either devoid of action or poisonous by chronic intoxication only to guinea pigs. An excellent record, so far. The species are clean, beautiful and inviting.

THE GENUS LACTARIUS

Lactarius contains some well known edible mushrooms—*L. deliciosus, volemus, corrugis,* being well liked. McIlvaine says that not a single species retains its pepperiness after cooking. Some of the genus tasted raw are horrible. *L. torminosus* "the griping milky," is charged with having caused fatal illness.[45] In Germany it is known as the "Birken"—or "Gift-reizker." Eleven were poisoned. Three children ate it fried, the youngest, aged two, died in twenty-four hours. Eight Polish laborers, including two women who ate most, prepared it. The women died after six day's illness, treatment coming late in their case. Symptoms came on in about five hours and consisted of nausea, headache, abdominal cramps, vomiting prolonged and even bloody; diarrhea was synchronous, violent and profuse and accompanied by tenesmus. Anuria and albuminuria followed. Skin dry and later jaundiced; pupils dilated; heart negative but weakening; respiration rapid, shallow, irregular and finally Cheyne-Stokes. Temperature normal. Liver somewhat enlarged. The remainder of the description, as well as the postmortem findings in the adults, suggests very strongly that *A. phalloides* was the cause and not *L. torminosus.* Atropin proved without effect in the therapy and the invaluable hypodermoclysis of normal saline solution was not used. No account of why or how *L. torminosus* was settled upon as the cause is given. Hockauf[11] doubts the diagnosis and says many authors (six are named) say *L. torminosus* is harmless when cooked. Krombolz has eaten it though the taste was bad. Huseman's two cases referred to the species fit *Amanita muscaria*. Great mycologists give conflicting reports. Kunkel says in Sweden it is used cooked and is poisonous only when raw, and this agrees with Ford's results.[22]—Ford found that its hemolysin and agglutinin were destroyed at 150° F. Though acutely fatal to both guinea pigs and rabbits which showed convulsive-like movements, with retraction of the head—a little like *A. muscaria* intoxication but with more somnolence—these toxic effects were not obtained when the extract was cooked one-half hour. Its safety or danger perhaps depends entirely upon the cooking. Maass[12] alludes to the presence in some fungi of drastically purgative resinous acids which may be decomposed by cooking processes and become foods. The milk of the Lactarii seems to be such a substance. "Insects eat both *L. torminosus* and *L. deliciosus*. They pronounce excellent what we find poisonous and vice versa" (Fabre). Hockauf regards *L. torminosus* and *L. zonarius* as poisonous and *L. plumbeus*, *L. chrysorrheus*, *L. vellereus*, *L. insulsus*, *L. pubescens*, *L. pyrogalus*, *L. fuliginosus* and *L. violescens* as suspicious or inedible. McIlvaine reports *L. insulsus* and *L. vellereus* as edible, as good as *L. deliciosus*. Murrill's list of forbidden mushrooms is headed by *L. rufus* and includes *L. torminosus*, *L. fuliginosus*, *L. vellereus*, *L. pyrogalus* and *L. theiogalus*—perhaps all condemned only on account of their taste when raw. Fabre's household finds *L. deliciosus* overrated, coarse and difficult to digest.

Lactarius uvidus extract was acutely poisonous to guinea pigs, fatal in forty-eight hours, but had no effect on rabbits. No hemolysin or agglutinin. Several authors rank it poisonous; the Boston Mycological Club pronounce it deleterious. With *L. torminosus* and *Clitocybe illudens* it is ranked as a violent gastro-intestinal irritant.

THE GENUS RUSSULA

Russula, one of the most difficult genera for reliable specific distinctions, appeals to the mycophagist because of the attractiveness, tenderness and abundance of its species. Members of the Detroit Mycological Club and the Institute of Science have for years eaten all the bright colored and peppery Russulas indiscriminately and believe that *Russula emetica* is a safe fungus to eat in Michigan. Hockauf says of the European *R. emetica* which is so often condemned, that our knowledge is insufficient and that exceptions can justly be taken to reports in the literature. Krapf was made ill by it (?) before 1800 and its bad name has followed in all subsequent reports which are based on this almost exclusively. Hockauf would take reports of many bad sorts with reserve. McIlvaine is very emphatic that about all Russulas are good, even *R. emetica,* identified by Peck. *R. foetens* smells ill, tastes worse and made Krombholz slightly ill. In 1817 ten deaths in Bohemia were credited to Russula. Murrill[7] includes *R. emetica* in his poisonous list and credits it with cholin, pilztropin and muscarin and puts down *R. foetens, R. nitida* and *R. fragilis* as mildy poisonous or suspicious. Warren (Port Huron) says, "I have eaten every kind of Russula I have gathered except *R. foetens* and no one would care to eat that. Never any bad effects. Greatest fault is that they are liable to be wormy. *R. vesca, R. virescens, R. cyanoxantha,* and *R. alutacea* are permitted in the Munich markets. The "fraglos giftig" *R. emetica* is eaten in the Baltic province Esthonia after parboiling. (Maass.[12])

Frey[16] says that poisoning by Russula should be classed among the greatest rarities. He reports two fatal cases, studied in the greatest detail and from every angle, with thorough autopsy. The clinical picture was not unlike that of *A. phalloides* intoxication, with gastro-intestinal symptoms dominant. The two boys that died (aged twelve and fourteen) ate the soup which they had prepared, on Sunday evening and Monday morning, were ill Monday night, attended school on Tuesday and became very ill that night, as did the father. They died on Thursday. Postmortem, the liver was not that of *A. phalloides* fatality and the gastro-intestinal hemorrhages and appearances were regarded as characteristic of the irritant action of Russula poison. It is assumed, in these two cases, that an essential change (spoiling) took place in the soup between the first and second meals. An official investigation of the abundant remnants of the fungi ruled out *A. phalloides* and placed the blame on spoiled Russula varieties.

THE GENUS MARASMIUS

Marasmius, the family of the internationally famous "fairy ring mushroom," has long been credited with having the poisonous *M. urens* and the doubtful *peronatus.* McIlvaine would clear both of suspicion. We have no data but we would again warn of the danger of getting *Clitocybe sudorifica* and *Clitocybe morbifera* cooked with *M. oreades.* The latter, moreover, has been found tough, leathery and entire in the vomited matter after a mushroom feast—illness *ex abusu,* a common form of spurious mushroom poisoning.

Conclusions on White-Spored Genera

Of some 50 families of Agarics about 23 are white-spored. Moreover, more than half of all species one finds belong to this section. Though the most dangerous toadstools belong to the Leucosporae, there are so many fine edibles that we do not wish to discard all the white-spored species. If we are to eat fungi at all we must expect to exercise discriminating observation on every specimen intended for the table. In Amanita, the edible *A. rubescens* is no harder to distinguish from the dangerous Amanitas than are *Lepiota naucina* and many others. Mixed lots of many varieties are a menace and should be used only by the trained student who knows the qualities of each species in the collection. The number of fatalities from fungi gathered by children tells its own story. Cases among students of mycology have all been due to the milder species, and have had the saving grace of adding real discoveries or valuable information to our knowledge. If such cases are duly published a real service and a duty are rendered to science. A synopsis of white-spored species which are definitely deleterious shows: About thirteen white Amanitas and a few nearer *A. muscaria* in their physiological action; one each in Amanitopsis, Lepiota and Tricholoma; three Clitocybes; at least one (and perhaps a half-dozen) in Lactarius; Russula uncertain. Lactarius and Russula are closely related genera, and will require much more investigation, both by eating and by laboratory studies, before the properties of the species will be known. Species closely related botanically are often widely separated toxicologically, and vice versa. This is seen in the contrasting qualities of *Amanita phalloides* versus *A. solitaria* and *A. rubescens; A. muscaria* vs. *A. frostiana* and *A. caesarea; Lepiota morgani* vs. *L. procera; Tricholoma venenatum* vs. *T. terreum* and others; *Clitocybe illudens* vs. *C. multiceps* and others; *Clitocybe dealbata* vs. *C. sudorifica; Lactarius torminosus* vs. *L. vellereus* and others.

The number of genera is small and some mycologists would avoid eating all species of the section. The common favorite *Pluteus cervinus,* or "fawn mushroom," has caused disturbance several times, attended by numbness and tingling in the extremities, mild general discomfort and an urticarial rash. Dr. Whetstone (Minnesota) has a record of the case of poisoning of an Iowa physician, attended by abdominal pain, nausea, and vomiting coming on three hours after eating. Cases like this should make one hesitate to recommend almost any species to the uninitiated.

THE GENUS ENTOLOMA

All species of Entoloma should be avoided by the mycophagist. They are seldom used. Warren says that you cannot cook the raw taste out of them. Vomiting, diarrhea, tenesmus, mental and physical depression are credited to them but no deaths.[22] Six species examined by Ford act identically, producing fatal chronic intoxication in guinea pigs or rabbits—sometimes in both. They vary somewhat in agglutinins and have no hemolysins. (*E. salmoneum, E. strictius, E. cuspidatum, E. nidorosum, E. rhodopolium, E. sinuatum* or *E. fertile.*) *E. grande* is under suspicion.[17] *E. modestum* and *E. subtruncatum* were negative.[41]

E. fertile (*sinuatum*)—¼ oz. nearly killed W. G. Smith (Stevenson, Vol I). It "harbors a virulent poison." The genus may have its own poison, as Amanita. According to a recent collection of cases by Sartory[46] in France *E. lividum* is an extremely dangerous fungus, causing severe illness, and occasionally death. He believes that *E. lividum* is nearly as poisonous as some forms of *A. phalloides.* Butignot refers four cases of violent illness to it,[52] though but few specimens were in the mixture eaten. Vomiting and abdominal pain, sweating and a vile diarrhea were the result.

These are not usually regarded as poisonous.

THE GENUS PHOLIOTA

"I have nothing but praise for the entire genus." (McIlvaine.) Recently *P. autumnalis* has arisen to claim high rank as a toxic fungus.[39]   In 1911 a mother and two children ate heartily of it. The children died.   Severe poisoning of three individuals is also reported from Minnesota.   Animal tests by Ford and Sherrick[41] on the Minnesota lot were negative on guinea pigs, rabbits and the frog heart, but a New York lot, although negative on blood corpuscles, was acutely poisonous to guinea pigs and rabbits even after heating.   Atropin did not neutralize the dilating effect on the heart.   Postmortem appearances resembled those of *A. phalloides* and the extracts were quite as poisonous.   It should be grouped with the deadly poisonous Agarics, with the nature of the poison unknown.[25]   *P. mutabilis* is approved in Munich.

THE GENUS INOCYBE

Absolutely negligible and uninviting as food, this genus has likewise recently taken an important rank toxicologically from laboratory studies.   The trouble began when Dr. Deming (once Vice-President of the New York Mycological Club) knowingly gathered *Inocybe infida* and mixed it, for cooking, with *Panaeolus papillionaceus* which he knew to be non-poisonous.   The chance taken was one in a thousand—but he lost.   (See 37, 47 and 48 in Bibliography.)   Five people were made ill.   Symptoms, which came on soon, were a sense of fullness in the head and a rapid pulse—as if nitroglycerin had been taken.   Sweating and warmth, no nausea or prostration; slight confusion, pressure and pain in the lower bowel.   Some patients vomited, some had diarrhea.   Recovery was complete in a few hours under simple treatment.   Conclusions[37, 48] are that *I. infida* contains a poison of the type of muscarin, acting more particularly on the nervous system and similar to the narcotic of *Inocybe infelix*. (See below.) Atropin acts as antidote. The relationship of the toxins of *I. infida* and *I. infelix* to those of *A. muscaria* is not yet clear.

Inocybe infelix, one of the most common Inocybes, closely related to the preceding, has not been tested for edibility, nor thus far been reported as toxic to man, but its poison seems definite and powerful. Ford and Sherrick[40] found it to contain a definite poison which resists dessication and boiling. Small doses produced a deep sleep in guinea pigs and rabbits from which they awoke well. A profound acute intoxication and coma, quickly fatal, followed large doses. The intoxication was such as is seen only with *Lactarius torminosus*, a somnolence with retracted head (rabbits), passing off in five hours. The action was not characteristically that of *A. muscaria,* though not inconsistent with muscarin, but that of a narcotic of some sort. Further work is promised. Autopsy on guinea pig showed hemorrhagic spots and perforating gastric ulcer. Generally the examination was negative. *Inocybe decipiens* has likewise no clinical record. Though its agglutinin is destroyed by heat, the heated extract in 2 to 4 cc. doses nevertheless kills guinea pigs acutely—even in 20 minutes—due to dilated heart. Smaller doses bring on lachrymation, salivation and nasal discharge, with labored respirations. These symptoms last a few hours and disappear, but the animals die in a day. Occasionally hemmorhage into the stomach is found postmortem. Dropped into the eye of rabbits, the pupil contracts—resembling *A. muscaria* and muscarin. Boiling the extract does not change its action. This significant record entitles this Inocybe likewise to a place among the more dangerous toadstools.[41, 1]

Inocybe sp. agrees in biologic pharmacology very closely with the preceding and the same conclusions are justified in this newest addition to a bad family. Agglutinin powerful, but thermolabile. A muscarin-pilocarpine poison.[50]

THE GENUS HEBELOMA

Hebeloma is closely related to Inocybe. The generic distinctions may be learned in order that the mycophagist may reject both genera as inedible. They never will be missed, anyway. Little is known about them. *Hebeloma sinapizans* is suspected (eaten with a gay mixture which included l'Amanita jaune citrone).[51] *Hebeloma fastibile* is related to Inocybe.[17] Kobert would class *I.*

rimosa and *H. fastibile* in the muscarin group.[1]   Ford[50] reports favorably on *H. crustuliniforme* and another closely related species, even though the former is called "poison pie" in England.

Summary of Brown-Spored Genera

In summarizing the brown-spored group we have to take strong exception to the recent idea that none are known to be poisonous. Pholiota has some edibles worth while but the importance that *P. autumnalis* (perhaps identical with *P. marginata*) has recently achieved as a dangerous species is an unexpected warning on the family.   Flammula has fair edibles and is free from suspicion at present.   Kauffman's long and careful studies on the glorious genus Cortinarius will now enable us to begin to record the qualities of its species with some hope of accuracy.   Past experience on its species warrants the statement that they are pretty safe esculents. The remaining brown-spored families should be rejected.

Hypholoma sublateritium is regarded as poisonous in Europe. It is sometimes bitter, and on this account alone, like many other fungi, has probably been wrongly labeled. Our Club members have occasionally found the "Bricktops" and others inedible, on account of taste. Kobert states that the "Falscher Stockschwamm," *H. fasciculare,* is not edible. Kunkel says it may be poisonous but not very. *H. instratum* and *Psilocybe cernua* both produce acute intoxication in guinea pigs, fatal in three days. Internal and subserous hemorrhages and enlarged glands were found postmortem. (*Morchella esculenta,* the Morel, produces similar findings). Edible properties are not recorded. No fatalities in man have been referred to Hypholoma and there are many edible species.

Agaricus or Psalliota—the meadow mushroom family—contains the most famous and most sought edibles, a number of species. Any one who knows of the woods-inhabiting species in the genus would probably know and avoid the deadly Amanitas growing among them. Though they do occur, it is very rare for the dangerous white Amanitas to get out into the open grassy haunts of *Agaricus campestris* and *Lepiota naucina.* But no one should rely on usual habitat as his safeguard. He should know well the appearances in detail of the plant he may safely use. We know that two of our Michigan fatalities were due to children wandering into the woods and adding *Amanita phalloides* to "the meadows" they had collected, and three other Michigan deaths were caused by mistaking the "Destroying Angel" for *Lepiota naucina.*

Ford, in 1907, stated that no cases of poisoning have ever resulted from the use of any of the purple-spored or black-spored Agarics. I am of the opinion that a good many cases of the milder type have been caused by both Coprinus and Panaeolus. It will come as a shock to the lovers of the old reliable "inkies" to find them candidates for the increasing cohort of poisonous fungi. Their reputation has been as fair as their spores are black. That of the "shaggy mane" has been traced back to Pliny.

In "Good Housekeeping" (October, 1910) Dr. Cleghorn tells of ten people in four families accustomed to using ink caps, being made ill on three different dates by *Coprinus comatus*. The appearance was as of one intoxicated. There was failure of muscular coordination, standing being difficult and walking impossible. Drowsiness, loss of emotional control, bloodshot eyes, enlarged pupils, incoherent or inappropriate speech were the symptoms coming on in a few minutes or hours after eating. There was no prostration and heart and lung action were strong and regular. One patient complained of the apparent bending and swaying of the furniture. One had a temporary complete paralysis of the left arm. Practically no food had been eaten but the ink-caps. Prof. John Dearness[58] suggests *Panaeolus campanulatus* as the cause in these cases but in view of the circumstances reported this hardly seems likely. Detroit cases of unpleasant effects—more than an acute indigestion—have been reported from taking beer with a meal of *C. comatus*. I have also known of four cases in which flushed face, bloodshot eyes and rapid and distressing heart action followed the eating of *C. atramentarius*. In two of these cases no alcoholic beverage had been taken. In the other two, only a very small amount to which the individual was accustomed. Further reports concerning the inkies are desirable.

Ford[22] has examined *Panaeolus retirugis* only. It is regarded as edible by all authorities but is similar to *P. papilionaceus* which though edible, has been known to produce a peculiar intoxication. He found no hemolysin or agglutinin. Fatal to guinea pigs and postmortem negative. *P. campanulatus,* classed as poisonous by Murrill, is eaten by McIlvaine. Its bad reputation goes back to

1816 and has not been taken seriously. A Minneapolis report says that two rather delicate ladies ate of it—two tablespoonsful of stew. Drowsiness came on quickly; a sensation of intoxication, dizziness, staggering, trembling, numbness, contraction of the jaw, stricture of the throat, precordial distress, headache with sensation of fullness, face flushed and eyes injected, no nausea. Delusions of sight accompanied insomnia—the patients saw big red automobiles in the room or queer figures on the wall paper. The eyelids in one case were temporarily paralyzed. Mild but irritant diarrhea. In one case the heart was intermittent for a week. Recovery was not prompt. A third and more vigorous patient only tasted the stew. Two hours later she complained of dizziness, ringing in the ears and dry throat.

P. papilionaceus, "The Butterfly," has flitted into and out of the questionable list. McIlvaine has seen it produce hilarity and other mild symptoms of intoxication, soon over. Moderate quantities have no effect. Murrill does not rank it as certainly bad. It is a small uncommon Agaric and may therefore be easily spared. In nine years experience in cultivating the gardener's mushroom I have not seen the Coprini or Panaeoli coming on the beds in amount sufficient to warrant the picking of them, but know that *P. subbalteatus* has thus occurred.

BOLETUS

Though these volumes deal only with the Agarics, or gilled fungi, a paper on mushroom poisoning would not be satisfactory did it fail to include some matter on the Boleti and on Gyromitra, especially since we have some positive data to report.

Ford[22] says that the definitely poisonous Boleti are not many, and that even the toxic, by reason of their bad taste or emetic or purgative action, protect the user from great harm. But few deaths have been traced to Polypores. Among the important esculents are *B. edulis, B. scaber* and *B. granulatus*. The majority are edible, but bitter and wormy varieties are common, and others produce vomiting and diarrhea. McIlvaine regards the genus as very safe. On the other hand, a gentleman at Walloon Lake, Michigan, after spending some weeks testing Boleti, said he had not found one variety that did not make him sick! Warren (Port Huron) says, "I never eat them and I tell others to let them alone. There are too many good kinds to bother with wormy Boletus." *B. satanus* and *B. luridus* are everywhere called poisonous, though the toxic principle is little known. Kobert found muscarin in the latter, but conservative Michael says it is edible. *B. clintonianus, B. cavipes, B. paluster, B. chrysenteron* var. *sphagnotum* were all found[22] free from muscarin or definite poisonous action on guinea pigs and rabbits. Variety *sphagnorum* has not been reported edible but *B. chrysenteron* and the other three are approved. McIlvaine, after years of testing by many people, is very positive that both *B. satanus* and *B. luridus* are edible. *Boletus felleus* is free from hemolysins and agglutinins and muscarin, but produces chronic intoxication in rabbits and guinea pigs, fatal in two or three weeks. Extract from the dried plant produced a steady emaciation in rabbits and progressive cachexia in guinea pigs. Probably to be classed as poisonous.[40] Very bitter and inedible.

B. chromapes: No hemolysin, agglutinin nor muscarin. Poisonous only to guinea pigs. Decision deferred. Edible (McIlvaine).

B. affinis and *ornatipes:* A thermolabile agglutinin destroyed at 150° F. No definite action. Edible (McIlvaine).

B. bicolor: An agglutinin; negative on hemolysin and muscarin. Non-toxic. One of the very best esculents (McIlvaine).

B. separans: An agglutinin requiring boiling for its destruction, non-toxic. Edible, McIlvaine and Hard.

B. ravanelli seems to be safe but not tested by actual use.

B. roxanae, similar to *B. separans.* Dietic properties unknown.

B. miniato-olivaceus should be regarded with suspicion because of the report on its var. *sensibilis* (below). Ford[40] finds it to contain a heat-resistant agglutinin and to be poisonous to guinea pigs by chronic emaciation. Rabbits were not affected. No evidence of muscarin. (Compare *Clitocybe dealbata* versus *C. sudorifica.*)

B. pachypus has a bitter taste and a bed-bug odor.[11] A case of poisoning which Hockauf would refer to cheese, has been credited to it. Murrill adds *B. ferruginatus, B. eastwoodiae, B. frostii* (edible, Peck), *B. morrissi,* and *B. rubinellus* to the uncertain or suspected. Fabre, in a chapter on insects and mushrooms, (Life of the Fly), records that his peasants eat *B. satanus* and other doubtful species after boiling them in salt water and rinsing.

Boletus miniato-olivaceus var. *sensibilis.* It will be seen from the above that our opinions on some species of *Boletus* are much at variance. The following case illustrates how effectively a student of mycology can add to our knowledge by *following up* thoroughly, *and reporting* cases of poisoning. Collins[59] records that a certain Boletus—found to agree with the erroneously-figured edible *B. subtomentosus* in Palmer's "Mushrooms of America"— was broiled and eaten for breakfast. Three persons ate sparingly and two ate freely. In two hours vomiting and then purging, with collapse calling for brandy and ether subcutaneously in one case, with narrowing or closing of the field of vision, coldness and helplessness, came on. There was no vertigo, headache nor acute pain. The action was mostly that of an irritant. Coffee was the principal stimulant used. One patient did not recover fully for several weeks. Fresh Boletus specimens were soon secured from the original spot and again one year later. These were identified by Peck as *B. miniato-olivaceus* var. *sensibilis.*

GYROMITRA ESCULENTA

This fungus is also known as *Helvella esculenta,* the false Morel, and the Lorchel. Our Michigan species may include *G. brunnea.* Dispute still rages around this fungus and this is characteristic of a species that contains a minor poison or an inconstant one or one that affects only a few individuals and these only at certain times. *G. esculenta* has a long criminal record in Europe. Nevertheless, it is not everywhere under the ban even there, for its sale, dried or fresh, is permitted in Berlin and Munich though forbidden in Austria. Dried, dusty, wormy (Anobium and Tinea), specimens are sold in the shops; old and inferior fresh ones at reduced prices in the markets. Several American authors say that only old specimens are dangerous. This is not true. The poison is very soluble in hot water and hence parboiling and rinsing may render the mushroom safe. Kobert says that all the Morchellas are safe but that the False Morel furnishes a record of over one hundred and sixty cases of poisoning. Hockauf[60] reports four cases with one fatality (girl of nine years) in April, 1905. Loevegren also has five cases with a fatality, in a girl of five years. Vomiting, colic, weakness, irregular respiration, tonic cramps of voluntary muscles, dilated pupils, jaundice and prolonged unconsciousness were the chief symptoms. Death may occur on the first day or in five days. The active principle has long been known as helvellic acid and has a true blood-dissolving action shown by the hemaglobinuria, icterus, and the pigmentation of the spleen. Nephritis and fatty degeneration of the liver are also found at autopsy. *Gyromitra esculenta* stands alone in producing a true hemolytic set of postmortem appearances. Frey says that this form of poisoning seems to have become very rare. *Amanita phalloides* does not produce it. Animal tests following Hockauf's cases were negative. Kobert says the fresh extract is very variable. Allen (California) reports *G. esculenta* plentiful there and one of the best edibles, but that it should be let alone. In Michigan it begins to appear on the edge of melting snow banks even as early as mid-March and I have seen a small fall crop in northern Ontario in September. It is common about Port Huron and is eagerly sought and even sold in the markets. Warren and Peck (letters) and Dearness[58] report a number of illnesses and at least one fatality due to Gyromitra. In the cases of Dearness the family were made ill after eating of the warmed-over cooking. Coma and death of one adult came on the fourth day. In the Michigan cases there were two groups of nine people each who ate, with two illnesses in each group. Symptoms came on in about six hours. Very violent vomiting and diarrhea, with much weakness and fear were the chief symptoms. Heart action was good. The acute illness lasted thirty-six hours, inability to take food three days, and recovery required about five days. "No other ill effects except that they don't want any more Gyromitras." The fungi were fresh and prepared as often before—and since. Warren says, "I know they may contain some kind of poison that affects some people at certain times."

Ford[41] has examined specimens of *G. esculenta* from Massachusetts. He found them entirely negative and harmless in every method of testing on guinea pigs, rabbits and the frog's heart.

CONCLUSIONS AND SUMMARY

Because of the growth of popular interest in the study of the mushrooms and toadstools, both as a "fad" and as a scientific pasttime, and because of the influx of foreigners accustomed to use fungi for food, the subject of mushroom poisoning is assuming increasing importance in America.

The white Amanita or Death-cup (*Amanita phalloides*) and its few closely related species are responsible for at least nine-tenths of all fatal cases of mushroom poisoning. In illness caused by this fungus the mortality runs very high. Symptoms are six to ten hours in coming on. Suffering is extreme, and death often does not occur until a week or more has elapsed, though the course is quicker in children. There is no antidotal treatment. Clinical course and post-mortem findings are characteristic.

The white Amanita group contains a toxin found in no other fungi. It is a poison which causes profound degenerative changes in the internal organs and in the cells of the central nervous system.

The white Amanitas are easily recognized and avoided.

In all cases of mushroom intoxication, it is the duty of physicians and of friends to make every effort to learn whether or not *Amanita phalloides* has been eaten or whether some less dangerous toadstool is causing the sickness. Such determination is important both in determining treatment and especially prognosis.

The yellow Amanita or "Fly Fungus," *Amanita muscaria,* is second in importance. It is much less poisonous. It produces characteristic symptoms unlike those of *A. phalloides,* coming on in three hours or less, showing prompt disturbance of the nerve centers, and a disease of shorter course and lower mortality. The degenerative changes seen in *A. phalloides* intoxications, do not occur. If fatal results occur, this outcome may be expected early.

A large part of the disturbances produced by *Amanita muscaria* are due to the muscarin constituent of the fungus. This poison can be counteracted by the drug atropin. Hence *A. muscaria* intoxication is somewhat amenable to treatment.

Physicians should be able to distinguish between these two forms of poisoning. Symptoms are not always definite enough to be relied upon, and specimens of the mushroom which has been eaten should be identified. Local or near-by botanical centers are always glad to be of service in such problems.

A number of minor poisonous species of mushrooms (about twenty) produce symptoms, when eaten, *which resemble the action of muscarin*. These species have not been given the importance and attention which they deserve. They usually also have an emetic action which prevents fatal consequences. Some of them are violent gastro-intestinal irritants and may thus add gravity to the illness. Deaths from them are almost unknown in healthy adults. Determination of the species is of great practical and scientific importance, since these minor cases are more numerous than is generally supposed.

Physicians and students of mycology should report cases in medical or botanical journals. Cases reported in the newspapers should be investigated.

Species closely related botanically may differ very widely in poisonous quality, though this is not usual. No variety should be eaten until its specific name has been determined by competent authority. If its edible qualities are not known or are in dispute, testing should proceed cautiously. The eating of mixed lots is to be condemned unless the user positively knows the reputation of each species to be good. Parboiling is a partial safeguard. None but clean, fresh specimens should be used, and these should be thoroughly cooked and indulged in only in moderation. Most mushrooms are not easily digested. Warmed-over portions are occasionally found to have developed toxic principles.

Good and abundant edible varieties are common, and the lover of fungi need take no chances. He can easily acquire a personal edible list, and can add new species to it as his knowledge and experience grow. Scientific mycology should precede mycophagy and increase one's pleasure in eating fungi.

Plate XCI.

INOCYBE CALOSPORA

Plate XCII.

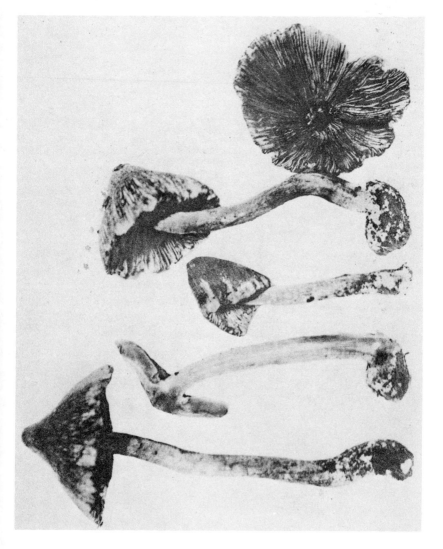

INOCYBE FRUMENTACEA VAR. JURANA.

Plate XCIII.

INOCYBE FASTIGIATA,

Plate XCIV.

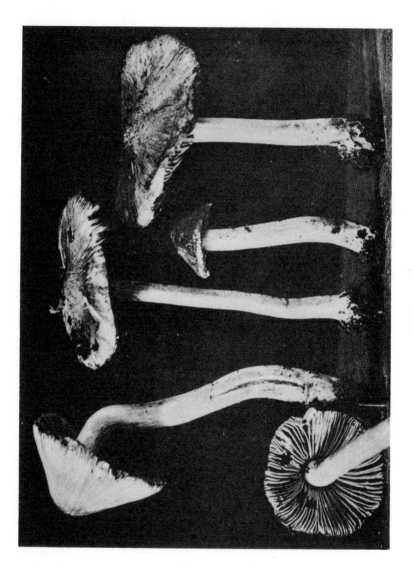

INOCYBE FIBROSA.

Plate XCV.

INOCYBE REPANDA.

Plate XCVI.

HEBELOMA SINAPIZANS.

Plate XCVII.

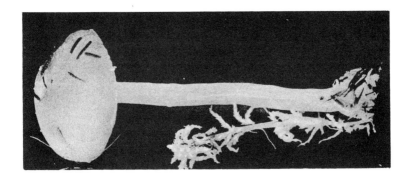

HEBLOMA CRUSTULINIFORME VAR. SPHAGNOPHILUM.

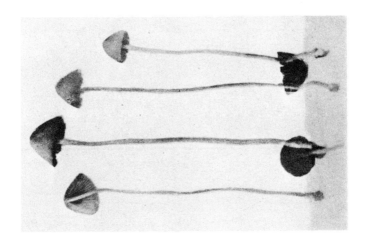

GALERA SP.

Plate XCVIII

PLUTEOLUS EXPANSUS.

Plate XCIX.

PLUTEOLUS RETICULATUS.

NAUCORIA SEMIORBICULARIS

Plate C.

VOLVARIA BOMBYCINA.

Plate CI.

VOLVARIA PUSILLA.

CHAMAEOTA SPHAEROSPORA.

Plate CII.

CHAMBEOTA SPHAEROSPORA.

Plate CIII.

PLUTEUS CERVINUS.

Plate CIV.

PLUTEUS LONGISTRIATUS.

Plate CV.

ENTOLOMA RHODOPOLIUM.

Plate CVI.

ENTOLOMA SERICEUM.

Plate CVII.

ENTOLOMA STRICTIUS.

Plate CVIII.

Plate CIX.

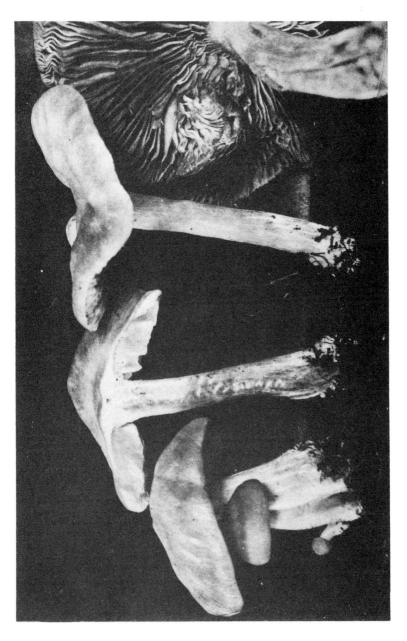

ENTOLOMA SPECULUM.

Plate CX.

ENTOLOMA CUSPIDATUM.

Plate CXI.

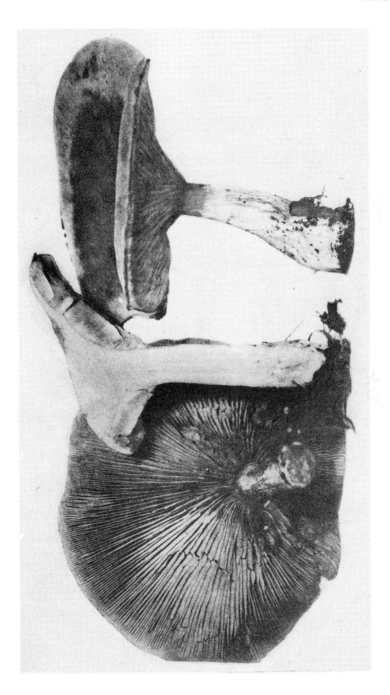

CLITOPILUS ABORTIVUS.

Plate CXII.

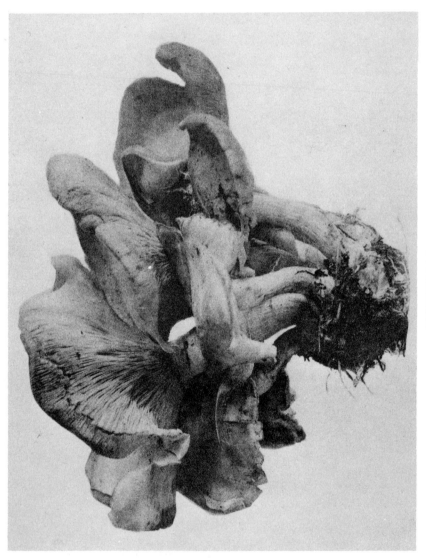

CLITOPILUS CAESPITOSUS.

Plate CXIII.

CLITOPILUS CAESPITOSUS.

Plate CXIV.

LEPTONIA PLACIDA.

LEPTONIA ROSEA.

Plate CXV

NOLEANA VERSATILIS.

CLAUDOPUS NIDULANS.

Plate CXVI.

AMANITA VERNA.

Plate CXVII.

AMANITA PORPHYRIA.

Plate CXVIII.

AMANITA SPRETA.

Plate CXIX.

AMANITA COTHURNATA.

Plate CXX.

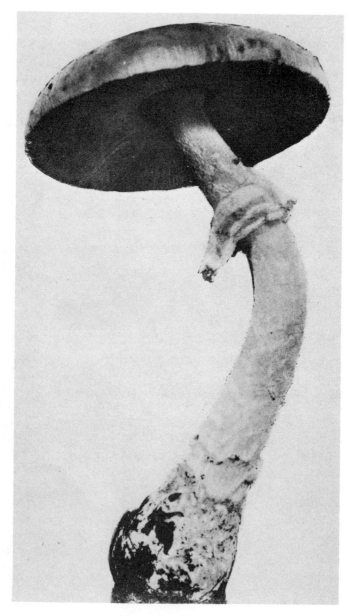

AMANITA CHRYSOBLEMA.

Plate CXXI.

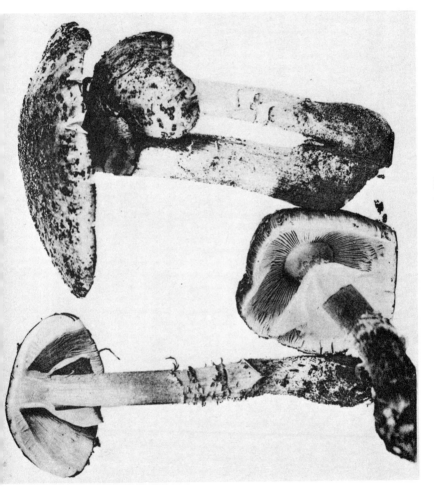

Plate CXXII.

AMANITA FLAVORUBESCENS.

Plate CXXIII.

AMANITA FLAVOCONIA.

Plate CXXIV.

AMANITA SPISSA.

Plate CXXV.

AMANITOPSIS VAGINATA.

Plate CXXVI

AMANITOPSIS VAGINATA.

Plate CXXVII.

LEPIOTA FISCHERI.

Plate CXXVIII.

LEPIOTA CLYPEOLARIA.

Plate CXXIX

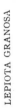

LEPIOTA GRANOSA

Plate CXXX.

LEPIOTA CEPAESTIPES.

Plate CXXXI.

FOREST FORM

LAWN FORM

LEPIOTA CRISTATA.

Plate CXXXII.

Plate CXXXIII.

FAIRY RING OF LEPIOTA MORGANI

Plate CXXXIV.

LEPIOTA MORGANI.

Plate CXXXV.

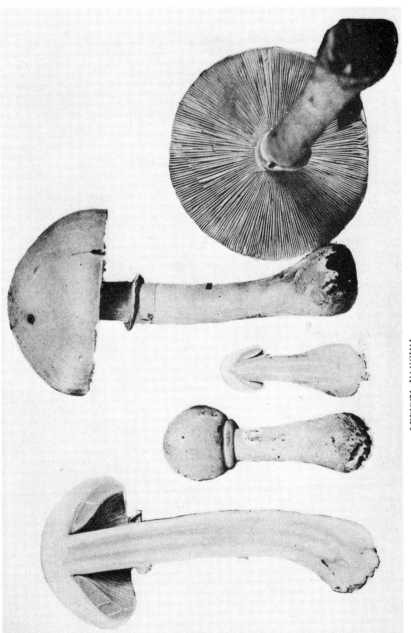

LEPIOTA NAUCINA.

Plate CXXXVI.

LEPIOTA NAUCINA.

Plate CXXXVII.

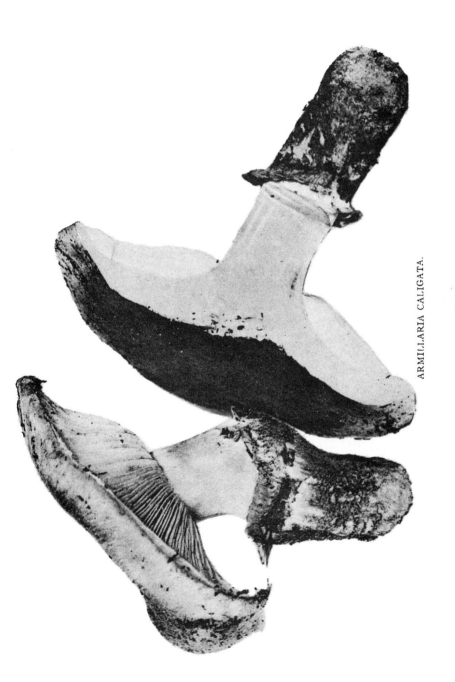

ARMILLARIA CALIGATA.

Plate CXXXVIII.

Plate CXXXIX.

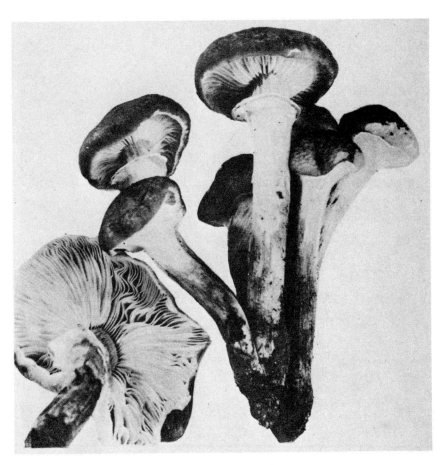

ARMILLARIA MELLEA.

Plate CXL.

Plate CXLI.

PLEUROTUS ULMARIUS.

Plate CXLII.

Plate CXLIII.

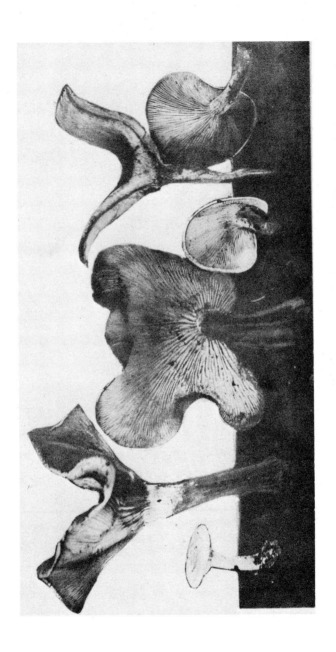

PLUEROTUS LIGNATILIS.

Plate CXLIV.

PLEUROTUS FIMBRIATUS VAR. REGULARIS.

Plate CXLV.

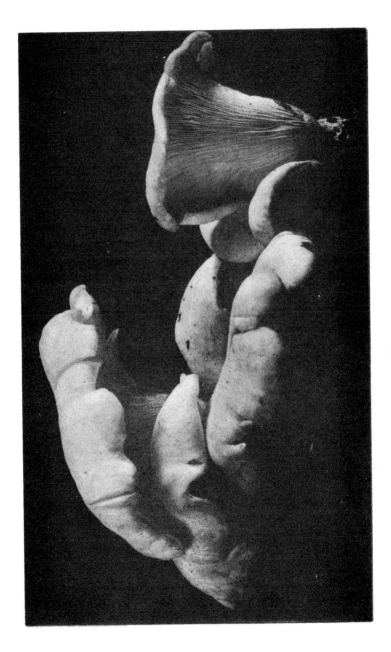

PLEUROTUS ALBOLANATUS.

Plate CXLVI.

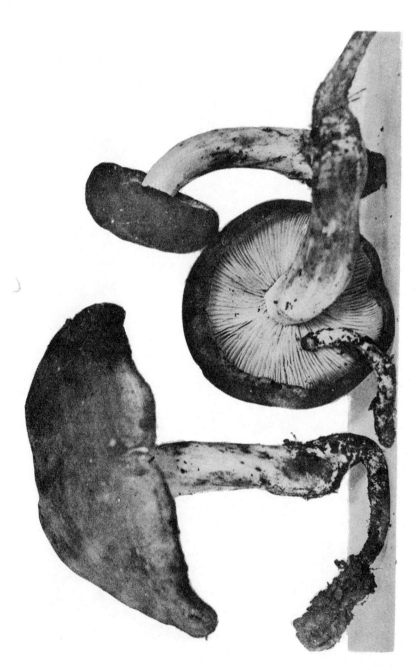

TRICHOLOMA USTALE.

Plate CXLVII.

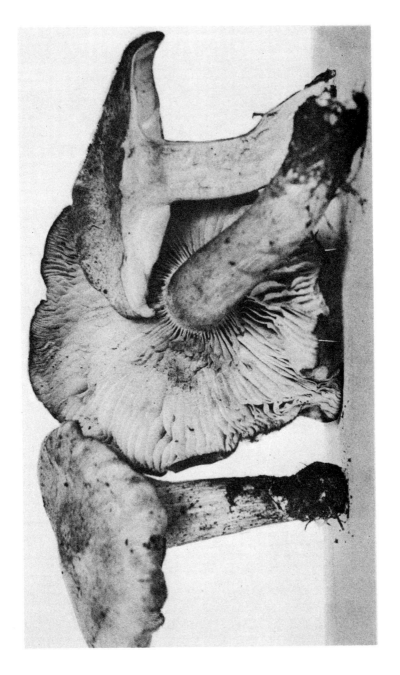

TRICHOLOMA NOBILE.

Plate CXLVIII.

TRICHOLOMA ACRE.

Plate CXLIX.

TRICHOLOMA TERREUM.

TRICHOLOMA FULIGINEUM.

Plate CL.

TRICHOLOMA LATICEPS.

Plate CLI.

TRICHOLOMA ACERUBM.

Plate CLII.

TRICHOLOMA TUMIDUM.

Plate CLIII

TRICHOLOMA CINERASCENS.

Plate CLIV.

CLITOCYBE PICEINA.

Plate CLV.

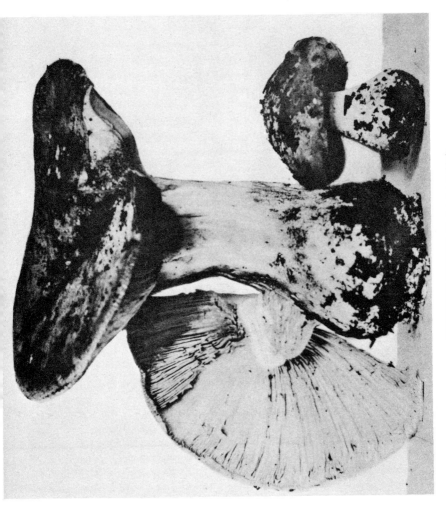

CLITOCYBE MAXIMA (Reduced one-third)

Plate CLVI.

CLITOCYBE PRAECOX.

Plate CLVII.

CLITCYBE MULTICEPS.

Plate CLVIII.

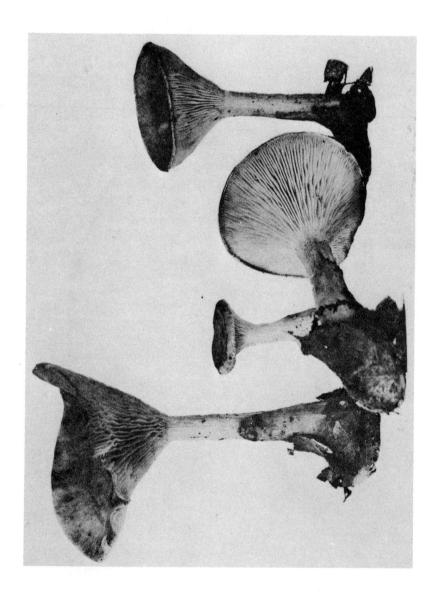

CLITOCYBE INFUNDIBULIFORMIS.

Plate CLIX.

CLITOCYBE CYATHIFORME.

CLITOCYBE MORBIFERA.

Plate CLX.

COLLYBIA DRYOPHILA.

Plate CLXI.

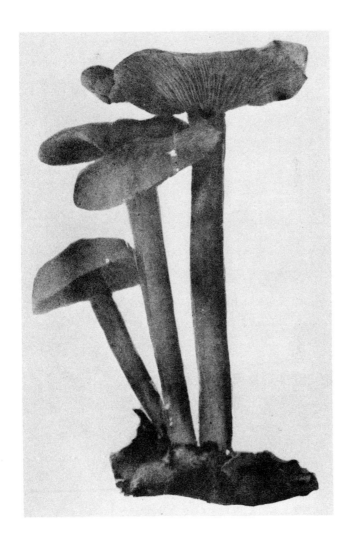

COLLYBIA STRICTIPES.

Plate CLXII.

COLLYBIA ALCALINOLENS.

Plate CLXIII.

COLLYBIA FAMILIA.

Plate CLXIV.

COLLYBIA HYGROPHOROIDES.

Plate CLXV.

COLLYBIA PLEXIPES.

Plate CLXVI.

COLLYBIA ABUNDAN S.

Plate CLXVII.

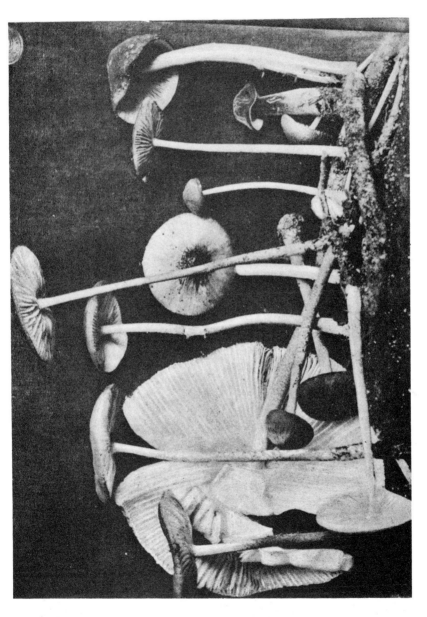

COLLYBIA RADICATA.

Plate CLXVIII.

Plate CLXIX.

COLLYBIA FLOCCIPES.

MYCENA SP.

Plate CLXX.

MYCENA INCLINATA VAR.

Plate CLXXI.

OMPHALIA EPICHYSIUM.

OMPHALIA GRACILLIMA.

Plate CLXXII.

OMPHALIA CAMPANELLA.

BIBLIOGRAPHY

(A) BOOKS CONSULTED

ATKINSON, GEO. F., Mushrooms, Edible, Poisonous, etc., 1900. Third ed. 1911. Very useful to the beginner; beautifully illustrated with photographs.

BARLA, J. B., Les Champignons de la prov. de Nice, 1859. With 48 colored plates of the common edible and poisonous species, with full descriptions. Flore Mycologique illustree Les Champignons des Alper-Maritimes, 1889-92. With 64 large, colored plates of species of Amanita, Lepiota, Armillaria, Clitocybe and Tricholoma.

BERKELEY, REV. M. J., Outlines of British Fungology. 1860. A manual, with 24 colored plates of many species.

BOUDIER, E., Icones Mycologicae ou Iconograph, d. Champignons de France, 1904. A series of the most accurate and most beautiful colored plates of fungi yet published; a relatively small number belonging to the Agarics. It is very expensive.

BRESADOLA, ABBE J., Fungi Tridentina, 2 vol., 1881-1900. Illustrated with 217 colored plates; a critical study of the rarer or confused species; invaluable to the specialist. I. Funghi mangerecci e. velenosi, 1906. Illustrated with 120 colored plates and descriptions in Italian of the more common edible and poisonous species.

CLEMENTS, F. C., Genera of Fungi. This is a useful book of keys to the genera, largely taken from Saccardo and adapted to those who cannot read Latin. It contains no descriptions.

COOKE, M. C., Handbook of British Fungi., 2 vol., 1871. With full descriptions of species. Not as helpful as either Massee or Stevenson. Illustrations of British Fungi. Eight volumes of colored plates illustrating practically all the Agarics of Great Britain; 1,198 plates in all. Necessary to the specialist.

COOKE ET QUELET. Clavis Synoptica Hymenomycetum Europaeorum. A useful little book with brief Latin descriptions of the Hymenomycetes of Europe, arranged in the form of a pocket manual.

CONSTANTIN ET DUFOUR. Nouvelle Flore des Champignons. A useful French book for beginners arranged in the form of keys, illustrated by 4,265, diagramatic line drawings. Mostly Hymenomycetes which are known in France.

"ENGLER AND PRANTL", Die Naturliche Pflanzen-familien. The volume containing the Basidiomycetes; one of many volumes covering an outline of the whole plant kingdom to the genera; profusely illustrated with woodcuts. Indispensable to the mycologist.

FARLOW, W. G., Bibliographical Index of North American Fungi, 1905. Giving the references to the literature for each species; only Vol. I, part I, has appeared to date.

FRIES, ELIAS MAGNUS. Systema Mycologicum, 3 vol. Vol. I. contains the Basidiomycetes, 1821. This volume and its date was made the starting point for the nomenclature of the Agarics by the International Congress meeting at Brussels, 1910. Epicrisis Systematis Mycologici, 1836-38. An extension of Vol. I of Syst. Myc. with changes and additional species. Monographia, 1857-63. Being a series of monographs of the genera of the Agaricaceae; nearly all the species mentioned in this work are illustrated by colored drawings which are now deposited in the Royal Museum at Stockholm. It includes only Swedish species, but the descriptions are

followed by commentaries and are invaluable to the specialist. Hymenomycetes Europaei, 1874. This is one of the most important and fundamental works on the Basidomycetes ever published. It represents the ripe
experience and best judgment of the master. Sveriges ätliga och giftiga
Svam par., 1862-69. A volume of large plates with colored figures of the
edible and poisonous species of Scandinavia. Icones, 1867-1884. Two
volumes of 200 large colored plates of the Basidiomycetes, selected from
the large number of drawings deposited at the Museum at Stockholm.

GIBSON, W. H., Our Edible Toadstools and Mushrooms, 1895. (Ed. new,
1903.) A book written in a delightful literary vein, containing popular
descriptions and discussions of some forty mushrooms; well illustrated
with colored drawings.

GILLET, C. C. Les Hymenomycetes, 1874. A manual with full descriptions and artificial keys to all the Basidiomycetes growing in France.
Very valuable. Les Champignons de France. A set of 712 colored plates
accompanying the preceding manual.

HARD, M. E., Mushrooms Edible and Otherwise, 1908. A popular book for
the beginner, profusely illustrated with photographs.

HERBST, WM., Fungal Flora, of the Lehigh Valley, Pa., 1899. This book
contains descriptions and 25 plates.

HUSSEY, Illustrations of British Mycology, 1847-55.

KARSTEN, P. A., Mycologia Fennica, 4 vol. Vol. 3—Basidiomycetes. A
manual of the flora of Finland.

LINDBLAD, M. A., Svambok, 1902, a popular manual in Swedish.

MARSHALL, NINA L., The Mushroom Book, 1905. "A popular guide to
the identification and study of our commoner fungi, with special emphasis
on the edible varieties." With photographs, many colored.

MASSEE, GEO., British Fungous Flora, 4 vol. 1892-95. A useful manual
for the English reader, but deals only with British forms. European
Fungus Flora; Agaricaceae, 1902. A compilation of all European species
of Agarics with only the essential characters given in brief description.
Text book of Fungi, 1906. A general discussion of matters of interest and
importance to the student of fungi, mostly of others than Agarics.

McILVAINE, CHARLES, One Thousand American Fungi, 1900. New ed.,
1912. A valuable compilation of descriptions of fungi formerly inaccessible to many. The last edition is well illustrated. An additional value
of this book is in the data concerning the edibility of mushrooms as tested
by the author.

MICHAEL, EDMUND, Führer für Pilzefreunde. 3 Vol., 1903-05. Containing
in all 307 beautifully colored plates of mushrooms, unusually true to nature
cheap and very helpful to the beginner.

MURRILL, W. A., Agaricaceae. North Amer. Flora, Vol. 9 et al., 1910.

OUDEMANS, C. A. J. A., Revision des Champignons dans les Pays-Bas,
1893. Vol. I contains synopses and descriptions of Hymenomycetes of
Holland; in French.

PATOUILLARD, N., Tabulae Analyticae Fungorum, 1883-89. A critical
study of many species, with numerous colored figures; invaluable to the
specialist. In French. Les Hymenomycetes d'Europe, 1887. Deals with
the general anatomy and classification of the higher fungi.

PERSOON, C. H., Synopsis Methodica Fungorum, 1801. One of the best
early efforts to place the classification of fungi on a scientific basis; in
some groups it is considered by some as more fundamental than the works
of Fries.

QUELET, L., Euchiridion Fungorum, 1886. A manual, in Latin, of the
species found in Middle Europe and France. Les Champignons de Jura
et des Vosges, 1872. Classification and descriptions of some 700 species
found in the mountainous regions of eastern France.

RICKEN, A., Die Blätterpilze (Agaricaceae). A manual, in German, of the
Flora of Germany, with excellent modern descriptions, and profusely
illustrated by colored plates. Appearing in parts; 1910-16. One of the
most useful and complete works of its kind, giving the microscopic
characters of most species. Invaluable to the student.

SACCARDO, P. A., Sylloge Fungorum. A work of huge scope including descriptions, in Latin, of all known species of the world, 1882—. It comprises to the present 22 volumes; Vol. V, and parts of later volumes, deal with Agarics.

SCHROETER, J., Die Pilze Schlesiens, 1889. A manual with full descriptions of the Agarics indigenous to Silesia.

SCHWEINITZ, L. de, Synopsis Fungorum.

SECRETAN, L., Monographie Suisse, 1833, 3 vol. Descriptions and classification of fungi growing in Switzerland.

SMITH, W. G., Synopsis of the British Basidiomycetes. Brief diagnoses and sketches of all Agarics of Great Britain; spore-size not given.

STEVENSON, REV. JOHN, British Fungi, 2 vol., 1886. A manual of the British Hymenomycetes, whose descriptions are largely those of Fries. Very useful to the student who reads only English. The same descriptions of many species are also found in McIlvaine.

SWANTON, E. W., Fungi and How to Know Them, 1909. A book for the beginner dealing in a popular way with all fungi, as well as Agarics; profusely illustrated with colored figures and cuts in black and white. The beginner will find it useful.

TAYLOR, THOMAS, Student Hand-book of Mushrooms of America, 1897. A series of fine pamphlets bound in book-form, with 14 colored plates dealing with a few common edible and poisonous mushrooms.

UNDERWOOD, L. M., Moulds, Mildews and Mushrooms, 1899. A small, compact text-book on the classification of fungi, with keys to families and genera, good bibliographies and explanatory notes on families; invaluable to the student who reads only English.

VITTADINI, Descriz. dei Funghi Mangerecci e velnosi d'Italia. Milan, 1835. A carefully written work of the mushrooms of Italy.

WINTER, GEO., Die Pilze Deutschlands, Oesterreichs und der Schweiz. A manual of the flora of the Basidiomycetes of Germany, Austria and Switzerland, with full descriptions; it is Vol. I, Part I, of Rabenhorst's Kryptogamen Flora.

(B)   JOURNALS OF MYCOLOGY CONSULTED

(For special papers in other journals, see (C) and text)

ANNALES MYCOLOGICI. Entirely devoted to fungi; articles are printed in various languages.

BULLETIN DE LA SOCIETE MYCOLOGIQUE DE FRANCE. Entirely devoted to fungi; in French. Started in 1885.

BULLETIN OF THE TORREY BOTANICAL CLUB. Containing some papers on fungi, especially the descriptions of new species by Dr. Peck of such as were sent to him from outside of New York State; an American Journal.

GREVILLEA. Published in England from 1892 to 1894. Devoted to Cryptogamic Botany and its literature; contains descriptions of the species in Cooke's Illustrations. Includes many references to American species.

HEDWIGIA. A German journal dealing with Cryptogamic Botany; 1852 to the present.

JOURNAL OF MYCOLOGY. An American journal devoted to fungi, superceded by Mycologia. 1885-1908.

MYCOLOGIA. Started in 1909; devoted to mycology; published by the New York Botanical Garden.

MYCOLOGICAL BULLETIN. A popular journal for the beginner which had a brief existence during four and one-half volumes.

MYCOLOGICAL NOTES. Published privately by C. G. Lloyd since 1898. Devoted to critical notes and synopses of the higher fungi.

REVUE MYCOLOGIQUE. A French journal for mycologists, started in 1879.

RHODORA. Published by the New England Botanical Club. Contains articles on fungi of New England.

TORREYA. Published by the Torrey Botanical Club, New York City. Containing occasional papers on Agarics, beginning 1901.

(C) STATE REPORTS, FLORAS, KEYS, LISTS, ETC.

ATKINSON, G. F., and STONEMAN, BERTHA, Key to the Genera of Hymenomycetes. Ithaca, N. Y.

BRADY, W. A., A Partial List of the Fungi of Wisconsin: Geol. of Wis.,
Vol. I, p. 396, 1883. (Includes 218 species of Basidiomycetes.)

BURLINGHAM, GERTRUDE S., Some Lactarii from Wyndham Co., Vt.:
Bull. Torr. Bot. Club, Vol. 34, 1907. (Contains a synopsis, list and new
species.)

BURT, E. A., Key to the Genera of the Basidiomycetes of Vermont: Con-
trib. to the Bot. of Vt., VI, 1899.

CLEMENTS, F. C., Minnesota Mushrooms: Geol. and Nat. Hist. Surv. of
Minn. Minn. Plant Studies, IV, 1910. (Published in book form for use
in schools with descriptions and keys; profusely illustrated with photographs.)

CURTIS, M. A., Catalogue of the plants of North Carolina, Raleigh, 1867.

EARLE, F. S., (collaborator), Plant Life of Albama: U. S. Dept. of Agr.,
Nat. Herbarium, Vol. 6, p. 150, 1901, (including a full list of the fungi
reported from Alabama). The Genera of North American Gill Fungi: Bull.
New York Botanical Garden, Vol. 5, p. 373, 1908. (Keys and descriptions
of genera, classified according to the rule of priority.) Keys to species
of various genera: Torreya, Vol. 2, (Russula, Hygrophorus, etc.).

FARLOW, W. G., List of Fungi found in the vicinity of Boston: Bul. Bus-
sey Institution, I, p. 430, 1876; II, p. 224, 1878.

FROST, C. C., Further enumeration of New England Fungi: Proceed. Soc.
Nat. Hist. Boston, Vol. XII, p. 77, 1869.

GLATFELTER, N. M., Preliminary list of higher Fungi, etc.: Acad. Sci.
of St. Louis, Vol. XVI, No. 4, p. 33, 1906.

HESS AND VANDAVERT, Basidiomycetes of Central Iowa: Proceed. Iowa
Acad. Sci., Vol. 7, p. 183.

KAUFFMAN, C. H., Michigan Fungi: Seventh Ann. Rep. Mich. Acad. Sci.,
p. 64, 1905. Unreported Michigan Fungi: Eighth Ann. Rep. Mich. Acad.
Sci., p. 26, 1906. Ibid: Ninth Ann. Rep., p. 83, 1907. Ibid: Tenth Ann.
Rep., p. 63, 1908. Ibid: Eleventh Ann. Rep., p. 55, 1909. Ibid: Twelfth
Ann. Rep., p. 99, 1910. Ibid: Thirteenth Ann. Rep., p. 215, 1911.

LONGYEAR, B. O., A preliminary list of the Saprophytic Fleshy Fungi
known to occur in Michigan: Fourth Rep. Mich. Acad. Sci., p. 113, 1904.
List of saprophytic Fungi: Rep. of Sec. to State Board Agr., 1898.

MACBRIDE, T. H., The saprophytic fungi of Eastern Iowa: Bull. Tab. Nat.
Hist. State Univ. of Iowa, Vol. I, p. 30, 1888. Ibid: p. 181, 1890. Ibid:
p. 196, 1890.

MOFFATT, W. S., The higher fungi of the Chicago Region: Nat. Hist. Surv.
of Chicago Acad. Sci., Bull. VII, part 1, p. 1, 1909. Descriptions and
24 photo plates; including 360 species of Basidiomycetes.

McKAY, A. H., Fungi of Nova Scotia; a preliminary list: Proceed. and
Trans. Nova Scot. Inst. Sci., Vol. XI, part 1, p. 125, 1904. Includes 284
species of Basidiomycetes.

MILLSPAUGH and NUTTALL, Flora of West Virginia: Field Columb.
Mus., Bot. Ser. I, p. 60, 1896.

MORGAN, A. P., The Mycologic Flora of the Miami Valley, Ohio: Journ.
Cinn. Soc. Nat. Hist., Vol. 6, p. 54-81, 97-115, 173-199. With descriptions
and six plates.

PECK, CHAS. H., New York State Mus. Reports, published in the Annual
Reports of the New York State Museum of Nat. Hist., and also separately
as Reports 27-54 consecutively, afterwards as Bulletins until 1912 when
Dr. Peck retired. The reports of Peck as State Botanist from 1870-1912,
include plants of all groups, but the greater portion is devoted to lists
of fungi found in New York State, to descriptions of new species, and to
synopses of many of the genera of Agarics. See also bibliography of each
genus. Fungi of Maryland: New York State Mus. Rep. 44, 1891. A list
prepared by Mary E. Banning of Baltimore and including about 100 Agarics.

REDDICK, D., A preliminary list of the Hymenomycetes of Indiana: Dept.
of Geol. and Nat. Resources of Ind., Rep. 32, p. 1193, 1907. A list including 88 Agarics.

SPRAGUE, C. J., Contributions to New England Mycology: Proceed. Bost. Soc. Nat. Hist., Vol. 5, p. 325, 1856; Vol. 6, p. 315, 1859.
STOVER, W. G., The Agaricaceae of Ohio: Proceed. Ohio State Acad. Sci., Vol. V, part IX, p. 462, 1912. Keys to the genera and species; comprising 540 species without descriptions.
UNDERWOOD, L. M., Report of the Botanical Division of the Indiana State Biological Survey: Proceed. Ind. Acad. Sci., p. 13, 1894; p. 144, 1895; p. 171, 1896.
VAN HOOK, J. M., Indiana Fungi: Proceed. Ind. Acad. Sci., p. 205, 1910; p. 347, 1911. Includes list of 347 Basidiomycetes.
WEBBER, H. J., Catalogue of the Flora of Nebraska: Rep. Neb. State Board Agric., p. 37, 1890.
WHITE, E. A., Hymeniales of Connecticut: Conn. State Geol. and Nat. Hist. Surv. Bull. 3, 1905; 15, 1910. Contain lists, keys to species and a few descriptions; illustrated with photographs of 28 and 39 plates respectively. Reference to 433 species of Basidiomycetes.

(D) MISCELLANEOUS BOOKS, PAMPHLETS, PAPERS, ETC.

ARTHUR, J. C., Three edible toadstools: Purdue Univ. Agr. Exp. Sta., Bull. No. 98, 1904.
ATKINSON, G. F., and SHORE, R. B. Mushroom growing for amateurs: Cornell Univ. Agr. Exp. Sta., Bull. 227, 1905. Mushrooms: Ibid, Bull. 168, 1899.
BADHAM, C. D., A Treatise on esculent funguses, 1847. (A British book, with 21 colored plates.)
BATES, Mushrooms—poisonous Amanitas, harmless Agarics (directions for cultivation): Amer. Florist, Vol. II, 1896.
BEACH, S. A., Mushrooms as a Greenhouse Crop: N. Y. State Agr. Exp. Sta., Bull. 88, 1895.
BIFFEN, R. H., On the biology of *Collybia velutipes:* Jour. Linn. Soc., Vol. 34, p. 147.
BRITZELMAYR, M., Materialen zur Beschreibung der Hymenomyceten: Bot. Centralblatt, Vol. 53-54, p. 33, 65 and 97, 1893; Vol. 62-63, p. 273, 1895; Vol. 71-72, p. 49, 1897. (Brief critical notes on European Agarics, with spore size.) Revision der Diagnosen zu den von Britzelmayr, aufgestellten Hymen. Arten., Bot. Centralblatt, Vol. 75-76, p. 129, 169, 203, 1898; Vol. 77-78, p. 356, 395, 433, 1899; Vol. 79-80, p. 57, 116, 1899. (Full description of the species described as new.)
BULLER, A. H. K., Researches on Fungi, etc., 1909, (a valuable study of spore expulsion in Coprinus, etc.).
BULLETIN, Boston Mycolog. Club, 1897, * * * (small pamphlets giving directions to amateurs, with brief descriptions of the species of some genera).
BURECK, A., Notes on enemies of mushrooms and on experiments with Remedies: U. S. Dept. of Agr., Entomol., 32-35.
DURT, E. A., Collecting and preparing fleshy fungi for the herbarium: Bot. Gaz., Vol. 25, p. 172, 1898.
COOKE, M. C., British edible fungi and how to distinguish and how to cook them. Edible and poisonous mushrooms; what to eat and what to avoid. (With 48 colored plates.)
CORDIER, F. S., Les Champignons, Paris, 1876, 4th ed. with 60 colored plates.
DAVIS, SIMON, Fleshy fungi of Stow, Mass.: Rhodora, Vol. 13, p. 57, 1911; Vol. 16, p. 45, 1914 (critical notes).
DUGGAR, B. M., The principles of mushroom growing and mushroom spawn-making: U. S. Dept. Agr., Bureau of Plant Ind., Bull. 85, 1905. (The best modern discussion of the subject.) The cultivation of mushrooms: Farmer's Bull., No. 204, U. S. Dept. Agr., 1904.
FALCONER, WM., How to grow mushrooms: Farmer's Bull., U. S. Dept. Agr., No. 53, 1897.
FAYOD, V. M., Prodrome d'une Historie Naturelle des Agricenes: Ann. des Nat. Botanique, 7 series, Vol. 9, p. 181.

FARLOW, W. G., Some edible and poisonous fungi: U. S. Dept. Agr., Bull. No. 15, 1898. Notes for mushroom eaters: Reprinted from Garden and Forest Magazine.

GAUTIER, L. M., Champignons, Paris, 1884.

GOWDY, J. K., Mushroom culture in France: U. S. Consular Rep. 66, p. 259, 537, 1902.

HARKNESS and MOORE, Catalogue of the Pacific Coast Fungi: Calf. Acad. Sci., 1881.

HASTINGS, SOMERVILLE, Toadstools at home: Gowan's Nature Series, No. 7, London, 1908. (60 photographic reproductions of fungi in their natural surroundings; excellent little primer.)

HAY, WM. D., Fungi hunter's guide, London, 1887.

HENDERSON, L. P., Mushrooms or toadstools, a natural food-product: Idaho Agr. Exp. Sta., Bull. 27, p. 27.

HESS, ALICE W., A few common fleshy fungi of Ames, Iowa: Iowa Agr. Exp. Sta., Bull. 61, p. 148.

HOGG, ROBERT and JOHNSON, G. W., A selection of the edible funguses of Great Britain, London.

HYAMS, C., Edible fungi of North Carolina: N. Car. Exp. Sta., Bull. 177, p. 27.

JONES, C. H., Composition of mushrooms: Vermont Agr. Exp. Sta. Bull., p. 196, 1903.

KAUFFMAN, C. H., Mushrooms: Nature Study Review, Vol. 8, p. 1.

LANGWORTHY, C. F., Mushrooms as Food: Plant World, Vol. 8, p. 134, 1899.

LONGNECKER, A. M., Mushrooms: Plant World, Vol. 5, p. 213.

LONGYEAR, B. O., Remarks concerning saprophytic fungi, etc.: Mich. Acad. Sci., Rep. 1, p. 97, 1897. Notes on Michigan Saprophytic Fungi: Mich. Acad. Sci., Rep. 3, 1901.

MARCEAU, L., Flore des champignons superior du Department de Saone-et-Loire, 1898. (A manual with extensive keys.)

MANGET, C., Tableux synoptiques des champignons comestible et venenaux, Paris, 1903.

MAY, W. J., Mushroom culture for amateurs, 1897.

MENDEL, L. B., Chemical composition and nutritive value of some edible American Fungi: Amer. Jour. Phys. 1, p. 225.

MOYEN, J., Les Champignons, Paris, 1889.

PALMER, JULIUS A., Mushrooms of America, Boston, 1885. About Mushrooms, Boston, 1894.

PECK, C. H., Descriptions of new species of fungi: Bull. Soc. Nat. Sci. of Buffalo, 1. p. 41, 1873. New species of fungi, (see Bot. Gaz). New species of fungi, (see Torr. Bot. Club Bull., Vol. 22-38). Mushrooms and their uses: Pub. by Cambridge Bot. Supply Co., 1897. The smooth Agaric: Country Gentleman, 1886, p. 833. Edible and poisonous fungi: N. Y. State Mus. Rep. 48, p. 203, 26 Plates, 1895. Report of the State Botanist on the edible fungi of New York State: N. Y. State Mus. Memoir, No. 4, p. 113, 24 Plates, 1900. Lists of all species described and named by Dr. Peck to 1908, see N. Y. State Mus. Bull. 131, p. 59, 1909. List of figures and illustrations of mushrooms published by Dr. Peck, see N. Y. State Mus. Bull. 139, p. 78, 1910.

RIDGWAY, ROBERT, Color standards and color nomenclature, Washington, D. C. 1912. (A series of 1115 named colors, invaluable for the future standardizing of the names of mushroom colors and tints.)

ROBINSON, W., Mushroom culture, London, 1870. (A full account of the older methods.)

SHEAR, C. L., Some common autumnal species of edible Fungi: Asa Gray Bull. 7, p. 93, 1899.

SICARD, G., Histoire naturelle des Champignons, Paris, 1883 (with colored plates).

SMITH, W. G., Clavis Agaricinorum, London, 1870 (Descriptions of families and genera with keys.)

STURGES, W. C., Edible and poisonous fungi: Rep. Sec. Connect. Board of Agr., 1895.

SYDOW, P., Taschenbuch der wichtigeren essbaren u. giftigen Pilze Deutschlands u. der Schweiz. (Pocket size, with colored figures.)
TAYLOR, EMMA L., Guide to the mushrooms. (Small primer, 200 pages and 66 plates.)
TORREY, JR., J., Raising mushrooms in a cellar: Rhodora, Vol. 3, p. 57.
TRELEASE, WM., Edible and poisonous mushrooms: Missouri State Hort. Soc. Rep., 1900, p. 224.
UNDERWOOD, L. N., Edible Fungi—A great vegetable food in Indiana: Trans. Ind. Hort. Soc., 1893, p. 62. Edible Fungi: Alabama Agr. Exp. Sta. Bull. 73, p. 337. Suggestions to collectors of fleshy fungi: Ala. Agr. Exp. Sta. Bull. 80, p. 271.
VIERMEYER, T. J., The Mycogone disease of mushrooms and its control: U. S. Dep. Agr. Bull. No. 127, 1915.
WEBSTER, HOLLIS, See Rhodora, Vols. 1, 2, 4.
WEEMS AND HESS, A study of the food value of some of the edible fungi of Ames, Iowa: Proceed. Ia. Soc. Prom. Agr. Sci., 1902, p. 105.
WILLIAMS, E. M., Common edible and poisonous Amanitas: Asa Gray Bull. Vol. 6, p. 80.
WINDISCH, E., Mushroom culture on an extensive scale, 1897.
WINDOR, D. K., The Mushrooms of Canada, 1871 (a little primer).
ZEGA, A., Composition of some edible Fungi: Chem. Zeitung, Vol. 26, p. 10, 1902. Mushrooms as food: U. S. Dept. Agr., Farmer's Bull. 79. Analyses of mushrooms: N. Y. State Agr. Exp. Sta. Rep. 1894, p. 134. Preliminary list of the edible fungi of Ohio: Ohio State Univ. Bull. 4, p. 30.

(E) ON MUSHROOM POISONING

BY O. E. FISCHER, M. D.

1. Ford & Clark—A Consideration of the properties of poisonous fungi: Mycologia, July, 1914, Vol. VI, No. 4.
2. Bagnall—Mushroom poisoning, with atypical cases: Boston Med. & Surg. Jour., July 16, 1914.
3. Ford—A clin. study of mushroom intoxication: Johns Hopkins Hosp. Bull., Vol. 18, 1907.
4. Gillot—Etude med. sur. l'empoisonement par les Champignons, Lyon, 1900.
5. Plowright—Brit. Med. Jour., Sept. 9, 1905, Vol. II, p. 541.
6. Pfromm—Med. Bull. Phila., Nov., 1905, p. 401.
7. Murrill—Poisonous mushrooms: Mycologia, Nov., 1910, p. 255.
8. Mycol. Bull., Vol. VI, No. 86, Feb., 1908, quoted from O. E. Jennings in Jour. of Mycol., Sept., 1907.
9 Barr—Letter. Kindness of Minneapolis Mycol. Club.
10. Schuerer—Kasuistischer Beitrag zur Kenntniss der Pilzvergiftungen: Deut. Med. Woch. Schr. XXXVIII, No. 12, Mar. 21, 1912.
11. Hockauf—Zur Kritik der Pilzvergiftungen: Wien Klin Woch. Schr., 1904, p. 731.
12. Maass—Berl. Klin. Woch., June 26, 1905, p. 814.
13. Ford—Jour. Infect. Dis., Vol. 5, 1908, p. 116.
14. Jour. A. M. A.—Vol. LX, 1913, p. 1154.
15. Abel & Ford—Arch. f. Exper. Path. u. Pharm. Schmiedeberg Festschrift, 1908, p. 8.
16. Frey—Zeit Sch. Klin. Med., 1912, p. 455.
17. Same as No. 7.
18. Ford—Jour. Inf. Dis., 1906, Vol. III, p. 191.
19. Abel & Ford—Poisons of *Amanita phalloides:* Jour. Biol. Chem., Vol. II, 1907, p. 273.
20. Schlesinger & Ford—Chem. Prop. of *A. phal.:* same as above, Vol. III, 1907, p. 279.
21. Ford & Prouty—Note on Amanita-toxin: Jour. Pharm. & Exp. Ther., Vol. I, 1907, p. 389.
22. Ford—Distribution of hemolysins, agglutinins & poisons in fungi: Jour. Pharm. & Exper. Ther., Vol. II, 1910, p. 285.

872   THE AGARICACEAE OF MICHIGAN

23. Coville—Observations on recent cases of mushroom poisoning in the District of Columbia: Circ. 13, Div. of Botany, U. S. Dept. Agriculture, 1898.
24. Prentiss—Phil. Med. Jour., 1898, II, p. 607.
25. Ford & Clark—Mycologia, July, 1914, Vol. VI, No. 4.
26. Harmsen—Zur Toxicologie des Fliegenschwammes: Archiv. f. Pathol. u. Pharmacol. Schmiedeberg, 1903.
26a. Ibid —. Bd. 50, p. 361, 1903.
27. Michael—Führer für Pilzefreunde. Zwickau, Sa., 1903.
28. Kennan—Tent Life in Siberia, New Ed., 1910, p. 198.
29. Sumstine—Mycol. Bull., Vol. IV, 56, Apr., 1906.
30. Tappeiner—Munch. Med., Wochenschr, Feb. 12, 1895, p. 133, J. 42, No. 7.
31. Ford & Brush—Note on properties of fungi from France: Jour. Pharm. & Exp. Ther., Vol. 6, No. 2, Nov., 1914.
32. Same—Action of Amanitas upon the frog's heart. Same as above.
33. Blount—A personal experience with mushroom poisoning, Med. Record, Nov. 23, 1901, p. 815.
34. Chestnut—Asa Gray Bull., Oct., 1900.
35. Webster—Rhodora, Jan., 1915, Vol. 17, p. 30.
36. Farlow—Poisoning by Ag. illudens: Rhodora, March, 1899, p. 43.
37. Clark & Smith—Toxicological studies on Clit. illudens & Inocybe infida: Mycologia, 1913, p. 224.
38. McIlvaine & Macadam—One thousand American fungi. Revised Ed.
39. Peck—Report of State Botanist, 1911, N. Y., Bull. 157.
40. Ford & Sherrick—Jour. Pharmac & Exp., Ther., 1911, II, p. 549.
41. Same—On Clit. sudorifica, etc., etc. Same as above, Vol. IV, 1913, p. 321.
42. Peck—As above, Bull. 150, p. 44.
43. Rabe—Zeitscher. f. exp. Phar. u. Ther., Sept., 1911, p. 352.
44. Bull. Soc. Mycol., de France, 1906, p. 22.
45. Goldman—Agaricus torminosus: Wien. Klin. Wochenschr, Mar. 21, 1901.
46. Sartory—Les empois. par les Cham., (Etc., 1912) Paris, 1912.
47. Murrill—A new poisonous mushroom: Mycologia, 1909, p. 211.
48. Clark & Kantor—Toxicological experiments with higher fungi: Mycologia, 1911, p. 175.
50. Ford—Further observations on fungi: Journ. Pharm. & Exp. Ther., Vol. VI, No. 2, Nov., 1914.
51. Bull. Soc. Mycol. de France, 1912, p. 28.
52. Same—1909, p. 25 and 1906, p. 22.
53. Jour. A. M. A., LXI, p. 1388.
54. Peck Report, 1895, p. 212. Same, 1901, p. 961.
55. Clark & Smith—Mycologia, 1913, p. 224.
56. Von Wedekind—Med. Record, Dec. 25, 1897, p. 919.
57. Step—Toadstools & mushrooms of the (British) country side.
58. Dearness—The personal factor in mushroom poisoning: Mycologia, Vol. 3, 1911, p. 75.
59. Collins—Rhodora, Vol. I, No. 2, Feb., 1899, p. 21.
60. Hockauf—Wien. Klin. Wochenschr, 1905, p. 1058.

(F) MONOGRAPHS, ETC., ARRANGED BY GENERA

AGARICUS. (See Psalliota).
AMANITA. Peck, N. Y. State Mus. Rep. 33, p. 38, 1880. Lloyd, compilation of the Volvae of U. S., p. 2, 1898. Boudier, Obs. sur.—especes d'Amanitas, Bull. de la Soc. Mycol. de France, Vol. 18, p. 251, 1902. Quelet et Bataille, Flora Monographie des Amanites et das Lepiotas, Paris, 1902. Beardslee, Notes on the Amanitas of the Southern Appalachians, Lloyd's Mycological Notes, Vol. I. See also: Fries, Saccardo, Gillet, Bresadola, Barla, Stevenson, Massee, Atkinson, McIlvaine, Morgan, Ricken, etc.
AMANITOPSIS. Peck, N. Y. State Mus. Rep. 33, p. 38 (under Amanita). Lloyd, compilation of Volvae of U. S., p. 8, 1898. Quelet et Bataille, Flore monographie des Amanites et des Lepiotas, p. 42, 1902, (under Amanita). See also: Fries, Saccardo, etc. (under Amanita in the older books).

ANNULARIA. (See Chamaeota.)

ARMILLARIA. Peck, N. Y. State Mus. Rep. 43 (Bot. ed.), p. 44, 1899. See also: McIlvaine, Morgan, Fries, Saccardo, Stevenson, Bresadola, Gillet, Stevenson, Barla, etc.

BOLBITIUS. See Fries, Gillet, Ricken, etc.

CANTHERELLUS. Peck, N. Y. State Mus. Bull. 2 (Bot. ed.), p. 34, 1887. See also: Saccardo, Fries, Gillet, Stevenson, Ricken, Morgan, Moffatt, McIlvaine, etc.

CLAUDOPUS. Peck, N. Y. State Mus. Rep. 39, p. 67, 1886. See also: Saccardo, Fries, Gillet, Massee, Stevenson, Ricken, Patouillard, etc.

CLITOCYBE. Peck, N. Y. State Mus. Bull. 157, (Bot. ed.), p. 59, 1912. See also: Barla, McIlvaine, Lloyd, Saccardo, Fries, Bresadola, Gillet, Stevenson, Massee, Morgan, Moffatt, etc.

CLITOPILUS. Peck, N. Y. State Mus. Rep. 42, (Bot. ed.), p. 39, 1880. See also: Saccardo, Fries, Gillet, Stevenson, Massee, McIlvaine, Morgan, etc.

COLLYBIA. Peck, N. Y. State Mus. Rep. 49, p. 32 (Bot. ed.), 1896, Lloyd, Mycolog. Notes, Vol. I, p. 33, 1900. See also: Saccardo, Fries, Gillet, Stevenson, Massee, Ricken, McIlvaine, Moffatt, etc.

COPRINUS. Massee, Revision of the Genus Coprinus: Ann. Bot., Vol. 10, p. 123, 1896. Daniels, E. A., Coprinus: Boston Mycolog. Club Bull. No. 15 and 16. See also: Saccardo, Fries, Stevenson, Patouillard, Massee, Gillet, Ricken, Atkinson, Peck's Reports, Moffatt, etc.

CORTINARIUS. Fries, Monographia Cortinariorum Sueciae. Upsala, 1851. Bataille, Flore Monographigue des Cortinaires d'Europe, Besancon, 1911. Kauffman, The Genus Cortinarius, Bull. Torr. Bot. Club, Vol. 32, pp. 301, 1905; The Genus Cortinarius with Key to Species, Jour. Mycol., Vol. 13, p. 32, 1907; Cortinarius as a Mycorhiza-producing Fungus, Bot. Gaz., Vol. 42, p. 208, 1906. Earle, A Key to the North American Species of Cortinarius, Torreya, Vol. 2, pp. 169 and 180. Britzelmayer, M., Revision der Diagnosen zu den von Britzelmayr aufgestellten Hymenomyceten-arten, Bot. Centralblatt, Vol. 73, p. 129, 169 and 203, 1898. Maire, R., Notes critiques * * * * Bul. de la Soc. Myc. de France, Vol. 27, p. 423, 1911; Notes critiques * * * ibid, Vol. 26, p. 176, 1910. See also: Saccardo, Gillet, Quelet, Stevenson, Massee, Ricken, Boudier, Karsten, Michael, Peck (N. Y. State Reports) Hard, etc.

CREPIDOTUS. Peck, N. Y. State Mus. Rep. 39, p. 69, 1886. See also: Saccardo, Fries, Gillet, Patouillard, Ricken, Massee, Stevenson, Moffatt, etc.

DECONICA. See Psilocybe.

ECCILIA. See: Saccardo, Fries, Ricken, Moffatt, Peck's Reports, Atkinson (Preliminary Notes on Some New Species: Jour. Mycol., Vol. 8, p. 113, 1902), etc.

ENTOLOMA. Peck, N. Y. State Mus. Bull. 131, p. 47, 1909. See also: Saccardo, Fries, Gillet, Stevenson, Ricken, McIlvaine, Hard, Atkinson, Moffatt, Morgan, Davis, etc.

FLAMMULA. Peck, N. Y. Mus. Rep. 50, p. 133, 1897. See also: Saccardo, Fries, Gillet, Stevenson, Ricken, Atkinson, Moffat, etc.

GALERA. Peck, N. Y. State Mus. Rep. 46, p. 61, (Bot. ed.) 1893. See also: Saccardo, Fries, Gillet, Ricken, Stevenson, etc.

GOMPHIDIUS. See: Saccardo, Fries, Ricken, Peck's Reports, etc.

HEBELOMA. Peck, N. Y. State Mus. Bull. 139, p. 67 (Bot. ed.), 1910. See also: Saccardo, Fries, Ricken, Stevenson, Massee, etc.

HYGROPHORUS. Peck, N. Y. State Mus. Bull. 116, p. 45, (Bot. ed.), 1907. Bataille, Flora Monographique des Hygrophores, Besancon, 1910. See also: Saccardo, Fries, Gillet, Schroeter, Ricken, Stevenson, Massee, Hard, McIlvaine, Atkinson, Moffat, Davis, etc.

HYPHOLOMA. Peck, N. Y. State Mus. Bull. 150, p. 73 (Bot. ed.), 1911.
Harper, Species of Hypholoma * * * * Trans. Wis. Acad. Sci.
Arts. and Let., Vol. 17, p. 1142, 1914. Morgan, North American
Species of Agaricaceae; Hypholoma, Jour. Myc., Vol. 14, p.
27, 1908. See also: Saccardo, Fries, Ricken, Atkinson, Moffatt, etc.

INOCYBE. Peck, N. Y. State Mus. Bull. 139, p. 48 (Bot. ed.), 1910. Massee,
Monograph of the Genus Inocybe, Ann. Bot., Vol. 18, p. 459,
1904. Bresadola, Fungi Tridentini. See also: Patouillard,
Saccardo, Gillet, Ricken, Hard, Moffatt, Davis, etc.

LACTARIUS. Peck, N. Y. State Mus. Rep. 38, p. 111, 1885. Burlingham,
Lactariae of the United States, Mem. Torr. Bot. Club, Vol.
14, p. 1, 1908. See also: Saccardo, Fries, Gillet, Bresadola,
Ricken, Massee, Stevenson, McIlvaine, Hard, Atkinson, Moffat,
Morgan, Michael, etc.

LENTINUS. Peck, N. Y. State Mus. Bull. 131, p. 42, 1909. See also: Saccardo, Fries, Stevenson, Bresadola, Patouillard, McIlvaine,
Hard, Moffat, etc.

LEPIOTA. Peck, N. Y. State Mus. Rep. 35, p. 150, 1884. Quelet et Bataille,
Flore Monographique des Amanites et des Lépiotes, Paris,
1902. Morgan, North American Species of Lepiota: Jour.
Myc., Vol. 12, p. 154, 195 and 242, 1906; Vol. 13, p. 1, 1907.
Lloyd, Myc. Notes, Vol. I, p. 4, 1898. Beardslee, The Lepiotas
of Sweden: Jour. Myc., Vol. 13, p. 26, 1907. See also: Saccardo, Fries, Gillet, Barla, Bresadola, Ricken, Schroeter,
Stevenson, Massee, McIlvaine, Hard, Atkinson, Moffatt,
Michael, etc.

LEPTONIA. See: Saccardo, Ricken, Stevenson, etc.

MARASMIUS. Morgan, North American Species of Marasmius: Jour.
Mycol., Vol. II, p. 201, 1905. Pennington, N. Y. State Mus.
Bull., 1915. See also: Saccardo, Fries, Stevenson, Massee,
Patouillard, Ricken, Hard, Moffatt, etc.

MYCENA. Peck, N. Y. State Cab. Rep. 23, p. 80 (Bot. ed.) 1872. See also:
Saccardo, Fries, Massee, Stevenson, Gillet, Ricken, Bresadola,
Patouillard, Atkinson, Hard, Moffatt, etc.

NAUCORIA. Peck, N. Y. State Cab. Rep. 23, p. 91 (Bot. ed.), 1872. See also:
Saccardo, Fries, Ricken, Moffat. etc.

NOLANEA. See: Saccardo, Fries, Gillet, Ricken, Stevenson, etc.

OMPHALIA. Peck, N. Y. State Mus. Rep. 45, p. 32, (Bot. ed.), 1893. See also:
Saccardo, Fries, Stevenson, Ricken. Patouillard, Hard, Moffat,
etc.

PANOEOLUS. Morgan, North American Species of Agaricaceae; Panoeolus:
Jour. Myc., Vol. 13, p. 59, 1907. See also: Saccardo, Fries,
Ricken, Atkinson, Hard, Peck's Reports, etc.

PANUS. Forster, Agarics of United States Panus: Jour. Mycol., Vol. 4,
p. 21, 1888. See also: Saccardo, Fries, Stevenson, McIlvaine,
Hard, etc.

PAXILLUS. See Atkinson, Hard, Saccardo, etc.

PHOLIOTA. Peck, N. Y. State Mus. Bull. 122, p. 141, 1908. Harper, Species
of Pholiota * * * * Trans. Wis. Acad. Sci. Arts and Let., Vol.
17, p. 470. See also: Saccardo, Fries, Gillet, Ricken, Hard,
Atkinson, McIlvaine, Moffat, etc.

PLEUROTUS. Peck, N. Y. State Mus. Rep. 39, p. 58, 1886. Webster, Bull.
Boston Myc. Club, No. 8, 1898. See also: Saccardo, Fries,
Gillet, Stevenson, Massee, Ricken, Patouillard, Atkinson, McIlvaine, Hard, Moffatti, etc.

PLUTEOLUS. Peck, N. Y. State Mus. Rep. 46, p. 58, 1893. See also:
Saccardo.

PLUTEUS. Peck, N. Y. State Mus. Rep. 38, p. 133, 1885. Lloyd, Myc. Notes,
Vol. I, p. 12. See also: Saccardo, Fries, Stevenson, Ricken,
Patouillard, Atkinson, Hard, etc.

PSALLIOTA. Peck, N. Y. State Mus. Rep. 36, p. 41, 1884. Smith, Rhodora,
Vol. 1, p. 161. Lloyd, Myc. Notes, Vol. 1, p. 25, 1899. (These

are given as Agaricus.) See also: (under Agaricus), Saccardo, Fries, Gillet, Ricken, Stevenson, Atkinson, McIlvaine, Hard, Moffatt, etc.

PSATHYRA. Peck, N. Y. State Mus. Bull. 150, p. 84 (Bot. ed.), 1911. Morgan, Jour. Myc., Vol. 13, p. 147, 1907. See also: Saccardo, Fries, Ricken, etc.

PSATHYRELLA. Peck, N. Y. State Cab. Rep. 23, p. 102 (Bot. ed.), 1872. Morgan, Jour. Myc., Vol. 13, p. 54, 1907. See also: Saccardo, Fries, Ricken, etc.

PSILOCYBE. Peck, N. Y. State Mus. Bull. 157, p. 94 (Bot. ed.), 1912. Morgan, Jour. Myc., Vol. 13, p. 246, 1907. See also: Saccardo, Fries, Ricken, etc.

RUSSULA. Peck, N. Y. State Mus. Bull. 116, p. 67, 1907. Kauffman, C. H., Mich. Acad. Sci. Rep. 11, p. 57, 1909; Ibid, Rep. 13, p. 220, 1911. Kaufmann, F., Die bei Elbing gefundenen essbaren u. giftigen Täublinge (Russula): Schriften der Naturforschenden Ges. in Danzig, N. F., Vol. 8, p. 21, 1894. Maire, Les bases de la classification dans le genre Russula, Bull. de la Soc. Myc. de France, Vol. 26, p. 49, 1910. Notes critiques * * * * Ibid., p. 167. Peltereaux, Etudes et Observations sur les Russules: Bull. de la Soc. Myc. de France, Vol. 24, p. 95, 1908. Battaille, Flore monographique des Asterospores, 1907. Barbier, Encore les Russules: Bull. de la Soc. Myc. de France, Vol. 24, p. 230, 1908. Romell, Lindblads Svampbok, p. 62. Hymenomycetes of Lapland: Arkiv för Botanik, Vol. II, No. 3, p. 5, footnotes. Denniston, Trans. Wis. Acad. Sci. Arts & Let., Vol. 15, p. 71. Macadam, Jour. Mycol., Vol. 5, p. 58 and 135, 1889. See also: Saccardo, Fries, Gillet, Quelet, Massee, Stevenson, Ricken, McIlvaine, Burlingham, etc.

STROPHARIA. Harper, Species * * * * in the Region of the Great Lakes: Trans. Wis. Acad. Sci. Arts and Let., Vol. 17, p. 1014, 1913, Morgan, North American Species of Agaricaceae: Jour. Myc., Vol. 14, p. 57, 1908. See also: Peck's Reports, Saccardo, Fries, Gillet, Stevenson, Ricken, Hard, Atkinson, etc.

TRICHOLOMA. Peck, N. Y. State Mus. Rep. 44, p. 150, 1891. See also: Saccardo, Fries, Gillet, Barla, Ricken, Stevenson, Massee, McIlvaine, Hard, Moffatt, Morgan, etc.

TUBARIA. See: Saccardo, Fries, Stevenson, etc.

VOLVARIA. Lloyd, Volvae of United States, p. 10, 1898. See also: Saccardo, Fries, Patouillard, Ricken, Peck's Reports, Hard, etc.

AUTHORITIES AND ABBREVIATIONS

The binomial botanical name of each plant is followed by an abbreviation, e. g. Fr., which refers to the person who named the species. According to the rule established by the International Congress at Brussels in 1910, no names are to be considered valid in the case of the Agarics, earlier than those published in the Systema Mycologica of Fries, 1821-1832. In case the name was used for the same species by someone before Fries, reference may be made to it thus: Fr. (ex. Pers.).

AUTHORS OF AGARICS

A. & S.........................Albertini and Schweinitz.
Atk............................Atkinson, Geo. F. (U. S.).
B. & C........................Berkeley and Curtis.
B. & Br.......................Berkeley and Broome.
Bann..........................Banning, Mary E. (U. S.).
Barla.........................Barla, J. B. (France).
Batsch........................Batsch, Augustus (German).
Beards........................*Beardslee, H. C. (U. S.).
Berk..........................Berkeley, Rev. J. M. (England).
Bolt..........................Bolton, James (Canada).
Boud..........................*Boudier, E. (France).
Bosc..........................Bosc, Louis (U. S.).
Bres..........................*Bresadola, Abbe J. (Austria).
Britz.........................*Britzelmayr, Max (Germany).
Bull..........................Bulliard, Pierre (France).
Burl..........................*Burlingham, Gertrude S. (U. S.).
Cke...........................Cooke, M. C. (England).
Clem..........................*Clements, F. C. (U. S.).
Curt..........................Curtis, Rev. M. A. (U. S.).
D. C..........................DeCandolle, Augustin P. (Switzerland).
E. & E........................Ellis and Everhart.
Earle.........................*Earle, F. S. (U. S.).
Ell...........................Ellis, J. B. (U. S.).
Fr............................Fries, Elias Magnus (Sweden).
Frost.........................Frost, Charles C. (U. S.).
Gill..........................Gillet, C. C. (France).
Henn..........................Hennings, Paul (Germany).
Herbst........................Herbst, Wm. (U. S.).
Kalchb........................Kalchbreuner, Karoly (Hungary).
Karst.........................*Karsten, P. A. (Finland).
Kauff.........................*Kauffman, C. H. (U. S.).
Kromb.........................Krombholz (Germany).
L. or Linn....................Linneaus, Carl von (Sweden).
Lev...........................Leveille, Joseph H. (France).
Lindb.........................Lindblad, M. A. (Sweden).
Lloyd.........................*Lloyd, C. G. (U. S.).
Longyear......................*Longyear, B. O. (U. S.).
Maire.........................*Maire, René (France).

Mass............................Massee, Geo. (England).
Mont......................Montagne, Camille (France).
Morg...............................Morgan, A. P. (U. S.).
Murr..........................*Murrill, Wm. E. (U. S.).
Pat............................*Patouillard, N. (France).
Pers...............Persoon, Christian Hendrick (Europe).
Pk...........................Peck, Charles Horton (U. S.).
Q. & S................................Quelet and Schulzer.
Quel..................................Quelet, L. (France).
Rav.............................Ravenel, W. H. (U. S.).
Ricken................*Ricken, Rev. Adelbert (Germany).
Rom............................*Romell, Lars (Sweden).
Roze...........................Roze, Ernest (France).
Sacc...........................*Saccardo, P. A. (Italy).
Schaeff...................Schaeffer, Jacobi C. (Germany).
Schroet.....................Schroeter, Julius (Germany).
Schw..............Schweinitz, Rev. Louis David de (U. S.).
Schulz................Schulzer, von Muggenberg (Europe).
Scop...........................Scopoli, Giovanni A. (Italy).
Sec.................................Secretan (Switzerland).
Smith..........................Smith, W. G. (England).
Sow..........................Sowerby, James (England).
Vahl.............................Vahl, Martin (Norway).
Vitt..........................Vittadini, Carlo (Italy).

Those names which are starred are living mycologists.

MISCELLANEOUS ABBREVIATIONS

Acad.. Academy.
Bot.. Botanical.
Bull............................Bulletin; a publication.
Cab .... Cabinet.
Cm... Centimetre.
Fig..................Figure, referring to an illustration.
Gaz .... Gazette.
Hist.. History.
Jour.. Journal.
Mem.......................Memoir, a publication.
Micr..............Micron, one thousandth of a millimeter.
Mm.. Millimetre.
Mus .... Museum.
Myc............................Mycology, Mycological.
Nat................................Natural, Nature.
No.........................Number of a figure or plate.
Op................................... Opposite (page).
p... Page.
Pl........................Plate; referring to illustration.
Rep............................Report; a publication.
Ridg...................Ridgway's Color Standards, 1912.
Sci.. Science.
Soc.. Society.
Sp. nov..New Species; described for first time by the writer.
Var.. Variety.

GLOSSARY

ABERRANT, differing from a certain species, genus, etc, in some respects, but not easily placed in another species, genus, etc.

ABNORMAL, (of a specimen), not properly developed.

ABORTIVE, (of a fruit-body or its parts), not perfect or entirely lacking.

ABRUPT, (of a stem), terminating suddenly.

ABRUPTLY-BULBOUS, (of the bulb of a stem), not rounded above.

ACICULAR, (of a stem or cystidia), bristle-shaped, very slender.

ACICULATE, same as acicular.

ACRID, (of the taste of a mushroom or its juices), biting on the tongue.

ACUMINATE, (of cystidia, or the ends of a lamella), gradually narrowed to a point.

ACUTE, (of cystidia or the edge of the gills), pointed; less than a right-angle; sharp-edged; not prolonged.

ADNATE, (of gills), see Fig. 1, 2; also (of the pellicle, scales, etc.), not capable of being peeled off or easily detached.

ADNEXED, (of gills), see Fig. 1, 4, narrowly attached to the stem.

AFFINITY, (of a species, genus, etc.), closely related by natural characters.

AERUGINOSE, (color), verdigris-green.

AERUGINOUS, same as aeruginose.

AGGLUTINATE, (of fibrils, hairs, etc.), as if glued together in tufts.

AGGREGATE, crowded close together.

ALLANTOID, (of spores), sausage-shaped.

ALLIACEOUS, (odor), like onions or garlic.

ALUTACEOUS, (color), light leather colored; isabelline; pale tan.

ALVEOLATE, (of the surface of pileus or stem), deeply pitted.

AMBIGUOUS, (of a species, genus, etc.), doubtful as to its place in classification.

AMYGDALINE, (odor or taste), like that of peach or cherry stones, cherry-bark, etc.

ANALOGOUS, similar in form, structure or appearance, but not necessarily related to.

ANASTOMOSING, (of gills, ridges, wrinkles, etc.), connecting crosswise, so as to form angular areas or pits bounded by the connecting gills, etc.

ANGULAR, (of spores), not regular in outline, not rounded; (of scales or pileus), when formed by cracking of cuticle, etc.

ANNULATE, (of stem), bearing an annulus.

ANNULAR, (of remains of veil on stem), resembling a ring.

ANNULUS, the encircling band or curtain on the stem, resulting from the loosening of the inner veil from the margin of the pileus. See Fig. 2, 5.

ANOMALOUS, deviating from the general rule.

ANTERIOR, (of gills), the end of the gills at the margin of the pileus; in front.

APICAL, (of stem), the portion near the pileus; referring to the apex.

APICULUS, (of spores), the short, often sharp papilla at one end of a spore, by which it was attached to the sterigma.

APICULATE, provided with an apiculus.

APPENDICULATE, (of margin of pileus), hung with fragments of the veil.

APPLANATE, (of pileus), flattened out or horizontally expanded.

APPRESSED, (of scales, fibrils, hairs, etc.), closely flattened down; same as adpressed.

APPROXIMATE, (of gills), free from but approaching the stem; closely; not remote.

ARACHNOID, (of the partial veil), cobweb-like.

ARCUATE, (of gills or margin of pileus), curved like a bow.

ARCUATE-DECURRENT, (of gills), extending down the stem.

AREOLATE, (of surface of pileus or stem), arranged in little areas.

ARGILLACEOUS, (color), clay color, resembling ochraceous-cinamon-brown.

ARID, (of gills), dry, somewhat parchment-like.

AROMATIC, (odor), of an agreeable aroma, reminding of drugs.

ASCENDING, (of gills), in the case of a conical-shaped or unexpanded pileus.

ASTRINGENT, (taste), causing more or less contraction or "pucker" of mouth membranes.

ATOMATE, (surface of pileus or stem), covered with minute, shining, point-like particles.

ATTENUATE, (of stem), gradually narrowed and thinner.

AURANTIACOUS, (color), of an orange color.

AUREOUS, (color), golden-yellow, reddish-yellow.

AXIS, (of stem), the central, interior portion.

AZONATE, (of surface of pileus), not zoned.

BASAL, (of stem), at the lower end.

BASIDIOMYCETES, see page 26.

BASIDIUM, (of gills), one of the large cells which collectively compose the hymenium and which bear each four spores.

BEADED, (of gills), applied to the row of drops exuding from the edge of gills.

BEHIND, (of gills), toward the stem.

BI—, of two, or twice.

BIBULOUS, (of surface of pileus), capable of absorbing moisture.

BIFURCATE, (of gills), forking by two's.

BISTRE, (color), blackish-brown.

BIOLOGY, the science of living organisms.

BIOLOGICAL, concerning the life of plants or animals.

BLOOM, (of pileus or stem), a minutely velvety surface.

BROAD, (of gills), a relative term, opposed to narrow; determined by experience.

BUFF, (color), pale creamy-gray.

BULBOUS, (of stem), enlarged at base. (See also "abruptly-bulbous", clavate-bulbous and round-bulbous.)

BULBILLATE, (of stem), provided with a small or obscure bulb.

BULLATE, (of pileus), with a rounded knob.

BYSSOID, (of mycelium), the condition when fine filaments spread from the base of the stem or fruit-body over the substratum.

CAESIOUS, (color), pale bluish-gray.

CAESPITOSE, aggregated in tufts but not grown together.

CAMPANULATE, (of pileus), bell-shaped or similar.

CANALICULATE, (of stem), furrowed or fluted.

CANDIDOUS, (color), shining-white.

CANESCENT, (surface), covered with hoary down.

CAP, the pileus.

CAPILLARY, (of stem), hair-like.

CAPITATE, (of cystidia), with a minute knob at the tapering apex.

CARBONACEOUS, (of tissue), of the texture of charcoal.

CARINATE, (of spores), furnished with a keel, boat-shaped.

CARNEOUS, (of trama), fleshy.

CARTILAGINOUS, (of stem, cortex or cuticle), tough-brittle, breaking with a snap.

CAULICOLOUS, growing on herbaceous stems.

CELL, (of fungi), the living, protoplasmic units into which the mycelium and hyphae are divided.

CERACEOUS, waxy.

CEREBROSE, (of surface of pileus), convoluted like a brain.

CHLAMYDOSPORES, (see secondary spores), thick-walled spores developed from hyphae but not on basidia.

CINEREOUS, (color), ashy-gray.

CINNABAR, (color), vermillion, red.

CINNAMON, (color), cinnamon-brown.

CIRCUMSCISSILE, (of volva). See page 593.

CITRINE, lemon-yellow.

CLAVATE, (of stem), thickened toward base, like a club; (of basidia and cystidia), thickened at apex, club-shaped.

CLAVATE-BULBOUS, (of stem), with a bulb which tapers gradually upwards.

CLAY-COLOR, argillaceous.

CLOSE, (of gills), halfway between crowded and subdistant; a relative term.

COBWEBBY, (of veil), composed of threads fine as those of a cobweb.

COCHLEATE, (of pileus), twisted like a shell.

COERULEOUS, (color), sky-blue.

COHERENT, (of stems), grown together.

COMPRESSED, (of stem), flattened lengthwise.

CONCAVE, (of pileus), round-depressed like a bowl.

CONCENTRIC, (of zonation, etc.), rings or zones within one another in a series.

CONCHATE, (of pileus), resembling an oyster shell in shape.

CONCOLOR, (of gills and stem), when of the same color as the pileus.

CONCOLOROUS, same as concolor.

CONFLUENT, (of flesh of stem), continuous with trama of pileus and of similar texture.

CONGLOBATE, (of base of stems), collected into a fleshy mass.

CONIDIUM, (see secondary spores), thin-walled spores developed on mycelium or on the hyphae of the fruit-body.

CONIDIA, plural of conidium.

CONIDIAL, relating to conidia.

CONIDIOPHORE, the specialized hypha bearing a conidium.

CONIFER, mostly evergreen trees bearing cones.

CONIFEROUS, said of forests or wood of conifer trees.

CONNATE, (of stems), grown together.

CONNIVENT, (of margin of pileus), converging on the stem.

CONSISTENCY, the firmness, density or solidity of the tissues which compose the parts of the fruit-body.

CONTEXT, the trama.

CONTINUOUS, (of stem), same as confluent.

CONVEX, (of pileus), regularly rounded, broadly obtuse, etc.

CONVEXO-PLANE, (of pileus), changing from convex when younger to flat when expanded.

CONVEX-EXPANDED, (of pileus), changing from convex and tending towards plane; the margin often remaining decurved.

CONVERGENT, (of trama of gills), in section the hyphae are seen to turn inwards to a median line.

CONVOLUTE, same as cerebrose.

CORIACEOUS, of a leathery texture.

CORNEOUS, of a horny texture.

CORRUGATE, (surface), coarsely wrinkled.

CORTEX, (of stem), the outer, denser rind.

CORTICAL, referring to the cortex.

CORTICATE, possessing a cortex.

CORTINA, the inner or partial veil in some genera of Agarics, the structure of which is cobwebby.

CORTINATE, provided with a cortina, or (of stem) covered by the threads of the cortina.

COSTATE, (of gills, etc.), veined or ribbed.

COTTONY, (of surface), covered by a soft cotton-like substance.

CRENATE, (of edge of gills or margin of pileus), scalloped.

CRENULATE, very finely crenate.

CRETACEOUS, (of color or consistency), like chalk.

CRISPED, (of gills), finely wavy.

CROWDED, (of gills), almost touching one another.

CRUCIATE, (of spores), having the general form of a cross.

CRYPTOGAMS, the group of plants which reproduce by spores and which include the fungi.

CRYPTOGAMIC, relating to cryptogams.

CUCULLATE, (of pileus), shape of a "high hat."

CUNEATE, (of pileus), wedge-shape.

CUSPIDATE, (of pileus or cystidia), tipped with a prominent sharp protuberance.

CUTICLE, (of pileus or stem), a differentiated thin layer of hyphae on the surface; same as pellicle.

CYATHIFORM, (of pileus), cup-shaped or bowl-shaped, flaring above.

CYLINDRICAL, (of stem or spores), of the same diameter throughout its length.

CYSTIDIUM, (of hymenium of gills), mixed with the basidia and usually projecting beyond them; large sterile cells.

CYSTIDIA, plural of cystidium.

DECORTICATED, of dead wood destitute of the bark.

DECUMBENT, (of stem), with the lower end lying against the substratum.

DECURRENT, (of gills), descending on the stem, see Fig. 1, (3).

DECURVED, (of margin of pileus), bent down.

DEBRIS, the mixture of fallen leaves, twigs, wood, etc., covering a forest floor.

DEFLEXED, same as decurved.

DELIQUESCENT, (of gills), absorbing water and dissolving at maturity.

DENTATE, (of gills), toothed on the edge.

DENTICULATE, (of gills), finely dentate.

DENUDED, (of pileus and stem), naked or glabrous by removal of the scales, flocci, etc.

DEPAUPERATE, undeveloped because of lack of favorable conditions.

DEPRESSED, (of pileus), central portion lower than margin.

DETERMINATE, having a fixed, definite limit.

DETERMINATION, assigning a plant to its correct place in the classification.

DIAGNOSIS, a distinctive description of a plant.

DIAPHANOUS, transparent or nearly so.

DICHOTOMOUS, (of gills), repeatedly forking in pairs.

DIFFERENTIATED, applied to portions or tissues of different character, all derived from a homogeneous tissue.

DIFFORMED, irregular in form.

DILATED, (of stem), enlarged.

DILUTE, (of color), reduced in strength.

DIMIDIATE, (of pileus), semicircular in outline, (of gills), that reach only half-way to stem.

DISK, (of pileus), the central portion of the surface.

DISCOID, (of pileus), with a noticeably marked, flattened disk.

DISCRETE, (of veil, scales, etc.), separate, not grown fast to and continuous with the surface.

DISTANT, (of gills), set far apart, especially toward the margin of the pileus; a relative term.

DIVERGENT, (of trama of gills), in section, the hyphae are seen to turn outwards from a median line.

DORSAL, (of pileus), the upper, back side.

DOWNY, (of pileus and stem), composed of fine hairiness.

DRY, not viscid nor hygrophanous.

EBENEOUS, (color), black as ebony.

EBURNEOUS, (color), white like ivory.

ECCENTRIC, (of stem), not attached in the center.

ECHINATE, (of scales, etc.), sharply pointed spines.

ECHINULATE, (of spores, etc.), with minute and finely pointed spines.

ELEVATED, (of pileus), raised up at the margin.

ELLIPTICAL, (of spores, young pileus, gills, etc.), longer than broad, usually more than twice as long as broad and curved in outline.

ELLIPTIC, ELLIPSOID and ELLIPSOIDAL, similar to elliptical.

EMARGINATE, (of gills), notched near the stem. See Fig. 1, (6).

ENTIRE, (of gills), edge not toothed, etc.

EPIDERMIS, see cuticle.

EPISPORE, the outer wall of a spore.

EPIPHYTAL, growing on leaves.

EQUAL, (of stem), of uniform diameter; (of gills), alike in length.

ERODED, (of gills), edge as if gnawed.

EROSE, same as eroded.

ESCULENT, edible, can be eaten.

EVANESCENT, (of veil, annulus, scales, etc), but slightly developed and soon disappearing.

EVEN, (of surface of pileus, stem, spores), without striations, elevations, depressions or unevenesses of any kind. Compare glabrous and smooth.

EXCENTRIC, see eccentric.

EXOTIC, foreign, not native.

EXPANDED, (of pileus), the opening out of the cap while maturing or ageing.

EXSICATTI, dried specimens kept in herbaria, often in sets.

"FAIRY RINGS," mushrooms appearing in circles. See page 4.

FAMILY, a term in classification, each family includes related genera; the scientific ending of a family name is *aceae*.

FALCATE, (of spores), sickle-shaped.

FARINACEOUS, (odor and taste), like fresh meal; (of pileus and stem), covered by mealy particles.

FARINOSE, like farinaceous.

FASCIATED, (of stems, pilei, etc.), grown together so that tissues are intimately continuous.

FASCICULATE, (of fibrils, scales, stems, etc.), crowded in bundles.

FERRUGINOUS, (color), rusty-red.

FIBRILLOSE, (of surface of cap and stem), provided with fibrils or clusters of small fibres composed of hyphae.

FIBROUS, (of flesh of stem), composed of toughish, string-like tissue.

FILAMENT, a thread, applied to the separate threads of the mycelium.

FILAMENTOUS, composed of filaments.

FILIFORM, (of stem), slender as a thread.

FIMBRIATE, (of gills), with the edge minutely fringed, due to presence of cystidia or sterile cells.

FISTULOSE, (of stem), tubular.

FLABELLIFORM, (of pileus), fan-shaped.

FLACCID, flabby; soft and limber; without firmness or elasticity.

FLARING, (of volva or annulus), spreading away from stem at upper margin.

FLAVESCENT, (color), becoming yellowish.

FLAVUS, (color), of Saccardo's Color Key; a light cadmium-yellow.

FLESH, the trama of the mushroom, especially of the pileus and gills.

FLESHY, of rather soft consistency, putrescent; as opposed to leathery, corky, woody, membranous, etc., referring to the consistency of the trama of most of the Agarics.

FLEXUOUS, (of stem), bent in an undulate manner.

FLOCCI, (of pileus or stem), small points or tufts resembling cotton.

FLOCCOSE, (of pileus or stem), provided with cottony substance on the surface.

FLOCCULOSE, finely floccose.

FLOCCULOSE-CRENULATE, (of gills), edge with minute flocculose decoration.

FOETID, (odor), ill-smelling, nauseating.

FRIABLE, easily crumbled or breaking into powder.

FREE, (of gills), not attached to the stem at any time.

FRONDOSE, said of a forest or the wood of broad-leaved trees.

FRONT, (of gills), the end toward the margin of the pileus; anterior.

FRUIT-BODY, the term applied to the mushroom as opposed to the mycelium.

FRUCTIFICATION, the fruit-body.

FUGACIOUS, disappearing early or quickly or (of color) fading soon.

FULIGINOUS, (color), smoky, sooty.

FULVESCENT, (color), becoming fulvous.

FULVOUS, (color), of Saccardo's Color Key; reddish-cinnamon-brown.

FUNGUS, applied to the individuals of a group of plants which lack the green chlorophyll and hence subsist on other plants, plant-remains or animals; they vegetate in the form of mycelium, and their fruit-bodies are also composed of mycelioid tissue.

FUNGI, the plural of fungus.

FURCATE, (of gills), forked.

FURFURACEOUS, (of pileus or stem), covered with bran-like particles; scurfy.

FUSCESENT, (color), becoming fuscous.

FUSCOUS, (color), a smoky drab; see Ridgway's Color Standards (1912). The term has been used in this report in a wider sense, including paler shades with more brown in them.

FUSIFORM, (of stem and spores), spindle-shaped.

GELATINOUS, jelly-like, applied to tissue whose hyphae become partially dissolved and glutinous in wet weather and when mounted in water under the microscope appear more transparent and wider, loosening from one another.

GENERIC, of the rank of a genus.

GENUS, a term in classification; each genus includes certain related species; the two names, viz. of its genus and its species, compose the binomial by which a plant is known in science, e. g. *Psalliota campestris.*

GIBBOUS, (of pileus), with an unsymmetrical convexity or umbo, or with convexity on one side.

GILLS, the knife-blade-like structures on the underside of the pileus; lamellae; collectively, the hymenophore.

GILL-TRAMA, the tissue of a gill between the two hymenial layers.

GILVOUS, (color), yellowish leather colored.

GLABRESCENT, becoming glabrous.

GLABROUS, (of pileus and stem), surface destitute of scales, hairs, etc., smooth.

GLANDULAR, with sticky drops or glands.

GLAUCOUS, (of pileus), covered with fine white bloom, easily rubbed off.

GLOBOSE, spherical or almost so.

GLUTEN, (of cuticle of pileus or stem, of universal veil), the dissolved gelatinous hyphae of certain tissues; very sticky and toughish.

GLUTINOUS, provided with gluten.

GRANULAR, (of pileus or stem), covered with granule-like substance.

GRANULOSE, same as granular.

GREGARIOUS, growing in company, scattered closely over a small area.

GROUP, a general term, applied indefinitely to a large or small number of plants whether classified or not.

GUTTATE, (of pileus), spotted as if by drops of liquid.

GUTTULATE, (of spores), containing an oily globule.

HABIT, the manner of growth of a plant.

HABITAT, the natural place of growth of a plant.

HAIRY, (of pileus), covered by an arrangement of fibrils resembling hairs.

HERBACEOUS, said of those flowering plants which perish annually down to the roots.

HERBARIUM, a collection of dried plants arranged systematically.

HETEROGENEOUS, applied to a structure composed of unlike tissues.

HIRSUTE, (of pileus), covered with rather long stiff fibres or hairs.

HISPID, (of pileus), covered with stiff bristle-like hairs.

HOARY, (of pileus or stem), covered with dense silky down; canescent.

HOMOGENEOUS, applied to structures composed of uniform tissues.

HOST, the plant or animal on or in which a parasitic fungus exists.

HUE, (of color), used here indiscriminately for "tint" or "shade." See Ridgway's Color Standards (1912) page 17, for correct usage.

HUMUS, the mixture of decayed vegetation and soil in the forest.

HYALINE, (of spores, gluten, etc.), colorless; transparent.

HYGROPHANOUS, (of flesh of mushrooms, or surface of pileus), watery in appearance, like the "water-core" of an apple, moisture disappearing rapidly accompanied by change in color, usually by fading.

HYGROSCOPIC, readily absorbing moisture from the atmosphere.

HYMENIUM, aggregation of the basidia in a continuous layer mixed with cystidia or sterile cells when present; the spore-bearing layer.

HYMENOMYCETES, the group of fungi possessing a hymenium composed of basidia which are exposed.

HYMENOPHORE, the portion of the fruit-body bearing the hymenium.

HYPHAE, plural of hypha; same as mycelium, composing also the fruit-body.

ICONES, colored plates illustrating fungi.

IDENTIFICATION, the study of the characters of a plant in order to determine its name.

IMBRICATE, (of pilei), overlapping one another, like the shingles of a roof.

INCARNATE, (color), flesh-colored.

INCISED, (of margin of pileus), as if cut into.

INCOMPLETE, (of annulus), forming a partial ring.

INCRASSATE, (of stem), thickened.

INCURVED, (of margin of pileus), same as inflexed.

INDIGENOUS, native, not foreign.

INFERIOR, (of annulus), below the middle of the stem.

INFLATED, (of cystidia), swollen like a bladder.

INFUNDIBULIFORM, (of pileus), funnel-shaped.

INNATE, (of scales, fibrils, etc.), a part of the surface tissue, not superficial.

INSERTED, (of base of stem), attached directly without "roots" or fibrils; instititious.

INSTITITIOUS, same as inserted.

INTERSPACES, (of gills), spaces between the attachment of the gills to the pileus.

INTERVENOSE, (of gills), veined in the interspaces.

INTERWOVEN, (of trama), intermingled arrangement of hyphae, not parallel, convergent nor divergent.

INTRODUCED, brought from another country and growing spontaneously.

INVOLUTE, (of margin of pileus), rolled in, especially when young.

ISABELLINE, same as alutaceous; pale tan-color.

LABYRINTHIFORM, of sinuous lines; like a labyrinth.

LACERATE, (of annulus, scales, pileus, etc.), as if torn.

LACINIATE, (of margin of annulus or pileus), cut coarser than fimbriate; slashed.

LACTIFEROUS, (of hyphae of trama), bearing a milky juice.

LACUNOSE, (of pileus or stem), covered with pits or indentations.

LAMELLAE, plural of lamella; same as gills.

LANATE, same as woolly.

LANCEOLATE, (of spores, cystidia or gills), lance shaped; many times longer than broad, and tapering.

LATEX, a juice, usually of milky color, but also applied to other colors.

LATERAL, (of stem), attached to one side of the pileus.

LENS, a hand magnifying glass.

LIGNATILE, growing on wood.

LIGNICOLOUS, same as lignatile.

LINGULATE, (of pileus), tongue-shaped.

LIVID, (color), like that of a bruise; bluish-black.

LOBED, (of pileus), with rather large, rounded divisions on the margin.

LUCID, clear to the understanding; transparent.

LURID, (color), smoky-reddish, sordid.

LUTEOUS, (color), dull egg-yellow; see Saccardo's Color Key.

LUTESCENT, (color), becoming luteous.

MACROSCOPIC, visible without magnification.

MACULATE, spotted.

MAMMIFORM, (of umbo), breast-shaped.

MARGINATE, (of pileus), with a distinctly marked border; (of bulb), with a circular ridge on the exterior upper angle where the universal veil was attached.

MARGINATE-DEPRESSED, (of bulb), provided with a narrow, circular, horizontal platform on the upper side.

MAST, the fruit of forest trees like acorns and nuts, often used of a heap of nuts.

MATRIX, the substance on or in which a fungus grows.

MILKY, of the color of milk.

MEDIAL, (of annulus), situated at or near the middle of the stem.

MEMBRANOUS, (of pileus, annulus, etc.), thin and pliant like a membrane; applied when the trama of pileus is quite thin.

MEMBRANACEOUS, same as membranous.

MICACEOUS, (of pileus), covered with glistening mica-like particles.

MIXED, referring to forests containing both conifer and broad-leaved trees.

MILD, (odor and taste), not with a distinctly marked peculiarity.

MICROSCOPIC, of a size requiring the use of a microscope to see clearly.

MICROSCOPICAL, same as microscopic.

MICRON, (measure), of the length of one-thousandth part of a millimetre; used to designate size as measured by the use of a microscope.

MICROMETER, a disc of glass ruled with lines forming a metric scale for measuring objects under the microscope in microns.

MICRO-CHEMICAL, referring to tests with chemicals on microscopic objects.

MOLDS or MOULDS, certain fungi whose vegetative growth appears mouldy.

MONSTROSITY, applied to a specimen of a very abnormal appearance.

MORPHOLOGICAL, pertaining to form and structure, often used in a phylogenetic sense.

MOVABLE, (annulus), that can be moved more or less easily up and down the stem.

MUCILAGINOUS, slimy.

MUCCOUS, slime.

MUSHROOM, a general term applied to the fleshy Agarics and fleshy species of other fungi; a mushroom may be edible, poisonous, unpalatable, tough, etc., but popular usage applies the term only to edible ones. See toadstool.

MYC., MYCET., MYCETO., MYCO., prefixes signifying fungus.

MYCELIUM, came as hyphae; the vegetative part of a fungus consisting of microscopic threads usually with cross-walls to form the cells which contain the living protoplasm.

MYCELEOID, (of base of stem), provided with a white mouldy growth of mycelium.

MYCOLOGICAL, relating to mycology.

MYCOLOGY, the term applied to the science dealing with fungi.

MYCOPHAGIST, one who eats mushrooms; an epicure concerning mushrooms.

MYCOLOGIST, one who is versed in mycology; a specialist in the study of fungi.

MYCORHIZA, the stunted rootlets of trees, when such rootlets are covered or permeated by the mycelium of fungi.

NAKED, (of pileus or stem), entirely devoid of fibrils, scales or other covering.

NARROW, (of gills), a relative term, the opposite of broad; determined by experience.

NIGRESCENT, (color), turning blackish.

NUCLEATE, (of spores), containing microscopically visible, oil-like globules.

OBCLAVATE, (of cystidia, spores, stem), a reversal of clavate.

OBCONIC, reversal of conic.

OBLONG, (of spores), twice as long as wide.

OBOVATE, (of spores, etc.), reversal of ovate.

OBSOLETE, (of annulus, scales, etc.), very imperfectly developed, hardly perceptible; (of terms), no longer in use.

OBTUSE, (of pileus, cystidia, spores), rounded or blunt; greater than a right angle.

OCHRACEOUS, (color), dingy ochre-yellowish.

OCHREATE, (of volva), sheathing the stem at base like a stocking.

OLIVACEOUS, (color), with an olive shade.

OPAQUE, dull, not shining.

ORBICULAR, (of pileus), circular in outline.

OVAL, (of young pileus, spores), having the shape of an egg.

OVATE, similar to oval but rather pointed at the narrower end.

OVOID, same as oval.

PALLID, (color), of an indefinite pale or whitish appearance.

PAPILLA, a small, nipple-shaped elevation.

PAPILLATE, (of pileus or spores), provided on surface with papillae.

PARALLEL, (of trama of gills), in section the hyphae lie continuously side by side.

PARASITE, an organism living upon another live organism and deriving food from it, with or without fatal effect.

PARTIAL VEIL, the inner veil, extending from the margin of the pileus to the stem. See page 4.

PATCHES, (of scales or remnants of the universal veil), flat, closely applied pieces.

PECTINATE, (of margin of pileus), resembling the teeth of a comb.

PEDICEL, (of cystidia) a slender stalk.

PELLICLE, same as cuticle, sometimes thought of as thinner and more definite.

PELLICULOSE, provided with a pellicle.

PELLUCID, translucent.

PELLUCID-STRIATE, (of pileus), when as the result of the thinness of the pileus the gills become visible thru it and appear as striae.

PENTAGONAL, (of spores), angular and five-sided.

PERIPHERY, the outer boundary or surface.

PERONATE, (of stem), booted; sheathed by the volva or universal veil.

PERONATE-SCALY, (of stem), when the sheath of a peronate stem is broken up and the parts persist.

PERSISTENT, retaining its place, shape or structure, not disappearing.

PETALOID, (of pileus), shaped like the petal of a flower, narrowed somewhat at base.

PHYLOGENETIC, pertaining to phylogeny.

PHYLOGENY, the history of the evolution of the group or race to which a species belongs.

PILEATE, possessing a pileus.

PILEI, the plural of pileus.

PILEUS, the cap or that structure of an Agaric which bears the gills on its under side.

PILOSE, (of pileus), covered with long, soft, hairy filaments.

PIPSHAPED, (of spores), shape of an apple seed.

PITTED, (of pileus or stem), similar to lacunose; with little depressions.

PITH, (of stem), the soft tissue in the interior, which often disappears so that the stem becomes hollow.

PLANE, (of pileus), with a flat surface.

PLIANT, not rigid nor firm; easily bent.

PLICATE, (of pileus), plaited; folded like a fan.

PLUMBEOUS, (color), like lead.

PLUMOSE, finely feathery.

POROSE, (of hymenophore), approaching the condition of possessing pores.

POSTERIOR, (of gills), behind, toward the stem.

PRAEMORSE, (of the "root" or base of stem), as if broken off abruptly.

PROLIFEROUS, (of stem), producing other stems on itself near the base.

PROTEAN, exceedingly variable.

PROTOPLASM, the living semifluid substance of the cells which is the basis of life.

PRUINATE, same as pruinose.

PRUINOSE, (on the surface), as if finely powdered.

PSEUDOPARENCHYMA, the tissue of fungi when its cellular structure imitates the parenchyma of higher plants.

PSEUDOPROSENCHYMA, tissue of fine elongated hyphae, somewhat resembling the prosenchyma of higher plants.

PUBESCENCE, a covering of short, soft, downy hairs.

PUBESCENT, provided with pubescence.

PULVERULENT, covered as if with powder.

PUNCTATE, (of pileus or stem), dotted with minute scales or other substance.

PUTRESCENT, soon decaying and becoming soft and mushy.

PYRIFORM, (of cystidia or cells), pear-shaped.

PYRAMIDAL, (of scales), pyramid-shaped.

QUADRATE, (of spores), angularly four-sided.

RADICATING, (of stem), imitating a root.

RAMIFICATION, branching.

REFLEXED, (of margin of pileus), turned up or back.

REMOTE, (of gills), free and at some distance from the stem; (of annulus), at some distance from apex of stem.

RENIFORM, (of pileus), kidney-shaped.

REPAND, (of pileus), wavy on margin and turned back or elevated.

RESUPINATE, (of pileus), with the upper surface reclining on the substratum, the gills facing outward.

RESUPINATE-REFLEXED, (of pileus), attached for some distance by the back surface, the other portion extending out like a shelf.

RETICULATE, (of pileus or stem), marked by lines, veins or ridges which cross one another as in a net.

REVIVING, said of a fruit-body which shrivels in dry weather and takes on its natural shape when wet.

REVOLUTE, (of margin of pileus), rolled back or up.

RHIZOIDS, radiating hyphae extending into substratum from base of stem.

RHIZOMORPHS, visible strands or cords of compacted mycelium, often dark colored, penetrating a soft substratum or between portions of it, as between bark and wood, etc.

RIMOSE, (of pileus), cracked.

RIND, same as cortex.

RING, same as annulus.

RIVULOSE, (of pileus and stem), marked with lines like a river-system on a map.

ROOTING, (of stem), an attenuated prolongation into the soil or substratum.

ROUND-BULBOUS, of a bulb not marginate.

RUFESCENT, (color), becoming reddish.

RUFOUS, (color), reddish, dull red.

RUGOSE, coarsely wrinkled.

RUGULOSE, finely wrinkled.

SACCATE, (of cystidia), shape of a meal-bag.

SANGUINEOUS, (color), blood-red.

SAPROPHYTE, a plant which lives on dead vegetable or animal matter.

SCABROUS, (of pileus), rough with short, rigid projections.

SCALES, applied to various decorations on the pileus and stem; torn portions of the cuticle or of the universal veil or of the volva; they may be membranous, fibrillose, hairy, floccose, hard, erect, flat, patch-like, etc.; often an important feature for identification.

SCALY, provided with scales.

SCLEROTIA, resting-bodies of small size, composed of a hardened mass of hyphae, from which fruit-bodies may develop.

SCISSILE, (of flesh of pileus), capable of being pulled into horizontal layers; this condition is most marked in a hygrophanous pileus.

SECEDE, (of gills), when at first attached to stem, i. e. adnate or adnexed, but separating from it later.

SECONDARY SPORES, not borne on basidia; conidia, chlamydospores, etc.; formed directly on the mycelium or on hyphae of the fruit body.

SEPARABLE, (of cuticle, pellicle, etc.), not adnate.

SEPARATING, see secede.

SERICEOUS, silky.

SERRATE, (of gills), with saw-tooth-like edge.

SERRULATE, minutely serrate.

SERRATULATE, same as serrulate.

SESSILE, (of pileus), without a stem.

SETACEOUS, (of stem), bristle-form.

SHAGGY, rough with long compact fibrils.

SILKY, covered with shining, close-fitting fibrils.

SINUATE, (of gills), a concave indentation of its edge near the stem.

SINUOUS, wavy, serpentine.

SLENDER, (of stem), very long as compared to its thickness; relative to stout.

SMOOTH, (of spores), not spiny, tuberculate, rough, nor angular, etc; (of pilus and stem), see glabrous.

SOLITARY, not growing in the immediate neighborhood of other individuals.

SOLID, (of stem), not hollow nor stuffed; of a texture in its central axis similar to that found in the rest of a cross-section.

SORDID, (color), dirty or dingy.

SPADICEOUS, (color), date-brown.

SPATHULATE, (of pileus), spatula-shaped; oblong with attenuated base.

SPECIES, the lowest term in classification; a group of individuals agreeing in certain characters which appear again in their progeny; one species differs from another in several marked characters agreed upon as sufficiently specific by tradition or by specialists in the group; a species is therefore a judgment, and has limitations imposed by an agreement of the judgments of scientific men. One or more species with certain common characters constitute a genus.

SPECIFIC, referring to characters which are used in designating or distinguishing species.

SPHAGNUM, a genus of mosses; bog-moss.

SPINY, (of spores), strongly echinulate.

SPHOEROID, (of spores), nearly spherical; similar to spherical.

SPONGY, (of stem), soft and tending to be water-soaked.

SPONGY-STUFFED, (of stem), with a spongy pith.

SPORE, the reproductive cells in Agarics borne four on each basidium; more accurately called basidio-spores. In other cryptogams the term is applied to reproductive cells or bodies of a great
variety of kinds. The basidio-spores when they germinate give
rise to mycelium.

SPOROPHORE, fruit-body.

SPURIOUS, false.

SQUAMOSE, (of pileus or stem), covered with scales.

SQUAMULOSE, minutely squamose.

SQUAMULE, scale.

SQUARROSE, (of pileus and stem), covered with recurved scales.

STAINED, said of any part which appears as if some coloring
matter had been spilled on it and spread on the surface.

STALK, an indefinite term for stem, pedicel, etc.

STELLATE, (of spores, scales), with extensions like that of a star.

STERIGMA, the tiny spicule-like extension at the apex of a basidium on which the spores develop.

STERILE, said of a fruit-body or hymenium which is immature or
produces no spores; or simply, without spores.

STERILE CELLS, term applied in this report to the slender cells
on the edge of gills which bear no spores and which cause the
fimbriate appearance of the edge as shown under a lens.

STIPE, technical term for the stem of mushrooms; see stem.

STIPITATE, possessing a stem.

STOUT, (of stem), relative to slender; not so many times longer
than thick.

STRAIGHT, (margin of pileus), when not incurved.

STRAMINEOUS, straw-color.

STRIATE, (of margin of pileus), radiating minute furrows or
lines; (of stem), longitudinal lines or minute furrows.

STRIAE, the lines or furrows when striate.

STRIGOSE, (of pileus or stem), with coarse or thick, long, rather
stiff hairs.

STUFFED, (of stem), when the axis is filled with a differentiated
pith which usually disappears in age leaving it hollow.

SUB—, prefix signifying "almost," "somewhat" or "under."

SUBGENUS, a term in classification; a grouping under a genus and
containing groups of related species. The subgenera of the mycologists of one generation are often raised to the rank of genera
by later students.

SUBICULUM, a more or less dense felt of hyphae covering the substratum, from which the fruit-bodies arise.

SUBDISTANT, (of gills), the spacing halfway between close and distant.

SUBDECURRENT, (of gills), when the attachment extends slightly farther down the stem than when adnate.

SUBHYMENIUM, a differentiated tissue just beneath the hymenium.

SUBSTRATUM, the substance in or on which the fungus grows, as soil, humus, fallen leaves, dung, wood, animal remains, etc. A better term than matrix.

SUBULATE, awl-shaped.

SULCATE, (of pileus and stem), grooved, more extreme than striate, less so than plicate.

SUPERFICIAL, (of scales, flocci, etc.), on the surface and easily removable.

SUPERIOR, (of annulus), attached above the middle of the stem.

SYNONYM, the name or names of a species or genus no longer tenable, either because of error in naming, rearrangement of the classification or as a result of "rules" promulgated by scientific men acting in agreement. Many of the long known plants have a number of such synonyms.

TAN, (color), leather-colored, similar to undressed leather; isabelline.

TENACIOUS, tough.

TERETE, (of stem), round like a broom-handle, not irregular.

TERRESTRIAL, growing on the ground.

TESTACEOUS, (color), brick-red.

TEXTURE, the arrangement of the components of the different tissues, as compact, loose, etc.

TINGED, with a tint of a color.

TISSUE, an aggregate of similar cells or hyphae.

TOADSTOOL, same as mushroom; popularly applied to those about which the user of the term often has no knowledge and which he therefore considers poisonous; a large number of so-called "toadstools" are edible.

TOMENTOSE, (of pileus or stem), densely covered with a matted wooliness or tomentum.

TOMENTUM, composed of long, soft, entangled or matted fibrils.

TOXIC, poisonous.

TOOTH, (of gills), decurrent by a tooth; see uncinate.

TRAMA, the fleshy portion of pileus or gills composed of hyphae.

TRANSLUCENT, capable of transmitting light without being transparent.

TRANSVERSE, cross-wise.

TREMELLOID, of a gelatinous consistency.

TRUNCATE, an enlarged portion ending as if cut off.

TUBERCLE, any wart-like or knob-like excrescence.

TUBERCULATE, (of spores), covered with minute tubercles.

TUBERCULAR-STRIATE, (of pileus), when the striae are roughened by small tubercles.

TUMID, (of stem), swollen, inflated.

TURBINATE, (of pileus), top-shaped.

TYPE, the original specimen or specimens from which the species was described and named.

TYPICAL, agreeing with the descriptions of the type or with the type itself.

UMBER, (color), almost tobacco-colored; see Saccardo's Color Key.

UMBILICATE, (of pileus), with a central, naval-like depression.

UMBILICUS, a naval-like depression.

UMBO, (of pileus), a raised, conical to convex knob or mound on the center.

UMBONATE, (of pileus), provided with an umbo.

UNCINATE, (of gills), provided with a narrow, decurrent extension at the stem.

UNDULATE, same as wavy.

UNEQUAL, (of gills), of different length, some reaching the stem, others shorter.

UNEVEN, (of pileus or stem), said of surfaces with striations, reticulations, tubercles, etc.; not even.

UNICOLOROUS, of the same color throughout.

UNIVERSAL VEIL, sometimes used for volva.

VAGINATE, (of stem), provided with a long volva or sheath at the lower end.

VARIABILITY, the state of being variable.

VARIABLE, capable of taking on a number of different shapes, forms, colors or other characters, while retaining its specific identity.

VARIEGATED, marked with a variety of colors, which are intermingled.

VARIETY, (a). Here used to refer to a form which a species constantly assumes, under definite conditions, e. g. climate, soil, artificial culture, etc. Such forms are often given names, as *Psalliota compestris* var. *hortensis*.

(b). Also used to designate forms which are not typical, but which are not sufficiently known to be designated by a specific name; such are given the name of the nearest species in this report followed by the abbreviation "var."

(c). When a variety is found to be constant in its characters and always distinct in some such characters from other species, it should eventually be given a specific name, but in rare varieties such constancy is not easily proven.

VEIL, see "partial veil," "universal veil," "cortina" and "volva."

VEINED, (of gills), with vein-like wrinkles or raised lines on the surfaces.

VELUM, see veil.

VENOSE, same as veined.

VENTRAL, on the under side of, opposed to dorsal.

VENTRICOSE, (of stem), swollen or enlarged in the middle.

VERRUCOSE, warty.

VERRUCULOSE, minutely warty.

VESICULOSE, referring to the trama of the Lactariae.   See page 83.

VILLOSE, covered with long, soft, weak hairs.

VINACEOUS, (color), of the color of red wine.

VIOLACEOUS, (color), of some violet hue.

VIRESCENT, (color), becoming greenish.

VIRGATE, (of pileus), streaked, usually by differently colored fibrils.

VISCID, sticky.

VISCOUS, gluey.

VITELLINE, (color), egg-yellow.

VOLVA, the universal veil of certain genera.   See pages 4 and 593.

WARTY, (of pileus, spores, etc.), covered by small wart-like excrescences.

WAVY, (of margin of pileus), alternately raised and depressed like waves.

WAXY, (of gills), of a consistency that can be partially or wholly moulded or compressed into balls.

ZONATE, (of pileus), marked with concentric bands of color.

ZONED, same as zonate.

INDEX

INDEX

A.

918   THE AGARICACEAE OF MICHIGAN

P.

A CATALOGUE OF SELECTED DOVER BOOKS
IN ALL FIELDS OF INTEREST

A CATALOGUE OF SELECTED DOVER BOOKS
IN ALL FIELDS OF INTEREST

AMERICA'S OLD MASTERS, James T. Flexner. Four men emerged unexpectedly from provincial 18th century America to leadership in European art: Benjamin West, J. S. Copley, C. R. Peale, Gilbert Stuart. Brilliant coverage of lives and contributions. Revised, 1967 edition. 69 plates. 365pp. of text.

21806-6 Paperbound $2.75

FIRST FLOWERS OF OUR WILDERNESS: AMERICAN PAINTING, THE COLONIAL PERIOD, James T. Flexner. Painters, and regional painting traditions from earliest Colonial times up to the emergence of Copley, West and Peale Sr., Foster, Gustavus Hesselius, Feke, John Smibert and many anonymous painters in the primitive manner. Engaging presentation, with 162 illustrations. xxii + 368pp.

22180-6 Paperbound $3.50

THE LIGHT OF DISTANT SKIES: AMERICAN PAINTING, 1760-1835, James T. Flexner. The great generation of early American painters goes to Europe to learn and to teach: West, Copley, Gilbert Stuart and others. Allston, Trumbull, Morse; also contemporary American painters—primitives, derivatives, academics—who remained in America. 102 illustrations. xiii + 306pp. 22179-2 Paperbound $3.00

A HISTORY OF THE RISE AND PROGRESS OF THE ARTS OF DESIGN IN THE UNITED STATES, William Dunlap. Much the richest mine of information on early American painters, sculptors, architects, engravers, miniaturists, etc. The only source of information for scores of artists, the major primary source for many others. Unabridged reprint of rare original 1834 edition, with new introduction by James T. Flexner, and 394 new illustrations. Edited by Rita Weiss. 6⅝ x 9⅝.

21695-0, 21696-9, 21697-7 Three volumes, Paperbound $13.50

EPOCHS OF CHINESE AND JAPANESE ART, Ernest F. Fenollosa. From primitive Chinese art to the 20th century, thorough history, explanation of every important art period and form, including Japanese woodcuts; main stress on China and Japan, but Tibet, Korea also included. Still unexcelled for its detailed, rich coverage of cultural background, aesthetic elements, diffusion studies, particularly of the historical period. 2nd, 1913 edition. 242 illustrations. lii + 439pp. of text.

20364-6, 20365-4 Two volumes, Paperbound $5.00

THE GENTLE ART OF MAKING ENEMIES, James A. M. Whistler. Greatest wit of his day deflates Oscar Wilde, Ruskin, Swinburne; strikes back at inane critics, exhibitions, art journalism; aesthetics of impressionist revolution in most striking form. Highly readable classic by great painter. Reproduction of edition designed by Whistler. Introduction by Alfred Werner. xxxvi + 334pp.

21875-9 Paperbound $2.25

VISUAL ILLUSIONS: THEIR CAUSES, CHARACTERISTICS, AND APPLICATIONS, Matthew Luckiesh. Thorough description and discussion of optical illusion, geometric and perspective, particularly; size and shape distortions, illusions of color, of motion; natural illusions; use of illusion in art and magic, industry, etc. Most useful today with op art, also for classical art. Scores of effects illustrated. Introduction by William H. Ittleson. 100 illustrations. xxi + 252pp.

21530-X Paperbound $1.50

A HANDBOOK OF ANATOMY FOR ART STUDENTS, Arthur Thomson. Thorough, virtually exhaustive coverage of skeletal structure, musculature, etc. Full text, supplemented by anatomical diagrams and drawings and by photographs of undraped figures. Unique in its comparison of male and female forms, pointing out differences of contour, texture, form. 211 figures, 40 drawings, 86 photographs. xx + 459pp. 5⅜ x 8⅜.

21163-0 Paperbound $3.00

150 MASTERPIECES OF DRAWING, Selected by Anthony Toney. Full page reproductions of drawings from the early 16th to the end of the 18th century, all beautifully reproduced: Rembrandt, Michelangelo, Dürer, Fragonard, Urs, Graf, Wouwerman, many others. First-rate browsing book, model book for artists. xviii + 150pp. 8⅜ x 11¼.

21032-4 Paperbound $2.00

THE LATER WORK OF AUBREY BEARDSLEY, Aubrey Beardsley. Exotic, erotic, ironic masterpieces in full maturity: Comedy Ballet, Venus and Tannhauser, Pierrot, Lysistrata, Rape of the Lock, Savoy material, Ali Baba, Volpone, etc. This material revolutionized the art world, and is still powerful, fresh, brilliant. With *The Early Work,* all Beardsley's finest work. 174 plates, 2 in color. xiv + 176pp. 8⅛ x 11.

21817-1 Paperbound $3.00

DRAWINGS OF REMBRANDT, Rembrandt van Rijn. Complete reproduction of fabulously rare edition by Lippmann and Hofstede de Groot, completely reedited, updated, improved by Prof. Seymour Slive, Fogg Museum. Portraits, Biblical sketches, landscapes, Oriental types, nudes, episodes from classical mythology—All Rembrandt's fertile genius. Also selection of drawings by his pupils and followers. "Stunning volumes," *Saturday Review.* 550 illustrations. lxxviii + 552pp. 9⅛ x 12¼.

21485-0, 21486-9 Two volumes, Paperbound $6.50

THE DISASTERS OF WAR, Francisco Goya. One of the masterpieces of Western civilization—83 etchings that record Goya's shattering, bitter reaction to the Napoleonic war that swept through Spain after the insurrection of 1808 and to war in general. Reprint of the first edition, with three additional plates from Boston's Museum of Fine Arts. All plates facsimile size. Introduction by Philip Hofer, Fogg Museum. v + 97pp. 9⅜ x 8¼.

21872-4 Paperbound $1.75

GRAPHIC WORKS OF ODILON REDON. Largest collection of Redon's graphic works ever assembled: 172 lithographs, 28 etchings and engravings, 9 drawings. These include some of his most famous works. All the plates from *Odilon Redon: oeuvre graphique complet,* plus additional plates. New introduction and caption translations by Alfred Werner. 209 illustrations. xxvii + 209pp. 9⅛ x 12¼.

21966-8 Paperbound $4.00

DESIGN BY ACCIDENT; A BOOK OF "ACCIDENTAL EFFECTS" FOR ARTISTS AND DESIGNERS, James F. O'Brien. Create your own unique, striking, imaginative effects by "controlled accident" interaction of materials: paints and lacquers, oil and water based paints, splatter, crackling materials, shatter, similar items. Everything you do will be different; first book on this limitless art, so useful to both fine artist and commercial artist. Full instructions. 192 plates showing "accidents," 8 in color. viii + 215pp. 8⅜ x 11¼. 21942-9 Paperbound $3.50

THE BOOK OF SIGNS, Rudolf Koch. Famed German type designer draws 493 beautiful symbols: religious, mystical, alchemical, imperial, property marks, runes, etc. Remarkable fusion of traditional and modern. Good for suggestions of timelessness, smartness, modernity. Text. vi + 104pp. 6⅛ x 9¼. 20162-7 Paperbound $1.25

HISTORY OF INDIAN AND INDONESIAN ART, Ananda K. Coomaraswamy. An unabridged republication of one of the finest books by a great scholar in Eastern art. Rich in descriptive material, history, social backgrounds; Sunga reliefs, Rajput paintings, Gupta temples, Burmese frescoes, textiles, jewelry, sculpture, etc. 400 photos. viii + 423pp. 6⅜ x 9¾. 21436-2 Paperbound $3.50

PRIMITIVE ART, Franz Boas. America's foremost anthropologist surveys textiles, ceramics, woodcarving, basketry, metalwork, etc.; patterns, technology, creation of symbols, style origins. All areas of world, but very full on Northwest Coast Indians. More than 350 illustrations of baskets, boxes, totem poles, weapons, etc. 378 pp. 20025-6 Paperbound $2.50

THE GENTLEMAN AND CABINET MAKER'S DIRECTOR, Thomas Chippendale. Full reprint (third edition, 1762) of most influential furniture book of all time, by master cabinetmaker. 200 plates, illustrating chairs, sofas, mirrors, tables, cabinets, plus 24 photographs of surviving pieces. Biographical introduction by N. Bienenstock. vi + 249pp. 9⅞ x 12¾. 21601-2 Paperbound $3.50

AMERICAN ANTIQUE FURNITURE, Edgar G. Miller, Jr. The basic coverage of all American furniture before 1840. Individual chapters cover type of furniture— clocks, tables, sideboards, etc.—chronologically, with inexhaustible wealth of data. More than 2100 photographs, all identified, commented on. Essential to all early American collectors. Introduction by H. E. Keyes. vi + 1106pp. 7⅞ x 10¾. 21599-7, 21600-4 Two volumes, Paperbound $7.50

PENNSYLVANIA DUTCH AMERICAN FOLK ART, Henry J. Kauffman. 279 photos, 28 drawings of tulipware, Fraktur script, painted tinware, toys, flowered furniture, quilts, samplers, hex signs, house interiors, etc. Full descriptive text. Excellent for tourist, rewarding for designer, collector. Map. 146pp. 7⅞ x 10¾. 21205-X Paperbound $2.00

EARLY NEW ENGLAND GRAVESTONE RUBBINGS, Edmund V. Gillon, Jr. 43 photographs, 226 carefully reproduced rubbings show heavily symbolic, sometimes macabre early gravestones, up to early 19th century. Remarkable early American primitive art, occasionally strikingly beautiful; always powerful. Text. xxvi + 207pp. 8⅜ x 11¼. 21380-3 Paperbound $3.00

ALPHABETS AND ORNAMENTS, Ernst Lehner. Well-known pictorial source for decorative alphabets, script examples, cartouches, frames, decorative title pages, calligraphic initials, borders, similar material. 14th to 19th century, mostly European. Useful in almost any graphic arts designing, varied styles. 750 illustrations. 256pp. 7 x 10. 21905-4 Paperbound $3.50

PAINTING: A CREATIVE APPROACH, Norman Colquhoun. For the beginner simple guide provides an instructive approach to painting: major stumbling blocks for beginner; overcoming them, technical points; paints and pigments; oil painting; watercolor and other media and color. New section on "plastic" paints. Glossary. Formerly *Paint Your Own Pictures*. 221pp. 22000-1 Paperbound $1.75

THE ENJOYMENT AND USE OF COLOR, Walter Sargent. Explanation of the relations between colors themselves and between colors in nature and art, including hundreds of little-known facts about color values, intensities, effects of high and low illumination, complementary colors. Many practical hints for painters, references to great masters. 7 color plates, 29 illustrations. x + 274pp. 20944-X Paperbound $2.50

THE NOTEBOOKS OF LEONARDO DA VINCI, compiled and edited by Jean Paul Richter. 1566 extracts from original manuscripts reveal the full range of Leonardo's versatile genius: all his writings on painting, sculpture, architecture, anatomy, astronomy, geography, topography, physiology, mining, music, etc., in both Italian and English, with 186 plates of manuscript pages and more than 500 additional drawings. Includes studies for the Last Supper, the lost Sforza monument, and other works. Total of xlvii + 866pp. $7\frac{7}{8}$ x $10\frac{3}{4}$. 22572-0, 22573-9 Two volumes, Paperbound $10.00

MONTGOMERY WARD CATALOGUE OF 1895. Tea gowns, yards of flannel and pillow-case lace, stereoscopes, books of gospel hymns, the New Improved Singer Sewing Machine, side saddles, milk skimmers, straight-edged razors, high-button shoes, spittoons, and on and on . . . listing some 25,000 items, practically all illustrated. Essential to the shoppers of the 1890's, it is our truest record of the spirit of the period. Unaltered reprint of Issue No. 57, Spring and Summer 1895. Introduction by Boris Emmet. Innumerable illustrations. xiii + 624pp. $8\frac{1}{2}$ x $11\frac{5}{8}$. 22377-9 Paperbound $6.95

THE CRYSTAL PALACE EXHIBITION ILLUSTRATED CATALOGUE (LONDON, 1851). One of the wonders of the modern world—the Crystal Palace Exhibition in which all the nations of the civilized world exhibited their achievements in the arts and sciences—presented in an equally important illustrated catalogue. More than 1700 items pictured with accompanying text—ceramics, textiles, cast-iron work, carpets, pianos, sleds, razors, wall-papers, billiard tables, beehives, silverware and hundreds of other artifacts—represent the focal point of Victorian culture in the Western World. Probably the largest collection of Victorian decorative art ever assembled—indispensable for antiquarians and designers. Unabridged republication of the Art-Journal Catalogue of the Great Exhibition of 1851, with all terminal essays. New introduction by John Gloag, F.S.A. xxxiv + 426pp. 9 x 12. 22503-8 Paperbound $4.50

A HISTORY OF COSTUME, Carl Köhler. Definitive history, based on surviving pieces of clothing primarily, and paintings, statues, etc. secondarily. Highly readable text, supplemented by 594 illustrations of costumes of the ancient Mediterranean peoples, Greece and Rome, the Teutonic prehistoric period; costumes of the Middle Ages, Renaissance, Baroque, 18th and 19th centuries. Clear, measured patterns are provided for many clothing articles. Approach is practical throughout. Enlarged by Emma von Sichart. 464pp.   21030-8 Paperbound $3.00

ORIENTAL RUGS, ANTIQUE AND MODERN, Walter A. Hawley. A complete and authoritative treatise on the Oriental rug—where they are made, by whom and how, designs and symbols, characteristics in detail of the six major groups, how to distinguish them and how to buy them. Detailed technical data is provided on periods, weaves, warps, wefts, textures, sides, ends and knots, although no technical background is required for an understanding. 11 color plates, 80 halftones, 4 maps. vi + 320pp. 6⅛ x 9⅛.   22366-3 Paperbound $5.00

TEN BOOKS ON ARCHITECTURE, Vitruvius. By any standards the most important book on architecture ever written. Early Roman discussion of aesthetics of building, construction methods, orders, sites, and every other aspect of architecture has inspired, instructed architecture for about 2,000 years. Stands behind Palladio, Michelangelo, Bramante, Wren, countless others. Definitive Morris H. Morgan translation. 68 illustrations. xii + 331pp.   20645-9 Paperbound $2.50

THE FOUR BOOKS OF ARCHITECTURE, Andrea Palladio. Translated into every major Western European language in the two centuries following its publication in 1570, this has been one of the most influential books in the history of architecture. Complete reprint of the 1738 Isaac Ware edition. New introduction by Adolf Placzek, Columbia Univ. 216 plates. xxii + 110pp. of text. 9½ x 12¾.   21308-0 Clothbound $10.00

STICKS AND STONES: A STUDY OF AMERICAN ARCHITECTURE AND CIVILIZATION, Lewis Mumford.One of the great classics of American cultural history. American architecture from the medieval-inspired earliest forms to the early 20th century; evolution of structure and style, and reciprocal influences on environment. 21 photographic illustrations. 238pp.   20202-X Paperbound $2.00

THE AMERICAN BUILDER'S COMPANION, Asher Benjamin. The most widely used early 19th century architectural style and source book, for colonial up into Greek Revival periods. Extensive development of geometry of carpentering, construction of sashes, frames, doors, stairs; plans and elevations of domestic and other buildings. Hundreds of thousands of houses were built according to this book, now invaluable to historians, architects, restorers, etc. 1827 edition. 59 plates. 114pp. 7⅞ x 10¾.   22236-5 Paperbound $3.00

DUTCH HOUSES IN THE HUDSON VALLEY BEFORE 1776, Helen Wilkinson Reynolds. The standard survey of the Dutch colonial house and outbuildings, with constructional features, decoration, and local history associated with individual homesteads. Introduction by Franklin D. Roosevelt. Map. 150 illustrations. 469pp. 6⅝ x 9¼.   21469-9 Paperbound $3.50

THE ARCHITECTURE OF COUNTRY HOUSES, Andrew J. Downing. Together with Vaux's *Villas and Cottages* this is the basic book for Hudson River Gothic architecture of the middle Victorian period. Full, sound discussions of general aspects of housing, architecture, style, decoration, furnishing, together with scores of detailed house plans, illustrations of specific buildings, accompanied by full text. Perhaps the most influential single American architectural book. 1850 edition. Introduction by J. Stewart Johnson. 321 figures, 34 architectural designs. xvi + 560pp.

22003-6 Paperbound $3.50

LOST EXAMPLES OF COLONIAL ARCHITECTURE, John Mead Howells. Full-page photographs of buildings that have disappeared or been so altered as to be denatured, including many designed by major early American architects. 245 plates. xvii + 248pp. 7⅞ x 10¾. 21143-6 Paperbound $3.00

DOMESTIC ARCHITECTURE OF THE AMERICAN COLONIES AND OF THE EARLY REPUBLIC, Fiske Kimball. Foremost architect and restorer of Williamsburg and Monticello covers nearly 200 homes between 1620-1825. Architectural details, construction, style features, special fixtures, floor plans, etc. Generally considered finest work in its area. 219 illustrations of houses, doorways, windows, capital mantels. xx + 314pp. 7⅞ x 10¾. 21743-4 Paperbound $3.50

EARLY AMERICAN ROOMS: 1650-1858, edited by Russell Hawes Kettell. Tour of 12 rooms, each representative of a different era in American history and each furnished, decorated, designed and occupied in the style of the era. 72 plans and elevations, 8-page color section, etc., show fabrics, wall papers, arrangements, etc. Full descriptive text. xvii + 200pp. of text. 8⅜ x 11¼.

21633-0 Paperbound $4.00

THE FITZWILLIAM VIRGINAL BOOK, edited by J. Fuller Maitland and W. B. Squire. Full modern printing of famous early 17th-century ms. volume of 300 works by Morley, Byrd, Bull, Gibbons, etc. For piano or other modern keyboard instrument; easy to read format. xxxvi + 938pp. 8⅜ x 11.

21068-5, 21069-3 Two volumes, Paperbound $8.00

HARPSICHORD MUSIC, Johann Sebastian Bach. Bach Gesellschaft edition. A rich selection of Bach's masterpieces for the harpsichord: the six English Suites, six French Suites, the six Partitas (Clavierübung part I), the Goldberg Variations (Clavierübung part IV), the fifteen Two-Part Inventions and the fifteen Three-Part Sinfonias. Clearly reproduced on large sheets with ample margins; eminently playable. vi + 312pp. 8⅛ x 11. 22360-4 Paperbound $5.00

THE MUSIC OF BACH: AN INTRODUCTION, Charles Sanford Terry. A fine, nontechnical introduction to Bach's music, both instrumental and vocal. Covers organ music, chamber music, passion music, other types. Analyzes themes, developments, innovations. x + 114pp. 21075-8 Paperbound $1.25

BEETHOVEN AND HIS NINE SYMPHONIES, Sir George Grove. Noted British musicologist provides best history, analysis, commentary on symphonies. Very thorough, rigorously accurate; necessary to both advanced student and amateur music lover. 436 musical passages. vii + 407 pp. 20334-4 Paperbound $2.25

JOHANN SEBASTIAN BACH, Philipp Spitta. One of the great classics of musicology, this definitive analysis of Bach's music (and life) has never been surpassed. Lucid, nontechnical analyses of hundreds of pieces (30 pages devoted to St. Matthew Passion, 26 to B Minor Mass). Also includes major analysis of 18th-century music. 450 musical examples. 40-page musical supplement. Total of xx + 1799pp.

(EUK) 22278-0, 22279-9 Two volumes, Clothbound $15.00

MOZART AND HIS PIANO CONCERTOS, Cuthbert Girdlestone. The only full-length study of an important area of Mozart's creativity. Provides detailed analyses of all 23 concertos, traces inspirational sources. 417 musical examples. Second edition. 509pp.   (USO) 21271-8 Paperbound $3.50

THE PERFECT WAGNERITE: A COMMENTARY ON THE NIBLUNG's RING, George Bernard Shaw. Brilliant and still relevant criticism in remarkable essays on Wagner's Ring cycle, Shaw's ideas on political and social ideology behind the plots, role of Leitmotifs, vocal requisites, etc. Prefaces. xxi + 136pp.

21707-8 Paperbound $1.50

DON GIOVANNI, W. A. Mozart. Complete libretto, modern English translation; biographies of composer and librettist; accounts of early performances and critical reaction. Lavishly illustrated. All the material you need to understand and appreciate this great work. Dover Opera Guide and Libretto Series; translated and introduced by Ellen Bleiler. 92 illustrations. 209pp.

21134-7 Paperbound $1.50

HIGH FIDELITY SYSTEMS: A LAYMAN'S GUIDE, Roy F. Allison. All the basic information you need for setting up your own audio system: high fidelity and stereo record players, tape records, F.M. Connections, adjusting tone arm, cartridge, checking needle alignment, positioning speakers, phasing speakers, adjusting hums, trouble-shooting, maintenance, and similar topics. Enlarged 1965 edition. More than 50 charts, diagrams, photos. iv + 91pp.   21514-8 Paperbound $1.25

REPRODUCTION OF SOUND, Edgar Villchur. Thorough coverage for laymen of high fidelity systems, reproducing systems in general, needles, amplifiers, preamps, loudspeakers, feedback, explaining physical background. "A rare talent for making technicalities vividly comprehensible," R. Darrell, *High Fidelity.* 69 figures. iv + 92pp.   21515-6 Paperbound $1.00

HEAR ME TALKIN' TO YA: THE STORY OF JAZZ AS TOLD BY THE MEN WHO MADE IT, Nat Shapiro and Nat Hentoff. Louis Armstrong, Fats Waller, Jo Jones, Clarence Williams, Billy Holiday, Duke Ellington, Jelly Roll Morton and dozens of other jazz greats tell how it was in Chicago's South Side, New Orleans, depression Harlem and the modern West Coast as jazz was born and grew. xvi + 429pp.

21726-4 Paperbound $2.00

FABLES OF AESOP, translated by Sir Roger L'Estrange. A reproduction of the very rare 1931 Paris edition; a selection of the most interesting fables, together with 50 imaginative drawings by Alexander Calder. v + 128pp. 6½x9¼.

21780-9 Paperbound $1.25

AGAINST THE GRAIN (A REBOURS), Joris K. Huysmans. Filled with weird images, evidences of a bizarre imagination, exotic experiments with hallucinatory drugs, rich tastes and smells and the diversions of its sybarite hero Duc Jean des Esseintes, this classic novel pushed 19th-century literary decadence to its limits. Full unabridged edition. Do not confuse this with abridged editions generally sold. Introduction by Havelock Ellis. xlix + 206pp. 22190-3 Paperbound $2.00

VARIORUM SHAKESPEARE: HAMLET. Edited by Horace H. Furness; a landmark of American scholarship. Exhaustive footnotes and appendices treat all doubtful words and phrases, as well as suggested critical emendations throughout the play's history. First volume contains editor's own text, collated with all Quartos and Folios. Second volume contains full first Quarto, translations of Shakespeare's sources (Belleforest, and Saxo Grammaticus), Der Bestrafte Brudermord, and many essays on critical and historical points of interest by major authorities of past and present. Includes details of staging and costuming over the years. By far the best edition available for serious students of Shakespeare. Total of xx + 905pp.
21004-9, 21005-7, 2 volumes, Paperbound $5.25

A LIFE OF WILLIAM SHAKESPEARE, Sir Sidney Lee. This is the standard life of Shakespeare, summarizing everything known about Shakespeare and his plays. Incredibly rich in material, broad in coverage, clear and judicious, it has served thousands as the best introduction to Shakespeare. 1931 edition. 9 plates. xxix + 792pp. (USO) 21967-4 Paperbound $3.75

MASTERS OF THE DRAMA, John Gassner. Most comprehensive history of the drama in print, covering every tradition from Greeks to modern Europe and America, including India, Far East, etc. Covers more than 800 dramatists, 2000 plays, with biographical material, plot summaries, theatre history, criticism, etc. "Best of its kind in English," New Republic. 77 illustrations. xxii + 890pp.
20100-7 Clothbound $7.50

THE EVOLUTION OF THE ENGLISH LANGUAGE, George McKnight. The growth of English, from the 14th century to the present. Unusual, non-technical account presents basic information in very interesting form: sound shifts, change in grammar and syntax, vocabulary growth, similar topics. Abundantly illustrated with quotations. Formerly Modern English in the Making. xii + 590pp.
21932-1 Paperbound $3.50

AN ETYMOLOGICAL DICTIONARY OF MODERN ENGLISH, Ernest Weekley. Fullest, richest work of its sort, by foremost British lexicographer. Detailed word histories, including many colloquial and archaic words; extensive quotations. Do not confuse this with the Concise Etymological Dictionary, which is much abridged. Total of xxvii + 830pp. 6½ x 9¼.
21873-2, 21874-0 Two volumes, Paperbound $5.50

FLATLAND: A ROMANCE OF MANY DIMENSIONS, E. A. Abbott. Classic of science-fiction explores ramifications of life in a two-dimensional world, and what happens when a three-dimensional being intrudes. Amusing reading, but also useful as introduction to thought about hyperspace. Introduction by Banesh Hoffmann. 16 illustrations. xx + 103pp. 20001-9 Paperbound $1.00

POEMS OF ANNE BRADSTREET, edited with an introduction by Robert Hutchinson. A new selection of poems by America's first poet and perhaps the first significant woman poet in the English language. 48 poems display her development in works of considerable variety—love poems, domestic poems, religious meditations, formal elegies, "quaternions," etc. Notes, bibliography. viii + 222pp.
22160-1 Paperbound $2.00

THREE GOTHIC NOVELS: THE CASTLE OF OTRANTO BY HORACE WALPOLE; VATHEK BY WILLIAM BECKFORD; THE VAMPYRE BY JOHN POLIDORI, WITH FRAGMENT OF A NOVEL BY LORD BYRON, edited by E. F. Bleiler. The first Gothic novel, by Walpole; the finest Oriental tale in English, by Beckford; powerful Romantic supernatural story in versions by Polidori and Byron. All extremely important in history of literature; all still exciting, packed with supernatural thrills, ghosts, haunted castles, magic, etc. xl + 291pp.
21232-7 Paperbound $2.00

THE BEST TALES OF HOFFMANN, E. T. A. Hoffmann. 10 of Hoffmann's most important stories, in modern re-editings of standard translations: Nutcracker and the King of Mice, Signor Formica, Automata, The Sandman, Rath Krespel, The Golden Flowerpot, Master Martin the Cooper, The Mines of Falun, The King's Betrothed, A New Year's Eve Adventure. 7 illustrations by Hoffmann. Edited by E. F. Bleiler. xxxix + 419pp.
21793-0 Paperbound $2.25

GHOST AND HORROR STORIES OF AMBROSE BIERCE, Ambrose Bierce. 23 strikingly modern stories of the horrors latent in the human mind: The Eyes of the Panther, The Damned Thing, An Occurrence at Owl Creek Bridge, An Inhabitant of Carcosa, etc., plus the dream-essay, Visions of the Night. Edited by E. F. Bleiler. xxii + 199pp.
20767-6 Paperbound $1.50

BEST GHOST STORIES OF J. S. LEFANU, J. Sheridan LeFanu. Finest stories by Victorian master often considered greatest supernatural writer of all. Carmilla, Green Tea, The Haunted Baronet, The Familiar, and 12 others. Most never before available in the U. S. A. Edited by E. F. Bleiler. 8 illustrations from Victorian publications. xvii + 467pp.
20415-4 Paperbound $2.50

THE TIME STREAM, THE GREATEST ADVENTURE, AND THE PURPLE SAPPHIRE— THREE SCIENCE FICTION NOVELS, John Taine (Eric Temple Bell). Great American mathematician was also foremost science fiction novelist of the 1920's. *The Time Stream,* one of all-time classics, uses concepts of circular time; *The Greatest Adventure,* incredibly ancient biological experiments from Antarctica threaten to escape; The *Purple Sapphire,* superscience, lost races in Central Tibet, survivors of the Great Race. 4 illustrations by Frank R. Paul. v + 532pp.
21180-0 Paperbound $2.50

SEVEN SCIENCE FICTION NOVELS, H. G. Wells. The standard collection of the great novels. Complete, unabridged. *First Men in the Moon, Island of Dr. Moreau, War of the Worlds, Food of the Gods, Invisible Man, Time Machine, In the Days of the Comet.* Not only science fiction fans, but every educated person owes it to himself to read these novels. 1015pp.
20264-X Clothbound $5.00

LAST AND FIRST MEN AND STAR MAKER, TWO SCIENCE FICTION NOVELS, Olaf Stapledon. Greatest future histories in science fiction. In the first, human intelligence is the "hero," through strange paths of evolution, interplanetary invasions, incredible technologies, near extinctions and reemergences. Star Maker describes the quest of a band of star rovers for intelligence itself, through time and space: weird inhuman civilizations, crustacean minds, symbiotic worlds, etc. Complete, unabridged. v + 438pp. 21962-3 Paperbound $2.00

THREE PROPHETIC NOVELS, H. G. WELLS. Stages of a consistently planned future for mankind. *When the Sleeper Wakes,* and *A Story of the Days to Come,* anticipate *Brave New World* and *1984,* in the 21st Century; *The Time Machine,* only complete version in print, shows farther future and the end of mankind. All show Wells's greatest gifts as storyteller and novelist. Edited by E. F. Bleiler. x + 335pp. (USO) 20605-X Paperbound $2.00

THE DEVIL'S DICTIONARY, Ambrose Bierce. America's own Oscar Wilde—Ambrose Bierce—offers his barbed iconoclastic wisdom in over 1,000 definitions hailed by H. L. Mencken as "some of the most gorgeous witticisms in the English language." 145pp. 20487-1 Paperbound $1.25

MAX AND MORITZ, Wilhelm Busch. Great children's classic, father of comic strip, of two bad boys, Max and Moritz. Also Ker and Plunk (Plisch und Plumm), Cat and Mouse, Deceitful Henry, Ice-Peter, The Boy and the Pipe, and five other pieces. Original German, with English translation. Edited by H. Arthur Klein; translations by various hands and H. Arthur Klein. vi + 216pp.
20181-3 Paperbound $1.50

PIGS IS PIGS AND OTHER FAVORITES, Ellis Parker Butler. The title story is one of the best humor short stories, as Mike Flannery obfuscates biology and English. Also included, That Pup of Murchison's, The Great American Pie Company, and Perkins of Portland. 14 illustrations. v + 109pp. 21532-6 Paperbound $1.00

THE PETERKIN PAPERS, Lucretia P. Hale. It takes genius to be as stupidly mad as the Peterkins, as they decide to become wise, celebrate the "Fourth," keep a cow, and otherwise strain the resources of the Lady from Philadelphia. Basic book of American humor. 153 illustrations. 219pp. 20794-3 Paperbound $1.25

PERRAULT'S FAIRY TALES, translated by A. E. Johnson and S. R. Littlewood, with 34 full-page illustrations by Gustave Doré. All the original Perrault stories—Cinderella, Sleeping Beauty, Bluebeard, Little Red Riding Hood, Puss in Boots, Tom Thumb, etc.—with their witty verse morals and the magnificent illustrations of Doré. One of the five or six great books of European fairy tales. viii + 117pp. 8⅛ x 11. 22311-6 Paperbound $2.00

OLD HUNGARIAN FAIRY TALES, Baroness Orczy. Favorites translated and adapted by author of the *Scarlet Pimpernel.* Eight fairy tales include "The Suitors of Princess Fire-Fly," "The Twin Hunchbacks," "Mr. Cuttlefish's Love Story," and "The Enchanted Cat." This little volume of magic and adventure will captivate children as it has for generations. 90 drawings by Montagu Barstow. 96pp.
(USO) 22293-4 Paperbound $1.95

THE RED FAIRY BOOK, Andrew Lang. Lang's color fairy books have long been children's favorites. This volume includes Rapunzel, Jack and the Bean-stalk and 35 other stories, familiar and unfamiliar. 4 plates, 93 illustrations x + 367pp.
21673-X Paperbound $1.95

THE BLUE FAIRY BOOK, Andrew Lang. Lang's tales come from all countries and all times. Here are 37 tales from Grimm, the Arabian Nights, Greek Mythology, and other fascinating sources. 8 plates, 130 illustrations. xi + 390pp.
21437-0 Paperbound $1.95

HOUSEHOLD STORIES BY THE BROTHERS GRIMM. Classic English-language edition of the well-known tales — Rumpelstiltskin, Snow White, Hansel and Gretel, The Twelve Brothers, Faithful John, Rapunzel, Tom Thumb (52 stories in all). Translated into simple, straightforward English by Lucy Crane. Ornamented with headpieces, vignettes, elaborate decorative initials and a dozen full-page illustrations by Walter Crane. x + 269pp.
21080-4 Paperbound $2.00

THE MERRY ADVENTURES OF ROBIN HOOD, Howard Pyle. The finest modern versions of the traditional ballads and tales about the great English outlaw. Howard Pyle's complete prose version, with every word, every illustration of the first edition. Do not confuse this facsimile of the original (1883) with modern editions that change text or illustrations. 23 plates plus many page decorations. xxii + 296pp.
22043-5 Paperbound $2.00

THE STORY OF KING ARTHUR AND HIS KNIGHTS, Howard Pyle. The finest children's version of the life of King Arthur; brilliantly retold by Pyle, with 48 of his most imaginative illustrations. xviii + 313pp. 6⅛ x 9¼.
21445-1 Paperbound $2.00

THE WONDERFUL WIZARD OF OZ, L. Frank Baum. America's finest children's book in facsimile of first edition with all Denslow illustrations in full color. The edition a child should have. Introduction by Martin Gardner. 23 color plates, scores of drawings. iv + 267pp.
20691-2 Paperbound $1.95

THE MARVELOUS LAND OF OZ, L. Frank Baum. The second Oz book, every bit as imaginative as the Wizard. The hero is a boy named Tip, but the Scarecrow and the Tin Woodman are back, as is the Oz magic. 16 color plates, 120 drawings by John R. Neill. 287pp.
20692-0 Paperbound $1.75

THE MAGICAL MONARCH OF MO, L. Frank Baum. Remarkable adventures in a land even stranger than Oz. The best of Baum's books not in the Oz series. 15 color plates and dozens of drawings by Frank Verbeck. xviii + 237pp.
21892-9 Paperbound $2.00

THE BAD CHILD'S BOOK OF BEASTS, MORE BEASTS FOR WORSE CHILDREN, A MORAL ALPHABET, Hilaire Belloc. Three complete humor classics in one volume. Be kind to the frog, and do not call him names . . . and 28 other whimsical animals. Familiar favorites and some not so well known. Illustrated by Basil Blackwell. 156pp.
(USO) 20749-8 Paperbound $1.25

EAST O' THE SUN AND WEST O' THE MOON, George W. Dasent. Considered the best of all translations of these Norwegian folk tales, this collection has been enjoyed by generations of children (and folklorists too). Includes True and Untrue, Why the Sea is Salt, East O' the Sun and West O' the Moon, Why the Bear is Stumpy-Tailed, Boots and the Troll, The Cock and the Hen, Rich Peter the Pedlar, and 52 more. The only edition with all 59 tales. 77 illustrations by Erik Werenskiold and Theodor Kittelsen. xv + 418pp. 22521-6 Paperbound $3.00

GOOPS AND HOW TO BE THEM, Gelett Burgess. Classic of tongue-in-cheek humor, masquerading as etiquette book. 87 verses, twice as many cartoons, show mischievous Goops as they demonstrate to children virtues of table manners, neatness, courtesy, etc. Favorite for generations. viii + 88pp. 6½ x 9¼.
22233-0 Paperbound $1.25

ALICE'S ADVENTURES UNDER GROUND, Lewis Carroll. The first version, quite different from the final *Alice in Wonderland,* printed out by Carroll himself with his own illustrations. Complete facsimile of the "million dollar" manuscript Carroll gave to Alice Liddell in 1864. Introduction by Martin Gardner. viii + 96pp. Title and dedication pages in color. 21482-6 Paperbound $1.25

THE BROWNIES, THEIR BOOK, Palmer Cox. Small as mice, cunning as foxes, exuberant and full of mischief, the Brownies go to the zoo, toy shop, seashore, circus, etc., in 24 verse adventures and 266 illustrations. Long a favorite, since their first appearance in St. Nicholas Magazine. xi + 144pp. 6⅝ x 9¼.
21265-3 Paperbound $1.75

SONGS OF CHILDHOOD, Walter De La Mare. Published (under the pseudonym Walter Ramal) when De La Mare was only 29, this charming collection has long been a favorite children's book. A facsimile of the first edition in paper, the 47 poems capture the simplicity of the nursery rhyme and the ballad, including such lyrics as I Met Eve, Tartary, The Silver Penny. vii + 106pp. 21972-0 Paperbound $1.25

THE COMPLETE NONSENSE OF EDWARD LEAR, Edward Lear. The finest 19th-century humorist-cartoonist in full: all nonsense limericks, zany alphabets, Owl and Pussycat, songs, nonsense botany, and more than 500 illustrations by Lear himself. Edited by Holbrook Jackson. xxix + 287pp. (USO) 20167-8 Paperbound $1.75

BILLY WHISKERS: THE AUTOBIOGRAPHY OF A GOAT, Frances Trego Montgomery. A favorite of children since the early 20th century, here are the escapades of that rambunctious, irresistible and mischievous goat—Billy Whiskers. Much in the spirit of *Peck's Bad Boy,* this is a book that children never tire of reading or hearing. All the original familiar illustrations by W. H. Fry are included: 6 color plates, 18 black and white drawings. 159pp. 22345-0 Paperbound $2.00

MOTHER GOOSE MELODIES. Faithful republication of the fabulously rare Munroe and Francis "copyright 1833" Boston edition—the most important Mother Goose collection, usually referred to as the "original." Familiar rhymes plus many rare ones, with wonderful old woodcut illustrations. Edited by E. F. Bleiler. 128pp. 4½ x 6⅜. 22577-1 Paperbound $1.25

Two Little Savages; Being the Adventures of Two Boys Who Lived as Indians and What They Learned, Ernest Thompson Seton. Great classic of nature and boyhood provides a vast range of woodlore in most palatable form, a genuinely entertaining story. Two farm boys build a teepee in woods and live in it for a month, working out Indian solutions to living problems, star lore, birds and animals, plants, etc. 293 illustrations. vii + 286pp.

20985-7 Paperbound $2.50

Peter Piper's Practical Principles of Plain & Perfect Pronunciation. Alliterative jingles and tongue-twisters of surprising charm, that made their first appearance in America about 1830. Republished in full with the spirited woodcut illustrations from this earliest American edition. 32pp. 4½ x 6⅜.

22560-7 Paperbound $1.00

Science Experiments and Amusements for Children, Charles Vivian. 73 easy experiments, requiring only materials found at home or easily available, such as candles, coins, steel wool, etc.; illustrate basic phenomena like vacuum, simple chemical reaction, etc. All safe. Modern, well-planned. Formerly *Science Games for Children*. 102 photos, numerous drawings. 96pp. 6⅛ x 9¼.

21856-2 Paperbound $1.25

An Introduction to Chess Moves and Tactics Simply Explained, Leonard Barden. Informal intermediate introduction, quite strong in explaining reasons for moves. Covers basic material, tactics, important openings, traps, positional play in middle game, end game. Attempts to isolate patterns and recurrent configurations. Formerly *Chess*. 58 figures. 102pp. (USO) 21210-6 Paperbound $1.25

Lasker's Manual of Chess, Dr. Emanuel Lasker. Lasker was not only one of the five great World Champions, he was also one of the ablest expositors, theorists, and analysts. In many ways, his Manual, permeated with his philosophy of battle, filled with keen insights, is one of the greatest works ever written on chess. Filled with analyzed games by the great players. A single-volume library that will profit almost any chess player, beginner or master. 308 diagrams. xli x 349pp.

20640-8 Paperbound $2.50

The Master Book of Mathematical Recreations, Fred Schuh. In opinion of many the finest work ever prepared on mathematical puzzles, stunts, recreations; exhaustively thorough explanations of mathematics involved, analysis of effects, citation of puzzles and games. Mathematics involved is elementary. Translated by F. Göbel. 194 figures. xxiv + 430pp. 22134-2 Paperbound $3.00

Mathematics, Magic and Mystery, Martin Gardner. Puzzle editor for Scientific American explains mathematics behind various mystifying tricks: card tricks, stage "mind reading," coin and match tricks, counting out games, geometric dissections, etc. Probability sets, theory of numbers clearly explained. Also provides more than 400 tricks, guaranteed to work, that you can do. 135 illustrations. xii + 176pp.

20338-2 Paperbound $1.50

MATHEMATICAL PUZZLES FOR BEGINNERS AND ENTHUSIASTS, Geoffrey Mott-Smith. 189 puzzles from easy to difficult—involving arithmetic, logic, algebra, properties of digits, probability, etc.—for enjoyment and mental stimulus. Explanation of mathematical principles behind the puzzles. 135 illustrations. viii + 248pp.
20198-8 Paperbound $1.25

PAPER FOLDING FOR BEGINNERS, William D. Murray and Francis J. Rigney. Easiest book on the market, clearest instructions on making interesting, beautiful origami. Sail boats, cups, roosters, frogs that move legs, bonbon boxes, standing birds, etc. 40 projects; more than 275 diagrams and photographs. 94pp.
20713-7 Paperbound $1.00

TRICKS AND GAMES ON THE POOL TABLE, Fred Herrmann. 79 tricks and games— some solitaires, some for two or more players, some competitive games—to entertain you between formal games. Mystifying shots and throws, unusual caroms, tricks involving such props as cork, coins, a hat, etc. Formerly *Fun on the Pool Table*. 77 figures. 95pp.
21814-7 Paperbound $1.00

HAND SHADOWS TO BE THROWN UPON THE WALL: A SERIES OF NOVEL AND AMUSING FIGURES FORMED BY THE HAND, Henry Bursill. Delightful picturebook from great-grandfather's day shows how to make 18 different hand shadows: a bird that flies, duck that quacks, dog that wags his tail, camel, goose, deer, boy, turtle, etc. Only book of its sort. vi + 33pp. 6½ x 9¼. 21779-5 Paperbound $1.00

WHITTLING AND WOODCARVING, E. J. Tangerman. 18th printing of best book on market. "If you can cut a potato you can carve" toys and puzzles, chains, chessmen, caricatures, masks, frames, woodcut blocks, surface patterns, much more. Information on tools, woods, techniques. Also goes into serious wood sculpture from Middle Ages to present, East and West. 464 photos, figures. x + 293pp.
20965-2 Paperbound $2.00

HISTORY OF PHILOSOPHY, Julián Marias. Possibly the clearest, most easily followed, best planned, most useful one-volume history of philosophy on the market; neither skimpy nor overfull. Full details on system of every major philosopher and dozens of less important thinkers from pre-Socratics up to Existentialism and later. Strong on many European figures usually omitted. Has gone through dozens of editions in Europe. 1966 edition, translated by Stanley Appelbaum and Clarence Strowbridge. xviii + 505pp.
21739-6 Paperbound $2.75

YOGA: A SCIENTIFIC EVALUATION, Kovoor T. Behanan. Scientific but non-technical study of physiological results of yoga exercises; done under auspices of Yale U. Relations to Indian thought, to psychoanalysis, etc. 16 photos. xxiii + 270pp.
20505-3 Paperbound $2.50

Prices subject to change without notice.
Available at your book dealer or write for free catalogue to Dept. GI, Dover Publications, Inc., 180 Varick St., N. Y., N. Y. 10014. Dover publishes more than 150 books each year on science, elementary and advanced mathematics, biology, music, art, literary history, social sciences and other areas.